POLITICS IN NEW GUINEA

POLITICS IN NEW GUINEA

TRADITIONAL
AND IN THE CONTEXT OF CHANGE
SOME ANTHROPOLOGICAL PERSPECTIVES

EDITORS

Ronald M. Berndt
Peter Lawrence

UNIVERSITY OF WASHINGTON PRESS

UNIVERSITY OF WESTERN AUSTRALIA PRESS

First published in 1971 by
University of Western Australia Press
Nedlands, Western Australia 6009

Published in the United States of America by
University of Washington Press, 1973

North and South America, Western Europe, the Middle East,
Africa, and the Caribbean: University of Washington Press
Seattle, Washington, 98195, U.S.A.

Eastern States of Australia and New Zealand: Melbourne
University Press, Carlton South, Victoria, 3053

Singapore, Thailand, Malaysia, Indonesia, Hong Kong, Philippines:
Angus & Robertson (S.E. Asia) Pty. Ltd.,
159, Block 2, Ground Floor, Boon Keng Road, Singapore 12

Library of Congress Catalog Card Number 73-172827
University of Washington Press   ISBN 0-295-95235-0
University of Western Australia Press   ISBN 85564-053-7

Printed in Australia by Frank Daniels Pty Ltd, Perth, Western Australia
and bound by Stanley Owen and Sons Pty Ltd, Alexandria, New South Wales

CONTENTS

MAPS, DIAGRAMS AND TABLES

FOREWORD

I

Fifteen anthropologists, from Australia, England and the United States of America, have contributed the thirteen articles that make up this volume on various aspects of socio-political structure and action in the Territory of Papua and New Guinea. Professor Peter Lawrence willingly accepted the onerous task of preparing an Introduction which provides a general perspective linking these separate studies; he draws out major social anthropological-sociological implications of significance to all who are interested in the Melanesian world and, especially, in the emergence of that Territory as a modern political entity.

All of the contributors have carried out field research in New Guinea, in an overall time span that extends over approximately thirty years: seniority in this respect rests with Professor Douglas Oliver and Dr Phyllis Kaberry. Although the language of this study is the language of Anthropology, and some of the problems dealt with here are perhaps more the concern of anthropologists than of other disciplines, what these contributors have to say is directly relevant to an understanding of what is happening in New Guinea today. The 'ethnographic present' of each chapter is now the past. In one sense, therefore, it is already 'past history'. But in another sense it is anything but that. It is not something that has been overridden and submerged by the continuing and often imperative demands of a new way of life. Things have not worked out that way. Possibly they were never expected, or intended, to do so. The strength of traditional values and institutions and the energetic and adaptable imaginations of the New Guinea people themselves, combined with the particular circumstances of contact with the outside world, have militated against attempts to impose or to seek answers in terms of simple 'Europeanization'. Traditional themes, variable and vulnerable as they are, have a decided bearing on contemporary political thinking.

One important development is the current upsurge of interest in a political identity for all New Guineans in the face of considerable socio-cultural diversity. The shaping of such a common identity must reflect in some way what is regarded as distinctive or unique to New Guinea: it must seek its roots in those elements which can loosely be called 'traditional' without being categorized as something that belongs solely to the past. In New Guinea the 'traditional' is an intrinsic part of the present, and likely to remain so. And this does not militate against change. In fact, conservative as they were in a number of fields, all the New Guinea peoples were very ready to accept change and innovation at the level of practical affairs— within certain limits. They turned to the past as a source of precedents and rules, but they were also forward-looking and adaptable where they saw practical advantages in being so (for example, in experimenting with new garden crops). Change and flexibility were a feature of their traditional orientation. This comes out quite plainly in the studies before us: and, as we shall see, these changes were (and are) located mainly in the spheres of economics and political action.

Politics are an essential ingredient of New Guinea traditional and contemporary socio-cultural living. It is true that, in the Territory generally, authority was diffused, restricted and localized, and often unsupported by sanctions. In fact, political organization was spatially limited. Yet, it is a mistake to believe that political consciousness is not widely significant, that authority always requires coercive force, that the presence of 'many leaders' necessarily implies political weakness, and that the absence of any fixed authority means anarchy. The most telling traditional examples which feed more or less directly into the present-day political scene are of two kinds. One concerns the idea and ideals and actual incidence of 'Big Men': men who, through personal achievement and energy and through manipulating others, maintain impermanent ascendency over those others, supported by them, until they are forced to yield ground to rivals who take their place and, in turn, go through the same process. The second kind of example relates to the ubiquitous Cargo Cult; for all its emphasis on the non-empirical, this, like its traditional counterparts, is basically a political type of enterprise focused on controlling both human and economic resources.

II

The thirteen chapters in this volume were originally published in *Anthropological Forum* between 1965 and 1970 (in Vol. I, Nos 3-4; Vol. II, Nos 1, 2 and 3). The history of the project was noted in an Editorial commenting on the first four contributions (see *Anthropological Forum,* Vol. I, Nos 3-4: 329-31), with further references in other editorials (e.g. *ibid.* Vol. II, No. 1: 1-2; Vol. II, No. 2: 155). But several of the points made there need to be repeated in this new context.

The idea of a book on New Guinea politics was originally conceived by Professor (then Dr) K. E. Read, now of the Department of Anthropology, University of Washington, Seattle, who was—in 1955—on the staff of the Australian School of Pacific Administration, Sydney. At that time eighteen Australian, English and North American anthropologists and others, all directly interested in traditional and changing social systems in New Guinea and Papua, promised to write papers on this topic. For various reasons, the publication did not materialize.

In 1965 (when I was overseas), as one of the original contributors and urged on by others, I began actively to make arrangements for rescuing as many of the original papers as possible and adding new ones. The success of the operation, and the degree of co-operation from individual specialists on New Guinea, can be gauged from the present result. Some of the original papers have been revised or substantially rewritten (e.g. those by Kaberry, Lawrence and Berndt); those by Burridge and Oliver remain virtually unaltered; others, by Chowning and Goodenough, Reay, Meggitt, Brown, Watson, Langness, Lowman-Vayda, Glasse and Lindenbaum have been specially written for this purpose. It is unfortunate that Professor Read himself was unable to participate.

Since 1955, when the project was planned, much research has been accomplished and an appreciable amount of material is now available in print. However, except for a plethora of articles and volumes on 'Cargo Cults', no single work has concentrated on New Guinea politics *per se*, except at the level of locally oriented studies. One object here has been to present a range of articles, all focused on what the anthropologist concerned considers to be 'politics': to see how these contributors approach this subject of political structure and organization—ideology and action— in the areas in which they have carried out intensive field research. Such studies, therefore, are important on two primary scores: in presenting new empirical material, and in posing and exploring theoretical questions of general anthropological importance.

In the journal in which these articles were published, each stands as a contribution in its own right. But they are spread over several years and their combined significance is to some extent diffused from the viewpoint of a prospective reader. We therefore decided (as noted in the Editorial to *Anthropological Forum*, 1965-1966, Vol. I, Nos 3-4: 331) that all of them should be collected and bound together as an Anthropological Forum Monograph, thus enhancing their anthropological value, with the addition of an Introduction. Professor Lawrence, as noted, kindly undertook to draw the main themes of the various papers together and look at them in general perspective, in relation to the implications both for political development in the Territory and for the broader issues of anthropological theory. He commenced this task while at the University of Queensland, and completed it at the University of Pittsburgh before returning to the University of Sydney where he has been appointed to the second Chair of Anthropology. Professor Lawrence is an Advisory Editor (Australian Panel) of *Anthropological Forum,* and becomes a co-editor of the present volume with myself as General Editor of *Anthropological Forum.*

The reprinting of articles previously published in a journal presents certain inherent difficulties when they are arranged in book form. The University of Western Australia Press has been accommodating in this respect, but limited funds have prevented a rearrangement of articles and a reordering of bibliographical references under a separate combined listing. Substantially, the articles follow their *Anthropological Forum* sequence, each retaining its notes and references: and these are preceded by the Introduction. We thank Mrs Geoff Allen for preparing the Index.

In this connection, it is necessary to acknowledge the enthusiastic response of all contributors. Also, in the background and responsible in varying degrees for the production of this volume are the editors of *Anthropological Forum*. *Assistant executive editors* over the 1965-1970 period have been: Dr D'Arcy J. Ryan, Dr Catherine H. Berndt, Dr Susan Kaldor, Mr John Wilson, Dr R. L. Rooksby and Dr Eric ten Raa; *Visiting Guest Editor*: Professor K. O. L. Burridge; *Advisory Editors*, Australian Panel: Emeritus Professor A. P. Elkin, Professor W. R. Geddes and Professor P. Lawrence; International Panel: Professor J. A. Barnes, Professor Raymond Firth, Professor Max Gluckman, Dr Phyllis Kaberry, Professor M. G. Marwick, Professor Claude Lévi-Strauss, Professor Robert Heine-Geldern (now deceased), Professor Helmut Petri, Professor Ward H. Goodenough, Professor Margaret Mead and Professor James Watson. In this connection, I would especially acknowledge the major editorial help of my wife, Dr Catherine Berndt.

III

Although it has not been our purpose to achieve a systematic comparative study of traditional New Guinea politics at the expense of flexibility in treatment and in subject matter, the result is, with the crucial introductory chapter, tantamount to such a study. From these accounts, in combination, it is possible to make some statements about the New Guinea region as a whole—the eastern, Australian-administered side—in relation to our specific focus. Of course, omissions are many, area-wise, as would be expected. The areas are to some extent selective, to some extent rather arbitrary, since they depend on where intensive research has been carried out and on the availability of anthropologists ready and able to contribute in this context. They in no way constitute a controlled sample of what is in fact available in the Territory and in Papua. For this we may have to go to the *Encyclopaedia of Papua and New Guinea*, which is being produced by the Melbourne University Press (the Anthropology section under the editorship of Professor Ian Hogbin: expected publication date, 1971).

Be this as it may, overall assessments of the Papuan-New Guinea area are rare. Of course, there have been some overviews like Professor L. P. Mair's *Australia in New Guinea* (1948), Professor W. E. H Stanner's *The South Seas in Transition* (1953) and Professor L. A. Mander's *Some Dependent Peoples of the South Pacific* (1954). But these look at the situation from the outside, as it were, and do not pay very much attention to the internal structuring of New Guinea societies and their responses to external pressures making for change. They concern, rather, the history of the Administration in that Territory in relation to contacts between local people and Europeans. Naturally, they are significant in broader terms, just as is such a volume as Professor S. W. Reed's *The Making of Modern New Guinea* (1943). Emeritus Professor A. P. Elkin's volume *Social*

Anthropology in Melanesia (1953) is of a different order—providing, as it did, a useful assessment of research which had been carried out in the past and research which needed to be done in the future. The South Pacific Commission, and other bodies, have continued to carry on this task. Of special importance in this connection is the *Ethnographic Bibliography of New Guinea* (Australian National University Press, 1968).

The first truly comparative study, limited to the Highlands of New Guinea, was published in 1954 by Professor K. E. Read (*Southwestern Journal of Anthropology*, Vol. 10: 1-43): this was compiled when the area was still virtually virgin country as far as social anthropological research was concerned, although it marked an important beginning. A second, much more ambitious attempt, and really the first of its kind since it brought together a number of workers writing on different aspects of the Anthropology of the Central Highlands, was 'New Guinea, the Central Highlands' (edited by Professor J. B. Watson), published as a special issue of the *American Anthropologist* (Vol. 66, No. 4, Part 2) in 1964. A third study is *Gods, Ghosts and Men in Melanesia* (1965), edited by Professors P. Lawrence and M. J. Meggitt, concerned with nine different New Guinea societies and focusing on indigenous religion. Together, these present a fairly close overall view of what religion means to these people, how it is socially and culturally integrated, what its structural components are, and what takes place when Christian evangelization is put into action in that context: and the separate chapters are bound together by a broadly based Introduction. Another is *Pigs, Pearlshells, and Women*, edited by Professors R. M. Glasse and M. J. Meggitt, and published in 1969. This is focused on marriage in the New Guinea Highlands and is therefore spatially much more restricted than is *Gods, Ghosts and Men* . . . Dr M. R. Allen's *Male Cults and Secret Initiations in Melanesia* (1967), on the other hand, covers a fairly wide range of New Guinea Highlands and coastal societies, as well as the New Hebrides, but it does not examine them in detail and is of a different order from the others. Like *Gods, Ghosts and Men* . . . , the present volume examines a cluster of related problems in some detail within a regional frame covering fifteen societies: it can be regarded in a sense as a companion to that, since the two can usefully be read in conjunction.

Finally, I repeat parts of an editorial comment of mine which appeared in *Anthropological Forum* (Vol II, No. 1: 1-2) in relation to these contributions. Most of them (as I said there) take into account the rapid changes resulting from increased involvement in the development of a new society—pressures which, while not as yet blurring individual cultural identity, are being felt in almost every aspect of indigenous life. A new, spatially much wider social unit is in the making: and one which concerns New Guinea political identity.* While the present overall focus in Papua-New Guinea generally is on Port Moresby as the seat of

---

* It is appropriate in this context to mention that a companion volume is being planned on contemporary political development in New Guinea.

government, in the shape of the House of Assembly, the real problems of political organization and, in long-range terms, political control, continue to lie at what used to be called the grass-roots level—in its segments, represented still and probably for some time to come by the separate socio-cultural and linguistic blocs rather than by electoral districts as such. It is on these segments or 'tribes' that our contributors concentrate. And any understanding we may achieve of how politics operate within the confines of these socio-cultural entities will ultimately provide us with clues to wider issues—broader political aims and aspirations, rivalries and coalitions.

The 'New Men' of Papua-New Guinea are still men with specific allegiances, with ties that link them quite closely with their own 'tribal' and family affiliations; they are products, in part at least, of their own cultural backgrounds. Understanding politics in New Guinea begins with understanding how political ideas are conceptualized in areas such as those that are dealt with in these studies.

This volume is, therefore, for the professional anthropologist, and for the student of New Guinea affairs. It is also for those who are vitally concerned with Papuan-New Guinea political administration and government: and, above all, it is for Papuans and New Guineans themselves—because within this volume is mirrored something of that heritage upon which a broader New Guinea identity could be built.

RONALD M. BERNDT
University of Western Australia

INTRODUCTION

The war of 1941-45 had two profound effects on South-East Asia and Oceania. First, as is now commonplace, it tolled the death knell of European imperialism. Second, it initiated a hitherto unknown mutual awareness among peoples of the region. The Japanese left in their wake a widespread spirit of nationalism, if not already established independent governments. Large numbers of Europeans, Asians and Oceanians were flung together and forced to have face-to-face dealings with each other, as either allies or enemies. These two changes have continued to reinforce one another. The first has led directly to the emergence of old colonies as new nations and the second to the need, especially on the part of the West, to understand the problems—above all, the political problems—which these nations face. It has fallen largely to the social sciences—in particular, Social Anthropology—to provide this kind of information.

Of all the European colonies in the region, perhaps none was affected more dramatically than Australian-administered Papua and New Guinea. At the beginning of 1942, few of the indigenous inhabitants had felt the impact of the West, which, in turn, knew little about them. There was a narrow coastal fringe of European settlement on plantations and in a few small towns. The people of the coast and immediate hinterland, although under full political control, had experienced few basic changes in their traditional way of life, while much of the interior, the great Central Highlands, remained unexplored. The bulk of the country was, anthropologically, *terra incognita*: with a few exceptions to be noted, most of the early studies had been concentrated necessarily in the coastal and sub-coastal belt, and limited to the examination of single villages.

Then, in 1942, the war brought Papua and New Guinea suddenly into the modern world. The country experienced Japanese occupation and witnessed bitter military campaigns. After 1945, the Australian government re-established and extended political control, and began to prepare the people for eventual self-determination. It introduced extensive economic, educational and political development, so that the territory now possesses many of the institutions of a modern nation-state. At the same time, social anthropological research has been conducted in many places throughout the whole country, greatly expanding knowledge of its people and cultures.

A large part of this recent research, following the lead of British Social Anthropology, and reflecting the needs of an expatriate administration aiming to establish immediately centralized authority, and ultimately an indigenous independent government, with a minimum of disruption, has been in the general field of traditional socio-political structure. Many post-war ethnographers, encouraged by the pioneer experiments of Williams (1938, 1940-41 and 1941-42), Fortune (1947a and b), and Vicedom (Vicedom and Tischner 1943-48) in the Central Highlands during the 1930s, have investigated traditional social and political relationships not merely within single local communities but also within whole linguistic groups—in some cases, between several adjacent linguistic groups.

Broadly, this is the subject of the present symposium. Yet the individual contributions show no regular pattern. The authors have tended to emphasize different features of the traditional political systems they have described, partly because of their own special interests and particular problems that seemed important in the field, and partly because of recent anthropological controversy concerning the principles underlying these political systems themselves. We now regard with circumspection—even suspicion—taxonomic categories which we accepted without question even a decade ago. This controversy has additional relevance because the research on which these papers are based was carried out at different times from the 1930s to the 1960s. Some of them were written in 1955-56 for a book on Melanesian political systems which was never published, and have been revised since then.

Both these considerations—academic debate and the post-war development of the territory—have helped to shape this Introduction. Its purpose is to offer the reader a synopsis of the forms and processes of traditional political systems in Australian-administered Papua and New Guinea as far as they can be delineated, against which he can interpret and assess both the essays presented here and the theoretical problems I have mentioned. It is designed also to give him an essential background to modern politics in the territory, about which there will be an increasingly large literature in the foreseeable future.

I discuss these issues in the following order. In the first section, I sketch the similarities and differences in approach between the contributors to the symposium. This does no more than indicate and summarize its contents. In the second section, I compare the principles underlying the state in Western society, on the one hand, and traditional Papuan and New Guinean political systems, on the other. I begin by outlining the Western state as a foil, and then present Papuan and New Guinean societies in greater detail from two points of view: the general typology of structural forms which anthropologists have used in the past but which is now, as indicated, being modified; and the ways in which these societies function as political systems. In the third section, I consider the interaction between traditional socio-political systems and the modern political institutions, which have been borrowed from the

Western state and introduced by the Administration. I do so only briefly because
virtually all the authors, in accordance with the original charter when the project
was first conceived in the 1950s, have concentrated on the traditional at the expense
of the contact situation.

THE CONTRIBUTIONS

All the peoples described in this volume inhabit the Australian Trust Territory,
reaching from Bougainville in the east through New Britain to the mainland—the
Madang, Sepik, and Eastern and Western Highlands Districts. Papua and West
(Indonesian) New Guinea are not represented. Each of the thirteen papers portrays
a separate socio-political structure, and one of them (by Brown) gives a table of
structural characteristics in the Highlands. Beyond that they follow no set course.
Kaberry's paper concentrates on the pattern and function of traditional political
relationships among the northern Abelam. Chowning's and Goodenough's paper
on the Lakalai, and my own on the Garia, stress traditional social control. Berndt
on the Kamano, Jate, Usurufa and Northern Fore (the Kainantu peoples) discusses not only traditional social control but also the political significance of
warfare, sorcery, intermarriage and leadership, ending with a section on changing
authority patterns after the establishment of the *Pax Australiana* in about 1950.
Burridge on the Tangu describes both traditional political functions, and Administration and mission institutions in 1952. Langness on the Bena Bena, Brown on the
Chimbu, and Glasse and Lindenbaum on the South Fore analyse leadership and the
political role of warfare. Watson on the Tairora, Meggitt on the Mae-Enga, and
Lowman-Vayda on the Maring concentrate on various aspects of leadership. Oliver,
adapting ideas from Leach (1954), writes about contrasting types of socio-political
systems that co-exist on South Bougainville. Reay on the Kuma examines the political
consequences of modern alienation and acquisition of land.

THE TWO POLITICAL SYSTEMS:
WESTERN SOCIETY VERSUS PAPUA AND NEW GUINEA[1]

By a political system, I mean the processes of validating, maintaining and
restoring order within a given framework of social relationships. The principles on
which these processes rest in Western society, on the one hand, and in Papua and
New Guinea, on the other, present a marked contrast. In Western society, the
relevant structure is the state: the official hierarchy of legislative, administrative
and judicial bodies (each vested with delegated and defined authority) or the
national polity geographically coterminous with the total social order. A traditional
New Guinea society lacks these institutions and cannot be regarded as a rudimentary
form of Western society. It is stateless: with few exceptions, it places no stress on
hereditary rank or leadership, and in no instance can it be described as a single,
unified body politic. I now describe the organization and political functions of each
type of society in turn, paying greater attention, as already indicated, to New Guinea.

From the present point of view, there are two important features of Western society: its increasing bias toward secularism; and its compartmentalization into analytically separate systems, each with a specialized function.

In the first place, Western man distinguishes clearly between the realm of the supernatural or transcendental—the world of God—and that of the natural, the physical world which he himself inhabits. In a formal sense, he may regard the social order as established and sanctified by God but, for all practical purposes, he treats it as if it belonged primarily, if not entirely, to the secular world. He views the possibility that the supernatural world, which has become increasingly remote in everyday affairs, should impinge directly on the social order as a matter of individual faith to be anticipated only at times of crisis. He regards his political system as fully secularized.

In the second place, it is necessary to conceive the Western social order as both a totality and a synthesis of separate specialized systems. As a totality, its nature is determined by the main emphases of its economic system: on specialization, expansion and continual change. Because of economic specialization, a Western society relies chiefly on occupation and rank, and progressively less on kinship, marriage and descent, as organizing principles. It consists broadly of a number of professional groups, each graded according to the importance publicly attributed to it, internally structured on the basis of status, and recognizing the authority of its own chief and officials, and finally that of the head of state. Moreover, because of the continual drive for economic expansion and the consequent shifts in the relationships between individuals, the social order must have an element of instability. State and group representatives must always make policies and decisions in the face of change.

There are three main specialized systems within Western society, each with its own structure, personnel, duties and functions: the economic, religious and political. Here we are concerned only with the last: the political system or state with its processes for validating, maintaining and restoring social order.

Most Western societies were established by force. Although, as in the case of Christian monarchies, they may be validated by reference to the Grace of God, their pragmatically effective sanction is popular acceptance. *Vox populi, vox Dei.* Yet the most important considerations are the maintenance and restoration of order, for which the state has three sub-systems: the legislature, which promulgates laws; the executive or public (civil) service, which administers them; and the judiciary, which upholds them through the courts.

The legislature relies on two principles: centralized and fixed authority, which we may define as *de jure* and expected command over the actions of others; and power or *de facto* and unexpected command over the actions of others (Nadel 1951: 169), coupled with influence and persuasion. Its deliberations and decisions have defined limits but, even within them, there is wide scope for political man- oeuvre, the art of manipulating people for specific ends within the framework of a popularly accepted moral system. As already suggested, the legislature's function is to determine policy in the face of problems which are never the same.

The public service should, in theory, eschew power, influence and political manoeuvre, and act entirely and impartially on the basis of centralized, delegated and defined authority. Its function is to direct human affairs according to accepted rules within the given structure of relationships, and to guarantee the provision of goods and services deemed essential for public welfare.

The judiciary consists of a hierarchy of courts which are convened and presided over by state officials (judges or magistrates), and which also rely exclusively on the principle of centralized, delegated, defined, and therefore limited authority to enforce the law and impose the punishments which it prescribes. The judiciary has a specific field of competence: it has no warrant to take action against all types of socially unacceptable behaviour. For instance, bad manners at a party come solely within the province of diffuse social penalization.

Especially in the administrative and judicial fields, the state rests on one concept: that of the citizen-isolate, the person who, by acknowledging his obligations to the state, to which he surrenders his title to use force in return for its protection, is automatically guaranteed rights and privileges equal to those accorded all other persons similarly accepting the state's authority. The essential principle is equality before the law: one law for all. The individual's rights and privileges should not be enhanced by his social status or his personal relationships with other members of society—especially those in political or official positions—which are deemed irrelevant. Each citizen-isolate should be indistinguishable and transposable, as it were, and the recognition of moral obligation universal. As in his rights before the law, the individual should have value to others purely as a human being. In law, the emphasis should be on the correct rule of behaviour as an end in itself, irrespective of social and political consequences. The ideal is abstract, impartial justice. *Fiat justitia, ruat coelum.*

As already suggested, New Guinea societies are based on principles in manifest contrast to those described above. In the first place, they cannot be regarded as having any bias toward secularism. Indeed, the concept of secularism does not arise because the people do not distinguish between the supernatural and natural but tend to confine all existence to a single physical realm. Gods and spirits are not seen as remote: they live on the earth near human settlements and have dealings with human beings. They are an integral part of socio-economic and political life: no major enterprise can succeed unless ritual is performed in their honour; and, as will be seen, they can be important in social control.

In the second place, these societies are generalized rather than compartmentalized. Unlike Western society, they can be analysed only as totalities and not into theoretically separate systems with specialized functions: economic, religious or political. Exactly the same groups or persons in specific relationships to each other carry out all economic, religious and political actions. Hence, what we designate as political action, instead of being the prerogative of a separate organization like the state, is merely one set of functions of the total, generalized social order. Moreover, it is impossible to classify many actions specifically as either economic, religious or political, as they belong equally to all three categories at the same time.

I now discuss two aspects of New Guinea societies in some detail: first, their structural forms and the recent debate about the principles on which these rest; and, second, the processes of social control, the functional equivalents of the Western state.

Structural Forms in Papua and New Guinea: The Problems of a Typology

The broad structure of New Guinea societies, also, is determined by the dominant features of their economic systems: relative lack of specialization and expansion, and relative stasis. Because of the lack of specialization there can be no occupational groups and society has to be organized primarily on those principles which Westerners are ceasing to regard as important: kinship, marriage and descent. A traditional society consists of a number of local groups, all of whose members perform virtually the same tasks. Most inhabitants of any one local group are linked to each other, and all of them are linked to a number of other people in different local groups, by kinship, descent or affinal ties. Yet by no means everybody in the society at large is connected in this way. There are always some persons—in his own settlement and particularly in settlements other than his own—with whom a man acknowledges no relationships of any kind and has few, if any, intimate dealings. There is an entire absence of centralized authority to give the total society political cohesion but rather strong emphasis on social equality. It is unusual to distinguish between kinsmen on the basis of hereditary rank and, although the economic systems of a few groups such as the Mae-Enga (Meggitt 1965a) and Tolai (T. S. Epstein 1968 and Salisbury 1970) may be said to provide examples of rudimentary capitalism, they are not so developed as to promote real stratification by wealth.

These general principles are expressed through a number of different structural forms which anthropologists have designated among the two million inhabitants and 700 language groups of the territory. The conventional method of classifying societies has been to refer to their dominant patterns of descent (cf. Wagner 1967: xxiii) and what are usually called the widest political groups (such as tribes or district groups), which combine for war and settle disputes between their members by means of negotiation rather than bloodshed (cf. Brown in this volume; Reay 1959; Hogbin 1963: 31-7; and Lawrence 1967 and 1969). The initial division is between systems with a patrilineal emphasis, which are found mainly but not exclusively on the mainland, and those with a matrilineal emphasis, which are found mainly but not exclusively in the islands. Beyond this, using the method I have outlined, and allowing for constant ethnographic revision and inevitable terminological variations, it is possible to tabulate some eleven general types of society.[2]

These are:

1. Patrilineage societies: West New Britain, Sio and Menyamya.
2. Matrilineage societies: Huon Gulf (Busama).
3. Patriclan societies: mainland coast and hinterland (Yam and Maring of Madang District).
4. Matriclan societies: islands off mainland (Trobriands), and parts of Bismarck Archipelago and Australian Solomon Islands (Bougainville).
5. Tribal or district group societies:[3] where a number of patriclans, without claiming a further common ancestor, form a named, war-making, political group, and the whole society consists of a number of such groups—south central Papua (Motu), north-eastern Papua (Orokaiva), Markham Valley (Adzera [Ngarawapum]), and Eastern Highlands (Siane, Gururumba, Bena Bena, Gahuku Gama, and Kainantu peoples). [N.B. Siane combine tribes with phratries.]
6. Patriphratry societies: where a number of patriclans, claiming a further common patrilineal ancestor, form a named patriphratry, which may or may not be a war-making group, and the whole society consists of a number of such groups—Western Highlands (Kuma and Mae-Enga[4]) and Eastern Highlands (Tairora, Daribi, South Fore, Manga, and Chimbu). [N.B. Chimbu combine phratries with tribes.]
7. Matriphratry societies: where a number of matriclans, claiming a further common matrilineal ancestress, form a named matriphratry, which may or may not be a war-making group, and the whole society consists of a number of such groups—New Britain (Lakalai).
8. Patrimoiety societies: in which all the patriclans in a society are divided equally between two halves or moieties, representatives of which are found in all local villages—Sepik region (Iatmül and northern Abelam).
9. Matrimoiety societies: in which all the matriclans in a society are divided equally between two halves or moieties, representatives of which are found in all local villages—New Britain (Tolai) and New Ireland (Lesu).
10. Double unilineal descent societies: in which every man and woman claims simultaneous membership in a patrilineal and matrilineal descent group—Rai Coast (Ngaing) and Wogeo.[5]
11. Cognatic societies: in which every man and woman claims simultaneous membership in a number of descent groups, through both males and females on both father's and mother's side—Western Highlands (Telefolmin), Southern Highlands (Huli), north-east Papua (Kunimaipa of Tapini),[6] Madang District (Garia of Bagasin

Area), Fergusson Island (Molima), Goodenough Island (Bwai-doga), and British Solomon Islands Protectorate (To'ambaita of Malaita and Choiseulese).

It is essential to introduce at once an additional factor of especial importance in unilineal societies. Because of the rule of exogamy, the main descent groups are linked by ties of kinship and affinity: lineage to lineage, and clan to clan, within village, tribe or district group, or phratry. Villages, and even tribes or district groups and phratries, can be linked through intermarriage. Hence, if it could be expressed in a suitable diagram, a more satisfactory model for these societies would be a congeries of descent and/or political groups knit together by a series of ego-centred kinship and affinal networks. This feature is more pronounced in cognatic societies.

This broad typology has proved satisfactory in the past as an introduction to New Guinea's peoples and problems. It stresses the differences not only between Western and New Guinea society but also between New Guinea societies themselves. Yet, during the last decade, it has been criticized on at least four grounds: the arbitrariness of emphasizing descent as a basic taxonomic criterion; the assumption that uniliny is a *de facto* reality rather than an ideal to which reality only approximates to a greater or lesser degree; the assumption that the different structural forms listed are discrete rather than stages along a continuum; and the lumping together of all cognatic societies. I review each of these criticisms and suggest how they modify our general conception of New Guinea societies.

The first criticism need only be mentioned. Wagner (1967: xixff.), using the analogy of racial classification, has argued that it is unrealistic to stress descent as the primary criterion for a structural typology without including other kinds of relationships. Yet he agrees with Schneider (1965: 78) in dismissing 'total system models', which try to include all possible structural features, as unmanageable, certainly until the computer can express them in more intelligible terms. For the time being, descent is our most convenient taxonomic criterion and we must continue to use it, even if as a stopgap label.

The second criticism is more stringent: the distrust of unilineal descent itself as a valid principle for classifying New Guinea societies. Most of the controversy has been conducted in the ethnographic literature of the Highlands but, *mutatis mutandis,* the arguments apply equally to other areas. The most quoted paper on the subject was written nearly a decade ago by Barnes (1962), who stated roundly that, in the Central Highlands, the African model of rigid agnation—the dogma of agnatic descent as the only principle of recruitment to local groups—which so far had been the lodestar of field research, was untenable. It was based on a misinterpretation of the work of Africanists and ignored reality.

Highlands societies, Barnes argued, did not consist of a hierarchy of pure patrilineal segments (lineages, subclans, clans and so forth), all political relationships being expressed in terms of the balance between them. A significant percentage of the members of local groups generally described as agnatic were not agnates at all but either affines (husbands of female agnates), non-agnatic cognates (children of female agnates living with their mothers' groups after their fathers' deaths), or agnatic descendants of non-agnatic cognates. In many cases, non-agnatic residents enjoyed rights virtually equal to those of full agnates, even aspiring to leadership.

This obviously affected local organization. Although there was no dogma of agnatic descent, most sons did choose to live with their fathers. Yet, because the lines of descent were punctuated so often with cognatic 'ring-ins', Barnes called this 'cumulative patrifiliation' rather than true patriliny. Moreover, many people preferred to live with their mothers' or other cognatically related groups. This could lead to either permanent residence with one group or temporary residence with a number of groups over a period of years, the individual enjoying considerable freedom in the selection of a settlement. Hence local populations in most Highlands societies (even setting aside the cognatic Huli), in spite of their claims to be entirely patrilineal, had only hard cores of agnates with clusters of cognates and affines.

Since 1962 there has been an increasing volume of literature on this theme. For the Highlands, de Lepervanche (1967-68) has demonstrated the general relevance of Barnes's argument and in this volume many authors—Reay, Watson, Langness, Glasse and Lindenbaum, Lowman-Vayda, Brown, and Berndt—specifically describe the same process, to a greater or lesser extent, among the Kuma, Tairora, Bena Bena, South Fore, Maring, Chimbu and Kainantu peoples respectively. In other publications, Ryan (1969: 160-1) and Wagner (1967) provide comparable evidence for the Mendi and Daribi.

There is one apparent exception: the Mae-Enga of the Western Highlands. In his other works (especially 1965a), Meggitt has described this society in uncompromisingly agnatic terms, using as his model Fortes's analysis of the Tallensi of Ghana (Fortes 1945). In his paper in this volume, although he tempers his position in some respects, he concedes very little to criticism levelled at his interpretation by McArthur (1967), Barnes (1967-68), and de Lepervanche (1967-68), all of whom claim that the Mae-Enga fit the African agnatic model far less neatly than he argues. The pure line of patrilineal descent is often broken by cognatic accretion, although patrilineal descendants of cognatic immigrants are agnaticized and finally treated as full agnates.

Yet, although the Mae-Enga may fall short of ideal patriliny, there is evidence that they are closer to it than the other Highlands societies cited. One index has been mentioned above: the granting of full agnatic status to the patrilineal descendants of cognatic immigrants stresses how much the people value the appearance of a uniform pattern of descent in their local groups. Another index is land: its availability and the nature of the titles to it. Meggitt (1965a) has argued a case in keeping with the theme of his paper presented here: that the Mae-Enga stress agnatic membership in local groups (localized clans or clan-parishes) whenever their land resources are short, and that the difficulty of acquiring land rights else-where restricts emigration from clan territory. The work of other Highlands eth-nographers is consistent with this position. For instance, in this book, Reay, and Glasse and Lindenbaum, and, in his monograph (1967), Wagner show that the Kuma, South Fore and Daribi, having sufficient land resources, have no marked preference for rigid agnation. Yet there is a further point which neither Meggitt nor his critics seem to have examined in full: the nature of cultivation rights, of which there are two kinds in New Guinea, individual and communal. It may be significant that the Mae-Enga jealously claim individual cultivation rights.

In future research, the different roles of individual and group land titles should receive more careful attention. The data now available are inadequate to solve the problem under discussion. Yet it could be argued that *individually held* and patrilineally inherited cultivation rights, as among the Mae-Enga, are not only an index of the importance people attach to agnation or cumulative patrifiliation as a principle—even if at times they modify it by adopting outsiders—but also a powerful weapon for maximizing agnatic reality by keeping unwanted non-agnates out of the group. Where land is short, the individual is more concerned with guard-ing his holdings than augmenting group membership. Hence, if he has them, he can use agnatically inherited and clearly defined *individual* titles as an argument to turn away people he regards as intruders. By the same token, the other Highlands groups mentioned in this context—the Kuma, South Fore and Daribi, who, as noted, have abundant land—appear to regard the size and power of local groups as more important than the protection of holdings, and either not to have or not to stress individual cultivation rights. In this situation, immigrants can easily be intro-duced to a group and allowed to plant on its communally held land: as there is no shortage and nobody's individual rights are being infringed, nobody has strong grounds for objection.[7]

As stated, the arguments of Barnes and the Highlands ethnographers are relevant to theoretically unilineal peoples in other parts of Papua and New Guinea. In this symposium, Kaberry, and Chowning and Goodenough show that patriliny for the northern Abelam and matriliny for the Lakalai have limited meaning. Northern Abelam patriclans are adulterated by non-agnatic cognates, including war refugees. The Lakalai have matriclans but tend to live patrivirilocally. Other scholars provide evidence of comparable situations among the Ngarawapum of the Markham Valley (Read 1950),[8] the Siuai of Bougainville (Oliver 1955), and Wogeo (Hogbin and Lawrence 1967 and Hogbin 1970). My own account of the Ngaing of the Rai Coast (Lawrence 1965) must eventually be modified to incor-porate these factors. The most interesting case is given by Groves (1963): the Western Motu, whose seven villages constitute a tribe internally subdivided into *iduhu,* which in turn may be described as either agnatic or cognatic groups ac-cording to context. For the manufacture of seine nets and fishing, they are strictly patrilineal groups: rights in both these fields are vested in, and restricted to, full agnates or those non-agnatic cognates who seek, and are accepted as having achieved, full agnatic status. But for the exercise of land rights, the *iduhu* becomes a cognatic group. Non-agnatic cognates are free to use *iduhu* land.

As unilineal descent is honoured in the breach sometimes as often as in the observance, we may well ask two questions: first, why, in the societies under discussion, do people still acknowledge and assert it as the primary qualification for group membership, stressing a unilineal ideology and implicitly describing their social systems in unilineal terms? Second, how are we to regard unilineal descent as a taxonomic criterion?

Wagner (1967: 200ff.) and de Lepervanche (1967-68: 184 *et passim*) provide the answer to the first question in their discussions of agnation. In effect, de Lepervanche argues that it is inadequate to typify or describe a society in real, objective, empirical terms without reference to its ideology: 'Ideology and action are not independent of each other. Ideological statements are part of social action.' In other words, a society's statistical pattern is meaningless unless it is viewed against the model which it claims to be but to which it only approximates. Agnation is ideological rectitude: it represents the correct form (' "proper" status within the group'), the ideal to quote and pursue. It makes things right: to fit the agnatic model is to possess a benefit. Hence, many self-styled agnatic groups have mechanisms for obliterating cognatic impurities. They falsify genealogies by turning distant female agnatic into male agnatic forbears, and have kinship terminologies in which the children of male cross-cousins call each other siblings, thereby eventually erasing irregularities of address in the cases of agnatic descendants of immigrant cognates. The law is preserved even when it is broken. The same logic applies equally to uterine descent groups.

This answers also the second question. The concept of unilineal descent is perfectly valid as an *ideal* taxonomic criterion: as when, in this volume, Brown typifies the Chimbu as 'quasi-unilineal', and Glasse and Lindenbaum indicate that the agnatic principle has symbolic importance for group unity among the South Fore, and when Wagner (1967: 70, 148ff., 190ff., and 200ff.) describes the Daribi as 'normatively agnatic', Rappaport (1969: 118) the Maring as 'putatively patrilineal', and Cook (1969: 97) the Manga as 'ideologically patrilineal'. In short, we have no alternative but to classify these societies according to the people's own assertions about their norms of descent, although we must not forget two factors already noted: that the actual invariably falls short of the ideal; and that even normative descent groups do not exist as isolates but always, as stated earlier and Langness makes clear, in association with a series of ego-centred networks, which link them person to person.

The third of the four criticisms of the general typology is now relevant: the tendency to regard it as consisting of societies which are qualitatively discrete rather than stages along a continuum. As the foregoing argument conveys, single unilineal, double unilineal, and cognatic systems are abstractions: in reality, they shade over into one another, each having in suppressed form certain characteristics of the others. Thus the normatively patrilineal Daribi (Wagner 1967: 65 and 69) and matrilineal Busama (Hogbin 1963: 17) recognize tacitly but not formally the principle of double unilineal descent. The Daribi believe that children inherit at birth maternal substance which is continually passed down the matriline.[9] Among the Busama, a man transmits land rights to his sisters' sons but those over movable property to his own sons. Yet the Daribi do not acknowledge uterine, and the Busama do not acknowledge agnatic, descent groups.

In the same way, as recent discussion of recruitment to local groups in the Highlands suggests, both single and double unilineal societies have points in common with cognatic societies. The ego-centred network, which is based essentially on bilateral kinship and affinal ties, is important in all three types of society: as is obvious in this volume and other publications for the Lakalai, Tairora, Bena Bena, Maring, Kainantu peoples, Gururumba (de Lepervanche 1967-68: 165), Manga (Cook 1969: 114), Mae-Enga (Meggitt 1965a), and Busama (Hogbin 1963), who are normatively single unilineal, for the Ngaing (Lawrence 1965) and Wogeo (Hogbin 1939b), who have systems of double unilineal descent, and for the Garia, Telefolmin (Craig 1969), and Huli (Glasse 1968), who are cognatic. Indeed, three Highlands ethnographers have borrowed the term 'security circle', which I coined for the Garia (Lawrence 1955-67): Strathern (1969) for the Siane, originally studied by Salisbury (1962) and, in this volume, Langness for the Bena Bena, and Berndt, with adaptations for a specific political and military situation, for the Kainantu peoples.

The same kind of argument is relevant to the fourth and last criticism of the general typology: that all cognatic societies should not be indiscriminately lumped together (cf. Hogbin 1963). All cognatic societies have certain features in common: the potential recognition of descent in many lines through both males and females together with the series of ego-centred kinship and affinal networks mentioned above. Yet, in Melanesia as a whole, they are by no means identical in structural form. Thus the Telefolmin (Craig 1969: 176ff.), Huli (Glasse 1968), and Molima (Chowning 1962), like the To'ambaita (Hogbin 1939a) and Choiseu-lese (Scheffler 1965) of the British Solomon Islands, emphasize the principle of fixed territoriality: local groups (admittedly with fluctuating membership) tied to specific tracts of land with definable boundaries. The Garia ignore this principle: they have no fixed territorial groups. No area of land is associated exclusively with any settlement. Rights to given strips and blocks are vested in individuals who live in villages or hamlets near the holdings they are currently using, and who therefore tend to be migratory, especially during early adulthood. Again, the Garia and Huli differ from the other peoples listed in that they have elaborate genealogical structures based on multiple descent names, which the individual uses as mnemonics for, and buttresses of, interpersonal kinship ties (cf. Gluckman 1950). Among the Garia, in the absence of fixed local groups, the right to use descent names is particularly important: they place a person in society.

Criticisms of this kind are inevitable after the collection and publication of local ethnographies, which make comparative analysis possible. They have already had some influence on current research, as is indicated by some of the papers in this symposium, and they will have an even greater impact in the near future. As was stated at the outset, the contributors carried out fieldwork at different times from the 1930s to the 1960s, some of us—Kaberry, Burridge, Chowning and Goodenough, Oliver, Berndt and myself—writing our papers during 1955-56 for a publication that did not materialize. The other contributors—Reay, Meggitt, Brown, Watson, Langness, Lowman-Vayda, and Glasse and Lindenbaum—wrote their papers after 1964. Of the first set of authors, Burridge, Oliver and myself were little affected by the issues discussed above and thus made few, if any, major revisions of our work before it appeared in *Anthropological Forum* after 1965. Kaberry, Chowning and Goodenough, and Berndt, however, amended their papers, making it clear that they were aware of the role of cognation in the formation of local groups among the normatively unilineal societies they had studied. Of the second set of authors, all have clearly been influenced by the recent debate, Langness, and Glasse and Lindenbaum making serious contributions to it, and even Meggitt modifying his previous emphasis on patriliny among the Mae-Enga by showing how cognatic and affinal networks become important at times when otherwise rival agnatic groups are prepared to relax and co-operate. Moreover, from now on we should expect younger fieldworkers wanting to make structural studies more precise, to pay the most careful attention to the processes by which local groups come into being. This may lead to greater reliance than in the past on statistical and historical analysis.

Finally, it is clear that we must modify our general view of New Guinea societies to this extent. Any broad classification of the kind I have sketched cannot be regarded as concrete. It must be qualified continually as new taxonomic categories are discovered and old ones revised. Moreover, it cannot represent structural forms perfectly realized but only ideal forms imperfectly simulated by actual examples. As such, it still has the same sort of introductory value suggested earlier. But allowance must be made for overlap between the three main structural types— single unilineal, double unilineal and cognatic—each of which, as we saw, may incorporate elements of the other two. As has been shown in the case of cognatic societies and can be seen in Brown's tabulation of social units in the Highlands, there is much local variation within each type. This emphasizes the essentially flexible nature of New Guinea societies. Whatever their forms, they all rest ultimately on common principles. Because of this, some neighbouring groups with overtly dissimilar structural forms can co-exist and interact with minimal difficulty, as is illustrated in this book by Burridge and Oliver for the Tangu and people of South Bougainville, and elsewhere by Harding (1967) for the peoples of Sio and its hinterland, and by myself (Lawrence 1964-67) for the inhabitants of the southern Madang district.

The Functional Equivalents of the State in Papua and New Guinea

Political action in traditional New Guinea societies is always suited to the various structural forms through which it is expressed. Yet, like these forms, it too can be reduced to common principles which are patently different from those found in Western society. To refer to an earlier comment, it is merely one function of the total, generalized social order, which lacks the essential institutions of the state, especially a graded hierarchy of authority derived from hereditary rank, wealth, or any other qualification, and vested in senior and junior officials. This does not mean, however, that there are no persons with authority for specific ends. Every society has its leaders—in some cases (such as the Trobriand Islands, Motu [Groves 1963], Tolai [Salisbury 1970: 329],[10] and island communities off the north-east mainland coast), petty chiefs or headmen whose positions are hereditary but, in most, Big Men[11] who have won them in egalitarian competition.

Leaders are, in a sense, microcosms of their societies. They are generalized rather than specialized, having to be pre-eminent in not one but many fields: agriculture, warfare, dancing, hunting, and organizing trade, feast-exchanges and initiation. Especially on the seaboard but also to some extent in the Highlands (Lawrence and Meggitt eds 1965: 18-20), as is illustrated by the papers on the Lakalai, northern Abelam, South Bougainville people, Garia and Maring, they have to master the ritual secrets which ensure the support of deities and ghosts in major undertakings, and even become sorcerers. Such men have distinct authority to take action in the fields enumerated and, as Salisbury (1964) and Watson (in this volume) have demonstrated, have at times also assumed very great, even despotic, power. Nevertheless, for two major reasons, collectively they have never constituted an official body like the state.

In the first place, unlike that of a state official, the authority of a Big Man in agriculture, warfare, and so forth is not coincident with the whole society but has a limited geographical range. A Big Man represents only one or two villages and would provoke conflict with his rivals were he to try to operate outside that sphere. In the second place, this kind of authority does not give him any real—at most, only embryonic—legislative, administrative and judicial functions. Because of the tendency to economic stasis rather than expansion and, in consequence, to the regularity of annual events, he cannot have an extensive role as a policy-maker. The range of the decisions he has to make is limited: he is not challenged by a constantly and radically changing situation. Again, he does not administer people on the basis of fixed, defined authority but rather, like a magnet, attracts to himself followers whom he may manipulate to varying degrees described later, but whose lives are regulated primarily by tradition. In the main, popular consensus is the basis of his authority: he sets in motion culturally prescribed activities so important to his followers that their co-operation is automatic. Finally, his authority (as against power and influence) does not spill over into the judicial field. It is difficult to substantiate instances where, like a Western judge or magistrate, he gives binding decisions in disputes. At most, enjoying greater power or influence than others, he can manoeuvre decisions to his own advantage, but even the extent to which he can do this is never constant. The Big Man among the Maring and Garia plays no special part in the settlement of disputes, whereas his counterpart among the Kainantu peoples, South Fore, northern Abelam, Lakalai, Kuma (Reay 1959: 126), Mae-Enga (Meggitt 1965a), Wogeo (Hogbin 1938), Busama (Hogbin 1963), and To'ambaita of Malaita (Hogbin 1939a), is apparently more effective. Yet, even in these cases, he does not act like a judge or magistrate but offers solutions only when he has weighed the socio-political consequences and is confident that he can satisfy all persons interested.

In the absence of any hierarchical organization comparable to the state in New Guinea, we must look for its functional equivalents within the total social order. We may begin by choosing one of two models taken from Fortes and Evans-Pritchard (Fortes and Evans-Pritchard eds 1940: 6-7).[12] First, there are those stateless societies in which political action is seen as a function almost entirely of unilineal descent, and only marginally of cognation and affinity. These are societies with 'the segmentary system of permanent, unilateral descent groups, which we call the lineage system [and which alone] establishes corporate units with political functions'. For them, 'kinship and domestic ties [i.e. cognatic and affinal relationships] have an important role in the lives of individuals, but their relation to the political system is of a secondary order'. Second, there are those stateless societies in which such a distinction cannot be postulated: '. . . very small societies . . . in which even the largest political unit embraces a group of people all of whom are united to one another by ties of kinship, so that political relations are coterminous with kinship relations and the political structure and kinship organization are completely fused' (cf. also Fortes 1970: 118).

For the last twenty years, especially in the Central Highlands, the first of these two models has been prominent in research but, as is implicit in the recent controversy over the reality of uniliny, we are now rejecting it. It is essentially the African model which Barnes and the other authors cited have shown to be inappropriate for normatively unilineal societies, and which is obviously irrelevant for cognatic societies, in New Guinea. We can no longer attribute overriding political significance to unilineal descent and relegate cognatic and affinal ties to a secondary role. To do this is to try to isolate a discrete political system comparable to the Western state, which, as we have seen, is fruitless. The second model—'the kinship polity' (Fortes 1970: 101-21) in which descent and/or local groups, on the one hand, and the cognatic and affinal networks that link them, on the other, have potentially equal importance—is closer to reality not only in cognatic but also in normatively unilineal societies in the territory. As Bohannan (1958: 65) says of the Tiv of West Africa, every intragroup, intergroup and interpersonal relationship has political consequence at some time. Thus, I examine political action within the broad framework of the second model, adapting Smith's (1956) ideas: the processes which validate the social order by proclaiming its legitimacy yet allow flexibility for

political manoeuvre, which maintain the social order by minimizing antisocial behaviour and maximizing social cohesion, and which restore the social order by providing means of settling disputes.

Obviously, popular support is essential for all New Guinea societies but, with
few exceptions, the people do not regard it as a final warrant. Most, if not all, social
systems are legitimized to some extent by religion. It is believed that creative spirit-
beings, either acting independently or incorporated in genealogies as superhuman
founders, gave men laws and customs. Throughout the whole territory, this belief
varies (Lawrence and Meggitt eds 1965: 12-16). Some peoples validate the total
social order in this way. Others do not: knowing no other, they take it for granted,
although they have myths that explain and buttress sensitive or key parts of the
social system—such as relationships that are continually under pressure and can
break down. The contributors to this volume have tended to ignore mythological
validation and concentrate on secular politics. Only Berndt, Kaberry and myself
refer directly to it, among the Kainantu peoples, northern Abelam and Garia,
while Meggitt alludes to it (in a diagram) among the Mae-Enga. Yet we have good
accounts of it in other publications: Meggitt (1965 a and b) for the Mae-Enga,
Valentine (1965) for the Lakalai, Wagner (1967) for the Daribi, Hogbin (1939b)
for the Wogeo, and myself (Lawrence 1964-67 and 1965) for the peoples of the
southern Madang District. Berndt (1962) gives a fuller description for the Kainantu
peoples.

As has been seen, individuals—even Big Men—have limited policy-making
roles because most activities are culturally prescribed. Mythological validation not
only places New Guinea societies within the conceived cosmic order but also reflects
the regular cycle of annual events made inevitable by the subsistence economy and,
by the same token, the consensual ideology of the people. Each society and each of
its major groups or associations (phratry, tribe or district group, clan, and network
or security circle) provides a man from birth to death with a fixed social milieu
controlling most of his behaviour and contacts. The outlook and interests of each
individual and group or association are identical: each has the same beliefs about
the world and the same ambitions, and hence can immediately anticipate other
people's reactions to specific events. In open debates on public issues, the aim is
always to achieve unanimity: to avoid division of opinion and offer a course of
action that wins automatic acceptance because it endorses already held values and
assumptions.

Nevertheless, people need elbowroom or latitude for political manoeuvre.
Even within the limits imposed by a consensual ideology there is still opportunity
for the interplay of personal power, influence and persuasion. People accept the
rules of their society as they stand but, whenever possible, manipulate them to their
own advantage. Thus the Garia, Tairora, Maring, Mae-Enga (Meggitt 1965a),
Mbowamb (Berndt 1964: 196), Daribi (Wagner 1967: 186), Yam (Hannemann
n.d.), and Dani of West New Guinea (O'Brien 1969: 210) deliberately create
affinal ties or exchange partnerships with groups and individuals who will be of

service to them by ensuring access to or even permanent rights over more land, by conferring other economic advantages, by granting protection from sorcery, and by cementing temporary or even steady military alliances. New Guinea ethnography affords many examples of local groups working hard to place their rivals under obligations through prodigal contributions of work and co-operation in important undertakings or through lavish hospitality. Such debts may not be repaid for years, so that the creditors may get continuous interest from their investment. As is illustrated by Meggitt's paper, life can be an unceasing play and counterplay for advantage around an ethic of equivalence.

Although New Guinea societies are strongly egalitarian and most adult males aspire to try their skill, in reality the Big Men are the most prominent in political manoeuvre. Thus, although military action is the culturally prescribed response to deaths in suspicious circumstances, it is the leaders who set attacks in motion, as is well illustrated by Watson's description of Matoto of Tairora. Northern Abelam and Kuma (Reay 1959) Big Men mobilize their followers to produce wealth which they exchange in their own names but for the renown of the clans they represent. Mae-Enga Big Men organize their clansmen to take land from their rivals by pressing trumped-up cases in Administration courts.

Throughout the territory, however, as already suggested, leaders are able to manipulate their followers and hence influence events to different degrees. Probably because of the manpower and wealth at their disposal, Highlands leaders seem to be the most aggressive. Watson, Glasse and Lindenbaum, Berndt (1962) and Salisbury (1964) show how Highlands Big Men on occasions modify, even break, rules to suit themselves. On the seaboard, there is no general pattern. Certainly, the Lakalai respected leaders who were 'men of anger' and, as Lowman-Vayda comments, the Siuai of Bougainville (Oliver 1955) used to have fierce war leaders. But elsewhere the impression is one of greater restraint. For instance, Garia Big Men have to behave with moderation because of the framework of cognatic relationships within which they operate. Because of the fluidity of local organization, they cannot represent stable groups. If they overreach themselves, their followers desert them for more amenable substitutes. With due allowance for structural differences, these factors probably obtain also in other coastal and island communities.

Political manoeuvre, however important, cannot be allowed to disrupt society. The social order must be maintained and, if necessary, restored. Maintenance of the social order entails not only the prevention of wrong actions which would make everyday life impossible, but also the provision of essential goods and services. We must take account of two kinds of wrong actions: first, offences against religion; and, second, offences against human beings, which in turn can be subdivided into wrongs of omission (such as the neglect of clanship, kinship and affinal obligations) and wrongs of commission (positive offences such as theft, rape, homicide and adultery). I deal with the first category only briefly but with the second in some detail.

Offences against religion are not standardized throughout New Guinea, but we may sum them up as: for men, non-observance of taboos and wanton disruption of ritual; and for women, discovery of the secrets of male initiation. Broadly speaking, few of these offences lead to human retaliatory action. It is believed that the deities and spirits of the dead, who instituted and preside over taboos, rituals and ceremonies, will punish the culprit with ill-luck, illness, or even death. There is one main exception: it is claimed that, in the past, women who by chance or design witnessed the secrets of male initiation were immediately killed to prevent them from passing on what they knew. In general, these sanctions appear to be effective, for wrongs in this category are infrequent.

The forces which check the occurrence of wrong actions against human beings and, in the absence of a public service, provide essential goods and services, are those which Nadel (1953) has summarized as self-regulation. The process stems from Malinowski's (1926) rule of reciprocity whereby, in spite of political man-oeuvre for group and personal advantage, gifts or co-operation must always be repaid in kind or in equivalent. Failure to repay will lead the original benefactor to withdraw his favours in future. Purely biological relationships within the kindred are of no significance unless reinforced by what Firth (1951: 27) has called 'cultural content': they are not maintained by any in-built altruism but must be based on mutual self-interest to persist. The parties to a relationship will maintain it only as long as they recognize that each can confer benefits on the other. There is no need to quote instances: New Guinea ethnography generally and the papers in this symposium in particular supply many examples. Yet I should cite one scholar's treatment of the subject: Burridge's analysis of the principle of equivalence both in his paper presented here and in other publications (notably 1960), which is probably the most sophisticated in the literature.

The rule of reciprocity may appear trite to Europeans but it is a genuine restraint in societies which lack cash economies and in which a man cannot buy immunity from direct physical co-operation with money. The only way to buy goods and essential services is to pay for them with counter-goods and counter-services. Co-operation, therefore, is the currency of these societies, so that a man is bound to the system by chains of interdependence. He must conform or, unless there are extraordinary circumstances, perish.

Yet, stated thus, the rule of reciprocity suggests that all social activities are of equal importance and confer equal advantage. This is clearly not so. Some are more important and advantageous than others: agriculture, land tenure and feast-exchanges, which are central themes in socio-economic life. They are what Nadel (1953) has called focal or multivalent activities, in that other activities can take place only if they have been carried out, and in that they have more than one capacity, serving also 'ends or interests other than the one[s] for which [they were] explicitly or primarily designed'. They are so important that the necessity to perform them ensures conformity among a large number of people in many spheres of life. Thus, Kaberry has shown how among the northern Abelam yam cultivation acts as a sanction for marital fidelity: successful cultivation brings great prestige but demands personal continence while yams are maturing in the ground, so that a man's wife is relatively safe from the attentions of his rivals during this period. Again, the *te* and *moka* festivals in the Western Highlands, trading systems throughout the country, and religious ceremonies such as the male cult among the Ngaing (Lawrence 1965) have comparable, if wider, secondary functions. They not only enable goods to move from one area to another and youths to be initiated into manhood but also ensure peace at regular intervals so that people can meet to fulfil their obligations to each other. Finally, in my essay presented here, I have analysed the importance of the pig exchange and the purchase of land rights among the Garia from this point of view.

The foregoing discussion implies three things. First, statements about good behaviour are phrased generally in terms of moral obligation: 'It is good to support your clansmen and kinsmen, distribute pork to them, and help them clear their gardens.' Yet they are really shorthand phrases for considerations of interdependence and mutual self-interest. A sense of moral obligation is not *sui generis*. As explained above, what is valued is not the nominal relationship but the real advantages which it confers. Moreover, to be effective, moral obligation must be internalized and buttressed. It is internalized by the conscious process of socialization or value-indoctrination, which is found in all New Guinea societies: children are taught from an early age to respect kinsmen, other people's property, and religion. It is buttressed by the feeling of shame often induced by public criticism or abuse, when, as soon as a man's offence is known, society reacts by condemning him in terms of its ideal moral code. This is a powerful sanction in small communities from which escape into anonymity is impossible: the culprit is always confronted by people who know him personally and censure his action. The shame induced can lead to either suicide or, more frequently, voluntary exile.

Second, as considerations of personal interdependence are its source, moral obligation is not, as it is theoretically in Western society, universal but is acknowledged only when there are positive social relationships to confer material benefits. Self-regulation does not operate (preventing offences, and ensuring the provision of goods and services) between all members of the society but, from an individual's point of view, only within a specified range of relationships determined by the form of the social structure: in unilineal societies, within his widest political group (tribe or district group, phratry, or clan-parish), and between himself, cognates, affines and trade partners outside it; and, in cognatic societies such as the Garia, between himself and members of his network or security circle. Beyond this range, where individuals and groups—even within the same society—are not linked by any formal or recognized relationships and therefore do not confer benefits on each other, self-regulation does not—cannot—operate. There are no forces to sustain it (cf. Read 1955).

Third, the process of self-regulation, although vital for social control in New Guinea societies, is not a discrete institution within the total social order. It has no separate existence of its own but is merely one facet of social relationships as they function in everyday affairs. The sanctions that it imposes (withdrawal of co-operation and public criticism) are examples of social penalization rather than punishment and, unlike the punishments handed down by Western courts, are not restricted to certain types of offences. All wrong actions come within its province.

It is clear that the process of self-regulation on its own is inadequate to maintain order throughout the whole society. Inevitably, there are loopholes. Some people (like Matoto of Tairora) have a limited sense of interdependence and moral obligation. In other cases, relationships supposed to be buttressed by self-regulation may have fallen into abeyance: considerations of short-term advantage may then tempt one of the parties to break the rules. Finally, as I have emphasized, there are some people within the society between whom the process cannot operate: those who are completely unconnected and belong to different political groups or networks (security circles). This situation can lead to the occurrence of positive offences (wrongs of commission) and necessitates some means of restoring order: personal or group retaliatory action. Although this is the functional equivalent of the Western judiciary or law, there are two strong differences between it and the type of action taken in our courts.

First, in Western society, a man who has been wronged takes his case to a solicitor but, after this initial step, relies very little on self-help, which is from then on minimized. Lawyers take over his case and, if it goes to court, a functionary of the state (a magistrate or judge aided by a jury) determines its conduct and settlement. The plaintiff, having surrendered his right 'to take the law into his own hands' in return for the protection of the state, is bound to accept the decision (subject, of course, to appeals to higher courts). But in New Guinea society, without state, head of state, and centralized and delegated authority, there can be no comparable court machinery for dealing with offences in this way. Thus self-help has to be maximized. The plaintiff must himself initiate and carry through retaliatory action with whatever support he can get from kinsmen, affines and other associates. He may call an assembly at which to air his grievances (as among the Tangu and Garia), or he may resort directly to preventive magic, sorcery, physical violence, homicide, military action, or (in some places) football as a substitute for the older forms of violence which are now outlawed.

Second, the principles controlling the conduct of disputes in the two situations are not the same. In Western society, the principle is centralized, delegated and defined authority. Court decisions and punishments are the prerogative of the state and should be, as stressed, strictly impartial because every citizen has equal rights before the law. Justice should have no strings: it is the nature of the offence that counts—not the status of, or personal relationship between, the disputants, or equivalent socio-political considerations. In cases involving close kinsmen or complete strangers, the culprit should be punished in exactly the same way.

Obviously, this kind of situation does not exist in New Guinea society. Just as the structure of stateless society is based on principles virtually diametrically opposed to those underlying our own, so also is the conduct of disputes governed by factors that Western law theoretically repudiates: the social range of relationships between all those interested—plaintiff, defendant and their respective supporters. Social range is computed initially in terms of the genealogical closeness or distance of kinship, descent and affinal ties, and of membership or non-membership in specific political groups (clan-parish, phratry, and tribe or district group). But it can be affected by other, more practical considerations: the extent to which a man knows and associates with his kinsmen, clansmen, tribesmen, affines, and so forth; the extent to which they are 'true men' willing and able to support him, and number in their ranks Big Men who are powerful warriors and orators, or are nonentities whose support is worthless; and the extent to which they live near him and can assemble in time to help him. Papers by Glasse and Lindenbaum (in this volume), Barnes (1962), Langness (1964), and de Lepervanche (1967-68), and my own work on the Garia (especially Lawrence 1955-67), stress the importance of common residence and economic association for reinforcing and even 'creating' kinship and affinal relationships.

In a word, to use Barnes's (1961) phrase, 'law' is unashamedly 'politically active'. With due allowance for variations in structural form, in most disputes in New Guinea society, the closer the effective relationship between plaintiff and defendant, the fewer people are likely to be involved, the less severe the retaliatory action taken, and hence the easier the settlement. Conversely, the greater the social range of the dispute—the more distant and tenuous the relationship between plaintiff and defendant—the more people are likely to be involved, the more severe the retaliatory action taken, and hence the more difficult the settlement.

These two statements can be illustrated by examining the conduct of disputes in the two distinct social situations previously indicated: those involving closely related or associated persons (in unilineal societies, of the same political group—clan-parish, phratry, tribe or district group—and, in cognatic societies, of the same network or security circle), among whom self-regulation should, but has now failed to, curb wrong action; and those involving unrelated, or only distantly related or associated, persons (of different political groups or networks), between whom self-regulation is not expected to be effective.

In disputes between closely related or associated persons, two factors are relevant. First, plaintiff and defendant should remember that their close tie in the long run represents mutual advantage and should have some sense of moral obligation toward each other. They are of the same political group or network: to cause one another irreparable harm would weaken their position against outsiders. Second, other people likely to be interested in the dispute also belong to this political group or network. Relatively few in number and closely related to both parties, they do not split into two groups, one on each side, but are swayed by the same considerations as described above. If, as sometimes happens, either litigant should lose restraint, they join forces to blanket the dispute and ensure an agreement as soon as they can. Hence, in these disputes, retaliatory action is usually mild and settlement easily reached. Only limited physical violence and mild sorcery should be used, and assemblies and football matches should be orderly. Even occasional cases of homicide at this social range should be settled by payment of compensation (pigs, valuables and food) rather than by further bloodshed.

When the social range is extended and disputes occur between members of different political groups or networks, the situation changes. As plaintiff and defendant are at best only distantly related or tenuously associated, they have no personal sense of moral obligation toward each other and nothing to lose by a breach. They feel free to kill each other. More people are interested now than in the previous case and, initially at least, form two opposing bands, one supporting the plaintiff and the other the defendant: clan-parishes, tribes or district groups, clusters of cognates and affines, and so forth according to the socio-political structure of the society.

This can lead to either limited blood feud or genuine warfare. A limited blood feud depends on one additional factor: the presence and effectiveness of a number of neutral kin. Some persons interested in a dispute may be related to both plaintiff and defendant, and also to some of the supporters of each. Clearly, they have divided loyalties. They have an obvious interest in the limitation and end of the conflict for reasons already given: they do not want either principal, who is their kinsman or associate, to be killed or injured, or their own relationships with members of either supporting group to be endangered. They may restrict battle casualties by avoiding relatives and associates on the other side or refusing to fight at all; or they may urge both sides to make peace either before or after fighting has begun. Their success as neutrals depends on several factors: their size as a group; their personal prestige; and their determination and physical ability to stop the fighting. In the last context, Meggitt (1965a) records that the Mae-Enga sometimes tie up neutral kinsmen to prevent them from warning enemies of an impending attack.

Disputes involving neutral kin are usually settled fairly easily and with limited violence—at most one or two deaths on either side—although certain differences should be noted. For instance, fighting tends to be more cruel when vital economic issues are at stake, as when a group sets out to take its neighbours' land by force. As such instances appear to be relatively infrequent, I reserve them for special comment below. Again, some societies appear to value peace less than others. Thus, Eastern Highlanders accept bloodshed with a measure of indifference, whereas the Garia are always at pains to arrest conflict. Even so—especially if one sets aside land disputes for the time being—for New Guinea as a whole one is left with the impression of a social order periodically disturbed yet by no means irreparably disrupted by hostility. What I have implied for the Garia in this volume probably holds for most other peoples. Major disputes tend to occur within a fairly close geographical range, which is also the area of the most intense interpersonal association and genealogical interrelatedness. Hence neutrals are always available.

This is not to deny that genuine warfare, with widespread killing and destruction of property, occurs when the kinds of restraints described are lacking. In some cases, persons technically neutral are unwilling to take or, as among the Mae-Enga, are physically prevented from taking requisite action. In others, disputes may occur between people who are not only themselves unrelated but also may have no supporters with kinsmen, affines or other associates on both sides. At least five groups —the Orokaiva (Williams 1930), the Gahuku Gama (Read 1955), the Huli (Glasse 1968), the Bena Bena, and the Mae-Enga (see note 13)—distinguish terminologically between warfare proper and the relatively controlled blood feud. Yet in spite of the claims of some informants—nowadays virtually our only source of information on this topic—it is debatable whether even warfare proper is always unrestricted. In most disputes, which involve homicide or adultery rather than serious economic issues such as land, Berndt's (1964) conclusions are probably right. In a most careful analysis of Highlands warfare he has found that, although it is a 'deadly game', it is 'never "total"', an all-or-none affair. For instance, among the Kainantu peoples (Berndt 1962: 252), groups which have driven their enemies away from their homes for reasons other than stealing their land often invite them to return so that the 'game' can continue. Yet more recent reports suggest that, when the end in view is economic—the increase of land holdings—warfare ceases to be a 'game' and becomes vicious. Everything is sacrificed for material gain: whole settlements are razed, their inhabitants annihilated, and otherwise venerated ties of neutrality ignored.[13]

My analysis of the settlement of disputes, and of blood feud and warfare, is derived from evidence from many societies in the territory: in this volume, the northern Abelam, Garia, Tangu, Lakalai, Bena Bena and Kainantu peoples; and, from other sources, the Chimbu (Brown 1964), the Huli (Glasse 1968), the Gahuku Gama (Read 1955), the Mae-Enga (Meggitt 1965a), the Melpa (Strathern and Strathern 1969), the Mendi (Ryan 1969), the Orokaiva (Williams 1930), the Ngarawapum (Read 1950), the Wogeo (Hogbin 1938), the Busama (Hogbin 1963), and the Dani of West New Guinea (O'Brien 1969). Inevitably, a general account can at most only allude to local idiosyncrasies but there is one that should be emphasized. Berndt (1964) makes a distinction between certain Highlands societies which, clearly, is important for the identification and enumeration of neutral kin, and which may apply also in other areas. Among some peoples—the Gahuku Gama, Chimbu, Kuma, Mendi and Huli—affinally linked groups rarely or never go to war: a man rarely or never marries into an enemy group. Strathern and Strathern (1969: 154) would place the Melpa in this category. Among other peoples—the Siane, Mbowamb, Kainantu peoples and Mae-Enga—affinally linked groups do fight one another, although individual affines and cognates avoid each other in battle.

We may now draw the final distinction between Western law and the New Guinea system of social control: the contrasting aims in the settlement of disputes. As mentioned, the aim of Western law is to guarantee or restore the individual and equal rights of the citizen-isolate, with emphasis on the nature of the wrong action and on abstract, impartial justice rather than on the relationship between those in conflict and the socio-political consequences of its disruption. In the New Guinea system, there is no concept of *fiat justitia, ruat coelum,* but a clear recognition that the sky must be kept up.[14] In settling a dispute, the aim is to vindicate the consensual ideology: to restore the social order by patching up relationships that have been damaged or broken. The nature of the wrong action is of secondary importance. What is important is that somehow, for the good of all, plaintiff and defendant must be made to resolve their quarrel. Hence, far from there being abstract, impartial justice, the forces of self-regulation, which Western law regards as irrelevant—even inimical—to court procedures, cannot be divorced from self-help or retaliatory action, which must, therefore, vary with every situation. They are its limiting or controlling principle, determining its nature and severity in accordance with the range of the dispute, and often preventing it from over-straining the social order.

TRADITIONAL POLITICAL SYSTEMS VERSUS MODERN POLITICAL INSTITUTIONS

It has already been remarked that the original charter for this symposium, when it was conceived a decade and a half ago, was that it should concern itself with traditional New Guinea political systems. The papers presented here do not lend themselves easily to the analysis of contact problems. They might seem to have only the most limited value for those who wish to concentrate on the politics of modern development and are tempted to turn at once to the works of political scientists in this field. It would seem reasonable to begin by studying current issues. Such an attitude is dangerous. Far from having been obliterated or changed out of all recognition by the impact of the West during the last century, New Guinea cultures have proved extremely durable and still have an influential role in contemporary politics. In particular, they shape the attitudes of New Guineans toward the Western political institutions recently introduced by the Administration—attitudes that untrained Europeans can describe but cannot understand until they have studied the elements of the traditional background. Hence, the symposium is important from this point of view: it provides an insight into New Guinea political values and processes in the emerging protonational situation.

As the papers themselves present so little material on contact issues, I have limited myself to a single problem that is crucially important for current politics: the effects of superimposing a centralized state structure on the stateless societies of Papua and New Guinea, or the interaction—often contradiction—between these two kinds of political system. I present the argument as I have done throughout. First, I outline the form of the new state structure: the legislative, administrative and judicial institutions of which it consists. Second, I suggest how traditional New Guinea political attitudes and processes may be obstacles to the immediate assimilation of the new institutions, especially with respect to the legitimacy and constitution of democratic legislatures, and the law.

New Guinea societies began to be incorporated within the new colonial state soon after 1884, the date of European annexation, but were themselves little changed during the next sixty years. Significant political change began only after the Second World War, when the country was properly explored and brought under control. For our present purposes it is most convenient to divide contact history into two periods: that from 1884 until 1945; and that since 1945.

After 1884, the British-Australian Administration in Papua and the German Administration in New Guinea had to establish themselves on two fronts. They had to create the major institutions of government and then make them effective throughout the country. Although in Papua there was early on a rudimentary Legislative Council, the main emphasis in both colonies was on administration: the creation of public service departments to deal with the most pressing problems—such as native affairs, health, land and agriculture—and of a judiciary; and the extension of direct rule to the villages. The people were allowed—indeed, were at that time able to carry out—only minimal duties within the new hierarchical structure. The Administrations appointed village headmen: village constables in Papua, and luluais, tultuls and medical tultuls in North-East (ex-German) New Guinea, whose functions were primarily executive but occasionally judicial. Taking orders from European officers, they were responsible for supervising work on roads and in the villages, and for guarding the health of their people. In North-East New Guinea, luluais were allowed to settle petty disputes in their villages until 1942. At the same time the Christian missions, although not an official wing of the Administrations, became most influential. They divided the country into local congregations and sent trained native helpers to the villages: catechists, evangelists and teachers, who, unlike village officials, usually came from areas far distant from those in which they worked.

Since 1945 the two territories have been under a joint Administration which, as part of the policy leading toward self-determination, has expanded and developed the legislative, administrative and judicial structure of the state. It has instituted local government councils and the House of Assembly, and has begun to indigenize the public service and judiciary. Above all, it has encouraged the people to participate in the government of their country, especially in the legislative field.

Local government councils have now replaced direct rule through village headmen in most of the country, and operate in the same way as their prototypes in Australia. The Administration proclaims council areas, which may include few or many linguistic groups depending on their size. Each large village or group of two or three small villages becomes a ward and returns a councillor. The council elects a president, vice-president and various committees, and employs its own clerk or secretary. It levies taxes and sponsors development projects within its area: schools, medical aid posts, roads, bridges and even commercial undertakings. The first elections for the House of Assembly, the proto-national parliament in Port Moresby, were held in 1964 and the second in 1968. The present composition of the House is as follows. There are ninety-four seats, of which ten are official (reserved for representatives or heads of departments), fifteen are regional (for which any inhabitant of the country with the local Junior Standard in education can nominate), and sixty-nine open to any inhabitant of the country regardless of educational attainments. In the public service, indigenes hold positions as medical officers, patrol officers, teachers, clerks, and recently, district officers. The Administration has created a hierarchy of courts from the Supreme Court to those at a district and sub-district level. Some indigenes have been appointed as magistrates.

There is no space here to discuss in detail the difficulties faced by the appointed village headmen in coming to terms with the colonial order. Yet, although their role was inadequate for the demands of modern government, they must not be dismissed as irrelevant to modern political enquiry. Their problems were in embryo exactly the same as those of their more sophisticated successors, to which they are therefore a useful introduction. Especially in the Central Highlands, where established Big Men were often appointed, there were examples of successful local officials. Yet, in general, the system was never a success. The principles underlying the old and new types of leadership were clearly incompatible. The old style was legitimized by religion and endorsed by a consensual ideology, and was frankly political. As we saw, Big Men could harness the power of gods and spirits, set in motion activities that the people regarded as essential, and manipulated their followers by playing on ties of kinship and affinity. Village officials were at an immediate disadvantage. Their position was entirely secular, for the Administration gave them no religious powers to legitimize their positions. They imposed tasks that the villagers disliked and did not regard as essential. They were expected to act as specialized, impartial officials on the basis of fixed authority in a generalized, kinship-oriented society. It was hard for them to take strong action against kinsmen and affines with whom they were linked in a network of reciprocal obligations but who refused to work on roads or village improvements. Although, as Burridge remarks, they were thereby restrained from tyranny, in settling disputes they were notorious for giving decisions in favour of those most closely and advantageously related to them. It is easy to understand why, in many places, they were overshadowed by the native helpers sent to the villages by the missions. These men were not handicapped in the ways described. Their positions were legitimized by a new and powerful religion thought to be the secret of European wealth (cargo), so that the activities they initiated (especially conversion and church worship) won immediate approval as the presumed means of improving the people's economic position. Again, working away from home, they were not restrained by kinship ties from behaving aggressively toward those in the congregation who disobeyed them (Lawrence 1964-67: 81-5).

These problems reappear, admittedly in a more complex form, in the people's reactions to the major institutions of the state, of which they have become increasingly aware during the last two decades. (I am not concerned here, of course, with the educated élite but with the majority of the people still living in the villages.) As suggested, these problems refer especially to the legitimacy and constitution of the democratic legislatures, and to the law.

Many villagers probably find great difficulty in granting legitimacy to local government councils and the House of Assembly, and tend to regard them merely as expressions of the Europeans' power to coerce. Clearly, as in the case of the former appointed headmen, they do not understand the principles on which these bodies rest. Traditionally, as we saw, they have never distinguished between the realms of the natural and supernatural but conceived all events as taking place in a purely physical environment ordained by creative spirit-beings in permanent reciprocal relationships with men. They cannot readily place the councils and House of Assembly in such a cosmic framework, and they search for a stronger than secular charter in keeping with their customary world-view—a charter of the kind that Mr Paliau Maloat, M.H.A. for Manus Open Electorate, was able to provide for his followers when he started his movement in November 1946. He told some 8,000 people that he was opening the meeting in keeping with 'God's instructions'. They should bow their heads and think on God in Heaven, who had made the whole universe (Maloat 1970: 148-9). I have described elsewhere (Lawrence 1964-67: 270) how the people of Astrolabe Bay in 1956 looked askance at the councils then being introduced, until the Lutheran Mission assured them that these bodies derived their authority ultimately from God, who had merely delegated it to the Queen and her Administration. At the national level, Dr Ilomo Batton, in a recent publication (1966-67: 75) in which he advocated renaming the joint territory Paradisia, also justified his choice by referring to God's creation of the world. I should stress that I am not alone in recognizing this problem. Mr A. C. Voutas, M.H.A. for Morobe Regional Electorate, who gained an intimate knowledge of his constituents when he campaigned among them on foot in 1966 and 1968 (Harding and Lawrence n.d.), has discussed with me the difficulty of winning popular endorsement for any national constitution. He did not dismiss my comment on the possible use of a religious sanction as mere 'academic theory', although we both recognized the risks involved in such a course. This need for a religious charter helps to account for continuing adherence to cargoism, which, as in the case of the mission helpers during the period of direct rule, provides explanations of, and offers solutions for, the current situation closely adapted to traditional socio-political values and epistemological assumptions (Harding and Lawrence n.d.).

The structure and procedures of the councils and House of Assembly also pose problems for ordinary people. Structurally, these bodies are specialized rather than generalized and the procedures we should associate with them tend to repudiate traditional consensual ideologies.This is best examined in the context of each type of legislature in turn.

In his own ward, the local government councillor faces the same dilemma as his predecessor, the village official. He, too, is meant to be a specialized, impartial representative of a generalized community organized on the basis of kinship. His election to office is often the result of local consensus: it is generally agreed beforehand that he is the most suitable person for office. He must always conduct himself, therefore, in such a way as, on the one hand, to justify this consensus and, on the other, to satisfy kinship obligations. His success in this difficult role may be influenced by the structure of his own society. Thus, in small, flexible societies like the Garia, his problem may be to hold the inhabitants of his ward together. Should he pursue an unpopular policy or antagonize his kin, people will desert him—as they deserted their Big Men and luluais in the past—for a councillor more to their liking.

In larger societies, as in the Central Highlands and New Britain, where council areas consist of only one or very few language groups, this problem may be replaced by that of local sectionalism. The suppression of warfare rarely leads to the loss of old friendships and antagonisms, which may continue to influence current affairs. The councillor can command the consensus of his ward only as long as he supports its traditional position. As a result, council meetings may become microcosms of traditional politics and fail to promote the people's interests in the modern situation. Voting may follow the inherited pattern of alliances and hostilities, and so prevent adjacent groups from co-operating to develop their land for cash crops. In this symposium, Reay gives an intricate example of this kind of sectional politics among the Kuma. Other publications indicate a similar picture for Bena Bena (Langness 1963: 151-70), Bundi (Harding and Lawrence n.d.), and the Tolai (Mann 1959).

The House of Assembly poses similar problems but on a wider scale. As national electorates are much bigger than council wards, the potential M.H.A. is less concerned than a councillor with local issues, which do not win him many votes, although they are important to him in one respect. He must project his image as a good villager, kinsman, husband and father if he is to impress his constituents. Beyond this, he has to overcome either of two difficulties. The first is again local sectionalism, which can be important in those electorates consisting of relatively few linguistic groups. The successful candidate must demonstrate that he represents the people as a whole and not merely a segment, as was apparent in the 1964 elections. At least three Europeans defeated indigenous rivals because they could convince the voters that they would not be partisan (cf. Reay 1964). The second difficulty arises especially in seaboard electorates which consist of many diminutive linguistic groups, in which traditional socio-political systems themselves have therefore only narrow relevance, but in which religion and cargo cult dominate popular reactions to current events (Lawrence and Meggitt eds 1965: 18-25). In this situation, the successful candidate has to win acceptance and votes in places where he is completely unknown. The danger is that, even if he scrupulously avoids presenting himself in this light, the electors will regard him as a cargoist demagogue. They will vote for him because they believe that he has the secret of acquiring new wealth, either directly from its source or indirectly through his amicable relationships with Europeans. However hard he may have worked on their behalf, he may lose the next election because he cannot satisfy their impossible expectations.

Traditional socio-political values have conditioned also villagers' reactions to the courts of law developed by the Administration and may frustrate the lawyers whose task it is to create a national legal code.[15] For several decades it has been recognized that at least 75 per cent of disputes in New Guinea are still settled by traditional processes of social control. Various explanations have been offered: the inaccessibility of courts, the complexity of the rules of taking evidence, the incomprehensibility of verdicts, and even the sartorial splendour of judges. But the real reason for the villagers' avoidance of European courts is probably once again their inability to understand the principle of centralized authority and abstract, impartial justice with its emphasis on standardized punishments, which are clearly antagonistic to their own system of 'sliding scale justice' (Lawrence 1969: 35). The Western legal system is too inexorable to allow the patching up of broken relationships, which, as has been stressed, is the aim of traditional social control and essential for the stability of traditional society. This is implicit in the Pidgin term *wetkot* ('white court'), which implies the foreignness of the institution, and the common view that to have a man put in gaol is equivalent to homicide.

Hence, villagers will not take cases to Administration courts if they are not prepared to face the socio-political consequences of a conviction. They rarely or never directly charge close relatives or in-laws: even taking to court a kinsman who has committed murder can strain personal relationships. The Chimbu may refer disputes with affines to patrol officers and their missionary, who have no judicial authority, but seldom to a judge or magistrate (Brown 1969: 94). The Kainantu peoples in the 1950s set up their own informal 'courts' in keeping with their own processes of social control to avoid this issue. Again, a Garia plaintiff avoids taking legal action against even an unrelated man if there is any chance that neutral kinsmen will upbraid him for having 'killed' their relative and threaten to turn a blind eye should the defendant resort to sorcery on his return from prison.

Indeed, Garia—like a number of New Guinea peoples—resort to Western law normally only when the litigants are so completely unrelated and geographically separated that there can be no neutral kin to create problems of this kind. By the same token, in other societies, people may seek ways to manipulate Western law to their own personal or group's advantage. Since the ban on warfare, 'fighting through the kiap' has become an established Sepik and Mae-Enga tradition. The Mae-Enga (Meggitt 1965a: 256-7) settle disputes between close kin locally but are less reluctant to take those at greater social range to European courts provided that no important exchange partnerships or other cross-linking relationships get in the way. As already mentioned, land-hungry patriclans work out elaborate—and apparently fraudulent—cases to put before Australian magistrates, whom they manoeuvre into giving judgment in their favour and thereby increasing their holdings.

The immediate conclusion is obvious. Until now, the traditional socio-political systems of Papua and New Guinea have stood their ground against Western society. Especially at the local and regional level, they continue to function and satisfy many of the people's needs. They regulate everyday life and settle most disputes in the villages. They are not without influence in many council areas and even in many national electorates. Finally, any national constitution not legitimized by a charter in keeping with these traditional polities may be shaken off as easily as the cloak of paternalist colonialism.

Nevertheless, we should be naïve to assume that this conservative picture will last indefinitely. There is yet one factor which may force New Guineans to desert their traditional norms—and also the norms that we might suggest to replace them. This is the spectre haunting the twentieth century: the population explosion now being reported from all over the country (cf. Salisbury 1970 and A. L. Epstein 1970). Surplus rural populations are being exported to the towns in search of jobs that do not exist, and in every urban area there is a fringe of mushroom growth shanty towns. Many of the emigrants cannot return home because indigenous systems of land tenure cannot carry the extra burden they represent. To deal with this problem, new urban societies based on what has become an international urban culture will have to grow up. The question will then be whether rural communities can perpetuate traditional cultures in isolation from the cities or whether they too will be forced to accept drastic change. As experience elsewhere suggests that the second alternative is more likely, it is possible that by the turn of the century the New Guinea we have known will have been transformed in ways that we cannot now imagine.

PETER LAWRENCE
University of Sydney

NOTES

1. I have treated this subject for non-anthropological readers elsewhere (Lawrence 1969). See also the paper by Sakora (1970), the first New Guinean to write academically about social control in his own country. His interesting and lucid account endorses and complements a great deal of anthropological analysis. For the sake of convenience, I have written about traditional society in two tenses: in this section, in the present tense because it is in keeping with the papers presented; and in the next section, which deals with contact history, in the past tense. For the sake of brevity, I have used the name 'New Guinea', as both a noun and adjective, to mean 'Papua and New Guinea'.

2. The ethnographic examples included in this rough typology are not intended to be exhaustive. I have included them largely because I have cited them in this Introduction.

3. I use the terms 'tribe' and 'district group' synonymously. Some ethnographers use the term 'tribe' and others the term 'district group' for what appear to be essentially similar socio-political formations.

4. Meggitt (1965a) describes sets of phratries which claim yet further common patrilineal ancestors and which he calls 'great phratries'.

5. Goody (1969: 112) designates these societies as 'patrilineal systems with named complementary uterine groups'. He cites the Wogeo as an example on the basis of Hogbin's earlier published work (Hogbin 1939b) and, for the purposes of this rough typology, I follow him. Yet Hogbin in his later publications (Hogbin and Lawrence 1967, and Hogbin 1970) denies that strict patriliny is a feature of Wogeo society. I refer to this briefly on p. 10, in this section, in my discussion

of the current controversy about New Guinea socio-political systems to which I have referred.

6. The Kunimaipa have been studied by Dr M. McArthur, Department of Anthropology, University of Sydney. As she has yet to publish her material I make no further reference to these people in this Introduction.

7. My argument is tentative and directed primarily to the Mae-Enga. I appreciate that evidence from other societies might force me to modify it were I to present it in a generalized form: as from the matrilineal Tolai, who, although short of land, smuggle cultivation rights to their sons, and the Chimbu, among whom the relationship between land rights, agnation and cognation is most complex (Brookfield and Brown 1963). Moreover, because of my own field experience, I have never assumed that land shortage only promotes uniliny but rather that it endorses a people's particular structural ideology, however it is phrased. Thus, the Garia stress cognation more heavily in the centre of their territory, where population density is greater and land consequently in shorter supply, because a man's recognized means of augmenting his holdings is to purchase cultivation rights from outside his patrilineage (Lawrence 1955-67). Strathern (1970: 156), arguing against Glasse (1968), suggests a similar case for the cognatic Huli. Kelly (1968), reviewing the problem in three Highlands societies, has stated the same general conclusion on the basis of more precise data.

8. H. A. and S. Holzknecht, Department of Anthropology and Sociology, University of Queensland, have reported a similar, but more pronounced, trend among the Amari, like the Ngarawapum, an Adzera-speaking group in the Markham Valley. (Personal communication.)

9. Cf. Goody (1969: 108) on the Tallensi of Ghana, a dominantly patrilineal people.

10. The Tolai appear to use both principles. Some clan leaders inherit their positions, although other Big Men win theirs by their own powers (Salisbury 1970: 329). R. M. McSwain, Department of Anthropology and Sociology, University of Queensland, who drew my attention to this point, has reported the same phenomenon from Karkar. (Personal communication.)

11. From now on, I use the terms 'leader' and 'Big Man' synonymously for both those with ascribed and those with achieved positions. In this general account, any distinction would be irrelevant.

12. For the sake of convenience, I have reversed the order in which Fortes and Evans-Pritchard (1940: 6-7) presented these two models.

13. For further comments on traditional warfare in the Kainantu area, see Berndt (1962: 240 and 412-13 *passim*). Professor M. J. Meggitt has kindly allowed me to quote the following passage from his article ' "Pigs are our hearts!": The Te Exchange Cycle among the Mae-Enga of New Guinea', included in a symposium on Highlands exchange systems which is being edited by Dr A. Strathern. It endorses my comments on the nature of warfare for strictly economic ends.

> The Mae distinguish between 'trivial' and 'serious' warfare. The former, although it involved the use of bows and spears, was the kind of skirmishing at a distance common throughout the highlands and did not occasion over many deaths. Usually it stemmed from minor quarrels and was confined to fraternal clans, who ideally were not permanent enemies. On the other hand, serious fighting, which was also frequent, generally arose out of disputes over land between clans of different phratries, and it was total warfare. The aim in such carefully planned invasions of coveted territory was to destroy the occupying group so that it could never reform and recover its land.

The invaders attempted to ensure complete victory by attacking at night with superior numbers, to which end they might induce another clan to join them with a promise of a share of the spoils. They burned houses (as many as 20 to 30 at a time) in order to incinerate the occupants, and those who tried to flee, whether men, women, or children, were mercilessly cut down with axes. Should the intended victims be forewarned of the attack, they in turn set ambushes and strived to kill as many of the invaders as possible. Taking both kinds of warfare into account, the resulting death-rate was probably relatively high for Highlands societies. Genealogies collected from the Mae suggest that, before about 1946-47, as many as 20 per cent of men died in battle or subsequently from the effects of their wounds. A surprising number of them were young (presumably militarily inexperienced) men, either bachelors or married men who had not yet reproduced.

14. I am indebted for this comment to Professor E. K. Braybrooke, Law School, University of Western Australia, with whom I was once privileged to give a joint course on this subject.

15. See also Lawrence (1969).

REFERENCES CITED

BARNES, J. A. (1961): Law as Politically Active: An Anthropological View. In Studies in the Sociology of Law (G. Sawer, ed.). Canberra: Australian National University mimeographed.
BARNES, J. A. (1962): African Models in the New Guinea Highlands. *Man,* Vol. 62: 5-9.
BARNES, J. A. (1967-68): Agnation among the Enga: A Review Article of *The Lineage System of the Mae-Enga of New Guinea* by M. J. Meggitt (q.v.). *Oceania,* Vol. XXXVIII, No. 1: 33-43.
BATESON, G. (1936): *Naven.* Cambridge: Cambridge University Press.
BATTON, I. (1966-67): Letter to the Community Leaders: What National Name and Why? *Journal of the Papua and New Guinea Society,* Vol. 1.
BERNDT, R. M. (1952-53): A Cargo Movement in the Eastern Central Highlands. *Oceania,* Vol. XXIII, No. 1: 40-65; No. 2: 137-158; No. 3: 202-234.
BERNDT, R. M. (1962): *Excess and Restraint.* Chicago: Chicago University Press.
BERNDT, R. M. (1964): Warfare in the New Guinea Highlands. *American Anthropologist* (Special Publication on New Guinea Highlands), Vol. 66, No. 4, Part 2: 183-203.
BOHANNAN, L. (1958): Political Aspects of Tiv Social Organization. In *Tribes without Rulers* (J. Middleton and D. Tait eds). London: Routledge and Kegan Paul.
BROOKFIELD, H. C. and P. BROWN (1963): *Struggle for Land.* Melbourne: Oxford University Press.
BROWN, P. (1964): Enemies and Affines. *Ethnology,* Vol. 3, No. 1: 335-356.
BROWN, P. (1969): Marriage in Chimbu. In R. M. Glasse and M. J. Meggitt eds (1969).
BURRIDGE, K. O. L. (1960): *Mambu.* London: Methuen.
CHOWNING, A. (1962): Cognatic Kin Groups among the Molima of Fergusson Is. *Ethnology,* Vol. 1, No. 1: 92-101.
COOK, E. A. (1969): Marriage among the Manga. In R. M. Glasse and M. J. Meggitt eds (1969).
CRAIG, R. (1969): Marriage among the Telefolmin. In R. M. Glasse and M. J. Meggitt eds (1969).
EPSTEIN, A. L. (1970): Autonomy and Identity: Aspects of Political Development on the Gazelle Peninsula. *Anthropological Forum,* Vol. II, No. 4: 427-443.
EPSTEIN, T. S. (1968): *Capitalism, Primitive and Modern.* Canberra: Australian National University Press.
FIRTH, R. (1951): *The Elements of Social Organization.* London: Watts.
FORTES, M. (1945): *The Dynamics of Clanship among the Tallensi.* London: Oxford University Press.
FORTES, M. (1970): *Kinship and the Social Order.* London: Routledge and Kegan Paul.
FORTES, M. and E. E. EVANS-PRITCHARD, eds (1940): *African Political Systems.* London: Oxford University Press.
FORTUNE, R. F. (1947a): The Rules of Relationship Behaviour in one Variety of Primitive Warfare. *Man,* Vol. 47: 108-110.
FORTUNE, R. F. (1947b): Law and Force in Papuan Societies. *American Anthropologist,* Vol. 49, No. 2: 244-259.

GLASSE, R. M. (1968): *Huli of Papua: A Cognatic Descent System*. Paris: Mouton.
GLASSE, R. M. and M. J. MEGGITT, eds (1969): *Pigs, Pearlshells, and Women*. New York: Prentice Hall Paperback.
GLUCKMAN, M. (1950): Kinship and Marriage among the Lozi of Northern Rhodesia and the Zulu of Natal. In *African Systems of Kinship and Marriage* (A. R. Radcliffe-Brown and C. D. Forde, eds). London: Oxford University Press.
GOODENOUGH, W. H. (1952): Ethnological Reconnaissance in New Guinea. *Pennsylvania University Museum Bulletin*, Philadelphia, Vol. 17: 4-37.
GOODY, J. (1969): *Comparative Studies in Kinship*. London: Routledge and Kegan Paul.
GROVES, M. (1963): Western Motu Descent Groups. *Ethnology*, Vol. 2, No. 1: 15-30.
HANNEMANN, E. F. (n.d.): Village Life and Social Change in Madang Society. Mimeographed.
HARDING, T. G. (1967): *Voyagers of the Vitiaz Strait*. Seattle: University of Washington Press.
HARDING, T. G. and P. LAWRENCE (n.d.): Cash Crops or Cargo? In *Papua and New Guinea 1968: The Politics of Dependence* (A. L. Epstein, R. S. Parker and M. O. Reay, eds). Canberra: Australian National University Press.
HOGBIN, H. I. (1938): Social Reaction to Crime: Law and Morals in the Schouten Islands, New Guinea. *Journal of the Royal Anthropological Institute*, Vol. 68: 223-262.
HOGBIN, H. I. (1939a): *Experiments in Civilization*. London: Routledge and Kegan Paul.
HOGBIN, H. I. (1939b): Native Land Tenure in New Guinea. *Oceania*, Vol. X, No. 2: 113-65. Reprinted in H. I. Hogbin and P. Lawrence (1967).
HOGBIN, H. I. (1963): *Kinship and Marriage in a New Guinea Village*. London: Athlone Press.
HOGBIN, H. I. (1970): *The Island of Menstruating Men*. Scranton, U.S.A.: Chandler.
HOGBIN, H. I. and P. LAWRENCE (1967): *Studies in New Guinea Land Tenure*. Sydney: Sydney University Press.
KELLY, R. C. (1968): Demographic Pressure and Descent Group Structure in the New Guinea Highlands. *Oceania*, Vol. XXXIX, No. 1: 36-63.
LANGNESS, L. L. (1963): Notes on the Bena Council, Eastern Highlands. *Oceania*, Vol. XXXIII, No. 3: 151-170.
LANGNESS, L. L. (1964): Some Problems in the Conceptualization of Highlands Social Structures. *American Anthropologist* (Special Publication on New Guinea Highlands), Vol. 66. No. 4, Part 2: 162-182.
LAWRENCE, P. (1955-67): *Land Tenure among the Garia*. Canberra: Australian National University Press. Reprinted in H. I. Hogbin and P. Lawrence (1967).
LAWRENCE, P. (1964-67): *Road Belong Cargo*. London and Melbourne: Manchester and Melbourne University Presses.
LAWRENCE, P. (1965): The Ngaing of the Rai Coast. In P. Lawrence and M. J. Meggitt, eds (1965).
LAWRENCE, P. (1967): Politics and True Knowledge. *New Guinea*, Vol. 2.
LAWRENCE, P. (1969): The State versus Stateless Societies in Papua and New Guinea. In *Fashion of Law in New Guinea* (B. Brown ed.). Sydney: Butterworth.
LAWRENCE, P. and M. J. MEGGITT, eds (1965): *Gods, Ghosts, and Men in Melanesia*. Melbourne: Oxford University Press.
LEACH, E. R. (1954): *Political Systems of Highland Burma*. Cambridge, Mass.: Harvard University Press.
LEPERVANCHE, M. de (1967-68): Descent, Residence, and Leadership in the New Guinea Highlands. *Oceania*, Vol. XXXVIII, No. 2: 135-158; No. 3: 163-189.
McARTHUR, M. (1967): Analysis of the Genealogy of a Mae-Enga Clan. *Oceania*, Vol. XXXVII, No. 4: 281-285.
MALINOWSKI, B. (1915): The Natives of Mailu. *Royal Society of South Australia*, Vol. 39: 494-706.
MALINOWSKI, B. (1926): *Crime and Custom in Savage Society*. London: Routledge and Kegan Paul.
MALOAT, P. (1970): History bilong mi taim mi bon na i kam nap tede. Canberra: Australian National University; and Port Moresby: University of Papua and New Guinea. Mimeographed.
MANN, A. H. (1959): Navuneram Incident, New Britain—Report of Commission of Enquiry. *Commonwealth of Australia, Parliamentary Papers*, 8.
MEGGITT, M. J. (1965a): *The Lineage System of the Mae-Enga of New Guinea*. Edinburgh: Oliver and Boyd.
MEGGITT, M. J. (1965b): The Mae-Enga of the Western Highlands. In P. Lawrence and M. J. Meggitt, eds (1965).
NADEL, S. F. (1951): *The Foundations of Social Anthropology*. London: Cohen and West..
NADEL, S. F. (1953): Social Control and Self-Regulation. *Social Forces*, Vol. 31.

O'BRIEN, D. (1969) : Marriage among the Konda Valley Dani. In R. M. Glasse and M. J. Meggitt, eds (1969).
OLIVER, D. L. (1955) : *A Solomon Island Society: Kinship and Leadership among the Siuai of Bougainville*. Cambridge, Mass.: Harvard University Press.
RAPPAPORT, R. A. (1969) : Marriage among the Maring. In R. M. Glasse and M. J. Meggitt, eds (1969).
READ, K. E. (1950) : The Political System of the Ngarawapum. *Oceania*, Vol. XX, No. 3: 185-223.
READ, K. E. (1955) : Morality and the Concept of the Person among the Gahuku Gama, *Oceania*, Vol. XXV, No. 4: 233-282.
REAY, M. O. (1959) : *The Kuma*. Melbourne: Melbourne University Press.
REAY, M. O. (1964) : Present-Day Politics in the New Guinea Highlands. *American Anthropologist* (Special Publication on New Guinea Central Highlands), Vol. 66, No. 4, Part 2: 240-256.
RYAN, D'A. (1969) : Marriage in Mendi. In R. M. Glasse and M. J. Meggitt, eds (1969).
SAKORA, B. B. (1970) : Administration of Justice at the Village Level. *Journal of the International Commission of Jurists*, Australian Section, Vol. 3: 9-18.
SALISBURY, R. F. (1962) : *From Stone to Steel*. Melbourne: Melbourne University Press.
SALISBURY, R. F. (1964) : Despotism and Australian Administration in the New Guinea Highlands. *American Anthropologist* (Special Publication on New Guinea Central Highlands), Vol. 66, No. 2, Part 2: 225-239.
SALISBURY, R. F. (1970) : *Vunamami*. Berkeley and Los Angeles: University of California Press.
SCHEFFLER, H. W. (1965) : *Choiseul Island Social Structure*. Berkeley: University of California Press.
SCHNEIDER, D. M. (1965) : Some Muddles in the Models: Or, How the System Really Works. In *The Relevance of Models for Social Anthropology* (M. Banton, ed.). London and New York: Tavistock Publications and Praeger.
SMITH, M. G. (1956) : Segmentary Lineage Systems. *Journal of the Royal Anthropological Institute*, Vol. 86, Part 2: 39-80.
STRATHERN, A. (1969) : Descent and Alliance in the New Guinea Highlands: Some Problems of Comparison. *Proceedings of the Royal Anthropological Institute for 1968*: 37-52.
STRATHERN, A. (1970) : Review of *Huli of Papua*, by R. M. Glasse. *Man*, Vol. 5: 156.
STRATHERN, A. and M. (1969) : Marriage in Melpa. In R. M. Glasse and M. J. Meggitt, eds (1969).
VALENTINE, C. A. (1965) : The Lakalai of New Britain. In P. Lawrence and M. J. Meggitt, eds (1965).
VICEDOM, G. F. and H. TISCHNER (1943-48) : *Die Mbowamb*. Hamburg: Cram De Gruyter, Vols 1-3.
WAGNER, R. (1967) : *The Curse of Souw*. Chicago: University of Chicago Press.
WILLIAMS, F. E. (1930) : *Orokaiva Society*. London: Oxford University Press.
WILLIAMS, F. E. (1938) : Report on Grasslanders, Augu, Woge, and Wela. In *Report of the Administration of the Territory of Papua*, Port Moresby, Government Printer.
WILLIAMS, F. E. (1940-41) : Natives of Lake Kutubu, Papua. *Oceania*, Vol. XI, No. 2: 121-157; No. 3: 259-294; No. 4: 374-401.
WILLIAMS, F. E. (1941-42) : Natives of Lake Kutubu, Papua. *Oceania*, Vol. XII, No. 1: 49-74; No. 2: 134-154.

PHYLLIS M. KABERRY

POLITICAL ORGANIZATION AMONG
THE NORTHERN ABELAM

ABSTRACT

This analysis of northern Abelam political organization has particular reference to the village of Kalabu and its neighbours in 1939-40. An outline is given of the distribution and size of villages, the language, economy, and major rituals. The description of village organization covers land ownership, principles of recruitment of members to the village, hamlet organization, qualifications for leadership and the situations in which this is exercised. Clan organization is analysed, showing fluidity of affiliation, the range of factors which determine this and their political implications. Lastly, the scale of political organization is discussed in terms of the nature and range of intervillage relations.

INTRODUCTION

Among the Abelam of the Sepik District of New Guinea the traditional autonomous political unit is the village, which occupies a defined stretch of territory and has relations of friendship and feud with neighbouring villages within a radius of some five to ten miles. Villages are subdivided into hamlets in which two or three patriclans are established. For purposes of initiation into the 'tamberan' cult and for the competitive exchange of long yams, men are divided into two non-localized sections or *ara;* ideally, each man should have a ceremonial partner (*tshambəra*) in the opposite *ara.*[1]

There is no village headman and no formally constituted council of elders; nevertheless, the village functions as a peace group, and within it fighting should never be carried to a point where it involves loss of life. There are recognized methods for settling disputes, such as restitution, compensation, and the exchange of long yams or shell rings. When a quarrel occurs, patriclan elders display a sense of responsibility in seeking to elicit the facts, in emphasizing the norms of behaviour, and in exercising a moderating influence to obtain a settlement.

The elders are treated with respect and wield considerable influence over their dependants; they control access to garden land and act as organizers and sponsors in the initiation ceremonies. When seniority in age is also combined with a reputation as a 'yam-grower' (*nəma wabi kwaban*), a man is referred to as *nəmandu* (literally, big man). The same term is used for 'elder sibling of the same sex'. Painters and carvers of renown are also described as 'big men' with reference to the tamberan cult; they come to the fore when a house-tamberan is constructed or when paraphernalia are required for initiation ceremonies. But it is those men who are skilled yam-growers who enjoy the greatest prestige and who play a dominant role in linked ceremonial and economic activities which affect their own clans, hamlets, and in some cases the village as a whole. All Abelam men own and plant yams; but a person described as a big yam-grower is one who has performed the rites during all stages of cultivation and has produced a surplus of fine yams.

Leadership in the village is, then, based on age coupled with achievement in those activities which are associated with male prestige and which have an economic basis in the management of land and the production and distribution of a surplus of yams and pigs. In analysing Abelam political organizations we shall be concerned with types of corporate groups, with the principles of recruitment to them, and with the situations in which members act together under the leadership of big men and elders. We shall consider the basis of efficient leadership, the methods by which younger men achieve recognition as potential leaders, and the extent to which they remain dependent upon the support and guidance of older men. Lastly, we shall examine the scale of political organization. Each village is linked to other villages in its vicinity by a variety of ties which can be classified in terms of type, incidence and range. This network of intervillage relations may be regarded as constituting a political system, and its extent can be defined only in relation to the village which, for purposes of analysis, is taken as a focal point.

These aspects of political structure will be discussed on the basis of data collected principally in the village of Kalabu, one of the northern Abelam villages, situated some four miles to the east of Maprik, the administrative headquarters of a subdistrict in the Sepik area in 1940. Brief visits were paid to nineteen other villages to the south and west of Kalabu, and some information on social organization and rituals was collected there. Despite slight variations in dialect and custom, the main features of social structure appeared to be similar throughout the region, but in this essay I am primarily concerned with the analysis of a political system of which Kalabu is the focal point of reference; my generalizations may not, therefore, be applicable in all respects to other village-groupings.

The vernacular terms in the text are those of the Mamu-kundi dialect spoken in Kalabu and five other villages. Fieldwork was carried out from May 1939 to May 1940, and a preliminary report on Abelam social organization (Kaberry 1941*a*), as well as a more detailed study of social control and political organization (1941*b*), has already been published.[2] In the latter article I adopted a very broad definition of legal sanction and, at one point, asserted that 'all sanctions are legal insofar as they contribute to the maintenance of socially defined rights and obligations' (1941*b*: 223). While I still consider that an analysis of the legal institutions of any one community requires an examination of a wide range of sanctions of a moral, religious and economic kind, I would now restrict the term legal to those sanctions which are organized, negative and involve the right to apply force. The status of agents who have the legitimate right to apply force will depend on the type of political structure; in an acephalous system, they may be the injured parties themselves or the heads of their respective kin or local groups who, once the guilt of the culprit has been established, obtain satisfaction for the wrong suffered.

With these qualifications, my earlier discussion of social control, including procedures for handling disputes, still stands; it is not my intention to traverse the same ground again in this essay. On the other hand, only a brief account of inter-village relations and of the basis of leadership was given there. The present essay, which was written in 1957 but revised in 1965, discusses these in detail and incorporates new data on local and clan organization. The use of the ethnographic present refers to the period of my stay among the Abelam in 1939-40.

ENVIRONMENT AND CULTURAL SETTING

Distribution

The Abelam inhabit about 120 villages in the region between the Torricelli Mountains (some 40 miles due west of Wewak) and the plains north of the Sepik River above Berui and Mindimbit. Villages vary in size from about 100 to 600 inhabitants. At the time of my research there was no map of the Sepik subdistrict and no census of population; but since then Antony Forge has carried out research among several Abelam village-groupings, and has kindly made available to me population figures based on the government tax-census for 1958/1959. The estimated population for the whole Abelam area was then 30,487. They have no collective name for themselves but they are called Abelam by the Arapesh. Linguistically they may be distinguished from their Arapesh neighbours on the north, west, and east who speak an entirely different language. According to Laycock (1961: 38-9), the Abelam language belongs to the Ndu-family, which also includes Iatmül, spoken on the Sepik River. Northern Abelam refer to the Iatmül as *Makǝro-kundi* (river-speech) and say they do not understand it. Culturally they have more in common with the Mountain Arapesh than with the Iatmül, but they also possess institutions which are either peculiar to themselves or reappear in a less complex form among the Arapesh.

It is clear, then, that boundaries drawn on the basis of similarity of language alone do not coincide with those drawn on the basis of shared culture traits. But the Abelam may be regarded as a distinct people on two grounds. In the first place, Abelam villages have more in common, linguistically and culturally, with one another than they have with the Mountain Arapesh and the Iatmül. Secondly, while the Abelam admit that some variations of dialect and custom occur among groups of villages, they nevertheless sharply distinguish these groups from the Arapesh and also from the coastal and Sepik River peoples. A myth of origin describes how the first human beings came out of a hole near a clump of bamboos south of the plains. One or two informants suggested that the Europeans emerged first, travelled north and disappeared. All agreed that the coastal peoples (*Yaus*) and the Arapesh (*Bugi-kundi*) preceded the Shamu- and Mamu-speaking sections of the Abelam; and most included some reference to the founding of their own villages. Despite variations in detail, accounts were consistent in distinguishing major linguistic and cultural groupings; in recognizing dialectical differences among the Abelam themselves; and in stressing the existence of villages as autonomous local units.

Abelam men have a focal point of interest in the tamberan cult and in the competitive exchanges of yams. Visits are made over a wide area to witness or participate in ceremonies; and, on an occasion such as a dance for initiation or the opening of a new house-tamberan, representatives from fifteen to twenty-five villages may be present. This is probably the most important factor in creating a sense of cultural identity among Abelam villages in contradistinction to neighbouring communities, which neither grow long yams nor have the same form of tamberan cult. Among the Mountain Arapesh there seems to be much more variation in the field of ritual and ceremony, and much less interaction among members of different villages, with the exception of those which have adjacent boundaries or which border one of the 'roads' leading to the coast (Mead 1938: 151).

Abelam Dialects

The Abelam villages which I visited recognize four groupings of villages which speak closely related dialects: Mamu-kundi, Shamu-kundi, Kamu- or Baisi-kundi, and Yambe-kundi. *Kundi* refers to speech or words; *Mamu, kamu* and *shamu* are variants of the term for 'what' and, when followed by the suffix *ban,* they indicate a speaker of the dialect in question, e.g. *Mamuban.* Lists of the component villages of these dialectical groups, which I collected from a number of informants in different villages, showed a high degree of consistency although sometimes the name or nickname by which a dialect was described differed from area to area. The main groups are given below; for the purposes of this essay, central and western sections are classed together as northern Abelam:

(i)   South-eastern Abelam: *Yambe-kundi* (also called *Tubo-kundi*). A list of eleven villages was obtained, but some informants included the border Plains Arapesh villages of Ulupu, Malinguena (Aunyelum), and Kwambigum.

(ii) Central Abelam: *Mamu-kundi.* Six villages: Kalabu, Malnba, Mogatugum, Naramko, Yanuko, and Waigagum (see Map 1). Estimated population in 1958/59 was 2,178.

(iii) Western Abelam: *Shamu-kundi.* Twenty-five villages. Kalabu sometimes refer to the area west of Maprik as Manja. According to some informants in Aupik (the most westerly of the Shamu villages), people in the villages to the west and south-west of Aupik speak *Mai-kundi,* a dialect of Arapesh.

(iv) Southern Abelam: *Kamu-kundi* (also referred to as *Baisi-kundi* or *Bulə-kundi*). Twenty-seven villages. These villages, mainly located in the plains, are collectively referred to as Toma by Kalabu.

Villages which belong to the same dialectical grouping say that they are *nagura kundi* (one speech), and refer to their dialect as *nəma kundi* (important or big speech). Related Abelam dialects are described as *magwal kundi* (small

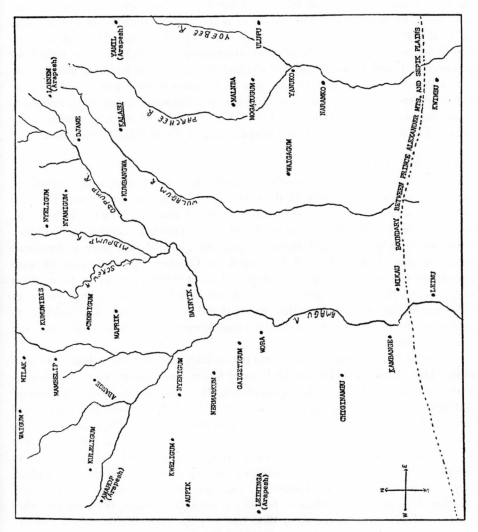

Map 1 Detail map of northern and central Abelam villages

Drawn after map of Department of Mines, Wau. Position of villages and rivers is only approximate. After Kaberry (1941a:235)

speech) ; but Arapesh (*Bugi-kundi*) is *na kundi* (another or different speech), and the same phrase is applied to dialects on the Sepik River. But although linguistic boundaries are defined with some precision by the Abelam, they do not coincide with political alignments. The dialectical group is not a political unit. Many men possess first-hand knowledge of thirty or more communities which they have visited for purposes of barter or to attend ceremonies; but their most frequent contacts are with villages within a radius of some five to ten miles of their home, and these do not always speak the same dialect or even the same language. Before discussing inter-village and intravillage relations, I shall give a brief account of those aspects of the culture which are relevant for an understanding of the political organization.[3]

Economy and Rituals

The Abelam practise a subsistence agriculture based on shifting cultivation; yams and taros are the staples, eked out by sago, bananas and breadfruit. The sago palm is important in the economy: it is a source of food when diet is rather lean, from November until March, and of materials for household articles and building. Palms are individually owned, rights are jealously guarded and, prior to European administration (first established in Maprik in October 1937), trespass on sago plantations was one of the most frequent causes of intervillage fights. In addition to gardening, the Abelam rear pigs and engage in a little hunting. Pigs are never killed for family consumption; they are bartered for shell rings or transferred to individuals in fulfilment of ceremonial commitments. Along with shell rings and yams, they constitute wealth.

Apart from carving, painting and pot-making, there is little technical speciali-zation. Men and women clear the bush, make fences, and garden, but women assume most of the responsibility for household crops. They also rear pigs, collect firewood and water, cook, make net-bags, and look after the children. Men hunt, build and carve, but their major interest lies in the cultivation of yams. There are two main types of yams: the long hairless species called *wabi* (of which the forked varieties are described as 'female') ; and the short hairy species, *ka*, which weigh from one to five pounds. The latter are usually intersown among other crops in the family plots; they are consumed by the household, and are also distributed at feasts and occasionally in subsidiary exchanges between ceremonial partners. *Wabi*, on the other hand, contribute little to the daily diet; but they are more highly valued and are planted in separate gardens. In this essay the phrase 'long yam' refers only to *wabi;* I shall use the vernacular term *ka* for the short hairy type.

The special gardens for long yams are made under the direction of elders. They are taboo to women, and men themselves may enter only if they have per-formed a minor rite to rid themselves of the impurities of sexual intercourse, which is regarded as inimical to yam growth and likely to provoke the anger of the spirits incarnate in the yams, as well as that of other spirits associated with the ancestors, sun, moon, forest and house-tamberan. All these spirits watch over yams and require sacrifices of coconut milk and pork fat, and the constant attendance of men in the gardens. The main rites are performed by elders, who must observe a taboo on sexual intercourse and certain foods for six or seven months. There is a close identification between a man and his finest yam: it is a symbol of his manhood and his industry. Many of the longest yams (five to ten feet in length) are not eaten: they are displayed at harvest, stored, distributed, stored again and eventually planted, except for a few unsuitable portions which are handed over rather grudgingly to the women for soup. After the harvest ceremonies, some are given away at girls' puberty ceremonies, male initiation, marriage and death; but the finest are normally reserved for presentation to a ceremonial partner once or twice a year; and one or two may be handed over to men in another village with which there is a relationship of traditional hostility. When a man dies, some of his yams are lashed to a mortuary frame by his grave and allowed to rot.

The complex of beliefs and activities focused on the cultivation and distribution of long yams may be termed a phallic cult. It is one which distinguishes the Abelam from other Sepik peoples and from most of the Arapesh, with the exception of border villages. It is also closely bound up with the tamberan cult which appears in variant forms throughout the whole Sepik district. Among the Abelam its especial features are the following. It is associated with spirits, *nggwalndu* (literally father's father's men), who are represented by faces painted on the façade of the house-tamberan and by carvings within it, and who watch over the gardens and promote growth. Each clan or subclan has a special relationship with a *nggwalndu*, and sometimes several clans have one in common. The same names for *nggwalndu* occur in widely separated villages, but they are linked with clans which have different names and totems.[4]

There are also a number of other carvings and ritual objects which are associated with stages of initiation and which are normally kept in huts on the edge of the piazza near the house-tamberan. In the northern and in some of the southern villages, *nggwalndu* and *wabinyan* (literally, 'yam-children'—small carvings bearing names said to belong to specific clans) are placed in tall peaked house-tamberans, which are triangular in vertical section and which may be forty to eighty feet high in front, although the ridge pole slopes down to a few feet above ground at the back. The lower part of the façade consists of patterned matting ornamented with attached masks and small carvings of animals, reptiles and birds. The upper section is made of sago spathes, brilliantly and spectacularly decorated with rows of faces (*nggwal-nggwal*) and geometric designs painted in red, black, yellow and white. Ideally, each hamlet should have its own house-tamberan, but some do not—especially in the smaller villages—and in that case they use one in another hamlet.

Although a house-tamberan is constructed in a hamlet under the direction of its most important man and is said to be owned by the hamlet, nevertheless the subclans and clans of the village under the leadership of their respective elders provide labour, and also building material from tracts of bush owned by them. The village acts as a corporate unit and takes pride in the skill, art, industry and initiative which are symbolized by the possession of a house-tamberan. The destruction of this building by an enemy village is an economic loss to the village as a whole and a blow to its prestige.

Again, neighbouring villages sometimes give a limited quantity of timber or sago palm thatch for building; or artists of pre-eminence may assist in the painting of the façade or the carving of *nggwalndu* and other ritual paraphernalia. These services are reciprocated later; what is important in this context is that some of these villages may be friends, and some may be traditional enemies with whom there is temporarily a truce.

Lastly, any male may enter a house-tamberan in his own village and in other villages, although he is not permitted to penetrate those sections at the rear which have been fenced off to conceal ritual objects from the uninitiated. For participation in the tamberan cult and yam exchanges, the males of the village are divided into two unnamed sections or *ara*: the men of one *ara* act as initiators to their ceremonial partners in the other *ara*. *Ara* are not localized, nor are they kin groups; but men frequently belong to the same *ara* as their fathers, and it is considered appropriate for the sons of two partners to be partners to one another and for the men of one clan to exchange yams with another clan. Ideally, the clans of a hamlet should belong to the same *ara* and have ceremonial exchange relations with an adjacent hamlet.

Initiation ceremonies involve men from a number of hamlets, and sometimes individuals from neighbouring villages who have made a contribution to the construction of the house-tamberan concerned or carved some of the ritual paraphernalia for it. In Kalabu there are several stages of initiation, some of which are believed to give strength in warfare to the initiated and to endow their hands with power in yam-growing. I was told that a year rarely passed without some ceremony being held. Kalabu was a large village, and in terms of resources could afford ceremonies more frequently than smaller communities. Nevertheless, the construction of a house-tamberan in 1939 was said by the men to have been a drain on time, labour and materials, and no other major ceremonies were held that year. Preparations were in train for initiation ceremonies in 1940, and the men had planted extra gardens for long yams and for subsidiary crops for feasts.[5]

VILLAGE ORGANIZATION

Land Ownership

Most of the northern Abelam villages are sited on ridges and are anything from one to three miles apart. No surveys had been made at the time of my visit in 1939-40 and any estimate of density of population would be sheer guesswork. But there appeared to be no shortage of land; in Kalabu itself most of the upper part of the settlement had been under bush about two generations previously. Fights between villages were not undertaken primarily for the conquest of territory, although they might result from quarrels over trespass on garden land and sago plantations near a boundary. If, however, the people of an outlying hamlet or small village were completely routed in a raid and their homes burnt down, they would abandon the site, and eventually the victors might make gardens near it or establish a hamlet of their own. For example, Malbimbil, about an hour's walk north of the main part of Kalabu (see Figure 1), had once belonged to an Arapesh group, but Kalabu had routed them many generations ago and made gardens there. The hamlet in 1940 was very mixed in its clan composition, and was something of a refuge for individuals from other parts of Kalabu who had found it expedient to change their residence for a short time. Most of these, however, also had houses in the hamlets in the main part of the village.

Villages are divided into hamlets and these again into named sections (see below), each of which is associated with a clan or subclan in the sense that its male members predominate. House-sites are handed down from father to sons, and also to married daughters who continue to reside in the hamlet. Many, though not all, of the sites owned by an extended family lie in close proximity to one another, and in the course of time they may come to constitute a separate section in the hamlet. Rights to sites in other sections of the hamlet are not necessarily waived. While most of the houses in a section belong to members of the same clan, a few may be occupied by individuals of different clans, who either have houses in other sections in the hamlet or have come from another hamlet to live near an affine or maternal relative. In the latter case, they retain rights to land in their former hamlet; but, if they or their sons do not resume residence, the sites pass to other members of their clan or, failing that, to other residents in the hamlet.

Each clan or subclan owns tracts of garden land and hunting bush in the vicinity of the hamlet and also farther afield. Management is vested in the most senior elder; but, if there are two or three elders who are cousins, some division of garden land usually occurs. Each elder then exercises full control over two or three tracts on behalf of his younger brothers, married sons, daughters, and any other persons who are affiliated to his group. He decides when bush is to be cleared and fenced for cultivation; and he subdivides the garden into plots and allocates them among his own dependants, as well as to one or two individuals who may wish to work with him. Should an extended family die out, the land is said to revert to other members of the clan.

Hamlets are corporate units, each having its own 'big man' and co-operating in a limited range of activities. Nevertheless, the village is more than a loose confederation of such units. In the first place, village boundaries are demarcated and are defended at the spear-point by members of the village. Secondly, the majority of marriages (73.4% in the case of Kalabu) occur within the village, so that a number of individuals are linked by cognatic and affinal ties, and have obligations to one another which often cut across hamlet and even clan responsibilities. Thirdly, the dual organization into *ara* for initiation and yam ceremonies establishes a relationship of mutual dependence between men of different descent groups and hamlets. And, lastly, the acquisition of prestige derives mainly from participation in these ceremonies, the conduct of which lies largely in the hands of the big men and other elders. Hence the younger men of the village occupy a subordinate position in relation to the old, and this is explicitly recognized in a number of situations: in the leadership assumed by the elders, in the deference paid to them, in the constant acknowledgment of their importance, and in the excuses made by men of some small hamlets who say that they have no old men to help them. Thus cognatic and affinal ties, generation differences, and the dual organization, crosscut localized descent groups and provide a basis for integration at the village level.

The identity of the village as a corporate unit is expressed in a number of ways: in its name, in its possession of a *djambu* (bird totem) to which reference is made mainly in the context of intervillage relations, and in myths which describe the founding of the village and the discovery of different kinds of food. The people of Kalabu have the crown pigeon as their village totem; they speak of their village as *Kalabu nggai* (Kalabu place), or of themselves as *Kalabumban* (Kalabu persons), or as *nanə Kalabu* (we Kalabu) or as *nanə, nagura nggai* (we, one place). They have a strong sentiment of solidarity in opposition to other villages; they boast of their numerical superiority, their prowess as fighters, and their skill as builders of house-tamberans and as cultivators of long yams—especially the *manbutap* variety, which is noted for its regularity of shape and the fine white texture of its flesh.

Recruitment of Members

Membership of the village is determined primarily by birth and marriage. In the latter case a man may also have a house in his natal village, spend some of his time there, cultivate one or two plots, and exploit sago palms which he has inherited or planted. Providing he continues to exercise these rights, he can transmit them to his children. Adoption of children from other villages does occur, but it is rare and normally involves the payment of shell rings. It is much more common for a childless man to ask a married sister for a son or, at a later stage, to persuade a sister's adolescent or married son to come and live with him. However, men from other villages who have suffered chronic misfortune, or who have been worsted in fights, may seek refuge in villages where they have cognates, affines or, more rarely, friends. If such a person decides to remain, he is lent a house-site and garden plots by his host, who consults neither the village at large nor even the big man of his hamlet, though he would obtain the approval of his own kin, with whom the newcomer would be expected to co-operate in economic and ceremonial activities. If the newcomer establishes a family and continues to reside in the hamlet, his rights of usufruct to land become rights to transmit it to his heirs; he may also be joined by kinsmen from his natal village. If he has brought a wife with him, his children are likely to retain his clan name, totem (*djambu*) and *nggwalndu*. On the other hand, if he marries a woman in his adopted village, his children frequently adopt her *nggwalndu* and her totem as their own, though later they (or the next generation) may take a new clan name and form a separate exogamous unit.

In Kalabu there were eighteen clans, of which seven were of stranger origin: four from Djame (Kalabu's main ally), two from Loenem (a friendly Arapesh village), and one from Waigagum (an 'enemy' village). The origin of the founders of these clans was remembered; occasionally a disgruntled man spoke of them in disparagement, but on the whole the 'newcomers' were a welcome accession to the strength of the village. The 'stranger' clans were fully incorporated in the village organization and some of their leaders played an important part in public affairs. Their respective members varied in the assiduity with which they cultivated links with their ancestral villages; some attended ceremonies frequently, selected wives from there, and occasionally collaborated in the making of the long yam gardens.

Hamlet Organization

The village in its relations with other villages will be discussed later. I shall now describe the interplay of political interests within it. The foci of political activity are the hamlets. The political identity of each hamlet is symbolized by its piazza or public square (*amei*), by its slit-gongs by means of which members send out messages to the rest of the village and to neighbouring villages, and, lastly, by its house-tamberan. The piazza is kept scrupulously clean and its borders are planted with ornamental shrubs and flowers. A few houses front on to it, but most are built to one side or along paths leading to gardens or other hamlets. The piazza is a forum for debate and discussion, a place for informal and formal assembly, for display and ceremony. People when stressing common membership of a hamlet say, 'We are one piazzo (*nanə nagura amei*).' The leaders of the hamlet are the elders of the component clans or subclans resident within it; and, among them, the big man of the founding clan is regarded as the big man of the hamlet. These men organize activities in connection with the long yam and tamberan cults and have particularly close relationships with the leaders in one or two adjacent hamlets, some of whom are ceremonial partners to them. The whole network of ceremonial exchanges is exceedingly complex if account is taken of every individual; but, if attention is directed to the major exchanges conducted by important men, it is found that usually adjacent hamlets are connected by relationships of ceremonial partnership. Moreover, in general conversation hamlets are frequently linked in pairs. Such statements also point to the concept of hamlets as corporate groups (irrespective of the divisions within them) and to the role of big men as representatives of these groups. The rough sketch plan (Map 2) indicates the relative position of hamlets in Kalabu, the existence of house-tamberans, and the main ceremonial links between hamlets.

A hamlet is generally divided into three or four named sections, each of which is associated with a clan or clan segment. The piazza is in the main section which gives the hamlet its name. In an earlier publication I used the term 'hamlet' for any named section, but distinguished between a 'parent hamlet' (i.e. main section) and those which were extensions from it and had no piazza of their own (Kaberry 1941*a*: 241-3 and fn. 5). It is more appropriate to reserve the term hamlet for a clustering of residential groups which share a piazza for their social and ceremonial life, and to describe the residential groups themselves as 'sections'.[6] The word for any place of residence such as village, hamlet, section or house is

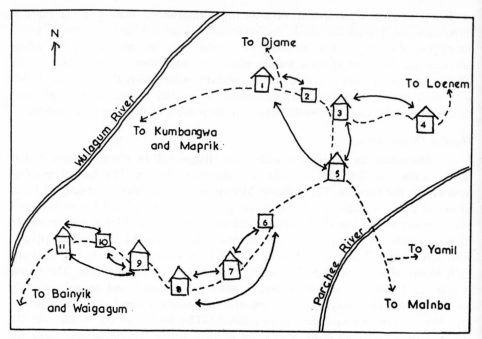

To Djame

To Loenem

Wulagum River

To Kumbangwa
and Maprik

To Yamil

Parchee River

To Bainyik
and Waigagum

To Malnba

Map 2 Sketch map of hamlets of Kalabu (1940)

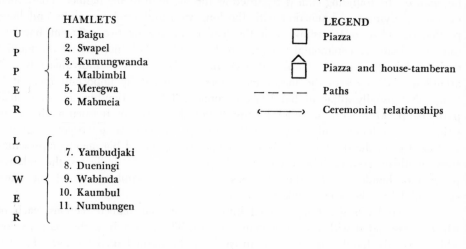

HAMLETS

U
P
P
E
R

1. Baigu
2. Swapel
3. Kumungwanda
4. Malbimbil
5. Meregwa
6. Mabmeia

L
O
W
E
R

7. Yambudjaki
8. Dueningi
9. Wabinda
10. Kaumbul
11. Numbungen

LEGEND

☐ Piazza

⌂ Piazza and house-tamberan

─ ─ ─ ─ Paths

←──────→ Ceremonial relationships

nggai; but a section may be distinguished from a hamlet as a 'little place' (*walgamu nggai*), and an ancestral hamlet is spoken of as *nggwal nggai* (father's father's place).

In a small village such as Malnba or Mikau there may be only three or four hamlets, and in this case villagers are brought into daily contact with one another. In a large village, particularly where settlement is somewhat dispersed, there is a tendency for hamlets to be divided into two or sometimes three groupings which over the course of generations may become separate villages, linked by ties of inter-marriage, ritual collaboration, and alliance in the face of a common enemy. Malnba with its offshoot Mogatugum is a case in point. In Kalabu there are eleven hamlets and these, with the exception of Malbimbil, are strung out along a horseshoe-shaped ridge. They are divided into two groups known as Upper (*Kwalə*) Kalabu and Lower (*Bapbap*) Kalabu. The former is the more recent settlement, but two of its ham-lets—Mabmeia and Meregwa—were founded at least four generations ago. It includes the following hamlets: Baigu (the most westerly in Kalabu and nearest to Djame and Kumbangwa villages), Swapel, Kumungwanda, Meregwa, Mabmeia and Malbimbil. Lower Kalabu consists of Yambudjaki (adjoining Mabmeia), then Dueningi, Wabinda, Kaumbul and Numbungen.

I could obtain no history of the gradual settlement of Lower Kalabu, but Numbungen is said to be the oldest settlement and lies approximately south-west of Baigu on the opposite side of the valley. The hamlets in Upper Kalabu had been founded by men who for various reasons had left their place of residence in Lower Kalabu. According to some of my more trustworthy informants, Meregwa was settled several generations ago by a man who belonged to the *Tshəmeigum* clan in Dueningi. His descendants took a new totem, a new *nggwalndu*, and a new clan name, *Kwarəngəm*, though that name contained the word for the totem of the parent clan, *kwarə* (hawk). The hamlet, a small one, consisted of three sections: Meregwa proper, Kalangwa and Kwandjaki; the last section was established by its present residents after they had suffered a defeat in a fight in their former residence at Yambudjaki. They belonged to the *Kwatməgəm* clan and one of them, Kulemini, was married to the father's brother's daughter's daughter of Kabmagioli, the big man of the hamlet and belonging to the *Kwarəngəm* clan. Kumungwanda hamlet was founded by a man of the *Luimugəm* clan, also an offshoot of the *Tshəmeigəm* clan in Dueningi. His son, Winandjui, built the first house-tamberan and, although an old man in 1940, he was still the most important elder there at the time of my stay in Kalabu. He and his own sons sometimes displayed their long yams on the piazza at Dueningi. The men of Swapel hamlet were a segment of the *Magnapatə* clan in Wabinda. Bailgu hamlet was somewhat anomalous in that it was not only close to Djame village but had been founded by a Djame man after he had married a woman of Kalabu, probably from Kumungwanda hamlet. He and his sons were joined by others from Djame, and together constituted the *Nyungwigəm* clan. They occupied the main section and Berangei section on the west; their big man was Patundu, one of the sons of the founder. The third section of Baigu was Djanggungwei, inhabited mainly by *Bugitshuagəm* and *Kundəgəm* clans (both of Arapesh origin). Wambegula was the most senior man in the former clan, and his mother had been a classificatory sister of the founder of the *Nyungwigəm* clan in Baigu. He had previously lived at Yambudjaki but, after a fight in which both he and the men of *Kwatməgəm* clan (see above) were worsted, he took up residence first at Kumungwanda and later at Baigu, near his cross-cousin Patundu. He and Kulemini (of Meregwa) had been ceremonial partners at Yambudjaki, and they had continued their relationship after the change of residence.

It is not possible within the scope of this article to trace further the ramifications of relationships between hamlets in Kalabu, but two points should be stressed. An individual has a range of kinship and affinal ties which link him with many persons throughout the village; these ties may be implemented by collaboration and assistance in certain situations. When a man changes his residence, he normally utilizes one of these links to obtain permission to occupy a house-site and garden plots. As against this dispersal of interests, there is a centripetal tendency of co-residents in a hamlet to constitute a corporate group symbolized by the name of their hamlet, the possession of a common piazza and, where possible, the erection of a house-tamberan on the façade of which are represented the *nggwalndu* associated with the clans of the component sections and those of clans which are in a ceremonial exchange relationship with them.

In 1940, the population of Kalabu according to my own census was 489, including 22 men away on indenture. (The population in 1958/59 had increased to 633.) There were 239 males (of whom 125 were married or had been married, and 114 unmarried), and 250 females (of whom 151 were married or widows, and 99 unmarried). The great majority of household heads were men, and the unit of production and consumption consisted of a man, his wife and unmarried children. Sons at puberty slept in the house-tamberan, but in all other respects were members of their father's household. Co-wives usually did not live in the same hamlet, or, anyway, in the same section. A few households had female heads: old widows living near a married son or brother; and younger widows who had children and were likely to marry again. The average size of the household was 3.2 persons; but if widows living alone are excluded, the average was 3.8 persons.

Hamlets varied greatly in size, and a calculation of their population was complicated by the fact that 22 men (most of them polygynists) had dual residence, although they regarded one hamlet as their main place. Since residence involved co-operation with neighbours, these men were active members of two hamlets; but, if account is taken of main residence only, the average size of a hamlet was 44.4 persons. The largest hamlet was Dueningi, with 74 persons; the smallest had 24. Most hamlets were divided into sections which ranged in size from very small ones with four to seven residents, at one extreme, and sixteen to thirty-seven at the other. It is possible that in such large sections as Kamagwa (in Dueningi) there were named subdivisions, but they were not sufficiently important to be in current use and did not come to my knowledge.

Members of the founding clan of a hamlet usually occupy two sections and, where formal segmentation had not already occurred, this reflects an incipient segmentation. Elders who are patri-cousins or more distant agnates and who have each their own little group of dependants, frequently live in different sections and they act independently of one another in small-scale undertakings. However for any major enterprise the big man of the clan in the hamlet comes to the fore and assumes responsibility. The subdivision of a hamlet into sections reflects one or both of two processes: (i) incipient or formal segmentation within a founding clan, sometimes leading to fission and the emergence of a new exogamous unit; and (ii) the accession of men who come to take up residence near a maternal relative or affine. If these men settle permanently and establish families of their own, they become the nucleus of a new section; they, in their turn, may be joined by agnates or sisters' sons and constitute a clan or subclan under its own elder.

In addition to the formation of new sections in a hamlet, new hamlets may originate when individuals build houses in the bush near outlying gardens; or when, as a result of some violent quarrel with neighbours, they go to an uninhabited part of the village where they already have land rights or can obtain them from a kinsman. If the new settlement prospers and attracts adherents, it will have its own piazza, engage in yam exchanges with neighbours, and eventually erect its own house-tamberan. But the component clans may still retain some ties with their respective ancestral hamlets: rights to trees and garden land are retained, and, once peace is made, there may be occasional collaboration for tamberan rituals, the cultivation of long yam gardens, a joint harvest display, and the exchange of yams with 'enemy' villages.[7]

The component clans of a hamlet may be classified as follows:

(i) *Founding clan,* usually the largest, and occupying two sections of the hamlet. If segmentation occurs, the new segment (subclan) changes its *ara* affiliation and frequently adopts another *nggwalndu,* although it regards that of the clan as its 'big *nggwalndu*'; intermarriage is not permitted.

(ii) *Detached clan,* a group which has hived off from the founding clan and become a separate exogamous unit, symbolized by the adoption of a new clan name. Sometimes the totem and *nggwalndu* are not changed for two or three generations. Members retain their original rights to house-sites, garden land and hunting bush; but they change their *ara* affiliation, and some may become exchange partners to men in the founding clan and/or in the accessory clan.

(iii) *Accessory clan,* originally linked to the founding clan by cognatic or affinal ties, more rarely by a tie of friendship. It has received house-sites and usually some garden land from the founding clan. Its leader belongs to the same *ara* as that of the founding clan and co-operates closely with it in the yam exchanges.

The hamlet is a corporate group, symbolized by its name and its piazza; members should live together in peace. Many are linked by kinship ties; but, even where an exact relationship cannot be traced, individual members may address one another by a kinship term, using age as a criterion and saying in explanation: 'we are one piazza' or 'we are one place'. If, however, relationships between two men are strained or they are in covert competition for status as a leader, they may refer to each other as 'my man' (*wuna ndu*). Marriage within the hamlet as well as between adjacent hamlets is common, and this reinforces neighbourhood ties. Of 207 marriages contracted within Kalabu itself by men over three or four generations, 56% were between adjacent hamlets and between sections of a hamlet. Exchange of women between clans is favoured and, of the 207 marriages, 14.9% were of this type. In a further 13.5% of marriages, the exchange was completed in the next generation. Marriage between full cross-cousins is regarded as equivalent to a marriage between siblings and is incestuous; but marriage into the mother's clan is permitted, and occurred in 6.2% of the unions recorded. Affines and cross-cousins should be friends, assist one another and work together. When leaders of two clans stand in the relation of affines or cross-cousins, or when their children have inter-married in the case of cross-cousins, co-operation in hamlet affairs is made easier. Moreover, the sharing of one piazza for gossip, fun and ceremonial occasions, the nearness of houses within sections and of sections to one another, and the consequent lack of privacy, compel the settlement of disputes. There is a considerable amount of informal assistance: women make gifts of food, lend tools and utensils, nurse one another's children, and often garden in adjacent taro plots. Each elder assumes moral responsibility for the conduct of his dependants; and if he thinks that a son, younger brother, or brother's son is guilty he berates him and demands that he pay compensation where the situation requires it. There is a certain amount of bickering among the women, but such squabbles either peter out or are brought to an end by the ridicule or rebuke of an older man or woman.

The most serious quarrels among men of different clans arise over adultery and accusations of sorcery. Men who suffer continual misfortune, or who have chronic illness in their households, suspect that a neighbour is practising sorcery and eventually move to another hamlet. Indeed, among the old men this was a reason frequently given for a change of residence and sometimes for a change of clan affiliation. In the case of a charge of adultery, members of the hamlet and other neighbours soon assemble. Where the guilt of the accused is not in doubt, the elders of the hamlet and of his own clan counsel payment of a shell ring in compensation. Where the evidence is not conclusive, two things may happen: either the plaintiff drops his charge; or, if he is convinced of the defendant's guilt, he challenges him to exchange long yams. Since performance of yam magic involves the observance of a taboo on sexual intercourse for about seven months, the implication of the challenge is that the accused is interested only in women and that his yams will be inferior in consequence. Each man will then have two exchange partners; but, over the course of time, the original partners may find it convenient to look for others and the pre-existing relationship will be dissolved by mutual consent. I give one example of a complex situation which resulted in some major realignments. Some years before my arrival in Kalabu, a serious fight had occurred at Yambudjaki hamlet which also involved some men of several other hamlets. A series of incidents —the remarriage of a widow, wife-stealing and adultery—had eventually led to a pitched battle which the elders were powerless to check. There were no deaths, but a few people were wounded and for a time Yambudjaki was largely deserted. Eventually 'peace' was made by the elders of the clans most directly concerned and many of the former residents returned, with the exception of members of the *Kwatmagam* clan who remained at Meregwa (see Figure 2). The main disputants became permanent ceremonial partners; but feelings of hostility persisted and, at a yam exchange in 1940, several spears were thrown before the elders and big men could intervene and restore order.

Leadership and Authority

The moral authority which elders exercise in discussion of public affairs and the settlement of disputes derives from the respect due to age, wisdom and a reputation for moral probity. In any casual gathering in the piazza they frequently sit together in the shade of the house-tamberan; and, when they take the floor, the younger men should listen with deference and remain in the background. At a feast in which they themselves are not the donors, they are served first and receive the choicest sprays of betelnut and leaves of tobacco. If quarrelling occurs in their presence, in their own hamlet or elsewhere, they may check it by ridicule or a joke; or, if it is more serious, they counsel moderation, remind the disputants of the misfortunes that have followed from fighting in the past, and assert the importance of ties of kinship. If fighting actually occurs, they wrest spears from those involved, and place the yellow *yauwal* leaf (the symbol of peace), in the centre of the piazza. In situations where an outburst of violence seems highly probable, they try to avert it beforehand by placing a *yauwal* leaf in the piazza and exhorting the younger men not to give way to anger. Six elders in particular were known throughout Kalabu in 1939-40 as peacemakers: two had a reputation as yam-growers, but the others enjoyed no especial pre-eminence, though they met their commitments to their respective partners adequately. On several occasions I saw them intervene effectively to check fighting.

The elders of a hamlet, then, have a joint responsibility for the maintenance of peace within it; and each elder has his particular responsibility toward his immediate dependants, whom he advises, assists and instructs. He manages garden land, and he always has some knowledge of agricultural and other types of magic which he hands on to the younger generation. But he is not necessarily a ritual specialist; indeed, his status as elder does not automatically confer on him the title of 'big man'. Ideally, each clan should have its own big man who excels in the growing of long yams and who may or may not be its most senior elder in terms of age. At the harvest display, the big man assumes titular ownership of all the yams for which he has performed magic, because he is said 'to have looked after them'. In other words, he takes the credit for the crop, although after the display individual owners take away their yams and control their disposal. Over a period of years he has established his reputation—one that is acknowledged by members of his hamlet, by the clan of his ceremonial partner, and by the village at large. His own clansmen entrust many of their yams to him, as may also sisters' sons, cross-cousins and affines. He is described as one who has a name: 'This name-man [man of renown], his *wabi* and *ka* are good. When he plants them they are abundant'; or he is one who 'has harvested big yams'. He has many garden plots and storehouses; he and his wife or wives produce a surplus of food for lavish distribution at feasts.

The big man of the founding clan is also the big man of the hamlet and is sometimes called *kumbu-ndu, kumbu* being the term applied to the tip of a yam or the top of a tree—the growing point. In an earlier article I took over the Arapesh phrase of 'trunk-man' for such a person, but entrepreneur is closer to the Abelam concept. He is sometimes spoken of as the 'owner' of the house-tamberan and slit-gongs of his hamlet; and, when an old house-tamberan is demolished, he has the right to utilize parts of the painted façade as a front wall for his yam storehouse, His authority rests on his status in his own clan, his moral reputation, his age, his achievements, his willingness to accept onerous responsibility, and his proven capacity for leadership. He cannot command force to secure compliance with his orders; but, once he has obtained the support of other elders for a project, he directs and supervises proceedings—whether it be for the construction of slit-gongs or a house-tamberan, the holding of initiation ceremonies, yam exchanges, or the making of a large yam garden. If he dies and has no immediate successor in his generation, the hamlet is said to lack a big man and its prestige in the village may suffer a temporary eclipse. However, in emphasizing the role of the big man of the founding clan in a hamlet, it should not be forgotten that he is primarily the entrepreneur and that the leaders and men of promise in other clans have opportunities for acquiring some prestige. The piazza is a forum in which they can display before an audience drawn from many parts of the village their own skill as orators and singers, as carvers and painters, and as the titular owners of yams for which they have assumed ritual responsibility. In the section that follows I shall give examples of leadership in the yam and tamberan cults.

Next to the construction of a house-tamberan and the holding of initiation ceremonies, the clearing of a large garden for long yams requires more organization than does any other Abelam activity. The initiative comes from the big man of a hamlet, the only person who can mobilize the labour required—which is given by his supporters (the elders of his own clan and of the detached and accessory clans of his hamlet), his ceremonial partners, and some of his kin and affines living in other parts of the village. The clearing and fencing of a garden for 30 to 40 large mounds takes eight to ten days, and the planting one day if a working bee of forty to fifty men plus boys is involved. Preparation of yam gardens begins in about mid-July and continues through October; during this period people are also concerned with house-building, some ceremonial yam exchanges, the harvesting of *ka*, the burning-off of old plots, and the preliminary clearing of undergrowth on land which has been under bush fallow and which will be used for planting crops for household consumption, although most of the work for the last is done at the end of the year and the beginning of the next. The organization of a team for a large yam garden demands, then, a considerable amount of consultation and careful planning beforehand. What are the rewards and expectations of those participating?

In the afternoon of the first day, when in fact most of the planting is completed, the workers are given a feast of short yams, taros, coconuts and betelnuts by the big man of the hamlet, who is the 'owner' of the garden, and also by one or two other big men who have associated themselves with him in the work and will have separate plots for a few yam mounds within the fenced area. Men of the hamlet of the big man who belong to his *ara*, and those from other parts of the village who are agnates, sisters' sons and affines, entrust some of their yams to him to be 'looked after'. He may have in his ritual care 15 to 25 yam mounds. Big men and elders of the other *ara* in his hamlet and from other hamlets are given small plots in the big garden, in which to plant a few seed-yams for which they will be ritually responsible. They will also expect some reciprocal assistance in the making of their own yam gardens later. Lastly, the entrepreneur himself can look forward to the display of yams cultivated in his garden: it is a display in which his whole hamlet can take pride, and it will be attended by men from the village who come to inspect the harvest and to place cordyline leaves on very fine specimens. Only yams which are five feet or more in length are displayed; they are lashed to poles and decorated with wooden or wickerwork masks, plumes, shell rings, flowers and leaves. The ritual specialists reap the glory of the harvest; they chant clan songs, boast of their prowess and belittle that of their ceremonial partners.

The successful termination of yam cultivation, from the point of view of those participating, requires the fulfilment of certain conditions: the performance of a series of rites during the various stages of yam growth; the safeguarding of the yams from all contact with women, and also with men who have had sexual intercourse without purification; and peaceful relations within the hamlet and between partners. Dissension is believed to anger the tamberan and yam spirits and affect the growth of the yams. Men should put aside their differences, and devote themselves to a task in which they have a common interest and from which they will ultimately derive prestige. In all these situations the big man of the hamlet has an important part to play.

Early in July, the big man of a hamlet which has held an initiation ceremony dons a mask and goes through the village with two or three men in attendance, imposing a taboo on some coconut palms, so that the fruit may be reserved for sacrifices in the yam gardens. Both the mask (a large conical wickerwork ornament which completely envelops the head) and the wearer are called *babatagwa*. He receives small gifts of taros, *ka*, bananas, betelnut and tobacco from prominent men in the hamlets which he then places in his house-tamberan to invoke the goodwill of the tamberan spirits toward all the crops of the village. *Nggwalndu* do not belong to one side of the dual organization or to the other; 'they stand midway', and the *babatagwa* acts both as their agent and also on behalf of the village as a whole. Some time later he and the other big men in the village place broken spears near the *nggwalndu* in their respective house-tamberans, as a symbol that fighting must cease during yam cultivation.

All the manual work in the yam garden—weeding, cutting of poles as stakes for the yam vines, repairing the fence, and keeping a watch against the depredations of wild pigs—is done by the actual owners of the yams, who observe a temporary taboo on intercourse while visiting their yams. When the vines in the large garden of the big man of the hamlet begin to twine up the stakes, he marks off an area with poles in front of his house-tamberan and makes it taboo not only to females but also to men who have not purified themselves after intercourse. In other words, not only is he the ritual guardian of the garden but he also has the right to interdict the use of the house-tamberan and its immediate precincts to all men in a state of impurity. During the period of cultivation, emphasis is placed on the antagonism between male and female principles rather than on the rivalry between men of the two *ara*. When the yams are harvested, the big men may once more adorn themselves and oil their ringlets to attract women; they may once more openly compete with their partners.

I have discussed the yam gardens in some detail because long yams, together with pigs and shell rings, constitute wealth: the acquisition of a fine harvest brings prestige to the owners of yams and enables them to play their part in ceremonial activities, which involve the distribution of wealth. In any set of exchanges, the leaders of the hamlet who belong to the same *ara* arrange that they and their respective dependants will transfer yams to their respective partners on the same day. If a young man has no yam which is a satisfactory equivalent for one already received from his partner, his elder or the big man is expected to make good the deficiency from his own storehouse, where he may have ten to fifteen yams, five feet or more in length. The prestige both of the big man and of the group participating in the exchange is at stake.

In addition to the yam exchanges which occur at various times throughout the village and involve all married males, initiation into one of the stages of the tamberan cult usually takes place each year in one of the house-tamberans. The 'owner' of the house-tamberan and the big men of the same *ara* from three or four hamlets collaborate to initiate their respective partners or the dependents of their partners who often reside in several hamlets in the village. Partners are thus mutually dependent and, over a period of time, render one another equivalent services: those initiated in one year incur the obligation to initiate in a subsequent year. But, when a ceremony is held, the initiators receive gifts of pigs, yams and coconuts as an immediate return for their services. All this entails consultation and careful planning many months in advance, since extra gardens must be made and pigs procured by the neophytes and by those who will assist and sponsor them, namely, the elders and big men. Unfortunately, no major initiation ceremony occurred during my stay in Kalabu; but, according to informants, ten or twelve married males (together with adolescent and young boys) may be initiated at one time; eighteen pigs may be transferred, and many more yams. On their part, the initiators, in addition to their own duties, make ritual paraphernalia—flutes, carvings, and also the beautiful feather head-dresses worn by the neophytes at the dance which brings the ceremony to an end, and which is attended by visitors from neighbouring villages.

The construction of a new house-tamberan involves the co-operation of all members of the village over a period of some three to four months. The big man of the hamlet concerned acts as entrepreneur and, with the other elders of the hamlet, secures the collaboration of all the big men and elders in the rest of the village. The latter in their turn are responsible for mobilizing their own dependants for the collection of materials from clan lands—timber, bamboos, cane, palm branches and spathes. In addition, neighbouring villages may provide timber and help to weave the matting for the lower façade; painters and carvers of renown may also lend their services. For example, in the construction of a house-tamberan at Numbungen hamlet, Djame, Loenem, Bainyik (all friendly villages), Malnba and Kumbangwa (both 'enemy' villages) each contributed one of the main structural supports.

Work had begun a few weeks before the date of my arrival, which was May 6th, 1939, and was completed on June 28th, 1939. Palm mats for thatching were prepared by men in their hamlets and carried to Numbungen. Clans and subclans were responsible for the thatching of sections of the framework, to which clan leaf emblems had been attached beforehand. The work for this began on May 23rd and was finished on the 24th. All the women provided bowls of soup and baskets of cooked vegetables for the male workers; but the ceremonial acknowledgment of the services given by the men of Kalabu and other villages consisted in the distribution of spathes, each containing about twenty portions of cooked long yams, a coconut, and sprays of betelnut. All told, nineteen spathes had been provided by the big men and elders of Numbungen: fourteen of these were laid out in front of the house-tamberan. The first eight were allocated to hamlets and sections of Upper Kalabu; the remaining six were given to Lower Kalabu (to which Numbungen belonged); and five had been set aside for the villages which had given some assistance. Lastly, white vegetable soup, served in three painted incised pots (obtained by barter from villages near Mount Turu), was eaten by the big men and elders.

During the following weeks, men in a shelter behind the house-tamberan stitched together the sago spathes for the upper part of the façade, which was some 50 feet high; others wove the patterned matting for the lower façade (some 20 feet high); others, again, carved birds, animals, masks and small figures. The painting of the spathes was done later in seclusion by the artists of the village, who observed a taboo on sexual intercourse during this period. On June 28th the painted spathes and then the matting were hoisted into position; slit-gongs were beaten; and a dance was held in the evening. The following morning a trellis was erected in front of the house-tamberan, and shell rings (linked together with cane) were attached to it. These were lent for the occasion by the men and women of Kalabu, as well as by people from the villages which had assisted. The big man of Numbungen, who had directed and supervised activities throughout, was the first to place his rings in position. The display of rings brought prestige to their owners, demonstrated the wealth of the village, and expressed its pride in the possession of a new house-tamberan. Visitors came from about fifteen villages, a dance was held in the evening, and for the first and last time women were permitted to enter the house-tamberan. Later, the building and its carvings were purified by rituals performed by the big man and elders of the hamlet.

Leadership in intervillage affairs will be examined in a later section; but we have already discussed a range of situations connected with the yam and tamberan cults which are recurrent, and which have a political aspect insofar as a number of men co-operate and contribute labour and resources under the direction and super-vision of leaders. These leaders are big men who have achieved pre-eminence as yam-growers and who have the personal qualities which assure them of the support of their own clansmen. The role of the big man is to act as the representative of his group and as entrepreneur in those activities which affect its relations with other groups. Within the hamlet, the big man of the founding clan enjoys a formal status superior to that of the other big men insofar as he is the prime mover in major concerns. On occasion, he may be able to enlist the support of big men from other hamlets for some enterprise in which he assumes command. But in this case his authority is temporary; there is no big man for the whole village, and no ranking of hamlet heads. Some enjoy more renown as yam-growers and artists and have a larger following, but in terms of formal status they are equivalent. Collectively, they are the big men of the village; as individuals, their relations with one another are mediated through hamlet and dual organization into *ara*. Big men of both *ara* collaborate in activities which affect the village as a unit; they render one another reciprocal services, as in the initiation ceremonies; and they compete for prestige, as in the yam exchanges. We shall now examine the way in which leadership is maintained and the processes by which new leaders emerge within the clan.

Clan Organization

The groups of individuals who act together under elders are clans and sub-clans. These clans are small, and range in size from three to sixteen males, the average being 6.8. But this figure applies to clans as exogamous units and takes no account of segmentation, which involves the emergence of corporate sub-groups, each under its own elder or big man. The average size of these smaller units is four or five married males, though three subclans had seven, eight and nine married males respectively.[8]

The Abelam apply the term *gəm* to named exogamous descent groups which have an agnatic core and which, in earlier reports, I described as patriclans. Most clan names have *gəm* as a suffix, and men who belong to one clan say they are *nagura gəm* (*nagura* meaning 'one').[9] They may also assert that their 'paternal forefathers (*nggwalyaba*) are one'. When fission occurs, the new group takes a new name, though not necessarily a new totem (*djambu*) and *nggwalndu*. It is the clan name which is diacritical of exogamy, and not the totem, though the latter is one of the clan symbols and is used in a variety of situations. For example, people may say: 'We are one totem'; or 'this ground belongs to hornbill'; or 'these yams are hawk's things'. In Kalabu, two clans may have the same totem and this may or may not indicate a previous agnatic or uterine tie; the same totems occur also in a number of Abelam villages but in association with different clan names and *nggwalndu*. In Kalabu and other villages I visited, no kinship link was postulated between the groups concerned and there was no obligation to extend hospitality to one another. Ideally, a person's *djambu* is that of his father, and the *djambu* is sometimes described as *nggwal na apwi* (father's father's bird) in contradistinction to *mbambu na apwi* (mother's father's bird). There is no taboo in regard to the former, but any contact with the latter is thought to cause minor illness unless that person has affiliated himself permanently with his mother's clan.

Each clan or subclan is associated with a *nggwalndu,* but the latter is exclusive neither to any one clan nor to any one *ara*: '*Nggwalndu* do not take sides; they stand mid-way.' They are invoked in yam magic, and a man may beg the assistance of the *nggwalndu* of his four grandparents. If, however, he grows a particularly fine yam he bestows on it the name of the *nggwalndu* of the clan with which he is actively affiliated; and, in the procession when yams are carried through the village at harvest, he chants 'I am *Mangiəla*' or 'I am *Təbmanggəro*', as the case may be, thus identifying himself and his yam with a particular *nggwalndu*.

Ara affiliation is not in itself a precise index of clan membership, but a change from one *ara* to another is an index of fission (and sometimes of segmentation) within a clan. Ideally, all members of a clan should belong to the same *ara* and should exchange yams with a clan in the other *ara*. If this were followed consistently, the clans of the village would be divided into moieties and would be paired in ceremonial relationships. But, quite apart from the fact that clans vary in size and that a large clan may have partners in two or more other clans, segmentation involves lack of co-operation in yam exchanges.

Clan names, totems, *nggwalndu* and, to a lesser extent, *ara* affiliation, are symbols which in conjunction serve both to distinguish clans and subclans and to indicate relationships among them. They are also symbols used by a person to express his relationship with individual members of a number of groups in terms of co-operation and the exercise of rights.

The clan or subclan is a landholding unit and this, with co-residence, is a factor making for its persistence as a corporate entity. In the large majority of cases (12 out of 18 clans), male members live together in one hamlet, though a few may have dual residence—i.e. subsidiary dwellings elsewhere. In the case of the remaining six clans, members are distributed among two or three hamlets. The clan or subclan always has an agnatic core and may consist of the leader, his sons, brothers, brothers' sons, paternal cousins and, more rarely, distant agnates, together with such adherents as sisters' sons, cross-cousins and daughters' children. Members of the clan should assist one another and co-operate in many activities. The need for peace within the clan is continually stressed by the elders: clansmen must not quarrel, or the clan will divide or break up.

Patrilineal descent is the ideal, and there is a patrilineal bias in clan membership. But my detailed analysis of genealogical, residential and case material (made since the publication of my earlier articles) show that in 1940 in Kalabu only 71.2% of the 125 married males were nominally affiliated with their fathers' clans, i.e. gave the name of their natal clan when questioned about membership. This 71.2%, however, included men who were no longer full corporate members of the groups with which they had first been affiliated; some had moved to other hamlets, acquired new ceremonial partners, and planted the bulk of their long yams in the garden of a maternal relative or an affine. Some had not changed their residence, though they no longer worked with other agnates in the hamlet; if they were young married men, they relied on a mother's brother, a wife's father or an elderly maternal cross-cousin to perform the magic for their long yams. All these persons occupied, as it were, an intermediate status: they had not broken off all relationships with their natal group; they had not finally committed themselves to full membership in another group. On some days they claimed one totem as their main totem, on other days another totem, thus symbolizing their links with at least two groups. If, then, we consider the composition of clans in terms of full corporate membership, we find that they comprise only 59.2% agnates. These data refer to Kalabu; I collected some genealogical material in other villages which indicated changes in affiliation, but my visits were too brief for me to obtain a detailed knowledge of the effective relationships of individual persons.

Clan organization in Kalabu presents certain parallels with the situation in some of the Central Highland tribes, and is probably similar to that among the Mountain Arapesh, but the theoretical problems cannot be examined here (see Reay 1959; Brown 1962; Berndt 1962 and 1964; Barnes 1962; Langness 1964; Meggitt 1965). However, the question will be asked: are we dealing with descent groups and, if so, are they patriclans? My previous discussion indicates that the people themselves think of gəm as descent groups. My quantitative data demonstrate a marked patrilineal bias; and, lastly, patrilineality is itself stressed as an ideal. Men desire sons who will inherit their land and trees: 'If there are not sons', they say, 'other people may steal the land.' They desire sons who will bear the personal names which are regarded as a clan heritage, the nggwal na yi (father's father's names): 'men are lost, but the names remain'. A man with many children is magnaban (literally, head or great one); the man who has no sons is yi-marəkban (a nameless person).

Kinship terminology and a number of other linguistic usages which cannot be discussed here all indicate that, at the formal level, descent through the father is distinguished from descent through the mother (Kaberry 1941a: 248-50) and that there is a preference for patrilineal inheritance. Nevertheless there are a number of situations in which a person may 'follow the road of the mother', or in which he may ally himself with his wife's people and thereby establish rights for his children who reside in her hamlet, without, however, surrendering his rights or theirs in his own natal clan. Clan affiliation is, moreover, reversible: that is, a person may change his affiliation more than once in the course of his life; he may co-operate in some measure with two or three groups; he may exercise full rights in one group and have latent rights in another; or he may, in exceptional circumstances, exercise some rights in two groups at the same time although he will regard himself as primarily affiliated with one. Men who are ambitious and who have changed their clan membership are sometimes referred to (or rather refer to themselves) as *nyinda-ndu* (middle-man): they look both ways. In private conversation, but particularly on public occasions, they stress their links with different individuals, saying 'we are one totem' or 'we are one clan'; they may intervene in quarrels, and grasp any opportunity to take the floor. They may entrust some of their longest yams to two or three big men in different clans; they may engage in two sets of yam exchanges; and, lastly, if they have two wives, they may place one in one hamlet and the other in another hamlet, and participate in the affairs of the two hamlets concerned. It should be stressed, however, that not all men who have switched from one clan to another behave in this manner. Provided that their relations with neighbours remain amicable and their affairs prosper, some are content to throw in their lot with only one group, although they continue to fulfil their obligations to individual kin in other parts of the village.

This is not the place to consider in detail the range of factors affecting clan affiliation. What concerns us here is that clans and subclans are small, that there is an element of optation in affiliation,[10] and that there is an implicit competition among them to attract new members. If the big men and elders are to retain the allegiance of their dependants, they must not only validate their own position as yam-growers but also show skill in composing quarrels, give assistance, and provide opportunity for the more ambitious among the younger men to play a prominent role on occasion.

In some circumstances a clan loses members through no fault of its leaders. I have already mentioned that a childless man may ask a sister who has two or more children for a son; again, a boy whose father has died may stay in his natal hamlet if his mother continues to live there, but it is highly probable that he will, when he is a youth, go to live with his mother's brother. The tie with uterine kin is particularly close; it is marked by co-operation throughout life, and it is to a mother's brother or senior maternal cross-cousin that a person is most likely to turn if he is left without a father or else quarrels with his agnates and other neighbours. But while his own father is alive and active, it is to the advantage of a youth to remain in his natal clan where he has an unchallenged right to garden land, building materials, house-sites and father's fruit trees, and where he can count on his father to assume prime responsibility for his welfare and protection. But as he approaches the age of marriage, a youth becomes increasingly sensitive to the prestige of his clan or subclan, to his standing within it, and to his relationships with others, especially those of his own generation.

In the first place, the big men and elders must be willing to help the younger members with gifts of long yams, shell rings and pigs in ceremonies which involve the transfer of some or all of these goods, i.e. in puberty rites for the fiancée, marriage, initiation and yam exchanges. Secondly, the leaders should try to ensure that their group as a unit not only meets its commitments to partners but retains the initiative by producing better and more numerous yams, thereby compelling its partners to enlist outside assistance to make an equivalent return. A clan which does little more than hold its own is in danger of losing its more ambitious members to other groups, and in particular those men who are not sons but younger brothers, brothers' sons, or parallel cousins to the most senior elder. An ambitious man who is dissatisfied with the leader in his own clan in his hamlet may ally himself with another segment of the same clan in another part of the village, or with the clan of his mother's brother or wife's father. Several factors may affect his choice: personal relationships; the prestige which the other clan enjoys and which will provide a forum for his own achievements; and, lastly, its age composition. The first two require no further comments; the third requires some amplification. If his mother's brother or wife's father has only young dependants, he is in a position to become the right-hand man and to succeed him when he dies or becomes too senile to play an active role. If, on the other hand, his cross-cousins or wife's brothers are already on the way to establishing some reputation as yam-growers, he has potential rivals. This may not prove a decisive factor, but it is one which enters into the calculations of some men who change their affiliation but do not fully commit themselves to one group to the exclusion of others.

This brings me to another aspect of effective leadership by elders. They should encourage and assist the more enterprising among the younger men to achieve skill as carvers and painters, to accumulate wealth in the form of pigs, rings and garden produce, and to assume some of the responsibility for yam magic. In other words, they must pave the way for their successors; and, with advancing age, they should be willing to remain more and more in the background.

During the early years of marriage, a man is mainly concerned with establishing a family, and with providing sufficient food for his household and the manual labour for the cultivation of his own yams and those of his own clan. With the assistance of neighbours, kin and affines, he builds a storehouse for his own *ka* and his long yams, of which he may have half a dozen fine ones and usually a number of small ones. But, if he is ambitious to become a noted yam-grower, he receives some instruction in magic from his father and another elder and makes a plot for a few of his longer yams which he has obtained from his partner, his elders or even an elder brother. For some of the rites, such as the application of particular kinds of herbs, he calls on the assistance of an elder. To begin with, his experiments are occasional, and limited as a rule to periods when he is already observing a taboo on sexual intercourse because his wife has a newborn child. Once the child begins to crawl, sexual relations are resumed; and, for a time at least, he is content to occupy a status of full ritual dependency on his elders. He will plant most of his yams in the garden of his clan or that of the big man of his hamlet; but he usually entrusts one or two to a mother's brother and/or wife's father. By distributing his longest yams, he insures against a complete failure of his crop; he maintains important ties; and, implicitly, he tests the skill of two or more ritual specialists.

If, however, the young man is an industrious gardener and continues successfully with his own experiments in performing all of the rites for his yams, he gradually acquires a reputation as a potential leader; and he is the more likely to be singled out for notice if he is subject to fits of possession by *Nyambabmu* (one of the tutelary spirits of long yams) during the planting season. While his elders are active, he cannot become the big man of his clan; he cannot compete with them for leadership. His energies are devoted to consolidating his own reputation and to securing the adherence of members of his own generation, to whom he should ideally stand in the relation of 'elder brother' or age-mate (*naui*).

In some clans there may be two or three younger men who are parallel cousins and who are regarded as promising yam-gardeners. Over a period of time one of them will demonstrate his superiority as a gardener and as a man of wealth in the eyes of his own clan and, what is equally important, in the eyes of his ceremonial partner (and his assistants), and other men in the village. When the elders who are big men die or become senile, he takes over the leadership of the clan, that is, becomes its big man; but his ability to hold the group together will depend to a very great extent on his personal qualities—his willingness to allow some credit to members of his own generation and to assist the younger men in their commitments. As long as he has some adherents and excels as a yam-grower he may, in the eyes of the community, be regarded as the big man of the clan. But if he is irascible, overweening and arrogant toward members of his own clan, then those who resent his authority may ally themselves with other groups; or they may constitute a separate segment in another part of the village; or they may form a new section within the hamlet, change their *ara* affiliation, and compete with him and his followers as ceremonial partners.

We have now examined the types of situation which involve leadership, the qualifications demanded of leaders, and the relations among leaders in the village. Within the co-residential clan (or subclan), the structure of authority involves the subordination of younger brother to elder brother, and of the younger generation to the senior generation, that is, to the elders who control access to land, to the tamberan cult and to ritual knowledge. These are the guardians, advisers and regulators. But the society also attaches value to achievement—to the production and distribution of wealth (particularly long yams), to skill in carving and painting, and to prowess in warfare. The elder who excels as a 'yam-grower' is a big man or *nəmandu*. He is the entrepreneur in activities involving the collaboration of his own clan and group in its relations with other clans both within and outside the hamlet. The status of *nəmandu* has two components: that of seniority in age (the same term is used for elder sibling), and that of outstanding achievement. In terms of the first component, nəmandu is a status which all men occupy in respect of those who are younger than themselves; it is one with which they may identify themselves. In terms of its second component—achievement—it is a status to which all may aspire in advanced middle-age, if not a little before. The rewards of this status are in the main intangible. It is true that a big man is able to enlist the labour and resources of a number of men in certain activities which are conceived to be of some advantage to them, but which also bring him particular prestige as the entrepreneur. But on his side, he must shoulder responsibility and produce a surplus of wealth for distribution among his dependants, temporary assistants, and ceremonial partners. By his own achievements he must constantly validate his pre-eminence and, at the same time, maintain the prestige of his clan as a unit. He must be willing to train and eventually to give way gracefully to his successors among the younger generation.

We have seen that only some 60% of the married men remain full corporate members of their natal clan, and that clans and subclans are themselves small. Nevertheless, hamlets and the village itself persist as corporate and relatively stable units. The stability of units larger than the clan would seem to derive from two principles of organization: the seniority and authority accorded to age on the one hand, and the dual or *ara* organization on the other. The society does not permit rivalry between generations. Competition for prestige occurs between men of the same generation who belong to different clans and, ideally, to different hamlets. In this we have the key to the ordering of political relations within the village. The pattern of leadership at the village level does not duplicate that within the clan or even within the hamlet: it is one of matched pre-eminence which is regulated by the *ara* organization. This emphasis on equivalence is one of the major themes of the culture, and finds expression in the term for age-mates (*naui*); in the symmetrical relations of brothers-in-law or of cross-cousins (as opposed to the asymmetrical relation between siblings); in the preference for an exchange of women between clans; in the pairing of hamlets in ceremonial relationships; in the exchange of shell rings to seal peace between disputants in the village; in the exchange of hostages to seal a truce between enemy villages; and, lastly, in the exchange of yams and pigs, both within the village and between villages.

Within the younger generation, dissidents may leave their natal clan, but they remain dependent on some elder for access to land, for assistance in yam magic, and for sponsorship in the tamberan cult. Moreover, a man's status and that of his children in the community depend on participation in the yam and tamberan cults: he must have a ceremonial partner; and he must ally himself with some group on one side of the dual organization or the other. The dual organization itself links together clans, however small, in relationships of a complex kind. Within its framework, rivals who are peers may compete for prestige in the yam exchanges; but they must also initiate one another in the various stages of the tamberan cult, and are therefore dependent on one another in some situations. Lastly, they must work together to keep in being the house-tamberans which are the centres of ritual and ceremonial life and the source of welfare for the whole village. They must combine to defend their village against aggression by neighbouring villages. We shall, therefore, turn now to the sphere of intervillage relations.

INTERVILLAGE RELATIONS

The people of Kalabu not only look upon themselves as constituting a close-knit community; they also regard other villages in their vicinity as corporate units. Some they describe as friends, *nggeindu* (literally, place-men), and others as *mama* (enemies—'people with whom we fight'). Among the former, one or two are called *nagura vi* (one spear)—allies who give assistance in fights against *mama*. The intensity and frequency of interaction among villages are largely a function of geographical distance: villages that are close friends or arch enemies are mainly those which have adjoining boundaries. If Abelam territory is surveyed as a whole, it is difficult to demarcate zones in which peaceful conditions obtain from others in which intermittent feud prevails. Nevertheless, if any one village is taken as a focal point, it will be found to have common boundaries with six or more other villages within a radius of some two to five miles. Two or three of these are friends, and three or more are enemies. Beyond this radius, there are other communities with which contact is less frequent and which are regarded as friendly neutrals, with the exception of those which are enemies of close friends and are therefore potentially hostile.[11]

The content of relationships between a village and its immediate neighbours may change over a period of years or generations. Intermittent fighting with *mama* may be punctuated by a formal truce during which yams are competitively exchanged and there is some collaboration in the tamberan cult. Again, a village which has been routed in an attack may abandon outlying hamlets, and some of its members may take refuge in a friendly village. More rarely, a friendly village may become an enemy: e.g. Malnba was at one time a friend of Waigagum; or a village may split as a result of fighting within it, and then one section moves off to become a separate village and may become for a time the *mama* of the parent village. But there is never an absence of political relationship among neighbouring villages; more positively, relationships are conceptualized by the people themselves as those of alliance, friendship, neutrality, and active hostility with occasional periods of truce. Any one village is thus the nexus of a system of political relations which embrace some eight to fourteen neighbouring communities having a total population of some 2,000 to 4,000. The system is not a closed one, since the range of political ties does not completely coincide even for adjacent villages which are allies. Nevertheless, political alignments among neighbouring villages tend to persist through generation after generation (unlike many other areas in New Guinea), and therefore justify the use of the term 'system' as a description of intervillage relations, if any one village is taken as a focal point. The content of these political relationships will now be examined in more detail.

Nggeindu

The relationship between villages which without further qualification refer to one another as *nggeindu* is not a formalized one involving defined rights and obligations, but it is associated with the ease and security which on the whole characterize relationships within the village itself, even when these are not reinforced by close links of kinship and affinity. In fact, the description of a friendly village as *nana nggeindu* (our place-men) or as *nana ndu-tagwa, ndei* (our men-women, they) implies that its members are in one sense regarded as belonging to the community. Visits are made for barter and for attendance at ceremonies; and, where individuals have personal friends (*pətə*), they normally look to them for hospitality or assistance in any major undertaking. Lastly, help may be given for the construction of a house-tamberan and ritual paraphernalia or for the holding of initiation ceremonies. For example, Djame, Loenem and Bainyik (all friends of Kalabu) contributed timbers for the building of the Numbungen house-tamberan in Kalabu.

In the case of *nggeindu* who are also 'one spear', there is an obligation to settle disputes without recourse to fighting, and also to give help against an enemy. Kalabu's main ally was Djame, a Shamu village sited on a ridge to the north, about half an hour's walk away. Kalabu had, at one time or another, been on terms of hostility with three other Mamu villages; and in some respects the people of Kalabu regarded themselves as middle-men (*nyindandu*), since they bordered both Mamu and Shamu dialect villages, and had some kinship usages in common with Djame. The other *nggeindu* of Kalabu were Loenem (an Arapesh village to the north-east), and Bainyik and Maprik (both Shamu villages, to the south-west and west respectively). With other villages again, such as Manbelip, Nemarkum, Naramko, Yanuko, Yamil, Nyeligum, Wora and Gaigetigum, contact was friendly but intermittent. The main enemies of both Kalabu and Djame were Kumbangwa, Malnba and Mogatugum, with all of whom they had common boundaries. But Kalabu also had an enemy in Waigagum, some two hours' walk to the south; and Djame itself had an enemy in Nyamigum on its own north-western boundary. Though Kalabu and Djame gave each other assistance in major fights with their respective enemies, geographical distance affected the degree of interaction between Kalabu and Nyamigum on the one hand, and between Djame and Waigagum on the other. In other words, the field of political relations for Kalabu and Djame was not co-extensive, although there was a considerable amount of overlap in view of their close spatial propinquity.

As far as I could ascertain, there was no deliberate policy of contracting marriages with certain villages in particular; when I enquired why men had taken wives from other villages, I was usually told that 'the women liked them'. In one case, the advantage of having a brother-in-law who was a renowned fighter was stressed. Nevertheless, it is significant that in Kalabu the majority of extravillage unions were with *nggeindu*. Of the 282 marriages contracted by Kalabu men over three or four generations, 75 (or 26.6%) were with women in other villages, and of these 51 (or 68%) were with *nggeindu*.[12] Among the 51 marriages with *nggeindu*,

31 (60%) were with Djame; the remaining 20 unions were distributed among seven other villages—8 with Loenem, 3 with Maprik, 3 with Bainyik, and so on. Marriages with women in enemy villages totalled 24: 9 with Waigagum, 9 with Kumbangwa, and 6 with Malnba and Mogatugum.

In the unions with enemy villages, ancestral links, geographical propinquity, and conditions of truce are factors to be taken in account. The high proportion of unions with the ally Djame is consistent with the type of behaviour which is required of affines and cross-cousins, and which normally involves friendship and close co-operation in economic and ceremonial activities. It will be recalled that, of the seven clans in Kalabu founded by immigrants from other villages, four were from Djame, two from Loenem, and one from Waigagum.[13] There were thus a number of men and women in Kalabu who had some kind of kinship or affinal link with people in Djame and, to a less extent, with people in Loenem. Whether a preponderance of marriages with Djame had led to the contracting of a political alliance, or whether an alliance had been followed by an increasing number of marriages, I was unable to ascertain. The former seems more probable; the people of Kalabu said they had always been friends with Djame. It is clear, however, that the formal relationship of alliance between the two villages as corporate units is reinforced by a network of dyadic kinship and affinal ties.

Kalabu men with relatives in Djame took an interest in its affairs and sometimes acted as peacemakers. For example, on November 22nd, 1939, a violent quarrel occurred in which some men in Lower Djame accused their ceremonial partners in Upper Djame of making heavy rains to hinder the yam-planting. Spears were thrown but there were no casualties, and eventually it was agreed that each side should display its unplanted yams. Early in the morning of November 23rd the yam houses were opened for inspection and, in addition, some sixty shell rings had been laid out as a symbol of wealth and of ability to buy pigs for distribution. Each of the men concerned in the dispute exchanged a shell ring, yams, and a section of pork with his ceremonial partner. Opportunity was also taken to distribute the remainder of the pigs killed to some of the big men in Kalabu, Loenem, Nyamigum and Kumbangwa, either as a settlement for debt or as a means of contracting a creditor relationship. But these proceedings did not pass without incident. *Yauwal* peace leaves had been placed in all the piazzas by the elders; but the actual disputants had placed wild taro leaves—symbol of anger—in their own yam-houses. Quarrelling occurred during the morning, old grievances were resurrected, and the elders of the village had frequently to intervene. Among the peacemakers were Walu and Kumban of Kalabu. Walu carried a *yauwal* leaf, and he told the Djame men not to quarrel: 'You must harvest yams; then you (Djame) and we (Kalabu) will send them to Malnba.' The appeal was made in terms of the common interest of men in growing yams and of the need for co-operation with Kalabu against their common enemy, Malnba, with which perforce as a result of European administration they had to observe a truce.

Mama (Enemies)

I never had any difficulty in eliciting from the men the names of villages which were *mama* of their own; indeed, as far as neighbouring villages were concerned, enemies sometimes outnumbered friends. Feuding had of course been forbidden by the Administration, which had established an administrative post at Maprik in October 1937; but hostile feelings had naturally persisted, previous fights were recalled with relish, and, on the occasion of a yam exchange, a few spears might be thrown before the elders could intervene. Apart from blood revenge, one of the main causes of fighting between *mama* was the cutting down of sago palms near a common boundary. With one exception, namely, that of Aupik, which was the most western of the Shamu villages, the Abelam denied that the abduction of women provoked feuds. 'Over women we fight not; over food we fight not; over sorcery, not. Only over sago.' Often men would also say: 'We fight because we are *mama*.'

Mama are alleged to commit sorcery, and this belief is consistent with the attitude that they are in general maleficent and fight to kill. They are, however, merely the technical experts who are called in by an outsider who has a grudge to settle against a fellow-villager. It is he who is said to obtain the sorcery materials—personal leavings of his intended victim—and send them to someone in one of the *mama* villages, where action may not be taken for years. The moral responsibility for the death of his victim, however, rests with him since, without his initiative in the first place, sorcery would not have been committed. If anyone falls seriously ill, *yauwal* leaves are placed in the piazzas by elders, and an appeal is made throughout the village for the unknown person (he who originally obtained the 'dirt' or personal leavings) to put aside his anger and send a shell ring to retrieve the 'dirt'. If death does occur, specific individuals may be accused or resort may be had to divination to establish the totem, and, through a process of elimination, the identity, of the culprit. But the accused will then assert his innocence and cite other disputes which the deceased had with other persons in the village over the years. The long delay which may elapse before sorcery is committed, the difficulty in isolating any one quarrel that might have provoked the theft of 'dirt', and lastly the belief that the sorcerer himself may belong to any one of several *mama* villages—all these are consistent with the fact that the village as a corporate unit does not avenge deaths attributed to sorcery. Nevertheless, the belief that *mama* are sorcerers does, without doubt, intensify feelings of hostility.

Mama were not always at feud; there were procedures for establishing a truce which might last for ten or more years. But sooner or later casualties would be inflicted during the ceremonial exchange of yams or, more commonly, in reprisals for theft from sago plantations or garden land near the common boundary. Within any one village, rights to sago palms were jealously guarded by owners and close kin; but, in the event of trespass by a fellow-villager, compensation would be accepted. If, however, members of a *mama* village were caught red-handed, spears were thrown and this usually led to a resumption of hostilities in which both villages became involved. The near kin (father, brothers, sons) of a slain man or woman had the duty of avenging his or her death, for which the village of the slayer was *collectively* held responsible. Any person—man, woman or child—could serve as a victim, and individuals working alone were liable to be picked off with a spear. Men went armed and on the alert while their womenfolk gardened; and, once the crop was harvested, plots were temporarily abandoned and others made in a more secure place.

Occasionally a party of men might make a surprise attack on a hamlet of a *mama* village; but, despite the insecurity and tension which must have existed, casualties appear to have been relatively few over a period of years. Old men in Kalabu who were renowned as fighters claimed to have killed only five to ten individuals during their lifetime; but their victims had sometimes belonged to three different *mama* villages and even included children. The heads of big men were taken and placed in the house-tamberan after ritual treatment. Sometimes a village would send a message, through a neutral village, challenging its *mama* to battle in an area midway between its own settlement and that of the *mama*. The big men, elders and warriors of reputation consulted and, if they accepted the challenge, sent a shell ring with a leaf twisted through it to their own ally with a request for assistance. The challengers then cleared half the proposed battle arena, and on a different day when the place was deserted the recipients of the challenge cleared the rest of the arena. On an appointed day (it should be noted that the arrangements were made by employing a neutral village as intermediary), all the able-bodied males, painted with charcoal and carrying yam ornaments in their mouths and shields in their hands, met for combat. Deaths might amount to no more than half a dozen. (For example, in an account of a battle between Kalabu and Malnba, I was told that four men had been killed and three wounded.) If both sides were evenly matched, a strategic withdrawal was made at the end of the day; but, if the men of one side were stronger, they chased their opponents from the arena, pursued them back to the nearest hamlets, and destroyed gardens and houses. Kalabu had inflicted major defeats on Kumbangwa and Malnba in the past and had burnt down their house-tamberans; Bainyik had been routed by Waigagum a generation previously and had abandoned an outlying hamlet. Refugees from Kwalingu, in flight after an attack by Tiyandegum, had been granted land and coconut palms by Waigagum; and a group from Nyindako village had, some three or four generations ago, fled from their village after its partial destruction by Mikau, and had established themselves as a clan in Gaigetigum to the north.

Kalabu and Waigagum, both large villages, had never been forced to abandon hamlets as a result of fighting. Size was an important factor in political relations, and refugees were welcomed as an accession to fighting strength. Conversely, dis-unity within a village left it vulnerable to its enemies: there was a strong reprobation of fighting among fellow-villagers which might eventually lead to deaths, feud, and the splitting of the community into two separate villages. Cases had occurred in the past among some of the Shamu dialect villages. As a result of severe fighting over women, Kuleligum had split off from Abange, and Nemarkum from Gaigetigum. In both cases, peace was eventually made, but the new village units remained separate communities and exchanged yams competitively as though they were *mama*.[14]

After two *mama* villages had been at feud for some years, a time would come when both wanted to clear and cultivate bush on their mutual boundary. A truce became a matter of expediency to both; the big men and elders would confer in their respective villages, and a neutral village would be asked to act as intermediary in arranging a meeting. The two sides then met on the boundary and exchanged hostages, who remained as guests for a few weeks. Such men were said to be *naui* to one another, that is, of approximately the same age and status. Thenceforth yams would be exchanged once or twice a year; members of the two villages attended dances and major ceremonies; and there was a certain amount of collaboration for the construction of house-tamberans, the carving and painting of ritual paraphernalia, and the holding of initiation rites. But such co-operation was intermittent, and appears to have varied in kind and extent from village to village. The contributions of Kumbangwa and Malnba to the Numbungen house-tamberan built in Kalabu have already been described (note that Waigagum did not assist). Similar cases of intervillage co-operation could be cited from other villages: thus Kwimbu received help from Kwambigum, Waigagum, Dumbet, Naramko and Tshuambigum; Waigamum had help from Bainyik, Malnba, Mogatugum, and Djame (all *mama*), as well as from its ally Kumbangwa. Some of the *nggwalndu* in Maprik were carved by Nyeligum, Abange and Djame; and the façade of the Mogatugum house-tamberan was painted by three men from Kalabu (its *mama*). If, however, collaboration in the tamberan cult did not always involve all *mama* with whom there was a truce, the ceremonial exchange of yams was regular and associated with competition for prestige and latent hostility.

These exchanges differed from those which took place in the village, in that the exchangers of yams did not stand in a *tshambəra* or ceremonial partnership to one another. There were several reasons for this. Participation demanded a surplus of yams over and above those required for commitments in the village, and even skilled yam-growers were not able to produce this every season. Hence the membership of the group which received and sent yams varied from year to year. Nevertheless in the case of a large village like Kalabu, which exchanged yams with two *mama* villages, responsibility was assumed by certain hamlets only. In this capacity they represented the village as a whole, and they were accompanied by a procession of armed men alert for any signs of treachery or ready to fight should a dispute arise over the yams. The following account illustrates the nature of relationships between *mama* villages, and also the pattern of leadership within Kalabu itself.

Kalabu's enemies were Malnba, Mogatugum, Kumbangwa and Waigagum; it exchanged yams with the first two (Mogatugum was in fact an offshoot of Malnba), and this entailed some division of responsibility within the village itself and with Djame. For example, on June 11th, 1939, eight yams and three sections of pig were collected at Kumungwanda hamlet and taken in procession to Malnba by about thirty men. A little later, Djame sent five yams to Mogatugum. In August, five yams and a section of pig were collected at Dueningi hamlet and despatched to Malnba. When I commented on the small number of yams, the men replied contemptuously that Malnba was a small place; its population was in fact about half the size of that of Kalabu. Apart from reminiscences about previous fights and a little good-humoured ridicule, the transactions were conducted amicably by both parties. On both occasions the big men remained in the background; the main donors of the yams were men in the middle range of leadership. They were in their forties, had each two wives, had achieved some reputation as yam-growers, and had ceremonial partners in Kalabu who were men of indifferent calibre. Most of them had changed their clan affiliation but had continued to participate to some extent in the affairs of their natal clan. These exchanges with Malnba gave them an opportunity to affirm publicly their ties with two hamlets in Kalabu, to demonstrate their skill as yam-growers, and to dispose of their surplus.

The exchanges with Kumbangwa were much more important and were conducted by the big men of the hamlets concerned in Kalabu. The Kumbangwa population was in fact only a little larger than that of Malnba, but fighting between Kumbangwa and Kalabu had occurred more recently than that between Malnba and Kalabu. On two occasions when yams were exchanged between Kalabu and Kumbangwa in 1939, spears were thrown, although no casualties resulted. The men said afterwards that this was merely 'talk-play' and was customary: 'Once we fought with spears; now we fight with yams.' The statement was one which I heard on many occasions, and was revealing. Exchange between *mama* villages was not merely a competition for prestige but a canalizing of hostility in symbolic terms. Kalabu did not exchange yams directly with Waigagum, which had its own extensive exchanges with its other enemies—Tiyandegum, Mikau, Kwimbu and Nemarkum. But, among the fifteen large yams taken to Kalabu by Kumbangwa on June 7th, three had been contributed by Waigagum; the latter had also made a part payment for the purchase of the black sow which was also presented.

Before leaving the home village, Kumbangwa had signalled on its slit-gongs the number of yams it was bringing to Kalabu; the news was received with some jubilation in Kalabu. But, when the yams were carried on to the piazza at Swapel hamlet in Kalabu about an hour later, the exchange of perfunctory compliments soon gave way to insults and skirmishing with spears. Ndigosha of Baigu hamlet, who was noted as an orator, artist and warrior, precipitated the quarrel by asserting that there were too many yams. Kumbangwa and Waigagum men retorted that Kalabu was afraid to accept the yams because it would be unable to produce an equivalent number for a return gift later. In a moment the men were prancing about with spears and it was some minutes before Kumban and Gumbidjara, who frequently acted as peacemakers in Kalabu, could restore order. The yams and pig were in fact accepted by Kalabu and, after some conversation, the Kumbangwa men returned to their own village.

The acknowledged leader in the events which followed in Kalabu was Walugwu, the big man of Swapel hamlet, but a number of other big men were also involved. These were Balumama, a resident of Swapel, parallel cousin to Walugwu and a noted yam-grower; Yagamun, the big man of Wabinda hamlet and a member of the same clan as Walugwu though belonging to another subclan; and, lastly, Ndungget, the big man of Yambudjaki hamlet who was a son-in-law of Walugwu, and whose father's mother had also belonged to the same clan as Walugwu. Walugwu, in conference with these men, shared out the yams received from Kumbangwa: they retained some for themselves and gave others to their younger clansmen. One yam was sent to Djame. After this first distribution, a second followed in Kalabu in which most men handed over yams to their ceremonial partners, the main recipient being Patundu, the big man of Baigu hamlet, who was ceremonial partner to Walugwu himself. Walugwu, Balumama, Ndungget and three young men of Swapel hamlet took the pig, having agreed beforehand to provide the six shell rings for the purchase of a large white sow which would later be transferred to Kumbangwa. On June 8th, Walugwu directed the butchering of the pig received from Kumbangwa: an uncooked section was handed over to Yagamun and a man of Kaumbul hamlet; but the bulk of it was given to Patundu and ceremonial partners of the men of Swapel. These recipients cooked it, carved it into small strips, and distributed them among their own kin and affines, some of whom lived in Djame.

On June 9th, a white sow, which had been purchased from its owners in Baigu hamlet, was lashed to a pole. Twenty yams, contributed by men of Swapel, Wabinda and Baigu hamlets, were first displayed on Swapel piazza; these were five in excess of those received from Kumbangwa. A procession of about seventy Kalabu men went to Kumbangwa, where the yams were accepted but the pig was rejected. Gumbidjara and Kumban again tried to keep the peace, but Kumbangwa men suddenly charged us with spears and most of us retreated down the hill. Some of the Kalabu men were then asked to return to Kumbangwa to discuss the matter further, but I was instructed to go back to Kalabu. About an hour later the rest of the Kalabu men returned, carrying the pig, which was immediately restored to its previous owners and the rings retrieved. Many of the participants in the yam exchanges were angry at what was deemed to be an insult to Kalabu; there was talk of making black magic to spoil the Kumbangwa yam gardens, and also of returning the yams already received from Kumbangwa on June 7th. But when tempers had cooled down, it was acknowledged that the Kalabu pig was white and not black, though it was alleged to be larger than that received from Kumbangwa. Walugwu was unable to find a suitable pig, and on June 12th, Yagamun sent a male black pig to Kumbangwa, which refused to accept it on the grounds that it was not a sow! On July 6th, Yagamun made a fruitless journey to Yamil village to inspect a pig, and in the meantime he publicly taunted Walugwu and others with their failure to produce one. It was not until July 21st that some men of Swapel and Baigu hamlets obtained a pig which was acceptable to Kumbangwa.

On October 19th, a few of the prominent young men in Baigu hamlet sent a section of uncooked pig and eleven yams to Kumbangwa. One of the yams was eleven feet two inches in length. *Yauwal* leaves were attached to the largest yams, and the elders in Baigu and Swapel ordered the yam carriers not to give way to anger: they were to be quiet men (*narandu*). Kumbangwa accepted the yams under protest, saying that it was too late in the year to plant them—a patent lie. Kalabu retorted that Kumbangwa was afraid that it would be unable to make an equivalent return in the following year. In Kalabu itself, some men of Baigu handed over yams to their ceremonial partners in Swapel, and also a section of pig which was equivalent to what they had received from them on June 8th.

The incidents which I have described reveal the state of tension and incipient hostility in which ceremonial exchanges between *mama* villages are frequently conducted, and the importance attached to yams as symbols of male prestige and leadership. The transactions are public, tallies of the length and number of yams are kept, and the exchanges should be approximately equivalent. Nevertheless, honour goes to the group that hands over yams which, within limits, exceed in size and number those received previously; and, while a truce obtains, the prestige of a village abroad is closely bound up with its participation and prominence in these exchanges. A village receives some help from its ally in these exchanges (e.g. Waigagum and Kumbangwa on the one hand, and Kalabu and Djame on the other); and such assistance, however minor, serves to symbolize and to perpetuate the traditional political alignment of neighbouring villages.

The incidents which I have described also throw further light on politics in Kalabu itself. In the important transactions, the entrepreneurs are the big men of certain hamlets; in those exchanges considered less important, younger men who have begun to establish a reputation as promising yam-growers have an opportunity to play a prominent part. Moreover, in any one exchange, men who excel in different roles come to the fore: the orators and singers, the owners of shell rings and pigs, the renowned warriors, and the peacemakers. Lastly, the exchanges provide a situation in which rivalry between leaders of subclans of the same clan and rivalry between ceremonial partners give way to consultation and collaboration in the need to maintain village prestige against a common enemy.

NOTES

1. Henceforth *tshambəra* will be referred to as ceremonial partners. With the exception of a few words like *ara, ka, mama* and *nggwalndu* (see below), I have avoided the use of vernacular terms in this essay. In some cases I have retained an anglicized version of Pidgin-English terms, e.g. house-tamberan (men's ceremonial house). 'Tamberan' is used among the Abelam for rituals, ceremonial paraphernalia and spirits connected with the men's ceremonial houses, entry to which is forbidden to women.

2. My research was financed by a fellowship from the Australian National Research Council. I should like to take this opportunity to acknowledge once more my debt to Professor A. P. Elkin, then Chairman of the Committee for Anthropology on the Council, for his generous help and encouragement.

3. For an account of the culture area of which both the Arapesh and the Abelam form a part, see Mead (1938). The Iatmül are discussed by Bateson (1932 and 1936).

4. For example, *Bira* is the name of a *nggwalndu* found in Kalabu and other Mamu villages, as well as in Kwimbu (Yambe dialect), Mikau (a Kamu village on the border of the grass plains), and in Abange (a Shamu village west of Maprik). The *nggwalndu* called *Manggiəla* is found in Kalabu, Malnba, Mikau, Gaigetigum, Aupik and Wosera.

5. Details of initiation vary among Abelam villages. For an account of a ceremony held in the Shamu village of Maprik, see Thomson 1952. Dr (then Mr) Anthony Forge in the course of his fieldwork witnessed a number of these ceremonies and is preparing his material for publication.

6. The account in this essay supersedes that given in my earlier article, which contained several errors in the alignment of particular sections and was written before I had completed a detailed analysis of genealogical and residential material (cf. 1941a: 241-3 and fn. 5).

7. In my first report (1941a: 242), I described new hamlets (or what in most cases were sections) as 'colonies', but the term is unsatisfactory since it ignores the complexity of relationships and suggest both homogeneity and clan membership and some dependence of a ritual and economic kind. It had some appropriateness in the case of Swapel and Kumungwanda where, in fact, the founders of the component clans originally derived from Wabinda and Dueningi respectively. But in the case of Malbimbil, Baigu, Meregwa and Mabmeia, the component clans in each hamlet derived from different hamlets in the village.

8. In an earlier article (1941a: 242 *et passim*), segments of clans were described as 'lineages' on the grounds that they were corporate shallow descent groups some three or four generations in depth. Since, however, exact genealogical connection between all members is not always known, these groups should be classified as subclans, in accordance with contemporary anthropological usage.

9. Some village names also have the suffix *gəm*. It should also be noted that *gəm* is employed in the context of dyadic relations. Persons who are descended from one of four grandparents say that they are *nagura gəm*. This usage is consistent with considerable fluidity in clan affiliation, and with situations in which one or both parties wish to stress amicable relations and co-operation in a particular enterprise.

10. Professor Firth (1957) has distinguished between *definitive* descent-group systems which do not allow choice in affiliation as regards membership through male or female links, and *optative* systems which do. I do not, however, regard Kalabu descent groups as ambilineal.

11. Journeys are also made to the coast to obtain salt, shell rings, and other articles. Only a few members of the village undertake such expeditions, and they have friends (*pətə*) in the villages through which they pass.

12. In my first article on the Abelam (1941a: 252), my preliminary estimate of extravillage marriage in Kalabu was 15%. This was based on material in genealogical charts only; but the analysis of other data in my notebooks revealed a much higher percentage of extravillage unions. (The figure given for polygynous unions in the earlier report, namely 12%, was also an underestimate: it should be 15%.)

13. In fights with Waigagum, men whose forebears came from that village collaborated with Kalabu but avoided injuring near kin in Waigagum. I collected some genealogical material during a week's visit to Waigagum, and discovered that

three of the immigrant clans there had been founded by men from villages which were allies to Waigagum, namely Kumbangwa, Kwalingu and Yanuko. There were cases of unions with women of other villages, but my data were not sufficiently complete to work out the proportion of these to intravillage marriages.

14. Among the Mountain Arapesh, abduction of women was one of the main causes of fights between villages. Battles were fought on the boundary between localities, but casualties appear to have been few. Fortune (1939) recorded that about 50% of the old men had each one or more victims to his credit. Within the sovereign locality (hamlet cluster), there was a repudiation of killing in interclan disputes.

REFERENCES CITED

BARNES, J. A. (1962): African models in the New Guinea Highlands. *Man,* Vol. 62: 5-9.

BATESON, G. (1932): Social structure of the Iatmül people of the Sepik River. *Oceania,* Vol. II: 245-91; 401-53.

BATESON, G. (1936): *Naven: a survey of the problems suggested by a composite picture of the culture of a New Guinea tribe drawn from three points of view.* Cambridge: Cambridge University Press.

BERNDT, R. M. (1962): *Excess and Restraint: social control among a New Guinea mountain people.* Chicago: University of Chicago Press.

BERNDT, R. M. (1964): Warfare in the New Guinea Highlands. In *American Anthropologist Special Publication:* New Guinea, the Central Highlands (J. Watson, ed.), Vol. 66, No. 4, Part 2: 183-203.

BROWN, P. (1962): Non-agnates among the patrilineal Chimbu. *Journal of the Polynesian Society,* Vol. 71: 57-69.

FIRTH, R. (1957): A note on descent groups in Polynesia. *Man,* Vol. 57: 4-8.

FORTUNE, R. F. (1939): Arapesh Warfare. *American Anthropologist,* Vol. 41: 22-41.

KABERRY, P. M. (1941a): The Abelam tribe, Sepik District, New Guinea: a preliminary report. *Oceania,* Vol. XI: 233-258, 345-367.

KABERRY, P. M. (1941b): Law and political organization in the Abelam Tribe, New Guinea. *Oceania,* Vol. XII: 79-95, 209-225, 331-363.

LANGNESS, L. L. (1964): Some problems in the conceptualization of Highlands social structures. *American Anthropologist Special Publication:* New Guinea, the Central Highlands (J. Watson, ed.), Vol. 66, No. 4, Part 2: 162-182.

LAYCOCK, D. C. (1961): The Sepik and its languages. *Australian Territories,* Vol. 1: 35-41.

MEAD, M. (1938): The Mountain Arapesh: I. An importing culture. *Anthropological Papers of the American Museum of Natural History,* Vol. XXXVI, Part III.

MEGGITT, M. J. (1965): *The lineage system of the Mae-Enga of New Guinea.* Edinburgh, London: Oliver and Boyd.

REAY, M. (1959): *The Kuma: Freedom and conformity in the New Guinea Highlands.* Melbourne: Melbourne University Press.

THOMSON, R. (1952): The Maprik Area Education Centre. *South Pacific,* Vol. 6, No. 8: 478-491.

PETER LAWRENCE

THE GARIA OF THE MADANG DISTRICT[1]

ABSTRACT

Garia society is cognatic or bilateral, with no easily recognizable political units, no system of rank, and a weak and localized authority system. This structural examination explores the ways in which social control is maintained. Of crucial significance in this situation is the 'security circle'. Within the context of the principles underlying socio-political action, central points of discussion are self-regulation, religious sanctions and retaliation, and factors influencing the conduct of disputes. Leadership is not important in this connection, but the security circle is. Made up of bilateral kindred, affines, and persons in special relationships, it represents the principal means of maintaining and restoring socio-political order.

With a few notable exceptions, such as Colson (1953), scholars who have analysed the socio-political systems of stateless societies have concentrated on those with unilineal segmentary structures. This paper is concerned with a cognatic or bilateral society, in which there are no immediately recognizable political groups or communities (such as tribes or clans), no system of rank, and only a weak system of authority with restricted geographical range. Although its political system—the means of inducing conformity to accepted norms of conduct and of settling disputes —shares many principles in common with those of segmentary societies, it expresses them through a different structural form. I approach the problem, first, by presenting a brief abstract of the people and their environment and, second, by examining their social structure and the methods they use to maintain and restore social order.

The People and their Environment

The Garia are one of several small linguistic groups inhabiting low mountain ranges, known officially as the Bagasin Area, about twenty to thirty miles west-south-west of Madang. Their neighbours are the Girawa, Yapa, Kopoka, and Sopu. These ranges overlook the Ramu River to the south-west and the Naru to the east. To the north and north-east they are bounded by the Gogol River.[2]

Garialand, about thirty to forty square miles within the Bagasin Area, is very rugged—a monotonous succession of mountain peaks, a little more than three thousand feet, and linking ridges, about fifteen hundred feet, above sea level. There is little or no flat land, and the whole area is covered with dense jungle except for patches of secondary growth where there has been native cultivation.

The people have a simple material culture. They depend for the bulk of their food supply on agriculture, so that climatic conditions are most important for them. The year is divided into two seasons, the dry and the wet. During the dry season (March-November), there is an abundance of food, and all important economic and social activities take place: the preparation of new gardens for the coming year, initiation ceremonies, dances, and pig exchanges. During the wet season (November-March), there is a shortage of food and little heavy work is done.

Population and Settlements

The Garia population is small (about 2,500) and is centred around fourteen major villages ranging from one to three hundred inhabitants each. These settlements are officially recognized by the Administration and have their own officials (luluais, tultuls, medical tultuls), and village books. Traditional local organization, however, was based on scattered hamlets, the largest of which had probably rather less than forty inhabitants. Villages were formed only during the 1920's and 1930's, when the Administration brought hamlets together at central points. Because of the dispersed distribution of landholdings,[3] large settlements are inevitably unstable in this society, and nowadays the people have adopted a compromise in their system of local organization. Most of them live for the greater part of the year in hamlets, clustered around the villages, which are used mainly as centres for assembly on important occasions, such as the arrival of Administration patrols.

In local organization, the basic residential unit is the elementary or compound family. Its members are nearly always in the same settlement and, although they do not all live under one roof, the houses they occupy are generally built close together. Husband and wife or wives have separate dwellings. The younger children and unmarried daughters sleep with their mother or mothers, and the adolescent sons in the settlement club house.

Otherwise no distinct principle is immediately apparent. Hamlets, almost without exception, consist of small and heterogeneous groups of people, most but not all of whom are in some way interrelated. But the population of no settlement is ever permanent, for the people are, within limits, essentially migratory. Individuals periodically move from one hamlet or village to another to make use of their scattered land interests.

The Political Region

Apart from their common territory, their common language, and their common allegiance to certain deities whom they claim to be exclusively their own, it is very difficult to treat the Garia as a discrete society. They do not express themselves as a single political body under common leadership or in terms of any common activity. They never assemble for any important ceremony such as group worship; they do not engage in joint enterprises, such as trading expeditions; and, what is most important, they have never united for purposes of warfare against their neighbours. Indeed, a marked feature of the social system as a whole is that Garia living on the borders have exactly the same types of relationships with members of other linguistic groups as they have with other Garia farther inland. In this way, the Garia social system can be said to be part of the wider social system of the Bagasin Area.

Moreover, as will appear later on, although groups based on unilineal descent do exist in the internal organization of Garia society, they are not emphasized to any extent and, with one exception, are less important in the settlement of disputes than bilateral kinship ties and other purely interpersonal relationships. Again, although common residence presupposes some degree of mutual interdependence, the inhabitants of a settlement (village or hamlet) do not express themselves as a closed group with political functions.

Nevertheless, it is possible to discover throughout the Bagasin Area as a whole regions within which there are systems of relationships with political functions in that they are effective for preventing or settling most disputes. Garialand can be regarded as one of these regions in so far as it is, for the people living at its centre, the widest possible range of political relationships of this kind. Yet these regions have no absolute boundaries and, as they can be defined only with reference to central points, they intersect with and overlap each other. Thus the inhabitants of any settlement can be placed in several of these political regions at any one time. To take an example, the people of Totoba village on the northern border belong to the political region which is coincident with Garialand, and to another which is coincident with Girawaland. But they are also the centre of a similar range of political relationships which crosses the border so as to include part of Garialand and part of Girawaland. Looked at in another way, the Bagasin Area consists of a series of these political regions—one of them being Garialand—which cut across one another at different points.

THE SECURITY CIRCLE

The organization through which political action is carried out is a system of interpersonal relationships which collectively can be called the security circle. The people who belong to a man's security circle are neither a distinct social nor a distinct local group. They are merely those individuals—close kinsmen, affines, and persons tied to him in other special ways—with whom he has safe relationships and toward whom he should observe certain rules of behaviour. These rules prevent intermarriage within the security circle, eating pigs, dogs, and fowls domesticated by its members, and the resort to all serious sorcery or physical violence. They enjoy mutual support and collaboration in time of need.

The composition of the security circle is as follows:

The Kindred

The general term for a man's kindred is *apuno*. This includes everybody to whom he can trace or claims to trace biological ties through either males or females both on his father's and on his mother's side. Two categories within the kindred are initially important:

a) Patrikin and Matrikin

(i) *Patrikin*—all those to whom a man is related exclusively through his father, including his sister's children, father's sister's children's descendants, and so forth.

(ii) *Matrikin*—all those to whom a man is related exclusively through his mother, including his mother's sister's children, and so forth.

b) Degrees and Grades of Relationship

The degrees of relationship recognized are: *immediate, close, quite close, quite distant, distant, and very distant.* These can be defined roughly in terms of generations but, for practical purposes, Garia usually refer to two general grades of kinship, the close and the distant.

(i) The close grade consists of the *immediate, close,* and *quite close* degrees of relationship, and includes all persons to whom a man acknowledges and can trace biological ties within the compass of the fourth ascending generation or a link marriage at that level.

(ii) The distant grade consists of the *quite distant, distant,* and *very distant* degrees of relationship and includes all persons to whom biological ties are claimed but cannot be traced within the compass of the fourth ascending generation or a link marriage at that level.[4]

Of these two grades, only the first belongs to the security circle. The members of the distant grade cannot be included in it except under special circumstances described below. Between a man and these persons kinship ties are never very effective and the rules of behaviour mentioned are not observed. In fact, kinsmen of the distant grade are hardly differentiated from unrelated persons, toward whom a man feels no obligations whatever.

Descent

A man's kindred can be divided also into a number of cognatic groups or stocks, each of which is associated with a descent name used by all its members. As membership is inherited both through males and females, he claims to belong to as many cognatic groups as he can remember descent names in his genealogy. Hence these groups are not segmentary but intermesh with each other.

Within the cognatic group, however, there are two categories of members: the *sawaibopi* and *uibopi*. The *sawaibopi* are the agnates within the group and can be termed a patrilineage in that they trace descent exclusively through males from a single common ancestor. Normally they reckon such links through about four generations and thus represent a small body of closely related persons, often a set of parallel cousins and their children. But there are some patrilineages which have greater genealogical depth and are thus comparatively large. Apart from common patrilineal descent, the agnates can be defined as a patrilineage in two other ways. They alone have the right to use the name of the cognatic group, of which they are the core, in perpetuity. They also possess exclusive corporate rights of guardianship over the land strips and agricultural ritual secrets which bear that name. Yet they are not a cohesive group in any other field of social action. They do not habitually live or work together, or assemble for any common ritual ceremony. The *uibopi* are those who trace their membership in the cognatic group at some stage through females. They belong, of course, to the agnatic cores of, or patrilineages within, other cognatic groups.

For our present purposes, it is more convenient to conceptualize the cognatic group as consisting of the full members of the patrilineage (*sawaibopi*) and its affiliated cognates (*uibopi*). The essential distinction between the two categories is that, on the one hand, the status of the full members of the patrilineage is not affected by time. They and their direct patrilineal heirs are always regarded as closely related and have, as noted, absolute rights to use the descent name described for ever. They are always the nucleus of the security circle of a man and his agnatic heirs. The status of the affiliated cognates, on the other hand, is affected by time. Their relationship to the full members of the patrilineage is close for approximately four generations, during which period they claim the right to use the descent name which the agnates transmit in perpetuity, to have effective ties with the agnates, and thus to belong to their security circle. But thereafter they progressively lose interest in the descent name, cease to recognize close relationship with the agnates, and so pay little regard to their membership in the cognatic group and drop out of the security circle of the patrilineage. The original tie continues to be remembered for a time but is of little importance, being emphasized only when occasion and advantage demand.[5]

Affinity

A man may not marry within the close grade of his kindred. He must take a wife from the distant grade or beyond, provided that she is not tied to him by any other special relationship.[6] Thus he marries into a class of persons with whom his relations are initially unpredictable. Affines, however, are included within the security circle, and the relationship, formally expressed in terms of rigidly enforced respect behaviour, requires the observance of the rules of conduct set out above, precluding further intermarriage, the eating of domesticated pigs, dogs, and fowls, and all forms of hostility.

Special Relationships

A man may have three kinds of special relationships with distantly related or unrelated persons, who on this account may be included in his security circle. They are:

a) Bush Brothers *(Sanawa'omei)*

A man calls bush brothers those people who have many land strips interdigitated with his own.[7] Bush brothers should not be biologically related to him except through common affiliations to other patrilineages, as intermarriage is barred. They are regarded as the equivalent of kinsmen of the close grade, and the special rules of behaviour must be observed toward them.

b) Exchange partners (*Sawaiya and Nalaiya*)

These are generally but not always members of the distant grade of the kindred or unrelated persons with whom a man has exchanged pigs. The relationship involves the observance of all the special rules of conduct within the security circle, with one exception: it does not preclude the further eating of domesticated pigs, dogs, and fowls.

c) Initiatory Relationships

These relationships are created during the period of a boy's initiation, which last from puberty till marriage. They are:

(i) *Sagamei*—those who are trained in sorcery together and undergo the operation of penile incision under the same practitioner.

(ii) *Mali'omei*—those who put on the bark girdle (*mali*) together for the first time during the *Abaiwala* initiation ceremony.

(iii) *Nawe'omei*—those who eat ritual food (*oitu*) together during the *Abaiwala* and *Ni* initiation ceremonies.

(iv) *Esiapei*—a reciprocal term for initiates and those who train them in sorcery, incise their penes, and dress them in the bark girdle for the first time.

In some cases, these initiatory relationships are coincident with kinship relationships of the close grade. But where this is not so, persons who initially do not belong to the security circle are included within it. The parties to initiatory relationships should avoid the use of each other's personal names, marriage with each other's *immediate* female relatives, eating each other's domesticated pigs, dogs, and fowls, and all expressions of hostility toward each other.

To return to a point made at the outset, a man's security circle is not a definable group. It is important to have some idea of its distribution within the political region surrounding his settlement. As stated earlier, the members of a man's patrilineage do not necessarily live together in one hamlet or village section. But his kinsmen of the close grade (including members of his patrilineage) and affines are to be found, generally if not invariably, within his immediate locality. This is due to a type of preferred marriage: where possible, a Garia will take a wife from a settlement near that of his father. This prevents his children's kindred from being excessively dispersed. Again, a man's bush brothers usually live within his locality, for he does not take up land so far away that he can never use it. Also, those with whom he has initiatory relationships are almost invariably within striking distance of his settlement, for people are initiated in the areas in which they live. The position of exchange partners is indeterminate: a man will create these relationships wherever it is most advantageous for him to do so—some within his immediate locality and some further afield.

Thus most members of a man's security circle are concentrated toward the centre of his political region, which is therefore the area of his most effective political relationships. Toward the outskirts of the region these relationships become fewer in number. In several but not all outlying settlements, a man may have a few close grade relatives, perhaps some affines, and some exchange partners.

Conversely, in spite of the high degree of interrelationship between people living in neighbouring settlements, a man does not include every inhabitant of his immediate locality—and still less of his political region—in his security circle. Some people—even those he meets every day in company with others with whom he has safe relationships—he must exclude. They are kinsmen of the distant grade and unrelated persons not tied to him by affinity or any of the special relationships. As noted, the rules of behaviour enforced within the security circle do not apply to these people and hence a man expects to have his most serious disputes with them.

To sum up the form of Garia socio-political structure, every individual is the nuclear figure of a security circle, the members of which are distributed within his political region, the majority tending to live nearer its centre and the minority toward its outskirts. At the same time, every individual is also a member of many other security circles, for there are as many security circles as there are people in the society. Thus, just as political regions overlap each other, in the same way security circles, which are their structural framework, intersect and link the population, settlement by settlement, in chains of interpersonal relationships. The system is not confined to Garialand. Because, in the peripheral areas, intermarriage and pig-exchanges between Garia and non-Garia are frequent, it crosses the borders and embraces people of different linguistic groups. Hence the socio-political organization described probably extends through a large part of the Bagasin Area.[8]

FORMAL AUTHORITY IN GARIA SOCIETY

If formal authority, following Nadel (1951: 169), be defined as 'expected' and 'de jure' 'command over the actions of others', then the authority structure of Garia society is very weak. It is apparent only in two fields and then it is so limited that it is of minimal significance for socio-political control.

The first field is individual leadership. 'Big men' (kokai apu) rise to the surface of affairs because of their skill in using ritual knowledge—the secret names of deities who, it is believed, invented Garia culture and still preside over it. Because of this knowledge, they have unquestioned authority to take the lead in certain activities: the practice and teaching of sorcery, agriculture, dancing, initiation ceremonies, pottery and, in the past, warfare.

Yet the authority of these 'big men' is limited. In the first place, it is restricted almost entirely to setting in motion the above routine activities. The leaders direct the stages by which gardens are made.[9] They impose food and sex taboos on novices during initiation. They supervise young men in sorcery training. But they are not hereditary or titular office bearers and they are unable to adjudicate or coerce. Although they use their influence in disputes as far as they dare, they cannot give binding decisions or judgments, and their only guarantee of obedience from their followers is the willingness of the latter to co-operate. They cannot inflict real and formal punishments on the insubordinate. At worst, they can only withdraw the benefits they normally confer. For instance, a garden leader cannot force his team to assemble for a fixed number of man-hours a day. He can only withhold agricultural ritual from the strips of those who lag behind in the work. But as each householder has several strips staggered in different gardens under different leaders, this would rarely spell economic ruin.[10]

In the second place, the leader's authority has a restricted geographical and structural range. In spatial terms, it rarely extends beyond one or two villages or a corresponding cluster of hamlets. Even within this area he will have several rivals. In structural terms, no leader can be said to represent a specific political unit, which is bound to him, and to which he is bound, by strict rules: one patrilineage, a particular group of patrilineages, or even the inhabitants of one particular settlement. Rather, he attracts around himself those people in his locality who wish to follow him in any special field because of his ritual and other abilities in it. These followers will include a heterogeneous collection of individuals from several settlements—kinsmen, affines, bush brothers, and sometimes persons who do not formally belong to his security circle. They have no permanence as a group, for individuals will change their allegiance as it suits them, especially when a leader gets a reputation for officiousness or seems to be losing his powers. This obviously curtails his scope for penalization by the withdrawal of benefits.

The second field of formal authority is that of the patrilineage over the land strips and ritual secrets bearing the name of the cognatic group of which it is the agnatic core. Rights to patrilineage land and ritual are of two kinds. First, there are personal rights, which involve actual use and may be vested in either the full members or the affiliated cognates. Second, the patrilineage claims for its full members, as a corporate body, exclusive rights to control the transfer of the above personal rights to outsiders and settle all disputes affecting the interests of both full members and affiliated cognates.

In this case also, the degree and range of authority is slight. The patrilineage is not by itself an effective unit for carrying out political action in matters outside this field, and land disputes are infrequent. Moreover, even with respect to its land strips and ritual secrets, the ultimate sanction for its authority is religious belief. It is assumed, in the last analysis, that the spirits of patrilineage forbears will punish those who transgress its rights by ruining their crops.

THE PRINCIPLES OF SOCIO-POLITICAL CONTROL IN GARIA SOCIETY

As formal authority vested in individual leaders and patrilineages is so limited, we have to look for the effective system of socio-political control in Garia society in other fields of activity. We must examine those forces which induce conformity to accepted norms, and the processes by means of which disputes are conducted and settled: religious sanctions; self-regulation (Nadel 1953); and self-help or retaliatory action.

Religious Sanctions

All Garia culture, including norms of everyday conduct, is generally believed to have been invented by the deities and to have its replica in the lands of the dead. The spirits of the dead are thought to lead the same kind of lives as do their living descendants.

In fact, however, few Garia quote their religion as a sanction for conformity in all aspects of behaviour. Apart from the special rights of the patrilineage already mentioned, only certain types of conduct, which refer to specific religious beliefs and observance, are invariably buttressed by religion. This involves the following types of offences: for both sexes, copulation in a garden; for males, knowledge of the secrets of the Male Cult before reaching the period of initiation (puberty till marriage), and non-observance of the food and sex taboos imposed during it; and for females, all knowledge of the secrets of the Male Cult.

These offences are the closest approximation to public delicts in Garia society. Those who are guilty of them are morally condemned by everyone in their localities and political regions who is aware of what they have done. Even afterward, when the scandal has died down, some stigma attaches to their names. In the past, women who witnessed Male Cult secrets were immediately put to death without any protection from their kinsmen. But, with this sole exception, apart from general moral condemnation, no human counteraction is taken by the leaders or anybody else against wrong-doers in this field. Only religious sanctions are thought to be effective. The real punishment is said to be the extreme displeasure—automatic and uninvoked—of the deities and spirits of the dead, who destroy the culprit's crops, cause him bad luck in hunting and blood feuding, or visit him with illness, deformity, or death.

Self-Regulation

Wrong actions against human beings can be classified as follows:
1. Neglect of social obligations toward all members of the security circle.
2. Offences which concern only the individual and can be settled with a minimum of social disturbance; theft and the killing of domesticated pigs.
3. Offences which affect primarily the individual but also involve members of his security circle: proscribed marriage, adultery, homicide or serious physical violence, sorcery, abduction of widows, and default in a pig exchange.

Initially, all these offences should be prevented within the security circle by the process of self-regulation: a system of reinforcing relationships by means of moral indoctrination and mutual self-interest or reciprocity. When self-regulation proves inadequate, people resort to self-help or retaliatory action.

In Garia eyes, all correct behaviour must be value-directed, and there is a distinct medium for expressing the idea. If you ask a man whether a certain member of his security circle will help him in a task for which he needs co-operation, he will reply: 'If he thinks (nanunanu) on me, he will help me. If he does not, he will not help me.' In this context, *nanunanu*, which is the normal word for 'thinking' or 'thought', has an affective connotation. It means 'to have a proper attitude' toward a person and so, by extension, 'to fulfil all the obligations' due to him. Every right action is prompted by good *nanunanu*, which is the quality of a good man. Every bad action is the result of bad or no *nanunanu*, which is the quality of a bad man.

The correlate of *nanunanu* is shame (*maya*), which a good man should experience should he purposely or inadvertently disobey the specified rules of conduct toward others. The feeling of shame should induce him to make amends as soon as possible. But where a man has no proper *nanunanu* or sense of shame, he can be prevented from doing wrong by the fear of public criticism and concern for his good name. Moreover, these two qualities cannot exist or arise by themselves. They have to be indoctrinated. Parents, elder siblings, and all close relatives take part in a child's early training, which is intensified after adolescence, when a boy or girl is prepared to take full adult responsibility in social affairs.

As has been implied, the social range of value-directed behaviour is the security circle. Value-indoctrination does not attempt to ensure that a man observes proper rules of conduct outside that limit. No sense of moral obligation is prescribed toward people who are not included in this category, although there can always be modifications to this generalization. A man may have cultivated associational ties with people with whom he has no formal relationships, if they happen to live in the same settlement as himself or have a few outlying land strips interdigitated with his own.[11] These associational ties may lead him to treat distant, partly remembered kinship links as if they were in fact close.

This means, of course, that all expressions of value-orientation or moral obligation (*nanunanu*) are not *sui generis*. They are shorthand terms for considerations of mutual self-interest or reciprocity. A man depends on the members of his security circle and those with whom he has associational ties for protection and co-operation in important tasks. If he does not fulfil his obligations to them, they will withdraw their support. He must, by his own good works, ensure that they 'think on' him. This brings into consideration the concept of the focal activity, defined by Nadel (1953: 267) as one on 'which a series of other [activities] depend . . . being incapable of achievement without the focal activity or impeded by any variation (through neglect or disregard) in the latter'. In short, some activities are socially more important than others and their observance will guarantee the fulfilment of reciprocal obligations in many other fields.

In Garia society, the most important focal activity is the giving and exchange of domesticated pigs. Where this activity has taken place, certain relationships within the security circle must gain additional content and strength. Where, however, it has not taken place, the relationships concerned are correspondingly weaker. This can be illustrated by examining its function in relation to each of the classes within the security circle.

a) The Close Grade of the Kindred

Within the close grade of the kindred, pig-giving promotes, over a period of several generations, a network of interlocking rights and obligations between a man and certain of his matrikin and patrikin.

A man has already existing, strong ties with the members of his patrilineage, based not only on common descent but also on the inheritance of guardian rights over land and ritual. Correspondingly, it is recognized that if he wishes to strengthen kinship sentiment and establish effective social, as against purely biological, relationships with his matrikin of the close grade, he must send them liberal gifts of pigs. The stated rule is that the first pig that comes to his hand should go to his true mother's brother and the latter's sons. Subsequently he should send pigs to the remainder of his close grade matrikin. None of these pigs need ever be returned in kind but the matrikin, having accepted them, are under an obligation to him and should always give him support in a crisis. It should be noted that where a man sends his own domesticated pigs to these matrikin, the latter may not eat them, but must send them elsewhere through the medium of the exchange. An alternative procedure is for a man to obtain pigs by exchange and send them to his matrikin, who may eat them. In either case, the act of giving pigs to matrikin sets up a chain reaction through the society, and results in the creation of exchange relationships based on mutual self-interest and hence expressed in terms of moral obligation.

This process has an important extension. A sister's son can send his true mother's brother a large number of pigs (over and above those already mentioned), in return for which he receives personal rights on some of the land strips and to the ritual secrets bearing the descent name which the mother's brother's patrilineage transmits in perpetuity. These rights are inherited by the direct patrilineal heirs of the sister's son, but they are limited to the actual use of the land and ritual spells. As has been seen, the patrilineage still claims residual guardian rights. The land and ritual must retain for the next four generations the name transmitted by the mother's brother's patrilineage. During this period, the affiliated cognates cannot alienate their personal rights without the corporate permission of the guardian patrilineage and, as already noted, must refer to its members all disputes arising over the land and ritual.[12]

Thus pig-giving can tie a man to his mother's brother's patrilineage by means of an interlocking system of rights and obligations connected with land. But over a period of several generations the system is extended beyond the *immediate* degree of the matrikin to the close grade of the patrikin. The personal rights originally acquired are inherited by the patrilineal heirs of the sister's son. This means that apart from those he receives directly through his father's patrilineage, a man may inherit personal rights on strips bearing the names transmitted by his father's mother's, father's father's mother's, and father's father's father's mother's patrilineages as well. He will be in exactly the same dependence relationship to their members as to those of his mother's brother's patrilineage. Furthermore, his sister's children, father's sister's children's descendants, and so forth may have a similar relationship with his patrilineage.

This system, however, does not account for all those who can be included in the close grade of a man's kindred. Personal rights are not often acquired from the mother's mother's patrilineage and beyond, and in some generations people do not bother to acquire them from their mothers' brothers. This inevitably leaves some biological relationships unreinforced. If they remain so, they will be more easily forgotten than those which are reinforced, and this is often the case. But this can be forestalled by the process already mentioned. As was seen, a man can buttress kinship sentiment with his matrikin other than those of the *immediate* degree by giving them pigs. This applies equally to those members of the close grade of his patrikin with whom he is not tied up in the system of land rights. He can either send them gifts of pigs or else enter into exchange partnerships with them.

b) Affines

Garia marriage has two basically important features. First, as already mentioned, a man must observe stringent respect behaviour toward his affines, which should preclude all friction between him and them. Second, at the time of his marriage and afterward, he must send his affines a series of marriage payments, consisting of pigs, taro, and valuables.

These marriage payments may serve a dual purpose. In the first place, they ensure harmonious relations between a man and his wife's kindred—people whom he previously could not formally include within his security circle and with whom he was on terms of mutual suspicion. He has married a woman from among them, and they have accepted his pigs. Both parties are under an obligation to each other, and therefore the possibility of hostility beween them should cease to exist.

In the second place, marriage payments may also set in motion for a man's descendants the process whereby the purely biological relationships within the close grade of the kindred are strengthened by the interlocking system of land rights. It is said that if the husband (father) sends pigs to his affines in excess of those stipulated as marriage payments, his sons will have to hand over fewer than would otherwise be the case, if they want to acquire personal rights on the land strips of their mother's brother's patrilineage.

c) Special Relationships

(i) *Bush Brothers*—The bond between bush brothers is not based primarily on pig-giving, although a man's bush brothers, being equated with his close kinsmen, will, if they live near him, co-operate with him in an exchange and share the pigs he kills. This helps cement the relationship.

Ultimately, however, bush brotherhood can be traced to the process of exchanging pigs for personal rights to land. Because of this, the geographical distribution of land strips bearing the name transmitted by a patrilineage is imperceptibly changing, generation by generation, and a man's personal holdings are mixed up with those of many people with whom he may have no consanguineal or affinal ties. From their number he chooses his bush brothers—those with whose land strips the majority of his own are interdigitated. This interdigitation of holdings is the main bond between bush brothers.

(ii) *Exchange Partners*—The relationship between exchange partners is based directly on, and cannot come into being without, the exchange of pigs. Exchange partners usually have no close biological links although, as has been mentioned, a man may create such relationships among his patrikin of the close grade should he consider that it would be advantageous to strengthen certain kinship ties. He normally establishes partnerships by sending out pigs to as many distantly related or unrelated persons as he can, as soon as he is satisfied that he has good rapport with his affines and close kinsmen. But in doing so he is, as already suggested, guided by reasons of expediency: he will single out for special attention those people within his political region who are influential and can be of particular use to him.

(iii) *Initiatory Relationships*—Within the security circle, initiatory relationships alone are not concerned with pig-giving or pig exchanges but are based entirely on the principles already described.

To sum up, self-regulation is the process which, in the majority of cases, maintains social order within the security circle. By means of it, relationships within the security circle are reinforced by considerations of mutual self-interest and hence become value-oriented. They thus have a greater chance of guaranteeing a man co-operation in everyday life, protection from hostility, and support in time of crisis. Where they are not reinforced in this way, they are more likely to be forgotten or ignored. Moreover, where self-regulation acts as the sole force to promote social conformity, it does not make use of any positive or direct sanction but only the indirect sanction of penalization. People who do not observe the rules of conduct prescribed for security circle relationships are handicapped by the loss of the benefits which these relationships normally confer. If a man treats his kinsmen, affines, and so forth badly, they will refuse to fulfil their obligations to him. They may even sever their relationships with him, thereby ceasing to function as members of his security circle, which will be correspondingly restricted in its range of effectiveness.[13]

Self-Help or Retaliatory Action

Self-regulation by itself cannot prevent all disputes between a man and the other inhabitants of his political region. Occasionally it may prove ineffective within the security circle itself: some people may disregard the rules of behaviour proper to certain relationships, especially if the latter have not been properly reinforced. But the most common reason is that self-regulation has too short a social range: as has been stressed, it has no bearing on a man's behaviour toward persons who live within his political region but do not belong to his security circle. In these two contexts, we must consider the kinds of offences that lead to open disputes and the forms of self-help or retaliatory action used to settle them.

Offences which concern only the individual—theft and the killing of domesticated pigs—are not in themselves important. Where such disputes occur between people who are not otherwise on bad terms, they are settled, as already indicated, with a minimum of social disturbance. Retaliatory action is negligible. It is only when they break out between persons already involved in some other feud that they are likely to embroil a large number of people and so contribute to a wider upheaval.

Where a man's garden or other property has been robbed and he does not know the identity of the thief, he may do either of two things. On the one hand, if the loss is slight, he will tie a *tanget* to whatever has been robbed, merely to indicate that he is aware of what has taken place and to shame the thief should he return. On the other hand, if the loss is heavy and recurrent, he will resort to preventive magic. He will put a spell on the *tanget* to bring illness to anybody who robs his property thereafter. Where, however, the identity of the thief is known, the plaintiff will demand compensation, which is usually paid at once. The affair rarely goes beyond the two persons primarily involved.

The rules concerning the killing of domesticated pigs are clear cut. They apply equally to members of a man's security circle and to people outside it. If a domesticated pig invades a garden, the gardeners may shoot it with impunity but the carcass is retained by its owner, who disposes of it as he wishes. But if a domesticated pig is shot either in a settlement or in the bush by anybody other than its owner, the shooter may keep and dispose of the carcass but must provide the owner with another live animal of the same size. These rules are generally observed. Where the pig is shot in a garden, the owner has no case; and when it is shot in a settlement or the bush, his demands for compensation are normally met at once by the shooter, who may explain that he mistook it for a wild pig. Again it is a personal issue.

The other offences previously listed—proscribed marriage, adultery, homicide[14] or serious physical violence, sorcery, theft of widows, and default in a pig exchange—are much more important in that they involve more people than the plaintiff and defendant, and hence cause greater social disturbance.

When one of these offences has been committed, the plaintiff may first summon the culprit to a 'court' or assembly: an acephalous gathering of people interested in the dispute because they belong to the security circles of either plaintiff or defendant, or both. Other people are not expected to attend. If they do so out of curiosity, they play no part in the proceedings. The plaintiff's most effective weapon, especially if he is a good orator, is vituperation of the defendant and the canalization of public opinion, hitherto only diffuse scandal and gossip, against him. As no leader presides over the assembly or can give a binding judgment, a decision is eventually reached by consensus of opinion. The following courses of action may be adopted:

1. For proscribed marriage: that the woman be given up.

2. For adultery, homicide, serious physical violence, and sorcery: compensation in pigs, valuables and, nowadays, money. Or if the offence has been committed by both parties by way of a feud, an exchange of the above items or, nowadays in the case of adultery disputes, a game of football.

3. For theft of widows: the return of the woman or compensation in pigs, valuables and, nowadays, money to the *immediate* relatives of her deceased husband.

4. For default in a pig exchange: that the defaulter make good his obligations.

If, however, the defendant refuses to appear at the assembly or to accept its decision, the plaintiff will resort to retaliatory action of the following kind:

1. For proscribed marriage: minor wounding of the husband and/or wife, or limited use of sorcery.

2. For adultery, homicide, serious physical violence, and sorcery: a retaliatory act of adultery, a fight, a blood feud, a sorcery feud or, nowadays, a challenge to a game of football.

3. For theft of widows: an attempt to retrieve the woman (which may lead to a fight), or a blood or sorcery feud.

4. For default in a pig exchange: a fight, or a blood or sorcery feud.

Where retaliatory action has resulted in a blood or sorcery feud, eventually both sides may be brought to feel that the dispute has gone far enough. They hold another assembly and arrange a peace settlement with an exchange of pigs, valuables, food and, nowadays, money.

Only one of the types of retaliatory action mentioned above needs further description. Football is based on Association Rules (which is played in native labour compounds at European centres), but it follows the pattern of older forms of organized hostility. Plaintiff and defendant choose sides of nominally eleven men each from their security circles. The contest may last two hours and its aims may vary. If either plaintiff or defendant wants to put the other to shame, he will try to run off with the ball after scoring the first goal or at any other time when his team is in the lead. This inflames the dispute still further, and leads to a brawl and a challenge for a replay. But if both parties want to settle, they will allow the scores to end up equal, the plaintiff being especially satisfied if his side kicks the coveted first goal, which gives him considerable prestige.

FACTORS INFLUENCING THE CONDUCT OF DISPUTES

A man may call together an assembly or resort to direct retaliatory action in disputes both with members of his security circle and with other persons in his political region with whom he has no formal ties. The effectiveness of such procedure depends on the amount of support he gets from other people. This support comes from those members of his security circle who consider that the offence against him is to some degree an offence also against themselves, that their relationships with him cannot be ignored, and that their interests will be served, or at least not seriously injured, by taking his side. These supporters do not represent an exclusive social group such as a patrilineage: they are generally an *ad hoc* heterogeneous collectivity of persons (patrikin, matrikin, bush brothers, and so forth). In an assembly, they will speak on his behalf and urge a settlement most favourable to him. In a football match, they will play on his side. In a feud, they will join him as active participants or openly declare their sympathy for him. The defendant is helped in the same way.

There are, however, three factors which significantly influence the conduct of disputes, by limiting the amount of direct support the individual will get and hence the severity of the retaliatory action he may take.

The first factor emerges from the structure of Garia society, and involves the value-directed behaviour and system of reinforced relationships on which it depends. It applies to all open disputes between members of the same security circle. It is the actual relationship between plaintiff and defendant. In theory, all serious disputes are banned within the security circle and should be prevented by the process of self-regulation. In fact, however, even within this social range, cases of adultery, sorcery, and theft of widows do occur. Moreover, there is one offence which can occur only within the security circle: proscribed marriage.

In all such cases, the close relationship between plaintiff and defendant, and everybody else concerned, should stop the emergence of large and clearly defined groups of supporters on either side, and should limit the severity of the retaliatory action taken personally by the plaintiff. Thus, in the past, where there was a dispute over a prohibited marriage, the security circle involved would hold a small assembly and try to prevent the union by means of moral pressure. If this failed, there were definite rules laying down the type of retaliatory action to which the *immediate* kinsmen of the bride could resort. The security circle would allow a true father, brother, mother's brother, or cross-cousin at most to wound her or her husband in the arm or thigh with a three-pronged arrow normally used for shooting birds, or use mild sorcery to cause minor illness. If the pair were still obdurate, the marriage was allowed to proceed. To shoot with a lethal arrow or use sorcery to kill was said to have been avoided by the bride's *immediate* kinsmen or at least to have been prevented by the other members of the security circle. The same restriction applied to all retaliatory action for the other offences listed, when they were committed within the security circle.

In principle, this represents a compromise between the plaintiff's normal desire to redress his wrong and his practical interest in, and hence value for, a close relationship. It would be to his detriment to eliminate a person from his security circle. This point of view is always shared by all others interested in such disputes, for they belong to the security circle of both plaintiff and defendant. Hence quarrels between formally related persons are generally of short duration and easily settled.

The second factor is an extension of the first. It is especially important in disputes between persons of different security circles: where there is no definite relationship (biological or social), no mutual self-interest, and hence no moral obligation, between plaintiff and defendant, and where both regard themselves as free to kill each other by physical means or sorcery. This factor is the number of persons who belong to the security circles of, and hence owe loyalty to, *both* plaintiff *and* defendant, together with the number of bridging relationships between the supporters of both parties.

This situation can occur because, as has been stated, a man belongs not only to the security circle of which he is the nucleus but also to many other security circles which link the population. The majority of disputes (involving adultery, homicide, serious physical violence, sorcery, theft of widows, and default in a pig exchange) originate between persons who do not belong to the same security circle but live within the same general locality. This is the geographical range within which their social contacts are most intensive and, as it is also an area of dense inter-relationship, there are always many people interested in a dispute who should observe varying degrees of neutrality. They may act as non-participants or as go-betweens and peacemakers. Or again, if they take sides, they may find relatives and so forth in the opposing party to whom they must behave with restraint.

Disputes of this kind result in greater social disturbance. They normally involve two mutually opposed groups: those who support plaintiff and defendant respectively. Yet they are rarely insoluble. In this respect, neutral and bridging relationships are especially important. They indirectly influence the actions of plaintiff and defendant by limiting the number of fully committed supporters on both sides so that only a relatively small cluster of close grade kinsmen and so forth can identify itself with one side to the complete exclusion of the other. Those who have to observe different degrees of neutrality exert a moderating influence and are thus essential for bringing about an ultimate settlement. In an assembly, they act as mediators, allowing a just settlement to be imposed, but seeing that it is not exceeded and that no material harm is done to the defendant. In a sorcery or blood feud, they will urge both sides to desist and make peace. In a football match, if they play on different sides, they will 'kick easy' or, if they are spectators, they will try to stop the game from degenerating into a brawl. The principle is the same as before: they do not want to see a member of their security circle eliminated or too seriously handicapped.

It is not usual for a man to have serious disputes with people living outside his immediate locality, on the outskirts of his political region. His contact with them is limited very often to meetings at times of pig exchanges, and such disputes as he has with them are caused mainly by his own or his partner's failure to produce the requisite pig. Such disputes are rare, but they are more difficult to settle than those between people living at close range. As already stated, settlements at a distance from each other are linked by relatively few relationships. Hence, in the event of a dispute at this range, each side can count on a larger body of supporters than in the previous context. But so great is the social and geographical separation that it is more difficult to arrange an assembly or even to resort to direct retaliatory action. The most likely possibility is a fight at the time and place of the exchange, but this never provides a satisfactory solution. There are fewer individuals to act as go-betweens and peacemakers. Hence disputes over pigs may be left unresolved for a considerable time until the parties concerned can be brought together by a few influential neutrals. Thus in these outlying areas, the system of socio-political control operates with minimum efficiency.

The third factor influencing the conduct of disputes is the degree to which members of a man's security circle are prepared or able to be involved in any conflict situation. The part an individual *should* play in a dispute is always phrased in terms of his formal relationship to plaintiff or defendant, or both. In many cases, this is a satisfactory explanation. Yet the attitude which an individual should adopt can be modified in various ways. There are those of weak character who, although nominally interested, avoid taking sides or acting as peacemakers. Geography may be important. Unless a day is announced well in advance for an assembly, football match, or peace ceremony, those who live in distant settlements may find it difficult to attend. Finally, some people who should remain neutral may favour one relationship at the expense of another for reasons of immediate short-term advantage.

CONCLUSIONS

The forces which maintain and restore socio-political order in Garia society can be summarized in these terms:

1. Leadership is not significant in this field. The 'big men' merely set in motion socially accepted routine activities, and in this sense are little more than intermediaries between deities and human beings. No 'big man' represents the society at large or any discrete group within it with judicial authority on the basis of which he can give binding decisions in disputes.

2. It is essential to conceptualize within the Bagasin Area as a whole a series of overlapping political regions, of which Garialand, from the standpoint of the people at its centre, is but one. The structural framework of a political region is not based on a balance between opposed segments (descent groups) of the same order as in unilineal segmentary societies. Except for the enforcement of patrilineage guardian rights over land and ritual, political action is not the prerogative of closed groups. Political action is merely one function of the generalized structural framework of which the most important feature is the security circle: the bilateral kindred of the close grade, affines, and persons in special relationships. Relationships within the security circle are strengthened by the process of self-regulation, which should prevent all serious disputes, and promote mutual collaboration and loyalty, between its members. The process of self-regulation is restricted to the security circle: it does not directly influence behaviour between persons who have no formal relationship with each other.

3. When self-regulation by itself proves inadequate for maintaining order, the individual who has been wronged calls together an assembly or takes direct retaliatory action, backed by those members of his security circle who feel that the offence concerns them also, and who are able and willing to become involved in the dispute.

Involvement is the result of individual choice and loyalty rather than of automatic allegiance determined by group membership. In this situation, the patrilineage does not emerge as a basic political unit. It will achieve unity in support of one of its members in a dispute with an unrelated person but may be too small by itself to carry much weight. It has to be augmented by non-agnatic cognates, affines, and so forth from the security circle so that it is no more than the nucleus of a heterogeneous cluster of supporters. Even then the dominant roles in conducting and settling a dispute are not necessarily reserved for its full members but can be assumed by other people depending on their personalities, and their skill in oratory, fighting, or sorcery. Moreover, when the patrilineage is large, it may fail to achieve unity in the face of cognatic affiliations. It is not regarded as abnormal for only some members of large patrilineages to be engaged actively in a dispute, while others remain neutral or act as peacemakers, because they are closely related to the other side. Large patrilineages would normally unite in disputes with persons on the outskirts of their political region but such disputes are so infrequent that they rarely do so.

4. Neutral and bridging relationships are essential for the restoration of order in dispute situations. They compensate for the absence of centralized authority. Where they are sufficiently numerous, they can blanket a dispute or prevent it from spreading too far. This function is formally recognized in the Garia phrase *obolo pulobu*, 'to remain in the middle', which refers specifically to the activities of neutrals, go-betweens, and peacemakers in situations of conflict and social tension. This, of course, means that the seriousness or ease of settlement of a dispute is in direct proportion to the actual degree of relationship between plaintiff and defendant, and to the number of available neutral and bridging relationships between the supporters of both sides. The closer and more numerous these relationships are, the less severe and more controlled will be the retaliatory action taken, and the dispute more easily settled. The most intense concentration of such relationships is within the security circle, so that quarrels involving its members alone are most quickly ended. Moreover the majority of disputes involving people of different security circles occur within a restricted geographical area, which is also a range of intense interrelationship. This ensures that in these disputes there are always sufficient neutral and bridging ties to facilitate a solution sooner or later. It is only when a man is at variance with persons living on the outskirts of his political region, where he has few formal relationships, that it is very difficult to maintain socio-political order and resolve such conflicts as arise. This is most important in the modern situation. As a result of pacification, people are able to journey far from their homes and have dealings with persons of other political regions. There is always the possibility of disputes breaking out. The traditional political system is inadequate in these cases. There are no neutral kin to ensure that the wrongdoer would attend an assembly or to act as go-betweens and peacemakers. The relevant security circles, far from overlapping, do not even touch. The only effective method of regulating and settling disputes such as these is for the parties concerned to turn to the Administration, the only neutral institution which can bridge the gap between them and ensure that a

case is heard. In the main, these are the only disputes brought to Administration courts. The others are usually dealt with by traditional means.

5. The above suggests an important theoretical principle. As an analytical device, self-regulation and retaliatory action have been described here as if they were discrete entities. In their actual function, this is true only of self-regulation when it is the sole force of control at work within the security circle. But in situations demanding retaliatory action as a means of restoring order, self-regulation interacts with it as an essential moderating mechanism. In nearly all open disputes, retaliatory action is kept in check, or limited to some extent, by the influences of value-oriented interpersonal relationships. Unlike impartial judicial authority in Western society, it cannot operate in isolation from self-regulation.

NOTES

1. The fieldwork on which this paper is based was carried out between 1949-53, which must be regarded as the ethnographic present. The original draft was written in 1955-56. The argument in the present version is the same, although I have revised certain passages.

2. For maps relating to this area see Lawrence (1964: 8, 20).

3. See Lawrence (1955).

4. This is the stated rule but, in effect, the dividing line between the two grades tends to fluctuate.

5. This subject will receive more detailed analysis in a full length monograph on the Garia.

6. See under Special Relationships.

7. For a fuller description, see Lawrence (1955: 35-6).

8. This was demonstrated by careful fieldwork for the peoples living on the Garia borders. For the Bagasin Area at large it was supported by general observation during journeys outside Garialand.

9. See Lawrence (1955: 3-8).

10. See Lawrence (1955:43).

11. Such persons are not classified as bush brothers, although a man has some degree of common economic interest with them. See Lawrence (1955: 36).

12. For fuller details, see Lawrence (1955).

13. A special case is, of course, proscribed marriage. A man who marries a woman from his security circle deprives himself and his children of definite advantages. He fails to augment his security circle by bringing in affines from outside it. In consequence, there will be fewer safe relationships in his own and subsequent generations. Nadel (1953: 269) makes the same point.

14. Wounding, homicide, and the blood feud are now outlawed. Cases of homicide are most infrequent and are dealt with by the Administration. What is said here about this subject applies only to the past.

REFERENCES CITED

COLSON, E. (1953): Social Control and Vengeance in Plateau Tonga Society. *Africa*, Vol. 23.

LAWRENCE, P. (1955): *Land Tenure among the Garia*. Social Science Monographs No. 4. Canberra: Australian National University.

LAWRENCE, P. (1964): *Road Belong Cargo*. Manchester: Manchester University Press.

NADEL, S. F. (1951): *The Foundations of Social Anthropology*. London: Cohen and West.

NADEL, S. F. (1953): Social Control and Self-Regulation. *Social Forces*, Vol. 31.

KENELM BURRIDGE

TANGU POLITICAL RELATIONS[1]

ABSTRACT

The development of relative unity among the people now known collectively as Tangu is outlined, with reference to such factors as residential mobility. The notions of reciprocity and equivalence are discussed as these are manifested through co-operative and exchange relationships, with special attention to the role of 'managers', and to the distinctive political activity known as *br'ngun'guni*. The place of both Administration and mission in Tangu is treated in some detail; and sorcery is seen as of paramount importance, pervading a wide range of circumstances, and a check on personal ambition not only in the traditional system but also in relation to Administration officials.

1

Before effective European penetration in the early nineteen-twenties, the people now known as Tangu[2] comprised four territorially distinct groups identified by neighbourhood appellations: Wanitzir, Biampitzir, Mangigumitzir, and Riekitzir.[3] The first missionary explorers adopted native usage,[4] but later comers—traders, recruiters and administrative officers as well as missionaries—seized on the name Tangu, which identified a small spur in Wanitzir, and used it in a general way to cover the four neighbourhoods. The usage was accepted not only because it was one used by the dominant power, but because the four neighbourhoods had for a number of years been becoming just such a unity as the name Tangu implied.

Today, each of the four neighbourhoods has one or more major settlements built on the spurs and crests of a single main horseshoe-shaped ridge whose axis, from forks to crown, is south-west to north-east. Eastward, the ridge shelves steeply into the broad Iwarum valley; north and north-west the slopes to the main stream beds are more gentle; south and west the main ridge proliferates into a series of heavily forested ridges which straggle into the swamps of the Ramu and its tributaries. While the major settlements contain the bulk of the population, there are numerous minor settlements and hunting lodges each of which is an alternative residence. Mobility of residence is a marked feature of Tangu life. No settlement is much more than a mile from another, many are within a few minutes' walk of others, and in two or three hours over rough country one may traverse the distance separating those farthest apart. Enclosed by, or pendant to, their main curving ridge, in their settlements Tangu represent a concentration of population not to be found elsewhere in the hills between the Ramu and Iwarum.[5]

Formerly, around 1870 say, the population was not only larger but more concentrated, grouped into four main assemblages of settlements. Sharing, so far as we know, a common language, members of the four neighbourhoods were inter-marrying, trading, bartering and making exchanges with one another. They were already becoming some kind of political unity. But, since some of the neighbourhoods were patrilineally biased, and others were matrilineally biased, intermarriages soon began to cause trouble in relation to the transmission of land rights. This, in a situation where the competition for prestige was also a competition for resources, seems to have led to a certain amount of disputing which, in turn, could not but hinge on beliefs in sorcery. Consequently, there were certain limited migrations from the main centres. Then there came into Tangu from the coast artificial dogs' teeth which the Germans had introduced for use as currency. These artificial teeth competed with, but have never found a stable value against, the natural dogs' teeth used in Tangu in bridewealth exchanges. The effect was to enable interested persons to dispute the validity of particular marriages. And since marital difficulties always could, and can, be channelled into sorcery and its implications, further fragmentation of the original settlement assemblages followed. Finally, at about the turn of the century, there was an epidemic sickness, the symptoms of which corresponded to those habitually diagnosed as' due to sorcery. Members of the four neighbourhoods now began to spill out of their original borders, taking over the lands of neighbours.

At least from the time of the sickness until the present day, settlement in Tangu has been highly mobile. And beween the sickness and the coming of the white man this mobility was accompanied by much internecine fighting, wife stealing, and vengeance raiding. Mobility, fighting, and sorcery beliefs seem to have been interdependent. Nevertheless, it also seems to have been the case that members of the four neighbourhoods, despite internal differences, banded together in defence against outsiders. Further, due to a variety of peculiarities in terrain and climate, resulting in each of the neighbourhoods having virtually exclusive resources or abilities for exploitation, the advantages of economic interdependence coupled with the neces-sary putative or actual kin connexion outweighed disruptive tendencies. From their mutual interactions Tangu began to form the basis of a common experience.

Beliefs in sorcery are, clearly, of paramount importance. Without them the intermarriages of patrilineal and matrilineal peoples, the competition for resources, the difficulties following the importation of artificial dogs' teeth, and the epidemic sickness might have had other consequences. And though one could point to certain tensions in the structure of social relationships—particularly those within the triangle Ego-Father-Mother's brother—which of themselves might have led to the same result, the fact is that to Tangu these tensions are inseparable from their expression in the idiom of sorcery.

Among Tangu a sorcerer has many facets of meaning.[6] But, at the expense of riding rough-shod over a variety of subtleties, we may sum up these meanings quite briefly. A sorcerer is a man, never a woman; a man who, considering himself unobliged by the moralities which bind other men, may kill or induce sickness in another simply because it is in him to do so. Combining the classical features of witchcraft, wherein the witch cannot help himself, and witchcraft accusations are a function of particular structural relations, and of sorcery, wherein the sorcerer is considered of his own volition deliberately to act so as to bring about an injury, Tangu sorcery beliefs are integral to their moral system: a system whose prime imperative is reciprocity of obligedness. Generally expected to be found in stranger or other communities, particularly where language difficulties do not permit of suitable solutions to issues, sorcerers are considered inimical, dangerous to life, health, and marital relations. Considered to be ultimately intractable and adamant, though most occasions today find them reasonably amenable to compounding an issue, sorcerers always unite a community against them. In the past, war and feud turned on accusations and suspicions of sorcery, and accusations and suspicions of sorcery were, and are, themselves closely bound up with trespass, the competition for resources, adultery, sickness and death.

Today, though feud and warfare have ceased, Tangu feel themselves most vulnerable to sorcerers who reside in the settlements of their outside neighbours. No Tangu will travel through or to these areas unless a friend, kinsman, or kinswoman is resident there. If an illness is diagnosed as resulting from sorcery, first suspicions place the sorcerer in these neighbouring areas. Strangers who pass through Tangu, particularly if they come from these places, are suspect. Generally speaking, the further one moves from home into the neighbouring areas the greater the danger; but once through them the strain decreases. Though Tangu on indentured labour are by no means immune from sorcerers, if they fall sick or die whilst working on some faraway plantation, and if sorcery is diagnosed, then the blame usually falls on co-labourers from the regions bordering Tangu. Not only is a sorcerer a man who may be dealt with, but suspicions of sorcery tend to fall on men who can be dealt with. Within Tangu, though the people of Wanitzir particularly are thought by those in the other three neighbourhoods to be prone to sorcery, suspicions generally settle on members of another neighbourhood, another settlement, on singular men who live by themselves, and on those who maintain close kin connections with Tangu neighbours. Sorcerers who live in the home settlement are believed to direct their malign intent against those in other settlements, other neighbourhoods, and on those who live outside Tangu. Unless there are special reasons, one is generally safe from the sorcerer who lives in the hut next to one's own. However, should a sorcerer be thought to be responsible for an injury, sickness or death within his own settlement, he is either forced to confess and make a compensation exchange, or is beaten up, or is forced to leave. In the last case, if the accused man has a strong following, or if the community is divided on his guilt, then the settlement will split—thus maintaining the axiom that an inimical sorcerer comes from another settlement.

It does not appear that Tangu were ever an organized and coherent unity. Rather are they a federation of peoples who, partly on account of geographical and demographical features, but mainly because of a shared historical experience and a virtually exclusive participation in a political activity known as *br'ngun'guni*,[7] remain distinct from their neighbours. The language Tangu speak is not exclusive to them, and there are considerable variations of pronunciation as between the four neighbourhoods. Other cultural features such as slit-gong signals, myths, dress, dances, size and shape of homesteads, decorative motifs, and hair styles are not only not exclusive to Tangu, but differ as between the four neighbourhoods. Kin links transcend linguistic and territorial barriers. In each of the neighbourhoods there are men and women with close affiliations with the outsiders nearest to them, and lines of ancestry may be traced through one neighbourhood to another and beyond. On the other hand, intermarriage between the members of the four neighbourhoods is more common than marriage outside, and the network of regularly maintained trading, barter, and exchange relationships within Tangu is very much more dense than those outside. Tangu insist they are one.

Tangu development since the time of the epidemic sickness has included European influences as integral factors in a continuing process of change. The name 'Tangu' provided the peoples of the four neighbourhoods with a symbol of community consistent with topography, population scatter, language, fighting alliances, and sorcery beliefs. The Society of the Divine Word, which commenced operations in Wanitzir in the nineteen-twenties, gradually established a church, schools, trade store and resident priest, and came to regard the four neighbourhoods as a convenient unit or parish centred on the station built almost on the spur of Tangu itself. The Administration, which followed the Mission, enforced the peace, controlled labour migration, appointed its representatives,[8] and insisted on habits of hygiene. It, too, began to regard the four neighbourhoods as a unity. And it was through the Administration and Mission acting in concert that Tangu clubhouses, ritual and cultural foci especially significant for boys passing through puberty, were abolished. While Tangu cling to the traditional ways their subsistence economy and prestige system force upon them, their minds have been opened to Christianity on the one hand, and administrative procedures on the other. But the sorcerer remains, and beliefs in sorcery effectively predicate the quality of Tangu political relations.

2

Tangu clear away forest or grassland every year to plant and harvest in rotation the main staples, taro, *mami*, and yams. Bananas, *pitpit*, sugarcane, corn and a variety of green vegetables are also cultivated in the gardens. Coconut, betel, and sago palms as well as breadfruit trees are planted and nurtured; wild leaves, breadfruits, nuts, grubs and frogs are gathered for use as relishes; pigs, cassowaries, wallabies, bush-rats and lizards are hunted for their flesh; dogs are used as hunting companions, pigs and cockerels are domesticated. Today, though the situation in the past may have been different, garden sites are widely scattered, and hunting lodges are even further afield in the bush. Tangu are a restive people. Households, basic working and productive groups normally consisting of a husband, his wife (or wives), their unmarried offspring—natural or adopted—together with, perhaps, an aged parent of either spouse, tend to move from their houses in a permanent settlement to garden shelters; whence they move off to their hunting lodges, returning in a few days to garden shelters or settlement. During the day the major settlements are usually deserted, and the bulk of the population is distributed over the surrounding countryside, gardening, hunting, or visiting relatives or friends. While dusk finds the majority of households secure in the settlement, many will have elected to spend one or several nights in the gardens or bush.

Apart from this habit of movement between established bases, the urge to found new settlements—associated with sorcery and bad feeling—continues.[9] But households themselves remain stable units: members help one another in the gardens belonging to the household, hunt, eat, travel, visit and live together. Second and third wives with children form parti-households centred on the common husband. Contract labour draws unmarried youths to the coast, whence they return in a few years with axes, knives, beads, cloth, knick-knacks and cash, the goods and cash being distributed among members of the household. When a youth or maiden marries, after spending some months with either or both parental households, the newly wed couple begin clearing a garden site of their own and form an independent household.

Each of the four neighbourhoods excels in producing commodities which are scarce in the others. Wanitzir and parts of Biampitzir monopolize the manufacture of clay cooking pots; Mangigumitzer and Riekitzir make the best string-bags; Riekitzir has plenty of betelnut and sago whereas Wanitzir has little of either; cash, European goods, and the best hunting dogs come from the coast through Wanitzir and Biampitzir; Mangigumitzir is short of tobacco but produces plenty of sago and yams. The mission trade store acts as a general exchange, selling a variety of goods for cash, and buying produce for resale or free distribution in times of shortage. Introduced by the Administration as a cash crop, rice, the production of which is organized by the locally appointed administrative officials, takes its place as a cash earning activity. But households, whose standing in the community depends on their productive capacity, take small interest in working a crop the fruits of which are equally divided irrespective of the work particular households may put into the task.

Distinct from sale and barter transactions between individuals and households—even though they usually take place within the same kinship categories—are the food exchanges which take place between households or groups of households linked to each other as brother and sister. The maxim that married siblings of the same sex should co-operate, and that married siblings of different sex should exchange, always holds good. For while the husbands of co-operating households are regarded, and categorized, as brothers, and the wives, similarly, as sisters, the husbands of households in exchange relationships are categorized as brothers-in-law, and the wives as sisters-in-law. As between two, or two groups of, households in exchange relationships, that is, the husband or husbands on the one side are regarded as the brother or brothers of the wife or wives on the other.

These food exchanges across the brother and sister link form the basis of the prestige system, and so of the political system. Because exchanges have to be equivalent, a capable and productive household gains prestige not only from its greater productive capacity, but from the greater number and range of exchange obligations in which it participates. For the same reason—and also because the range of exchange obligations is finite—the able are forced to exchange against the able, and the less productive must needs exchange against a similarly productive household. As a further consequence, groups of households in exchange relationships tend to be roughly of the same size, and major settlements tend to bifurcate into two roughly equivalent exchanging halves. Within this basic pattern the competition for prestige, and so for political influence, takes place between independent households which seek to ally themselves now with this household or group of households, now with another, as advantage and circumstances serve. Shifts in alliance, and the ambiguity in relationships which goes with such shifts, are essential to the dynamic of relative prestige and political influence. Since, too, prestige is measured, first and basically, against productive capacity in garden and bush, not only are cash earnings largely irrelevant to prestige, but those who would wish to withdraw from the basic subsistence activities must needs withdraw from the prestige system. Politically almost worthless, money is not yet a basic measure of the man among Tangu; and full-time specialist activities, necessarily dependent upon money being a basic measure of man, are inconsistent with political significance.

3

For Tangu all exchanges should be equivalent. If they are not they may be seen as slights or insults, and as a consequence they will provoke quarrels and bring trouble from sorcerers. The same set of notions operates in sale and barter transactions, so that wherever a transaction is deemed by one or other party to be unfair, over-generous, or mean, an injury is deemed to have been suffered. What may seem at first sight to be a particular and contingent donation is in fact always one of a series of donations and counter-donations: returns have to come back, and if they are not made, or if they are improperly made, or if, for example, in the many obligations a man has he chooses one sister rather than another—leaving his obligation to the latter to a later date—bad feeling, a quarrel, or a major dispute is probable. Since, too, there are insuperable practical difficulties in making a truly equivalent exchange of foodstuffs, the ideal of equivalence results, quite naturally, in a highly critical attitude. But while Tangu watch one another closely, insisting that others should conform to normative expectations, each individual covets that reserve of power and ability which will enable him to be rather more than equivalent to others. Formally, a particular cycle of continuing obligation is brought to an end by the households concerned becoming *mngwotngwotiki*—equivalent, neither obliged nor unobliged. And on becoming *mngwotngwotiki* households practise avoidance, cease to have anything to do with each other.[10] Nevertheless, in a small community such as Tangu are, opportunities present themselves, and it is not long before those households which have become *mngwotngwotiki* re-engage with one another.

Though all transactions are dominated by the notion of equivalence, the critical attitude resulting from the ideal of equivalence is at its most acute during feasts, which are accompanied by dancing and an activity known as *br'ngun'guni,* a talking in public assembly, a political activity. In each major settlement, in any one feasting year—coinciding with the horticultural cycle—the same groups of households, forming approximately half the total number of households in the settlement, are regularly recruited to provide food, or dance, for the remainder who, in their turn, dance, or provide food, for the others. And the two groups of households are regarded as related to each other as brother and sister. Other kinds of feasts, occurring on contingent or special occasions, recruit settlement in opposition to settlement, groups of brothers and sisters in opposition to each other irrespective of settlement allegiance, and groups of brothers and sisters in opposition as representatives of different settlements. But whether the feast seems to be evoking territorial rather than kin issues, or *vice versa,* every feast is a political occasion, every feast is phrased as an exchange across the brother and sister link, and in every feast individuals watch one another closely with an eye to the future.

Most feasts carry on from dusk until dawn. Only a few dances may be danced during daylight hours. Still, even though dancing caps the proceedings, every feast is implicitly if not explicitly a political occasion. For it is during the intervals between different phases of the dance, as food is placed before the exhausted dancers, that the opportunity is taken for *br'ngun'guni.* In the regular intracommunity feasts, *br'ngun'guni* tends to be rather more subject to convention. A speaker accompanies his delivery with staccato beats on the hand-drum, a nervous trotting to and fro— or a slow walk—and high leaps into the air and mighty thwacks on his buttocks to emphasize his points. The statements themselves, made by the leading men of either group of households, are often boasts regarding their own prowess in gardens or bush. Swashing the buttocks may turn modesty into outrageous boasting, or praise of another's production into scorn. Yet speakers may also remind one another and the assembled company that it is time to harvest yams, to clear fresh sites for new gardens, to plant the first taros. Proposals are put forward for the date of the next feast. Administrative officials take the opportunity to point out that the paths are overgrown, or the rice fields neglected. Catechists extol the benefits of children attending school. There may be argument: grievances are made public whether they relate to hunting or fishing rights, administrative, Mission, or kin matters, exchange obligations, or suspicions of sorcery. Visitors attend feasts in other settlements not only because they like a party, but because *br'ngun'guni* allows them to submit an issue to public discussion, because by so doing they may force an opening which they believe to be of advantage to them.

All feasts provide opportunities for *br'ngun'guni,* but the activity of *br'ngun'-guni* is not always accompanied by feasts. It may arise *ad hoc* out of an incident such as a theft, a trespass, an accusation of sorcery, or the announcement of a betrothal. In such cases the initial complaint, accusation or announcement is called a *vierkakaki;* and only when the parties concerned descend from their homesteads on to the central dancing space, face each other, threaten, argue, and call the evidence, does it become *br'ngun'guni.* Boast leads to counter-boast, accusation to counter-accusation. And here, as in the formal *br'ngun'guni* at feasts, the issue between the participants can only finally be resolved by relating grievances, ambitions or desires to the production and exchange of foodstuffs. The end of one *br'ngun'guni* is but the springboard for another session. Whatever the basis of disagreement—and this can only relate to a breach of equivalence—a feast or series of feasts is projected. Brothers are recruited or re-recruited to either party, their households co-operate in the preparation of a feast, dancers repair their finery. At the feasts themselves more *br'ngun'guni* occurs. Only by thus explicitly 'quarrelling it through' may households in mutual opposition gain that mutual respect for each other which is involved in being *mngwotngwotiki,* truly equivalent.

It should be emphasized that *br'ngun'guni* does not merely express the critical or competitive values inherent in a feasting exchange taking place within the ideal of equivalence. It is a deliberative device providing the implicit authority for a series of activities; and it is a mechanism for initiating, continuing, or even resolving disputes. Apart from the determination to continue disputing, decisions are rarely explicit: it is up to each individual present to gauge the shifts in the distribution of power that appear to be taking place, and to take his own most appropriate action within the requirements of equivalence. Since all wrongs in Tangu may be seen as, or may be reduced to, a hampering or reduction of food-producing potential, such breaches of equivalence are restored by food exchanges and *br'ngun'guni* through which a true equivalence, or a state of *mngwotngwotiki,* may be realized. The irreconcilable breach of equivalence, which usually involves the suspicion or outright accusation of sorcery, results in one or other household and adherents moving out to form a new settlement elsewhere.

As a social institution *br'ngun'guni* is not exclusive to Tangu—though under that name it is exclusive to Tangu speakers. And it may happen that outsiders will come to *br'ngun'guni* in Tangu—usually to state a case of trespass or sorcery.[11] Conversely, on several occasions during the period of fieldwork some Tangu expressed the resolve to go and *br'ngun'guni* outside their borders. But the events found these same men snug in their homesteads. Within Tangu, *br'ngun'guni* is most frequent between the members of a major settlement—and for most purposes the statement includes all those outlying settlements which regard themselves as attached to the major settlement for feasting purposes. It often happens that members of different settlements in the same neighbourhood become involved in *br'ngun'guni,* and rather less frequently, though not at all unusually, representatives from different neighbourhoods are involved. Still, there are local differences within

Tangu. In Wanitzir, though each of the major compact settlements is divided into two approximately equivalent halves for feasting purposes, and all households participate, consistent with the patrilineal bias there, co-operating brothers tend to be brothers by kinship as well as political brothers, and the brother and sister link is political rather than one of kinship. In Mangigumitzir, on the other hand, the correspondence between kin and political relationship is close. And here, since the neighbourhood consists of a single large settlement with a couple of outliers, in any one year approximately a third of the total number of households stands down from community feasting. Members of these households attend the feasts and participate in *br'ngun'guni,* but they neither provide food, nor eat, nor dance—unless specifically invited to do so.

In Wanitzir, Mangigumitzir, and Biampitzir community feasts take place through each successive annual horticultural cycle. But in Riekitzir, where there are three major settlements and many smaller ones, community feasts are held only every alternate year—though this does not prevent *ad hoc br'ngun'guni* in a non-feasting year. Though each of these major settlements is divided into two approximately equivalent halves for any feasting year, and outlying households and groups of households generally find a place in one or other half of a single major settlement, unlike Mangigumitzir and Wanitzir where the basic referents are respectively the sisters and the brothers, and where the co-operative groups are reasonably stably aligned from year to year, in Riekitzir particular households co-operating in one year may be in exchange relationships two years later. In Biampitzir, as in Riekitzir, the reference point may be either brothers or sisters. But groupings in Biampitzir tend to be more stable than groupings in Riekitzir.

4

Br'ngun'guni emerges as a political, not merely jural, institution which defines the smaller and existential political group on the one hand, and, because virtually only Tangu participate in *br'ngun'guni* in Tangu, members of the different neighbourhoods being entitled to *br'ngun'guni* together, it defines the larger political community on the other. While kin relationships provide the basic criteria for recruiting co-operative groups in opposition to each other, thus providing the situation in which *br'ngun'guni* may take place, and although the kin idiom is always used to describe alignments, the actual alliances depend on how far the leaders or managers of a possible co-operative group of households are able to realize their potential. In each of the neighbourhoods a co-operative group represents a group of brothers who have been made effectively such by their co-operative relationship. Rather than being a group of brothers who co-operate, a co-operative group consists of co-operators whose brotherhood is emphasized because they co-operate. And the managers or leaders of co-operative groups are those who, basically in virtue of their prowess in garden and bush, can make brothers for themselves, brothers in deed as well as in name.

A manager is required to participate in *br'ngun'guni,* and he is expected to put on a good show. He is expected to take the initiative in organizing feasts. He must be married, industrious, and skilled in gardening and hunting lore and techniques. He should have children, for the usual pretext for initiating a series of feasts is to do so in the name of a child, or to celebrate the life crises and anniversaries of children. A manager should be firm and even a little hard-hearted, for brothers who are lazy will attempt to milk him and he should not allow such a drain on his resources. He should be mean so as to conserve what he has, and cunning, so that he may show overwhelming generosity at precisely the right time. A manager cannot afford to waste his substance on people who cannot repay in full, and who in any case, because they cannot repay in full, may have recourse to sorcery against him. A manager should have a wide knowledge of, and ability in, dances: and to achieve this he must attend as many feasts as possible and make his contribution. He should be wise, knowing the myths and stories of his community, and he should be able to evaluate public opinion, have a sure knowledge of social situation. A manager should know when to be aggressive and emphatic, when to withdraw.[12] Taking his cue from community feelings, balancing his own ambitions and desires against it, he influences, guides or steers but does not give orders.

Tangu call a manager a *wunika ruma* (big man). And although any man who works hard and produces quantities of foodstuffs for exchanges may earn this label, effective power and influence is a function of inter-managerial rivalries. Co-operators are as much rivals as those in exchange relationships, and it takes managerial skills to contain the rivalries within a co-operating group. On the other hand, it may be more advantageous to break the co-operative relationship and engage in exchanges. Certainly, if the most able men in the community happen to be co-operators, then, because they cannot otherwise make such significant exchanges, they will break the co-operative relationship and enter the exchange relationship. In *br'ngun'guni* the rising young man finds his experience and perfects his techniques. Industry or productive capacity is the primary qualification which entitles a man to a hearing and respect, but wit and skill in oratory and repartee give point to managerial claims. While anyone may participate in *br'ngun'guni,* and be witty, lacking the evidence of productive ability he earns only laughs. Anyone may rise to his feet and make suggestions, but the weight these suggestions carry does not depend on their inherent wisdom: it depends on the proven achievement of the man who makes them, and on the way in which the achievement is advertised. While oratorical skills distinguish those with added capacities from the simply industrious, industry distinguishes the witty from the capable.

Whether *br'ngun'guni* occurs *ad hoc,* or in the course of feasting and dancing, participants are put on their mettle, watched closely. Because managers are able men, and in the competition for prestige must needs be subtle and cunning, they are the more readily suspected of having recourse to sorcery, or sorcerer-like means. Hence, the more they expose themselves in public, the more they are forced to be explicit, the more they are forced to commit in public such reserves of power as they may be keeping to themselves, the better for all concerned. Equivalence should be seen and made public; equivalence is not consistent with secretive and sorcerer-like ways of getting even with a rival. Nor are these requirements of maintaining equivalence without their burden of anxieties. Since men, particularly managers, and not women bear the weight of political decision, only men are considered to have relevant dreams, only men have encounters with ghosts or dream-images of their fathers or elder brothers, and inspection shows that most dreams and encounters with ghosts are politically relevant. While a dream always carries an imperative to action, and such action usually has political consequences, it is also given that a dream may deceive. Though it is hoped that a ghost will give useful advice, it is accepted that the advice may be misinterpreted or a deliberate and mischievous deception. So that, to succeed as a manager, the outward and positive skills of industry in the gardens and bush, oratory, persuasiveness, and knowledge of people and situation should be matched by a knowledge of the self. A manager should be able so to wrestle with his conscience that he can shun the temptation to sorcery and to secretive means of getting even, and he should be so aware of himself and others that he can draw benefit rather than disaster from his dreams and encounters with ghosts.[13]

It may be presumed that in the past groupings of households were rather more permanent than they are today, and that many more characteristics and abilities went into the making of influential men and managers. Clubhouse life may have blunted the sharper edges of the current cut and thrust in *br'ngun'guni*, and would certainly have provided a greater if more complex knowledge of the factors to be taken into consideration in any particular set of circumstances. It is possible that the productive ability on which so much stress is laid today was qualified by warrior values and numerous ritual or other specialist skills. No doubt a man could always depend on a core of loyal kinsfolk or near neighbours who could be counted on to help him when in trouble. But today nowhere in Tangu is the managerial role dependent on kin affiliation at the expense of productive and other managerial capacities; and although co-operating brothers build their homesteads next to each other, they move off when the co-operative relationship becomes irksome. If a manager's son is to become a manager in his turn, he himself must engage in food exchanges, he himself must be capable of producing the food which all may see, he himself must be able to talk well, he himself must steer clear of the suspicion of sorcery. No man can help him interpret his dreams, no man can prevent him from following the disastrous advice of a mischievous ghost. He himself must learn how best to react to the storm which washes away his crops, the trespasser who takes his game, the sorcerer or adventurer with designs on his wife or daughters, the opponent who exceeds his equivalence in *br'ngun'guni*.

While capabilities outside the process of producing and distributing food-stuffs carry limited kinds of influence in certain restricted fields of action, since becoming a manager and maintaining the role is contained within *br'ngun'guni*, and the latter is itself linked to feasting and more *br'ngun'guni,* power as expressed in the co-operative support of other households and a readiness to defer or accord respect remains dependent on competent and industrious food production, combined with those skills which will advertise the production most effectively. It follows, too, that a manager whose muscles stiffen with age, or who suffers an accident or sickness which disables him, or who is otherwise prevented from performing his task in bush and gardens, falls from grace. Where a younger man must needs take energetic measures against sorcerers, the older man retires, becomes a passenger in the household of one of his sons, and tends to live out the remainder of his days in quiet solitude. The label *wunika ruma* sticks for a while, then 'old man' is substituted for 'big man'. Though a manager who is also believed to be a sorcerer retains much of the power he might otherwise lose, using his reputation as a sorcerer to persuade others to work for and with him, as time passes he becomes more and more isolated, and the fear of co-operating with him and encountering his moodiness as well as the spleen of rival sorcerers overcomes the dread of non-co-operation.

While managers remain active and fit, warding off the sickness which, Tangu feel, emanates from wrong-doing as well as from sorcerers, apart from influencing a group of households the role carries little more than a general prestige and renown. Managers are expected to entertain and impress visitors, their names become well known in the region round about. Their advice may be sought in a variety of matters, and they are expected to appear to take the initiative in village affairs. At the same time, competitors are close; at the first sign of failing powers allegiances tend to shift; no one may become a tyrant or exercise authority. The cycle 'productivity-challenge-*br'ngun'guni*-feast-productivity-challenge-*br'ngun'guni*' remains tight. Managers are not able to rest on their laurels since the power to influence others, to guide or steer the behaviour of households in a co-operative alliance, is attached, not to an office or kin status, but to character, the capacity to produce quantities of food, and certain other skills. The role carries no kind of immunity that is not written in the present personality and abilities of the manager himself. He is an open target for sorcerers, and a flagrant breach of equivalence in an exchange will scare those allied to him even if he is reckless on his own account. Equivalence and egalitarianism as they are expressed in Tangu mean not only that one man is as good as his neighbour, but that no man can afford to seem better than a neighbour. Scrupulous observance of equivalence is even more necessary in a manager than in others. For if in the poor man neglect is merely comic or disgraceful, in the rich man it is culpable. To maintain contacts and keep out of unnecessary trouble; to work hard but not isolate himself in the gardens and bush by so doing; to compete with a rival without breaching equivalence; to treat with a poorer man on a level of equality; to be diplomatic when need be, and forthright when opportune; to be a good husband, father, brother, and friend; to guide without ordering; to command respect without office or rank—the role is a difficult one. At best, it expresses an enviable ideal of what a man should be. And sorcery maintains it.

5

Food production, exchanging, feasting, *br'ngun'guni* and managerial roles exist within, and relate to, a wider power structure which includes administrative officials and servants of the Mission as well as varieties of European. Further, activities in Tangu occur within a self-conscious historical perspective which has seen the diminishing importance of the larger kin group, the disappearance of the clubhouses, and the emergence of new settlement patterns; it has included two world wars, an ever widening horizon of communication with diverse peoples, and cargo cult activity.[14] To ignore the powers conferred on some Tangu through their involvement with the open and greater society would be unduly to distort the situation. Whatever the political system might ideally have been, nobody can now report its operation in a situation where war and peace were not decided by European authorities. And these issues, war-making and peace-making, are surely the most crucial in any political community.

European patrol officers with a section of policemen come to Tangu from sub-district headquarters at Bogia about once a year, and, communicating in Pidgin, inspect the major settlements, take a census, listen to complaints, and carry out any special tasks or investigations. Otherwise, the initiative for making contact with administrative officers lies mainly with the locally appointed officials, luluai, tultul, and 'doctor boy' or medical attendant—who must walk down to Bogia to do so. And since Bogia is a comfortable day's walk from Tangu, to go there means an absence of some three days—three days during which much can happen, three days lost to the gardens in any case. A luluai has general supervisory duties, and he is aided in his work by the tultul who, nominally the village constable, is regarded by Tangu as the former's lieutenant. Between them the two officials are responsible for seeing that the village and roads leading to it are kept clean and in good repair. When a patrol visits the area, they are responsible for the good behaviour and correct muster of the villagers in their charge. They should keep the peace, apprehend wrongdoers and escort them to Bogia for an investigation of the case.[15a] They are custodians of the village book, and they should report any circumstances of sorcery or foul play which may come to their notice. Finally, it is for them to choose a suitable site for growing rice, and they have to organize working parties for clearing, sowing, weeding, harvesting and transport to the coast for sale. The medical attendant tries to supervise the general hygiene of the village, organizes the digging of latrines, maintains the medicine hut, reports to the base hospital from time to time to replenish his stores, and reports cases of sickness to the European medical authorities. Although there appears to be a sharp division of function as between supervisor, constable, and medical attendant, from day to day these native officials tend to spread their various duties among themselves, so that Tangu have come to regard them as forming a quasi-ranking order without the necessary attachment of particular powers.[15b] Thus, though a medical attendant is expected to succeed a tultul, and the latter a luluai, in Tangu the respect accorded an official depends not on his place in the ranking order but on his managerial capacities.

Few of the tasks demanded of the native officials have any traditional sanction. Failure or inefficiency may earn a reprimand, dismissal, or even imprisonment; and the reward for faithful and efficient service may be a commendation or even a medal. Spokesmen for their villagers, native officials are also instruments of the Administration. That is, they often have to serve conflicting interests. Though, in theory, they may bring the full battery of sanctions wielded by the Administration to bear on the community, they themselves are subject to the same sanctions, and since contacts between the officials and European officers are very limited, in most circumstances the officials act as members of their communities rather than as servants of the Administration.

Despite friendly encounters without number, force characterizes the relations between Tangu and the Administration at all levels. Whether in day to day administration, or on patrol, the request for attendance at court, for carriers, for food, or whatever it might be, has always behind it the possible use of policemen and subsequent detention in prison. That there exist appropriate channels of approach, complaint and appeal is beside the point; that administrative officers use their powers with restraint and responsibility is highly commendable. But the fact remains that the checks on administrative authority are lost in the complex of Tangu expectations from, and attitudes towards, the Administration. Tangu expect to be coerced by force or the threat of force, and the mildest of invitations or suggestions from administrative officers have, for Tangu, this sanction behind them. In all their contacts with the Administration, Tangu have uppermost in their minds the fear of imprisonment.[16]

Tangu relations with the Mission are more numerous, more essentially reciprocal. The European priest, resident in Wanitzir, has to maintain his station, teach, convert, and maintain close relationships with the bulk of his parish. He communicates in the vernacular as well as in Pidgin. His native teachers or catechists, distributed through the five schools in the four neighbourhoods, receive a small monthly stipend which is regarded by the Mission not so much as payment but rather as compensation for the time lost from the gardens whilst the teachers are engaged in their duties. Although the training of a catechist is costly, and, being nimble-minded above the ordinary they are subjected to many temptations,[17] most of them remain within the Mission organization which, in turn, considers itself amply repaid if the vocation is faithfully and conscientiously fulfilled. Mission boss-boys, recruited from the major settlements on account of their managerial abilities, and employed on a retainer basis, recruit, organize and direct working parties which build or maintain Mission property. Terms of payment for the working party are discussed beforehand, and the boss-boy is paid a little more.

Unlike the Administration, which is not obliged to accept the resignation of an official, and which can imprison an official for laxity, the Mission counters to the rebel teacher or unwilling boss-boy can only be diffuse. A stoppage of stipend means nothing to a teacher who is willing to leave his village, and only a little to one who prefers to remain with his kin. Since the priest cannot personally supervise all the schools, the teachers must be taken on trust. And, lacking contracts of service binding on both parties, the priest must also come half-way to meet the demands of the boss-boy, who himself must go at least as far to meet the requirements of possibly recalcitrant labour. Force and the Administration may at times be invoked, but since doing so destroys the basis on which relations between the Mission and Tangu are built, the missionary might as well go home. Further, if the Administration is called in, while a point may be gained for the nonce, there are many ways of retaliating. Life for the catechists can be made unbearable; pupils may be instructed by their parents not to attend school; petty pilfering of Mission property may occur; Mission buildings may be damaged; malcontents may take it in turn to sit outside the Mission station to laugh, jeer, and sneer at the missionary, or throw stones on the tin roof of his sleeping quarters during the night. And this kind of thing the Administration is powerless to prevent over an extended period of time.

There are, then, three logically separable systems concerned with the management of affairs in Tangu, each often grating on the others. An official who is also a manager may use traditional techniques in certain situations, and in others, such as when a patrol comes along, he may draw on the reservoir of force which the Administration places at his disposal. And he may combine his full potential to steer a particular situation to a desired end. But he is vulnerable to sorcery, he cannot depend on the Administration to help him out of trouble, he has a garden, kinsfolk and exchange obligations, and administrative duties necessarily interfere with these tasks and responsibilities. Hence, though officials may gather gossip and news on their visits to Bogia, and doing so may give them some temporary renown, their interests tend to centre on their own personal and community affairs. Mission teachers, on the other hand, educated and trained at Alexishafen, are socially and economically part of a total New Guinea ambience in a way in which other Tangu are not. They are aware of, and they are interested in, affairs having a wider reference than the immediate locality. They read books, and newspapers when available. They converse with the missionary, learn from him of policies and outside affairs, and rely on his personal help and support in many situations. Among themselves, too, teachers form a solidarity: they can and do bring pressure to bear on the missionary who directs their activities.

Administrative officials do not form a solidarity, nor can they bring pressures to bear on the Administration. Involved as they are in community affairs, they are rivals who may easily extend their rivalry into their administrative roles. Whereas Mission teachers, full-time specialists, cannot enter significantly into the prestige system based upon productive capacity, feasting and exchanging, and while they may, on application to the missionary, move out of possible fields of conflict, the errors of administrative officials will come home to roost. Yet teacher and official are often useful to each other. While the teacher does not aspire to managerial status in the traditional sense, and is thus not a rival, because he has a fund of information concerning Administration and Mission intentions he may enable officials to plan ahead and reconcile their often conflicting roles of manager and

official. On the other side, by persuading householders to send their children to
school and religious instruction, officials and managers can enhance the catechist's
reputation within the Mission organization, and can advance their own and their
community's reputation in the eyes of both Mission and Administration.

The production of rice for cash neatly demonstrates the traditional and administrative systems in action. Officials set aside one day in the week when households are expected to 'work for the government', as it is phrased. The problem is
to find adequate labour. The best workers make themselves scarce, disappearing
into the surrounding country to tend their own gardens or hunt—activities which
serve personal, kin, economic and political ends within a known frame of reference.
While administrative officials are not unaware of the general benefit that might
proceed from successful rice production, they know the difficulties attendant on
sharing out such cash as might accrue from a sale, and they know that those
managers who are not officials are presently stealing a march on them. If they were
to go to Bogia and report the recalcitrants, they might be inviting sorcery, and they
know that an administrative intervention will give satisfaction to no one and annoy
everyone. While some officials have tried to incite competition with other administrative units, thus bringing the activity within a more familiar ambience, few
Tangu—knowing that such intercommunity rivalry can only encourage sorcery too—
can view such attempts with equanimity.

If an official is also a manager in his own right he may achieve a measure
of success in his role as official. But, in the rice situation, managers who are officials
tend to prefer traditional renown and, in the crux, are prepared to let the rice field
go hang. Officials who are not managers are faced with organizing households in an
unfamiliar way to work for ends which do not appear valuable in opposition to men
who have proved their worth in garden, bush and *br'ngun'guni*. And the only effective means of doing so is to invoke sanctions of force—rice growing is 'government
work'. But by such action he disburdens himself of the personal responsibility which
is the essence of the managerial role. Disputes which involve officials who are not
managers with managers who are not officials usually end with the latter carrying
the day—temporarily. Community support goes to the managers who represent
activities and notions with forseeable ends which have value for Tangu. At the
same time the community generally fears the administrative forces which the official
may call in to help him. So that while the official is always vulnerable to the threat
of sorcery, rice growing tends to be backed by those who lack the essence of
managerial ability, by those who want a short-cut to power, by those whom Tangu
themselves respect least.

Separation of the roles of manager and native official is clearly obnoxious, and
where the roles are so separated rice growing has been a dismal failure. Combination
of the roles, on the other hand, goes far toward creating an acceptable office. The
relative stability of social relationships in Wanitzir, and the more or less successful
production of rice there, is due partly to the combination of roles, and partly to the
facts that there the Mission is strongest, the proportion of officials to population is

greater than elsewhere in Tangu, and the settlements are compact. In Riekitzir, where rivalry between managers is strongest, settlements are scattered, the proportion of officials to population is smallest, and the combination of roles is rare, rice production is negligible.[18]

6

Mission roles, complementary for the most part to the needs of administrative officials as well as traditional managers, spring from a basically reciprocal system. Within the system actions may be approved or disapproved, but the extent to which they can actually be encouraged or stopped depends on a common submission to moral notions within which advantage and loss are dependent on pragmatic bargaining positions—each party having something to give the other and consequences to look to in default. No point is made or surrendered without having its effect on others within the system. Indeed, the consequences are felt by, and obtain reactions from, all Tangu as well as the European missionary. These features give the Mission system common ground with the traditional system which, working within the notion of equivalence in exchange, requires that managers depend not only upon their own productive ability, public criticism and approval, and the number of households they can persuade to lend aid in a particular situation, but upon a necessary opposition. The quality of a manager, that is, depends as much on those sisters' households which can be organized to exchange with him, as on those households of brothers he can persuade to help him. Managers mature on, and find their full scope in, opposition. Administrative roles, on the other hand, though they must interact with others, are authoritative, order-giving roles. Within the system itself, checks on officials are dependent on whether the European officers concerned come to know of a particular default, and upon their own personal initiative both before and after the event. The potential of a virtually uncheckable dominance is there.[19]

In practice, however, what might easily become a tyrannous role does not in fact do so because the officials are Tangu, living in Tangu, subject to their own traditional checks, and out of immediate contact with the European officers on whom they must depend. More importantly there is, too, the fear of sorcery. Whether a man is an official, a manager, a teacher, a boss-boy, or just an ordinary fellow going about his affairs, he has to tread warily with an eye to the interests of others lest he fall sick or die as the result of breaching equivalence, lest he incur the envy of a man willing to employ a sorcerer, lest he incur the wrath of a sorcerer for no reason that he can make out. Meanness is self-defeating; it leaves a man bereft of those who might otherwise help him. To be over-generous is to behave with contumely, to invite the attentions of a sorcerer. Overtly, equivalence rules, and should be seen to be observed. Covertly, each man covets an edge over his fellows: sorcery is his means, sorcery checks him. Paradoxically, while beliefs in sorcery appear as integral to the maintenance of the traditional system of checks on ambition, preventing any single man from gaining an outright dominance, and although the Administration is as emphatic as the Mission in its efforts to eradicate beliefs in sorcery, the administrative system as such in Tangu is almost entirely dependent on sorcerers for checking the activities of its representatives in Tangu.

NOTES

1. This essay was first written in 1954. Based upon fieldwork carried out in 1952 as a Scholar with the Australian National University, it was originally presented as a chapter in a symposium on Melanesian Political Systems. That symposium having miscarried, it is offered now in a form only slightly different from the original.

2. Located 4° 25′ South, 144° 55′ East, about fifteen miles inland from Bogia bay in the Bogia Subdistrict, Madang District, New Guinea.

3. The suffix *-itzir* or *-tzir* carries the meaning 'people of'. The total population of all four neighbourhoods together is just under 2,000.

4. See, for example, Georg Höltker 1945, 1950.

5. Tangu account for 27% of the total population living in the hills between the Ramu and Iwarum and occupy 9% of the total area.

6. See, for example, Burridge 1965: 226-238.

7. See Burridge 1957: 763-780.

8. See Burridge 1960: 14-24, 73-85.

9. Both Mission and Administration have always attempted to encourage concentration into larger settlements. Their failure was complete until Yali (a well known cargo activist in the Madang District) advised Tangu to concentrate. After Yali was imprisoned, Tangu again began to disperse.

10. On the level of kinship, becoming *mngwotngwotiki* is also the occasion for children of the two households to marry each other. On the whole, once the marriage has been consummated and the couple have begun to form an independent household of their own, the state of being *mngwotngwotiki* ceases.

11. Such an occurrence happened only once during the period of fieldwork— and then the 'stranger' or 'outsider' was a native of the settlement concerned, who had married out.

12. For example, when faced with a novel situation, such as the arrival of the author in Tangu, managers retired to the bush. Since there existed no precedents on which they could base predictions, it was wise to vacate the situation altogether. Only when opinion had 'firmed', when the situation had settled somewhat, did they return and make up their minds as to what they should do.

13. See Burridge 1965: 238-248.

14. See Burridge 1954: 241-254; 1960 *passim*.

15*a*. and *b*. There are often arguments between the three officials as to which of them is to go to Bogia and leave his garden untended or miss a feast. Sometimes it is a good idea to be away for several days on 'official duties', sometimes it is not. But if they cannot agree among themselves, then it is best not to go to Bogia at all.

16. As of the time of fieldwork, 1952.

17. Since native teachers are generally capable and educated, they are in a position to accept posts with European commercial enterprises which carry greater remuneration, an enviable ration scale, and the opportunity for living in the larger centres rather than in the bush.

18. On rice growing in Tangu, see Burridge 1960: 260-263.

19. Cf. the case of Bumbu, in Hogbin 1946: 38-65.

REFERENCES CITED

BURRIDGE, K. O. L. (1954) : Cargo Activity in Tangu. *Oceania*, Vol. XXIV, No. 4.
BURRIDGE, K. O. L. (1957) : Disputing in Tangu. *American Anthropologist*, Vol. 59, No. 5.
BURRIDGE, K. O. L. (1960) : *Mambu: A Melanesian Millennium*. London: Methuen.
BURRIDGE, K. O. L. (1965) : Tangu, Northern Madang District. *In* Lawrence and Meggitt, eds., 224-49.
HOGBIN, H. I. (1946) : Local Government for New Guinea. *Oceania*, Vol. XVII, No. 1.
HOLTKER, G. (1945) : Ethnographia aus Neuguinea. *Annali Lateranensi*, Vol. IX.
HOLTKER, G. (1950) : Ein Papuanisches Zwillinspaar beim Stamm der Tanggum in Neuguinea. *Anthropos*, Vol. 45.
LAWRENCE, P. and M. J. MEGGITT (eds.) (1965) : *Gods, Ghosts and Men in Melanesia*. Melbourne: Oxford University Press.

ANN CHOWNING and WARD H. GOODENOUGH

LAKALAI POLITICAL ORGANIZATION[1]

ABSTRACT

This discussion of the large Lakalai dialect group of New Britain focuses attention on patterns of co-residence and co-operation, with special reference to leadership and social control. The main bases of leadership are age, wealth or control of wealth, knowledge, industry, magical power, and ability in warfare; and the processes through which men achieve prestige, obtain adherents and assume authority are examined in some detail. Seniority is seen as fundamental in this society. Elders institutionally dramatize their authority, impressing upon the community the power that lies behind it. This traditional political organization has relevance also in the present-day situation.

INTRODUCTION

The Nakanai-speaking peoples inhabit one hundred miles of the central north coast of New Britain island (see Map 1). The Lakalai, who numbered 2,700 people in 1954, are the westernmost and most numerous dialect group among them.[2] They occupy twenty villages on the Hoskins Peninsula (see Map 2), where together with the non-Nakanai-speaking Xarua and Kapore they form the West Nakanai subdivision of the administrative district whose centre is at Talasea on the Willaumez Peninsula.

The region where the Lakalai live is a flat plain between the sea and an arc of mountains which includes the active volcano Mt Pago. All but three villages are on the coast, as the fresh water supply is largely confined to small streams that emerge only a few yards from the beach. The rain forest of the interior is replaced near the coast by bush, the dense second growth of fallow garden land. In this bush the Lakalai make their villages and gardens.

A village consists of one or more hamlets. Each hamlet normally contains from four to six dwellings, a men's house, and a feasting ground in a grove on the edge of the clearing. Hamlets belonging to the same village are traditionally separated from each other by narrow strips of bush, often nowadays reduced to a stand of areca (betel) palms or only an invisible line. Several neighbouring villages linked by paths and maintaining peaceful relations with each other form what we shall call a territory. Territories are separated by stretches of bush or climax forest without connecting paths. Relations between them used to be chronically hostile.

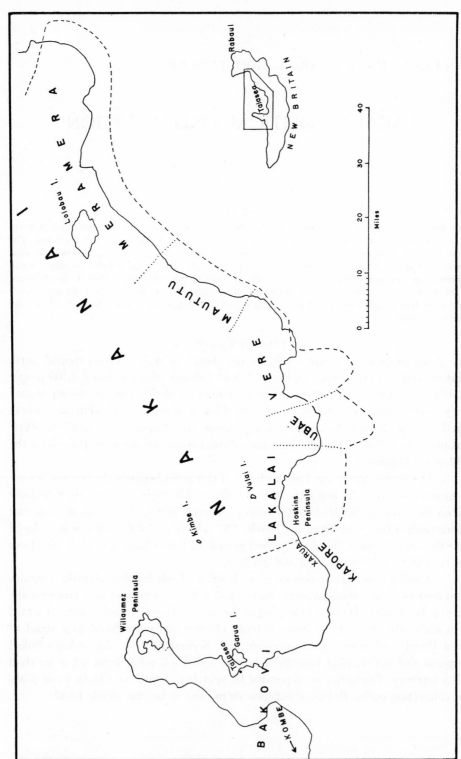

Map 1 Linguistic and ethnic divisions of the north coast of central New Britain

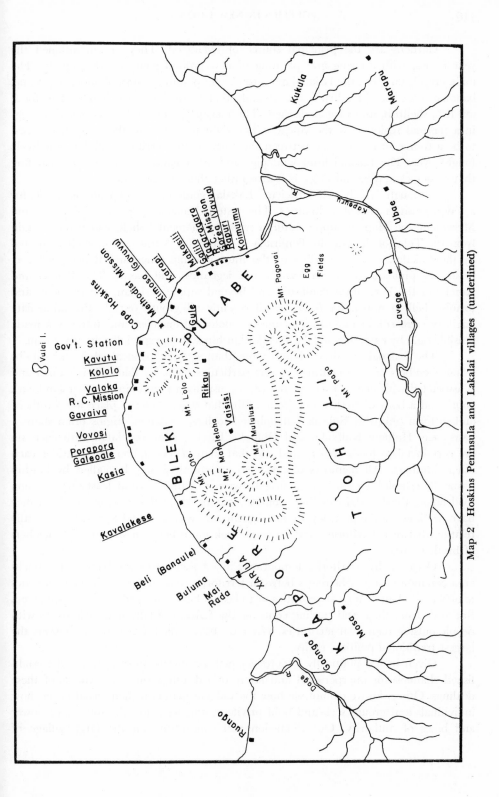

Map 2 Hoskins Peninsula and Lakalai villages (underlined)

Gardens are the principal source of livelihood. They are maintained the year round, with clearing and planting of new ground going on continually. The main crop is taro, but the Lakalai also grow sweet potatoes, yams, manioc, sugarcane, bananas, coconuts, breadfruit, and several other fruits. The principal protein foods are fish, shellfish, and megapode eggs. The megapodes or 'bush fowl' lay their eggs in a thermal region near the volcano. The right to collect in these egg fields used to be a source of controversy between the surrounding territories, and was actively fought over. The Lakalai hunt wild pigs and other game, but all meat, including that of domestic pigs and dogs, is festive rather than ordinary fare.

Although largely self-sufficient, Lakalai communities depend on trade for a few necessities as well as luxuries. The eastern Nakanai (especially Maututu and Meramera, see Map 1) supply *bubu,* a type of ornamental shell, which they obtain from the Tolai of the Gazelle Peninsula in return for *Nassa calossa* shells collected by the Lakalai. From the tribes of the interior come songs and dances, tobacco, cassowary pinions, woven wristbands and legbands, and basalt. The Bakovi and Kombe of the Willaumez Peninsula and beyond supply obsidian, red pigment, and tortoise-shell in return for *bubu.* Until recently all groups outside the immediate territory were considered to be enemies or potential enemies, and trade was made possible only by extensions of the Lakalai kinship system, especially the sib system.

The Lakalai are divided into more than sixty matrilineal sibs[3] and subsibs whose members are not confined to any particular territory. Each sib is named and is associated with one or more sacred places, usually a mountain or other landmark (*olu*) and a body of fresh water (*lalu*). Sibs that share a sacred place are 'brothers' and so form phratries. Subsibs remembered to have common origins often share a name, e.g. Holuolu Kaiboibo and Holuolu Tatoha. Also associated with each sib are certain taboo foods (*lelea*) and sibs that share a food taboo also consider each other 'brothers'. All members of one's sib and phratry may be called by kinship terms. By establishing correspondences between sibs that have at least one common food taboo, the Lakalai can find 'sibmates' among all of the tribes with whom they have dealings. In the past, loyalty among sibmates was supposed to transcend hostile relations between territories, and all trade took place between sibmates or members of brother sibs.

Occasionally, territories temporarily allied themselves for large-scale attacks on a common enemy. Marriages between territories were arranged through sibmates to offset imbalances in local sex-ratios or to keep a landowning sib locally represented. But aside from these and trading contacts, the Lakalai usually had little to do with people outside their own territories. What we have called a territory represents the largest traditional political entity.

Given such a politically underdeveloped society, we must examine the established channels for interpersonal and intergroup dealings and the contexts of these dealings. Otherwise we cannot see how the Lakalai maintain their social order, how individuals and groups seek and hold privilege, and what are the sources of power and bases of authority. Our discussion will concentrate on the large village of

TABLE 1

Population of West Nakanai Subdivision, based on Census in August, 1954, by Patrol Officer Ernest Sharp

Village	Men	Women	Children	Absent	Total
Lakalai-speaking					
Koimuimu	41	32	53	4	130
Rapuri	21	21	33	5	80
Gorea (Vavua)	32	36	84	7	159
Galilo	64	59	125	17	265
Makasili	33	21	30	2	86
Karapi	55	54	119	9	237
Kimoso (Gavuvu)	38	35	66	4	143
Gule	20	25	48	12	105
Rikau	28	40	54	4	126
Kavutu	21	21	33	4	79
Kalolo	21	18	11	18	68
Valoka	42	46	53	52	193
Gavaiva	46	49	71	3	169
Vovosi	20	25	34	22	101
Porapora	37	39	41	36	153
Galeoale	40	46	69	11	166
Kasia	30	48	92	18	188
Kovalakese	37	38	55	17	147
Vaisisi	36	21	37	3	97
Totals	662	674	1,108	248	2,692
Kapore-speaking					
Beli (Banaule)	50	41	80	14	185
Mosa	47	49	87	7	190
Gaongo	18	19	24	4	64
Totals	115	109	190	25	439
Xarua-speaking					
Buluma	71	65	136	16	288
Mai and Rada	67	67	134	16	284
Totals	138	132	270	32	572
Grand Totals	915	915	1,568	305	3,703

Galilo (Table 1), which has long been a centre of Lakalai population and has also remained aloof from the 'cargo' movements[4] in which most other Lakalai villages have actively participated.

KINSHIP

Kinship considerations are implicit in almost all Lakalai relationships. They may be overshadowed by other social bonds, such as partnerships, but, in contrast with societies in which kinship encompasses only a few of the persons with whom one deals, for the Lakalai kinship extends indefinitely. As a result, they find it necessary to ignore their kin obligations in many instances in order not to be exploited unduly by others.

Although a Lakalai can apply at least one kinship term to anyone with whom he has daily contact, i.e. to any member of his village, he is unlikely to be able to trace genealogical connection with him. He seldom knows the names of ancestors more remote than his grandparents. He deduces his relationship to others from sib membership, from the relationship his parents had with their parents, and from the relationship he and they have to a common kinsman.

Because kinship is readily extended in this way to encompass virtually all peaceful social relationships, the Lakalai distinguish an inner circle of kinsmen with whom there are many mutual obligations from those who are outside this circle. We shall speak of kinsmen within the circle as a person's 'near' or 'close' kin and refer to those outside it as his 'distant' kin. A further distinction separates consanguineal kin, what the Lakalai call 'true' kin, as those persons whose genealogical connections to oneself are known, from nominal kin, other persons, such as sibmates, who are called by the same terms as consanguineal kin. The consanguineal kin of a spouse are the persons with whom a man incurs obligations through marriage, and these constitute his affines.

What we are calling a Lakalai's near kin consist primarily of his consanguineal kin, fellow villagers who belong to his sib or subsib, and the other residents of his hamlet. Adoption may add to their numbers. As long as they live in his village, the near kin include all persons with whom a man's parents and grandparents were joined in 'sibling sets' together with their descendants. Ideally, a sibling set consists of uterine siblings, but practical considerations frequently lead remoter consanguines who are already classed as 'siblings' in the kinship terminology to form a sibling set in which they act as if they were uterine siblings.

We need not consider Lakalai kinship classification in detail, but it will be advisable to note a few of the more important distinctions and obligations.

In his own generation a Lakalai differentiates siblings and parallel cousins sharply from cross-cousins. Among the former he further distinguishes older from younger relatives. Siblings in the same sibling set are supposed to help and support each other in all undertakings; the property of one may be freely borrowed by another without asking permission; the older should be responsible for the younger, and, in return, the younger is expected to be dependent upon the older and to respect and obey him. Joking between such persons is considered improper. Remoter kinsmen classed as siblings show more camaraderie and engage, moreover, in practical joking. Nominal siblings of opposite sex are expected to be lovers. Cross-cousins are not allowed to use each other's names, enter one another's houses, joke, quarrel, insult, scold, or make requests of each other, or engage in mutual sex relations except in marriage. There should be a strong sense of mutual responsibility, each giving support and material aid to the other without being asked.

In his parents' generation, a Lakalai refers to kinsmen on his father's and mother's sides respectively by different terms, but in his personal dealings with them there are no marked contrasts in general attitude and behaviour. He should show respect and obedience to all, and they are responsible for his welfare. But there are two kinds of responsibility, one associated with the family and the other with the sib. The first includes the responsibilities one has toward children in connection with food, education, marriage, and ceremonial preparation for adult life. The second includes protection of property rights, protection against attack or other injury, and avenging a death. All of a Lakalai's senior kinsmen share both sets of responsibilities, but they do so in varying degree. His father and father's immediate brothers have primary responsibility in relation to the first set. Maternal uncles play a secondary role here, but will assume these duties fully if necessary. Maternal uncles and elder sibmates take primary responsibility for the second set, but the father's brothers and sibmates will do so when necessary. While relations with consanguineal kinsmen of the father's generation are marked by respect and obedience, those with nominal kinsmen who are younger than one's father are easy and informal.

Respect is required of a Lakalai in most exaggerated form in dealing with his older affines, especially his parents-in-law. It is particularly important not to call the latter by name, touch them, or use disrespectful language in their presence. A young man's father-in-law can demand labour from him at any time. A husband should also help his wife's brothers, but they, like cross-cousins, make no direct demands. Relations between brothers-in-law are expected to be harmonious, and usually are. Few marriages take place without the consent of both families, and exchanges in which a brother and sister marry a sister and brother are common. Ideally, brothers-in-law should garden together. They should also support each other in quarrels or feuds (except where their own sib allegiances forbid).

Despite different emphases in the several kin relationships just outlined, they are all characterized by the general feeling that seniors are self-sacrificing in relation to juniors, who should be respectful and obedient in return. (Although in one sense the relation between a man and his parents-in-law appears as an exception, it can also be viewed as one in which the young husband and father is being initiated into his role as a responsible and self-sacrificing parent.) Parents deliberately withhold favours from disobedient and disrespectful children, as do senior kinsmen from junior. The threat of not providing a wife is especially potent, since a man is not accorded the privilege of adult status until he has married and become a father.

Junior kin, on the other hand, often exploit their dependent position by demanding that their elders care for them or protect them from danger in situations where they are in fact quite able to care for themselves. Pleading youth and inexperience is an acknowledged device for avoiding difficult tasks and getting extra favours.

As kinship connections become remote or nominal, obligations become weak and are often ignored. This seems to result in an ambivalent feeling about remoter kinsmen. As kinsmen, they are presumably to be trusted, but their remoteness makes them in fact less reliable. The joking relationship, which obtains between less immediate kin, seems directly connected with this ambivalence. In joking, one uses language that, if spoken seriously, is a curse or insult to anyone who hears it. Thus joking is itself ambivalent—cursing with a smile. At the same time, a joking relationship is proof to remoter kinsmen that each is placing trust in the other. Close relationships require no such affirmation.

PARTNERSHIPS

Relationships between individuals who are not consanguineal kinsmen are frequently formalized in partnerships. There are several types of partnership, all characterized by the use of special terms of address and reference instead of personal names. They fall into two major categories: those involving an exchange of goods or services and those based on sharing an experience.

Mutual rights and obligations are at once more specific and more limited in partnerships concerned with exchanging goods and services. For example, men who call each other *gauli* exchange snared bush fowl (megapodes) and keep an accurate count of the number exchanged. If one man dies before the account is even, his son must settle it for him. This relationship assures the participants of a supply of bush fowl, because the taboos associated with the use of hunting magic prevent a man from eating birds that he has snared himself. It also affords an opportunity for friendly rivalry between hunters, but it does not affect their other dealings with one another. Similarly, if a man is away from home when his brother dies and another man digs the grave, the first man calls the gravedigger by a special term and is obliged to return the favour when he can, but has no other obligations toward him. It can be said of exchange partnerships generally that they are highly formalized, contractual in nature, and specific as to mutual rights and duties.

Sharing partnerships are usually broader in scope. Although some of them make specific demands of the partners, others have the character of formalized friendships. People who like to work or play together or who share a sleeping mat in the men's house begin to call each other by special terms and thus publicly assume the responsibilities of the corresponding partnership. They are, in effect, pledged to provide companionship and to offer aid whenever it is needed. All close friendships are eventually formalized in this fashion. Other sharing partnerships result from fortuitous associations and involve specific obligations. Their further development depends on the congeniality of the partners. For example, youths who on the same occasion received the headdress symbolizing the achievement of young manhood call each other *vikilipi* and are supposed to share their sexual adventures. If they are congenial, they may also join forces in other enterprises such as night fishing and egg collecting. Since a man usually has several *vikilipi,* he can stress the relationship with the one whom he likes best. Similarly, men who are paired in a dance at a memorial feast for the dead become *maroto* and help each other in clearing their respective gardens. If they wish to, they may share other activities.

The only partnership involving persons of opposite sex is that between *samura.* A man's *samura* is any woman, other than his wife, mother, sister or daughter, with whom he works a garden plot. He may initiate the relationship for various reasons, including pity for a family that has too few men. If the girl is unmarried, he receives a share of the brideprice when her subsequent marriage deprives him of her services. His *samura* cooks the food from their joint garden and sends him a share. The relationship is particularly valuable to a man whose wife is ill, pregnant, or inclined to express resentment by refusing to cook for him.

Sharing partnerships may affect kin relationships in several ways. For example, an older man removed the avoidance obligations of a youthful kinsman who had become a partner of his son. Another man adopted his son's orphaned partner. Men seek aid from their partners when their close kin cannot or will not provide it. A child whose father cannot afford to buy him a bead necklace asks the man for whom he is named, because the name-sharing partnership obligates the older man to fulfil all requests.

A man's partners usually live in hamlets other than his own, sometimes in other villages. Consequently they add to the number of persons on whom he can rely. The Lakalai ordinarily suspect the motives of fellow villagers whose confidence they do not regularly enjoy—that is, those who are not consanguineal relatives or hamlet mates. They trust their partners, however, and a man feels more secure when he has increased through such relationships the number of people on whom he can depend for aid and support. By the time they are thirty years old, most Lakalai men can count as partners of one kind or another from six to ten of their contemporaries in their village and territory.

WRISTBAND SOCIETIES

A special type of partnership involves co-membership in a wristband society. There are several such societies, each with a distinctive wristband, the generic name for which is *mileki.* Some are more important than others. Two are especially important politically. They are the *savarasi* and *suara* societies, the former associated with hamlet leadership and the latter with leadership in war. Membership in the *suara* society is also a prerequisite to selection for the highest political office, that of *valipoi.* We shall have frequent occasion to refer to *savarasi* and *suara,* but must postpone our account of them and of wristband societies generally until after we have examined the processes by which men achieve recognition as leaders in Lakalai society.

SIBS

Sib membership is conferred by birth and is not changed by adoption. It is retained by the dead, whose spirits continue to protect and aid living sibmates and close relatives, though they may also cause death by stealing their living kinsmen's souls in order to enjoy their company. A man who knows the proper spells can summon the spirit of a dead sibmate to reside in his hunting dog and help him hunt pigs; or he may call upon such a spirit to cause a woman whom he wishes to seduce to be obsessed with thoughts of him. Each sib has a fund of myths that account for its acquisition of food taboos and its special association with cultural items. Tobacco, for example, is said to have been given to a man of the Holuolu sib by one of its taboo animals. These animals may be malevolent to others but aid the sib's members. These mystical ties with ancestral spirits, sacred places, taboo animals, cultural objects and myths emphasize that the bonds between sibmates are independent of human wish or contrivance, forming a part of the natural and spiritual, indeed cosmic, order. This attitude affects everything connected with sibs, including sib-owned property.

Sib property includes its sacred places and, often, scarce goods found at or near these places. Sibs also may be said to own cultivable land and some reefs, to both of which they have what appears to be an inalienable title. When a Lakalai clears virgin forest, he converts it into cultivable land, and it remains such as long as it is recleared frequently enough to keep it from reverting to climax forest. The cleared land, it is said, becomes the property of his sib in the sense that all its members have right of access to it, whereas non-members have no such right. But prior right is held by the clearer, his consanguineal matrilineal kin, and their lineal descendants in the female line. Within this lineage, as we shall call it to distinguish it from the larger sib, the senior male holds ultimate authority. No one outside the lineage may garden or build on it without his consent.

Cultivable land is regarded as inalienable from the sib to which the controlling lineage belongs. If this lineage dies out, the one most closely connected with it in the sib assumes authority. As long as there are living members of the controlling lineage, however, they continue to have prior rights, regardless of where they may be residing, a fact that will be important when we consider the problem of territorial citizenship. If no member of the controlling lineage resides in the territory where its land is located, its interests are administered by the senior member of another lineage of their sib. If their sib is unrepresented, any locally resident children or grandchildren of its men exercise control; but they must surrender it when a member of the controlling lineage or its sib moves into the territory.

Other items that may be sib-owned are mask designs and the dances and trick costumes associated with memorial feasts for the dead. They are usually 'discovered' in inspirational experiences, which sometimes involve dead sibmates. The discoverer establishes his copyright by killing a pig. He may give or sell his copyright, but in either case the recipient is required to validate his ownership in the same way. All of the copyright holder's sibmates have free performance rights or use rights to these dances and masks. If the copyright is not sold, it becomes in time general sib-property under the control of its senior members. Unlike land, copyrights continue to be alienable.

Personal insult or attack is a problem to be dealt with by one's entire sib. Very rarely, indeed, does a sib withdraw support from one of its members or turn against him. A recent case of father-daughter incest, which resulted in court action against the man by his own sib as well as his daughter's, is our only recorded actual example. No matter how justifiable the punishment of a person may seem to other members of the community, there is always a chance that his sibmates will resent it and attack the punisher.

Most deaths are attributed to malevolent action by evil spirits or human beings. Where death is not due to violence it is often attributed to sorcery. Death due to neglect and suicide as a result of humiliation are also regarded as manslaughter. Most deaths, therefore, are felt to call for reprisal, either by direct attack on the killer or one of his sibmates, or by sorcery directed against the sib of the persons responsible (whether their identity is known or unknown). Because all of a sib's members are held responsible for a crime committed by one of them, children are warned against strangers and, in former times, were told never to leave their hamlet alone. A woman of childbearing age is an especially satisfactory victim in reprisal killings and feuds, because her death keeps her from adding her children to the numerical strength of her sib. On the other hand, the very fact that the deed of one man may endanger all of his sibmates leads them to try to control his actions. They may threaten to withdraw their support if he persists in causing trouble.

Offences involving the principle of collective responsibility include killing another person, directly or by sorcery; killing someone's pig; rape or attempted rape; wife-stealing; and, finally, showing contempt for someone who has died by failing to honour mourning taboos. In such cases, a member of the offended sib may seek to kill the offender or one of his sibmates, confident that his own sibmates will support his action. Although there are established procedures for terminating them, sib feuds may last for generations, indeed long after the original offence has been forgotten.

Sib affiliations, as already noted, become more important to a person who has no close consanguineal kin or who, for one reason or another, is not on good terms with them. If his parents are dead, he can expect his sibmates to help him obtain a wife. A man who has neither sibmates nor parents can demand that member's of his father's or grandfather's sib provide him with magical knowledge.

In summary, sib membership defines a man's basic place not only in his social world but in the whole cosmos. He can never relinquish membership nor be immune from the liabilities to which membership exposes him. Neither can his sibmates ever fully disown him. While a man may have to flee his hamlet or territory, he need never flee his sibmates. As long as he has sibmates in other communities, he is assured of shelter and such safety as it is within their power to give.

We stress this because only between sibmates and consanguineal kin do the Lakalai treat rights and duties as transcending the acts and wishes of men and thus, as it were, 'divinely' or 'naturally' given. Rights and duties otherwise, as in the case of partnerships, become effective by virtue of mutual agreement, as the result of covenants among men. Where no covenants have been made, and when the terms of established covenants have been broken, men are automatically enemies. This means that Lakalai live together in hamlets, villages, and territories only insofar as they individually show their willingness to abide by a social contract whose unwritten but traditional terms constitute the Lakalai 'common law'. As we shall see, this has important consequences for social control and for political structure and process.

PROPERTY

We have already discussed sib property, and we shall have occasion to treat certain aspects of property again in connection with the special items subject to hamlet and village control. Here we are concerned with personal property in the sense that the parties to property relationships are individuals as distinct from corporate bodies such as sibs and lineages.

There are many things subject to personal ownership, some of them highly and others lightly valued. They include gardens (as distinct from land), houses, fishing platforms, fishing and gardening huts, fruit-bearing trees, trees whose wood is prized, tools, weapons, canoes, nets, food, cut timber, domestic animals, personal ornaments, paraphernalia for ceremonial adornment, wealth-tokens, magic and other esoteric knowledge, and all newly acquired goods of European origin, such as bicycles, cloth, and Australian money. Items of particular interest here are wealth-tokens, ceremonial paraphernalia, domestic pigs, nets for hunting wild pigs and turtles, and special knowledge.

Anyone who produces an object of value through his labour and skill becomes its owner, unless his labour and skill are paid for by someone else in a contract sale. Where several men jointly make a canoe, for example, they are all its co-owners, each having personal title to a share. If one of them expects to be sole owner, he must pay his helpers for their labour, unless they are people on whose labour he has a proper claim, e.g., his son-in-law. Similarly, a person has title to any objects of value he discovers, such as wild fruit trees or mask designs.

Once established, an owner's title consists of a set of clearly defined rights, powers, duties, and liabilities.[5] It is his privilege to dispose of what he owns as he sees fit, and his right that such disposition be accepted by other members of the community. Disposition is subject to certain limitations, however, for he must be of age and must not disregard kinship obligations or other encumbrances. There are, for example, minimum provisions that a man must make for his children. Until they are made, his children have what amounts to a lien on his property. An owner has the power to obligate others by making them gifts, which they cannot refuse without offering insult to the giver. While an owner has the right to use his property and enjoy its fruits, he does not have exclusive right. Provided he is not himself using it, certain specific consanguineal kinsmen, such as own brothers and their children, also have use rights. They are free to take his tools, for example, or gather nuts from his almond trees without asking permission. Somewhat remoter kin and certain of his sharing partners are accorded use privileges, provided they ask his permission on each occasion. Persons accorded use privileges, and non-owners with use rights, are expected to acknowledge their indebtedness to the owner by giving him a share of whatever has been acquired through the use of his property. Borrowing as just outlined, whether by right or by permission, is not to be confused with rental. When a man lends his canoe to kinsmen to go fishing, he expects a share of the catch as a courtesy; but when he rents his canoe, as to someone wishing to make a trip to the government station or to visit kinsmen in east Nakanai, a fee is negotiated in advance (or a fixed rental is understood to apply), payable in wealth-tokens or Australian money.

Title may be acquired by purchase, that is, by an exchange of goods that is agreed upon in advance of the transfer of title. With items of no great value such exchanges are on a barter basis. The higher the value of the goods or services sold, the greater the likelihood that they will be compensated, at least in part, by wealth-tokens.

These tokens consist primarily of goldlip pearl shells (*tuali*), spears (*gata*) that have been decorated with cockatoo feathers and *Nassa calossa* shells, tortoise-shell arm bands (*sasa*), and strings of cut shell beads (*bubu*). The raw materials for all but the spears are not locally available and must be imported through trade channels. Australian money is freely used in place of local currency at the present time, but in important transactions the Lakalai feel that at least some traditional wealth-tokens should be employed.

Wealth-tokens are required in the sale of pigs, and play a special role in gift transactions, as we shall see. They make up a significant portion of the bride-price. Compensation for manslaughter must also be paid in prescribed forms of currency. Lakalai wealth-tokens, therefore, have value as something more than a medium of exchange, in that no important jural process is possible without them. It is their transfer that validates a marriage contract, a title to special knowledge, or settlement of a feud. Only the transfer of currency can give the results of major property and social transactions the status of full legality.[6]

We must consider two types of gift. In the first, called *vararapu*, gifts are given as expressions of goodwill in the expectation of receiving similar tokens of goodwill in return. But no strict accounting is kept, nor is there any formal claim against a person who fails to reciprocate. Consanguineal kinsmen, sharing partners, affinal kinsmen, and hamlet mates regularly engage in this kind of mutual giving. Tobacco, food, betelnut, tools, and ornaments may all be given in this way. Valuable items that are normally reserved for the second type of gift may be given as *vararapu*, but only to very close kinsmen, e.g., a sister's son. Senior kinsmen regard it as a part of their responsibilities to make gifts to their junior relatives. Such behaviour enhances their general reputation for generosity. It also provides a rationale for the demand that junior kinsmen respect and obey their seniors.

Gifts of this type, usually involving items of small value, may be given in the interests of hospitality, of maintaining strategic nominal kin ties, and of neighbourliness between village and territory mates. A return gift or favour should be made at the first natural opportunity in order to avoid offence.

To make the second type of gift is to *vuivuti*. Gifts of this type consist of wealth-tokens and large cuts of pork. To offer such a gift is to accord formal social recognition. To accept such a gift is to assume a legal obligation to repay in kind at the first opportunity. While one has the privilege of refusing to accept such a gift, to do so is ostensibly to shame the giver. The actual consequences of refusal, however, depend on the circumstances behind the original gift and on the ability of the refuser to repay it. In breaches of the social code, for example, the offended person acknowledges offence and offers to restore cordial relations by presenting the offender with a wealth-token. Refusal to accept indicates that the offence was intended. Acceptance and return payment resolve the issue. When, under other circumstances, an intended recipient refuses a gift because of his inability to repay in kind, he is himself shamed. For this reason men sometimes *vuivuti* to persons who they know cannot repay, in order to humiliate them. If they accept and then fail to pay back, they incur public censure; if they refuse, they confess their poverty, a condition the Lakalai attribute to laziness. In either case they are revealed as of no account, as 'rubbish men'. Thus, while in one sense a way of honouring the recipient, *vuivuti* may also be an aggressive act intended to dishonour him. Through this form of gift, therefore, wealthy persons have power to humiliate others.

The majority of *vuivuti* are transacted with cuts of domestic pig killed on ceremonial occasions. To have enough pigs to initiate such transactions in addition to repaying debts incurred in them, one must actively engage in pig raising. One may not buy pigs from village mates, moreover, but must purchase them from outside. Since pigs require individual attention, no one family on its own is capable of raising the necessary number of pigs for an important ceremony, at which as many as twenty may be slaughtered. Anyone intending to sponsor a ceremony, therefore, turns his young sows over to others to raise. Each recipient is obliged to kill the sow (or a substitute pig) when the giver requires, but has title to all other offspring of the sow in payment for his services.

Although it is common for Lakalai men to dispose of much of their personal property by testament or gift before death, there are definite rules of inheritance. All one's personal property rights pass intact to one's children and those of one's sibmates who are consanguineal kin. The children have priority in that their marriage needs and foreseeable obligations must be met before sibmates claim a share. If a man has no children, his sister's children have first claim. When children inherit, they equally acquire rights to use the property and enjoy its benefits, but actual title is vested in the eldest male (eldest female if there are no males), and only he has disposal rights. But if, before his death, a father gave a fruit tree, for example, to a younger child, that child acquires title.

Lacking writing, a man must transmit his knowledge to his heirs before his death, or to someone who will hold it in trust and teach it to them when they are of an age to use it. Although most of the special knowledge that is personal property cannot ordinarily be used by women, men often teach it to their wives, sisters, and daughters to hold in trust for their male children. Trustees, even when women, may, at the owner's discretion, receive the privilege of using the knowledge, but they may not dispose of it to anyone other than the designated heirs.

Testamentary disposition of knowledge and other property allows a man to show favouritism among his children. The rebellious child receives the minimum that is in keeping with a father's duties, while the dutiful and attentive child receives the lion's share as well as many other attentions. Such favouritism does not deprive children of their right, as siblings, freely to use each other's tangible property or to call upon each other's special knowledge free of charge, but it prevents their having something to pass on to their heirs.

Objects most often inherited without prior testamentary disposition are a man's wealth-tokens. These are held in trust by a senior male kinsman: the eldest brother among the heirs, one of their paternal or maternal uncles, or their step-father, depending on who is or becomes available as the most appropriate trustee. The trustee normally sets portions of the wealth aside in the name of each male heir, according as it will be needed for a future marriage or other known obligation. He also holds a portion of it in their collective name in reserve against future commitments.

Very wealthy men do not like all their wealth to go to their heirs. It is customary for such men to have destroyed what they do not want passed on. Although concerned that enough remains to take care of the marital and other fixed needs of their children, the Lakalai say that they do not want anyone else to enjoy a reputation for being wealthy unless he has earned it himself.

TRUSTS AND POOLS

We have just indicated in connection with inheritance that wealth-tokens are normally held in trust for a man's heirs by a senior kinsman. The Lakalai follow the principle that as long as a man is not himself fully 'adult' he should entrust his wealth to his closest senior kinsman or to the person to whom the latter entrusts his own wealth. The result is the formation of trust groups consisting of one man as trustee and those of his junior kinsmen who regard him as the most appropriate person to whom to entrust their wealth.

As long as a man lives, his sons always belong to his trust group, whether or not he is its trustee. As long as a man has an older brother, he will entrust at least some of his wealth to him or to whoever is the older brother's trustee. It is disrespectful for the younger to be independent, for it implies that he trusts neither the integrity nor judgment of his older brother. When a trustee dies, each member of the group entrusts his wealth to another senior kinsman, who may or may not have been a member of the earlier trust group and who may or may not already be a trustee.

What is held in trust in these groups consists entirely of wealth-tokens, ceremonial paraphernalia, and, nowadays, Australian money. A trustee not only keeps the wealth physically in his possession but also keeps track of what is available for financing the marriages of junior members of his group. He also tries to make sure that there is sufficient cash on hand to pay taxes and fines incurred by the group's members. He must, therefore, give his consent to any transactions by junior members that require expenditure of wealth. He also safeguards the ceremonial paraphernalia and controls their use. If he thinks that a junior kinsman cannot afford the financial obligations stemming from participation in a ceremony, for example, he will deny him the use of the necessary equipment. He has, therefore, considerable power over those for whom he is trustee.

As a man accumulates wealth through receiving his share of brideprice paid for female relatives, through trade or, nowadays, through selling copra or going out to work for wages, he turns it over to the head of his trust group. If he is dissatisfied with the way his trustee operates, he does not withdraw what he now holds, but gives the bulk of his future income to another trustee. A man who entrusts his own wealth to someone else may himself be a trustee for others. He may start holding wealth for his sisters' children, for example, long before he holds his own. In the course of time, a man can gain considerable influence and power as he becomes trustee for a growing population of junior male kinsmen. His chances of doing so, however, are virtually eliminated as long as he has a living older uterine brother. His chances for gaining power through trusteeship are also limited by the number of his junior male kinsmen.

The system of trusts, with its stress on seniority, inevitably tends to concentrate financial power in the hands of a limited number of older men. It also provides channels for the exercise of power across sib and hamlet boundaries, for membership in a trust group is not confined to a single sib or hamlet.

Pools, also, unite people across sib and hamlet lines. They exist in connection with the large nets used to hunt wild pigs and turtles. Pig nets may be as much as one hundred fathoms long. They are actually composed of several smaller nets, which are separately owned and inherited but are joined together more or less permanently for hunting purposes. The senior of the several owners is head of the pool. He is in charge of the magic performed on the entire net. He is also its physical keeper (unless he is unmarried) and is in charge of disposing of game taken in it. Since in theory, though not in fact, there is only one pig net to a hamlet, invitations to feasts are sent to a pig net owner in each hamlet. Ideally, he would be the head of the pool, but another owner may receive the invitation in his stead. The net-owner, in turn, extends the invitation to his hamlet mates, and all the net-owners, under the direction of the pool heads, decide when they will hunt for pig to be contributed to the feast. In fact, only rarely would all the men of a single hamlet own shares in the same net. The head of a pool has no power over the disposition of the sections of net belonging to other members of the pool. They have the privilege of withdrawing from the pool and seeking to join another.

Turtle nets are pooled and administered in the same way as pig nets, but the separate pools do not join together in turtle hunts as they do when hunting pigs.

HAMLETS

Physically, each hamlet is a cleared space containing a group of family houses and a men's house. Adjacent to the men's house is a small grove of shade trees, called a *malilo*, under which the men gather to talk, eat, or prepare for ceremonies. There is a central open area in which feasts and dances can be held. Houses stand around it in no set pattern. Also felt to be physically part of a hamlet are its dump and the place to which its men retire to make special ceremonial equipment, both places being located in the immediately adjoining bush. Paths lead to the beach, the spring, the gardens, and to other hamlets of the village and territory. In the past, hamlets in danger of attack were sometimes palisaded, but usually it was considered sufficient protection to leave a watchman to guard the children and to signal the approach of strangers by beating the slit-gong.

Hamlet membership is based directly on men's house affiliation, which becomes especially significant at marriage. A married man always belongs to his father's men's house and resides in the same hamlet with him for as long as his father lives. In former times, his wife lived in his father's house until she had several children, at which time he built a separate house for her beside his father's. This practice is still followed by Methodists but runs counter to the desires of the Catholic Church that each couple have a separate house immediately upon marriage. It is evident, however, that many Catholics still follow local custom. If a man was raised by a step-father, he joins the latter's men's house and resides in his hamlet just as if he were his real father.

When his father (or step-father) dies, a married man's choice of residence varies according to circumstances. He may continue to reside in his father's hamlet, especially if he belongs to a lineage that controls no land in the territory while his father's lineage does. He may also join a hamlet in which his senior sibmates are concentrated or the one in which his lineage controls the land. Brothers in a sibling set are especially likely to stay together, and, together with their brothers-in-law, they most frequently form the nuclei of new hamlets. If a man's father dies before his marriage, he has strong obligations to whoever finances his marriage in his father's stead. These obligations are even greater if the same person assumed other obligations of parenthood, such as sponsoring his ceremonial initiations. The more completely a person has stood in *loco parentis*, the greater the likelihood that the young husband will treat him as a father substitute for purposes of hamlet affiliation. A father's younger brother or an older sister's husband most frequently serves as father substitute. Half of the men in Galilo village whose fathers or step-fathers died before they married and whose marriage sponsors were still living in 1954 were affiliated in the same hamlets with these substitute sponsors.

In summary, then, we may say that a Lakalai man has the *duty* of living with his father or father surrogate (the strength of the duty depending on the degree to which the surrogate substituted for his father) for as long as either lives. He has the *right* to live where his lineage controls the land, or where he has senior sibmates, or where he was raised. He may, by agreement, reside where his father's grand-father's, or brother-in-law's lineages control land.[7]

In founding a new hamlet, the Lakalai consider it desirable to have more than one sib represented. Normally, the initiative in establishing a new hamlet is taken by a man with sufficient junior relatives to follow him: younger brothers in his sibling set, sons, persons to whom he is a father surrogate. If he can, he persuades others who are less dependent upon him to help him establish the hamlet, such persons as sibmates, cousins, or siblings-in-law. He either settles on land that his own lineage controls or seeks permission from his wife's lineage to settle on its land. In the former instance, it is desirable for his sister and her husband to join him, since his own children cannot inherit land rights from him; in the latter instance, he is likely to be joined by his wife's brothers. There is a tendency, therefore, for hamlets to be composed of varying combinations of brothers, brothers-in-law, and cross and parallel cousins in the senior generation, together with their respective adherents from among their junior kin.

Within each hamlet, then, there are several households, which vary in com-position and recency of establishment. A long-established household will consist of a man, his wife or wives, his married sons and their wives, and his unmarried children and grandchildren, plus various old unmarried dependants and those married men to whom he has been a full-fledged father surrogate. As his grandchildren multiply, his sons build separate houses directly beside his. Dependent relatives of the sons' wives may become attached to their houses, and, in due time, the sons' sons bring their wives there, too. Eventually, when the old man dies, his several married sons will each be the head of relatively independent households. A brief description of two Galilo hamlets will provide concrete illustration of how the system works out.

Peduma (see Map 3) was the newest hamlet in 1954, and its founders were still living there. Head of the hamlet was Tovili, who led the exodus from the hamlet of Barilae. In his house were his two wives, his three unmarried children, and a married daughter (with her two children) whose husband was away at work. The recently married son of his wife's dead sister was reared by Tovili and stayed with him when he returned to Galilo on holidays from his missionary post. Tovili's step-son Bagou, child of one of his present wives, lived with his wife and children in a house next to Tovili's. Galia, Tovili's oldest son, had a house on the other side. In Galia's house, in addition to his own wife and children, were a widowed aunt of his wife and the children of his wife's dead sister. Second in importance to Tovili was Loua, Tovili's 'brother'. Loua was left without close senior kinsmen in Galilo at an early age. He joined with Tovili to form a sibling

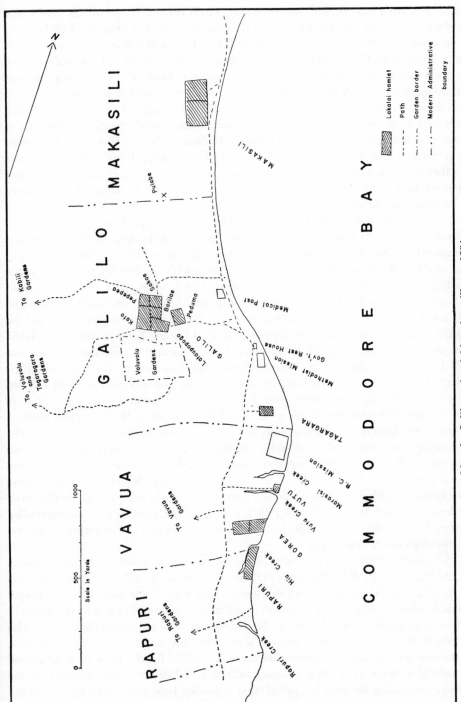

Map 3 Galilo and neighbouring villages, 1954

set because their fathers were lineage mates. Tovili became trustee of his wealth and sponsored his marriage. Living with Loua were his wife, her unmarried children by a previous marriage, and her children by Loua. Loua's children by his former wife were living with Galia, whose wife was their mother's sister. The remaining two Peduma houses were occupied by Loua's younger 'brother' Uoso (their mothers were own sisters) with his wife and children, and the married daughter of Loua's current wife (with her husband and daughter). Also affiliated with Peduma, when they were home on leave from their jobs, were Loua's wife's younger half-brothers, Loua and Laveliu, who were also brothers' children to Tovili's first wife. They were both married and had several children each. The younger Loua's wife came from another territory, and her brother, a widower, had decided to affiliate with Peduma in partnership with his brother-in-law. Tovili had agreed to supply his brideprice if he remarried locally.

Kato was older than Peduma. In 1954 it was occupied by the children and grandchildren of its founders and founders' sisters. The nucleus of the hamlet was composed of five sibmates: four own brothers and their mother's sister's son. The last of these, Kulei, was the senior male member of his sib and lineage and was the leading man of the hamlet as well as being luluai (chief government-appointed official) of Galilo. His household was exceptionally large. It contained his wife and his and her children by previous marriages, including Kulei's married son and his family. It also included the married son of a dead lineage 'brother' for whom Kulei was now father surrogate. Kulei's maternal aunt, mother of his four cousins, was still living. She resided in a separate house with her current husband and their crippled son. His sons, married and unmarried, by his first wife, and her four married sons by her first husband, now dead, had their houses around hers. The eldest of the four shared his house with his wife's married half-brother. His wife's and brother-in-law's step-father, an old widower, occupied a separate house by himself. The remaining household in Kato included the daughter of Kulei's maternal uncle, who was one of Kato's founders, together with her husband, unmarried children, and married son with his wife. The as yet unmarried sons of Kulei's dead sister were also affiliated with Kato's men's house. Except for the old widower, the senior male or female of each household was a close consanguineal relative of a corresponding person in the other households, and Kato was consequently composed of an exceptionally close group of kin.

Lakalai hamlets, then, consist of several households whose heads are members of the lineage controlling the land, or whose fathers or grandfathers were members of that lineage. These men form the hamlet's nucleus. There may be other households headed by some of their sibmates and siblings-in-law. Control of the hamlet's affairs is primarily in the hands of the older men who are family heads and who belong to the nuclear group as defined above. Various factors, to be discussed later, determine their relative influence and make it possible for the head of a peripheral household to have more than ordinary influence. While the senior member of the lineage controlling the land has jurisdiction regarding land matters, he has no greater voice in hamlet affairs than any other man of comparable seniority within the nuclear group. There are hamlets, therefore, whose affairs are managed jointly by several elders of roughly equal stature, while there are others that are dominated by one man. The former seemed to predominate over the latter at the time of observation. In relation to outsiders it frequently happens that one man has prestige and influence far exceeding that of his fellows. This gives him somewhat greater influence in the internal affairs of his hamlet, but not to a degree commensurate with his outside reputation. The fact is that each of the several household groups within the hamlet has considerable autonomy in its own affairs. Joint action by the entire hamlet membership is largely a matter of voluntary co-operation between these household groups. A hamlet is essentially federal in its structure, whereas a household is not. Within a household, its senior man has some rights vis-à-vis its other members that he alone possesses. This may be but is not necessarily the case for any one household head vis-à-vis the others.

When it is the case, one or more of three different considerations may be responsible. First, one household head may have authority over the others by virtue of his kinship position as uncle or older brother. Secondly, he may overshadow the others as a truly 'big man' by virtue of his accomplishments as a warrior and feast giver. Finally, he may have been inducted into one of the more important wristband societies.

One wristband, named savarasi, is specifically associated with hamlet leadership. It is large and elaborate, so much so that the wearer, also called savarasi, cannot put his hand into the basket in which he carries his personal equipment. When a man becomes prominent in his hamlet, he asks the members of this wristband society to invest him with the savarasi, which he wears on his left wrist. At the same time, he acquires another, smaller wristband for the right wrist. Putting on the savarasi indicates that the man is now freed from heavy labour, for which he depends on others, though not from all work. He also has a special ability to stop quarrels. This ability seems to derive in part from fear of the spirit in the wristband and in part from the backing of other men who have the same wristband. There may be from one to four savarasi in a hamlet, and they are given pay by the leaders of other hamlets when they go to visit. Investment with the savarasi, then, formally ratifies a man's position as a hamlet leader and joins him in a special partnership with other hamlet leaders, who owe and normally show him a great deal of formal courtesy. It also enhances his authority within his hamlet, giving him magical peacekeeping powers.

Even greater power and authority belong to wearers of the suara wristbands. These wristbands, however, are more specifically associated with leadership in war and will be discussed later.

To be noted now is the absence of an exclusive office that can be labelled 'hamlet chief'. There are social ranks based on age, kinship, accomplishment, and membership in wristband societies. A hamlet may be headed by one man who clearly outranks all others or by several men of roughly equal rank.

As our account of hamlet structure has implied, the ties uniting the several households of a hamlet are based on kinship connections between their respective heads. Whatever may be the actual degree of kinship, hamlet mates ideally treat each other as if they were consanguineal or affinal kin. They do not operate in the roles appropriate to nominal relationships. The feeling that the members of a hamlet form a group of close kinsmen finds concrete expression in connection with hunting and gathering activities. Every adult man is under a direct obligation to supply food to all of the children of his hamlet, whenever he is so fortunate as to obtain enough for more than his own family's immediate needs. Every large catch of fish, bag of game, or collection of eggs or mussels is divided by those obtaining them among all of the hamlet's households for general distribution. Like close kinsmen, hamlet mates are not supposed to fight or conspire against each other, even if they belong to sibs that have an unsettled feud between them. Occasionally a man's enemies persuade one of their sibmates who lives in the same hamlet with him to steal something that has been in contact with him so that they can use it to make sorcery against him. Anyone guilty of such a betrayal is called the 'rat' of the hamlet. He has done injury to one who trusted him as if he were a consanguineal kinsman.

Thus the members of one's hamlet, whatever their actual relationship, are automatically included, together with one's consanguineal and affinal kin and one's sib and lineage mates, within the circle of relatives with whom one expects to maintain more than nominal kin ties. These are the people who together comprise a Lakalai's close kin.

VILLAGES

Rarely does a hamlet form an independent unit within a territory. One-hamlet villages have usually contained the remnants of several hamlets, which united following depopulation, or they represented the start of new villages, which would soon grow into clusters of several hamlets.[8] Commonly, a group of neighbouring hamlets, from two to six in number, form a village. On occasion villages have consisted of two or more clusters of several hamlets each, as when a daughter hamlet within the village maintains especially close ties with its parent hamlet. Each village not only forms a distinct hamlet group physically, but is recognized as forming a definite unit in Lakalai thinking. Thus, each village is named, sometimes for one of its hamlets, sometimes for a nearby stream or other geographical feature.

Membership in a village is based on residence in one of its hamlets, regardless of whether the residence is by right or by arrangement. Both territories and villages are small enough so that all adult members know one another by name; But only in his own village can a Lakalai designate everyone by the proper kinship term, recognizing everyone as at least a nominal relative. He cannot readily do so for all members of other villages in his territory.

In the past, a strip of uncleared bush separated the coastal villages from the beach. Since the end of warfare, a few villages are now built on the water's edge. Village grounds include the strip of bush and the stretch of beach fronting on it. A village also claims for its residents exclusive rights to fish on offshore reefs, to build fishing platforms in the shallows, and to collect shellfish, saltwater, sand, and hearthstones from its waterfront. Whenever possible, each village has its own fresh water supply, where the village's women are also free to fish with hand nets. Rights to draw water temporarily are readily granted to neighbouring villages if their own supply becomes brackish, but fishing rights are jealously guarded.

Village property may also include exclusive rights to distant areas as well as to resources within its physical bounds. The four large villages at the eastern end of the Lakalai coast have, through some mutual agreement in the past, divided up the megapode egg fields and stands of nipa and sago palms along the Kapeuru river (see Map 2), so that each village has an area reserved for its members to dig eggs and collect thatch.

The several hamlets of a village regularly make their gardens together. Hamlet affiliations are observed in that hamlet mates tend to clear adjacent plots. Consanguineal and affinal ties across hamlet lines, however, prevent a perfect correlation of hamlets and garden subdivisions. The modern village of Galilo, being a composite of two older villages, still retained two village gardens in 1954. With few exceptions, people continued to garden in one or the other depending on the former village association of their respective hamlets. Sometimes two small villages within a territory make their gardens side by side for purposes of defence and companionship.

Each plot is separately worked by a man and a woman as gardening partners: a husband and wife, brother and sister, parent and child, or pair of *samura* partners. Mutual aid in clearing depends upon individual arrangements among kinsmen. The two services that are connected with gardening and that individuals contribute to the entire village community are fencing against wild pigs and garden magic. Each man is responsible for the garden fence beside his plot. Others criticize him if he fails to keep it in repair.

The unity of the village garden appears more clearly in connection with taro magic. In each village there is one person who is recognized as garden magician. While others know some garden magic, only one person holds the office of garden magician in a village. The office passes to the senior person among those of his heirs to whom he teaches the necessary rites. Many of the rites are performed in secret, but some are public and require the participation of everyone under the magician's direction. It is within the magician's power to cause crops to wither as well as to flourish. But since his spells affect all plants in the garden equally, he cannot injure the crops of others without destroying his own at the same time. In 1954 Galilo had one principal garden magician, Kulei, head man of Kato hamlet and village luluai. He performed the magic for one of the two village gardens, the one with which he was himself associated. He had taught the rites to the husband of his older brother's daughter to hold in trust for her children, and this man acted as magician for the other garden, in which he had his own plots. Unlike many other specialists who charge for their services, a garden magician performs on behalf of the village without pay. We may, therefore, designate his as a public office.

Other specialists who perform for the entire community without charge, and whom we may designate public officials, are the leader of wild pig drives, done with nets, and the war leader. The former is, presumably, always the head of a pig net pool. He appears to be selected by the heads of the other netting pools as the one among them who is the most knowledgeable pig hunter, from both the practical and the magical standpoints. The office of war leader is a thing of the past. To fill it, a man had to prove his ability as a fighter and war magician and, if possible, he was also a wearer of the *suara* wristband. In former times a village of any size could usually count several *suara*. Ideally, each sib that owned land locally had a *suara* among its members. Their great supernatural powers made *suara* effective settlers of disputes as well as formidable warriors, and they played an important role in maintaining order within their village. Apparently the most skilled among them was the village's war leader. He directed military operations in which the village as a whole was involved.

There are other specialists, such as weather magician and diviner, who provide services that the Lakalai feel should be available in every community. They ordinarily expect a fee, however, except when performing for sibmates and consanguineal kinsmen. On the other hand, a Lakalai expects the fee to be higher if he must import a specialist from another village. The larger the village, the greater the likelihood that all of the essential services will be available to its residents from a fellow villager, who is expected not to refuse to serve when asked, nor to over-charge. A one-hamlet village is at a disadvantage and must often do without the benefit of specialists. Whether they function as public officials or not, the presence of the various specialists and the demand for their services emphasizes the interdependence of the several hamlets in a village and contributes to the sense of community among them.

Most important for village unity was the now defunct office of *valipoi*. Selected from among the local *suara* by unanimous consent of the village's prominent men, the *valipoi* had the power to make ultimate decisions regarding war and peace, the settlement of internal disputes, and other matters directly affecting the collective safety and welfare of the village's members. We may properly speak of him as the village chief. The place of the *valipoi* in recent years has been largely taken by the government-appointed headman or luluai. Indeed, Galilo village's last *valipoi* was also appointed its first luluai, upon nomination by his village mates to the appointing officer.

TERRITORIES

Each Lakalai territory contains a group of hamlets or villages that are at peace with one another and are interconnected by paths. It used to be bounded by uncleared bush in which there were no paths leading to the next territory.

Occasionally a territory may consist of a single large village containing many hamlets. Usually, however, it comprises several smaller villages. The brief histories obtained for three territories indicate tendencies for the population to vacillate between relative consolidation in large villages and dispersal in scattered hamlets and small villages. In order to show these tendencies and reveal the internal structure of a Lakalai territory, we shall sketch the recent history of Pulabe, to which the modern villages of Galilo, Makasili, and Tagaragara belong.

Pulabe is reputed to be the place from which all the present villages of Pulabe territory are commonly derived. About one hundred years ago, the name Pulabe had come to be applied to a group of hamlets that had grown out of this supposedly original settlement. They were all situated close together and may have formed one large village or a cluster of villages. In addition to Pulabe proper and some hamlets to the north whose names we did not record, there were the hamlets of Mautulaba, Kohogi, Kasesese, Mapopopo, Lapele, old Kato, Gagae, old Sokoe, Beho, old Pepepea, and Barilae (see Map 4). Further removed was the village of Tagaragara, established by men of Pulabe who wanted to be closer to its fresh water supply.

Mautulaba was soon abandoned, following an epidemic (a customary reason for leaving a hamlet site). But quarrels and feuds were responsible for the more important changes. The first resulted when a man from one of the original hamlets killed a pig belonging to a man of Gagae. In the fighting that followed, various hamlets tended to join one side or the other. Those in the immediate vicinity of Pulabe hamlet supported the pig slayer and eventually moved to the site of the present village of Makasili, which they established. In 1911 it had three hamlets, since reduced to two.[9] Hamlets taking the opposite side were Mapopopo, Kasesese, Lapele, Gagae, and Beho. Together with old Pepepea, old Sokoe, old Kato, and Barilae, they formed a distinct village called Kabili or Galekabili. On settling their differences, Kabili and Makasili kept paths open between them and maintained peaceful relations.

It was not long before a feud developed within Kabili when a man of the Gararua sib killed a man of the Kevemumuki sib. The Kevemumuki people were stronger, and the Gararua people decided to flee the territory. Among them was the village's garden magician, who executed rites to destroy Kabili's gardens, whereupon all of Gararua took refuge with sibmates among the eastern Nakanai. A year later, a delegation of kinsmen from Kabili begged them to return and undo the effects of the garden magic. After their return, the Gararua people settled a new hamlet— the present Lataupopogo, then called Voluvolu—next to Barilae. Meanwhile, the feud had resulted in the abandonment of Kasesese, Lapele, old Kato, and old Pepepea, so that there were now two distinct clusters of hamlets in what had been Kabili: Voluvolu, containing Barilae and Lataupopogo, and Kabili, containing Beho, Gagae, Mapopopo, and old Sokoe. Voluvolu soon had a third hamlet, new Kato, which was added following a quarrel in Lataupopogo. In Kabili, the hamlet of old Sokoe was abandoned in favour of the new hamlet of Marako next to Beho, and Mapopopo was also abandoned, most of its residents moving to neighbouring Gagae. This, then, was the situation about twenty-five years ago, each village having three hamlets (see Map 4).

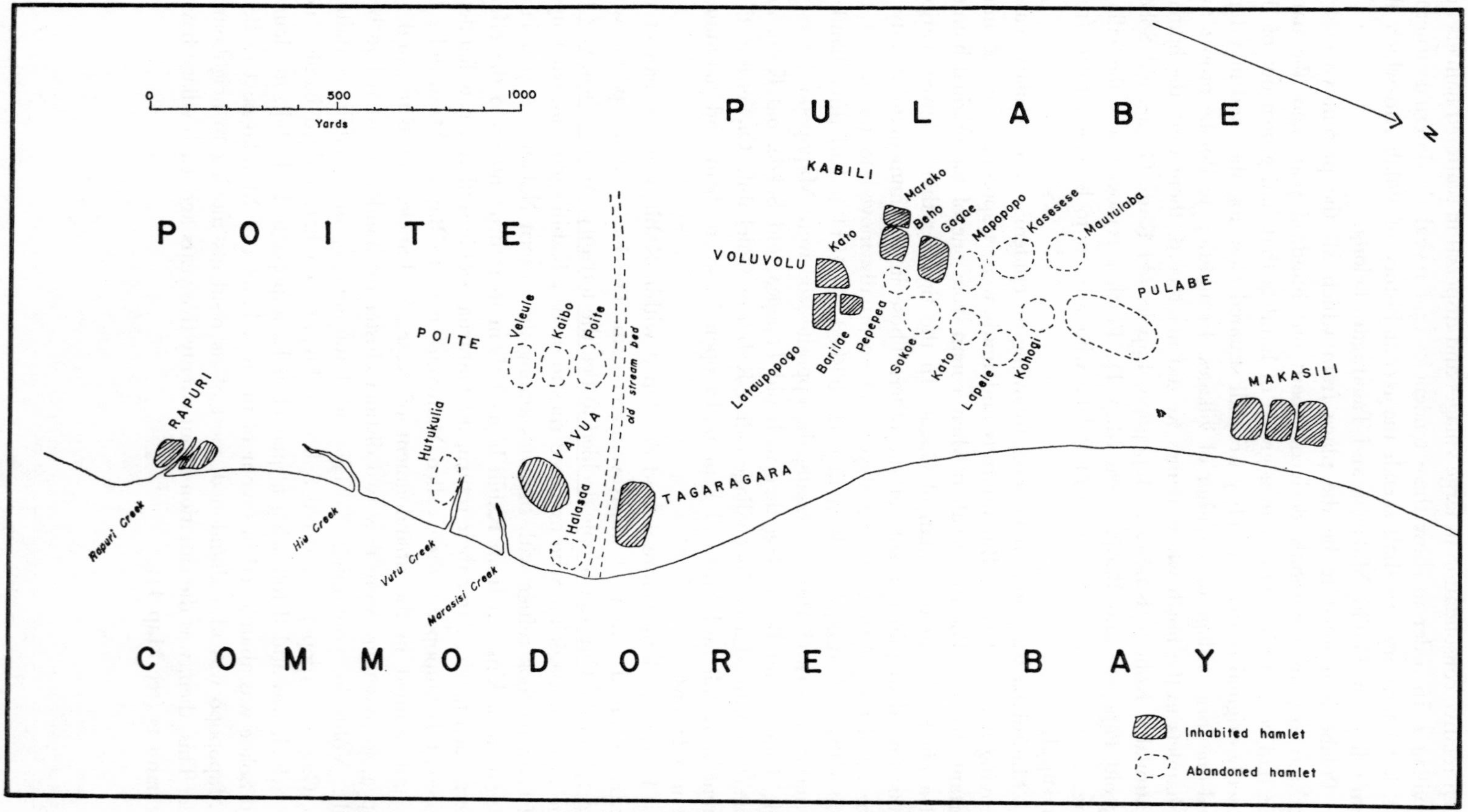

Map 4 Pulabe and Poite circa 1925

Subsequently, a patrol officer ordered the Kabili people to move to Voluvolu and form a single village. In this move, the bulk of Kabili's residents consolidated in one hamlet, new Sokoe, while others joined kinsmen in the existing Voluvolu hamlets. After World War II, two new hamlets were formed: new Pepepea and Peduma, as outgrowths of Sokoe and Barilae respectively. The resulting six hamlets formed the village of Galilo as we encountered it in 1954. Within it, especially close relations existed between Sokoe and Pepepea (representing the older Kabili and themselves only recently separated) and between Barilae and Peduma (also only recently separated).

In 1954 Galilo was the largest of all Lakalai villages. There were indications that it was held together by pressures, real or imagined, that the people felt to emanate from both the government and the Methodist Mission. Left to their own devices, they would probably have broken up into two or even three smaller villages, centring on Kato, Peduma, and possibly Pepepea. Indeed, Peduma had removed itself physically from the rest of Galilo, maintaining the traditional strip of bush between it and the other hamlets, which physically merged. That the Pepepea and Sokoe hamlets continued to maintain the separate garden they had when they formed the village of Kabili is also significant. There were many indications that this was a matter about which the people felt strongly.

By virtue of its location close to the beach, the village of Tagaragara was always vulnerable to attack. It was necessary for its inhabitants to seek refuge in Voluvolu and Kabili during periods of fighting with neighbouring territories, as when the people of Tubisu raided Tagaragara for its abundant coconuts. The village had contained at least two hamlets in the past, but by 1954 was reduced to one very small one. When an eruption of Mt Pago around 1910 obliterated the stream that separated Pulabe and Poite territories, Tagaragara was directly affected. Because it had been located on one side of this stream, it was no longer separated by a natural barrier from the Poite hamlets of Vavua and Halasaa on the opposite bank. A Catholic Mission was established at the site of Halasaa not long afterward, and both the Vavua and Tagaragara people came directly under its influence. The result was considerable intermarriage between the two villages and the breakdown of territorial barriers between them. The government treated them as a convenient unit because of their proximity to each other and appointed a single luluai for both. After World War II, when the Vavua people wished to move to their present location at Gorea, most of the Tagaragara people joined them, the luluai for the two villages being a Tagaragara man. Two brothers remained behind, but one of them later moved to Sokoe in Galilo. The remaining brother and his numerous children and grandchildren made their gardens with the Voluvolu hamlets in Galilo. Those Tagaragarans who moved to Gorea made a special point of preserving their village identity, however. They also continued to garden beside the Voluvolu gardens, whereas the original Vavuans gardened elsewhere. Since 1954 Tagaragara has expanded again with the return of most of its members who had gone to Gorea.

Like the Tagaragarans, the people of Makasili also joined the Roman Catholic Church. But Kabili and Voluvolu have remained Methodist. There is, consequently, a basis for religious antagonism between Galilo and the other Pulabe villages. Nevertheless, ties between them remain close. Neither religious differences nor governmental regroupings have been sufficient to override the bonds of territoriality among these villages.

This brings us directly to the question of what comprise these territorial bonds.

It is evident from the foregoing account of Pulabe territory that the common derivation of all its villages from a specific place provides one kind of bond. Similar common derivations have been noted for other territories as well. In each, the people symbolize the bond by referring to themselves collectively by the name of the place from which their villages and hamlets all derive. The people of a territory are, as it were, all hamlet and village mates once or twice removed. This bond is reinforced by the maintenance of face-to-face relations, the sharing of certain interests and common participation in certain activities.

Common interests include preservation of the equal rights of all territorial residents to hunt and gather throughout the territory, to travel within its confines unmolested, to enjoy the support of other villages in war and take refuge with other villages when attacked. The members of any hamlet or village undertaking an important ceremony expect attendance and active participation from all their territory mates. Every act of mutual support in ceremony and war serves to promote feelings of territorial unity.

Such feelings receive additional reinforcement in connection with organized contests. The Lakalai do not compete with each other for fun but in order to win. To lose is to suffer shame and humiliation which can be alleviated only through violence. For this reason, contests between villages or hamlets within the same territory are likely to lead to intraterritorial fighting and are, therefore, avoided. They are held between territories, instead, and although not conducive to peaceful interterritorial relations, they promote esprit de corps within the territory, as all its members jointly share in victory or defeat. One type of contest consists of riddling and puzzle solving. The more important, however, is canoe racing. In former times, almost every hamlet had a racing canoe, but it engaged in races only with hamlets from outside the territory. Paddlers were recruited from the entire territory to which the hamlet belonged. Fights between competing crews were not uncommon. While the owner of a victorious canoe enjoyed special prestige, the entire crew and territory shared in the glory.

Not all residents of a territory have the same legal relationship to it. We must distinguish between the status of resident and that of 'citizen', as we shall call it. A territory's citizens are all those people who belong to lineages presumed to be derived from the original clearers of the sib-owned tracts within its confines. In other words, a territory's citizens are the people who have primary rights in its lands. This means, of course, that people are often citizens of territories other than the ones in which they reside. They continue to assert their priority of right to their ancestral lands, and no one can dispute their right to settle there or to take advantage of all the rights enjoyed by the territory's residents. One young resident of Galilo, for example, was explicitly told by his mother that he could go to another territory in which his lineage controls land and gather betelnuts, coconuts, and *Nassa calossa* shells without asking permission of anyone.

A territory's residents who are not citizens are said not really to belong to the territory. Informants repeatedly pointed out to us that this or that resident of Galilo really belonged somewhere else, where his lineage controlled land. Thus, the luluai of Galilo, Kulei, was not a citizen of Pulabe territory but of Bubuu in the Maututu region of east Nakanai. Although Galilo had become the place where almost all members of Kulei's sib were concentrated, they remained citizens of Bubuu, where their land was located. In Galilo in 1954 there were representatives of what appeared to be at least thirty-six different lineages of twenty-one sibs and subsibs. Of these seven, and possibly only five, controlled lands within Pulabe territory. On a per capita basis, the land-controlling lineages accounted for only a slightly larger proportion of the population, sixty-four out of 266 persons or about twenty-five percent.

The nucleus of a territory's population, then, consists of its resident citizens, who control adjoining tracts of land and found new hamlets and villages on these lands. Associated with them in their hamlets are sibmates who are citizens of other territories and other persons who are descended from women brought in as wives from outside the territory. The latter, by marrying back into land-controlling lineages, as inevitably they must, become the fathers, wives, and siblings-in-law of the territory's resident citizens. The bulk of resident non-citizens are the citizen's consanguineal or affinal kinsmen. Few residents cannot count at least one grandparent from among the land-controlling lineages.

The distinction between citizen and resident is significant for eligibility to leadership positions. Only resident members of landowning sibs are eligible, at least in theory, for induction into the *suara* wristband society. Since *suara* provided leadership in war, played a major role in the settlement of disputes, and were alone eligible for a village's highest office, that of *valipoi*, this restriction tended in the past to force resident non-citizens into follower roles and to keep them dependent politically, as well as economically, on resident citizens with whom they had close kinship ties. Non-citizens can and do gain political power, especially now that warfare has ended, but it is more difficult for them. In the past, at least, the distinction between territorial citizen and resident non-citizen was politically significant.

THE ORGANIZATION OF PRODUCTIVE ACTIVITIES

For bare economic necessities, the basic co-operating unit consists of an adult man and woman, though it is possible for one adult to subsist alone. Gardening, cooking, most hunting, gathering, and the production of most consumer goods do not require the joint efforts of a larger group. The fact that many of these activities are carried out in groups arises from a desire for companionship and considerations of defence. The work itself, however, is done individually and is not co-ordinated. Thus, the great majority of economic activities and those that occupy the bulk of a Lakalai's time require little organization. Each hamlet, of course, provides a fixed group within which to get these seemingly *ad hoc* working parties together. Indeed, they are almost always composed of a nucleus of hamlet mates plus various of their respective consanguineal and affinal kin or sharing partners who may reside in other hamlets within the same village.

There are, to be sure, some economic activities that require the co-ordinated efforts of more than two people. All are essentially masculine activities. They include building and repairing houses, using large nets in hunting and fishing, making and decorating canoes, going on trading expeditions, slaughtering domestic pigs, and bringing in heavy catches of game.

In these activities we may distinguish four types of participants: 1) the person initiating the activity, 2) the persons whose labour he commands, all junior to him, 3) persons who volunteer their labour but whom he does not command, and 4) such experts as may be necessary. A person must have access to essential equipment, sufficient labour, and expert knowledge, before he can initiate any of these activities. This means that he must be old enough to command labour for which he need make only token payment or be wealthy enough to hire labour. He, or an immediate kinsman, must have the necessary knowledge, or he must be able to afford its hire. The persons whose labour he commands are his junior hamlet mates, especially the unmarried young men, and his junior consanguineal and affinal kinsmen (excluding his siblings-in-law and cross-cousins). He gives orders to these people. Persons whose labour he does not command, but whom he expects to volunteer their help, include his senior hamlet mates, his senior consanguineal kinsmen, and his siblings-in-law and cross-cousins. The amount of actual help they give is up to them, and the activity's initiator does not give them orders. To both sets of helpers the initiator is expected to give token payment in the form of a *vararapu* of tobacco and betelnut. The products of the activity belong to the initiator. Within the limitations already noted, moreover, he is the person generally in charge of the activity. When someone else provides the expert knowledge, however, the expert assumes direction of whatever portion of the work involves his services.

When Tovili, the senior household head and founder of Peduma hamlet, wished to repair his house, he sent for all the other men of Peduma and for his half-brother's son, a junior sister's son, and the husband of his grandniece, the last three being those of his close kin whose labour he commanded who were residents of other hamlets. Tovili joined the workers for a while and then sat and gave directions. When the job was finished, he distributed tobacco to all who had helped.

On another occasion, when Tovili wished to slaughter pigs for a memorial ceremony he was sponsoring, the same group with one or two additional in-laws helped him round up and kill the pigs. While he and his daughter did the actual meat-cutting, all of his helpers as well as the adult women of the hamlet joined in the discussion of how the cuts were to be distributed. In the case of pigs that he did not himself own, Tovili usually accepted the recommendations of the owner. The children of the hamlet, who carry messages and run errands, helped deliver the cuts of pork, at least one of which had to go to each hamlet in the village. Other cuts were distributed to each household in Peduma and to Tovili's grandniece (the only other member of his matrilineal lineage resident in Galilo). The cuts distributed to other hamlets were large. Each represented a *vuivuti* to a person whom Tovili and his helpers had chosen to receive the gift on behalf of his hamlet. While this either obligated the recipient or paid off an old obligation to him, he was expected to distribute a share of what he received to the other households in his hamlet. By contrast, the cuts distributed among Tovili's hamlet mates and grandniece were small and did not have to be repaid. They were a *vararapu,* representing their share of the available luxury food in recognition of the help they had given and of their rights as members of his kindred.

The use of fish and turtle nets involves the same people, again. Tovili was the only person in Galilo in 1954 who knew how to make these nets and who could perform the magic required in their use. All such nets in Galilo were owned by Tovili's children, who were residents of Peduma. All the men of Peduma and the Galilo men who were married to Peduma women went out together with these nets under Tovili's leadership. He sat in a separate canoe and directed the fishing, which was surrounded with taboos. The participants could have no dealings with any other netting group while fishing, for example. Like most magicians, Tovili and his sons, who assisted him, could not eat any of the food taken by means of their magic. This enhanced their role as benefactors of their hamlet. The in-laws from the other hamlets provided the necessary additional man-power, a large group being needed to set up the nets and conduct the drive.

The foregoing examples of pig-killing and net-fishing show how the organization of any activity productive of tangible goods is geared to considerations of property rights. The people who work together are those who have the right to use one another's property without asking or who expect that their requests to use it will not be refused. These are the same people who have a right to one another's surplus food, who have at least some responsibility generally for one another's welfare, and who regularly exchange labour and food with one another on a *vararapu* basis.[10]

Just who these people are differs to some extent for every individual. The co-operating group varies in its make-up according to who is playing the initiator's role. Since it always includes one's hamlet mates, however, each hamlet supplies the core of co-operating personnel for every group activity initiated by any of its members. Who the others are depends on their kinship with each initiator. Thus, the hamlet stands out as the relatively fixed unit of group activity.[11]

The only economic activity that requires co-operation by a larger group is hunting wild pigs with nets. The chances of success increase in proportion to the length of the net. Such hunting, therefore, normally takes place with all the netting pools in a village working together. Occasionally, the several villages in a territory combine in this type of hunting. The number of participants depends on the person initiating the hunt.

Feasts are the occasions for these co-operative hunts, which are initiated by whoever is feast sponsor. He sends tobacco and betelnut to the net leader, usually the head of a netting pool, in each hamlet. Each hamlet receiving this gift of tobacco is thereby notified that its members are invited to participate in a feast and at the same time asked to help catch the necessary pigs. In other words, it is understood that the several hamlets of a village help each other in such undertakings on a *vararapu* basis. The initiator's *vararapu* of tobacco and betelnut in advance (to be followed by his *vararapu* of food in the feast itself) indicates the terms upon which he is requesting aid from other hamlets.

The hunt is directed by a hunt leader, whom we have already mentioned in connection with village officials. He is himself head of one of the netting pools, and serves as leader of the hunt because of his recognized practical skill and magical knowledge in this type of hunting. The hunters consist of the crews associated with each net and a gang of beaters.

Each net crew is made up of the several owners of its parts, their children who are of appropriate age, and such of their consanguineal kinsmen as are not more directly associated with another net. The several nets are suspended end to end from short stakes so as to make a long line curving inward very slightly toward the ends. The men in each crew station themselves just inside the net at intervals of about thirty feet, spears in hand. The beaters are boys too young to be stationed at the net, and men who are not members of a netting crew. When a pig, driven by the beaters, runs into a net, it is pounced upon by the net watchers to either side and trussed up to be carried alive, if possible, into the village. Its disposal is entirely in the hands of the owners of the particular net in which it is caught, unless it is a domestic pig which has run wild. For the moment, that pool owns the pig. If it is an exceptional pig, a prize boar for example, the members of the pool may dedicate it to their men's house. In such event, the pig is not turned over to the sponsor of the feast, but members of the pool and their crew of helpers and hamlet mates sponsor a feast of their own. Any other game caught in these hunts, such as cassowary, belongs to the members of the pool in whose net it was taken. Usually, however, the pigs caught are turned over to the feast sponsor who initiated the hunt. As soon as a pig is taken, the hunters return to the village. Each net has a song connected with it. The returning hunters sing the song of the net in which the pig was taken, announcing to the villagers the identity of the triumphant netting pool. The wives of the men who are co-owners of the successful net cook a special taro pudding which they give to all members of the netting crew.

The hunt's organization, then, amounts to a joint action by several distinct co-operating groups of the sort we have already encountered in connection with other activities. In each of these groups, the head of the pool is the initiator for its net's crew. Upon notification from the feast's sponsor, he calls together the other owners of his pool and all other members of the crew, i.e., those of his and the other owner's hamlet mates and kin who are not more closely connected with another net. When we consider that ideally there is one netting pool per hamlet, it is even more clear that the Lakalai conceive of a netting crew in terms of the same organizational model that provides the basis for other group activities: the initiator's hamlet mates and consanguineal kin.

The hunt leader's role is to co-ordinate the efforts of the several netting crews. He performs magic on behalf of the entire hunt. He leads the net bearers through the bush, decides where the nets shall be placed and in what order of arrangement, and supervises the placement. If a pig escapes the nets, he decides how to pursue it and leads the hunt to new areas of bush. Here his responsibilities end.

It appears, then, that all productive activities in which Lakalai engage in groups are organized in terms of the same principles. The co-operating work group consists of the people who regularly exchange food and labour with the initiator of that particular activity, plus those of his junior hamlet mates and kinsmen whose labour he commands. The labour contributed is a *vararapu* to the initiator who must acknowledge this with a *vararapu* in return. Since all members of the same hamlet are in such exchange relationships with each other, hamlets stand out as constants in what would otherwise be work groups whose personnel changed with every initiator. While most work groups of this kind operate on their own, hunting with pig nets requires that they co-ordinate their efforts. In doing so, they maintain their separate identities. They all bear the same formal relationship to the feast's sponsor, the initiator of their work on a village scale, that individual members of a work group bear to its initiator. Their efforts are co-ordinated by a public official, who is the village's leading specialist in the activity concerned.

THE ORGANIZATION OF FESTIVALS

As with productive economic activities, the basic co-operating group for preparing a festival consists of the hamlet mates and consanguineal kinsmen of the festival's initiator or sponsor. This is true regardless of the festival's scope as defined by the number of participants in its consummation.

The sponsor calls upon the labour he commands, and is voluntarily helped by those of his hamlet mates and consanguineal kin whose labour he does not command. The more labour he commands, the easier it is for the sponsor to broaden a festival's scope. An old man who has many junior kinsmen, who is head of a large trust group, and who is senior man in his hamlet, is in a position to command the labour of many. Those of his close kin and sharing partners whose labour he does not command are likely to volunteer help because of his prestige and position, as are the many younger men whose marriages he has helped to finance. Nominal relatives who wish to strengthen their ties with him will help out, also. A young man, on the other hand, has few junior kinsmen, controls no one else's finances, is without sons-in-law, has helped finance few if any marriages. His senior kinsmen and sharing partners are willing to volunteer help only as befits a modest undertaking in keeping with his station. A festival's scope, therefore, is limited by the way in which organizational principles apply in its sponsor's particular case. The only other limitation is the sponsor's ability and willingness to sustain the necessary effort.

We may conveniently classify festivals under two headings: those in which the sponsor's relations with guests and participants are entirely on a *vararapu* basis, and those in which distributions of *vuivuti* type also occur. In the latter, domestic pigs are slaughtered so that large cuts of pork may be sent to individuals in other hamlets. In the former, food distributed does not include such special gifts of pork over and above the portions appropriate to serving people at a festive meal. Normally the *vuivuti* of domestic pork occurs in feasts of village scope or larger, where at least several hamlets other than the sponsor's are involved. Typically, the killing of numerous pigs and the *vuivuti* of cuts of pork to hamlets in other villages and territories are associated with the main feast in memory of a dead man. Also associated with this feast are special performances in which individuals are carried on litters through the village. Each man on a litter performs some trick or wears a special costume. The memorial feast is also the standard occasion for performing group-rehearsed dances. Such elaborations, however, may accompany any festival of wide scope in which several villages participate when invited by a gift of pork to their leading men. Dances and litter parades have become associated with the festivals sponsored by the government and the Roman Catholic Mission. They mark any festival as a major social event.

With the foregoing principles in mind, we may now examine the organization of various festivals in greater detail. The first group to be considered comprises those that are initiated by a hamlet's senior men as essentially hamlet affairs. Though they may extend in scope beyond the hamlet, they are largely sponsored by the hamlet itself.

When a tree in the *malilo* (hamlet's sitting place) dies, the senior men of its hamlet send the younger men to gather eggs and tell the women to prepare taro. When the food has been gathered, the young men cut down the dead tree and use its wood to make a fire in the *malilo*. The women bring taro to the *malilo*, and the men roast the eggs in the fire there. The senior men of neighbouring hamlets are invited to the feast thus prepared.

Another occasion for a small feast exclusively for men is the killing of a pig that has been dedicated to the men's house. An owner may decide to dedicate a young domestic pig or the members of a netting pool may dedicate a pig caught in their net. The hamlet's senior men set the time for the feast and issue invitations to the senior men of other hamlets.

When a man brings home the first megapode eggs of the season, the senior men in his hamlet may decide to hold an egg feast. Again, they send all the young men to collect eggs, tell the women to prepare taro, and invite the senior men of other hamlets. If there are many eggs to be gathered, they inform the entire village, all of whose men go out egg collecting, and the feast becomes an affair in which the entire village participates, though it is still held in the hamlet initiating it. Its senior men may also order the slit-gong beaten to inform other villages in the territory that eggs are plentiful. And, if possible, they send them bundles of eggs as *vararapu* gifts.

In addition to these feasts, there is a type that gives people a chance to enjoy scarce foods. On hearing that a hamlet has just received a good supply of some specially valued food, such as whitebait, the senior man of another hamlet may send a messenger to his counterpart in the first one to announce that his hamlet is coming to visit and wishes to be provided with food of the sort just acquired. The self-invited hamlet's men and women, dressed in full ceremonial costume, descend on their hosts and are duly feasted as requested. Afterward, they entertain their hosts by singing and dancing for them. At a later date, when the host hamlet learns that the other one has acquired a supply of some delicacy, its members return the visit.

None of the feasts so far mentioned provides much opportunity for an individual to gain prestige as a feast maker. They are associated with the sudden or long anticipated availability of some prized food, a psychologically appropriate occasion for celebration; and they function to affirm neighbourly relations among hamlets within a village in that every such celebration should include as guests the senior men, at least, of the village's other hamlets or else be part of an exchange of feasts between two hamlets. They are conducted on a *vararapu* basis.

The festivals to which we turn next are sponsored by individuals. Occasionally a man gives a small feast in his own name, without any pretence of honouring others. For example, he may collect green bananas, wrap them in scented herbs and bark, and store them in his house until they are ripe. Then he summons people and dispenses the bananas along with tobacco and betelnut. This feast is also a *vararapu*, and the giver intends only to spread his reputation, feeling his prestige enhanced by the knowledge that people are mentioning his name when discussing his gifts. More often, however, feasts are connected with the fulfilment of kinship obligations. A dutiful father, for example, celebrates with a feast every important event in the childhood and adolescence of his first-born child, whether son or daughter. He also celebrates a few events in the life of each of his children. A grandfather may similarly sponsor feasts for his grandchildren. And when a man dies, his nearest surviving relatives should sponsor a festival in his memory.

The first menstruation of a daughter provides an occasion for such a feast. On being informed of the event, a girl's parents and aunts and uncles make special gardens to provide sufficient food, especially if her father plans a village-wide feast. When the gardens mature, the time for the feast is set. The father kills a domestic pig that he has been saving for the occasion, but this will not provide enough meat to feed the whole family. Therefore, he sends a packet of tobacco and a branch of betelnut to the heads of netting pools in each hamlet, who arrange a hunt to supplement what the girl's father provides.

Feasts for children may be larger or smaller in scope than the one just outlined, depending on the father's resources and inclinations. If he limits the feast to include only his hamlet mates and the child's consanguineal kin and territorially resident sibmates, he can expect the guests to bring some food of their own. (They are the same persons who would be helping him if he were giving the feast on a larger scale.) This obviates the necessity of making extra gardens beforehand. The domestic pig killed and eggs collected by the father's hamlet mates also suffice. On the other hand, a father may decide to make a major celebration if he is in a position to do so. At the ear-piercing of a Galilo girl who was an only child, her father decided to make a very large feast involving several villages and accompanied by the *vuivuti* of quantities of domestic pork. The festival was of such scope that it was accompanied by dancing and litter parades.

Because they are sponsored privately by a specific individual rather than by a hamlet through the person of its senior man, feasts of this sort can provide a major avenue for gaining prestige and, through the *vuivuti* of pork, power as well. A man loses face if he completely fails to celebrate those occasions that it is his duty as a father to honour. By going beyond the call of duty, he makes a bid for special recognition. In this respect, there is one festival that brings the greatest prestige to its sponsor and all his hamlet mates. It requires years of planning and preparation and far greater outlay than any other festival. It is essentially a memorial ceremony for a prominent dead man, but ambitious men use the death of any relative, man or woman, as an occasion.

The sponsor is always a close kinsman of the deceased. In former times, after the body had sufficiently decomposed, he surreptitiously exhumed it and removed the left humerus, which he hid in his house. Nowadays, he saves some object that was closely identified with the dead man, such as a section of his walking stick. Whatever is kept is still called the 'bone'. Having secured the bone, the sponsor chooses a sow for breeding purposes. When she litters, he gives her offspring to other men, his hamlet mates, consanguineal and even nominal kinsmen to raise. When he is satisfied that a satisfactory start has been made in raising the necessary pigs, the sponsor announces his possession of the bone to his hamlet mates. They help him build a special platform in the men's house on which to put it. He then gives the bone, which he has painted and wrapped in barkcloth, to a sorcerer, whose services he hires. The sorcerer places the bone on the platform with the appropriate spells, while the men of the hamlet shout, blow conch shells, and beat the slit-gong. For four days thereafter it is forbidden to make any kind of noise near the men's house. Those who disobey are made sick or killed by the sorcerer or, according to one informant, by the spirit of the dead man, which is residing in the bone. On the fifth day, the strict taboos are lifted, but the bone remains in the men's house until the main festival. The sponsor pays the sorcerer on the fifth day and makes the usual gift of tobacco and betel to the heads of the netting pools in his village or territory. They hunt pigs while the women in the sponsor's hamlet prepare the necessary taro for the feast that the sponsor makes to celebrate the lifting of the taboos and the formal announcement that in due time a memorial festival will be held.

At the same time, the sponsor 'places the slit-gong' by putting it outside the men's house. If he does not own a slit-gong, he borrows or rents one. From now until the main festival, while the pigs are maturing, members of neighbouring hamlets throughout the territory come to sing and dance around the slit-gong. As the number of pigs increases, the sponsor notifies the men of his hamlet, village, and perhaps territory, if the intended scope of the festival warrants, that they should plant special gardens for the approaching feast. Then, early one morning, he kills several pigs and beats a special rhythm on the slit-gong. This is the signal to begin dance rehearsals. Cuts of the pigs killed go to the senior men in all the hamlets and villages that the sponsor can afford to invite. They provide the food for the feast that marks the screening of the *malilo*. The purpose of the screen is ostensibly to conceal the dance rehearsals from the eyes of women. A *malilo* is screened in every village to which the sponsor has sent pork. Each of these villages prepares dances to perform in the festival.

The main show consists of rehearsed dances and processions of litters in which costumed men often perform some sort of trick, such as pretending to eat raw taro or to be on fire. Ordinarily, each hamlet of the sponsor's village or territory presents a dance and a procession, whereas in the case of remoter guests, each village or territory presents one. At least one dance performed must belong to the sponsor's sib, and he frequently buys the rights to a new one for the occasion.

While the rehearsals are going on, the sponsor hires an expert to cover and decorate the bone. A close relative of the sponsor will wear it in a dance or carry it in the litter parade.

To announce the end of the rehearsal and the date of the festival, the sponsor kills more pigs and distributes meat to each hamlet and village that received it at the beginning of the rehearsal period. On this occasion, too, first-born sons of members of the sponsor's hamlet are admitted into the screened *malilo*, given their first dance skirts, and initiated into the dance. In the three or four days remaining before the festival begins, the sponsor's hamlet mates and others of his kindred build platforms in his hamlet's square. At the last minute they pile them with pork, eggs, taro, and betelnut. Only if all the sponsor's helpers work hard can a satisfactory amount of food be provided, and the women say that they never rest during this period. The hamlet fills with visiting relatives, nowadays from all of Lakalai and east Nakanai as well, some of whom may stay for days or weeks.

On the first day of the actual ceremonies, the firstborn children of men in the sponsor's hamlet conduct all residents of the village into their hamlet, where they perform a dance called 'stirring up the dance ground'. Then the women of the participating hamlets and villages lead out the various dancing groups and litters in turn, while everyone else gathers to watch. The performances continue through the second day and end with a dance by the village girls who have not yet borne children. On each day of the festivities, the sponsor provides a special men's feast.

The next day is devoted to slaughtering pigs, and the sponsor sends portions as *vuivuti* to at least one man from every hamlet within his village or territory (and from every village or territory otherwise that attended the ceremonies). He also pays the rain-magician he hired to prevent rain from spoiling the festival.

In former times, after distributing the pork, the sponsor held a small feast to celebrate the drilling of a hole in the bone. He hired a specialist to perforate the bone and attach it to the butt end of a spear, which he gave to an outstanding warrior, preferably a close relative of the dead man. All of the territory's men accompanied the warrior as he set out to kill with the spear the first foreigner from another territory whom they met. For this service the sponsor paid the slayer. The spear would thereafter be especially effective in war.

After this cycle of ceremonies, which now omits 'blooding' the spear, the sponsor is thenceforth known as *la-buru-la-galamo,* 'patron of the slit-gong'.

The planning that a memorial festival requires is obviously considerable. Its sponsor must have ample resources in wealth-tokens to pay for the services of the several necessary experts: sorcerer, bone decorator, rain magician, bone driller, and warrior. He must calculate all the occasions for which he will have to kill pigs and the number of hamlets and villages he plans to invite, and then see to it that there will be enough pigs to meet these requirements before formally announcing his intention to sponsor the festival. He must at the same time have enough resources in wealth and pigs to meet the other obligations that come his way in the normal course of events, such as making feasts for a daughter's first menstruation or a son's achievement of maturity, financing a junior kinsman's marriage, or repaying others for *vuivuti* that he receives from them. He must also be in a position to enlist the active support of his fellow villagers as well as hamlet mates, for they must be willing to assume the burden of extra gardens. A lazy, improvident, or no-account man cannot hope to sponsor such an undertaking successfully.

These are reasons why the successful sponsor of a memorial festival gains tremendous public stature. The fame of his hamlet and village is similarly enhanced. Although the ostensible reason for sponsoring the ceremonies is to honour a dead kinsman, a major incentive for assuming the attendant burdens is to increase the prestige of the sponsor. Ambitious men actively compete to give more and bigger memorial ceremonies than their rivals can manage.[12]

WAR AND PEACE

Warfare used to be a major activity. Fighting occurred between sibs, as represented within a territory, between hamlets, villages, territories, and even temporarily allied groups of territories. Immediate causes of hostilities varied from the desire to redress an injury to the desire for economic gain. Manslaughter, rape, and killing another man's pig caused inter- as well as intraterritorial conflict. The desire for scarce goods was a frequent cause of raiding between territories.

Military organization comprised small companies of kinsmen. Sibs, the principal units of collective responsibility, provided the nuclei around which these companies were organized—in any given territory the land-owning sibs, whose members were the territory's citizens. A company also included the resident non-citizens who were associated with the citizen sib, residentially and in land use, by virtue of close kin ties. The company's leader was the sib's outstanding warrior, although presumably the leadership role might also be filled by an exceptionally able warrior from among its associated kinsmen. If the sib had a *suara,* he was its leader. Members of the *suara*'s sib had to obtain his permission before going to war. In intervillage and interterritorial fighting, the several companies seem to have been associated much like the several net pools in pig drives, the most distinguished of the several company leaders (always a *suara* if there was one) serving as commander in the field. He it was to whom we referred earlier as a village's or territory's war leader.

Fighting within a village seems never to have been planned. The fights we recorded seem to have developed out of individual quarrels that became free-for-alls as others joined in. They will be discussed further when we take up the maintenance of internal order. Here we shall consider intervillage and interterritory hostilities. They took basically two forms: the surprise raid and the formal battle. Intermediate between them were fights in which the group attacked had reason to expect trouble, as when its members had stolen a woman from another village, and was prepared to meet it.

A raid's organization depended on the intention behind it and on the initiator's ability to rally support. Many raids were triggered by an offence against a sib, such as manslaughter (responsibility for which could be established by divination if it was not already public knowledge). The offended sib's *suara* or leading warrior took charge. If time permitted, he sent messengers to other hamlets to ask his sibmates to join him. In his own village he could expect support from his hamlet mates and from his affines, provided they did not belong to the enemy sib. He could also, if necessary, recruit members of his phratry, who were under no obligation to volunteer help but could not refuse it when it was asked.

A small raiding party often tried simply to kill any member of the offending sib it might encounter. Frequently it sought to ambush such a victim along a path and, with luck, did not have to deal with other enemies at the time. When such a raiding party returned home, however, it announced its victory by beating a special rhythm on the slit-gong. It followed that, unless the sib was especially large and powerful, it had then to muster its forces against a retaliatory attack.

A raid against a village demanded a larger force and was not usually undertaken unless the enemy was outnumbered. Villages, which sometimes were palisaded, were guarded by sentries in time of war, but precautions clearly were relaxed often enough so that surprise raids were possible. The raiders might try only to kill one or two men and get away again before being discovered, or, in extreme cases, they might try to wipe out the enemy village. A raid of the latter sort by one village against another required the prior consent of all the raiding village's men, because it involved suspending sib loyalties. All the men had to take part and had to agree to kill even their own sibmates, first performing a kind of magic that was intended to blind them to the identity of individual enemies. The ideal was to leave no one alive to take revenge, except for any sibmates of the person whose death was the occasion for the raid. The leading warriors had the duty of chasing down and killing anyone who sought to flee the village. On such raids, the attackers silently entered the village at night and began the actual attack at first light, before the villagers were fully awake.

One occasion for a raid was a girl's eloping to another village during the night. Organizer of the ensuing war party was normally her father, who was joined by members of his own and his daughter's sib. Sometimes a serious attempt was made to get the girl back, but more often the participants used the raid as a means of working off their anger, flinging a few spears without seriously trying to wound anyone. It also helped persuade the groom's family to part with a large brideprice.

Actual kidnapping, as distinct from elopement, was handled differently. The girl's brothers had the primary responsibility of rescuing her, but any kinsman present when the kidnapping was discovered was likely to collect available help and go after her at once, rather than waiting to gather the proper group. Theoretically, such raids were extremely dangerous, since they involved invading an already alert enemy village during the daytime. In fact, however, if there was no great delay in pursuit, the kidnappers were unlikely to have had time to mobilize their own people, summoning them from the gardens and their other activities, and rescue attempts were sometimes successful.

Raids were also made against enemy groups when they were known to be assembled away from their home villages. A long period of fighting between Galilo and Ubae was touched off when a group of young men from Ubae went to the egg fields to dig megapode eggs and attacked some Galilo men who were there for the same purpose, mistaking them for hereditary enemies. In the ensuing war, the Galilo men, who outnumbered Ubae's, occasionally raided the Ubae villages; but generally they found it safer and simpler to attack the Ubae men at the egg fields, where, of course, they were themselves attacked in return.

In raids of this sort, scouting parties approached on the enemy's flanks. Each was led by a proven warrior. When the scouts located a party of the enemy, they sent a messenger to inform the main group that waited for their report. After surrounding the enemy insofar as was possible, they attacked. If they greatly outnumbered the enemy, they closed quickly; otherwise they attacked more cautiously. Indeed, much of the attack consisted of making threatening gestures with shields by shaking and kicking them. The war leader displayed his bravery and the power of his protective magic by carrying no shield. The attackers took care to avoid directing their spears against any sibmates among the enemy. A battle between evenly matched groups consisted of throwing spears (the only weapons) back and forth, the fighters singing songs of rejoicing as they did so, until everyone was exhausted. Few men were killed, and in many skirmishes both sides withdrew without having inflicted damage on the other. In fights between smaller groups within the same territory, this was the usual pattern. To kill one of the enemy was normally sufficient to insure victory.

Most fighting was conducted in the manner just described, even in formal battles, although the preliminary organization of the latter was different. Raids might be led either by a sibmate of someone already killed by the enemy or simply by a warrior eager for more glory. Usually the initiator of the raid also led it, and there was no complexity of command. A formal battle, by contrast, required more careful planning. We have no satisfactory information on the specific conditions that led to a formal battle rather than a raid, except that the formal battle was normally held only between groups that believed themselves to be evenly matched, whereas raids were undertaken by those who thought they could either overwhelm the enemy or manage to kill by stealth without serious risk of being overwhelmed themselves in a pitched battle.

A formal battle took place in an area between the warring villages. The *valipoi* of one village sent a message to the *valipoi* of the other, proposing battle. The message was carried by one of the village's *suara,* who as a messenger was not to be molested. If the second *valipoi* accepted the challenge, he set a date for the battle by putting knots in a leaf to mark the number of days thereafter that the battle should occur. He kept one such leaf himself and sent the duplicate off with the messenger. The several *suara* on each side then assembled their followers. The groups thus assembled on one side set up camp together, and sent out scouts to assess the strength of the enemy village and see if its *valipoi* was present. If he was, a battle could not be fought—since no conflict could take place in the presence of a *valipoi*—and the group simply went home again. Presumably this convention permitted last-minute changes of mind, as when a *valipoi* could not assemble enough men. If a group found itself outmatched it did not, as far as we know, withdraw— to do so would have been disgraceful—but presumably could use the time to seek out additional allies, or perhaps, to summon its own *valipoi* from his position well behind the lines.

Leading warriors and sib heads performed war magic for the military party before it set out, but individuals also recited private spells at the battlefield. Special leaders, weaponless, arranged the lines of battle while the scouts guarded them, though theoretically they were immune from attack. When both groups were assembled, all the men joined their specific company lines, and the battle began, with some lines attacking first. The killing of one man spurred others on to avenge his death, but if a *suara* saw that his line was weakening, he instructed his men to break and flee at once. They were not usually pursued by the enemy.

At home, the warriors met with a reception that varied according to whether anyone had killed or been killed. Defeat was shameful, and usually led to new battles as soon as they could be organized. If an equal number of men from each village was killed, however, it was considered a fair exchange, and no grudge was supposed to be borne. In any event, payment had to be given for each dead man before peace could be established.

If the score stood even, if there had been a long period of fighting, or if for any reason one side wished to discontinue the feud, the *valipoi* or other leader of the party suing for peace sent a messenger to the enemy village—to its *valipoi*, if it had one, or otherwise to a sibmate who could pass the message on. The messenger carried a croton leaf in which knots had been tied to indicate the number of days before the formal peacemaking. If the other side agreed to the truce, both groups set about getting together the wealth-tokens necessary to pay an indemnity for each man they had killed in the fighting. This was primarily the responsibility of the sibmates and consanguineal kin of the men who had actually done the killing, including, of course, the trust groups to which they belonged. When everything had been collected, all the warriors of both sides went to the prearranged meeting place. They assembled about one hundred yards distant from each other. With them came their women, adorned for dancing and carrying baskets of food. The war leaders and one or two outstanding warriors from each side, usually members of the sibs who had lost men in the fight, danced forward, flourished a spear in one hand and a goldlip shell in the other. They measured the shells against each other, returning to their groups to get others until the shells were equal. Then they broke the spears to signify the formal termination of hostilities. There were exchanges of wealth between the sibs of the killed and the killers. Each man's death was compensated with a goldlip shell, a set of tortoise-shell bracelets, and a string of shell beads or a length of pig net, which symbolized, respectively, his head, ribs, and intestines.

When this exchange was finished, the older men who were warriors sat down together to parley until sunset, unravelling all the causes of the fight, figuring out just who had been killed, and making sure that all payments were complete. They also decided who would act as hostages, choosing several grown men to go and live in the enemy village for a while. Meanwhile the younger men, still in opposing groups, braced themselves for attack by the women of the other side. The women attacked them with sticks and stones, a procedure regarded as sexually arousing and indulged in on a number of formal occasions, such as weddings. The men tried to dodge the missiles or fend them off, but could not strike back. These attacks ended in some couples, exhausted and excited, withdrawing to the bush together, and in some cases marriage resulted. At sunset, the older men interrupted the activities, and a general feast was held with the food that had been brought by the women. After the feast, the women again attacked the men, and this time the older men joined in.

The next morning, people returned to their own villages, taking the hostages and any wives acquired during the night (having paid brideprice for the latter on the spot). The hostages stayed long enough for everyone to be sure that all was well. One village then set a time for them to return home. In the case of Ubae and Galilo, Ubae men came to Galilo at the appointed time, bringing some of the Galilo hostages, to whom they had given additional wealth in the form of ornaments. The Ubae hostages and visitors were feasted in each of the Galilo hamlets, and all were given valuables. Then some of the Galilo men escorted them home to Ubae. There they and the remaining Galilo hostages were similarly feasted and given wealth. With their return home the formal peacemaking ended.

Although the peacemaking ceremonies were now over, the men who had taken part in them were thenceforth participants in an exchange partnership. The men in the one village no longer addressed or referred to those in the other by personal name, but substituted the term *tahalo*. They avoided having any physical contact with each other, but repeatedly exchanged gifts of food, and one year after the peace they exchanged pigs. Avoidance of names and of physical contact lasted for the lifetime of the peace partners. Any violation of these taboos was regarded very seriously, and to attack one's *tahalo* was outrageous. If the *tahalo* relationship resulted from settlement of an intersib feud, its violation was so serious as to be grounds for the offender's repudiation by his sibmates.

LEADERS AND 'BIG MEN'

The foregoing accounts of how Lakalai activities are organized and conducted require us to distinguish between two types of leader. There are, first of all, the prime movers, the initiators and sponsors of activity, regardless of the degree to which it requires expert direction. Secondly, there are the directors or managers, the men who assume command of group activities and co-ordinate the participants' efforts. Frequently, the two roles are played by the same individual. Most activities, in fact, require little co-ordination. Everyone participating knows what has to be done and assignment of a task or two at the outset is sufficient to set things on their proper course. Any senior can direct any junior to where he is most needed. It is only in a few group activities—hunting and fishing with large nets, warfare, and some types of garden and weather magic—that co-ordination becomes critical and requires expert knowledge. Under these conditions, the managerial role is assumed by the person acknowledged to be the outstanding expert in the activity in question. In situations where ordinary seniority does not suffice, we may say that the qualifications for managerial leadership are based entirely on recognized technical competence. A manager is respected for his skill, but is not necessarily a prime mover in community affairs generally nor looked upon as a truly 'big man'.

The usual term for a leader, *tahalo uru* ('big man'), designates several different types of person depending on the context. In sib affairs he is the senior man, in hamlet affairs the senior householder. The term may refer to any old man (*uru* means 'old' as well as 'big' or 'important'), any one in authority, any expert, and the manager of an activity while he is directing the work of others. It also refers to the community's principal prime movers, the two or three men in a village or territory who are recognized by all as its most prominent residents. It is with the last, the 'big shots' of the village and territory, that we are presently concerned. To distinguish them from other so-called 'big men', we shall refer to them as the village magnates.

To become a magnate, a man must possess a variety of qualities of which seven are essential: age, industry, wealth, responsibility, courage, knowledge, and in former times membership in a land-owning sib of the village. In addition, he must be ambitious. No Lakalai can achieve much prestige without trying to do so. There is no hereditary rank. Although some of the foregoing attributes are more important than others, they all contribute to the making of a magnate.

We have already seen how important seniority is generally as a basis for authority and respect in Lakalai relationships. It is only with age that a man can hope to be taken really seriously. He must show that he is a good father and a man who can and will fulfil his obligations to his junior relatives. Significantly, a Lakalai is not considered fully adult until he has had several children, nor can he be a truly responsible member of the community until he becomes a grandfather.

While men learn new bits of magic and new specialties from youth on, they acquire important knowledge only with age. There are, or used to be, some types of knowledge to which only old men had access. The older a man becomes, the better are his chances of being recognized as the community expert in connection with such important matters as weather control, gardening, hunting, curing, love, war, and sorcery. Of one thing a young man can always be sure: whatever he knows, there are older men who know more. Ordinarily only men of mature years controlled the magical powers accompanying the *savarasi* and *suara* wristbands and, until recently, only old men were eligible for membership in the *valuku* society, about which we shall have something to say shortly.

Because it is important to the Lakalai that they have ready access to the services of experts, they value their presence in their villages. The value of their services, in some instances, is heightened by the fact that a magical practitioner cannot himself consume the goods that his magic helps to create. The head of a pig-net pool, for example, cannot eat any pig caught in his net, because he has made the magic over it. Some forms of magic require the practitioner to suffer physical privation. For as long as a rain magician is operating, for instance, he must fast. During the three to four days when he is active in a memorial festival, he sits on a platform in the hamlet and has nothing to eat. He is paid for his services, to be sure. This does not alter the fact that it is an ordeal for him to practise. It seems reasonable to conclude that the taboos surrounding the exercise of their skills help to cast experts in the role of public benefactor and serve subtly to put the community in their debt. Many experts, of course, have the power to do harm as well as good, and a sorcerer has real power. Although few men dare to practise sorcery openly, the mere suspicion that they know how to do so can be quite effective. In this regard, it is a Lakalai axiom that all old men know at least some sorcery and many of them know a lot. It was particularly important for an ambitious man to know benevolent magic, and it seems that a *valipoi* was specifically forbidden to practise sorcery.

Knowledge and age, then, tend to go hand in hand, each reinforcing the other as a basis of authority and respect. But these attributes are not sufficient in themselves to create a village magnate. It is essential that he be in possession of wealth and that he use his wealth to place others in his debt. Thus, it is important that he be head of a trust group, a position for which young men, once again, are ineligible. In control of wealth-tokens and pigs, a man has the resources to finance marriages, to buy the services of specialists, to purchase for himself and his children rights to the more important forms of knowledge, to sponsor festivals, and to make *vuivuti* gifts. Without wealth he can do none of these things.

To become wealthy a man must be industrious. Industry is a characteristic on which the Lakalai pride themselves. Both men and women judge one another by the amount of time they spend gardening. A hard worker is a 'real man', a credit to his parents, and a desirable son-in-law.

A magnate displays his superior industry by assuming extra responsibilities. He not only makes gardens with his wife and daughter, he asks other girls from needy families in the community to garden with him as his *samura*. Thus he helps to feed families with inadequate man-power. He assumes the responsibilities of a father on behalf of orphaned relatives, not just close consanguineal relatives to whom he owes this as a duty but nominal or affinal ones as well. He contributes handsomely to the brideprice of all of his kinsmen. In former times, especially, but even today, he is likely to have more than one wife. Polygyny brings prestige for several reasons. It is a conspicuous display of industry, for it takes a 'strong man' to garden for two or more wives and support two or more families. A polygynist, moreover, has as many first-born children as he has child-bearing wives. Each first-born must be honoured with the numerous festivals required to celebrate important events in his or her childhood. At each such occasion wealth-tokens have to be transferred to the child's matrilineal kinsmen, the husband's affines. Polygyny, therefore, requires more than usual wealth. We should add that Lakalai women do not show any great willingness to see their husbands acquire additional wives. Several of our informants had experimented unsuccessfully with polygyny, its failure in each case being largely due to the stubborn resistance of the first wife. A successful polygynist, therefore, proves himself to be the sort of man who is both master in his own house and capable of handling difficult social situations.

A would-be magnate's industry must be more than sufficient to produce food and other goods for his dependants' immediate needs. He must produce surplus goods in order to engage in trade and import wealth-tokens. If, for example, he can organize his junior kinsmen to collect quantities of megapode eggs and can then lead a trading expedition to the eastern Nakanai, he can exchange the eggs for wealth-tokens. In former times, such trips were highly dangerous, and their leader needed courage as well as industry. He also had to have the courage to visit other territories, where he had sibmates, in order to claim his share of brideprice received when women of his sib married.

One of the most dramatic ways in which a Lakalai displays his industry is successfully to sponsor a large-scale memorial festival. To do this and to engage successfully in trade, he must not only show personal industry but also be able to call upon the industry of others. He must have a following. If he is blessed with many junior kinsmen whose labour he actually commands, he is under less pressure to build up a following. If he is not so blessed, he must acquire his following by assuming responsibility for the welfare of remoter kinsmen. By displaying all of the necessary attributes of a responsible leader, by dutifully sponsoring festivals on behalf of his children, by being ready with wealth to meet his obligations to his in-laws, by buying magic and dances for his children, by assuming whatever burdens he can feasibly carry, he makes himself attractive to older and younger kinsmen alike. The former teach him more than they otherwise would, give him needed advice at critical moments, and do him favours in order to obligate him to take charge of the affairs of their own children later on. His younger kinsmen court his support by volunteering to help him in his undertakings, by cheerfully obeying his calls to work, and by catering to his wishes. They tend increasingly to entrust their wealth to him as trustee in preference to some other senior relative.

An ambitious man offers his followers security in return for their loyalty and obedience. His industry, knowledge, and wealth are all sources of security to others. So also, in former times, was his ability as a warrior. Indeed, no man could hope to become a village magnate unless he had proven himself an outstanding fighter. In this regard, we should note that the Lakalai regard displays of violent temper and physical aggression as properly in keeping with masculine nature.[13] Those with reputations as risk-takers and 'men of anger' take pride in the fact. Many men used to cultivate the epithet 'man of the spear', and no one who was not a man of the spear could hope to achieve the status of magnate. Although the best warriors were frequently quarrelsome and difficult, and although some of them spent years moving from hamlet to hamlet to escape the consequences of their actions, they were persons to be reckoned with. People avoided crossing noted warriors. The more stable among them, moreover, were ideally suited to operate as keepers of the peace in the community. As they settled down in later years, their reputations were sufficient to allow them to break up quarrels. They were also persons who would not be afraid to champion the rights of their dependants whenever they were infringed by others. Such persons were ideal candidates for induction into the *suara* wristband society.

Proof of all the qualities necessary for leadership can come only with time. By exhibiting them continuously over the years and on an increasingly impressive scale as he gets older and commands more resources, a Lakalai builds himself a reputation as a 'big man'. In every village there are a number of older men who have achieved good reputations in this way. A hamlet may contain more than one such person, though one of them is usually recognized as 'bigger' than the others. These men represent their respective hamlets in dealings with other hamlets. They are the ones who receive invitations to festivals and to whom are sent *vuivuti* of pork for distribution to their hamlet mates. It is they who make the important decisions in their hamlets, who settle disputes among their hamlet mates and other followers, who are regularly consulted for help and advice, and who initiate the major undertakings calling for group effort. While they are not tyrants, they have earned the right to give advice and to have it taken seriously. They are obeyed because their followers feel indebted to them and dependent upon them, respect their superior age, knowledge, and past deeds of prowess, fear the consequences of their wrath, and desire the advantages of their favour. The *savarasi* wristband symbolizes their authority and power.

Among such men in a village, one or two tend to stand out above the others. They are the village magnates, the men with the biggest followings, who have always demonstrated their industry, wealth, knowledge, courage, and responsibility more forcefully and dramatically than any of their age mates, and who now as older men have no rivals left except one another. These are the men who, if they were also *suara,* used to be eligible for selection as *valipoi.*

SUARA AND VALIPOI

The Lakalai regard as temperamentally best suited for leadership roles men who are extroverted, who deal with their world vigorously and aggressively. Competition for leadership is primarily in activities where these temperamental qualities are most advantageous. These qualities are also intimately linked with Lakalai ideals of masculinity, as we would expect. Competition for leadership is an extension of the process by which Lakalai seek to become self-respecting men.

At the time of our study, it was primarily as financiers and feastmakers that men competed for distinction. Warfare was no longer possible. But it was obviously of great importance for such competition in the past. Indeed, of the several activities in which men formerly sought to prove themselves, warfare was one in which they all engaged and at an age when they were still too young to compete in other ways. Concern for increasing one's personal masculine power, one's effectiveness as a man, was intimately linked with war. This concern found institutional expression in the wristband societies.

Chief symbol of membership in a wristband society is the broad, plaited wristband called *mileki*. Each of the several such societies has its own *mileki*, distinctive in name, shape, and associated taboos. The Lakalai divide the various wristbands into two major categories: plain wristbands, or *mileki* proper, and wristbands decorated with cockatoo feathers, the *suara.*

When a boy reaches physical maturity, he is invested with one of the minor types of plain wristbands, which he wears as an ornament on ceremonial occasions. His father pays for the boy's investment and, if he can, may buy him two or three types of *mileki*. The senior member of a society leads its investment ceremonies. If a man pays for his own investment, he acquires special rights, which include receiving a share of the pay every time another man is given the same type of *mileki*.

Each individual wristband contains the spirit of a dead ancestor of the man who made it. This spirit requires and enforces the taboos that surround the recipient. Not only must he observe restrictions himself, but no one else may disturb him by 'playing' near him, jostling him, or awakening him. Anyone doing so is struck down by the spirit and will not recover consciousness until the wearer of the wristband recites a spell over him.

With most plain wristbands, these taboos and restrictions last only for several days immediately following the induction ceremony. The person who conferred the wristband then lifts the taboos. The spirit departs and from then on seems to have no further interest in the wristband wearer. According to informants, the permanent benefit gained from a *mileki* is that it helps its possessor to be a successful warrior. Although warfare had been discontinued for some time by 1954, fathers were still purchasing investments for their sons. The *mileki* appear, therefore, to be a magical means of enhancing what continue to be regarded as important manly powers.

Most important of the plain *mileki* is the *savarasi*. As we have seen, only hamlet leaders were eligible for membership, and it appears that they customarily financed their own investment. They had to be successful financiers to manage this. The *savarasi* was hedged with a permanent taboo on quarrelling in the presence of a man who was wearing the wristband. The *savarasi* wearer thus had magical power to intervene in quarrels and demand their settlement. In this way the *savarasi* was not only recognition of leadership, it further enhanced the leadership capacity of its wearer by the additional powers it gave him.

The *suara* wristband used to be conferred on men who had already proved themselves to be outstanding warriors and who were at the same time members of landowning sibs within their territories. A man who showed exceptional promise as a fighter might receive the *suara* when he was still young, but normally he had to prove himself many times over first. The suppression of warfare and lack of opportunity to prove oneself is the apparent reason why no new investments are being made. Men with ambitions in this direction made a point of joining organized war parties. Either alone or with the help of a single companion they frequently attacked strangers. They might even act as hired killers. When a man had many killings to his credit and otherwise behaved as a magnate should, he was invested in an extremely elaborate and expensive ceremony. His person was thereafter surrounded with permanent taboos whose breach was punished magically. It was forbidden to make a disturbance in his presence, or to sit close to him. His house might not be entered. Children might not play near him. If men fought in his presence, he was offended, and had to be paid with wealth tokens. If he was present at a feast, he distributed the food. If there was trouble in the village, people fetched him, and, at his command, the trouble-maker stopped what he was doing. The *suara*'s natural influence, as a warrior and 'big man', was heavily reinforced by the magic associated with the wristband. The spirit in it was especially powerful and remained in it permanently. It gave the *suara* his enormous strength as a warrior, and punished both him and others for any offence against the taboos associated with the wearing of the wristband.

A *suara* was, above all, a sib leader and war leader. As a sib leader, he controlled his sib's land and wealth. Not only his sibmates, but those men whose sibs had no land locally and who gardened and resided on the land of their fathers' or grandfathers' sibs, owed allegiance to the *suara* who controlled it. In spite of this, we should note that a man could be sponsored for induction as a *suara* by members of his father's rather than his own sib. The one *suara* presently living in Galilo was so chosen, although his own sib as well as his father's paid for his induction. It is also possible for a sib to have more than one *suara* in one village, since all such men have a joint interest in promoting the welfare and solidarity of the same sib. Our only instance of a sib having more than one *suara* in Galilo, however, involved a pair of brothers who, as members of the same sibling set, co-operated in virtually every enterprise.

As war leader, each *suara* led a separate band of warriors into battle. This was recognized as divisive, and there normally seems to have been little co-operation among *suara*. Because sib membership often cuts across hamlet lines, thanks to the association of fathers and sons in residence, the *suara* system helped to unite members of different hamlets. Ties to village land, moreover, probably influenced the *suara* themselves to try to avoid conflicts that would lead to the breaking up of residence groups. Nevertheless, our evidence suggests that the *suara*, as leading warriors, tended to be hot-tempered trouble-makers and killers who were extremely useful to the community in time of war, and to their own sibs during conflict with other sibs, but who were something of a threat to peaceful intravillage relations. The solution, if it could be reached, lay in elevating one *suara* to the position of *valipoi*.[14]

The *valipoi* was always a *suara*, and indeed some of our data are confused because informants do not always distinguish plain *suara* from *valipoi*, describing either as being 'like a king'. But only the *valipoi's* position could legitimately be called that of a chief. He was elected by general agreement of all the 'big men' of the village. If, after discussion, agreement could not be reached, there was no *valipoi*, but such a situation was undesirable. As one informant said, 'Villagers like to have a *valipoi* because he settles all quarrels and behaves well, setting an example to all.' As soon as he was elected, word was sent to inform other villages of his identity. The *valipoi* of different villages seem to have had a partner type of relationship, for they called one another *taho*.

Alone of all leaders, a *valipoi* was responsible primarily to the entire village, not to its separate hamlets or sibs. He also represented the village in its negotiations with others. Fights between villages could take place without a *valipoi*, but what his position facilitated was the re-establishment of peace. Despite his role in warfare, his principal function was to keep the peace, both with relation to other villages and within his own. The visible sign of this responsibility was that, from the time of his election on, he might not hold a weapon. Having fully proved himself as a warrior, he was now above such things. When he needed protection, as when travelling, the *suara* of his village accompanied him and acted as his bodyguard. They also carried messages for him and enforced his orders. Their loyalty to him balanced their duties to their sibs; for if they had not been prepared to support him, they would not have approved his election (or remained in the village). The *valipoi* himself profited from his position not only in the enormous respect and prestige received, but in being freed from all normal work, which was performed for him by others. Labour was also donated to *savarasi* and ordinary *suara*, but not to the extent of permitting them to remain idle. The *valipoi's* wives, who were not as privileged as he, did their gardening in partnership with other men. His job, however, was no sinecure. It could even be galling to a man of action. One Galilo *valipoi* abandoned his position and went out to found the hamlet of Tagaragara by the stream that supplied Galilo with water, specifically in order to guard Galilo women and children against foreigners who might attack them there. But his case is not typical, and the position seems normally to have been held for life.

When a *valipoi* felt that he was near death, he designated a successor, who was either a son or a sibmate, and gave him a special belt decorated with feathers to indicate this choice. As far as we can judge, he was only marking a likely successor; the recipients of the belt simply had a better chance than other *suara* to be chosen *valipoi*, but had to go through the full process of proving himself first. In view of the support that the controversial present luluai of Galilo has received, however, it may be significant that he is the son of a *valipoi* who was the first government-appointed luluai of the village, and that he himself received the belt from his father. On the other hand, he does not belong to a land-holding sib, and the belt was presumably delivered to him after pacification, so that the whole affair may have been abnormal. Another Galilo resident, who received a belt from a different *valipoi*, is not even a 'big man'. Certainly none of the major positions of leadership in Lakalai was hereditary.

The system of formal titles associated with the *mileki* and *suara* wristbands occasionally made it possible for younger men to achieve nominally important positions in village affairs. The one remaining *suara* in Galilo, for example, was chosen for investment while he was still a young man (and in preference to his older brother) because of his enormous physical strength. But he has never had a chance to prove himself in battle, and his being a *suara* is considered virtually an empty title. He is accorded the little privileges that go with it at feasts, but he does not rate as one of Galilo's really 'big men'. By contrast, the last man said to have held the title of *suara* in Rapuri village (he was probably a *valipoi*) was so influential that many residents of his village accompanied him every time he moved to a new hamlet and followed him in his terminal illness to the government hospital in Talasea, far from Lakalai country. As these contrasting instances reveal, wristbands do not in themselves make someone a 'big man' or magnate. They are something to be acquired by men as a part of the process of becoming magnates, and they serve as a means of giving more formal substance to a magnate's position as such. Only one who had already become a village magnate could hope to be a *valipoi*, and this seems to have been the ultimate in recognition and power that he could achieve.

Pacification and introduction of the government-appointed luluai and tultul have eliminated the *valipoi* and *suara*. To the best of our knowledge, there are neither *valipoi* nor active *suara* (ones who have really proved themselves) now alive.[15] But even without these titles, a village magnate is still treated with great respect. He is not usually referred to by name but as 'our big man', and 'father of so-and-so'. People speak softly and walk quietly in his vicinity and are careful not to waken him. Children are warned to stay away from him as much as possible. The reason given is that 'big men' generally, and magnates especially, have uncertain tempers and control powerful magic.

INTERNAL ORDER AND SOCIAL CONTROL

At every turn, as we have examined Lakalai social structure, we have encountered the principle that seniors are responsible for their juniors and that juniors owe seniors loyalty in return. In practice, this means that juniors owe special loyalty to those among their seniors who assume major responsibility for them. Some responsibility is assumed as a duty, as in connection with close consanguineal kin. Other responsibility is assumed as a privilege. The result from a structural standpoint is that a Lakalai village consists of several elders, each having one or more types of following. Each type of following is composed of persons for whom he has the same set of responsibilities. As sib elder he has a following of sibmates; as head of a trust group he has a following of kin whose wealth he controls; as head of a hamlet he has a following of hamlet mates; as an older person, he has a following of consanguineal kinsmen generally. A man's several followings tend to overlap in membership, and men differ as to the type of following they enjoy. These followings form the constituent groups within a village. They are held together as a community to the extent that the elders they follow are willing to form a community. Thus, each village, and territory as well, can be viewed as a federation of elders and their followings. The number and size of a man's followings are indicative of the degree to which he is a 'big man'. In this respect, some men are more prominent in a federation than others. The most prominent among them are what we have called a village's or territory's magnates.

Rivalry between prominent elders makes it difficult for them to remain in the same federation. When two prominent men in the same hamlet become rivals in hamlet affairs, one of them is likely to secede and form a new hamlet of his own, taking his following with him. If he builds the new hamlet next to the old one, he and his following continue to remain in the same village with his rival. The breach between them is only as hamlet mates, no more. If the rivalry between village magnates becomes intense, one of them will take his following and build a new hamlet or group of hamlets at a greater distance from the first, indicating thereby the autonomy of the new settlement at the village level. In a breach between two villages, and this invariably follows armed conflict, one of them is likely to move so as to increase the distance between itself and its rival. If the breach is of long duration and intense, intercourse between the two villages may be so reduced as to lead them to operate as independent territories. There is reason to suspect that Poite became independent of Pulabe as a territory in this way. The fissive tendencies generated by rivalries among prominent men are countered by the tendency for people to align themselves with the most prominent men. As new magnates emerge, therefore, they draw to them more and more individuals, first their own kinsmen and then the kinsmen of their kinsmen, including lesser leaders and their followings. Thus, as old villages break up, new ones grow.

While the rivalries between men for influence and following are not altogether incompatible with the maintenance of peace and internal order within Lakalai communities, they produce fierce loyalties and much bitterness, especially when the more ambitious men push hard and cause others humiliation. Thus, when someone's legal rights are violated, strong emotional outbursts result. The intense feelings engendered by rivalries within and between communities are now free to express themselves in righteous wrath. Any serious offence by one Lakalai against another immediately produces an explosion of emotion that leads, automatically, to at least a show of physical violence. Thus, every offence seriously endangers the peace, and major offences result in outright breach of the peace.

It is in this structural context that we must review the problem of social control in Lakalai. As in every society, it has two major aspects, the prevention of disorder and, when prevention fails, the restoration of order.

Lakalai parents and elders constantly tell their children and young people what are the likely consequences of improper action. Emphasis is laid on the liabilities to which failure to perform one's duties and to which violating the rights of others expose one, and this is consciously exploited as a device for preventing disorder.

One consequence of misconduct is ridicule and public humiliation. A Lakalai suffers shame (*mahela*) when he is the object of public discussion. He avoids approaching a group of village mates without invitation, so that if they are talking about him they and he will not be embarrassed. It is painful, therefore, when others deliberately make sure that a man hears himself talked about. Knowledge that others know and disapprove of his behaviour may, it is said, drive a man to suicide. In the absence of other coercion, it is shame that makes a man fulfil his obligations to his kinsmen and partners, defer to his elders, care for younger kinsmen and hamlet mates, and repay his debts.[16] A person who behaves improperly is usually scolded only by his close relatives; but the fear that others are laughing at him or talking disapprovingly of his conduct may affect him more strongly than the scolding. A lazy man who does not do enough work to feed his family properly is admonished by all the men in his hamlet if the pleas of his close kin fail. Although some men ignore such general admonition, demonstration of disapproval by the wider group is sufficient to bring most men to a proper sense of shame. Men who are cowardly, ignorant, improvident, or undutiful are not 'true men' and may be called 'women'. For a woman, especially, to disparage a man is to humiliate him in the extreme.

In addition to scolding and admonishing, senior kinsmen threaten to withdraw support from recalcitrant juniors. No one will allow a kinsman to starve, but a man may well refuse to help buy a wife for someone who is dishonest or lazy or who has mistreated a former wife. The head of a trust group has it within his power to make life difficult for younger kinsmen who do not behave themselves. In fact, if a really lazy gardener is married to a hard-working woman, the head of the hamlet in which they reside may encourage another man to elope with the wife, and will perform the love-magic for the wife stealer. The hamlet head then smooths over the resulting quarrel and persuades his hamlet mates to contribute to the financial settlements, including the new bridprice, because all of the hamlet will now benefit from the woman's labours.

Another thing elders impress upon young people is that giving offence exposes one to physical attack or sorcery. They tell constantly how in their youth the slightest offence was likely to result in the offender's being speared on the spot, and they seek generally to create the impression that all but one's close kinsmen are not averse to doing one injury. While sorcery and spearing were more to be feared in former times than they are today, it is evident that talk of it is greatly exaggerated for effect.

These, then, are the several techniques by which people seek to control the behaviour of others: shaming, scolding, threatening withdrawal of support, and dwelling upon the dire bodily consequences of giving offence.

Within a hamlet, they are quite effective in most cases. If a person continues to cause trouble, and his hamlet mates actually indicate withdrawal of support and go so far as publicly to shame him, he has little recourse but to leave the hamlet and seek shelter in another. There is, however, no formal ceremony of ostracism, nor is there any way to force a man to leave his hamlet if he refuses to do so. In the latter event, however, others leave the hamlet in preference to living with the trouble-maker.

The village's chronic trouble-maker is either someone excessively quarrelsome and given to violent action or, as is the more usual case, someone who is overly active in extra-marital love affairs. The Lakalai do not disapprove of such affairs provided certain conditions are met: the woman should not be married; her identity should be kept secret (women are not virgins at marriage but should have good reputations); and, above all, she should not become pregnant. A man who flouts these rules is liable to a beating by the girl's relatives. (In the past, he was liable to being killed by them.) Continually to have affairs with married women makes one liable to united action by their husbands, husband's kin, and kin of the women as well.

In former times, a trouble-maker was usually advised by his senior kinsmen to leave the village or territory and join sibmates elsewhere when it appeared that he was in danger of becoming an object of attack by assault or sorcery. Death at the hands of aroused members of the community or exile to escape it were the ultimate prospects for the antisocial individual. While collecting information as to past hamlet affiliations of persons in the Galilo genealogies, we encountered several cases of men who, our informants said, were never able to stay in one place for long. Constantly in trouble, they moved from village to village and territory to territory until they died by sorcery or by the spear. The labour recruiter provides a convenient refuge for men in trouble today. School is also useful. In 1954 two young men implicated as possible fathers in the pregnancy of an unmarried girl suddenly acquired an interest in advancing their education and slipped away to the government school in Talasea.

Fear of sorcery was unquestionably a powerful deterrent to improper behaviour in former times. Lakalai complain that young people fear it less today and that their behaviour shows it, but sorcery is still practised and still feared. It is especially effective as a deterrent to theft from gardens and fruit trees, which are away from the village and unguarded. Owners frequently place a spell on them designed to make a trespasser ill. To be cured, he must confess his fault and ask the owner to be merciful. The owner, after administering a scolding, usually nullifies the effect of the spell with the warning that he will not be so forgiving another time. Another deterrent is the thief's knowledge that his victim may hire the services of a diviner to learn his identity. Even where his identity is not known, he is still liable to sorcery. There is a spell that finds out and attacks the guilty party, whoever he may be.

We turn now from general deterrents to disorderly conduct, and from the personal liabilities of offenders to consider the social consequences of an offence.

As a violation of the accepted rules of conduct, every offence nullifies the rules in the relations of offender and offended. They must re-establish their relationship as one subject to customary law if they are to have peaceful dealings with each other thereafter. An offence is, in effect, a breach of the peace between the parties concerned, an abrogation of the social contract. It makes them overt enemies, and they will continue as such until a formal peace is re-established between them. This requires an exchange of wealth-tokens. Thus, if a person breaks a taboo, as by speaking the name of his cross-cousin, stepping into the garden of a man that he calls *tahalo,* or eating the kind of food last eaten by a dying man, the injured party, with whom the privilege of restoring the peace now lies, sends him a *vuivuti* in the form of a wealth-token. By accepting the gift and repaying it with wealth-tokens of his own, the offender completes the exchange by which normal relations between him and the other are re-established.

In more serious offences, such as manslaughter, assault, rape, theft, or killing someone else's pigs, fighting of some sort almost invariably occurs between the parties concerned before there can be a settlement. If one man catches another stealing, for example, the two are likely to fight with clubs. In former times, men who had a falling out would stand a safe distance apart and throw spears at each other until they were physically exhausted. After the offended person expends his immediate anger in violence of this sort, he and the offending party then discuss the issue, exchange at least token payments, and restore order to their relationship. It is the duty of the *suara* and *valipoi* to help compose these differences.

A man guilty of homicide or rape was likely to be killed outright in former times by his victim's kinsmen, if they caught him before he could gain the protection of his hamlet and sibmates. Otherwise the sibmates, hamlet mates, and other close kinsmen of the victim attacked the hamlet and sibmates of the culprit. Standing at some distance, they exchanged volleys of spears until they were tired. If the injured side then withdrew still threatening the other side, it was evident that fighting would continue, and it behoved the culprit and his sibmates to leave the village and territory until such time as a peace could be negotiated. If, after its initial outburst, the injured party was willing to negotiate, then a peace settlement such as that already described in connection with warfare was concluded. Spear fighting is prohibited nowadays, but fighting with sticks is still a common consequence of such offences as assault and wife-stealing.

In making a settlement, no restitution or payment in compensation for the injury inflicted is normally required, homicide being the one exception. But there must be an exchange of payment, which makes the settlement legally binding. While this removes any legitimate cause for further action by the offended party, the Lakalai say that they often continue to nurse grudges covertly. Therefore, if the two groups were formerly living in close proximity, it is a strain for them to continue to do so. Consequently, after a peace there tends to be a greater physical distance between the opposing parties than formerly. If brothers have a falling out, although they compose their differences, they tend to reside thereafter in different hamlets. Where different sibs or hamlets in a village are involved, they become the nuclei of distinct villages following settlement of their differences; and when different villages are the disputants, they tend to increase the distance between them, as in the founding of Makasili village at an increased distance from Kabili, which we discussed in connection with the history of Pulabe territory.

As long as the immediate parties concerned are able to negotiate directly, there is a minimum of interference from others. Usually, however, the offices of a third party are required.

The proper person to intervene is always the senior or most prominent member of the most immediate group to which the principal disputants both belong. Within a household, it is the household head who settles differences; within a hamlet, its senior 'big man' or leading warrior; within a sib, its senior member. These men have authority if no *savarasi, suara,* or *valipoi* is present. The latter three all have specific obligations to keep the peace within the village, by force if necessary, and it is their duty to intervene when they know of a quarrel or of a source of conflict such as an adultery case, and to try to settle it before it leads to killing.

This duty falls to the *savarasi* first. If he is not wearing his wristband when he hears of a quarrel, he puts it on. He then walks between the opposing parties, hand uplifted. If one of them persists, he hits him on the jaw with the uplifted hand. This should bring him to his senses. But if it does not, the *savarasi* takes the disputants to the *suara,* who lectures on proper behaviour. His mere presence should, of course, produce an end to the quarrel. As a last resort, they are taken to the *valipoi.* In former times, according to one informant, a man who refused to listen to the *suara* or *valipoi* and remained in the village was speared by his own village mates the next time a general fight was in progress. Presumably, this method of execution was employed in the hope of avoiding retaliation from the culprit's sibmates.

Peacemakers used to derive their powers from several sources. First, they were likely to have been leading warriors. Except for the *valipoi,* they were in all probability dangerous men in their own right. A man who had a reputation as a warrior, even if he was not invested with a wristband, demanded respect from others, who should not make disturbances or quarrel in his presence. Interestingly, something that most offended such men was wife-beating. A warrior's hot temper, which he carefully cultivated, might easily get out of hand, so much so that a 'big man' might use magical means to quieten him. But within limits the warrior was an influence for peace in the community. A second source of a peacemaker's power was his being himself a 'big man' if not a true magnate. He had a considerable following, whose support he could command. A *savarasi* could count on the support of his entire hamlet, a *suara* on his usually locally powerful sib and its dependent kin, and the *valipoi* on all the residents of his village as well as his sibmates. Undoubtedly of great importance was the support that *savarasi* and *suara* received from their fellow wristband wearers. As an elevated *suara* who commanded the support of the other *suara* in his village, a *valipoi* was in an especially strong position to punish, with death if need be, a persistent trouble-maker. Added to their physical and social power was the magical power that derived from the spirits inhabiting their wristbands. There was plenty of reason to be very circumspect in one's dealings with these men.

As adjudicator, whoever he was, the intervening 'big man' exerted his influence over both parties to persuade them to negotiate. If need be, he advised the litigants as to how they should arrange their future relations. Thus, when there was a dispute across territorial lines within the Gutumaigigi division of the Kabilimomosi sib a generation or two ago, the disputants took the matter to the senior man in the sib, who was also a *suara.* He established the terms of settlement and declared that thenceforth there would be a further subdivision of the sib, each to be known by the names of the principal litigants, and each comprising the matrilineal descendants of their respective supporters.

Within the village there was an established procedure by which offences were settled. The important man most closely associated with the injured person held a council-of-war to plan an attack on the offender and his sib and hamlet mates. Kinsmen to members of both parties brought word of this meeting to the intended victims. A representative of the latter group then went to the hamlet of the opposing leader. Standing in the middle of its cleared space he loudly asked who was planning a fight with his sib or hamlet. After he repeated this question several times, the opposing leader called back, publicly announcing his intention to fight and reciting the injury that his group expected to redress. It was at this point that he peacemaker intervened, though token fighting might have to take place before the injured party was willing to negotiate.

When someone committed an offence against a resident of another village, the victim's village was likely to take up the dispute. Its warriors would descend on the other village and, in the heat of their anger, might kill any of its residents whom they encountered on the way. Negotiating a settlement between villages was more difficult because there was unlikely to be a person of sufficient stature in the territory not committed to either side who could act as adjudicator. Furthermore, it is possible for someone to operate as adjudicator, whatever the nature of the disputing groups, only as long as both parties are committed to remaining a part of some larger grouping and are willing, therefore, to respect the authority of its 'big man'. Until the government and missions entered the scene and prior to the development of large scale 'cargo' movements there was, of course, no one who could act as adjudicator in the negotiation of peace between territories. What was crucial here was the ability of opposing *valipoi* to treat with one another as fellow *taho* within the same wristband society and as men whose duty was the regulation of conflict.

THE *VALUKU* SOCIETY

We have seen how Lakalai communities are federations of elders with their followings and how these same elders are the agents of social control, in that their authority prevents disorder and helps to settle disturbances of the community's peace. We have reviewed the sources of their power in wealth, knowledge, and military prowess, and we have observed the processes by which men develop stature in the eyes of their fellows, acquire followings, and establish their right to authority. We have seen the crucial role of the wristband societies in the traditional system of social control. In all of this we repeatedly found that seniority is fundamental. Only elders can really hold power, and age automatically brings an increase in power for most men, however else it may be augmented by personal achievement. We now consider the means by which the elders collectively dramatize their authority and vividly impress upon the community the power that lies behind it. Their instrument is the *valuku* society.

The arrival of dry weather following the three-month rainy season marks the beginning of relative abundance. The megapode eggs become plentiful, as do the canarium almonds, so important in Lakalai festive cookery. This is the season of festivities, and all major festivals are planned to occur within it. During this season, also, the members of the *valuku* society become active.

The *valuku* are masked figures. Spirits are said to enter the masks when they are made and to remain there until the masks are dismantled and destroyed. Mask designs are numerous, and copyright to them is owned both by individuals and by sibs. There are several myths to explain the *valuku*. According to one, they have a special connection with the Gararua sib. To indicate it, we must say something about its apparent historical, as distinct from mythological, origin.

At the base of the Hoskins Peninsula on the extreme west are the villages of Mai, Rada and Buluma (see Map 2). Their inhabitants speak a dialect of the

Bakovi language spoken on the Willaumez Peninsula. They call themselves 'Xarua'[17] or 'Garua', which is the name of an island half-way up the Willaumez Peninsula near Talasea (see Map 1). According to tradition among their Kapore-speaking neighbours, the Xarua people came from this island and tried to settle farther east on the Hoskins Peninsula. They were unable to maintain themselves, however, and were harried westward until they settled in their present location. The Gararua sib (Lakalai plural of Garua) presumably derives from Xarua women who married Lakalai men. It would appear that the *valuku* may have been introduced to the Lakalai by the Xarua. The Xarua still control whether or not the *valuku* will be active at all in a given year. Because the usual abode of the spirits of the Gararua sib is the Dage River, *valuku* impersonations must begin in the village nearest the Dage and be taken up village by village eastward around the Hoskins Peninsula. The Xarua villages are those closest to the Dage, so it is the Xarua who start the *valuku* each year.

Until the missions discouraged secrecy and sorcery, only old men knew how to make the masks. They protected their knowledge jealously, using sorcery to kill any person who infringed the taboos surrounding the *valuku*. Each year, a few of the older men (presumably men in their forties) were initiated into the mysteries, one of the most important of which was the method of constructing the frames of the several masks and the nomenclature of their parts. The new initiates were invested with masks to which they had rights at a special ceremony, and had to kill pigs for the other men to eat.

The exact time to start the *valuku* impersonations was decided by the senior men in the society in each village—with due regard to the fact that the villages immediately to the west had already started. Late one afternoon the society's members built a special hut in a suitable *malilo* in the village. They screened off the hut's immediate environs, and only the society's initiates were allowed within the screen. Here they constructed the masks and other paraphernalia to go with them. The completed masks were kept on special racks within the hut. While the masks were there, there was a strict taboo on loud noise in the vicinity, especially during the day. Children were not to cry nor adults to quarrel. If they did so, the old men would make them ill or even kill them through sorcery. It was also forbidden for women to see the paraphernalia partially dismantled or to look inside a mask. Any woman who did so was killed, as was the man careless enough to let her see it.

Nowadays, the age of initiation has been so greatly reduced that all adult men and even teen-age youths take part. The feeling of secrecy about the mysteries is still strong, but the fear of sorcery as punishment for violating the taboos is greatly reduced. In other respects, however, the *valuku* continue to operate much as in the past.

The period of activity lasts for several weeks. During this time, any initiate may put on a mask and, with his body completely concealed by coconut leaves, walk through his village's hamlets and about his territory's paths. Sometimes masked men go in groups. There is a definite progression in the types of masks worn. Some masks may be freely worn by all members of the *valuku* society. Wearing them early in the *valuku* season, the society's members chase and beat women and children whom they meet on the paths or find in the hamlets. They are careful not to molest first-born children, however, because any one harming a first-born must sponsor a feast for him. Women carrying babies or water bottles are usually left alone, too, but younger girls and children are often badly frightened. Later in the *valuku* season, the initiates begin wearing more elaborate masks, which are copyrighted. Most of these are harmless, and women can demand of one kind that its wearer bring them food. There is a mask form, however, whose wearer has the privilege of raping any women he encounters on a path. The duration of activity depends on the inclinations of the society's senior men. When they decide to end it, they destroy the hut and all the masks.

Lakalai men say that they regard the *valuku* impersonations as nothing more than enjoyable sport, and it is evident that other residents of the villages are entertained as well as frightened. In most cases, the observers have no difficulty in recognizing the wearer from his feet and manner of walking. The beatings administered are not supposed to be punishments, but a man who dislikes another may make a special point of persecuting his womenfolk. On the other hand, if a husband and wife quarrel violently during the *valuku* season, the society's members don masks, attack them in a body, and break up their household goods. Otherwise, the society does not operate as a village police force nor as an agency administering punishment for breaches of the peace.

Nevertheless, the *valuku* society has obvious political functions. In former times, when membership was limited to a village's older men, the masked impersonations of spirits forcefully dramatized their authority and the power behind it—especially the latter. Only the old men, through the society, could take such liberties as beating people and sexually assaulting women. And concentration of the knowledge of sorcery in their hands was emphasized by the taboos surrounding the *valuku* and the consequences of their violation. The *valuku* society is an institutionalized expression, in a relatively harmless manner, of the 'teeth' in the seniority system of authority relationships. Above all, it emphasizes and dramatizes the solidarity of the community's elders *vis-à-vis* its other members. Whatever the differences and rivalries among them, they are united in enforcing their authority.[18]

EPILOGUE

Introduction of Australian Government control immediately following the First World War, conversion to Christianity, and new economic wants and opportunities have created new problems for the Lakalai while at the same time eliminating some old ones. Not only has Lakalai political and social organization undergone change as a result, it has also been developing its potential for larger scale organization through a succession of 'cargo' movements.

To detail these changes in culture and circumstance, to review the history of contacts with Europeans, to describe the 'cargo' movements, and to draw their implications for Lakalai political organization and its potentials for development are beyond the scope of this account.[19] We hasten to add, however, that what we have described here obtains in large measure today. Most luluais, government-appointed headmen, qualify as 'big men' in their villages. Except for the cessation of warfare and de-emphasis of warrior skills, with consequent disappearance of initiated *suara* and *valipoi*, political life within the villages follows much the same pattern as before.

Furthermore, in order to understand the bases of leadership in the larger modern movements, knowledge of the traditional sources of authority and of the roles of managers and prime movers, as we have called them, seems to be essential. Indeed, much of the authority of cargo leaders seems to derive from their recognition as experts qualifying them for managerial direction of the social reforms that many Lakalai believe will lead to the better life summed up in the one word 'cargo'. While this account does not deal with these matters, which have recently been of much concern to the Lakalai and those who administer them, it should provide an essential part of the background for their understanding.

NOTES

1. The writers spent six and five months respectively in 1954 among the Lakalai as members of an anthropological expedition sponsored by the University Museum and Department of Anthropology of the University of Pennsylvania and assisted financially by the American Philosophical Society and the Tri-Institutional Pacific Programme. Ann Chowning returned briefly in 1962 and 1964 for periods totalling six weeks, the trip being financed respectively by grants from the Columbia University Council for Research in the Social Sciences and the National Science Foundation. Other members and associates of the 1954 expedition were D. B. Swindler, Wenner-Gren Pre-Doctoral Fellow in Anthropology at the University of Pennsylvania; C. A. Valentine, Fulbright Scholar at the Australian National University; Edith O. Valentine; and A. Floyd, land ecologist with the Department of Forests of the Territory of Papua and New Guinea. This report owes much to the work of our colleagues, especially that of C. A. Valentine, on whose data we have drawn freely. We are especially grateful for the many courtesies afforded by the territorial administration and for the help and hospitality so freely given by the European residents of Cape Hoskins, who proved warm friends and good neighbours. To our Lakalai friends and helpers our debt is enormous. We hope they will forgive us the shortcomings of this report.

2. Since the name Nakanai becomes Lakalai in their dialect, we have chosen to refer to them by this designation. Their western neighbours call them 'Muku', and the eastern Naganai call them 'Bileki', which the Lakalai themselves use in reference to the villages to the west of the Methodist Mission near Cape Hoskins. For convenience, we shall designate speakers of all Nakanai dialects other than Lakalai as 'eastern Nakanai'.

3. Because of the several uses to which anthropologists have put the term clan, we follow Lowie (1920: 105), who proposed the less ambiguous term 'sib' for unilinear descent groups in which actual descent from a common ancestor is not directly traceable. For a fuller discussion of Lakalai kinship and related matters, see Chowning (1958), and in *Anthropological Forum*, Vol. 1, Nos 3 and 4, pp. 476-501.

4. Modern Melanesian utopian aspirations are widely symbolized by the material goods of Western civilization, collectively called 'cargo' in Pidgin English. There have been many social movements and religious cults aimed at implementing the coming of cargo in Melanesia. See, for example, Berndt (1952-53, 1954), Worsley (1957), Burridge (1960), Schwartz (1962) and Lawrence (1964). For the Lakalai see the brief accounts by Goodenough (1956a, 1963) and Valentine (1963b).

5. We use these terms in the Hohfeldian sense, as outlined by Hoebel (1954: 48-9).

6. We may say that in Lakalai a person's property, marital, or other interests are legal if encroachment on them by others in the judgment of 'disinterested' public opinion is a violation of social contract and properly suspends peaceable relations between them until there has been an exchange of wealth-tokens to renew the social contract. Cf. Hoebel's definition of legality (1954: 27-8).

7. Cf. the discussion of Lakalai residence by Goodenough (1956b: 25-7). For a more recent and fuller discussion, see Goodenough (1962).

8. Cf. Hees (1915-16: 52). Hees is our only published source on the Lakalai prior to the period of intensive European contact.

9. Cf. Hees (1915-16: 42).

10. People who regularly co-operate in these ways also include cross-cousins and siblings-in-law, who, of course, cannot make free use of one another's property nor request its use of each other, but who are expected to offer its use whenever it is evident that it is needed.

11. Because the obligations of hamlet mates to one another are those of near kin, the Lakalai hamlet is a kin group as well as a local group. See the discussion by Goodenough (1962).

12. For an illustrated account of memorial festivals, see Goodenough (1955).

13. For a description of Lakalai ideas about personality and temperament, see Valentine (1963a).

14. An informant from beyond Pulabe mentioned an official called the *palamali*, who sounds so similar to the *valipoi* that we assume that the terms are synonyms.

15. For this reason some of our data are ambiguous. For example, we were told that the *suara* wore long braided beards and lived in especially large houses, which were avoided by women and children. When intervening in fights, attending ceremonies, and visiting other villages, they wore and carried special paraphernalia, such as painted armlets and net bags, both hung with rattles, and carved canes (if they were elderly). We do not know whether these and other marks of distinction were shared by all *suara*, or whether, as seems likely, some of them were reserved by the *valipoi*.

16. The compelling force of shame is revealed by a man's suicide said to have been occasioned by his realization that people were discussing his extramarital affairs. The Lakalai assume that shame is the principal reason for suicide for men, or that it used to be before the opportunity to go away to work outside the area offered escape from the situation.

17. The letter 'x' is used here to represent the so-called Melanesian 'g', which is a voiced spirant. This sound is not represented in the Lakalai language. Lakalai speakers regularly convert it into a voiced stop, the normal 'g'.

18. For an extended account of the *valuku* masks and the myths associated with them, see Valentine (1961).

19. For general discussion of these matters, see Valentine (1958, 1963b).

REFERENCES CITED

BERNDT, R. M. (1952-53): A Cargo Movement in the Eastern Central Highlands of New Guinea. *Oceania,* Vol. XXIII, No. 1: 40-65; No. 2: 137-58; No. 3: 202-34.

BERNDT, R. M. (1954): Reaction to Contact in the Eastern Highlands of New Guinea. *Oceania,* Vol XXIV, No. 3: 190-228; No. 4: 255-74.

BURRIDGE, K. O. L. (1960): *Mambu: A Melanesian Millennium.* London: Methuen.

CHOWNING, A. (1958): Lakalai Society. Ph.D. dissertation, University of Pennsylvania (microfilm).

GOODENOUGH, W. H. (1955): The Pageant of Death in Nakanai. *University Museum Bulletin* (Philadephia), Vol. 19, No. 1: 1943.

GOODENOUGH, W. H. (1956a): Some Observations on the Nakanai. *Papua and New Guinea Scientific Society Annual Report and Proceedings,* 1954.

GOODENOUGH, W. H. (1956b): Residence Rules. *Southwestern Journal of Anthropology,* Vol. 12: 22-37.

GOODENOUGH, W. H. (1962): Kindred and Hamlet in Lakalai, New Britain. *Ethnology,* Vol. 1: 5-12.

GOODENOUGH, W. H. (1963): *Co-operation in Change.* New York: Russell Sage Foundation.

HEES, F. (1915-16): Ein Beitrag aus den Sagen und Erzählungen der Nakanai. *Anthropos,* Vol. 10: 34-64; Vol. 11: 562-85, 861-87.

HOEBEL, E. A. (1954): *The Law of Primitive Man.* Cambridge, Mass.: Harvard University Press.

LAWRENCE, P. (1964): *Road Belong Cargo.* Manchester: Manchester University Press.

LOWIE, R. H. (1920): *Primitive Society.* New York: Liveright.

SCHWARTZ, T. (1962): *The Paliau Movement in the Admiralty Islands,* 1946-1954. Anthropological Papers of the American Museum of Natural History, Vol. 1, Part 2.

VALENTINE, C. A. (1958): An Introduction to the History of Changing Ways of Life on the Island of New Britain. Ph.D. dissertation, University of Pennsylvania (microfilm).

VALENTINE, C. A. (1961): *Masks and Men in a Melanesian Society: The* Valuku *or* Tubuan *of the Lakalai of New Britain.* University of Kansas Publications, Social Science Studies.

VALENTINE, C. A. (1963a): Men of Anger and Men of Shame: Ethnopsychology and Its Implications for Sociopsychological Theory. *Ethnology* Vol. 2: 441-77.

VALENTINE, C. A. (1963b): Social Status, Political Power, and Native Responses to European Influence in Oceania. *Anthropological Forum,* Vol. I: 3-55.

WORSLEY, P. (1957): *The Trumpet Shall Sound.* London: MacGibbon and Kee.

MARIE REAY

STRUCTURAL CO-VARIANTS OF LAND SHORTAGE AMONG PATRILINEAL PEOPLES

ABSTRACT

One point of difference among New Guinea Highlands peoples hinges on whether, and how far, warfare was linked with territorial gains. Among the Kuma of the Wahgi Valley, land conquest was apparently not an issue before European contact. This paper shows how they are now moving to re-form their old phratries, and finding the disposal of clan land useful in political competition between pacified clans. Comparisons are drawn between Kuma and Central Enga, with special attention to availability of land, agnatic descent, recruitment, and marriage.

This paper presents a tentative analysis of some innovations in Kuma society which may be associated with scarcity of land suitable for coffee holdings in certain groups. This is a recent development and, at least by October 1965, few groups seem to have been substantially affected. Nevertheless, the response of a patrilineal people to a novel scarcity of land of a certain type may shed some light on the difficulties in comparing two Highlands societies (Chimbu and Central Enga) which have been chronically short of arable land.

CLAN LANDS AMONG THE KUMA[1]

In discussing land tenure in earlier writings (1959*a*, 1959*b*), I have drawn attention to the abundance of land and the fluidity of the system controlling its use. Since the Kuma did not consider land an important enough asset to fight over, I did not feel it necessary to specify when referring to 'clan territory' that this signified land in which a corporate group had corporate rights. Since I had already stressed the Kuma's eagerness to incorporate non-agnates, I did not feel it necessary to emphasize that gifts of land to individual outsiders never alienated that land from the clan, and that the granting of land to refugee segments of defeated clans (or occasionally to whole refugee clans that seemed unlikely to swamp their hosts) expressed also the hosts' hopes that they might eventually swell their own numbers by absorbing these groups.

Land conquest was evidently unknown among the Kuma, although border-lands between a few pairs of clans belonged definitely to neither and the use of such land by one clan led easily to quarrels over pigs with their neighbours. Inspection of such borderlands by Europeans with a view to purchasing them through the

Administration sparked off what were probably the first land disputes among the Kuma for hundreds of years. In 1953-5 I found no tradition that clans fought over land even in the days before warfare and disease depopulated the arable Wahgi flats and hostilities had divided the phratries. Supernatural sanctions ensured that land conquest could not result directly from martial victory. Sorcery traps (literally 'wooden bones') guarded clan lands from unauthorized occupancy until they rotted, and the clan expressed an intention of returning by renewing them.

GROUP REPRESENTATION IN MODERN POLITICS

About the turn of the century, the Komban clan was routed in warfare, fled eastward from Tombil (a site four miles west of Minj township), and did not find haven until its members reached Gumine in the Eastern Highlands district. They did not renew their sorcery traps and, after these had rotted, the Berebuga and a satellite clan from their northern Anbugka phratry fled from Banz, crossed the Wahgi River, and eventually settled on the old Komban territory.

In 1963 the Berebuga were trying, in common with other clans, to increase their numbers dramatically in order to secure enlarged representation on the Native Local Government Council. When they learned that land was scarce at Gumine and the Komban's title to the territory where they had settled in the last few generations was insecure, they invited the erstwhile refugees to come back and settle with them on the ancestral lands. A suggestion from a patrol officer that the Berebuga should grant a continuous and compact territorial block to the Komban in order to avoid later disputes over individual parcels of land was uncongenial to them since they saw that this would lessen their chances of absorbing the Komban into their own political community. Disputes did occur after the Komban had planted their gardens among those of the Berebuga and the pigs of each group trespassed upon and damaged the crops of the other. In the course of the disputes the Komban learned of the Berebuga's real motive for inviting them back. They responded to this knowledge by becoming ambitious to achieve independent political representation. The Berebuga leaders had been urging the kiaps (Administration officers) and the councillors of other clans that the people of Tombil were numerous enough, since the resettlement of the Komban, to elect two council members instead of one as previously; and they were determined that both councillors should be Berebuga men. Now the Komban luluai expressed publicly his own wish for the people of Tombil to have two councillors, but he specified that one should be Komban. The 'big' councillors, nearly all Konumbuga, agreed that this would be equitable and expressed the opinion that the Berebuga would elect one council member and the Komban another. The local government advisory officer, who was hoping that the two groups would ultimately accept joint representation by a single member, agreed that the people of Tombil could elect two members between them to the new council.

The Minj (South Wall Wahgi) and Nangamp (North Wall Wahgi) Native Local Government Councils had been operating since the end of 1961. At Council meetings in December 1964 resolutions were passed to amalgamate the two into a multi-racial Wahgi Council embracing the entire Middle Wahgi region. Early in 1965 it was well known that the plan entailed reducing the number of councillors holding office. Groups that had been agitating for increased representation on the Minj Council proceeded to try to increase their numbers with redoubled vigour under the threat of being deprived of the representation they now had as soon as the Wahgi Council was established. When two or more groups were required to elect a single member between them, the argument ran, he would represent only the group to which he himself belonged and the other groups would be deprived of representation.

The Komban luluai was well aware that the Berebuga would be voting for candidates of their own and that his group was in danger of not being represented at all, despite the kiap's assurance to the contrary. He responded to this knowledge by asking Mazi, the councillor of a small North Wall Wahgi clan at Kerowil, to make land available to the Komban for renewed resettlement. Mazi realized that his own clan, Baiman, was too small either to merit a separate council member when the amalgamation occurred or to return a candidate for membership in competition with a candidate from a larger clan. He and his clansmen agreed to the Komban settling with them in the hope that the immigrants would be persuaded to accept land that was interspersed with their own, rather than being distinguishable as a territorial block, and would be absorbed into the Baiman for electoral purposes. These negotiations broke down when the Baiman learned that the Komban were intending to insist on a territorial block and had already sent messengers to Gumine to persuade more immigrants to come and swell their numbers. The Komban had also realized the advantages of separate representation.[2]

I have described these negotiations in some detail, not because I am intending to discuss innovations in these particular groups (on whom I have had little opportunity to gather case material) but to indicate the manner in which Kuma see the disposal of clan land as being useful in modern political competition between pacified clans. While the Komban were trying to re-establish themselves as a distinct group large enough to warrant a separate councillor, other clans that had broken apart some generations ago were sending envoys to groups now independently established in the Jimmi and Chimbu regions, urging them to return. A Minj youth gained the approbation of his clansmen by reporting to them that he had told a fellow patient in the native hospital at Kundiawa that the latter and his entire tribe, reputedly short of land, were welcome to come and settle on the rich and abundant lands of his own clan. These moves were being made long after the electoral boundaries for the Wahgi Council were officially settled.

Under the influence of missions and Administration, sorcery traps protecting clan territories from unauthorized occupancy have long been allowed to rot when they have not been deliberately removed. Groups are restrained from squatting on other clans' territories by a realistic assessment of their chances in the judgment of the kiaps, not by a supernatural sanction. A few clans, however, whose traditional territories lay wholly in the higher side-valleys and who have long had permissive usufruct of lower land for pig grazing are trying to establish claims to the lower land on the basis of long uninterrupted residence there, in order to derive a cash income from growing coffee.

Kugika clan, whose members count its failure to warrant a separate council member as a temporary political defeat, began to discuss plans to offset this as soon as the October 1965 elections demonstrated that the larger clan with which they were required to combine, Ngeni-Muruka, could outvote them. The former Ngeni-Muruka councillor, who was re-elected to represent both groups jointly, had already proved to be unscrupulous in his dealings with the smaller clan, and some of the Kugika devised a scheme to secure his dismissal and force a by-election. A parcel of borderland had long been regarded by both clans as part of their territories and, although neither group had any pressing need to use it until the Ngeni-Muruka decided in recent years that it would be suitable for grazing some cattle they had bought, occasionally one group or the other would try to redress some injury done them by the other by urging the Administration to settle the boundaries in their favour. Well aware that the boundaries determined by the Administration on these several occasions supported their own claim to this land, and that the Ngeni-Muruka have never accepted this repeated decision, some Kugika suggested that members of Koimamkup subclan living near this land should engage some of the adjacent Ngeni-Muruka in a dispute over entitlement to it and let the freshly re-elected Ngeniga councillor adjudicate the dispute. Since he could be expected to decide the matter in favour of his own clan, the Kugika would then appeal to the kiap and the councillor would be dismissed for both flouting an administrative decision and showing favouritism toward his own clan. Important leaders of the Kugika told me that they were not encouraging the Koimamkup to proceed in this way because they thought the councillor would realize at once what the Kugika were trying to do.

ANCIENT ENMITIES AND NOVEL NEEDS

The Kuma phratries were originally, according to tradition, territorial groups that waged war upon each other. The North Wall Wahgi people were still organized in tribes that included whole phratries and parts of phratries up to the introduction of administrative control, but the southern phratries had long been fragmented into clans that warred independently with each other and formed alliances that shifted as they contended with different foes. Territorially the phratries were widely dispersed and their only significance at the time of my first fieldwork in the Wahgi Valley appeared to be historical. Traditional intraphratry enmities were continually renewed in ritual.

The aggressive aspects of war-magic had declined considerably even by 1953-5. Few sorcerers waited to sacrifice a pig and smear its blood on their magical material before rattling their spears at or starting a brawl with a hostile clan. The prime function of the war-magic houses had become defence against any aggressive magic an enemy's clan's sorcerers might be using, although whenever an enemy died through illness or accident the clan's most eminent sorcerers strutted and allowed clansmen to credit them with the death.[3]

In 1961 the Roman Catholic mission 'exorcized' the war-magic houses of many clans between Kup (to the east) and Minj, burning weapons and perishable materials and confiscating prehistoric stones that had formerly been used in war-magic. Members of groups that had been taken by surprise and yielded their magical materials expressed anxiety later when they learned that some of their enemies retained magical means of injuring them. One leader who had time to organize his group to resist is said to have asked the missionary rhetorically whether the Australians had let the mission burn their weapons of defence during World War II.

In 1965 the Swiss Evangelical Brotherhood had been urging the Minj people to let them 'exorcize' the remaining war-magic houses. The local government advisory officer, who was concerned with establishing the new Wahgi Council, had asked councillors to consult their constituents about the most desirable way of combining with other groups to elect members representing a larger population. The councillors called meetings, as instructed, and introduced discussions of electoral wards. Each meeting I attended in two clans reached rapid consensus that whilst it would plainly be appropriate for certain other groups to obtain reduced representation it was out of the question for the group directly concerned to have any less than its present representation. The men then removed themselves a little distance from their womenfolk and discussed the matter that preoccupied them currently: whether or not they should allow the missions to exorcize their war-magic; if not, what excuse they could give the missionaries which the latter might accept; if so, whether the Swiss or the Catholics should do it.

The discussions were mostly inconclusive. The idea of the missions exorcizing war-magic houses was attractive because it offered a safe means of removing taboos on sharing food cooked at one fire which had become extremely inconvenient in the circumstances of modern life. The simple ignoring of these taboos would not suffice, since flouting them was believed to invite death. Most adherents of traditional religion expressed the opinion that it would be desirable to get the Catholics to remove the fire taboos, since they did not discourage the performance of the Pig Ceremonial as the Swiss did. Each meeting discussed the feasibility of hiding the more important objects of war-magic while allowing the missions to exorcize the fire taboos along with war-magic of less defensive significance. It was evident that the men generally believed that since the missions were fully determined to exorcize the magic nothing could prevent this from happening.

The attribution of final effectiveness to simple determination came to my attention in another context during 1964-5, which I shall relate here as a digression because of its relevance to land shortage in modern times. Baiman clan had long been settled at Kerowil but had originally been part of a larger group in the Chimbu region that had suffered defeat in warfare and been scattered, some remaining east of Kup while this segment fled to the Middle Wahgi and settled on a vast tract of land that had long ago been depopulated in similar circumstances. In the late 1950s or early 1960s a neighbouring clan was in need of more land after underestimating the amount it required for itself and receiving a large sum of money from the Administration for a tract of its territory. The Baiman made available to this clan a tract of land they themselves were not using and received in return some traditional valuables and a small amount of cash. The other clan planted coffee on this land and by 1964 it appeared that a good income would soon be assured from it. The Baiman now found themselves relatively short of land that was suitable for coffee production. That is to say, both they and some non-agnatic adherents had enough for their own planting but they realized that if they had the other land back they could attract enough new adherents (from clans that were becoming short of coffee land) to develop into a politically important community with increased council representation and money to buy vehicles and increase their influence. Baiman clansmen began to grumble that the land already planted with coffee was really their land, and Councillor Mazi approached the leaders of the other clan with a naïve-sounding proposition. This was that the Baiman should buy back the land for the precise number of valuables and amount of cash that they had received for it. Predictably, the leaders refused. Men of Mazi's clan and some of their wives and relatives told me confidently, however, that the Baiman would certainly obtain the land back in this way because it was rightfully theirs and Mazi was 'determined'.

Late in May 1965 the missions exorcized the war-magic houses in the region of Minj. By early July, persons in different clans who had opposed the decision were reassured by rumours (some founded in fact, and some not) that the choicest weapons and the magical materials crucial for the welfare of the clan had been hidden; that a couple of ancient cassowary bones from a cave up the Minj River had been surreptitiously substituted for the human bones held by one lineage; that only a fragment of a particularly important object had come to light. The fire taboos, however, had disappeared; the only persons still observing them were men whose actual fathers had been killed in battle. By late September, just before the Local Government Council elections, young people whose clans had been traditional enemies had experimented with holding courting ceremonies for each other and youths occasionally visited hoping for assignations; older men who still bore scars from each other's spears were addressing each other face-to-face as 'distant agnate' (*tabi,* literally the tree from which war-shields were made); and rumour was rife that the two worst traditional enemies, Kugika and Kondiga, were shortly going to contribute to each other's marriage payments and were even thinking of ultimately forming themselves into a single clan. In tracing the origin of this rumour, I discovered an innovation which may be a structural co-variant of land shortage among a patrilineal people.

REPATRIATION OF A CLANSMAN

X (Kugika)'s FFW was captured in warfare by the Kondiga, together with her baby son. She lived out her life as the wife of a Kondiga man, who reared her son as his own. The child, X's actual FB, grew up, married, and himself had a son Y who was as old as X (about 48 in 1965) and a daughter who was much younger.

When the Kugika and the Kondiga held peace-making ceremonies at the instigation of the missionaries, X's FBS sought him tearfully. He had been born in Kondiga territory, he said, but the Kondiga regarded him as an outsider because his F, who had been with them from infancy, had been born a Kugika. He himself had displeased the Kondiga by his failure to give his sister to a particular clan (Berebuga) as arranged. The girl had run away to a lover of another clan (Kumnga) and her brother had been unsuccessful in trying to get her back because the kiap's court had insisted that she could marry whom she wished. This had upset the exchange of women between the Kondiga and the Berebuga, and the former told Y that he should have guarded his sister more closely. They began to plant coffee. Their subclan lived up the Minj River, where they had abundant high land but little level ground of good quality suitable for coffee growing. Other subclans living adjacent to the government station had none to spare, since they had sold more and more parcels of land for extensions to the government station during the years before a native coffee industry was established.

When Y's adopted relatives were berating him for failing to dispose of his sister in the desired way, some of them remembered that his father had been born a Kugika and began to jeer at him for being not really a Kondiga at all but a Kugika, one of their traditional enemies. Later, when they found they were short of land for coffee holdings, they told him that they themselves needed the excellent garden land they had granted his father, and they banished him to a less favourable site. Y told X of his pitiful plight, saying that a man without a clan was nothing.

X told him that the Kugika had plenty of land they would be pleased to share with their recovered agnate. As soon as he himself had given the marriage payment for his elder son's Konumbuga wife, he would get his subclan to decide what land to give him initially to plant with sweet potatoes. Later they could grant him some land for planting coffee, but first it was necessary to get him settled with them. When his sweet potatoes came up he could come and settle as a Kugika with his wife, a widow he had inherited from a Kondiga man. (When he had failed to dispose of his sister in the desired way, they had baulked at helping him find marriage payments for a bride who had not been previously married.) Y expressed his intention of acting as if the young man were his own son and contributing to the payment now that he and X were 'true brothers'.

The news of this incident was circulated mainly by youths of both clans who were not aware of the actual relationship of X and Y and of the history of Y's father's separation from his natal clan. Some older men of other Kugika subclans, hearing that the Kodiga and the Kugika were intending to contribute to each other's marriage payments, did not doubt the authenticity of the rumour but said simply that now that the old enemies were 'one fire' it would be logical enough for them to re-form as a single clan. At the time of the Local Government Council elections, some expressed the opinion that if they were to combine with the Kondiga instead of the Ngeni-Muruka they would be able to elect one Kugika councillor along with one Kondiga councillor, instead of the Kondiga themselves having two councillors as already determined. 'The Kondiga are our brothers,' they said. 'We are all Kuma (naming their phratry), whereas the Muruka are only Ngeniga.'

From the time the Wahgi Council had first been discussed and the Minj people had first known that the Kugika were being required to combine with another group instead of having their own councillor, the neighbouring Konumbuga had been urging them to combine with Konumbuga, rather than with Ngeni-Muruka as the kiap had suggested. The Kugika, however, expressed their hope that if they were sufficiently determined not to join with the Ngeniga the kiap would allow them to elect their own councillor as before. The Konumbuga had tried to persuade the Kugika that it would be more appropriate for them to join a clan of the same phratry than an outsider clan. These discussions had not led to agreement, since both the Konumbuga and the Kugika were well aware that combining with a group already large enough (with its adherents) to warrant the retention of three of the six former councillors would be 'coming inside' it (i.e., being politically absorbed by it) and thereby losing their own representation. The idea of combining with a Kuma group rather than with a clan outside the phratry lingered, however, and when a Ngeni-Muruka councillor had been elected to represent the uneasy combination of that clan and Kugika some of the latter followed the electoral team as far as the Kondiga's polling centre in an attempt to vote again in company with their 'distant agnates'.

KUMA AND CENTRAL ENGA

A number of striking differences between Kuma and Enga society may be related to land abundance in the former and land shortage in the latter, especially when some Enga-like innovations can be discerned among the Kuma at a time when various clans among them are growing short of arable land suitable for coffee. The standard ethnographic accounts of the two peoples (Reay 1959a; Meggitt 1965) tend to obscure the similarities between them because of the authors' contrasting emphases on variations from the ideal in the one case and pervasiveness of the ideal in the other. Both Kuma and Enga stress patrifiliation with segmented, named, corporate descent groups and also virilocal residence at marriage. They differ radically in some of the means they use to express this common emphasis. Asterisks in the notations below indicate areas in which Enga-like characteristics have been emerging in a limited way in Kuma society.

Enga	Kuma 1953-5	Kuma 1963-5
(1) short of land	land abundant	some shortage of coffee land*

	Enga	*Kuma 1953-5*	*Kuma 1963-5*
(2)	warred over land	did not war over land but used it as a political tool or lever	(fringe Kuma) retrospective claims to have conquered land*
(3)	over-populated	short of people	one territory overpopulated (through immigration); land disputes in this territory*
(4)	discourage non-agnates	welcome non-agnates for political advantage	continue to solicit settlement by non-agnates despite lesson of (3)
(5)	concern with physical paternity	concern only with social paternity	distinction between social and physical paternity*
(6)	slight incidence of births to unmarried women	no births (but some early pregnancies) to unmarried women	slight incidence of births to unmarried women*
(7)	no war over women	warred over women as potential mothers of agnates	litigation predominantly over women
(8)	some incidence of 'absolute' divorce (women re-marrying into other than their first husbands' clans)	no 'absolute' divorce (levirate operating in divorce as in widowhood)	some incidence of 'absolute' divorce*
(9)	slight incidence of permanent spinsterhood	no permanent spinsterhood	no permanent spinsterhood (though slight incidence of delayed marriage for women)
(10)	men reluctant to marry	men eager to marry	youths try to delay marriage*
(11)	no permanent bachelorhood	some incidence of permanent bachelorhood	some incidence of permanent bachelorhood
(12)	phratries with political functions	phratries without political functions; these attributed to them in remote past	some attempts to re-establish phratries as political entities*

Some kind of pattern is discernible in the sets of traits listed above. The Enga see themselves as being short of land. Since the land immediately available to them is inadequate for their needs, they do not see themselves as being short of people.

They warred over land, which was important to them. The Kuma, on the other hand, have traditionally regarded land as plentiful and not worth warring over. Land conquest was ruled out by supernatural sanctions and does not ever seem to have been contemplated. Patrol officers investigating entitlement to land on the Wahgi flats in 1963-5 have encountered retrospective claims to land conquest in the region of Aviamp (near the borders of South Wall Wahgi and Hagen-type people). In one case I heard about, this was plainly a telescoping of events, with those events omitted that might detract from the group's claim to the rich coffee lands in question. (In the event of the Government's buying the land, the owners could expect to receive enough cash to purchase a profit-making truck and in the event of the purchase falling through they could expect to obtain eventually a sizeable cash income from their own coffee.) The 1955 version: Group A chased Group B from the latter's territory. B dispersed with various segments finding temporary refuge with other groups, but was unable to re-form before the sorcery traps protecting a large part of its territory had rotted. Group A had returned to its own territory after demonstrating its victory over B, but later engaged in warfare with C and was defeated. C routed A and, fleeing from its own territory, this group settled on unused land which B had vacated earlier and had failed to protect by returning to renew its sorcery traps there. Leaders in Group A were expecting to return eventually to their former territory, although various administrative officers and interpreters had tried to convince them that clan boundaries were permanently frozen in accordance with the pattern of settlement found on the Administration's arrival. The leaders' 1965 version was that A had migrated eastward and, finding B occupying this land, had annexed it by conquest, forcing B to flee elsewhere while they themselves settled permanently on B's former territory; they admitted to having fought with B over women, but did not mention the sorcery traps, the time interval between the rout of B and their own settlement there, nor the relation between their war with C (again over women) and their taking up of uninhabited land.

The Kuma see themselves, however, as being short of people. What needed to be defended from foes was not the abundant clan land but the agnatic descent group itself, which could otherwise face extinction. The Wahgi flats, which are now valued so highly, were regarded as undesirable sites for settlement. The typical pattern of settlement on the spurs and foothills between the valley basin and the side-valleys of the ranges was of men's houses hidden in plumes of bamboo and clumps of sugarcane on the points of hills and the highest rims of ridges, with the women's houses exposed and accessible to attack much farther down the slopes. Men who had to live down on the flats were as unprotected as their womenfolk, who were judged to be worth defending only if they were young enough to bear sons. A further reason for finding the Wahgi flats undesirable for settlement was the incidence of disease there (mainly malaria). Nevertheless, the flats were populated within living memory by clans and phratries that have died out. Refugees from these groups (including a whole clan of one extinct phratry) found refuge with others on higher ground. It seems doubtful whether they would ever have settled voluntarily on the lower flats, and indeed I have found no legends that ascribe the origins of particular groups to land lower than the spurs and foothills. Assuming that the groups that perished on the Wahgi flats settled there only when driven from higher ground, it is possible that healthy and defensible land may have been short enough to fight over in the heyday of the phratries which are said to have fought as units in the olden times, much further back than living memory.

The South Wall Wahgi people never fought over land nor ever annexed land by conquest according to the accounts I elicited in 1953-5. They did fight bitterly and often over women, whom they did not value as persons but saw as possible mothers of future clansmen, additional agnates who could defend their group from hostile outsiders and also help to perpetuate it by themselves acquiring women to continue their line. The Kuma saw themselves as being short of people: the more brothers and sons a man had (both in a personal sense and also in a collective sense of clan 'brothers' and clan 'sons'), the greater were his chances of personal survival. Also, with other clans dying out from disease and warfare, the greater were the chances of his clan surviving and even increasing.[4]

Land as a treasured possession of the Central Enga may account for their emphasis on exclusive rights to it and their consequent discouragement of outsiders from settling among them. Land for the Kuma, however, was plentiful enough to be used as a political tool or lever in the practical expansion of descent groups who were out for their own safety and continuance and could therefore afford to incorporate outsiders to help them. Non-agnates were incorporated, and quasi-agnates bred, by a nearly identical process among Kuma and Enga (Reay 1959a: 50-1; Meggitt 1965: 31 ff.). A radical difference between the two is that in Kuma the group took the initiative in attracting and securing non-agnatic adherents and in resisting any tendency on the part of an individual to desert his natal group, whereas in Enga the individual took the initiative in seeking absorption in an exclusive group in full knowledge that his natal clan was only too anxious to get rid of him. This difference is clearly a consequence of relative abundance and scarcity of land. It does not, of course, imply any difference in the 'agnatic emphasis' of the two societies. Given a significant emphasis on agnation (or patrifiliation to named, corporate descent groups) in both, the Enga discourage the admission of non-agnates to land they want for themselves whereas the Kuma see the incorporation of non-agnates and the subsequent assimilation of quasi-agnates as a means of swelling the effective male strength of the clan and fought, not over land, but over women as the potential mothers of agnates yet unborn. I would guess the Enga to be a more courageous people than the Kuma, since they had something to fight for besides themselves. Wahgi Yu (speech) has no word for 'courage', and descriptions of rare courageous acts are marked by a word meaning 'stupid' or 'silly'.

Valuing motherhood as a means of increasing a group of men, the Kuma could not afford to allow women to remain permanently unmarried; nor could they permit women to bear children in circumstances which obscured their social paternity. Meggitt reports a slight incidence of both these features among the Central Enga. In recent years, however, Kuma girls have been able to baulk the men's arrangements for their disposal and to resist being given in marriage unless they themselves find this congenial. In consequence a number of girls have borne children out of wedlock, though they have all married subsequently. The child is accepted, predictably, as a member of its mother's group but when she marries later its domicile and group identification are settled by mutual agreement between the men arranging the marriage. The Kuma have learned (from missionaries and others) the importance most Europeans attach to physical paternity and, instead of maintaining the fiction that a bride in early pregnancy simply looks as if she may be fertile and that her husband is the child's one and only father, they now acknowledge publicly that she is pregnant either to a particular other man or to 'all men'. She is still counted as a useful acquisition to the group. Pregnancy and even childbirth are in no way bars to marriage. The reverse side of the incidence and absence of permanent spinsterhood in traditional Enga and Kuma societies is the contrast between the incidence of permanent bachelors in every Kuma clan community and what may be a total absence of permanent bachelorhood among the Central Enga.[5] If this is so, it may be related to what is evidently a contrast in the practice of divorce in the two societies. Kuma divorce (as distinct from annulment—the termination of marriage before spouses settle down to performing their usual roles)[6] seems to have come about only at the initiative of husbands, whereas Enga women left their husbands more often than the men sent them away. Leaving a Kuma husband did not initiate divorce but simply brought about a temporary separation that made him undertake to correct his fault and get his wife restored to him. A case cited by Meggitt (1965: 151) of a woman returning home because her husband broke her arm while thrashing her is exactly paralleled by a Kuma woman going home in identical circumstances until her husband indemnified her agnates for the injury he had done her and took her back. Similarly, a Kuma woman would not initiate divorce by returning home when her husband failed to make a payment (*ibid.*): her agnates would use her attempt to do so as a ploy to induce the husband to bring his payments to them up-to-date. It is probably as true for Kuma as for Enga that 'Men are able to punish their wives physically when they misbehave, so have little reason to seek divorce. Women cannot use force against husbands who are at fault. They can only desert, or try to induce their own kinsmen to remove them from their husband's control' (*idem*: 152-3). But a woman of the Kuma finds it exceedingly hard to convince her kinsmen that she has left her husband with a good enough cause to make him content to leave the balance of marriage payments with them, and with a good enough cause to make them willing to terminate their own valued association with their affines. In the rare case where they cannot persuade themselves that their own kinswoman was partly at fault (and this involves an admission by the man's clansmen that he was grievously to blame), they insist that he himself settles with them where they can keep a watchful eye on her interests. Although people are agreed that the rules allow a woman to leave a husband who is unusually lazy or brutal and, further, that he has no just claim in such circumstances to a return of the bridewealth he has given, everyone is aware that in the event of his wife's relatives insisting on her remaining with them he will demand the return of marriage payments and, when this is not forthcoming, will take the woman back—if necessary by force. It is probably no exaggeration to say that in traditional Kuma society there was no 'absolute' divorce in the sense of the dissolution of a marriage involving a permanent loss of a woman on the part of a particular clan with which she has habitually performed the role of wife to a member. A woman could be 'divorced' from a particular husband, but not 'absolutely' divorced from his group. A woman convicted of anti-human magic against some member of her husband's subclan is married off to a man in another subclan who needs a wife, rather than being surrendered to another clan, now that the death penalty for witchcraft has been abolished. Considering that both Kuma and Enga have polygyny in conjunction with a high masculinity rate, this difference in divorce practice may help to account for the incidence and absence of permanent bachelorhood in the two societies.[7]

Of the 12 contrasts between traditional Kuma and Enga society listed at the beginning of this discussion, changes have occurred in numbers (2), (3), (5), (6), (8), (10), and (12) in the direction of Enga-like traits in contemporary Kuma society, and these have occurred during the development of coffee as a cash crop with the subsequent high valuation of land suitable for coffee growing and a new Enga-like shortage of land of a particular kind, noted above as '(1)'. I am not suggesting that land shortage has led to the development of these Enga-like traits among the Kuma, apart from (2) and (3) being regionally limited consequences of (1). My list notes no change in (4), and it is true that many clans continue to solicit non-agnates to settle with them on their clan lands in order to obtain political advantage for their groups. Y's subclan, however, mentioned above in 'Repatriation of a Clansman', had plainly acquired an Enga-like exclusiveness and, far from trying to attract new non-agnates to join its ranks, was even pruning itself of birth members who were known to be only quasi-agnates. This was done as a direct consequence of the scarcity of land suitable for coffee growing. The current introduction of tea as a cash crop is likely to have similar consequences, unless a new industry such as timber or nut cultivation can be established on ground not suitable for subsistence agriculture.

The other Enga-like characteristics, however, have appeared in response to other factors. Changes in (6) and (8) have come about through women's ability to have some say in their own disposal by appealing to modern courts and conciliators who insist on recognizing laik bilong meri ('what a girl wants') as a more important principle than laik bilong papa ('what [her] father wants'). A girl may now bear a child without having to marry and give it the blessing of social paternity from birth onward. And if her husband wishes to divorce her she can appeal against the 'leviratic' tradition of being passed on to a clansman and marry into a different clan; she may even sue for divorce on her own account with some hope of success if her husband neglects and ill-treats her. Courts and conciliators existed, of course, in 1953-5 but it is now much easier than it was then for a woman to reach the government station without interference and in the event of the case being heard by interclan tribunal she knows that the councillors have to endorse the kiaps' law of *laik bilong meri,* whereas in 1953-5 the only conciliator to whom she could appeal off the station was the luluai of her husband's (not her own) clan, who would be concerned with preserving the marriage or at least ensuring that she remained married to some member of the clan.

The change in (10)—the decline in the eagerness of youths to marry, and their modern attempts to delay marriage as long as they can—must be attributed to their reluctance to settle down to a provincial life of coffee and pigs and continual indebtedness when there seem to be exciting alternatives offering. Many a youth would prefer to delay marriage until he has acquired enough money (through employment for Europeans, either within the Wahgi Valley or beyond) to pay for his own marriage, contribute generously to those of his age-mates, buy a coffee-pulping machine of his own which he can allow men from other subclans to use for a cash consideration, buy a bicycle which he can use for quick transport for himself and for favours to and sometimes cash return from others, and buy some shorts in the pockets of which he can expect to have loose cash to jangle. Some manage to delay marriage for two years by joining the Highlands Labour Scheme, though others who find employment locally run the risk of receiving, sooner or later, a deputation of their age-mates who have come to take them back to attend to brides who have arrived for them.

The change in (5), the distinction now overtly made between social and physical paternity, whereas previously only social paternity had been publicly acknowledged, has probably been influenced by the dramatic increase in the number of alien contacts both within the Wahgi Valley and outside it and also by the solicitousness of missionaries for the welfare of unmarried girls who appear to be pregnant. The change has some relationship to land shortage, however, as the Kondiga's acknowledgment of Y and his father as Kugika despite uninterrupted residence with their own clan shows.

Finally, the innovatory attempts to re-establish the Kuma phratries as political entities—trait number (12) above—have been a direct response to political dilemmas, not to any scarcity of agricultural resources. Moves to re-establish the phratries would not have been possible without the abolition of traditional enmities that had long divided them. The enmities were formally abolished when the missionaries' removal and burning of war-magic materials were followed by clansmen and former enemies ritually eating food cooked on a single fire, thus lifting, at the missionaries' instigation, the fire and food taboos that had long served to emphasize and perpetuate social separation.

Although the moves to re-form the old phratries were in no way motivated by a shortage of coffee land, I do not believe that the association between politically a-functional phratries and abundance of land in the traditional Kuma system was accidental. If land had been scarce, some kind of 'tribal' organization such as the phratries offered would have been expedient, for the defence of clan territories might have required the setting up of enduring alliances. There is an obvious comparison, which I shall not attempt here, with the tribal alliances of Chimbu, a society that has many Kuma-like structural features but has settled for a system of alliances that transcends phratry affiliations, using or ignoring them as circumstances dictate.

NOTES

1. For 'Kuma' readers may substitute 'Minj' or 'South Wall Wahgi'. I follow here, for brevity and consistency, my earlier adoption of the North Wall Wahgi people's 1953-5 habit of referring to the southerners by the name of their largest phratry. This habit has been discarded.

2. In the elections for the Wahgi Local Government Council in October 1965, the Berebuga and the Komban were included in a single ward but required to return two members. An overwhelming majority (809 of 892) of formal votes were cast for solely Berebuga or solely Komban candidates. The winners on the third count (one Berebuga and one Komban) were the two who gained the highest number of first preferences. If, however, equal weight had been given to the first two preferences in a simple 'first two past the post' count (on the assumption that when a voter knows that two candidates are to be elected he allots his first two preferences to those he wishes to elect) a second Berebuga candidate would have been elected instead of the Komban. This reflects the numerical superiority of Berebuga voting strength.

3. Aufenanger's excellent account (1959) of war-magic houses in adjacent regions may be taken to apply equally to the South Wall Wahgi area (Kup to Aviamp), although his sketchy information on the house belonging to Kondingagɔm subclan of Kobanka clan is wholly inaccurate. At least one lineage (and sometimes more) in each subclan had such a house which had as its guardians the males of one minimal descent line or mat-mat group. Aufenanger's account of the status of the guardians of such houses in the Kobun region of the Jimmi ('The old wardens of the war-magic houses, who used to hold an all-important position, have lost their reputation') does not apply here, since the guardians were only socially important at the time of battle unless they were also war sorcerers, as they sometimes were, and had high status on this account. (The two roles were quite distinct.) All such houses held weapons of historic interest (e.g. shields and spears that had been used successfully in important battles) and the overt function of the war-magic houses (the story told to women and minors) was the storage of weapons. Included as weapons were net bags and leaves containing magical materials individual members of the lineage had obtained from war sorcerers elsewhere. The guardians of one house placed there in 1949 some cartridges obtained during the cargo cult at that time. Relatively few war-magic houses held materials in the form of prehistoric stones or human bones that were judged to be crucially important for the defence of the clan. Many of these materials were chance found within living memory by members of the lineage or by affinal relatives who presented them in great secrecy to help them in extended clashes with their enemies. Some others had been in the possession of the lineage for two or three generations. Aufenanger's statements on 'beliefs' (ibid.) should be treated with caution, since those concerning the identification of stones with ancestors and the distinction between 'male' and 'female' stones are made in the Minj region as purely symbolic statements, not as

statements of belief, and the story of the legendary birds coming at night before a battle was here used simply as a rationale, for the benefit of women and children, for the whistling noises coming from a men's spirit seance. The lively interest taken in the war-magic houses by missionaries of two sects during recent years led to a widely expressed opinion in 1963-5 that human bones in various houses were really the bones of Jesus and that the clan that gathered and protected them would be assured of political eminence both now and when the white people left. The expectation was that Jesus would then be resurrected: land was allotted to him in advance in case he turned out to be a black man, but if he turned out to be white he would summon a helicopter from Mount Hagen and fly back to Heaven. (The white people were to leave their material equipment behind, as had been expected in 1949.)

4. This paper is based on material collected up to late 1965. Subsequent events have confirmed the main trends noted here. Attribution of land conquest has become commonplace in foreshortened accounts of warfare, and a theme of land pressure experienced by expanding populations has been introduced into some of the legends of origin. Candidates for a regional seat on the Wahgi Council have won votes from former traditional enemies by reminding them of common phratry membership, and an attempt was made to pack the election of committee men in one ward with phratry fellows of one small group nominating a candidate.

5. Meggitt (1964, 1965) reiterates that Enga men enter marriage unwillingly and postpone it as long as possible from fear of sexual contamination, but says nothing of the incidence of permanent bachelorhood. In assuming that it may be absent altogether, I follow Bowers (1965: 28), who says of Enga men: 'Finally, however, they do marry (Meggitt, personal communication)'.

6. My earlier discussion of divorce (1959a: 85) is marred by a failure to distinguish between the two. Brides who are driven away by resentful co-wives before they have had a chance to perform the everyday role of wife can hardly be considered to be divorced. Meggitt also fails to make this distinction and there is nothing to indicate whether the Enga woman who was 'driven away by her senior co-wife' (cited as a case of 'jural divorce', 1965: 151) would be properly a case of 'divorce' or 'annulment' in this sense.

7. Cf. Bowers 1965: 29-32. I am not, of course, suggesting this as a full explanation. The Enga situation allows women more mobility between clans but mobility within a single clan-community does nothing to reduce the incidence of permanent bachelorhood in Kuma. Both permanent bachelorhood and absence of interclan mobility for females are due to the high valuation of female fertility which is evidently absent in Enga.

REFERENCES CITED

AUFENANGER, H. (1959): The War-Magic Houses in the Wahgi Valley and Adjacent Areas (New Guinea). *Anthropos*, Vol. 54.

BOWERS, Nancy (1965): Permanent Bachelorhood in the Upper Kaugel Valley of Highland New Guinea. *Oceania*, Vol. XXXVI, No. 1.

MEGGITT, M. J. (1964): Male-Female Relationships in the Highlands of Australian New Guinea. In *American Anthropologist Special Publications*: New Guinea, the Central Highlands (J. Watson, ed.), Vol. 66, No. 4, Part 2.

MEGGITT, M. J. (1965): *The Lineage System of the Mae-Enga of New Guinea*. (M. Gluckman, gen. ed.), London: Oliver and Boyd.

REAY, Marie (1959a): *The Kuma: Freedom and Conformity in the New Guinea Highlands*. Melbourne: Melbourne University Press for the Australian National University.

REAY, Marie (1959b): Individual Ownership and Transfer of Land Among the Kuma. *Man*, Vol. LIX, No. 109.

M. J. MEGGITT

THE PATTERN OF LEADERSHIP AMONG THE MAE-ENGA OF NEW GUINEA[1]

ABSTRACT

Taking as its starting point the problem of achievement-and-ascription in New Guinea societies, this paper focuses on traditional leadership among the Mae-Enga of the western Highlands. Here, followers demand and create leaders rather than *vice versa*. In times of stress, structural oppositions of agnatic segments at various levels discourage the persistence of factions within them by demanding corporate action; but periods of peace afford opportunities for choice, manoeuvring and change in leadership. It is suggested that the composite model based on these two alternating states may be applicable not only elsewhere in New Guinea but also in Africa.

Antiphon
Sempronius: . . . the better part of honour is liberality or openhandedness. It is tarnished by amassing of crude worldly goods, but enhanced to the utmost degree by liberality and magnificence. What profit is there in keeping things that bring one no profit? To use wealth is undoubtedly better than to possess it. How glorious it is to give, and how miserable to receive! And as to act is better than to possess, so the giver is nobler than the receiver . . . some say there is merit in nobility that is based on the deeds and lineage of one's ancestors, but I say there is no glory in reflected light, if a man has none himself.

La Celestina, Act II.

INTRODUCTION

As long ago as 1891 Codrington reported that, although in Melanesia chiefs "never [have] so much importance in the native view as they have in the eyes of European visitors" (p. 46), nevertheless in most of the islands they do have "place and power"; and he examined the institution of chieftainship among societies in the Solomon Islands, the Santa Cruz group and the northern New Hebrides in an attempt to discover the source or support of this power and authority.

His brief but incisive analysis of observations made over a period of twenty-five years led him to conclude that in these small-scale societies the three main props of chiefly status were the control of supernatural powers, of wealth and of retainers. By the first Codrington meant the putative knowledge of techniques of magic and sorcery that were thought to enhance personal *mana*, strike down opponents and enlist the aid of ghosts. Because a chief commonly passed on this information to a kinsman of his choice (usually a son, nephew, or grandson) "a semblance of hereditary succession appeared" (p. 52), although often enough the nominated successor was unacceptable either to the villagers at large, who then selected their own man, or to the leader of a rival clan or faction, who then put himself forward as chief. By control of wealth Codrington meant the ways in which important men, helped by relatives and exchange partners, manipulated supplies of food, pigs and locally defined valuables (such as shell-, mat-, or feather-money) in order to advance themselves and their protégés in the secret societies and clubs that were widespread throughout Melanesia. As Codrington pointed out, ". . . social eminence is maintained by [shell-money] because the moneyed man has his debtor under his thumb, and by the power he has of imposing a loan he can make rising men his debtors and keep them back" (p. 327). In addition, the chief could by those means attract young men ". . . who hung about him, living in his canoe-house, where they were always ready to do his bidding. These fought beside him and for him, executed his orders for punishment or rapine, got a share of his wealth, and did all they could to please him and grow great and wealthy with him" (p. 52). This demonstration that chiefly position in Melanesia was defined in terms of achievement rather than of ascription implies that the incumbent needed constantly to validate his occupancy with successful performance. Codrington recognized this when he said, "The power of a chief naturally diminishes in old age, from inactivity, parsimony, and a loss of reputation . . . In any case someone was ready, it might be by degrees, to take the place of one whose force (*mana*) was waning" (p. 53).

Since 1891 a great many anthropologists have worked in Melanesia (including coastal New Guinea) and, although not all of them have been specifically concerned to examine the institution of leadership, they have built up a relatively extensive body of descriptive material bearing on this topic. By and large their results are compatible with Codrington's original propositions about achievement and chiefly position.

I shall not here attempt to summarize the evidence for this kind of view but instead I direct the reader to the surveys made by Hogbin (1958) and by Sahlins (1963) which bring out clearly the contingent, optative nature of the relationship between leader and follower in Melanesia, such that both parties must recognize and constantly exploit factors of friendship and greed, persuasion and bullying, in their attempts to achieve their own ends. Thus Hogbin remarks, "In the majority of islands this office (of headman) was open to all, and anyone could rise to the top if he displayed the appropriate qualities to an outstanding degree. He had to be a natural leader and organizer of men, to be even tempered, tactful and industrious, and it was advisable for him to have shown resourcefulness and strength in battle. Often a reputation as a sorcerer helped. The procedure to secure advancement was to accumulate wealth . . . [and use it] for the benefit and entertainment of the rest of the people . . . [who] were thus in a permanent state of debt to him and felt obliged to acknowledge him as their superior . . . [but] a headman who ignored the wishes of the community and tried to act arbitrarily was quickly removed" (1958:158-9).

Sahlins, in comparing Melanesian political arrangements with those of Polynesia, also emphasizes the relative precariousness of the Big Man's position. "The attainment of Big Man status is rather the outcome of a series of acts which elevate a person above the common herd and attract about him a coterie of loyal, lesser men. It is not accurate to speak of 'big man' as a political title, for it is but an acknowledged standing in interpersonal relations" (1963:289). But "the personal quality of subordination to a centre-man is a serious weakness in factional structure. A personal loyalty has to be made and constantly reinforced; if there is discontent it may well be severed" (p. 292).

The main difference between the accounts given by Hogbin and by Sahlins, it seems to me, concerns their views of what is likely to cause a Big Man's followers to desert or to rebel against him. Whereas Hogbin implies that a successful leader is most liable to alienate his supporters by becoming overbearing and careless of their moral expectations, Sahlins emphasizes economic discontent in particular as a primary stimulus to defection. He argues that a Big Man, in order to remain widely known, must divert an increasing amount of his followers' resources outside the local community, a deprivation that in time inevitably costs him their support. Although this sequence may occur, I think Sahlins has failed to perceive that generally the more successful a Big Man becomes, the more widely ramified are his exchange relationships and the more wealth (food, pigs, or valuables) flows through him back into the community—that is to say, the gravy-train effect is no less significant here than at Tammany Hall.[2]

However that may be, a survey of the Melanesian literature indicates that in most of these societies, whatever supplementary attributes and skills men exploit to emerge from the ruck, they maintain their positions as leaders and spokesmen by being the most efficient entrepreneurs or managers in their local communities. Moreover, such men tend to take the lead not only in purely economic affairs but also in the whole range of activities that the group considers to be important, whether these concern planning military attacks or negotiating truces, arranging the ceremonial calendar or co-ordinating duties in communal feasts, inaugurating trading voyages or commissioning the performance of magic or sorcery, match-making or mourning. In short, leadership in these societies generally is multiplex as well as achieved.

Nevertheless, as Hogbin and Sahlins note in passing, there are a few Melanesian societies in which the invocation of particular ascriptive requirements more or less limits the pool of potential leaders. In Manam and Wogeo, for instance, only the men of certain families are able to be headmen (Burridge 1960:139; Hogbin 1967:passim), whereas in the Trobriands the system of rank "restricts eligibility to compete for political leadership in any given locality to the members of the highest ranking matrilineal descent group or sub-clan associated with it" (Powell 1960:118; Uberoi 1962:passim). In some of the societies, particularly those along the Papuan Gulf, the status of the leader has become associated with an enduring corporate group and its definition so narrowed that we may properly speak of hereditary succession to office. Thus, in each localized section of a Western Motu clan, "status is ascribed and jural authority vested in a leader who usually succeeds by agnatic primogeniture" and who organizes enterprises connected with the group's most important assets: fishing nets, trading vessels and ancestral rites (Groves 1963: 118). Among the natives of Orokolo Bay the number of hereditary positions of authority is multiplied so that each long-house (or even each half of it) may boast a 'chief', while in the larger Purari Delta communities hereditary village 'chiefs' and village 'priests' may direct the activities of the corresponding officials in the several long-houses (Maher 1960: *passim;* Williams 1924, 1940: *passim*).

Although in these societies the recognition of hereditary succession to offices, however rudimentary these may be, pre-ordains the identities of leaders on specific occasions, in none of the societies (so far as we can tell) is the system all-embracing. Instead, we find operating in conjunction with such ascriptive devices the normal Melanesian pattern of Big Men, managers who through skilful manipulation of wealth and social relationships have created personal followings that help to maintain them in positions of influence. It is common then for the 'hereditary' leaders and headmen to use entrepreneurial competence to augment their 'ascribed' supporters in struggles among themselves and with ordinary (that is, 'non-hereditary') Big Men, while the latter frequently try to usurp the positions of established leaders and found their own dynasties. Unfortunately, in the earlier Melanesian literature, there are relatively few analyses of those societies in which systems of achievement and ascription of power co-exist, so that the ways in which they interact remain something of a mystery to us.

It is with this problem in mind of the balance or interpenetration of achievement and ascription in New Guinea societies that I present here a brief examination of the traditional pattern of leadership among the Mae-Enga of the Highlands of Australian New Guinea.[3]

At first sight the Mae data might suggest that leaders there are to be characterized simply as Big Men, cast in the common Melanesian mould, that is, shrewd and able men who, through the manipulation of traditionally defined valuables, place people in their debt, create *ad hoc* followings or factions, build up networks of exchange relationships and thus temporarily exert influence in their local communities. But further analysis indicates that individual men, no matter how cunning or forceful, do not really achieve the position or reputation of Big Man in this relatively random or arbitrary manner.

On the contrary, certain constraints inhere in the situation to restrict the range of choice, degree of freedom and even the identity of the acknowledged, successful leader—in particular, qualifications imposed by the nature of the social structure. What is significant among the Mae is the way in which the segmentary lineage system can function to pre-define the personnel of the groups of followers even before they possess leaders. That is to say, 'followers' (who are largely allocated in agnatic terms) are the constant; it is they who demand and create leaders, rather than the more usual Melanesian pattern whereby leaders emerge by recruiting followers. A further consequence of this process is the way in which the inevitable structural oppositions of agnatic segments at the various levels of the hierarchy of groups serve to limit the likelihood that politically active and opportunistic factions or cliques will survive within such descent groups.

DESCRIPTION

The Enga, who number more than 100,000, live west of the Hagen Range among mountains that rise from 6,000 to over 11,000 feet above sea level in the Western Highlands District of the Australian Territory of New Guinea.

The culture of the western Enga differs to some extent from that of the eastern Enga. The western people are generally called the Mae and those to the east the Laiapu. Further cultural subdivisions exist within these categories. The largest are the Yandapu and the Mae proper in the west, with some 30,000 people, and the Syaka and the Laiapu proper in the east, also with about 30,000 members. These four regions make up the central Enga, whose population density is considerably higher than that of the surrounding fringe Enga; it averages more than 90 per square mile and in some localities along the upper Lai River is as much as 350 to 400 per square mile.[4]

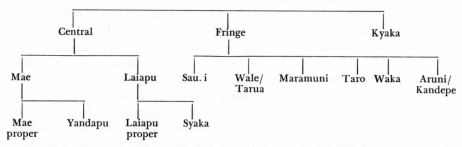

Diagram 1   The distribution of Enga-speaking people

The central Enga are sedentary gardeners who also keep pigs and fowls. Hunting has little significance. The staple crop is sweet potatoes, grown in a system of intensive tillage and supplemented by other root and leaf vegetables. The growth of the more important crops is markedly conditioned by variables such as the altitude, slope, drainage and fertility of the land and the prevalence of frosts. Consequently, a considerable area of central Enga-land is, in terms of the traditional technology and crops, horticulturally useless to the people. Inasmuch as each gardening unit or household needs access to about five times as much arable land as it currently cultivates in order to meet its long-term food requirements, the remaining suitable land of the lower slopes and valleys (the 5,000 to 8,000 feet zone) is subjected to exceptionally heavy population pressures. Intergroup disputes over land are consequently very common and until recently were the major cause of warfare.

The terms Mae, Yandapu, Laiapu and Syaka do not in any way refer to confederate or tribal entities. The members of such a cultural category never in any circumstances assemble as a whole to act together; they have neither a unified political organization nor a centralized administrative authority.

The Mae, like other central Enga, belong to named and localized patriclans that ideally (and usually) are exogamous and politically autonomous. The mean size of the Mae clans (in 1955-57) is 350 members, and the range is from 100 to 1,000 members. Clan territories are on the average between one and two square miles in area and are compact in shape. There are no clan or other villages; the people comprising the clan-parish (that is, the clansmen, their wives and their unmarried children) live in houses dispersed through the clan territory. Men and women have separate dwellings.

Rights to land in clan territories are inherited patrilineally and, ordinarily, should not be alienated from the patriclan. Affines and matrilateral kinsmen may, however, occasionally be granted temporary and specific usufructuary and residential privileges on the understanding that, while they are there, they should support their hosts politically and economically on all occasions. An outsider who hopes to settle permanently with the host clan should demonstrate his good faith by relinquishing claims to patrimonial land in his natal clan territory; but, because of the prevailing demand for land, such men may try to keep up gardens in both territories. These attempts, naturally enough, are likely to anger both the agnates and the hosts of the man concerned; bitter disputes and forcible evictions may follow.

In short, a Mae-Enga man who moves away from his natal patriclan to live elsewhere may condemn himself to a relatively precarious future, one in which his claims to important resources are seriously impaired. In the new community he may become something of a second-class citizen, a mere associate member. It is not surprising, therefore, that in the traditional political system men living away from their fellow clansmen rarely receive the title of kamunggo, Big Man or Organizer and Leader.[5]

The kinds of activities in which a patriclan is corporately concerned may be briefly noted: warfare, both within and between phratries; payments of compensation for the killing of members of other clans and for the deaths of allies; distributions of pigs, pork and other valuables at various stages in the great te ceremonial exchange cycle; and irregularly held rituals to propitiate the ancestral ghosts of the clan.[6]

The phratry, which is the largest patrilineal descent group recognized by the Mae, comprises a number of clans (the mean is 8, the range from 4 to 19) whose putative eponymous founders are thought to be the sons of the eponymous founder of the phratry (see Diagram 2). Normally, the territories of the component clans of a phratry lie side by side along a river valley. The phratry, which is not an exogamous unit, rarely engages in corporate activities. When, however, one clan enacts a ritual for its ancestral ghosts, its fraternal clans have the right to participate. Similarly, a clan seriously threatened by invasion by a clan of another phratry may rally all of its brother clans to its defence. Phratries also occasionally challenge each other to relatively formalized battles or tournaments in order to test their opponents' strength and to enhance their own prestige.

Each Mae patriclan in turn contains several subclans whose eponymous founders are taken to be the sons of the clan founder; the mean number of subclans per clan is 4 and the range is from 2 to 8. The arable land, including fallow, in a clan territory is exhaustively divided among the constituent subclans of that clan. In many cases, the land-holdings of the subclans interpenetrate and their houses are scattered seemingly at random; in others, however, the subclan lands and houses may be sharply separated and the boundaries clearly marked. The latter condition is generally a sign of population pressure and land shortage within the clan, a situation likely to lead to clan fission or splitting.

The activities that concern the subclan are the holding of mortuary feasts for deceased members and the exchanging of valuables with their matrilateral kinsmen, as well as making compensatory distributions of valuables to the matrilateral kin of members who have been ill, injured, or insulted. Also, the purificatory ceremonies carried on in seclusion by bachelors are generally organized on a subclan basis.

The sons of the subclan founder are regarded as the eponymous founders of the constituent patrilineages, of which there are on the average 2 per subclan; the range is from 1 to 4. As before, the land belonging to the subclan is exhaustively divided among the patrilineages, whose plots and houses almost always intermingle.

Although the members of the patrilineage are involved with other groups in the arrangement of marriages and the accompanying public prestations of brideprice and return gift, the patrilineage is in other respects a quasi-domestic grouping that keeps its affairs to itself. The other situations that particularly concern the patrilineage are the provision of help to fellow members in garden cultivation and in house building.

Finally, to round out this description of Mae social structure, mention should be made of the families that make up the patrilineage group. The mean number of families per patrilineage is 7; the range is from 1 to 14. The land of the patrilineage is shared among all the heads of families in that patrilineage. Even though spouses reside in separate dwellings (the men's houses having a mean of 5 occupants each), the elementary or nuclear family remains the important hearth group. It is the basic unit in domestic economy, including gardening and pig-raising, and provides the actors in the rituals intended to propitiate domestic ghosts. The family head may also represent and act for all of his dependants in public distributions of wealth at the patrilineage, subclan, or clan level.

ARGUMENT

Even so brief a sketch of Mae society indicates that its members are constantly caught up in a range of activities of varying complexity, many of which demand considerable co-ordination of the actions of the participants. In addition,

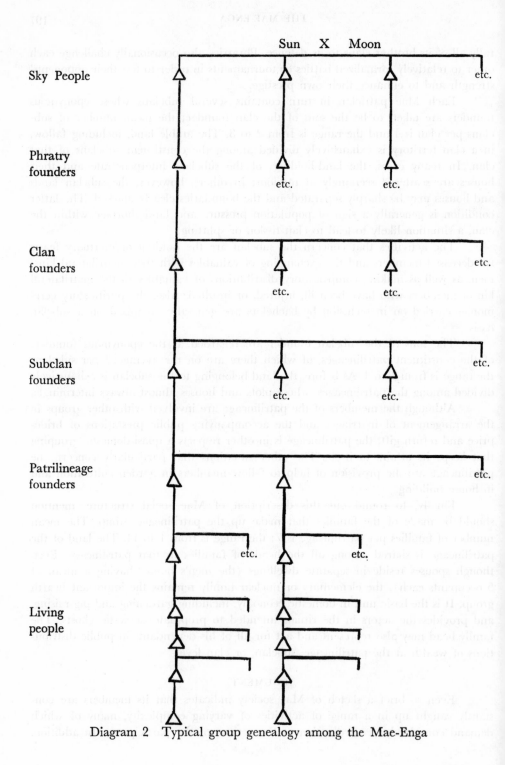

Diagram 2 Typical group genealogy among the Mae-Enga

the same situations frequently generate intragroup disputes that, in the interests of technological efficiency, economic advantage, or simple political survival, require settlement or compromise. Obviously the daily life of the Mae has ample room for leaders who not only can skilfully organize their fellows but also can arbitrate among them.

Moreover, it is plain that on most occasions the definition of the personnel of the appropriate action groups is consistent with the hierarchical arrangement of the patrilineal descent groups. That is to say, clansmen fight wars, pay compensation for homicide, celebrate the *te* exchanges, propitiate the ancestors; subclansmen stage mortuary feasts and distributions, indemnify matrilateral relatives; patrilineage men build houses, co-operate in gardening, organize marriage presta-

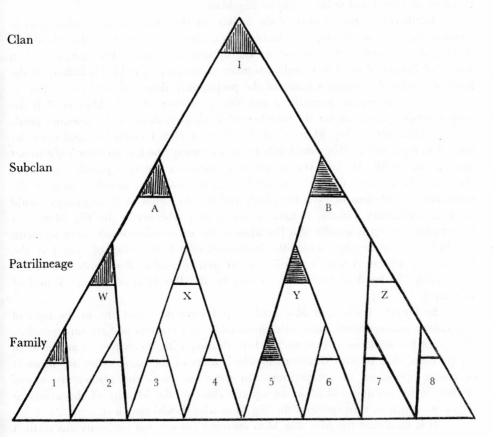

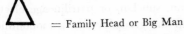 = Family Head or Big Man

Diagram 3 The formal structure of Mae leadership

tions. Given this social division of labour, leadership among the Mae might perhaps be regarded merely as an ascriptive function of the segmentary lineage system.

To some extent this is so. The recognized leader or Big Man of a particular segment in the agnatic hierarchy finds his 'power base' primarily among the members of that segment and not elsewhere because, in terms of the Mae ideology of descent-group definition, outsiders cannot legitimately be obliged or expected to provide the corporate support he needs. Thus, in Diagram 3, the head of a family No. 1 in patrilineage W cannot command the aid of members of other families in the patrilineage unless he is also the acknowledged Big Man of the latter. Similarly, the Big Man of lineage W cannot command other members of subclan A unless he is also the Big Man of A, and the Big Man of subclan A cannot command other members of clan I unless he is also its Big Man.

Furthermore, the identity of the activity or the situation in question may, in terms of the popular ideology, be invoked to define the segment(s) that should be concerned in it and, hence, to specify the appropriate leader. For instance, when a man of lineage Z of clan I weds a woman of another clan II, his father, as the head of his family, arranges many of the preliminary details of brideprice; but, as marriage prestations are normally a patrilineage matter, the Big Man of Z is the proper public spokesman for the members of Z vis-à-vis those of the woman's patrilineage. Although the Big Man of subclan B or of clan I could be (and often is) invited to represent Z, this would only be as a courtesy; he has no clear right to act thus at this point. If, however, negotiations between the two patrilineages meet obstacles, the ensuing dispute can quickly expand to bring in other men of the superordinate subclans or even the clans, and the Big Men of these groups should enter as arbitrators. Finally, it may be noted that whoever is the Big Man in a higher order group is usually also Big Man of the successively lower order segments of which he is a member. Thus, the individual who is Big Man of clan I is also Big Man of subclan A and of patrilineage W and is head of the family No. 1; and analogously the head of family No. 5 may be the Big Man of lineage Y and of subclan B.

So far, the features of Mae leadership I have described are, in the light of segmentary arrangements, eminently predictable and correspondingly uninteresting. The point to emphasize is that we are here dealing with the system in action or in compression, that is, with situations in which units of the same order are in overt or covert opposition or competition. On these occasions the segmentary system defines, in an unequivocal idiom of agnatic descent, the identity of the actors as followers, which in turn specifies the Big Men who should now lead.

It is then that the Mae Big Man exercises his greatest authority (as distinct from mere influence) as the acknowledged representative of his group. The individual member, on the other hand, has at such times little or no freedom of choice; he must support whatever course of action his clan, subclan, or patrilineage elects to pursue. That is to say, on these occasions when the group acts as a monolithic unit in opposition to other, like groups, there is no room for internal factions or cliques. In a peculiarly panglossian fashion the current leader is the best possible leader—for now.

But if we ask how, in a system of segmentation expressed in terms of uni-lineal descent, non-hereditary leaders emerge or are replaced, a rather more interesting ethnographic situation appears. We are now concerned with the system 'at rest' as it were, during the periods of peace, relaxation, or decompression, when segments are not obviously in opposition. These are the times when individuals have much more freedom in choosing whom they will support with valuables or services or whom they will patronize. Now the structural equivalent of factions may operate briefly within lineage segments; now men may extend their dealings with non-agnates. It is through these kinds of activities that leadership may be confirmed or it may change.

Let us look first at the situation within the agnatic unit at a given hierarchical level. At any time there is in this group not only the Big Man who is its recognized leader but also the Big Men and heads of its component units.[7] The more ambitious of these, by volunteering help or patronage in situations that do not specifically concern them, may take every opportunity to persuade their fellows of their skill and suitability as potential leaders. Thus (returning to Diagram 3), the Big Man of patrilineage Z may contribute substantially to brideprices paid by men in lineage Y, or the Big Man of subclan B may establish a series of obviously favourable *te* exchange relationships with men in subclan A. In such ways lesser Big Men can announce to their fellow agnates their intentions of supplanting the current leaders of Y (and hence of B) and of A (and hence of I) respectively. At the same time members of the corresponding segments who have for any reason become dissatis-fied with the leadership offered on earlier occasions by the existing Big Man of B or of I may actively solicit the advances of the would-be usurpers and may use them to signal their own withdrawal of support.

So, whereas the individuals in periods of war or active intergroup competition have little choice but to back the Big Man currently in power as the representative of their group or segment at any level, they can subsequently act in times of peace or relaxation to manoeuvre another Big Man of a parallel, lower order segment into an advantageous position. Then, by the time the next round of intergroup opposition occurs, the new man may be accepted as the proper leader of the larger unit.

An interesting consequence of this technique is that an outgoing or declining Big Man is not usually replaced by a close agnate, such as a man of his own patri-lineage. Instead, the position tends to oscillate among the segments within the superordinate unit. For instance, in Diagram 3, the successor to Big Man I almost certainly will not be a man of patrilineage W and probably will not be a member of subclan A. Most likely, Big Man B, if he is able and not too old, will be the new clan leader, while the odds favour Big Man X as the new leader of A.[8] Clearly, if this process of oscillation operates generally within the Mae clans, it could, by emphasizing the oppositions of the segmentary system, be a significant factor in preventing the emergence of any chiefly lineages of the Polynesian kind within the localized descent group; and this presumably would make the development of 'conical' clans unlikely.

Although this kind of shifting of the positions of incumbents and aspirants seems to be a perennial process, it is nonetheless a gradual, almost imperceptible affair. In the ordinary way a Big Man, particularly if he is the leader of a subclan or of a clan, may maintain his place for as long as a decade or more. This relatively slow turnover of the occupants of these statuses is in large measure a function of the effectiveness of the selection process itself.

Most aspiring Big Men are tested so often in the course of their careers that those who survive the initial weeding out go on to be shrewd and efficient representatives of their groups; once they are in control, their fellow members generally have little reason to be dissatisfied with the choice—at least, not until advancing years and illness disable the incumbent. On the other hand, the expectations of the group members naturally exert a steady pressure on the current Big Man to continue to validate his position by demonstrating his qualities as orator, planner, arbitrator, negotiator and exchange agent, not only on occasions of intergroup opposition but also when peaceful conditions obtain. It is in this context that the network of extra-group and extra-agnatic connections of the Big Man is significant.[9]

That is to say, the Big Man, in order to meet the demands and to hold his position, needs to draw on support, including wealth, not simply from his clansmen but also from various outsiders—from his non-agnatic cognates, from his affines and even from those unrelated men who are his *te akali,* partners in ceremonial exchange cycles. Thus, the Big Man has to be able to demonstrate to people who are not his clansmen that, in certain situations which do not jeopardize the welfare or the ends of their own agnatic groups, it is in their interests as individuals to back him economically and politically. This means that any man, in times of 'peace' for his own clan or subclan, is largely free to choose those of his extra-clan relatives or partners to whom he will give support or those from whom he will accept favours.[10]

An important characteristic of the acknowledged Big Man, then, is that not only do his agnates continue to support him in peace as well as in times of conflict but also other people outside the clan commonly treat with him, because he has previously shown that he can manipulate credit arrangements in the total network of economic and prestige transactions to the advantage of anyone who has invested valuable or services through him. The 'profit' in pigs, pearlshells, or prestige which returns to such extra-clan investors through the agency of the Big Man he can, and does, translate into further obligation on their part. The next time his own clan is likely to be embroiled in warfare or competitive prestations, the Big Man may call on these outsiders, albeit on an individual basis, for military or material contributions.[11]

Thus, the men of a clan try to exploit the opportunities offered by times of peace and relaxation and by the talents of the Big Men they have selected in order to secure for their group a high reputation and a commanding position in the universe of ceremonial exchanges. If the clansmen are successful in this, several important consequences follow. The clansmen believe that their actions are pleasing to the ancestors of the clan; therefore (*sic*), ghost-caused calamities are less likely to occur and to this extent the future seems more secure. Self-confidence and group solidarity stand high. The wealth that passes through the hands of their Big Men into the clan, together with the expansion of their credits, enables the men to acquire more wives. So more children are born to the clan, the daughters of which will bring in more brideprice. In addition, all these marriages create more affines and lead to more exchanges of valuables; hence they furnish wider fields of operation for the Big Men. The circulation of wealth speeds up and credit expands. This in turn enables the Big Men to create more debtors abroad, and more extra-clan individuals are motivated to provide economic and military aid to the clan in order to protect their investments. Other clans, which are potential enemies, recognize this and are less likely to launch attacks on this group, a respite that in turn gives it more opportunities to pursue the same course of activities.

In short, nothing succeeds like success—but only up to a point. The spiralling process as it involves a particular descent group carries in it the conditions for its own change. Given the ecological situation of the Mae-Enga clans, the increase in group size that follows or goes with such success generally builds up the pressure on land resources. Almost inevitably a critical point is reached where the expanding clan (whatever internal segmentary changes it may be experiencing) has to attack its neighbour(s) to secure more arable land.

Invasion is always a risky operation and miscalculations are common. The aggressors may be totally defeated and dispersed, so that their clan no longer exists as a social entity. The individual survivors can only hope to find refuge with relatives in other clans, on whose bounty they will henceforth depend as they live as attached members of the clan parish. Or, allowing that the invaders are able to occupy some or all of the coveted land, they may lose so many men, including current or potential Big Men, that their position in the exchange system becomes seriously and permanently weakened. In addition, they are also obliged to offer compensation for any allies who have been killed while helping them, as well as to make restitution to the matrilateral kin of their own casualties.

Even if the invasion is wholly successful and the attacking force loses few of its members, it has still secured only a postponement of events. The military victory further enhances the prestige of the clan, the expanding credit of the group attracts still more women who produce more children, and the population growth of the clan is even more likely to outrun the rate at which the needed arable land can be acquired. In one way or another the clan splits to form two or more smaller clans, each of which has to begin anew the process of selecting suitable leaders and of building up its position in the network of exchanges and military standoffs. Often enough, the new units are too small and too weak to survive the external pressures.

CONCLUSION

Essentially my argument has been that a simple synchronic account of leadership among the Mae-Enga is inadequate. Only a diachronic analysis of the data reveals the full complexity of the pattern. Within the life history of any given clan and its subordinate segments, we must recognize that there is a more or less regular and predictable alternation of conditions defining the form of leadership at any time.[12]

On the one hand, there is a condition of diastole, a period when an extended network of relationships is significant. This is a time of relative peace and relaxation within the group and *vis-à-vis* other groups, during which men set up fairly free, contractual, dyadic relationships of exchange and aid with each other, including non-agnates. It is then that aspiring Big Men try to improve their positions, while incumbents strive to maintain their own. At the same time, their fellows can also work to unseat or to confirm them as leaders. In short, this is the period in the cycle when all the observed events are most compatible with the usual 'Melanesian' or Big Man model of leadership.

But economic and political conditions, and through them demographic conditions, do not remain stable for each group. Diastole gives way to systole. The expansive, relaxed period is succeeded by (and in part contributes to) a state of opposition, or actual conflict, between segments, especially between clans. Situations of segmentary opposition demand corporate activity and support. The free dyadic relationship of Big Man and partner is replaced by the constrained, obligatory relationship of group leader and follower. The situation of stress or compression now defines in agnatic terms the identity of the action group and hence confirms the authority of the leader. Now an 'African' or segmentary model is appropriate.

I wonder how widespread is this condition of alternating systole and diastole? I suspect that the composite model I am proposing will be valid elsewhere—not only in other parts of the New Guinea Highlands or even of Oceania, but perhaps also in sub-Saharan Africa.[13]

NOTES

1. I undertook fieldwork in the Highlands of New Guinea in 1955-57, 1960 and 1961-62 under the aegis of the Research Committee and the Department of Anthropology of the University of Sydney. I thank the University of Sydney for its financial support. I am also most grateful to my colleagues Roy Rappaport and Marshall Sahlins for their critical comments on this paper, some of which I have tried to incorporate in the final draft.

I must emphasize that I am here concerned simply to suggest an argument about Mae-Enga leadership, not to present a detailed ethnography of the institution. The field evidence available to me to document the latter would fill a book—a long one, which one of these days I may even write.

2. It may be that here I am not doing full justice to the complexity of Sahlins's argument; much turns on what each of us takes 'economic' to include.

3. It is important, as Sahlins has reminded me, to recognize clearly a possible ambiguity in the use of the terms 'achieved' and 'ascribed'. That is to say, in

some contexts in the literature the terms may refer simply to the manner in which potential incumbents enter given social positions; in other contexts they may be taken to indicate qualities or characteristics of the positions themselves, as in 'achieved/personal/informal' and 'ascribed/general/official'. Compare Sahlins 1963: 295.

4. Compare C.S.I.R.O. (1965) and McAlpine (1966).

5. See Meggitt 1965a:39 ff. for data. I should point out that, in the present paper, I am not writing about those men to whom the Mae occasionally refer as *kamunggo* merely because they are active warriors, killers of enemies of the clan and clever at setting ambushes. Such men are rarely the true *kamunggo*, who plan military strategy and direct tactics from behind the lines. Indeed, many Mae believe that the very quality of unreflecting violence that distinguishes a man in battle may make him a great nuisance at other times; they echo Clemenceau in arguing that the fruits of war are too important to be left in the hands of warriors.

6. For more details see Bulmer (1960), Bus (1951), Elkin (1953) and Meggitt (1957, 1958, 1965a, 1965b).

7. Mae terminology distinguishes between the 'really' Big Man (*kamunggo erete, kamunggo andaiki*) and the 'mere' Big Man (*me kamunggo, kamunggo kore*), that is, between the acknowledged and powerful leader and the aspiring or potential leader, between the clan leader and the subclan or patrilineage leader. It is the former who is *sauwu pinggi,* the first in order or the first in the line. We could perhaps call such a Big Man the *maximan,* with maximanic as the corresponding adjective.

8. Something of this logic carries over into the post-European contact situation. Thus, if subclan A produces the luluai (the official Administration representative) of clan I, his tultul (official lieutenant) will most probably come from subclan B. If the latter then succeeds as luluai of I, the new tultul will be a man of subclan A.

9. The difference between the Big Man and the ordinary man is very clear in this respect. Thus, of two Big Men I knew at one time, one had 146 *te* exchange partners, representing 18 clans, in his network, while the other had 49 partners from 10 clans in his. Compare these leaders with a sample of 12 other men whose *te* networks averaged only 21 members each, representing 5 clans. The significance of Big Men as channels along which wealth flows in and out of the clans is also apparent in the following figures. In 6 cases of homicide compensation paid by clans, 108 men gave 325 pigs; more than half of these pigs (183) were donated by only 21 men, mainly Big Men. Similarly, in 4 cases of compensation received by clans, 119 men were given 273 pigs; 120 of these pigs came in through the hands of only 18 men.

10. I want to stress here the temporary nature of, and the self-concern apparent in, such relationships. That is, we are dealing with an *ad hoc* consortium, the short-term co-operation of several interests to effect a common purpose. Perhaps a better analogy is the Sicilian *consorteria,* a loosely organized regional network of *mafiosi,* in which the head of the most powerful *cosca* or local coalition is dominant for the time being.

11. Although the Mae hold the Clausewitzian view that military action is simply another way of extending economic, political and even diplomatic pressures in the arena, they see that this extension is a matter for agnatic groups as such, especially clans. In this the Mae differ from, for instance, the Swat Pathans, among whom "the activities of (political) groups are discussed in terms of the actions of

their leaders" (Barth 1959:71). For the Mae the reference is always to 'our clan' or 'our subclan', never to 'my Big Man' or 'our Big Man'.

12. Does this oscillation inhibit the development among the Mae of any significant ritualization or sacralization of the status of the Big Man, the absence of which in turn facilitates the alternation? Note, too, that the Mae ritual expert, like the noted warrior, is rarely a Big Man. Compare this state of affairs with that in the Trobriands (and in parts of Polynesia) where the chiefly status is highly ritualized and stably defined.

13. Experts in systems analysis will, of course, have no difficulty in perceiving that here I am dealing with a larger or basic feedback system (the life cycle of the descent group) with which is integrated a lesser feedback in the form of the diastole-systole epicycle. No doubt some systems buff could reduce all of this to an elegant flow chart—I wish him joy of it.

REFERENCES CITED

BARTH, F. (1959): *Political Leadership among the Swat Pathans.* London: Athlone Press.
BULMER, R. N. H. (1960): Political Aspects of the Moka Ceremonial Exchange System among the Kyaka People. *Oceania,* Vol. XXXI, No. 1.
BURRIDGE, K. O. L. (1960): *Mambu: A Melanesian Millennium.* London: Methuen.
BUS, G. A. M. (1951): The Te Festival or Gift Exchange in Enga . . . *Anthropos,* Vol. XLVI, No. 2.
CODRINGTON, R. H. (1891): *The Melanesians.* Oxford: Clarendon Press.
C.S.I.R.O. (1965): *Lands of the Wabag-Tari Area, Papua and New Guinea.* Melbourne: Land Research Series No. 15.
ELKIN, A. P. (1953): Delayed Exchange in the Wabag Sub-District . . . *Oceania,* Vol. XXIII, No. 3.
GROVES, M. (1963): Western Motu Descent Groups. *Ethnology,* Vol. II, No. 1.
HOGBIN, I. (1958): *Social Change.* London: Watts.
HOGBIN, I. (1967): Land Tenure in Wogeo (1939). In *Studies in New Guinea Land Tenure* (I Hogbin and P. Lawrence, eds.), Sydney: Sydney University Press.
McALPINE, J. R. (1966): *Land in the Wabag Sub-District, Territory of Papua & New Guinea.* Division of Land Research Technical Memorandum 66/8. Canberra: C.S.I.R.O.
MAHER, R. F. (1961): *New Men of Papua.* Madison: University of Wisconsin Press.
MEGGITT, M. J. (1957): Mae Enga Political Organization. *Mankind,* Vol. V, No. 3.
MEGGITT, M. J. (1958): The Enga of the New Guinea Highlands. *Oceania,* Vol. XXVIII, No. 4.
MEGGITT, M. J. (1965a): *The Lineage System of the Mae Enga of New Guinea.* Edinburgh: Oliver & Boyd.
MEGGITT, M. J. (1965b): Mae Enga Religion. In *Gods, Ghosts and Men in Melanesia* (P. Lawrence and M. J. Meggitt, eds.), Melbourne: Oxford University Press.
POWELL, H. A. (1960): Competitive Leadership in Trobriands Political Organization. *Journal Royal Anthropological Institute,* Vol. 90, Part 1.
ROJAS, Fernando de (1499/1964): *La Celestina.* (The Spanish Bawd: J. M. Cohen trans.) Harmondsworth: Penguin Books.
SAHLINS, M. D. (1963): Poor Man, Rich Man, Big Man, Chief. *Comparative Studies in Society and History,* Vol. V, No. 3.
UBEROI, J. P. S. (1962): *Politics of the Kula Ring.* Manchester: Manchester University Press.
WILLIAMS, F. E. (1924): *Natives of the Purari Delta.* Port Moresby: Anthropology Report No. 5.
WILLIAMS, F. E. (1940): *Drama of Orokolo.* Oxford: Clarendon Press.

PAULA BROWN

THE CHIMBU POLITICAL SYSTEM[1]

ABSTRACT

The current Chimbu pattern is one of dispersed settlement and land-holding, easy individual mobility and tolerance of divided loyalties, especially within the tribe. Structurally, this is a segmentary system in the form of a patrilineal mechanical model, but genealogies show many inconsistencies. Taking war or hostility to strangers as a pervasive feature of highland New Guinea, this paper sees group cohesion as resting on intergroup rivalry and a common interest in self-protection. Two kinds of leadership are indicated (war-leaders, and 'managers'), both lacking in continuity. A table lists the main units in thirteen New Guinea Highlands societies.

The Chimbu are a New Guinea Highlands people. Their traditional home is in the centre of the Chimbu River valley and from there they claim to have spread in all directions, but farthest to the south and west. In 1933, at the time of discovery, people speaking the main Chimbu dialect of the Central Language Family were as far west as Nondugl in the middle Wahgi, south to the Wahgi and at a few places across it, east of Mt. Kerigomna, north of Iwam pass and north of the Bismarck Mountains. At their farthest extent, they mingled with other peoples: to the south and west, people of the Central Language Family, and to the north and east, people of the East Central Language Family of the East New Guinea Highlands Stock (Wurm 1961). In this expansion, the Chimbu language has often dominated. A language spoken mostly on the eastern bank of the Chimbu River has almost disappeared, and some of the Wahgi valley people now speak the main Chimbu dialect rather than another which they spoke previously.

In the earlier reports, Chimbu was often called 'Kuman', meaning south and west. Now 'Chimbu' is generally accepted by both natives and Europeans, and often applied to Central Highlands people speaking other languages.

Directional and relative altitude terms are often used by Chimbu to refer to aggregates of tribes above, to the west, to the south, etc. of the speakers. Nowadays Local Government Councils include populations of ten thousand or more. But traditionally, the largest political unit was the tribe, a named group occupying a distinct territory, holding pig ceremonies and occasionally other large ceremonies at one time and sometimes acting as a war unit.

New Guinea Highlands people have been the subject of no little research and speculation in recent years. As I see it, three of the subjects of discussion and disagreement are of relevance to the political organization.

1. The introduction of sweet potatoes as the staple crop cultivated under a form of intensive agriculture is assumed to have brought about rapid population expansion of the Highlands peoples during the past 300 years (Watson 1965). Sweet potatoes reached several parts of Polynesia before European explorers began to spread American and European plants to the Pacific Islands. But sweet potatoes are believed to have been introduced to the western Pacific by Spanish and Portuguese explorers in the 17th century and to have reached New Guinea from the Philippines. The process by which they became the main crop, cultivated in the New Guinea Highlands by such special methods as ditching, tilling, mounding, composting, etc. remains uncertain. Sweet potatoes now provide about 90% of the diet of Highlanders and it is difficult to conceive of the dense population of Chimbu without them. However, new archaeological evidence indicates that the ditching techniques now used for the predominantly sweet potato agriculture have existed in the Wahgi valley for about 2,000 years (Jack Golson, personal communication). It is thus likely that the Highlands has supported a large population for a considerable period of time. Chimbu traditions of fighting, expansion, migration and the whole pattern of movement and settlement support the hypothesis that the population has increased, but the early phase of this may pre-date the dominance of sweet potatoes. Such demographic data as are available show little population increase today (Brown and Winefield 1965).

2. The basic social units in the New Guinea Highlands are quasi-unilineal groups in which the incorporation of non-agnatic kinsmen and affines is easy and frequent. Group ideology is nearly everywhere of patrilineal descent with phratries, clans and their segments. Genealogies are rarely precisely kept. The segment called a 'patrilineage' by some authors discussing Highlands people (Berndt 1962; Meggitt 1965; Newman 1965; Read 1959, 1965; Salisbury 1956, 1962) usually has no inclusive genealogy. For the smallest significant group, in the Central Highlands variously called subclan section, subsubclan, men's house group (Brookfield and Brown 1963; Reay 1959; Strathern 1966), there is a general claim that the men are all interrelated as 'one-blood' or 'father-son'. But not all the men who reside with the group and/or participate in its activities claim to be agnatic descendants of the group's founding ancestor. Non-agnatic kinsmen and affines with their families are commonly incorporated in these small groups. Such genealogies as are known account for only part of the members of a clan segment. In Chimbu, while the closest patrilineal kin are known by a genealogy extending to the fathers or grandfathers of present day adults, the connection between this small genealogy and others is not known by most people.

3. New Guinea Highlanders combine in larger political units than those found in most other parts of Melanesia, but there was no centralized authority in these groups nor any organized procedures for internal control. The Highlanders are

notable for being quick to fight with people and groups outside their localities, if not also within them. There is no regular mode of succession to the prestige position of Big Man. Leadership of larger groups is achieved by wealth and success in the exchange system, oratory and sometimes in fighting. Followers outside the group of close agnates must be attracted by the leader from amongst his kinsmen and affines and those of his clan or segment. But the leader cannot coerce his followers, and only succeeds through popular support.

EXPANSION OF THE CHIMBU PEOPLE

While no archaeological work has yet been done in Chimbu, there is evidence of their expansion over recent centuries. All Chimbu agree that the traditional home is in the Chimbu Valley at Womkama. The central and upper Chimbu valley has the densest population today—over 350 per square mile (Brookfield and Brown 1963). The traditions of nearly all tribes and groups trace their origin to this home and recount a number of pauses, settlements, fights, removals and recombinations of groups taking them to their present territories. The traditions are rich in local detail, describing the planting of trees, the use of ceremonial grounds, cemeteries, battlegrounds, and building of shelters and houses.

Place names and songs commonly refer to these events in the past: the persons or groups who were there and/or the events which took place, the plants which were grown and so on. Places will be named after, for example, a spot where a girl of Singauga subclan stopped, a rock in the former territory of the Bandi, a place where members of Komukngaumo were defeated, where a bamboo was planted. The symbolic correspondence of names is complex—animals, birds and plants are common names for persons and places. Further, group names are often personal names with a suffix meaning line or descendants. Thus Chimbu things, places, persons and groups are associated and interrelated by their names. Group names are often joined into a pair to indicate alliance.

There is a common form to the traditional tale of origin of a Chimbu tribe as told by one of the leading older men. The several elements are not always present, but the general form is this: At Womkama, there were a man and his wife. They had no fire to cook food, no holes for their mouth, nose, ears, vagina, etc. Then a man came. He showed the woman how to make fire and made holes for her mouth, nose, ears and vagina. When the husband discovered this he was angry. They fought. One of the men left, the other man remained with the woman. This tale accounts for the origin of certain basic physiological and cultural characteristics of the Chimbu, the propensity to fight over women and property and the need for the defeated to seek a new home.

The origin story is only vaguely linked to traditions of fights and movements in recent history. These are often specific as to the source of the quarrel and nearly always name places and individual persons and groups involved. More recent traditions of migration frequently detail the route and stopping places with additional events and encounters with other groups. But Chimbu are very imprecise about quantities and time: it was never possible to obtain a good estimate of the number of people involved in any event or to date any event before living memory. The fights and movements during an informant's lifetime could be only approximately dated, as ages of persons can only be estimated. Even the dates since 1933 when the first patrol went through Chimbu are uncertain. In their expansiveness, the Chimbu are inclined to say "the Gena fought" if only a single man of Gena tribe was present.

We have a great deal of evidence that groups have grown and segmented. Exogamous groups have divided in two; individuals, families and small groups have been incorporated into host groups and alliances have formed between groups. With these several mechanisms for growth and change in group composition, it is difficult to estimate the size of the originally migrating group. Traditions of movement to the south and west of the Chimbu valley link nearly all the present inhabitants to the traditional place of origin through a series of stops and realignments. Often a group's name links it to a group still in the valley. In general, groups move distances of several miles and retain few ties to past localities except by legend and name. There are just two groups whose traditions suggest that they may have been living outside the central Chimbu valley before this large expansion: Endugwa, some of whose branches speak a different dialect, and Wauga, who claim origin at their present home whence some of them have migrated westward. These show slight differences from the valley Chimbu in custom and vocabulary. The Endugwa 2 and 3 tribes, as listed in the government census, have a traditional link to Endugwa 1 but speak a different dialect. I classify Endugwa 2 (Nauru) as Chimbu since they are in the Waiye Council, but not Endugwa 3, who live south of the Wahgi river, and have little contact with the others.

Some Chimbu groups have migrated south and westward into the Wahgi valley and adopted the Wahgi valley language and culture. Others went up the Koronigl and into the Kuno to the northwest. Those who went east and north of the Chimbu valley have intermarried with other peoples and adopted some other customs. The approximately 60,000 people who speak the main dialect of Chimbu today extend west to about the boundary between Chimbu and Western Highlands Districts and south to the Wahgi River. To the southeast where there is no mountain barrier, Chimbus adjoin people of closely related languages. Within Chimbu proper, slight dialectal differences distinguish people of the west, south and east.

All Chimbu recognize a common culture and traditions interrelating the groups. The traditions are mostly of expansion with occasional disasters, the loss of people in warfare or disease, and migrations, which were mostly forced through conquest by larger and stronger groups. Many traditions say that new territory was found uninhabited. The prevalence of border disputes made many groups live well within their borders, using the land between tribal settlement concentrations for grazing pigs, and occasional gardens. While the Chimbu have a scattered pattern of settlement, men's houses are especially concentrated toward the centre of tribal territory at lookout points and both gardens and women's houses are dispersed around them (Brown and Brookfield 1967).

The traditions of all groups recount fights, movements and alliances continuing up to the arrival of the Taylor, Leahy, and Spinks expedition of 1933. Administrative policy has been to maintain the tribal territorial units as they were in 1934 with some adjustments made by the Lands Commissioner after hearings. The nineteen tribes vary in population from 1,000 to over 5,000, with an average of 2,400, and in area from three to fifteen square miles, averaging nine. They all include several clans. Quite commonly, also, the tribe is an alliance of two groups with separate traditions of origin. Sometimes the tribe name joins the two parts, as in Siambuga-Wauga. The main components of the tribe are subtribal territorial units. A subtribe is sometimes also a clan; where it is made up of several clans, these clans claim common ancestry, growth and fission into two or more exogamous units. They rarely have fully distinct territories (Brookfield and Brown 1963).

Tribes were the largest units recognized by Chimbu. In addition to their territorial unity, they co-ordinated the largest ceremonies, the pig feast and the vegetable distributions and fought as a loosely co-ordinated unit in attack against neighbours and in self defence.

THE SEGMENTARY SYSTEM

The Chimbu ideology of group structure is agnatic—they call their main groups 'father-son' (nem-angigl). A very wide group which I call a phratry is composed of several of the groups I call clans. This is expressed as a set of brothers, not always with an inclusive name for the father of them all. Clan names are taken from the founder's name with a suffix meaning line or rope. The phratry need not have any corporate property or functions, but when several clans which are associated as all or part of a phratry are in addition localized, they usually have a territorial block and form all or part of a tribe. Many such subtribes have a tradition of recent fission from a single exogamous clan.

Different informants in the same tribe often give different versions of phratry composition. There is substantial agreement about the brotherhood of the several founders of clans now associated in a tribe or subtribe but connections to those outside may vary. Thus all our informants in Naregu named the three clans Pentagu, Numambugu and Kombaku as brothers. But their conception of the relation of Naregu to Siku and Kombuku, now some miles away, and Gamgani, now a small group mostly attached to one subclan of Numambugu, differed.

Clans are segmented in a number of ways. Often there is a division into two sections and within each section certain groups are closely associated as pairs with linked names, for example, Bau-Aundugu. However, the more or less fixed named groups which I call subclans are regularly identified as brother groups. Thus the Chimbu's general model ignores the clan sections and subclan linkages and identifies phratry, clan and subclan, the main named groups.

The Chimbu segmentary system takes the form of a patrilineal mechanical model: the segments are viewed as having the nesting characteristics of a unilineal descent system. Each set of son groups is said to be descended from a set of brothers whether or not a founding father can be named for the more inclusive group. In Chimbu this series does not have many clear levels and some groupings which can be observed in action and in reference are not depicted as levels of the descent model. To this point, the Chimbu model of their structure has many characteristics of a lineage system.

The clan, with an average population of 600-700, is the usual unit of exogamy. Chimbu state of some groups that they were formerly parts of an exogamous group and have only in the past one or two generations begun to allow marriage between the segments. In these cases, as with other exogamous groups, each present exogamous group is named as a 'brother' of the others—the clans as viewed today are parallel. Chimbu are unconcerned about questions of past relationships of segments, and do not attempt to systematize their accounts of the structure. In different contexts a different level of segmentation may be relevant—consistency is not sought for the system as a whole. Brother clans in a local phratry, tribe or subtribe are bound to one another by many ties of kinship and affinity. They make prestations to one another. Within the clan, joint action in fights and in prestations is often taken by clan sections and linked pairs of subclans. These may also co-operate in local enterprises such as erecting fences. Such activities are mainly co-operative works for local residents, done often in the name of groups. Subclans are more common activity units. They are the main organizing units at marriages and funerals, and undertake some joint agricultural activities. Nowadays the pattern of co-operation is much affected by government-directed work on roads, cash crops, and public works, organized in units under government-appointed officials or elected councillors. These changes have affected the people's view of their groups. In one case a small clan is joined with a subclan of a large clan. While there are many relations of kinship and affinity among them, they also act as a political unit.

The patrilineal segmentary model is not consistently carried within the subclan. The resident population of a subclan varies from about 50 to 250, composed of 15-60 men and their families. The major divisions of subclans are irregular. Chimbu are reluctant to admit that the subclan is internally subdivided and the subgrouping may shift from time to time, on different ceremonial occasions, or for local activities. In some groups a division is attributed to a past quarrel after which subgroups use different cemeteries or ceremonial grounds. Divisions are not clear-cut. Residence in men's houses, neighbourhood, farming co-operation and contributions to prestations may cut a subclan differently. Some subclan section land blocks are discernible and expressed in men's house groupings (Brookfield and Brown 1963). Chimbu refer to the subclan section as a men's house (*yagl ingu*) or 'one-blood' (*boromai suara*). It is conceived as a group of close agnates or lineage mates and is relevant in fixing the prohibition on marrying into the mother's 'one-blood' group.

Most of the members of about half of the 'one-blood' groups in the Mintima area could be organized on an inclusive genealogy of some sort known to a few old men in the group. When these genealogies were given, they were not usually connected to the clan-subclan father-son tie. Rather, the 'one-blood' group began with a subclan section founder and named his sons, carrying the genealogy through males and occasionally wives down to living men in a number of generations. These varied in size from 12 to 40 men and in the form of the lineage. One group was said to be descended from one man with four wives, with living men as his grandsons; another listed seven brothers, whose sons and grandsons are now adult men; and still another consisted of a founder, four sons who are now old men and their sons. A more lineage-like form of three to seven generations was given for other groups. In these genealogies, many inconsistencies and confusions appeared, and the Chimbu custom of naming boys after their fathers' fathers or fathers' brothers contributes to this.

As recited, these were all patrilineages with no non-agnatic branches. They did not contain any men who were not patrilineal descendants. But the groups all had as resident and active members men who were not mentioned in the genealogy. Only further inquiry could link these men to the genealogies and some discrepancies were never cleared up. There were many cases when a man was, as far as I could determine, a fully accepted member of the group, yet not listed in the lineage. Such men were often either the son of a man who lived uxorilocally or had been adopted in childhood as an orphan or the son of a divorcée, most often by his mother's brother, but sometimes by another kinsman or affine. Such men were related to the patrilineal group as sons of female members, or occasionally sons' sons of female members. However, there were some other relations, such as that of wife's brother or wife's sister's son, linking such a man to the group. Accretion is not masked by fictional agnation. Persons become participating members of groups in which they reside as husbands or women's sons, or other non-agnatic kin or affines. The descendants of females who have become so affiliated, and of others, are classed as members. Several men who have long lived in the Mintima groups, but whose fathers were known to be born members of other groups, were prominent leaders, and one was a very successful local government councillor.

In other 'one-blood' groups, no general genealogy was known, the only traceable genealogical ties being from the living to their parents or grandparents and some collateral relatives. A large proportion of the living members of the groups could be identified by their ties in these small genealogies and the majority of the male members of these groups were said to be linked by descent through a line of males.

Throughout, among the men patrilineally related to resident members are some who have lived elsewhere closely associated with their matrilateral kin or affines for many years. Most of these men are well-known to their agnatic relatives and visit or meet now and then. They often attend funerals and contribute to marriage payments. But if they live farther than about two miles from the centre of subclan settlement, they rarely use land agnatically inherited. In only a few cases where some land was not much more than a mile from the man's home was any land used for gardens or houses. We also know many men who are natal members of groups elsewhere and live temporarily or permanently in the Mintima area. The same situation holds: they occasionally visit their agnates but rarely use land.

Individual movement follows marriage patterns. Most marriage takes place within the tribe (44%) and in neighbouring tribes (46%). Matrilateral kin and affines are mostly within about four miles of a man's home (Brown 1964). Visits and even long residence with matrilateral kin or affines rarely take a man out of reach of his own subclan. Quarrels or accusations of sorcery often force a temporary move. In the past, defeat in fighting made some individuals and families seek refuge with more distant relatives, and in recent years the development of cash crops, especially coffee which grows only in the lower altitudes of Chimbu, has brought some movement. We have a number of cases of men who have their own and their wives' houses on land of their non-agnatic kin or affines but maintain close ties with their own agnates and participate in all their activities, and a few instances of men who have become estranged from their agnates, retain some of their natal land and spend most of their time with kinsmen in nearby clans.

There are a number of common circumstances of movement. Illness, fear of sorcery or accusation of sorcery might make a woman take her children and leave her husband's group and live in her own with her father or brother. She is given garden and house land. If this move leads to divorce or brings her husband to dwell uxorilocally, it might be prolonged so that the children are regarded as members of their mother's group. Widows also bring their children home quite often. A leading man attracts followers, most often his wives' brothers and daughters' husbands. They are given land and help in their payments and often remain in the adoptive group. Leading men may also take in widows and other women as additional wives, adding dependants and building up a following in this manner. People regard the main contribution to a man's marriage payment as defining the man's group membership. Thus, when a non-agnate who lives with an adoptive group is given the bulk of his marriage payment by that group, they consider him a member. They do not expect him later to return to his agnates, but I have seen this happen in a number of cases.

Chimbu nowadays have several ways of reckoning membership in groups which did not exist in the past. Before 1959, each local group, usually a subclan, had a census book held by the tultul. More recently there have been tax lists for the Local Government Council and a voters' list for the House of Assembly. At the time of the census, elections and tax collection, a few individuals and families request to have their names transferred and thus assert their membership. These are returning agnates or kin or affines who wish to be associated with different groups. To the prevailing wish to enlarge the group and thus enhance its importance is now added the expectation of increased tax income to encourage immigration.

The rapid development of coffee production in the Waiye Council area attracted people from remote places.

Nowadays men leave the area for work, usually without their wives. However, taking employment provides a change from regular participation and satisfies some of the functions of visits to kinsmen. In collecting a sample of residential histories, I found few men who had never lived outside their own subclans. Within a tribe, territories are intermingled so that, even moving within his own territory, a man may associate more closely with kinsmen and affines in some locations. Chimbu welcome visitors, offer them land and house space and do not expect exclusive loyalty. Rather, they give and receive the same kind of assistance and participation with kin and affines as with agnates. In the eight years that we studied the people of the Mintima area, 60% of the adults resided outside their own subclan territory during at least one of our survey periods (Brown and Brookfield 1967).

No simple criterion of membership is possible in Chimbu as the people recognize different kinds of association with groups. We collected information on genealogies, land holdings, residence and, less systematically, participation in group enterprises for the people around Mintima—parts of two clans, a population of about 1,000 in six subclans making up 11 'one-blood' or subclan section groups and one subclan which cannot be divided into such sections. Of these, six 'one-blood' groups were given with an inclusive genealogy of from three to seven generations from adult men. The others, and the one undivided subclan, were made up of a number of unconnected two or three generation genealogies. In comparing the proportions of members present, participating and absent in groups with and without inclusive genealogies, no significant difference could be found.

The following is an analysis of the residential history of 255 men in the Mintima area. In all subclan sections, some men (26 of 255) were agnates who lived outside their groups throughout the eight years I studied the area. A few others lived nearby, used patrilineal land and participated in some group activities. About twice as many men (57) were non-agnatically related kinsmen or affines of men on the genealogies and lived with the groups at least part of the time. Some of these (19) were adopted in childhood or the sons of men who joined the group, and such men were not associated with any other group. They are comparable to the 26 members of genealogical groups who have lived elsewhere. I was unable to see any distinction in status between these adoptees or their sons and the true patrilineal members of the 'one-blood' group.

In every group there are some non-agnatic residents. For a few of these (6) no tie of kinship or affinity with other members is known, but the majority have some tie to a host. Thus some 38 men were non-agnates living with the Mintima group apparently as guests for part of the period studied. They were attached to individual hosts, most often affinally to their wife's father, wife's brother, sister's husband or daughter's husband. It at first seemed as though adoptees could be distinguished from visitors, but further visits to the area showed me that some 'adoptees' return to their natal groups and some 'visitors' remained throughout the period of my study. I found: of all the men who were active participants, resident in or near the group with which they were associated, at least part of the time, 78% were recognized agnates, 22% were non-agnates.

LEADERSHIP

In most segmentary acephalous political systems, the co-ordination of small group leaders in joint action is not automatic. This is especially so when there is no tradition of succession or stratification of subgroups.

Status differences among Chimbu youths are hardly discernible except perhaps as they vary in their skill in singing and dancing and success with girls. Nowadays a boy with more schooling, leading to a job with some status such as medical aide, clerk, carpenter, truck driver, agricultural extension worker, or mission teacher, has a higher status but all of these are very new opportunities. A youth, even if he has earned some of his marriage costs, is heavily in debt to his kinsmen after his marriage, and in order to gain status in the traditional system, he and his wife must work hard for several years to provide vegetable food and pigs for prestations and to enter into exchanges of valuables.

While land is limited in Chimbu, every man can acquire by inheritance, loan or gift as much as his household can use—it is his own energy and ambition that really determine his achievement. The Chimbu have no ranking system for men but recognize as the lowest status 'rubbish' men or 'nothing' (yogo) men—most of whom have failed to keep a wife, but in any case they produce little and take only a small, if any, part in exchanges or distributions. No more than 10% of the men would be so classified. The majority of men produce adequately for their family needs and meet their obligations in exchanges and distributions—I call these 'ordinary' men. The category includes young married men, who may later become prominent, old men who were formerly prominent but are now less active, and the majority of married men between 30 and 45, the prime age of Chimbu leaders.

Perhaps two status levels above these can be distinguished. The first I shall call 'prominent' men: they are more active and productive than the average, initiate new gardening work, house building, fencing and such local activities, speak up in discussions, make speeches in subclan affairs and often have some dependants and followers attached to their household. Such men would have had at least two wives in earlier times, but now most men in the Mintima area are adherents of the Catholic mission. Nowadays they may employ workers. Perhaps 20% of the men are 'prominent'. Few men become prominent before they are thirty, and a man can hardly maintain his prominence if he has only one wife and no other attached persons. Prominent men over fifty usually have their daughters and daughters' husbands, wives' younger brothers and their wives, or other attached younger families to contribute food and labour to their enterprises. Chimbu do not make a clear and consistent distinction between this status and a higher one. They may call any prominent man a Big Man (yomba pondo), especially if he is in the speaker's own group. However, it seems more in keeping with Chimbu behaviour to distinguish a status of Big Man as those, perhaps 5%, one or two in each subclan, who are more than prominent, who often make speeches at their clan prestations and meetings when the main organizers are of a different subclan, who speak at tribal ceremonies, initiate important tribal and clan enterprises and whose disapproval is likely to stop any plan from being carried out.

In all small groups, joint tasks are somehow accomplished and some leaders can be discerned. Chimbu aften speak of men's house heads, more or less equating the men's house group with a 'one-blood' group. The men's house is ideally a permanent group occupying a traditional site which serves as a centre for gardening, minor ceremonies and defence against raids. But during my period of fieldwork, this did not hold and I doubt if it ever had. All the large houses have some residents who are not members of the 'one-blood' group—both kin and affines of members, and members of other clan segments. Hardly half of the men's houses in the Mintima area can be said to be headed by prominent men. Some houses are associated with two or three men of ordinary status and also occupied by a few younger men, and some have only two or three men. There are also houses occupied by only one man and some boys, frequently his sons.

Sometimes the impetus for building a men's house comes from one man who brings together some members of his 'one-blood' group and some personal followers to construct the house. A house does not keep its exact occupancy group throughout its lifetime of perhaps four to nine years, but commonly has a core of men who work together on domestic tasks, contribute when payments are to be made and are most active at marriages and funerals of the group. Such groups vary considerably in size and also fluctuate in size all the time. Men tend to be attached to a single men's house, but when it is convenient, they sleep elsewhere. When their local interests change they may become attached to another house. In Chimbu some men live apart from a men's house group and rarely participate in its activities, while some of the important leaders keep separate establishments. During the eight years of my study there, there was an almost complete turnover of houses but many were rebuilt on the same sites and changes in leadership were not dependent upon men's house groupings.

Whether or not the men's house group has a leader, several men are prominent in each subclan and most 'one-blood' groups have one or two such men. Small group leadership has at different times had a different place in the larger activities of Chimbu. To some extent, different abilities have been required of leaders.

In the days before Australian administration, the daring fighter was much admired although he did not always gain a following. He was rather of a type called 'hard' by Read (1959:433). This was a bold man, quick to anger and attack. He bragged, threatened, intimidated, assassinated unwary men, women and children and was ever eager to lead a raid against people, pigs and property of other groups. When many other men in his group wanted to attack or avenge a killing, such a man became a leader. But this was not a lasting position. Some former warriors became native officials, but on the whole their interests were inimical to the Australian Administration. One ex-tultul told me, regretfully, "Chimbu men used to be strong fighters before the white man came, but now they are like women and children." Some former warriors sufficiently changed their aims and manner of leadership to serve satisfactorily as native officials.

The more popular leader is a 'manager' or 'director' (as described by Read 1959; Reay 1964; Salisbury 1964; Strathern 1966). His style might sometimes resemble that of the bold warrior, as it was an essential part of his pose to demand respect for the group he represented. Beyond his own small group he is highly regarded as a man of wealth, oratory and judgment. He succeeds in gaining widespread support for the enterprises he urges as a result of taking up popular causes, wise timing of activities to support, or wise choice of occasion. The large-scale feasts of Chimbu can be carried out only under favourable conditions for expanded gardening, pig raising and pandanus ripening. Co-ordination is essential. The clan and tribe's reputation rest on the showing they make in these festivities. A successful group is also strong and co-ordinated enough to withstand attacks from other tribes. Occasionally intertribal fighting dissipates all this and the tribe breaks up to migrate and form a new alliance. Successful leadership keeps the tribe together to make an impressive display and prestation and to withstand attacks.

These conditions did not bring about any permanent leaders. The individual leaders can lose their following as they age and are unable to keep up their activities or fail in any enterprise. There is no accumulation of property or inheritance and little opportunity to provide for descendants. Land is inherited, but additional land can be acquired, and inherited land can be lost if rights are not defended (Brookfield and Brown 1963). Personal pride is asserted when men claim that their fathers had been Big Men, but in fact I saw little continuity of leadership.

In Naregu tribe I knew many ageing leaders. While some of them had encouraged their sons to get some sort of training for new occupations, many had no sons and none of them had sons who showed promise of becoming Big Men. The prominent men I knew had all achieved their positions by their own efforts. However, in two neighbouring tribes, the most powerful leaders had passed on their influence to their sons. Yet the situations were very different. Siune was a traditional Big Man, who as luluai in the 1950's built a large coffee plantation. Kerenga, his son, was elected councillor but never had his father's influence. Kawagl had been a very powerful man and had brought Father Schaeffer into the area. He became a hanger-on at the Catholic mission and passed the luluai-ship to his son Asiwe.

In Naregu the first luluai was a traditional type of Big Man and was replaced by Kondom, a government supporter who introduced a more modern style of leadership by his own economic enterprise and organizing group work activities. Later, the Local Government Councillors were mostly men intent on development through education and economic enterprise. Tultuls in Naregu were an intermediate type. Some traditional Big Men and fighting leaders who adapted badly to the new requirements were overpowered by Kondom. The Local Government Council permitted a turnover to the managerial type of leader whose interests were concentrated upon new works (Brown 1963).

CONFLICT AND COHESION

There are many unstable characteristics in the Chimbu political system: the population was expanding and the frequent conflicts led to the disintegration of groups, migration and new alignments; the relations between phratries, clans, and their segments can shift with movements and clan fission; leadership is achieved—there is no regular means to transfer positions of prestige or power. Indeed, the normal characteristics of corporate groups do not seem to be present. Yet political units, most particularly tribes and clans, have names, more or less fixed territories, traditions of unity and continuity and carry out some joint actions in self-defence, attack against outside tribes, rituals and prestations.

In this political system, group cohesion is achieved through intergroup rivalry. The need for unity has often been put forward as an explanation of war in modern states, but I am claiming that war or hostility toward strangers is a pervasive feature of New Guinea Highlands society; one of the most important ties which holds tribes and clans together is their common interest in self-protection against all other tribes.

One aspect of Chimbu intertribal rivalry is competitive displays and feasts. The high point of every feast is the entrance of armed dancers in pantomime of attack. The pandanus nut or oil feasts are held for one single tribal recipient. The pig feast is given for all exchange partners in all tribes in an area. While the clan carries out some independent large food distributions and sometimes fought as a unit, it more often collaborates with some or all of the other clans in the tribe. Ceremonial grounds where the pig feast is held are used by parts of one or more clans—but the tribal co-ordination of a pig feast is more important that the separate activities at each ceremonial ground. In all large-scale and important activities, it is the tribal name that is used even when some segments of the tribe do not participate. The enhancement of tribal reputation is the aim of all large-scale activities.

Intergroup competition is focused on the present—the display and size of prestation at a feast, the success of a raid, the following of the leaders; nothing is passed on to future generations and few references are made to successes in the past. This contemporary interest is compatible with the lack of concern for genealogies, easy individual mobility and incorporation into groups. When a group loses a fight and has no strong leader to hold it together, it disperses. The success of large groups, especially of tribes, is a product of co-ordination of individual action through the collaboration of leaders and segments. Internal strife is always possible. Interpersonal conflicts might at any time flare up into intergroup fights, but the protagonists need to gather their supporters. When the tribe is working toward a major enterprise, internal conflicts may not be supported. The universal desire for the enhancement of tribal reputation may override private interests.

The tribe can succeed in its competitive relations with other tribes only by the co-ordinated efforts of as many people as can be brought in to produce a display of strength and wealth. Each group tries to keep the men who were born into it and also to bring in men born elsewhere—competition for members is one aspect of Chimbu politics, but the main political effort is the competition between tribes for land, wealth and prestige.

Chimbu accept visitors and encourage them to become group members by giving them land and financial assistance even when local resources are limited, and are not concerned to define the status of persons. Unlike the Enga, they can tolerate divided loyalties, especially within the tribe. I think that the dispersed settlement and land holdings permit flexibility in land acquisition and possible transfer or dual group membership. It is possible for men to participate in the affairs of two groups, especially when they are within one tribe. The existence of tribes containing several clans is thus crucial, and an important difference between Chimbu and several other New Guinea Highlands societies. This also affects alliances and oppositions in war, ceremony and marriage.

Table I shows the main units[2] and a number of their characteristics in thirteen New Guinea Highlands societies, using information given by several authors (see References Cited). Although there are many gaps, some comparison is possible. Units called by the same name differ in size and in the many criteria of corporate activity; co-ordinated activity of the largest groups varies in type and frequency. Thus some scholars regard the main political unit as a clan, having occasional joint activities with other clans of the same tribe or phratry, while other scholars consider the tribe as the most important political unit even though the component clans frequently take independent action. Territory and defence, fighting alliances and oppositions, ceremonial co-ordination, and the realm of influence of a Big Man are all important, and may vary from place to place, and from time to time in the same place.

NOTES

1. Fieldwork on the Chimbu was carried out from 1958 to 1965 in a series of trips, all sponsored by the Australian National University. Some of the research was done in collaboration with H. C. Brookfield; he and J. A. Barnes made helpful comments on an earlier draft of this paper. I am also indebted to many people for stimulating discussion about the political systems of the New Guinea Highlanders.

2. For three other tables showing a rough equation of social units in the Highlands, see Reay (1959:35), Brown (1960:32) and R. Berndt (1964:187)

REFERENCES CITED

BARNES, J. A. (1967): Agnation among the Enga: a review article. *Oceania*, Vol. XXXVIII, No. 1: 33-43.

BERNDT, R. M. (1962): *Excess and Restraint: social control among a New Guinea mountain people*. Chicago: University of Chicago Press.

BERNDT, R. M. (1964): Warfare in the New Guinea Highlands. In *American Anthropologist Special Publication:* New Guinea, the Central Highlands (J. Watson, ed.), Vol. 66, No. 4, Part 2: 183-203.
BROOKFIELD, H. C. and P. BROWN (1963): *Struggle for Land.* Melbourne: Oxford University Press (in association with the Australian National University).
BROWN, P. (1960): Chimbu Tribes: Political Organization in the Eastern Highlands of New Guinea. *Southwestern Journal of Anthropology,* Vol. 16: 22-35.
BROWN, P. (1963): From Anarchy to Satrapy. *American Anthropologist,* Vol. 65: 1-15.
BROWN, P. (1964): Enemies and Affines. *Ethnology,* Vol. 3: 335-56.
BROWN, P. and H. C. BROOKFIELD (1967): Chimbu Residence and Settlement. *Pacific Viewpoint,* Vol. 8: 119-51.
BROWN, P. and G. WINEFIELD (1965): Some Demographic Measures applied to Chimbu Census and Field Data. *Oceania,* Vol. XXXV: 175-90.
BULMER, R. N. H. (1960): Leadership and Social Structure among the Kyaka People of the Western Highlands District of New Guinea. Ph.D. thesis, Australian National University.
GLASSE, R. M. (1962): The Cognatic Descent System of the Huli of Papua. Ph.D. thesis, Australian National University.
LANGNESS, L. L. (1964): Some Problems in the Conceptualization of Highlands Social Structures. In *American Anthropologist Special Publication*: New Guinea, the Central Highlands (J. Watson, ed.), Vol. 66, No. 4, Part 2: 162-82.
MEGGITT, M. J. (1957): Enga Political Organization: a preliminary description. *Mankind,* Vol. 5: 133-7.
MEGGITT, M. J. (1965): *The Lineage System of the Mae-Enga of New Guinea.* Manchester: Manchester University Press.
NEWMAN, P. L. (1965): *Knowing the Gururumba.* New York: Holt, Rinehart and Winston.
READ, K. E. (1951): The Gahuku-Gama of the Central Highlands. *South Pacific,* Vol. 5: 154-64.
READ, K. E. (1959): Leadership and Consensus in a New Guinea Society. *American Anthropologist,* Vol. 61: 425-36.
READ, K. E. (1965): *The High Valley.* New York: Chas. Scribner's Sons.
REAY, M. (1959): *The Kuma. Freedom and Conformity in the New Guinea Highlands.* Melbourne: Melbourne University Press for the Australian National University.
REAY, M. (1964): Present-Day Politics in the New Guinea Highlands. In *American Anthropologist Special Publication*: New Guinea, the Central Highlands (J. Watson, ed.), Vol. 66, No. 4, Part 2: 240-56.
RYAN, D. J. (1959): Clan Formation in the Mendi Valley. *Oceania,* Vol. XXIX: 257-89.
RYAN, D. J. (1961): Gift Exchange in the Mendi Valley. Ph.D. thesis, University of Sydney.
SALISBURY, R. F. (1956): Unilineal Descent Groups in the New Guinea Highlands. *Man,* No. 56: 2-7.
SALISBURY, R. F. (1962): *From Stone to Steel.* Melbourne: Melbourne University Press, for the Australian National University.
SALISBURY, R. F. (1964): Despotism and Australian Administration in the New Guinea Highlands. In *American Anthropologist Special Publication*: New Guinea, the Central Highlands (J. Watson, ed.), Vol. 66, No. 4, Part 2: 225-39.
STRATHERN, A. (1966): Despots and Directors in the New Guinea Highlands. *Man,* Vol. 1, No. 3: 356-67.
VICEDOM, G. V. and H. TISCHNER (1943-8): *Die Mbowamb: Die Kultur der Hagensberg-Stämme im Ostlichen Zentral-Neuguinea.* 3 vols. Hamburg: de Gruyter.
WATSON, J. B. (1965): From Hunting to Horticulture in the New Guinea Highlands. *Ethnology,* Vol. IV: 295-309.
WURM, S. A. (1961): The Languages of the Eastern, Western and Southern Highlands Territory of Papua and New Guinea. In A. Capell, *Linguistic Survey of the South-Western Pacific.* (Revised ed.) Nouméa: South Pacific Commission.

TABLE 1   CHARACTERISTICS OF THIRTEEN HIGHLANDS SOCIETIES

People	Main Units	Population/ Composition	Territory or Localization	Belief in Common Agnatic Descent	Exogamy	Ceremony	Fighting Unit	Restriction on Internal Fighting	Alliance with Larger Group
SOUTH FORE	subclan		+	+	+			+	+
	hamlet	12-20 houses	+	+				+	+
		2-4 subclans							
	clan-parish	several hamlets	+	+	−	large food distribution	+	+	some
	phratry	3-10 clans		+	−		+	slight	some
KAMANO USURUFA JATE	patrilineage		+	+	+			+	+
	clan-village	12-20 houses, 1 or more lineages	+	+	+	age grade, pig feast	+ defence	−	some
	district	50-480 pop.	+	+	−		+ offence	−	changeable
BENA BENA	subclan	ca. 230 pop.	+	+	+		+	+	+
	clan		+	+	+		+	+	+
	tribe	2-5 clans		−	−	initiations pig feast			
GAHUKU-GAMA	subclan	village or village section	+	+	+			+	+
	clan	1 or more villages-100 pop.	+	+	+	+	+	+	+
	subtribe	200-500 pop.	+	+	+	initiation, pig feast	+	feud	−
	tribe	2 sub-tribes	+	+	−		+	feud	some
GURURUMBA	subclan	village	+	+	+	arrange marriage	+	+	+
	clan	67-587 pop.	+	+	+	+	+	+	+
	tribe	2-6 clans	+	+	−	pig feast	−	+	+ fixed
SIANE	subclan-ward	200 pop.	+	+	+			+	+
	clan-village	2-3 clans	+	+	+	+	+	+	+
	phratry subtribe	2-9 clans, 400-1500 pop.	+	+	+	3 year	+	feud	+
	tribe		+	+	−	pig feast	+	feud	+

	Level	Population					Function				
CENTRAL CHIMBU	subclan	30–400 pop.	scattered in clan	+	+	+		+	+	+	+
	clan	av. 600–700 pop.	several blocks in tribe	+	+	+	arrange marriage	+	slight	+	+
	tribe	av. 2400 pop.	part, some	–	+	+	pig & food distribution	+	–	occasional	+
	phratry	2–9 clans	+	+	+	–	–	–	–	+	+
KUMA	subclan	50–500 pop.	+	+	+	+	arrange marriage	+	+	+	+
	clan-parish	100–1700 pop.	+	+	+	+	pig, nut feasts	+	+	some; brother clan	+
	phratry	2–9 clans	+	+	–	–	–	–	–	+	+
MBOWAMB & HAGEN	subclan	30–395 pop.	+	+	+	+	+ ceremonial grounds	+	+	+	+
	clan	700–3500 pop.	+	+	+	+		+	+	+	+
	tribe	258 men	+	+	+	–	+ pig feast	+	+	some	some
KYAKA ENGA	settlement						ceremonial grounds	+	+	+	+
	clan-parish	50–550 pop.	some	+	+	some	fertility, initiation	+	+	+	+
	great clan	av. 800 pop.	+	+	+	+	some	+	+	changeable	changeable
CENTRAL ENGA	subclan	av. 90 pop.	partly localized	+	+	some	+	+	+	+	+
	clan	2–7 sub-clans, av. 350 pop.	+	+	+	+	fertility	+	+	occasional	occasional
	phratry	4–19 clans, av. 2290 pop.	+	+	some	+	fertility	occasional	–	occasional	occasional
MENDI	subclan	1–100	+	+	+	+		+	+	+	+
	clan	**2–6 subclans**	some	+	+	most	payments	+	+	+	+
	clan cluster	2–4 clans	some	+	+	+		+	+	some	+
HULI	**parish section**	500	+	cognatic	+	+	+	some	+	**some**	+
	parish		+	agnatic	+	+	+	some	+	some	changeable

KEY—
+ Characteristic present.
Some characteristics present in some groups only.
— Characteristic absent.
Where information is not available the space is left blank.

JAMES B. WATSON

TAIRORA: THE POLITICS OF DESPOTISM IN A SMALL SOCIETY

ABSTRACT

Traditional leadership in the Tairora area of the Eastern Highlands is discussed with specific reference to one strong man whose reputation is well and widely established in recent tradition. Local reports of his career are examined from various angles, in relation to: socio-cultural context, including the place of a strong man in a moral system with an egalitarian emphasis; historicity and validity; and the nature, conditions, and limitations of influence and authority in a small-scale society.

This paper has a single central purpose expressed in its title. It is to consider the place of leadership, especially despotic leadership, in very small societies. It will approach this task from the vantage point of a particular society and a particular leader. The paper is divided into three parts. The first part is a brief ethnographic sketch. In the second part I shall consider the legend and historicity of a despotic leader whose career largely furnishes the focus of the paper. In the third part I shall examine the community in which this man held sway. Ancillary questions with respect to each of these parts will be introduced in the context of the discussion rather than in advance.

ETHNOGRAPHIC SKETCH OF A TAIRORA COMMUNITY

In the following ethnographic sketch I shall focus upon a Tairora-speaking community called Abiera (see map). The people of this local group are the nearest to being the immediate heirs of a strong man named Matoto. Their description of him furnishes the central topic of the paper. Matoto (accent on the first syllable) spent most of his life in what is essentially the territory today occupied by Abiera. His sister and several of his contemporaries were living at Abiera in 1964. Some of his children and two former wives were then living at Bontaqa (see Note at end of this contribution), a nearby local group closely connected with and largely colonized from Abiera. The effects of Matoto's activity still constitute a major portion of the remembered history of the area, and Matoto's own figure is more vivid in the minds of many people of Abiera and their neighbours, probably, than any other of his time or before him.

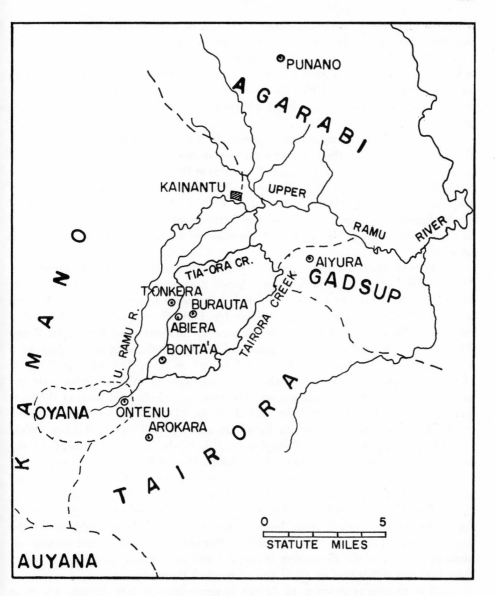

Yet modern Abiera represents neither a specific settlement where Matoto
ever lived nor a settlement exactly like the one where he lived. There have been
many changes since his death, the most enduring ones attributable to the coming
of the Australian Administration in about 1930. In identifying Matoto with Abiera,
therefore, I am strictly following local practice: he belongs to their history and hence
to Abiera. Accordingly, it matters little that the settlements of his day were Kambuta, Bahiqora, and others no longer in existence. It matters much, however, if one

wants to use Abiera in talking about Kambuta or Bahiqora because of the considerable changes that have occurred in the meantime. I will thus employ a flexible approach to the ethnographic background of the immediate pre-contact period, referring to the Abiera of 1964 where I think it is relevant, but sometimes pointing to the obvious differences which have arisen in the three and a half decades since Matoto's death. In either case, I will always speak of Abiera as Matoto's stamping ground.

'Abiera' is the designation employed by the Australian Administration for these people as well as their former name for themselves. Either their own current name or the government name has to them almost the same connotations of (1) the settlement where they reside, (2) the residents, and (3) the immediate territory they exploit or claim. Abiera is located in what is today the Kainantu subdistrict of the Eastern Highlands District of the Territory of New Guinea. It is some six to eight miles south of the town of Kainantu, the administrative subdistrict headquarters.

Present Abiera territory seems to coincide approximately with the territory of Matoto's lifetime. It is a rough, oblong-shaped area some three to four miles from east to west by a mile to a mile and a half from north to south. Most of the area is grassland, spanning Tia-ora Creek, a sizeable, north-flowing stream, and bounded on the east by Tairora Creek and on the west by headwaters of the Upper Ramu River. The settlement itself lies in grassland on the gentle, west-facing slope of a low mountain or ridge crowned by a small 'island' of bush. This bush at the back of the village and numerous casuarinas, planted singly or in small groves, are the main exceptions to the prevailing grass. The most intensively used parts of the local territory are (1) the residential site, (2) the bush, (3) the gardens, located mainly on the lower western slopes of the mountain and especially along Tia-ora Creek, and (4) pig ranges scattered throughout much of the territory exclusive of the gardens and the immediate village. A similar pattern of land use prevailed during Matoto's life, slightly modified according to the location of the settlements of the time and the residential division of the local group between two settlements.

The Abiera of both that day and this regard themselves as a grassland or 'kunai' people and distinct from 'bush' people, as some of their neighbours to the south and west are characterized. Besides differences of resources and certain exploitative practices, the distinction between 'bush' and 'kunai' peoples also sometimes connotes differences of ritual and of magical knowledge.

The present population of Abiera is approximately 200. It may not have been the same at all times during Matoto's life as one of his major political achievements was the recruitment of a sizeable group of refugees. In any case, I seriously doubt it ever exceeded greatly, if at all, the present figure.

All available evidence indicates that the forebears of the Abiera people had been living in the present vicinity for perhaps a hundred years or more at the coming of the white man. An immigrant ancestor and his two brothers are said to have founded their lineage, entering the area from a point to the east. Allegedly he found the country he settled empty of other people. Today most of their immediate neighbours, as well as the Abiera, claim derivation from the original settlement and take the name of one of their social divisions from it. Since the remembered settlement (there were quite possibly others now forgotten) was called Tairora, all of the people asserting descent from the residents of Tairora think of themselves at one level as 'Tairora'. The loose grouping that results can conveniently be identified with a phratry. The phratry today embraces somewhat more than a thousand people, occupying some five or six territories, and residing in eight to ten or more settlements, depending upon how the lines are drawn. The territory and settlements of the Tairora phratry lie in a rough, north-south line for perhaps eight miles along a valley—sometimes therefore called the Tairora Valley.

The government appears to have taken the collective name of this series of related communities to designate the entire ethno-linguistic group who speak dialects of the same language. Thus an ethno-linguistic congeries of roughly 10,000, as well as its language, is also today called 'Tairora'. To avoid confusion, therefore, I shall speak of 'Tairora phratry', 'Tairora language', or 'Tairora ethno-linguistic group' according to what is meant at any given point.

Abiera territory lies within a narrow, northern salient of the area occupied by the Tairora ethno-linguistic group. Since they are on one of the peripheries of their own speech community, the people of Abiera live within social range of communities of several other languages. Indeed, the Abiera have now and in the past have had intercourse with peoples variously speaking Auyana, Oyana, Kamano, Agarabi, and Gadsup. None of these languages is intelligible to a speaker of Tairora unless he happens to be bilingual.

Despite the linguistic multiplicity of their neighbours, the Abiera have much in common with them in respect of the general appearance of their settlements, their dwellings, and their means of subsistence. Basically, they exemplify what is by now doubtless thought of as an Eastern Highlands pattern of subsistence, founded on pigkeeping and the intensive cultivation of sweet potatoes, bananas, sugarcane, taro, yams, greens, and winged beans. Hunting plays but a small part in the diet of grassland groups like Abiera. Like all their neighbours, the Abiera live in concentrated settlements surrounded by country where fenced gardens and open pig ranges are found. The dwellings are sufficiently clustered and some settlements so small that it would still be possible to surround them with the palisades of yore. The houses are the familiar, round, conical-roofed, dwellings of the area. The men's house differed from the houses of the women and children principally in its larger size, interior apartments, and the symbolic protrusion of its tall centre pole through the peak of the thatched roof. Today one can see at Abiera structures resembling a men's house, but there is no longer an institutionalized residence for the men and initiated youths. The village now contains, moreover, not only houses with plaited bamboo walls (instead of bark or palings with straw insulation) but some that have rectangular floor plans. Both of these features are post-contact innovations in the area.

The Abiera settlement is surely like those of former days in being connected to the bush, to the gardens, and to the places where water is obtained in the valleys below by a network consisting of main paths and feeder paths. Some paths are used by but a few people, such as a path to the pig shelter or a section of forest belonging to a particular owner. Main paths ascend to the forest above where firewood and construction material are obtained, as well as betel nuts and pandanus nuts in season. Main paths also descend to the valleys which lie on three sides of the settlement site and where the gardens are principally located. These paths fan out to particular gardens, stands of banana, or other resources, or they lead away to neighbouring communities with whom there is interterritorial traffic. Departing from the village, one could follow some of these paths for many miles as network connects with network, settlement with settlement, in almost every direction.

The image of the paths and the network is most appropriate to an understanding of the social connections linking the sedentary individuals and local groups of this part of the world. Any individual or local group occupies at a given time a particular point on a network. His various uses of the network lie within a certain, roughly radial perimeter. The most intensive use of the paths is in connection with the exploitation of the local territory. This use ordinarily involves little interaction with the occupants of other territories and much with those of the local territory. Beyond the local territory is a zone in which are found friends, allies, agnatic or affinal kinsmen, and enemies in other local groups. Though the occupants of this zone have a variety of relations with the given group, none is likely to be that of neutrality. Beyond this zone is one in which less frequent use is made of the network. It contains groups where trading partners live, occasional allies, occasional adversaries, former hosts or potential future hosts when asylum is needed. At the outer perimeter of the zone are probably local groups whose social colouration is not very clear though something may be known of such a group besides the name. Beyond that are perhaps at most a few place names or areas that have either an extraordinary character or none. The outer perimeter of the network used by any one local group might not lie more than ten or fifteen miles from the local territory. The perimeter could be elongated in the direction of local groups or local goods of unusual interest. At Abiera, stone axes, salt, plumes, and bows were goods of unusual interest because of their importance and the limited distribution of their sources. The perimeter could be foreshortened by the interdiction of natural barriers or large, perennially hostile groups.

There is as yet no clear measure of the degree of foreshortening of a social perimeter by the presence of groups speaking another language. It is plain that a language boundary neither blocks the development of social links nor permits only links of one sort. Bilingualism is typical of most interlinguistic borders. Yet before the existence of a *lingua franca* in the area, language almost certainly exerted some influence, barring or facilitating linkages in a given direction.

The case of Abiera and doubtless some other communities cannot be covered by simple generalizations about language boundaries. With a perimeter including groups speaking four or five different languages, it would not be likely that social relations were equally extended to them all or included all kinds of relationships in equal degree. It is quite possible at least for groups to fight when neither understands the language of the other, but it is less easy to traffic with them in other ways. It is thus the case that Abiera's traditional relations with the nearby Oyana speakers (see map) seem to have been predominately hostile, as they have also been with the Gadsup speakers in the opposite direction. With local groups of the Kamano language that lie within their range to the west, relations have apparently been nearly as diverse as with groups of their own Tairora language. The same may be true of local groups to the north who speak Agarabi. Although there has within recent memory been more intensive contact with Kamano-speaking communities, the culture of the Abiera and other groups of the Tairora phratry contains many obvious suggestions of long and intimate relations with Agarabi. I shall only mention at this point the Auyana ethnolinguistic group as a discussion of one such group figures later in this paper.

Since the politics and sociology of Abiera are very much a part of the paper, I shall present here only some terms I think essential for initial description and discussion. The first two terms are *territory* and *local group,* which I have already used. A local group is the largest aggregate of people with a sense of identity recognizing common access to a single continuous territory. Thus the two terms are reciprocal and mutually defining. Local groups in the vicinity of Abiera at the present time average around 200 persons. This may be somewhat more than in the past. Within a single territory there are one to several *settlements.* These are what are sometimes called *hamlets* or *villages.* The term *hamlet* has been used especially to describe one of several closely related settlements within a given territory, that is, a residential segment of one local group. Settlements in the area of Abiera are nucleated, not isolated dwellings or farmsteads. The settlements or hamlets of a given territory can probably be related to each other, historically, in one of at least three ways. One settlement may be derived from another directly, hence its colony or daughter. Or each may trace its immediate origin to a separate source in former linked hamlets of the same territory. Or one of the hamlets may have been founded largely by an immigrant group, usually refugees who have come to lodge in the territory more recently than the other and perhaps will stay for a shorter time. Sometimes the hamlet settlements are so close as to seem only sections of a single village. This is the case with Abiera at present but not apparently in the remembered past.

It is of course generally true in connection with a human community in space and time that the situation of a given moment is but a transition from a previous situation to a future one. Certain patterns of transition, or processes, can be stated for Abiera and its neighbours, and it will be a part of my concern to discuss them later in the paper.

I spoke earlier of the Tairora phratry and its origin. The Tairora phratry is made up not only of local groups and their respective territories. From another point of view it includes several categories of people which I shall call *sibs*. The members of each sib assert a common origin that ties them together, giving them certain claims and expectations in respect of each other. I prefer to call these constituents of the phratry 'sibs' rather than 'descent groups'. The word 'group' is likely to be overworked in an ethnographic paper, and the status of a Tairora sib as a group can also prove troublesome. The sibs of Tairora phratry are named, and their members claim descent through male progenitors to a common ancestor, usually male, or more often a group of ancestors, who lived at a certain place. What I am calling the phratry is in this sense simply a larger 'sib' including lesser sibs. It also has a name and the members of its component sibs claim a common origin and ancestry. No present Tairora sib, to my knowledge, is completely localized, although each is represented by more members in some territories and local groups than in others. There is probably no Tairora sib, moreover, without some representatives in every present local territory of the phratry, but there may be some sibs without *male* representatives everywhere. The modern situation is not necessarily a perfect match in all of these respects for the situation of Matoto's day with which this paper is principally concerned. Indeed, Matoto seems to have been instrumental in recruiting one of the sibs of Tairora and perhaps is creating another.

It would be possible at present to recognize Tairora sub-phratries and sub-sibs. In my opinion, to do so would convey a false sense of hierarchical orderliness. Nor would it bring us much closer to an understanding of the processes of segmentation and of fusion that have led to the present array of sibs and the phratry link among them. These processes, in other words, can be more efficiently approached by other means.

Residence in a Tairora territory is patrivirilocal, but individual movements within the territory or the colonization of new settlements may often put sons in different settlements from their fathers, brothers, or other sib mates. The flight of refugees can result, for a given interval or in a given generation, in the residence of numerous men outside of their natal territory, whether or not in the territory of their mothers, wives, sisters, or daughters. At the present time, after nearly 40 years of the *pax britannica,* patrivirilocality is probably more prevalent in the villages of the area at large than it was at any time in the immediate past.

The Tairora phratry is not exogamous but marriage is—and probably was in the pre-contact period—normally between members of different sibs. Since members of two or more sibs were normally found within a given territory, sib exogamy did not necessitate local or territorial exogamy. Figures from the past are not obtainable, but in modern Abiera and one other community I have studied over half of the marriages are between spouses born in the local territory, although perhaps not in the same settlement. The index of territorial exogamy may have been higher in the past, but there seems to be no reason to think exogamy was the jural or statistical norm, except for the sib.

Polygyny is and was practised for as long as anyone now living remembers. At the present time, no man at Abiera has more than three wives, and there are only two such men. The great majority of men have but one wife at any time, and probably this was also true in the past. A major difference, however, is that some men of the past had many more wives than three. One of these was Matoto, the subject of the present paper. Matoto's wives numbered perhaps as many as sixteen or more, according to the names that living contemporaries could recall.

THE LEGENDARY MATOTO AND THE HISTORICAL MAN

Figures of awesome and arbitrary men of great power are not common in the literature of small-scale and 'primitive' societies. Other kinds of leader figures, how- ever, are frequently described. There seems to be a disposition to believe that small group leaders are or were typically anything but powerful, and some scepticism may therefore surround the few reputed despots of which there is some account (Read 1959; Brown 1963; Salisbury 1964; Strathern 1966). The fewer or the more dubious the accounts, the more important it is that further reports be as full as possible. Thus the type, if and where it occurs, can be recognized and its circum- stances known.

In addition to wishing to examine a small-group despot himself as a figure, I have another problem to which to attend. This arises from the fact that Matoto, the figure with whom I am concerned, was dead some years before I heard of him. I learned quite a bit about him, but some of what was said of him or ascribed to him might well strike the sceptical reader as fabulous. Some of the reports of Matoto may perhaps have this character. My initial reaction was to reject much of what I heard. I do not now think my reaction was correct, but the fact remains that I must deal with the legend of Matoto in order to deal with him as an historical figure. The need to deal with a legend is not wholly detrimental, of course. What- ever else one may conclude, it is true that Matoto's heirs conceive of him in a certain way. This at least tells us something of his heirs, however convincingly it tells us of Matoto. One can thus get some insight into the process of legend-building and the relations between history, tradition, and cultural values in this part of the world.

Matoto's reported image is more a miscellany of details, incidents, and qualities than a biography. It is not a *vita* but almost a mélange of attributes. There is much consistency among the various statements made about Matoto, but I am unable to order them as a nicely unfolding career. I shall largely take them, then, as describing a *persona*. Though some of the incidents obviously occurred in the early part of his life, they are probably events or deeds that were recalled after he became outstanding and thus became as much a part of the *persona* as some- thing he did yesterday or was doing at the moment.

I believe I first heard of Matoto when his name came up in an Abiera genealogy. Someone in the group who were helping me in recalling names spon- taneously remarked, "A bad man." Other names before Matoto's had evoked occasional comments or nods of recognition and remembrance, but his produced the most forthright comment and the largest amount of nodding. I found nobody, moreover, who had not heard of him or could not place him, although that was surely not true of some of the members of his generation. I found many persons, moreover, who enjoyed telling me about Matoto.

Matoto had died just prior to 1930. The date can be estimated because all informants agreed Matoto was alive when the first white man visited the Abiera. In fact, Matoto drew his bow at that European but was restrained by some of his fellows, so people now say, from shooting him. Recollection of this incident brought smiles as it was to these men so characteristic of Matoto. Between that time and the establishment of an administrative post (Upper Ramu Post) at Kainantu around 1930 Matoto was killed in an ambush. Thus he ended his career with his reputation as a 'strong man' (buhàribainti) unsullied by either declining years or the indignities and loss of initiative that might have come with the introduction of the pax britannica. The point is probably worth bearing in mind in assessing Matoto's legend.

In subsequent conversations about Matoto, most of all in conversations with some of his living contemporaries, a number of pieces of his image accumulated. Through the eyes of these informants, we see Matoto as a man of tremendous stature and physique. I am a good six feet, but informants—including some, it must be admitted, who never saw him—insisted he was substantially taller than me. From the position of their hands, I would conclude he was perhaps six feet-six or so. I did not believe it and don't, and my informants sensed my doubt. They assured me by saying that they could produce some of his bones from which I could see beyond question how big he was. Some vertebrae, apparently, were in the possession of one man and the skull was kept by a woman in another village, closely related to Abiera, where one of his sons lives. Other bones were said to have found still other owners. Unfortunately, I never saw these bones. An aged sister of Matoto living at Abiera in 1964, however, was a woman of considerable size by local standards. This tends to suggest that Matoto was at least not small by the standards of his group. His son is also a good-sized man, though no six-footer; but people who professed to know said the son was no match for the father. I have seen a few very large men in the area of Kainantu, especially among the Agarabi to the north of Abiera, but nobody of nearly the size claimed for Matoto.

The question of size is interesting for two reasons. For one thing, there is an unmistakable connection in the mind of the Abiera and other people of the area between prowess and renown, on the one hand, and physical size and strength, on the other. Doughty small men are noted and some of them seem notable, but the emphasis upon their qualities suggests that they were men to be reckoned with despite small stature.

The second reason for noting beliefs about Matoto's size is that one encounters in various parts of the Kainantu vicinity a general belief that the men of the past were all larger than men today. There are no men today as large physically as those before. Indeed, people assert that the pigs of the past were also larger, the grass taller, local groups more populous, gardens more extensive, and food more plentiful.

A connection is plausible between the perceived decline in size of familiar things and the loss of initiative and local autonomy in the control of affairs under the *pax britannica*. Whether or not this is the entire explanation for so widespread a belief, it is probably a part of it. While superfluous as far as discounting claims for Matoto's oversized physique is concerned, this belief, as a valid instance of social perception, helps to confirm the close connection in the local mind between size and power.

The keeping of Matoto's bones is a part of the legendary image. The bones themselves seem to afford the possessors strength and security. It was reported that the skull was brought forth during an eclipse of the sun that occurred in the early sixties in this part of New Guinea. Word of the eclipse had been circulated by the Administration for weeks in advance in an effort to forestall anxieties among the villagers. One effect of advance notice was to give people ample time to be concerned about the crisis and to prepare emergency measures. Displaying Matoto's bones in a public ceremony was one such measure.

Matoto is remembered as a fearless and independent youth. Even as a boy, it is claimed, he was unconcerned where night might overtake him. If away from the village or other shelter, he would simply sleep where he happened to be, alone and in the open, in the grassland or the bush. To Abiera people such a practice is unmistakably associated with cold courage and indifference to fear. The same indifference is attributed to certain other men in proclaiming their prowess. A local tultul, for example, speaks with pride of having slept beside the road one night when drunk. The village was not far, but his courage was such that he did not care. Besides the pre-contact possibility of an encounter with marauding enemies, there may be lurking sorcerers, ghosts, or other supernaturals who could cause serious harm. Even within the village, there is an elaborate arrangement for blocking a doorway when people sleep at night. Leaving the house to relieve oneself produces anxiety. Women, especially, are accused of fearing to go out into the night for such a purpose, and their houses are for this reason sometimes said to be contaminated and unhealthy for men. That a mere youth did not care whether he slept in a house or in the company of others would be extraordinary evidence of strength.

Some informants claim to believe that the death of Matoto's mother had a part in his becoming a ruthless fighter and killer. She was apparently killed by enemies from the Kamano area. During Matoto's initiation into the male cult, he was allegedly harangued about her death and exhorted to bear it in mind for future vengeance. This much is wholly credible, but one cannot believe that such an experience was out of the ordinary for a youth in this society. Probably most boys had one or more close kinsmen whose deaths they might be concerned to avenge. There seems little question, moreover, that the initiates were publicly reminded of such obligations during the course of their initiation, as well as on other occasions.

Approximately 60 years or so ago, say about 1900, the Abiera people were driven from their territory. This was apparently before Matoto reached fighting age, perhaps while he was still a child. In departing from their territory, as is now retold by some Abiera informants, they stood on the ridge overlooking the empty settlements and gardens, singing and shaking their shields and promising to return. The refugees found asylum in a territory several miles to the north where they stayed for an undetermined period, probably for several years. In the meanwhile, their former dwellings and gardens were despoiled by their enemies, especially the people of Ontenu, an Oyana-speaking group to the southwest.

Returning from exile some years later, the people re-established themselves in their former territory. There is no suggestion that they had to oust anybody else, but they obviously had to be prepared to defend themselves against renewed attack. They built new settlements on new sites. The names and locations of these settlements, like all subsequent ones, are readily recalled. From this point on, whatever may have been the case previously, there seem to have been two settlements at all times. Even so, informants are practically unanimous in asserting that the residents of each settlement were mixed, neither settlement—nor men's house—having all or only the members of a single sib. The settlements were close—within calling distance of each other. Indeed, both settlements were in the same general part of the claimed territory, not far from the present village. The point is that the settlements were obviously located in close proximity to each other, far closer than they need have been to remain within the local territory. One material reason for their proximity was, surely, to have access to the small island of bush previously mentioned. Probably a more compelling reason was the need for common defence and the close social ties between the two hamlets. For, at least from Matoto's day to the present, the two residential divisions have been regarded as integral parts of Abiera.

It was after their return from exile, according to some informants, that Matoto began to gain a reputation. Whether or not this was his first fighting, it was now that he became recognized, by both friend and foe, as no ordinary man. His recognition appears to have been rapid. I could, in any case, obtain little sense of development from informants. It may well be a retrospective halo effect that has dimmed the memory of what other fighting men contributed, but some now see Matoto's prowess as what uniquely assured the Abiera local group of stable possession of their territory following their return. He is said to have struck fear into the hearts of the Ontenu, a principal enemy at this time, with his style in battle.

The question of why or how Matoto was so fearsome is one that produces immediate and elaborate answers. People who never saw him as well as those who did, friend and foe alike, not only speak of his manner but actually pantomime him! I have witnessed such a pantomime by young men who had obviously obtained their impressions at second hand. The imitation of Matoto by an elderly adversary of his and Abiera's, however, differed from that of the young men only in being somewhat more detailed and vivid—perhaps the touch of authenticity. To judge from the pantomime I saw, Matoto would have been a glowering, scowling man who looked straight through one, imperturbable and unresponsive to word or gesture—unless he decided a gesture were threatening. For this last reason men—even his own fellow villagers—were again and again reported to conduct themselves with care lest they unintentionally excite him or attract his unfavourable attention. In his presence people were said to move slowly, to keep their eyes averted or on the ground. Sometimes they spoke with lowered voices. He, meanwhile, was apparently full of quick, nervous moves, ever darting glances here and there, watchful and wary. A man whom he transfixed with his eyes would apparently be extremely uncomfortable. A stranger to him could hope for nothing better than to avoid his notice altogether.

Clearly, to informants it was more than an awesome mien that evoked such caution. No one doubts that Matoto liked to kill, nor that killing was nearly always on his mind. To those who feel they knew Matoto, the very question would seem simple. If this was not in fact his nature, therefore, he played the role superlatively for he succeeded in convincing those around him that he killed for pure pleasure, or simply because it was innate in him to do so. Spotting a visitor in the village, he would become agitated, demanding to know of a kinsman, "Who is that? Let me kill him!" A local style of story-telling, to be sure, makes words of a man's supposed thoughts. Word or thought, however, modern informants believe Matoto's killer-lust was insatiable and depict his contemporaries as constantly concerned to restrain him.

The brother of a woman married into an Abiera settlement was cited in a hypothetical example of the caution required of the prudent. Should the man wish to visit his sister, it was said, he might have to sneak into the village and stay in his sister's house all the while he was there. Only by keeping out of Matoto's sight and leaving furtively—though others might know of his presence—could he be sure to avoid possible trouble. Such graphic illustrations tend to give the local picture of Matoto some credibility.

There is no reason, so far as I know, to believe that Matoto in fact shot down large numbers of people indiscriminately. He is almost invariably described as a bad man, but no one ever suggested to me that he was mad. I do not believe that is what people now think of him, and certainly those of his contemporaries I could query thought no such thing. I have already cited the instance in which Matoto was said to have drawn his bow at the first European to visit Abiera. He was restrained on this occasion, apparently, by his fellows. Perhaps such threats, or the appearance of threat, were as common as reports suggest. If so, his close associates were surely aware of it. As in the case of the European, it may have been their public role to restrain Matoto.

In battle, Matoto was easily recognized because of his commanding stature and great black shield. It was the purpose of every warrior, in attiring and ornamenting himself, and in comporting himself in a fight, to be as flamboyant and frightening as possible. Black charcoal and white lime are used to paint fierce patterns on the face, the white especially around the mouth and eyes. The tall, rectangular shields of albizzia are shiny black from smoke. They carry a thin staff, mounted at the top edge and standing perhaps two to three feet above the shield, which supports a spray of cassowary plumes. At the top of the staff are tied one or two weighted splints of springy bamboo, with feathers attached. The warrior often moves as a dancer, dramatizing himself and taunting his enemy. As he shakes his shield in their faces, the sprung weights with their feathers bob violently about, adding to the total effect of movement, vigour, and aggressiveness. Men of the Tairora phratry had a special sort of grunting cry or guttural song they used as they danced back and forth before their adversaries. They themselves said, if asked, that they had no equals for *sang froid* among the men they met in fighting, and other traits of theirs tend to make the claim at least feasible. After hearing members of another ethnolinguistic group describe Tairora fighting behaviour, I suspect it deserves some credence.

Matoto would have had all of this cold bravado besides his name. In most local groups with which a community is apt to be at war, the strong man is a known figure, both by appearance and by reputation. Indeed, he is as a rule intimately known, for the contending groups are small, relatively close to each other in space, and almost invariably connected through a network of persons, kinsmen or co-residents, who provide an active chain of communication. Matoto's former enemies, for example, usually felt no handicap in describing him to me in detail. An ideal and a prime feat of fighting is to kill an enemy strong man, a man who has gained renown. The loss of such a man was a serious blow. People knew who they were and could single them out, even in the midst of a mêlée. Indeed, it is quite likely that a man with such a reputation would announce himself, or be announced, to the enemy. Matoto, once famous, would thus have had little trouble in being recognized. As an established strong man, moreover, he might never face an adversary who was not psychologically handicapped by the reputation of his opponent. In fact, an old man whose local group had often fought against Abiera said men simply did not stand before Matoto. They avoided him or fled as it was impossible to do otherwise.

No one was prepared to attempt a tally of Matoto's fighting victims. While insisting they were "plenty" or "too many to count", informants could give me but few names. Accordingly, I have little idea of the number of men he may have killed. Of itself this does not require that we reject the local view of his score, however, for names are soon forgotten. Even the names that one would hope to obtain in local genealogies are often hard to come by, and the names of men of outside groups might thus in most cases be beyond recall. Sheer enumeration, not surprisingly, is little developed in Tairora culture. A man himself or his contemporaries might recall his exploits on certain occasions, perhaps counting his claimed killings; but if so, this is apparently a part of tradition which rapidly fades. Despite a notable resemblance to other cultures in patterns of male aggression and prowess, there may be in Tairora nothing that matches the counting of coups or the notching of pistol butts. I have discovered no trophies or other artifacts associated with the mnemonic representation of killings. The number of arrow points embedded in a shield is sometimes claimed to represent the fighting in which the owner engaged; but these are presumably enemy arrows. Arrows taken from the bodies of the enemy fallen, to be sure, are placed on the graves of one's own lately deceased or sent as debts or credits to other groups. There may be many arrows from a single victim, however, as well as the arrows of more than one archer. No tally is thus implied. A single death, so to speak, does multiple service. Without skulls, scalps, feathers, bones in a necklace, or links in a belt, the statistics of prowess or victory, if they ever were kept, are soon lost.

The actual achievements underpinning the reputation of Matoto as a killer are hard to assess, leaving open the question of how much was sheer fact, how much the aura of fame. The same general question applies to the killings attributed to other Tairora killers: how much was a great reputation necessarily based on a large number of victims? What in local terms, is a large number? I have insufficient data to support a firm answer, but I would suggest that an impressive killer need not have had a tremendous score. I do not wish to imply that a fierce manner empty of achievement was alone enough to support a strong man. Substantial numbers of people were killed—to judge from genealogies—and presumably those with the reputation did most of it. I am certainly not suggesting, therefore, that Matoto was merely an actor, much less a fraud. It seems quite conceivable to me, however, that an awesome personal style, combined with an apparent or real taste for aggression, might rapidly expand a reputation initially established on the basis of very few killings and perhaps found an entire career encompassing not more than a dozen or two.

Whatever the actual number of Matoto's 'outside' killings, a good proportion were apparently by stealth or ambush. In the Kainantu area, indeed, it is likely that more people met violent death in this way than in open fighting. Matoto is said to have been very fond of stalking victims. A man in his late sixties still living at Abiera in 1964 claims to have been Matoto's constant companion, a sort of aide-de-camp to him. Many times, he recalls, Matoto would summon him saying, "Let's go and wait in the reeds by the water-hole of that village. Perhaps we can shoot someone." This was a common danger against which the people of any village must always be wary. On one occasion when the two were in hiding, they overheard people on the path asking each other whether Matoto might be lying in wait for them! Matoto is also described as striking off on his own, going alone sometimes to distant places to take some person by surprise. Later he might report a killing to his group.

Matoto's best remembered victims are insiders, residents of the local community. This seems likely enough and does not mean that his killings were mostly at home. It need mean no more than that local events and local victims are longer remembered than outsiders. One victim was a wife of his. He shot her while she was at work in her garden for a reason I have not been able to learn precisely. The killing suggests that he may have suspected her of adultery, which is perhaps the case, but no one could recall such a thing. Some suggested a lesser fault, in fact, no more than a minor slight or dissatisfaction, indicating how little they believed would move Matoto to kill her. Two of the victim's brothers, according to informants' accounts, were near enough to the scene to hear their sister's mortal cry. It is a brother's obligation to come to the aid of a sister and to avenge her unless a serious fault on her part can be shown. Instead, these men fled. Matoto ordered the immediate interment of the woman, without feast or ceremony, thus forestalling the possibility of any embarrassment with her kinsmen. Under ordinary circumstances kinsmen would have come to keen the deceased and view her corpse, and would have received substantial food and other payments as Matoto's affines.

It is generally supposed that Matoto received payment on various occasions for coming to the aid of other groups against their enemies. He would thus be approached, often by representatives of a distant group in the Kamano area, to induce him to come and to bring Abiera men to help them. The negotiations are supposed to have been carried on quietly so that only Matoto might know of the agreement. If the negotiations were successful and the promises kept, payment would be covertly made—often at night. No one could suggest how often such arrangements occurred, but it is assumed that they were common. Thus it would seem that Matoto and some of his associates saw considerably more fighting than may have been required merely for the defence of their own territory or the oppression of enemies immediately threatening them. It is further suggested that Matoto assumed the right to speak for certain other men in concluding agreements to fight abroad. The reason for secrecy was perhaps in part to protect Matoto from the suspicion of personally benefiting from the arrangement but also probably to protect those offering the payment and possibly to preserve an element of surprise when the enemies suddenly confronted Matoto in the van.

Some of Matoto's personal killings are also said to have been prearranged and to have been carried out in exchange for payment. In one such instance, men from another community wished the death of a man residing in Matoto's territory. The man himself was an outsider, but the wife was a local woman. He had got into trouble in his own community and thus decided to live with his wife's people—that is, uxorilocally. Nevertheless, so it is reported, those who wished his death knew they could not obtain it without Matoto's approval. They therefore approached Matoto secretly, to obtain his permission or to induce him to do the killing himself. Matoto assented. Some are convinced that he readily agreed to the killing, finding the prospect, as always, attractive. Payment, it is supposed, was surreptitiously brought to Matoto so as not to alert the community or the intended victim. On the given day, there were various people about the settlement. The marked man himself was seated making a pig rope in the dooryard of his wife's house. Matoto approached him and discharged an arrow into him at close range. As is claimed in nearly all such shootings by strong men, the victim died "at once". Matoto dragged or threw the body of the dying man into the house and leapt to the roof to kick in the thatch preparatory to setting it afire and charring the corpse. (The Tairora say this was a favourite gesture of theirs in attacking an enemy village.) The wife and other kinsmen of the dead man pleaded with Matoto not to fire the house but to give them the body, which he did.

Again, the deceased was buried without the usual observances. These tend to be not only emotional but protracted, often lasting several days, according to the importance of the deceased. The interval also allows word to reach distant kin and gives them time to come to the funeral. A funeral thus offers ample opportunity for an overflow of feelings that could lead, in cases where the killer must face the victim's kinsmen, to serious trouble. A major topic at funerals, moreover, is the cause of death. A funeral is plainly a manifestation of solidarity among the bereaved, who may live scattered among several local groups. A central expression of their solidarity is in determining steps for revenge as well as in an implicit promise to the deceased and to each other to carry it out. Accordingly, dispensing with the funeral was probably not solely the whim of a powerful man but a decision which the would-be mourners and the larger community could themselves welcome as imperative. It was usual for the killer of an insider to flee the community. Since this was presumably unthinkable in Matoto's case, the conflict of roles during the funeral would probably have been socially insupportable.

None of my informants suggested that Matoto had any grudge or reason, other than the negotiated agreement, to kill this particular man. It is of course pertinent that the victim was not among his own agnates or long-time co-residents. He was probably an affine of Matoto's. The courage or cold blood of the deed did not consist primarily in shooting a defenceless and unsuspecting individual, however, who was in any case away from his home community. That sort of thing is common enough, of course, and is certainly not considered discreditable in a strong man. Even the killing of an enemy child or a woman is praiseworthy, though obviously it means less than the killing of a prominent man. The audacity, the degree of penetration of the arrow, whether only a single arrow is used, whether it finds a vital spot, and how fast the victim succumbs are all measures of prowess, quite apart from the identity of the victim. In this case, an additional measure is that the victim was at least among affinal kinsmen, including brothers-in-law. Yet Matoto's stature was apparently such that he could perform an act that would make a lesser man liable to serious threat of retaliation from some of these kinsmen.

Were Matoto's reputation solely that of a fighter and killer, he might still be a noteworthy example of Tairora male character, although as such perhaps of less general interest. There is no question about the fascination of informants with his audacity and the fear he inspired. Killings and intimidation, however, are not the only achievements credited to Matoto. He is also reported as a peacemaker. On one occasion, after their return from exile, fighting broke out within the Abiera group. As it is now remembered, the hamlets of Bahiqora and Kambuta fell out over some difference. Tempers were frayed, weapons appeared, and in the ensuing mêlée a man was killed. A similar situation might easily lead to a disruption of the community and the departure of a sizeable segment of it to another part of the territory. If serious enough, it might even cause them to flee as refugees to another territory. In cases where a killing is attributable to one or two individuals, the social fabric can sometimes be repaired by the flight of those responsible. The present altercation is described as a pitched battle, with lines drawn, men on both sides skirmishing in the grass, and arrows flying. This is the behaviour of an armed confrontation between enemy camps. Responsibility was apparently collective with no individual culprit whose flight could quell the sense of outrage. The death of a man was probably not intended and it was certainly not inevitable. It doubtless occurred by unfortunate chance. Since it occurred, however, matters at once became critical. Matoto is said to have intervened directly at this point, walking or standing between the fighting parties and demanding that they stop. If they continued to fight, they would have him to contend with. As modern informants see it, this singular act preserved the integrity of the Abiera local group and the call for vengeance was effectively quieted. No doubt, saving the community was vital to Matoto's career, for the community was his base; but in recognizing this as his possible motive, one is at the same time recognizing that he was no mere killer with an uncontrollable thirst for blood.

A major political feat of Matoto's lifetime concerns one of the two major sibs at Abiera today, the Poreqorxntx.[1] The name 'pore' referred locally to the Auyana ethnolinguistic group or other peoples that lie in a southwesterly direction from Abiera. Though younger members of the sib deny it, older men remember that their name is no coincidence. Their ancestors came from Auyana country, speaking that language, and settled as refugees in Tairora territory. Their life in exile was apparently turbulent and they were again driven from their settlements to seek asylum in still other territories. During the worst of it, one elder Poreqorxntx recalls, members of the group were scattered among several Agarabi and perhaps Kamano, as well as Tairora, communities. He believes that these people and their children have never all rejoined the nucleus of the group and now will never do so. Matoto is said to have promised the Poreqorxntx—if by then they were called that—security in Abiera territory. Those that were scattered might safely return and become a part of the Abiera local group.

A decision to give asylum to a group of refugees is a recognized pre-contact move in the Tairora area, as it probably is in much of New Guinea. Basically, therefore, the invitation to the Poreqorxntx had ample precedent. Arrangements of this kind were of necessity made when a group of refugees sought the acceptance of a host group in order to settle in their territory. Such a thing must be decided; it could not simply happen or it would leave the refugees more vulnerable than ever—their hosts always having the option of making common cause with their enemies. In this case, the decision seems to have been attributed to a single man. Whether Matoto acted as a spokesman of authority or as a mere mouthpiece for his group would be important to know. It would give clear evidence as to his personal power in the sphere of politics. If he were more than a man who expressed the *vox populi*, it would also raise the question whether Matoto himself had precedents in this area of supposed small-group democracies.

From one point of view it might matter less whether Matoto, indeed, single-handedly conceived and engineered the decision to give asylum to the Poreqorxntx —or enforced it upon reluctant members of the community. (The latter is not an impossibility, by the way, as Abiera men appear to have been among those harassing the refugees until just prior to accepting them within the territory. Some Abiera, therefore, may have had to be curbed or at least obliged to discontinue their previous hostilities toward the aliens.) Regardless of the facts, as long as the decisions were credited to him, Matoto would appear in the role of a benefactor of the Poreqorxntx, and they would be beholden to him personally. At the very least, it is reasonable that some credit for the decision might go to Matoto, as the approval of a powerful man would be essential to a workable decision. His opposition to it, in other words, would be sufficient to invalidate the agreement. It is no wild leap of fancy, moreover, to suggest a reciprocal relationship between Matoto and the refugees. The more Matoto was given singular credit (whether or not deserved) for recruiting and guaranteeing the Poreqorxntx asylum in Abiera territory, the more they would depend upon and support him in the interest of their own security. The more support they gave him personally as his clients, the more powerful he would be and hence, in turn, the better able to keep the agreement. The mutual relationship of collective and individual interests suggested here is probably a classical instance in the politics of pre-contact New Guinea. Although in this respect the emergence of the key, single figure has seldom been suggested in the Central Highlands and even less often, to my knowledge, in the Eastern Highlands, there are ample suggestions of it in the politics of other parts of Melanesia.

The dynamics of the relationship are too obvious and inevitable, surely, to have escaped a man with the ambition, the power, and the intelligence to play a strategic part. Matoto lived, above all, in a system where a network of personal obligations is both the means and the measure of a man's success. The potential benefits of the relationship were not likely to be lost, either, upon a group like Poreqorxntx: its fortunes were already at an extremely low ebb and unlikely to improve without incurring some such obligations. Matoto was not of the Poreqorxntx sib or he would probably never have been able to act on their behalf. He belonged to a resident Abiera sib, a part of Ondaburx, now locally called Komohorxntx. Far from being an obstacle to enjoying their full support, the agnatic opposition of the Poreqorxntx to his own group, together with their affinal reciprocity, would probably be advantageous to an ambitious leader. It is indicative that in 1964 an older Poreqorxntx man, Matoto's contemporary, was one of his most notable enthusiasts.

Even without crediting Matoto with initially devising the Poreqorxntx asylum or for being the first ambitious man ever to see in such an arrangement a personal opportunity, I think one must recognize in his recruitment of this group a role well transcending that of the 'hot' killer. Here, even if false in taking credit for the move, he played the astute politician. The incorporation of outside people is a more rapid means than any other of enlarging the personnel and fighting manpower of a community. Another most important consequence is in recruiting brides for young men. Obtaining women has a double advantage under the circumstances: it increases the supply of a scarce and valuable good, and it cements ties between hosts and refugees, making them affinal kinsmen of each other. Matoto's part in Poreqorxntx's recruitment, moreover, suggests an intervention for which either the strength or the wit were previously lacking. These refugees from the Auyana ethnolinguistic group did not enter Tairora territory for the first time in Matoto's day. Their asylum among Tairora predates him. For whatever reasons, therefore, it may be that nobody immediately prior to Matoto had sufficient foresight or influence to join the refugees stably to the local community. From here on, in any case, they became permanently resident in Abiera territory. Their commitment today is unquestioned.

Even earlier, possibly before Matoto's rise to power, the Abiera lost a group of residents subsequently known as the Baqe. Through colonization and later hostilities this group left the parent community and became alienated. When members of the Baqe segment killed a man from the Tairora phratry, apparently one from Abiera, open fighting broke out and the Baqe were driven into refuge with a group to the east. Thus the ranks of Abiera suffered a depletion. The process is fairly common in this area, but the result no less serious for the local group affected. Such a depletion in due course doubtless made the recruitment of the Poreqorxntx all the more desirable or necessary.

We may fairly assume that among peoples like the Abiera long periods of military quiet were few. Fighting may not have been 'constant' as it is sometimes described, if by that is meant a weekly affair. There can seldom have been whole seasons, however, let alone years, without interterritorial skirmishes or killings, or larger scale hostilities. A given community might rise or decline, but it probably did not hold its own for long without constant effort. I do not imply solely military effort, of course, but there is little reason to think that other efforts—exchanges, reciprocal giving of brides, and so forth—could be used, no matter how assiduously, in full substitution for a continuous, visible, and convincing show of strength and vigour. Beleaguered communities are well known, local groups driven from their own territory. In at least one case I have studied this seems to have happened as many as a dozen times in roughly a century. Numerous groups have disappeared as separate social or territorial entities once they were driven into exile. It is claimed by some informants that there are groups—Oqinata for one—that completely went under. Their members allegedly were hunted down to the last man, none of them able to find refuge. I am reluctant to believe in the complete annihilation of many groups under the circumstances which prevailed in Tairora. Local society, both sociologically and ideologically, is singularly open. Nevertheless, I take the case of Oqinata as some measure at least of the extent to which the balance could shift against a weakened local group.

Abiera—and Tairora—fortunes rose to unusual heights during Matoto's lifetime. The nucleus of the community was not obliged to leave its territory again, following their return at the beginning of his career, until they were attacked in the early 1930's by constabulary of the Australian Administration. Such stable tenure is not unique, to be sure, but there is ample other evidence for speaking of Abiera's outstanding military position. Indeed, Abiera ascendancy and that of the Tairora are still well remembered in the vicinity and testimony seems remarkably consistent.

There is little doubt that Matoto's career was a part of the prestige and fighting reputation of Abiera and the Tairora phratry during the decades immediately preceding Australian control. There can be no argument, moreover, that Abiera simply happened to be blessed with a run of good luck for that period, or somehow escaped the usual problems of maintaining a forceful stance in the face of recurrent challenge. I do not know specifically how the various challenges arose nor how many arose during Matoto's life, but Abiera was not unchallenged. A major challenge came from within the phratry itself. One of the three main sibs (or sub-phratries) of Tairora today is Onxmantxqa. Today the members of this sib live largely in the settlements of Tonkera and Burauta. (A handful live at Abiera.) Both of these settlements, however, were established in post-contact times, under the guarantee of the Australian Administration. Modern Tonkera (also Tongkera or Tongera) was established in the late 30's or early 40's and Burauta not until about 1958. The people who settled both present communities had previously lived within the area of the Tairora phratry, occupying a territory immediately adjoining Abiera's. They were driven into exile by Matoto and his people prior to the arrival of the Australians. When the Administration began to sort things out in the Kainantu area, a substantial bloc of Onxmantxqa was discovered living among Kamano- and Agarabi-speaking villagers to the west and north. With Australian protection, many of these people returned, as indicated, to found the new settlements inside their former territory. (The prevalence of Kamano bilingualism among the Tairora-speakers of both Tonkera and Burauta, by the way, is notable. It is sufficient, in fact, that Lutheran catechists of the Raipinka Mission address the villagers in Kamano since few catechists speak Tairora.)

The expulsion of Onxmantxqa elements from their lands provides evidence of major hostilities during Matoto's lifetime on the immediate borders of Abiera. It split the phratry in a way which might not have been repaired but for the intervention of an outside agency, the Administration. Matoto's recruitment of the Poreqorxntx almost certainly had a bearing on relations with Onxmantxqa. Even today, a majority of the members of the Poreqorxntx sib are uneasy with the residents of Tonkera and Burauta. Many are unwilling to visit either village. Sorcery is often suspected or attributed to them. It is obvious that this enmity stems from the past and it therefore supports the claim by Poreqorxntx informants that it was ancestors of the Onxmantxqa who were largely oppressing them at the time Matoto allegedly offered them asylum. As to whether the offer and the acceptance produced or only deepened a rift between Abiera people and Onxmantxqa, I could not obtain direct information, but a reasonable inference can be drawn from similar cases. In providing asylum to a dislodged group, the hosts must consider the possible entanglements involved. Such an act, though friendly to those who seek refuge, is not neutral to others. The group which has driven them from their lands may not take kindly to others which offer the refugees aid and protection, especially when the enemies and the host group share a common boundary. From the point of view of the refugees, moreover, there is little comfort in an asylum among hosts friendly to one's principal enemy. Too many opportunities for betrayal exist, and too many temptations. It seems reasonable to conclude, therefore, that the Poreqorxntx were recruited in part as allies against a common adversary, or else it was recognizable that their recruitment would make of Onxmantxqa a common adversary of Abiera hosts and recruits, and the decision was thus probably one involving a risk that had to be calculated. The rest of the affair between Onxmantxqa and their neighbours is reasonably solid history. Onxmantxqa contemporaries of Matoto's say it was no one but him who drove them into exile.

Although furnishing vivid accounts of much about Matoto—even a pantomime of his mannerisms—informants nevertheless provide little description of his efforts as an Abiera statesman. Facts of this kind have to be ferreted out. The facts I have reported above are essentially correct, I believe, and of course they are obtained from the information of local people, judged in the light of the recent and modern political alignments of the area. Matoto's own impact on many of the events of his lifetime is seldom explained. When informants allude to political matters, it is commonly in military terms. It is with the implication that Matoto was so powerful he could intervene between warring factions, give solid assurance to distressed refugees, scatter his enemies, and in general have his way with friend or foe. It is the sheer force and power of the man from which people apparently think all else flowed. No one points to any astuteness of Matoto's, only to his ability to do uncommon favours for his supporters, great harm to his opponents. He is overwhelming as a fighter, frightening as a man. It is as if he had no need to be clever. If the skewing of this picture reflects an unbalanced view of Matoto, I suspect it nonetheless fairly reflects local stereotypes.

Still other things remain to be said about Matoto that indicate the stature he achieved as well as suggesting some of the specific expressions and sources of power among the Abiera. All informants agreed that he had many wives. A conventional number was 'twenty'. I finally concluded that nobody knows precisely how many women could at one time or another, in one sense or another, be called wives of Matoto. I do not doubt that the total number was large, and perhaps twenty is reasonable. Matoto's self-styled aide-de-camp, with the help of one or two other men, could recall the names of 16. All of the men were sure there were other wives but said that they could not recall their names because the women from distant places had returned to their own territories after Matoto's death. The implication seems to be that Matoto not only had far more wives than other men but obtained them from more distant places.

In the Tairora area, it is conventional to say that women find irresistible a strong man and a great fighter. (Vigorous and stylish dancing, closely allied to fighting, is also said to 'kill' the spectators, especially women.) Since Matoto travelled widely throughout the area, he encountered many women who, according to informants, therefore wanted to become his wives. There is more than a hint that the communities Matoto visited were often glad to give him women, thus affording them the access of affinal kinsmen to some of his decisions and actions. Quite probably the wish to make a kinsman and ally of Matoto, as much as the susceptibilities of women themselves, built his extraordinary menage. It must also be noted that Matoto is credited with a limitless sexual appetite, or at least one that he displayed rather notoriously. There is evidence, too, that he was plainly proud of the number of women who belonged to him. An elderly man in a village at some distance from Abiera vividly recalled a journey Matoto once made through the area. He was accompanied on that occasion by a number of his women—eight or nine, I believe—and he boastfully called out to my informant to see the number of wives who were with him and count them!

Women seem to have been in perennially short supply, that is, women of the right age, appeal, and working and child-bearing capacity for the men who wanted them. The supply of widows past child-bearing is scarcely relevant. The cost of a wife was considerable, though the value of a good one clearly exceeded it. The economic problem was not whether a good woman was worth as much as she cost, but the scarcity of women. Younger sons of a man with several sons are sometimes said to have had to fend for themselves, their father's and kinsmen's resources having been exhausted in providing brides for elder brothers. In particular, the stone axes that were a normal if not necessary part of the brideprice were hard to obtain. Unlike much of the other wealth that went into the payment for a bride, they were not produced locally but came from the west through trade. The supply was consequently limited, like the supply of nubile women.

There is thus no question that a man with many wives possessed not only a large quantity of a scarce and extremely valuable good but commanded the services of producers who could furnish him with much of the wealth—pigs, garden crops, bark, mats, and net-bags—he might need in furthering his career. In addition, a bevy of wives was a highly conspicuous symbol and a public tribute to a man's virility, his attractiveness as a male, or his importance. Men sometimes boast that the women of other territories yearn to come and marry them. The women not only stand for the magnetism of a man to females, furthermore, but for the esteem in which he is held by their kinsmen. Even the ability to manage and keep peace among several wives testifies to a competence not all men profess. A long series of payments to affinal kin is set in effect by a marriage. Obtaining the goods to maintain one's obligations under this system would itself be no mean accomplishment when multiplied by a large number of wives. One does not know whether, with a man like Matoto, such obligations were scrupulously adhered to. It is possible that he was even more generous than others, however, for his wealth and hospitality are a plain though only a background part of his legend. There is a suggestion by informants that Matoto may have had relatively less to do with some of his wives than with others, and perhaps he failed to consummate a union with some of them. Matoto's children in the immediate vicinity of Abiera are not unusually numerous. One does not know, of course, the number of children who returned—or stayed— with their mothers to live among kinsmen in distant groups. There is no indication, however, that Matoto bestowed any of his wives upon clients among his younger followers, though this was perhaps the case. It seems, in any event, that Matoto had wives residing in a number of communities and that at the peak of his career women were often simply proffered to him, at the urging of their kinsmen if not because they themselves wished to marry him. Through his wives, his access to pigs and garden food must have been considerable.

I have already hinted at another aspect of Matoto's career, his ability to travel much more widely than others in the hinterlands of Abiera. This ability is evident both directly and indirectly in the stories about Matoto. We hear of him participating in fighting at surprising distances from Abiera, where he apparently went at the urging of local combatants. His contemporaries believed that he would travel great distances to stalk and kill people. The distant sources of some of his women have been noted. I was able to record that he visited Punano territory in the Agarabi ethno-linguistic area, a distance of 12 to 15 miles from Abiera, requiring travel through parts of perhaps five or six intervening territories. (This may not have been his most distant visit but simply one which, through chance, I happened to discover.) Some of these journeys, at least, were in the nature of personal visits, not expeditions on which he was accompanied by numerous followers. The precise purposes of such visits might vary. In general, journeys of this kind were necessary to acquiring or proving a big name, but they surely involved specific missions, the receiving of hospitality, the maintenance of a large personal network, and some- times the making of political arrangements. Such feats are not only atypical of ordinary men but are specifically recognized as a measure of a big man's stature among the people of his community and in the larger area. I have heard of lesser men than Matoto whose importance was claimed in part on the basis of the distances to which they could travel and the territories they could visit with impunity—or at least ones that they dared to risk visiting. Some fearlessness is clearly implied, as well as a large network of contacts and reciprocities and the stature it connotes.

The situation of the present day is by no means comparable. After nearly 40 years of administrative control and the building of 'government' roads, some of them regularly used by vehicles and by total strangers to the area, many men of Abiera have now seen places more distant than any ever seen by Matoto. Even so, I know from personal experience that it is often still not easy to induce villagers to travel in small parties in alien country. It is even less easy to induce them to stop inside a settlement with which they are unacquainted and where they have no friends or kinsmen. In the midst of a government patrol accompanied by con- stabulary the situation is no doubt different, but that has nothing to do with the parties of which I am speaking—and, of course, it has even less to do with Matoto's journeys.

How was Matoto able to do this? The answer is probably twofold. On the one hand, he had, as noted, more numerous and widely scattered exchange partners and affines than other men. These individuals could give him some assurance of safety. On the other hand, Matoto doubtless had considerable protection or immunity thanks to his very reputation. I would not like to suggest, nevertheless, that his journeying was without risks. It is very well to say that, if one were Matoto, he could do such things. One knows the importance attached to killing, however, especially to killing the strong men of an enemy group. Many men, in accomplishing the death of a strong man, not only would do themselves credit but could put others in their debt. Indeed, as I shall describe, Matoto's own death ultimately supports the argument that his wide-ranging personal movements were not free of risk.

Matoto's reputation was even more widespread than his journeying. His travels and his fighting exploits were apparently not equally extended in all directions, but his name was known—and still is known—in places where it is said he never went. In fact, some of the knowledge of Matoto at a distance was even stylized, giving it a character distinct from chance hearsay. I note one saying in particular which I have heard in a number of places: "Matoto is in the Tairora." This phrase seems to have the character of a stock expression. When asked what it meant, people usually told me that it was something they often heard during Matoto's lifetime. There is no difficulty in understanding Matoto's linkage with "the Tairora". At a distance the phratry would almost certainly be named rather than the Abiera local group. Beyond Matoto's phratry-identification, I can only guess at the meaning of this conventional remark. I suspect it had to do with political considerations involving Abiera or Tairora. Either Abiera or Tairora was a formidable roadblock to hostile plans or an exceedingly desirable ally. It is not unlikely that the saying even conveyed a sense of Tairora invincibility. The exaggeration of some local claims of prowess is patent, but I do not think the suggestion is altogether absurd. Some of Matoto's adversaries, as noted previously, say that no one dared oppose him in a fight. The Abiera-Tairora record in the decades just before contact seems almost wholly one of political and military success. I think it is at least worth considering, therefore, that this saying about Matoto referred to Abiera (or Tairora) invincibility during the height of his career. This connotation might not be clear to men at a distance or of a later generation, though the shibboleth itself might survive. .

The first time I heard of Matoto, he was characterized as a 'bad man'. The characterization 'baqubainti' occurred over and over again, almost as often as I found myself talking with someone who had not previously described Matoto to me. It was usually spontaneous. This was clearly the most prominent part of his stereotype.

What Matoto did abroad was generally good—good, at least, for Abiera— while the bad deeds were mostly done at home. One of the familiar examples of Matoto's misdeeds concerned a knoll above the former site of an Abiera settlement.

Here Matoto was said to sit for hours, watching over the territory and the people at work. The men of the past spent much of their time as guards or watchmen, accompanying the women to the gardens to defend them from ambush, or manning posts at strategic points from which they could detect an enemy party. (Cf. the watchtowers of the Dani of West Irian.) Such strategic points, especially the tops of grassy ridges, are still known today in many local territories. Matoto's traditional knoll commanded one of the main paths from the settlement to the gardens. In the late afternoon men and women would pass along the path on their way back to the village. According to present informants, Matoto frequently saw a woman to whom he felt attracted at the moment and without a word would motion the others, often including her husband, to continue on their way. Then he would take her into the grass to enjoy her sexually.

These demands of Matoto evoked no challenge, according to modern informants. The men whose women were chosen simply submitted, seemingly because they had no recourse. It was said that Matoto took such liberties entirely according to his whim and regardless of the husband in question. I suspect that the cuckolds may not have included a random selection of the community, however, for there is no reason to believe that the Tairora of Matoto's day were all sheep but him. Other strong men are remembered, men with a number of wives and with reputations for being 'hot'. One can only speculate now whether these men would risk an open confrontation with Matoto, or whether Matoto, even if he dared, could afford a serious breach with close associates and prominent followers. As far as I could determine, sexual licence was not the recognized prerogative of a strong man, and Matoto's liberties were based simply on the fear of reprisal against any who might challenge him. Modern informants naturally cite Matoto's behaviour as proof of his complete intimidation of his contemporaries.

Even in the village, some also asserted, Matoto might enter a woman's house at will. If her husband were present, he would motion him outside while he copulated with the wife. I have no idea how common were such incidents. Younger informants implied that they were as common as they were notorious. There is some tendency on the part of the younger men, however, to suggest that Matoto's sexual liberties were more outrageous, as well as more germane to his character, than some of Matoto's contemporaries make them seem. His self-styled aide-de-camp did not deny that Matoto did such things. However, he seemed to treat them as secondary if perhaps inevitable expressions of Matoto's power, regrettable but not the most memorable things about the man.

The question arises why Matoto engaged in such flagrant violations of village mores as well as in such flagrant sexuality. As a man with a large number of wives and presumably with the possibility of additional ones if he wanted them, what need did he have of further sexual outlets? Or, if his appetite were as nearly boundless as modern informants believe, why was it necessary or desirable to satisfy it publicly and at such apparent cost to the self-esteem of other men? Covert adulteries are well known in Tairora society and it is generally assumed that numerous women are willing partners. Since the male-female avoidances of many Central Highlands peoples have now been noted (Read 1954; Meggitt 1964), moreover, the question might even arise whether a strong man like Matoto did not risk his virility or his strength in excessive sexual contacts—or if Tairora views differ from those of other Eastern Highlands peoples. Informants seem to feel about Matoto's sexual behaviour that he simply wanted a given woman at a given time and so he took her. With his power and the fear in which he was held, in other words, he could do so. I find it difficult to believe that the motivation was wholly or even largely libidinous. After all, as suggested, Matoto could have engaged in discreet adulteries like other men. In fact, since he apparently had no fear of retaliation, he could easily have expected the silent consent of the husbands. There is ample suggestion that, even with ordinary adulterers, some Tairora men are more concerned about the exposure or the shame than with the fact of their wives' infidelity. One could, of course, counter that it would be grossly out of character for a man like Matoto to be sneaking about in gardens or in the bush to meet another man's wife. The implication that he must avoid an encounter with her husband would presumably have been quite unacceptable to one whose whole *persona* was based on audaciously and recklessly taking or seeming to take what he wanted.

I shall argue that Matoto's open freedom with other men's wives, whether or not it had an appreciable libidinous component, was a symbol of the very things Matoto stood for. In order to succeed as a symbol, it had to be flagrant and notorious. His behaviour could not therefore spare other men's feelings any more than it could stay within the mores of the community—or be fobbed off with some rationalization or other. The violation of other men's rights, the offence against the mores, and the wanton disregard of all the conventional cautions about male strength and female sexuality, I submit, were just what they were meant to be. They established Matoto's immunity to ordinary restrictions, to the rules that inhibited ordinary men. I further suspect that this behaviour was at once the boldest and—for its boldness—the least disruptive possible under the circumstances. Bolder still, perhaps, would have been the large-scale destruction of property or the killing of members of his own local group—something which is not reported of Matoto. (A wife and one outside man are the only local victims of which I heard and, while there may have been others, there is no suggestion of wholesale 'inside' killings.) Such acts would have been seriously disruptive, striking at the physical well-being of the group and its vital manpower. Matoto's sexual behaviour, in fact, may have given men whose wives were forced into public adulteries less reason for shame than if the adultery had been covert or the adulterer a lesser man. Perhaps this point, which may escape younger informants, helps to explain the more matter-of-fact attitude of Matoto's aide-de-camp concerning his sexual behaviour.

In addition to boldness and impunity, Matoto's reputation for unbridled sexuality is consistent in at least one other respect with his *persona*. As do peoples elsewhere in the Eastern Highlands, the Tairora conventionally accept the need to restrict their contacts with women, above all sexual contacts. Men are thought to weaken or die, and young men to fail to develop properly, from excessive feminine contact or from contact at the wrong times in a man's life or during a woman's menstrual or birth cycle. As with other types of avoidance and dangers, however, older men are less susceptible than young men and strong men less so than lesser men. Were there space here, I believe a convincing case could be made that Tairora practice differs appreciably from their profession—and perhaps Tairora differed also from some of their neighbours with regard to women and sexuality. Nevertheless, this is not to suggest that no importance whatever attaches among the Tairora to such beliefs and restrictions. Matoto's sexual behaviour could thus well be a symbol of his immunity, as a man of unparalleled strength, to the magical and physiological restrictions that governed men of ordinary caution.

What of Matoto's power in local affairs? What authority did he have in allocating the resources of the community or the efforts of the people? One hardly looks for a tightly managed system in the Eastern Highlands, but rather one that operated by personal influence, exchange, and mutual obligation. Nevertheless, a figure like Matoto is an undeniable source of power, whether based on fear of physical reprisal or fear of his ability to withdraw support. His arbitrariness is clear enough in some matters already noted, at least, to raise the question whether it extended into spheres unexpected in a small-scale society. One informant stated that everything in the village belonged to Matoto and that people would not cut down so much as a tree without advising him of it in advance. Another felt that no marriage could—or would—be arranged without Matoto's consent. Still another indicated that in the morning, before anyone left the settlement, the movements of the group for the day would be decided in accordance with Matoto's views. In fact, he might tell several men to go and repair a fence, send them to guard women at work in the gardens, or despatch them on some other assignment.

Depending on how these points are taken, the impression of central regulation or co-ordination may be considerably at odds with the autonomy of individual decision among present Tairora villagers. Yet modern conditions differ radically from pre-contact conditions and practices might also therefore differ. The pressure of enemies and the importance of fighting have disappeared or taken new forms, and one can hardly judge the behaviour of villagers or the authority of outstanding men of yore from that of any figures of the moment—other than the figure of the kiap. (He, incidentally, is often seen as a fighter *par excellence* and his authority, in the eyes of many, is based on this quality.) No mechanical, evolutionist preconception about the course of political development, at any rate, should stand in the way of considering whether central authority within the village may have been greater in the past. Nor shall I argue whether for sheer power Matoto is outmatched by latter-day leaders and the so-called 'satraps' of colonial administration (Brown 1963). I think it is out of the question. I am rather concerned with whether, as informants suggest, village activities only loosely regulated or not regulated by authority at present were more centrally controlled in Matoto's day.

A strong inferential case can be made for greater central co-ordination in the past. The men's house, now gone from many villages of the area, was a nerve centre and a clearing house for the affairs of a settlement. Anyone living in the men's house would probably know, without making a special effort, whether someone intended cutting down a tree. Whether a Matoto would have any reason to oppose it—or how he would do so—is a question to which I do not have the answer. Anyone concerned would be able to express his approval or withhold it from a given marriage. The approval of a Matoto, moreover, might not be negligible, as he could throw his support behind the arrangement in the form of a substantial contribution. Whether he could literally veto it—or would often find himself in a position where he wished to do so, I cannot say. As to despatching daily task groups in the morning, it was explained to me, such co-ordination of movements was a purely practical matter. A solitary individual was vulnerable to ambush, and in order to induce compliance, my informant supposed, Matoto would have to do little more than indicate the consequences of a refusal to adjust to the movements of others. Otherwise a leader could threaten not to come to a man's defence should he be attacked. But this seemed frankly hypothetical to the informant, who doubted that anyone would act so wilfully.

Better institutions and more urgent conditions may thus have existed in the past for a man like Matoto to influence even the quotidian affairs of the village. Logical inference would further suggest that a man so much more powerful than any today, who made peace between warring factions and whose prowess was so much a part of Abiera's own ascendancy, was something more than a neutral factor or a mere agile arbiter of public opinion. After all, a manager of consensus, if that is a reasonable description of Matoto (!), may find that those whose views he samples have a marked tendency to gravitate toward his own position, although the usual implication of this sort of role is a process in which the ostensible leader continually adjusts *his* views to those of the many. It is clear that in the men's house were made such decisions as the time of ceremonies, when to fight, whom to seek for allies, whom to accept as refugees. A formal council is scarcely indicated, but the voice of a powerful man—if he were interested to take a position—would hardly be likely to be ignored. It does not stretch a point to suggest that Matoto took positions! The men's house and the imminent danger of attack are gone today, as is the need to co-ordinate with each other's movements for safety within the local territory and in fighting abroad. The Administration has usurped much of the local community's initiative as well as disfranchising leaders like Matoto. I do not think, therefore, one should be intimidated by the weakness of present leaders in viewing those of the past.

I found some who believed that the community worked for Matoto. Besides the constant suggestion that no one dared deny him anything or oppose him in anything, there was an implication that the people of Abiera were regularly at Matoto's disposal or were obliged to give him their labour toward the production of goods for his use. The community—indeed, a much larger community than

Abiera—gave him a surprising number of women who would more than obviate any need of labour or production in the female sphere. This is clearly the major sphere of production, moreover, including a majority of the garden crops, pigs, bark and bark clothing, sleeping mats, net-bags, and some forage foods and materials, not to mention children. There were still men's tasks, however, such as housebuilding, providing firewood, and ditching and fencing gardens. While I doubt that Matoto was ever completely exempt from such labour, it seems impossible for a single man unaided to dig all the ditches and build all the fences needed for the gardens of a large number of wives, to say nothing of keeping them in daily firewood. (The division of labour would presumably place an inescapable limitation on the number of wives a man could have without some supplement to his own effort in complementing the economic efforts of these women.) Matoto can hardly have done without the help of kinsmen, perhaps brothers-in-law in the case of wives resident in other communities.

One informant pointed out a special form of help allegedly available to Matoto. Some men were, for one reason or another, of no use in fighting. A man might have little stomach for it or he might simply lack the skills, be unable to see well or run, or he might be handicapped in some other way. Accordingly, my informants said, such a man would say to Matoto, "You fight for us, keep the enemy at bay, and protect our territory, gardens, and pigs. You are busy and away all the time with this fighting and therefore cannot help your wives in their gardens. I will stay behind while you are fighting, help your wives, and look out for them, so you will not need to worry about your fences and your ditches."

I would not expect more than a loose division of labour between fighting men and non-fighters. A formal arrangement seems altogether too neat and too complex for the sanctions and exchanges such systems as Tairora appear capable of supporting. Though monolithic in his own way, Matoto was probably very far from resembling the manager of an Abiera plantation! A man of his means, however, could work in other ways. Unless some of his wives were idle or very poor producers, he would have had an extraordinary quantity of garden food, pigs, and other goods at his disposal. It requires little imagination to see the reciprocities of the system employed so that other men supply his wives with firewood or the help they need in the making of gardens. If his own prestige did not of itself command these services, it would nevertheless tax Matoto little to pay for them in the form of food exchanges, contributions toward brideprice, and pigs for ceremonial occasions. The economics of Matoto's position, I therefore suggest, are centrally focused upon the large number of women he had as wives and whose production he could consequently command. With such a resource at his disposal, there seems little need to imagine him constantly torn between the urgencies of domestic labour and the pull of political affairs that took a man of renown afield.

The lack of spontaneous emphasis by informants on Matoto's commissary or on his giving feasts or organizing exchanges is in itself interesting. Questioning made it clear that this part of his behaviour was by no means deficient. "He fed us well," I was told. In fact, from one account, Matoto was a punctilious host, refraining from eating during a feast. While his guests ate, he simply sat smoking and watching. This was seen as an aspect of strength and self-discipline as well as a nice point of etiquette. If Matoto measured up with respect to hospitality, why was so little said of it without prompting by the interviewer? Possibly it is simply obvious to a Tairora that a man like Matoto would fulfil these qualifications, whereas he was far more outstanding with respect to the qualities they spontaneously emphasized. Matoto is remembered for how he impressed and intimidated others, accordingly, not for how he looked after them or indebted them to himself. The perceptual selectivity of informants thus favours the 'hot' qualities of the man, not the generosity or solicitousness of the provider. Indeed, it may not be too much to say that the latter qualities are almost literally crowded out by the former.

A field marshal would be out of place in Tairora. Beyond a few rudimentary tactics such as stealth, surprise, and ambush, co-ordination was more concerned with the alignment and consolidation of kin and allies against given adversaries. These largely political or diplomatic manoeuvres were important, to be sure, but would hardly afford scope for the accumulation of power or the conquering ambitions of a Tairora Alexander. Enmities and amities developed in the immediate context of interterritorial, sib, and phratry relations. No doubt the sphere of action could be widened, as witness Matoto's forays into Kamano. Dominance could not add substantial occupied land nor subjects, however, though it could sometimes empty a nearby territory of enemies, and a position of strength could confirm allies or attract refugees or other immigrants. The stage for Matoto's exercise of power was thus very small by the standards of 'civilized' empire-builders, even in the field of his greatest renown.

For several reasons it would be difficult to say how many persons could ever securely have been counted under Matoto's banner. The names of local groups peripherally involved with him are particularly elusive. Pre-contact populations are usually a mere guess. And loyalty or allegiance must have varied in given cases from fairly constant to highly contingent as well as from active to marginal. In round numbers, the Tairora phratry today (with the Onxmantxqa repatriates) is roughly a thousand people. Allowing a maximum of five to six hundred for Matoto's day and perhaps thrice that number for his more visible clients or cohorts outside, we would have no more than 2000 to 2500 people who may sometimes have fought or thought of themselves as a part of Matoto's enterprises. With *their* friends and kinsmen, no doubt, the number would be larger, but here the problem of definition and boundary becomes truly formidable. As it is, my figures can be no more than suggestive.

I have previously noted that Matoto was much involved in arrangements for fighting abroad and that emissaries came to him, even from distant groups, to seek his assistance and allegedly to pay for it (p. 238). Perhaps this is as near to a maximum expression of military authority and central leadership as is possible in a community like Abiera. One also sees Matoto, through the eyes of one informant, despatching a group of Abiera fighters to attack Ontenu, a traditional enemy. He told them to find and kill an important man, not just anyone they might happen to meet. "Come back and report to me you have killed a big man and I will give you pork to eat," he was paraphrased as saying. "Come back and name some rubbish man and I will give you nothing!" Queried about this, the same informant said that, after Matoto became renowned, he did not go on every fighting expedition himself but would send out others. This image of Matoto, furnishing (or threatening to withhold) the feast for the returning fighters, also helps to confirm his control and disposition of garden food and pigs well beyond personal needs, and particularly suggests their employment in a redistributive pattern associated with central authority.

Matoto died in ambush in Arokara territory some time around 1930. The ambush was well prepared. A friend or kinsman sent him an invitation to come to the borders of Arokara to receive a present of betel nuts. The Arokara are traditional enemies of Abiera and of nearly all the Tairora phratry, but presumably it was an individual friendship that made the invitation conceivable. As the story is recalled, a confederate of Matoto's exchange partner prepared a small space inside a stand of reeds at the spot where Matoto was to collect his gift. The reeds were parted sufficiently for an arrow to travel from the hidden archer to the victim. When Matoto appeared, he was manoeuvred into position and shot. He died either on the spot or on the way back to Abiera, some three or four miles to the north. He is said to have died from a single arrow, thus in a sense violating the convention that strong men are difficult to kill, dying only slowly, even after being struck by many arrows.

Matoto's strength nevertheless made itself manifest to the last. The body, according to several informants, lay out for 'nine days' while his many kinsmen and cohorts came to participate in the funeral. Despite the protracted period of mourning, so it is recollected, the body did not deteriorate or even begin to smell. It was finally laid to rest between the roots of a great tree in the forest above Abiera. I was shown the place, but the bones had been removed by people who wanted them for the power that inheres in them.

Matoto's death strikes one as too simple. Was it not even stupid? How could a man who all his life had been laying traps for others blunder into such a trap himself? My informants viewed it differently. They saw it as treachery, for Matoto would not have responded to the invitation of an obvious enemy. He would have known he had many enemies at Arokara, a traditional enemy of Abiera, all of them wishing his death. The one who drew him into ambush was necessarily a man he trusted, and one he should have been able to trust. For the informants it follows that Matoto was simply betrayed.

There are, however, other views. A sorcerer at Aiyura, a Gadsup-speaking traditional enemy of Abiera's to the north, asserts he was making sorcery against Matoto at the very time of his death and thus claims the credit. Matoto's death was procured at Aiyura, according to this man, and only incidentally occurred in the

Arokara territory, eight or ten miles distant. While the claim suggests again the 'international' stature of the man, the alleged sorcery seems to be unknown to the Abiera. Whether or not they might accept it if they heard of it, I do not know. Some probably would.

No one suggested that Matoto died a victim of his own reputation, although this seems most plausible to me. Like the champions of all ages, I suggest, Matoto is Matoto because he never refuses a risk, never turns from a fight or a challenge. I have already observed that Matoto felt obliged to undertake unusual journeys abroad. He could not have sat at home or kept to visits no more hazardous or far afield than his fellows. As long as he enjoyed the role he played, this was a part of the price. More than the style of the strong man was surely at stake. In the competition with rival strong men of his own or other communities, there was an advantage in a larger network and in wider contacts. The man with more numerous and diverse political resources had more to call upon or combine in support of a given enterprise.

Matoto may well have made his trips without reluctance or fear, confident and self-assured. I do not know, and I doubt that it would be possible to find an informant who would consider the question moot. Not only his contemporaries, moreover, but he himself may have believed in his extraordinary power and immunity. One who had dared so often and always succeeded might, if he had once been cautious, ultimately become less so. Keeping the appointment at Arokara, I would therefore contend, was neither stupid nor out of character. It was essential to the *persona*. For the Tairora to recognize that the *persona* created its own victim, however, would be too much. It would be for them to deny the validity of the *persona*. Their image of Matoto makes plain they could hardly accept such a view. If there are sceptics or scoffers concerning Matoto, I did not encounter them.

Compared to the magnified figure of the strong man, his death, at least to others, will seem disproportionate. It is only a limitation of Tairora culture, however, that makes it so. Heroes of many groups die insignificant deaths. But the insignificance is disguised by attributing death to the anger of some supernatural or perhaps to a curse upon the hero's birth. The hero may be transported to heaven in a goddess's chariot or on clouds of fire. The Tairora do not have miracles, however, only magic. A corpse that does not rot for nine days represents in the Eastern Highlands the strength of a man, not a divine intervention.

If his death seems an anticlimax to such a life, moreover, Matoto's ghostly existence has been a better match. I have already noted some of the attention given his bones (pp. 232-3). A recent incident involving Matoto's ghost throws further light upon the importance of the man.

The ultimate destination of Tairora ghosts is somewhat ambiguous. Like some of their neighbours, the Tairora speak of a ghost country or community located in the Finisterre Range north of the Markham Valley. According to many, ghosts eventually disappear from the midst of the living to take up their abode in this land of ghosts or afterworld. Matoto's ghost, however, appears to have figured in the lives of his descendants on more than one occasion. In 1964, while I was living at Abiera, a prominent man of the village reported losing his way in the forest one day. He wandered helplessly for hours, he says, unable to find his direction out of the trees and into the clear. Blundering about in this state, he stumbled over rocks and roots, bruising and scratching himself. He began to hear ghostly voices, which he recognized as those of Arokara. The voices kept urging him to take a certain path which, they said, would lead him out of his difficulties. He found it almost impossible to resist their urging, though sensing it was malicious, and he finally stood looking down into a narrow, steep canyon with a stream of water at the bottom. "Come down here," said the voices. "It is a beautiful place." He knew he would have to obey as his resistance was almost gone and he knew he might never again find his way. At that point, a voice he recognized as Matoto's told him, "Do not go down there or you will not come back. They are deceiving you. This is the way to the village." Matoto thus prevented him from entering the canyon, being strong enough to counter the numerous enemy ghosts. Matoto pulled him back, showed him the way, and saved his life, for the canyon led to the after-world. Had he entered it, he would himself have become a ghost.

The patch of forest in question is quite small and naturally quite familiar to the people of Abiera. There is scant likelihood ordinarily of becoming lost in it. Everyone knows that it contains no canyon and the right path, when found at last, was obvious and familiar. My informant attributed his hysteria to the influence of hostile ghosts. It is more significant for the present purpose that he attributed his salvation to Matoto. As in the case of Matoto's bones, the 'bad' man seems to be the source of good to his people. I think the ambivalence is of some interest.

THE HISTORICITY OF MATOTO

Informants do not appear to make Matoto grossly larger than life though, paradoxically, he may seem so to many of them. No one like him is conceivable in Abiera today, and informants born since 1930 find the life of Matoto's day itself increasingly difficult to conceive. To them the men and things of the past seem bigger. There may thus be little temptation to confect a more fabulous Matoto because, in a sense, he is already quite fabulous. Seeing Matoto in the sort of life milieu in which he arose tends on the other hand to domesticate him, as it were, exchanging heroic perspective for mundane. Finding congruences between the figure and the milieu frequently validates the claims of informants but may, at the same time, challenge the implications they draw from them. Certain attributes of Matoto which to younger informants are superlative or unique prove not to be unprecedented. In making the figure credible, however, it has not been my purpose to find in Matoto an everyday sort of man, not even an everyday sort of strong man. It is obvious that he was not one. Were a figure like his more common, we would surely hear of others equal to him, or we would hear less of Matoto. Since I do not believe Matoto was unique of his kind, however, I must argue that he arose not as an anomaly but in a community capable of producing such a man and that he found there the scope with which to operate as Matoto reputedly operated. I thus take the position that in essential respects the Matoto described to me at Abiera in 1964 is not the invention of either his contemporaries or his heirs.

In this section I wish to deal with a few final points concerning the historicity of Matoto. They will be quite brief, for if the picture that emerges from the preceding section still leaves a heavy question mark, I am not likely to erase it here.

Undeniably, Matoto's career terminated at a rather significant historical moment. The beginning of the *pax britannica* was a point beyond which no more men like him would arise in Abiera. There could thus be no newer rival for the attention of Abiera chroniclers. Other things being equal, this is presumably a propitious condition for legend-making. Matoto had been dead only about three decades, however, when I collected information about him. In so short an interval it might be wondered how much legend could develop, that is, *legend* as distinct from Tairora imagery and Tairora perceptions of masculinity, strength, and power. As I encountered it, Matoto's life was far from having been moulded into a closed account, a single statement containing nearly all available information in conventional form. Conventionalization is evident, but closure is not. Talking to more people tends to yield additional information. Particular background details can be ferreted out if the right informant is discovered. There is a limit to this kind of information, no doubt, but the limit is not that of a completely encapsulated tradition. It is imposed rather by a dwindling number of first-hand witnesses to historical events.

A second argument I would make concerning Matoto's historicity is that, if my informants or those who informed them have invented very much of the Matoto story, there exists in the Tairora mind a most extravagant image. Such an image would raise a problem in the interpretation of Tairora culture: what experience or imagination did the Tairora possess for conceiving of it? The simplest answer is, I think, Tairora politics and especially Matoto himself. The supposition that the image is unaccountable or mere hyperbole is hard to defend.

I am probably belabouring the point. I may be over-concerned about not having known Matoto or having talked to him, though that might not in fact have answered many questions. He would have been an old man living under radically different conditions from those of his prime. Only seeing him in action, I believe, would answer questions satisfactorily, and it is rare, not only in New Guinea but everywhere, for the anthropologist to arrive at the high noon of indigenous politics and untrammelled military activity.

The only primary documents of Matoto are his living contemporaries, some his family and kinsmen, some his associates, some his adversaries, and some people who met him once or twice or knew of him from afar. There is confirmation in their respective testimony. On the whole it varies only in the amount of detail each person can provide, according to his closeness in time or space to Matoto. The local memory is surprisingly good, I believe, on topics of interest. I once recorded, for example, a report of an incident of early contact that my informants said involved Mr. Jim Taylor, one of the pioneer government officers in the Central Highlands. Taylor was only briefly in the Kainantu area. Their recollection was not of some peculiarity such as a piece of his costume or something about Taylor's manner. They recalled a confrontation at a particular point between particular people during which certain things were said and done. In taking it down I wondered if the report were *too* graphic, that is, more detailed than a memory of 25 years could be expected to be. I later met Taylor. Recalling the report I had been given, I asked him about it. He was amazed. "Do they remember that?" he exclaimed. "I'd forgotten all about it, but that is just the way it happened!" Matoto's killing of the man with the pig rope, for example, is equally graphic. Such detail and vividness are quite 'historical' in character.

There appear to be no serious inconsistencies in the composite account of Matoto. I have omitted no large segment of the information I possess for failing to be able to fit it to known facts. Vagueness about quantities and time sequences, rather than inconsistency, is the more typical shortcoming. Since the magnitude of Matoto—his real power and the manner and extent of its use—is after all the basic question, one would sometimes prefer numbers and cases to adjectives.

The sociological and demographic effects attributed to Matoto are quite visible and consistent with the account. The alien Poreqorxntx refugees are now an integral part of Abiera and neighbouring local groups. In fact, they are by far Abiera's largest sib. The Onxmantxqa people whom Matoto expelled from their territory did not return from exile until historical times. The claims regarding Matoto's part in these events are corroborated by both friend and foe. All agree that Matoto was instrumental in these changes, which reorganized the Tairora phratry.

The military reputation of both Matoto and the communities under his sway is still today notable in the Kainantu vicinity. Everywhere in the area certain communities stood out as dominant while others had a client status or an unmistakably precarious hold on their territory. Many communities, surely, did not carry their fighting far abroad. In these matters, I know of no local reputation that exceeds Tairora's. Measured simply in miles from the seat of his activity, moreover, Matoto's personal reputation seems unmatched in the vicinity. His role after death—the power ascribed to his mortal remains and his ghost—is perhaps no more than suggestive, but the ghostly Matoto does at least reflect the mortal reputation.

A final point that makes Matoto credible largely as he is reported is that the pattern he represents is not unique. The outrageous liberties, the taste for killing, the bullying and intimidation, the large-scale polygyny, the fierce presence and the convincing semblance of fearlessness—in a word, the mystique of the strong man as its components emerge from the account of Matoto—can each be seen in kind, if not in precise combination or in degree, in other remembered figures of the Tairora area, some of them still alive. There is sometimes, indeed, the same attitude, that these are 'bad' men. When it exists, the attitude appears to have the same basis in flagrant violations of community mores or individual rights. More than merely supporting Matoto's credibility, the existence of the pattern shows his general relevance. The question of Matoto's milieu becomes, then, not a matter of how Abiera accommodated to an unparalleled event but how the milieu produces such strong men, the role of strong men, and the suitability—or vulnerability—of the milieu to a man of great strength.

MATOTO'S MILIEU

I will organize my closing remarks under three general headings: (1) the sociology and the politics of Tairora life; (2) Tairora economics, particularly the role of leadership in the allocation of labour and goods; and, finally, (3) the moral system.

(1) *Sociology and Politics.* Every Abiera man operates within a network consisting of the individuals who are personally connected to him and who interact with him in some way, from minimal to intensive. These include the affinal and consanguineal kinsmen with whom he interacts, as well as others, such as co-residents, people raising pigs for him or for whom he raises pigs, exchange partners in other groups, age-mates and friends, or those whom he leads or follows. The network of an individual may be large or small. One could devise more refined measures for such a network, such as spatial range of the network, frequency or intensity of interaction, and possibly a scale of different kinds of interaction. A man whose network is limited to his immediate co-residents, for example, might have more prolonged or intensive relations with them than a man whose network was larger, just as a man with a single wife might have more to do with her and her brothers than a man with several wives. It is clear that Matoto had a personal network both wider in spatial terms and larger in number of individuals involved than lesser men. These dimensions serve as a measure of a man's magnitude, just as the areal extent of the network is actually a conventional symbol of his importance.

A personal network is obviously ego-relative, and even a small network must necessarily cut across two or more of the divisions of the larger society, its recognized units or segments. These divisions, the basis upon which they are discriminated, and their relations with each other constitute the usual subject matter of social structure. The Abiera local group, the Poreqorxntx sib, and the Tairora phratry illustrate such divisions. The personal network of an individual may include interaction with some but not all of the members of a given division. The network of an influential man such as Matoto involves relations with members of more divisions and with more of the members of a given division, as a rule, than that of a man of small influence.

Although a man of influence may have connections with all or nearly all of the members of a given division, it is not those connections that typically define a division. The connections of a founder or founding ancestor to a division are exceptions, but in the case of a living founder these connections are not likely to define anything larger than a local group or even a settlement; and in the case of a founding ancestor they are not the same sort of connections, obviously, as among contemporaries. Nevertheless, if influential, a man can provide a strong connecting link between two or more divisions. The more members of his own division he includes in his personal network and the more of those of another division, the more a strong man may be able to move either division to act and hence to move them to act in concert or to develop mutual interests. With respect to politics, a close relationship therefore exists between the division to which a man belongs through birth or residence and those other divisions in which he is influential through his network. The influential man is often a key political factor because of a network that permits him to represent or make commitments in some sense or degree on behalf of more of the individuals of his own division *vis-à-vis* more of those of other groups—and probably also with respect to more other groups.

Beyond an individual's personal network are persons who know of him and in whose choices and decisions his reputation or activities may play a part. These are largely persons who are connected in various ways to members of the given individual's network but who are not themselves directly included in it. These persons could be called a fringe zone and the reputation and influence of the given individual among them his aura. The aura of a man of slight influence would be narrow, just as that of a man like Matoto, even on today's evidence alone, was unusually broad. There is in theory a quasi-exponential relationship between the size of a personal network and the breadth of an aura. There is a feedback between the ability of a strong man to initiate large-scale activities at the centre of his network and the number of persons, in and beyond his network, among whom his capacity to initiate and achieve given purposes is credited. Capacity feeds upon reputation, just as reputation feeds upon activities and achievement. In speaking of aura, the Tairora are likely to use the metaphor of a 'big name'. As large-scale achievements both contribute to and are to a degree guaranteed by a big name, a large and favourable aura is by no means merely an incidental measure of a strong man's influence.

The residence- and descent-based divisions of Tairora society are variously interconnected. They combine for certain common purposes or certain periods, are independent for others; and they stand opposed for still other purposes or at other times. Despite fluidity and change, there is continuity. From the local point of view, there are reasonable expectations without which terms like 'traditional enemy' or 'traditional friend' would be meaningless. Poreqorxntx and Komohorxntx (the latter the current name of the sib of which Matoto was a member) largely comprise today's Abiera. These two divisions are counterpoised as clusters of mutual affines in an intensive connubium, but as 'Abiera', a residential group occupying a single territory, they tend to stand together *vis-à-vis* certain outside groups.

The local groups of Tairora society, like the individuals that constitute them, could be rated on a scale of importance or influence. A local group, like an individual, could be said to have a network, larger or smaller, tighter or looser than that of other local groups, and varying over time, according to its importance and its influence. It also has an aura or 'name'.

There is probably no simple sense in which a strong man (or a man with a large network) makes an influential group (or a group with a large and active network). Nor does a strong group make a strong man. The occurrence of strong men is governed in part by factors—e.g., genetic—that are independent of the factors of group strength. The occurrence of a strong group at any given time is likewise in part governed by factors—e.g., local history, demography, disease— which are quite accidental from the point of view of a given individual. Yet some of the factors of collective political and military strength and of individual prowess and renown do overlap, are mutually reinforcing, and work in parallel fashion. A potential Matoto in a weak community (or one with more powerful rivals) might not become the same man as in a community already large, relatively stable, and with a current position of influence in its vicinity. Nevertheless, he would probably make his community stronger than if he had not occurred. Lest we forget, Matoto's Abiera was just returning from exile at the dawn of his career. Matoto made Abiera strong both because he was a formidable champion and because he supported advantageous political decisions, e.g., recruiting manpower through incorporating the Poreqorxntx. That his *persona* and his personal network both aided and bene- fited from such moves seems plain.

In these points and in much of the earlier discussion of Matoto's career, the importance of military events and political decisions in determining the composition of Abiera is clear. The Poreqorxntx became a part of Abiera not because their fathers or their mothers were a part of it (they were not, in fact) but because it was mutually advantageous to these refugees and to Matoto, if not to all of his local group, that they should become fully a part of Abiera. As there is no reason to consider this development extraordinary, it is not too much to say that the local group is in large measure not only a key political unit but one whose composition or membership may be, from time to time, substantially altered by political means. A sense of common descent develops rapidly in Tairora groups, though probably not quite as rapidly as a sense of common polity. This is tantamount to saying that in the formation of Tairora social divisions, politics plays a larger role than con- ventional consanguinity, or perhaps better, plays a prior role.

To a leader whose rise to power and whose influence is based on political and military success such a system gives relatively great scope and manoeuvrability. His career may be short, but the effects of his movements and decisions are rapidly felt in shaping the divisions of society. He need not confine his search for cohorts to the consanguineal accretions of generations, and, in bringing in other cohorts, he is not only adding personnel but extending coventional consanguinity to those not formerly included.

The strong man, like Matoto, influences policy through his renown and through the size of his personal network. The two factors would in fact be difficult to separate analytically. With his influence he is able to mobilize many more individuals than the ordinary man. People may, on the one hand, be afraid not to join him but, in joining him, on the other, are at least not afraid of being committed to a weak or dubious effort. Strength attracts strength. Obligations to a Matoto are likely to be widely respected because it is rewarding to respect them, dangerous to neglect them, and obligations to him are likely to be widely incurred because Matoto is in a strategic position (with his prowess as a killer and his control of substantial production through his wives) to obligate numerous people.

As Matoto becomes identified with Abiera, the personnel he mobilizes on his behalf are mobilized on behalf of what are largely Abiera objectives as well. What is accomplished, e.g., against Matoto's enemies or for his friends, is also accomplished against Abiera's enemies or for its friends. Besides a congruence of objectives, there is a feedback relationship between personal power and community support: the more powerful a Matoto, the more he becomes spokesman and leader of the largest social unit structurally accessible to him. Members of that group simply cannot ignore or deny him. It is not just because they are intimidated that they acknowledge him, though they may be intimidated. They acknowledge him because, if in both mystique and the size of his reciprocal network he is strong enough to intimidate them, he must likewise be strong enough to be of great benefit to them, individually and collectively, through his activities. There is potentially a great congruence in Tairora society between the purely individual ambitions of the man of strength and the group in which he is based. There is a clear *quid* of the community for the *quo* of the individual. The more Matoto becomes *de facto* spokesman and leader of Abiera, the more, through their backing, his power increases.

In fine, though not without cost, a Matoto is an unparalleled asset to a local group. It is difficult to conceive of a single individual who, under the circumstances, could do more of the things that, under the circumstances, were important to be done for the community. The costs of a Matoto include the indignities suffered by individuals upon whose rights he may trample, the insecurity of marginal persons or those who cannot gladly play the game his way, and the frustrated ambitions of other local strong men who may perhaps aspire to greater prominence but find their best chances foreclosed. Ambitious men must choose thus between being prominent collaborators of Matoto's or withdrawing from the group to seek an independent status. Further costs include the women given to a strong man as wives and the labour services he apparently receives from certain men. Pragmatically, it seems clear, the individuals and collectivities are quite prepared in a case like Matoto's to support these costs. One could argue that some persons have no choice, and at least the illusion of having no choice is a part of the leader's power. The difference may be of little practical consequence as long as Matoto's use of power is not largely terroristic—a use for which, despite the appellation 'bad man', there is no irrefutable suggestion in the Abiera account of Matoto.

The Tairora field in which Matoto flourished is populated by local groups which, even today, average little more than 200 persons. There is no reason to think they were larger in the recent past, and they may well have been smaller.

The several factors governing local group size—ecological, sociological, political, and ideological—would be interesting to consider but they are beyond the scope of the present paper. Groups of such small size are inherently unstable demographic units. The fluctuations in births and deaths (from all causes to which they are subject) would be of much less consequence in a larger group, of course, but are magnified in a small one. To these fluctuations must be added the possibility of rapid loss to a local group through flight to asylum or internal dissension, colonization, and segmentation. On the other hand, there is the possibility of a rapid increase through the recruitment of outside refugees or allies. It is not difficult to see the importance of an interterritorial system in which, through exchanges and alliances with other groups, some cushioning of a given group's power fluctuations is often possible.

As has been recognized by various students of Eastern Highlands societies, a local group often takes to flight, not through some dramatic defeat involving heavy losses, but through the loss of a man or two and the realization that further losses against a given adversary are consequently likely, in view of the balance of manpower and outside support between them. In a group in which the loss of one or two fighting men can loom so large, it is patent that the presence of one man of extraordinary prowess or repute is at least equally decisive. The recognition of this principle is no exclusive insight of the ethnographer: the fighting objectives and ideals of the Tairora area are quite clear in their recognition of it. Hence the constant aim of killing the strong man of an enemy group, despite the general awe of confronting him openly. (Although I am no longer arguing the historicity of Matoto, it is such considerations that make me reluctant to dismiss as megalomania some of the emphases of the Abiera account of him.) The very dependence of the group upon—or their vulnerability to—such men, it seems to me, makes their cost to their own community, however high (or bad) it may be, slight as compared to the cost to their enemies. Even if Matoto is, as I suspect, at the far extreme of possible individual power in a Tairora leader, he highlights the politico-military nature and conditions of the leadership of pre-contact times.

I have no evidence that Matoto introduced specific political or military innovations. The case is complicated, however, in at least two ways. If he did introduce innovations, on the one hand, they would probably not have survived both his death and the political changes made since 1930 by the Australian Administration. On the other hand, it is possible that Matoto's power was itself an innovation, in other words, an increase in the degree of political centralization over anything previously experienced. This is what most informants seem to imply with their view that there was never before anyone like Matoto. I have tended to reject their view, not only seeing Matoto as a strong man who devised no radical new methods but remaining to be convinced that he realized and activated the existing political possibilities of his time to a radically new degree. This position naturally does not resolve the question of whether his leadership was innovative in a total sense, if not in the sense of particular ideas. Thus one cannot rule out the possibility that Matoto may have represented political novelty in the form of personal magnitude. There was an unmistakable and immediate reflex in the part of the regional power structure where he happened to live and which he used for a base. Through astuteness, he made Abiera a very powerful collective point in the regional network, just as he made himself a very powerful individual point in the network. However, my supposition is that, even if Australia had not burst upon the Tairora at just this moment, Matoto could have bequeathed to his followers and heirs little beyond a name, an aura, a reputation for strength—his own and theirs collectively. I doubt that he could have left them either a durable or a different sort of political system from the one which he found, unless, possibly, his use of personal power established precedent and in that sense prepared the way for more powerful subsequent leadership. In any case, he did not leave them a system less dependent on the rise of successive strong men—or less vulnerable to the whims of those it might succeed in producing. Despite Matoto's legacy, Abiera's bright reputation would be dimmed as fast as the community failed to maintain a posture of strength before its rivals, and strength expressed in practically the same terms which Matoto found when he began to express it. Only the Australian Administration changed that.

(2) *Economics*. The economic aspects of Matoto's leadership are little stressed by Abiera informants. Even his activity as a giver of feasts and a provider, as noted previously, is far from being highlighted. I have suggested by way of possible explanation (p. 242) that the Tairora strong-man mystique lays greater stress on fighting competence and aggressive masculinity than on the possession or use of wealth. Or it may be better to say that aggressive masculinity is defined rather in such terms than in terms of wealth.

In this respect the Eastern Highlands as a whole may differ from areas such as Mt. Hagen where, according to Strathern (1966), important men qualify primarily as manipulators of wealth. The *moka* exchanges and the wearing of necklaces that commemorate a man's economic exploits, rather than fighting prowess, measure his standing. In fact, ". . . the big men were not brave in warfare, but put the bachelors in the front lines, while they themselves stayed at a safe distance" (Strathern 1966: 363). There thus appears to be a contrast between two parts of the Central Highlands with respect to status and leadership. Not only Matoto, but Kavagl of Chimbu (Schäfer 1938; Salisbury 1964), Upper Chimbu leaders (Criper 1966), and Siane leaders (Salisbury 1964) seem to be men whose status is based in large part, if not centrally, upon audacity, a capacity for violence, or an awesome *persona*. I do not argue that all of these groups are as little concerned with the leader's economic skills as the Tairora account appears to make Matoto. Nevertheless, the qualifications of Tairora leadership seem to have appreciably more to do with physical prowess than Strathern indicates is true of Mt. Hagen peoples. Indeed, the quantities of wealth employed by the Tairora are smaller, there is no development of *Moka* or equivalent ceremonial exchange, and necklaces or comparable economic tallies reflecting status are lacking. The almost complete preoccupation of informants with Matoto as a man of strength thus cannot be dismissed.

The difference is properly one of emphasis, probably not an absolute difference. In Tairora as elsewhere, the man of little means tends to be a little man— 'rubbish man' in the current Pidgin; and the man of great means is likely to be a great man. There is no call to dichotomize wealth and fighting prowess in considering the basis of leadership. For a community as well as for a prominent man there is a complementary relationship between them. A leader would by local standards probably have both wealth and power. Yet in Tairora ultimate control of one's own destiny as well as that of others rested in the hands of individuals and groups who could muster fighting strength and deploy it, convincingly and with political skill. To the outstanding ones among these individuals, ample control of wealth and production appears to have been assured. But it was apparently based on fighting and political competence, not on adroitness in the manipulation of goods. As previously noted, the wealth which came to strong men took the form notably of women in marriage, and it could hardly have taken a more meaningful economic form since women are the prime producers of goods—other than imported goods.

For purposes of discussion, I will sketch an economic system in which Matoto might have operated as a redistributive central hand (Polanyi 1957). As noted, the community—indeed, a larger community than that of the local territory—bestows numerous food producers upon him in the form of wives, and provides 'garden men' and male kinsmen, such as brothers-in-law, to help the women and hence Matoto. This donation is in recognition of and in exchange for his spectacular skill and specifically his power to be of help to those who thus favour him—or to cause serious harm to those who do not. In such a system, on the one hand, people would be purchasing or ensuring security with wealth—above all, women. On the other, the fighting force or allies upon which they depend would be centred upon the leader who, through his sizeable establishment, could furnish considerable quantities of food to others, presumably including those who fought beside him. The men's house would make an ideal physical point for the centralized provisioning of the fighting men, through the daily sharing of food brought there by the wives of the leader. The occasional feasts given by the leader would be only high points in the commissary round, since the occupants of the men's house would receive the leader's food (and also share with him their own) almost continually.

In constructing such a scheme from the few suggestions of several decades ago, one can do little more than point to its plausibility. Some of the most crucial conditions no longer obtain. The men's house is gone, for example, as are both power and extensive polygyny comparable to Matoto's. There would be little justification today for placing great wealth in the hands of a war leader, even if it were possible for men to qualify as such. Some valuables remain as before—notably women and pigs—but others are of little present significance. New valuables, above all, money, have replaced them. In acquiring wealth in this new form, new means are required. Through wage work and cash crops, the relative importance of 'garden man' roles and strong man roles has been all but reversed. Durable forms of wealth such as shell and stone axes perhaps once played a part in the economics of status differentiation, but it could scarcely be inferred from conditions today. Stone axes are no longer imported or in circulation, and according to one report (J. K. McCarthy, personal communication) the aboriginal value of shell was practically destroyed through catastrophic inflation when large quantities were imported into the area by Europeans during the period of initial contact. Incidentally, these dramatic economic changes may suggest an additional reason why the economics of strong man leadership are so opaque to—or through—the eyes of informants. They make it impossible to use present conditions as testimony for a strong man economy of the sort I have sketched.

There does in any case remain to consider the concentration of female producers—wives—in the hands of Matoto. What use was made of their production? In placing such numerous producers under the control of a single man, it would be remarkable if the comunity did not receive in return some of their production through the central position of the leader. If Matoto did not use much of it in this way, moreover, it is not easy to imagine what use he could have made of his wives' output. In one form or another, therefore, the local group presumably benefited from the leader's extraordinary menage. (1) They may have received some of the women as brides secondarily passed to Matoto's clients; or (2) they may have benefited from their services if Matoto placed his wives as co-residents with the wives of other men to work in conjunction with them; or (3) in the most general sense, at least, the community benefited from the sheer addition to its numbers, its labour force, its child-bearers, and its productivity.

(3) *Morality*. Politics and morality are certainly not alien to each other. As "the art of the possible", or as the means of making and carrying out decisions affecting the life of a group, politics is only partially defined. Goal, direction, or guidelines are also necessary. Politics is clearly not concerned with everything possible nor with all conceivable decisions. It is concerned with decisions or possibilities that afford individuals and groups some approximation to what they consider desirable. Matoto's career overtly raises the question of morality. People from within his own community over and over again call him a bad man. The standards of behaviour they invoke are therefore of interest. I believe, moreover, that Matoto peculiarly highlights Tairora morality and politics, revealing not only emphases but what may be a major vulnerability.

I do not consider Matoto anomalous in the moral ambience of Abiera. The question of moral ambience, to be sure, applies in a double sense: it is the ambience that produced Matoto, whatever he became, and it is the ambience in which Matoto is judged and survives in a popular image. Failing to observe the congruence between Matoto and the morality of his group, I feel, would be a loss to understanding the morality as well as Matoto.

In the light of the position I have just stated, how should one take the statement that Matoto was a bad man? Is it in part an idiomatic convention to speak of a strong man in this way, comparable perhaps to saying of an impressive dancer that he 'kills' his audience with his performance? Certainly one finds that a number of the strong men of the Tairora are described as bad. The men themselves in some cases acknowledge that they are bad. To take this as entirely a convention, however, would imply that Matoto (and his congeners) did not in fact do anything the community could seriously reprove. Matoto's reported excesses seem to preclude such a view.

The bad deeds in Matoto's case are surely not his aggressions against outsiders. They are his threats and intimidations against his own people, his infringements of their rights and dignity. Can this behaviour be regarded as incidental to his role as strong man, or should it be seen as an instrumental to the role? Did Matoto commit outrages, in other words, because of the temptation to do so and since he expected to get away with it, or were the outrages an effective—even a necessary—part of the strong man *persona*? (I have already given my views of Matoto's flagrant adulteries, pp. 248-9.) Leaving aside his own motives, did Matoto's excesses contribute to his effectiveness as a leader or diminish it? I doubt that his bad behaviour seriously detracted from his effectiveness as a strong man. I would further argue that his behaviour, whether or not instrumental to the role, was a logical and consistent extension of some of the very qualities and tendencies which made Matoto strong. These are not simply contradictory acts, somehow out of character with the 'good' in Matoto. Becoming an outstanding politico-military asset to Abiera may or may not have led directly to his bad deeds, but the source of the two has much in common. I am therefore questioning the possibility in Tairora of an equally effective leader whose character combined benevolence toward insiders with relentless aggression toward the outside. I am arguing that what may be boundary in Tairora morality from a community point of view—social control—is continuation from the point of view of Tairora ideals of masculine character, that is, from an individual point of view.

Matoto and others like him logically epitomize the masculine ethic of Tairora. Taken with the legendary accretions, the figure of Matoto is almost its perfect realization. I do not believe, therefore, the *de facto* rules of the Tairora power game differ entirely from the recognized rules. The man, like Matoto, who reaches the top does not do so primarily through perceiving some sort of deception, while his competitors remain duped and lesser figures for supposing the game to be actually what it seems. Such a view makes dominance depend too much upon insight, in other words an essentially intellectual quality. I believe it is not that the real rules for winning are obscure but that key attributes of dominance are unequally distributed among acknowledged competitors. Matoto and other dominant men do not beat the game, I should say, but play it better.

The Tairora masculine ethic can be described in either concrete or abstract terms. Abstractly it has much to do with strength, forcefulness, indifference and hence immunity to fear or threat, and with unconcern for the normal consequences of acts involving danger. The strong man transcends many of the usual restrictions of life since, if he *is* strong, this is one of the principal ways in which to demonstrate it. Others do not control a strong man or manage his affairs by holding him to standard prudence or propriety. More concretely, the strong man is indomitable and ruthless with his adversaries. He is, at his peak, so much stronger than they that they cannot even confront him. Aggression and killing are such a part of a strong man like Matoto as almost to resemble a reflex. He must constantly be forestalled by the mildness or circumspection of those who do not wish to provoke him, including his fellow villagers, or by the sympathetic intervention of his associates when a stranger has innocently done so. The strong man is 'hot'. The energies of life are powerfully present and undilute in him. People understand this: he is simply that way. It is intrinsic, not a matter of his studied resolve. He could not, therefore, be appealed to and thus deflected. A hot man *is* hot, not someone who chooses to be. He is like a force of nature. He is often hence a terrible man. He could not be so terrible to his enemies if he were not, in fact, terrible: it is because he embodies so much of the power and danger of the world which other men have in smaller measure. He is kept within limits that are, as far as possible, socially positive for the group, but this must be accomplished through a willingness of the community to overlook transgressions or at least through their failure to challenge them. His group are relieved, on the one hand, not to have to face such a terrible man among their enemies. His presence tends to put the community at large well above the level of its neighbours. Their name is ascendant. On the other hand, the terrible man is no light burden to them nor one that all of them bear gratefully. In the final analysis, they do not have him because they choose to—or they are in doubt whether they have a choice. He is rather a fact of life, like friends and enemies. Like them, he must be dealt with, and if he brings them good, he likewise brings them some harm.

Matoto, I would argue, is a fuller embodiment of the emphases of the male cult than most apprentices can ever become. Hence he is logically a *better* man. He is no bizarre phenomenon outside the system but fulfils in unusual degree the teachings and exhortations given to Tairora youths, especially during their initiation and early residence in the men's house. As a man who is strong, fearless, unfeeling with his competitors, and pitiless with enemies, he is the system's ideal—as so many men are clearly not. He is the logical result toward which the education of young men seems largely pointed. At the same time, he is probably a result that can only now and then be achieved in such full measure. Were men like Matoto more common, they might succeed in modifying the system into one better adapted to the threat. The system produces strong men frequently, but few of such strength. It consequently lacks appropriate checks and elaborations. As Salisbury suggests, the salvation of the system is that a despot does not live forever and that his prime years are relatively brief (1964: 227). I would add that there is further salvation in that despots of Matoto's calibre are not able to bequeath their full power to others, nor are they likely to be succeeded regularly by others equally despotic.

Local groups like Abiera are very small. One of Matoto's surviving contemporaries said that Matoto's own immediate group—probably the men's house group—had only 'ten men'. The figure is probably conventional, but it is clearly in line with the demographic facts. Even the 1964 population of Abiera, probably larger than in Matoto's day, had only 12 youths between 10 and 20 years of age. These would formerly have been the raw material for making fighting men. Ten or twelve chances per half generation is not many for producing an outstanding strong man. The elder men act as if they would like each youth to become as hot and relentless in persecuting the group's enemies as Matoto. To this end boys will be frightened, cut, beaten, bled, sweated, purged, anointed, and fed pork, salt, and special herbs in the course of growing up and being initiated. Impressive and secret physical measures for men, such as nose-bleeding and cane-swallowing, will be invoked to promote their masculinity and aggressiveness. They will be subjected to oratory and exhortations. But it is nevertheless impossible to control the outcome. Some of the youths will be sickly or small and many of them mean-spirited despite all efforts.

The stakes are high for the community, certainly, but for the individual as well. It is not melodramatic to say that the question of developing strong men is one of life or death for the community, though the individual can normally seek a fate apart from the community, if it disintegrates, by availing himself of asylum among receptive people with whom he is connected. Whether in his natal or another community, however, the individual male always has an interest in being able to forestall slights and to cope with challenges to his claims. He must be able to assert his rights against competitors from within—or resolve not to compete and accept the resulting status. Thus on his own behalf he needs strength and competence in the techniques and symbols of aggression and masculine comportment. As the community's needs are in this respect strikingly congruent with those of the individual, the measures for making ideally aggressive men from material that is rarely perfect are drastic indeed, as they have often been portrayed. Against the enemy, at least, the problem is hardly ever an over-supply of aggressive men nor one of individual men who are over-aggressive. The footing of these communities is perennially warlike, and a community which finds itself possessed of several warrior-killers or of an unusually formidable one, other things being equal, would be a community whose fortunes were bound to rise. Their enemies can be oppressed or dislodged; their friends can be grateful; their allies can be unwavering and can increase in number.

Within the community the astute warrior can avail himself of rewards unmatched by those for any other form of achievement. If ever the morality of the system were in doubt, its economics need only be noted. Women, as already remarked, are its most valuable good and a naturally scarce good as well. They are simultaneously a measure of and a means to wealth and high status. Women are lavished upon a Matoto. Though the reasons are multiple, the effect is singular. His power is thereby confirmed and augmented even in being recognized.

Truly formidable men for fighting on the outside may rarely be in surplus in a given local group, but men oriented toward domination may from the inside view be over-numerous or over-powerful. Men like Matoto seem in some respects uncontrollable, and others, differing only in degree from him, are relatively plentiful for a game with one winner. These men, if they compete, as they are likely to do, keep each other on edge, in effect forcing each other to extremes that tend to escalate the competition. Some of the terrorizing of the local community may in fact arise from such competition. The situation can at least be viable in the short run if the gap is great between the leading man and his next most powerful competitor; if no clear and preferable alternatives are present for the second-rank men; if the dominant man is astute; or if opportunities for the expression of ambition and aggression beyond the immediate community are available and ample to occupy enterprising men. A Matoto is patently too big for the local community, as his exceedingly large personal network reflects. Yet he needs the community for a base and it cannot afford to alienate him. Even with a large external outlet for his energies, however, there is some local backwash from his power, and that to his critics is bad.

Women seem a particularly vulnerable and frequent object of the aggressions of powerful men. Killing wives is not a commonplace in Tairora, to be sure, but Matoto's killing of his wife (p. 237) is not unique, even for Abiera alone. Hamxnti, a contemporary and sib-mate of his, also killed one of his wives. Hamxnti's grounds —adultery—were better at least than any grounds now recalled in Matoto's case. Like Matoto, Hamxnti was a strong man. Indeed, after Matoto's death, he was probably the nearest equivalent to a successor. Like Matoto's, Hamxnti's deed went without retaliation.

Women have been described elsewhere in the Central Highlands, of course, as the pawns of men (e.g., Reay 1959; Berndt 1962), and the killing of wives by big men, in the Highlands and elsewhere in New Guinea, is reported often and widely enough to suggest elements of a common pattern. Common conditions, some of them easily recognized, probably account for the similar behaviour of prominent men toward women in Abiera and beyond. Some of these conditions are (1) violence and aggression as a part of male character; (2) the status vulnerability of a man, especially a big man, to damage through insubordination or disloyalty on the part of a wife; (3) the vulnerability of a woman to unrestrained physical violence from a more powerful male; (4) a wife's jural inferiority to her husband; (5) the failure of the community to provide adequate protection or to ensure retaliation for a woman when her attacker is a man of power; and (6) that violence against women, especially women from outside groups, is often less disruptive or costly to the community than equal violence against other residents. A strong man in particular can often afford the loss of a wife through killing or suicide, for he may possess several wives. The powerful husband, unlike ordinary men, moreover, has access to many women and is able to acquire additional wives through his status and power. Thus the personal consequences to him are not as great in losing a wife or alienating her kinsmen as for an ordinary man. The wife of a man with many wives may have a greater temptation to seek extra-marital sexual outlets, e.g., if she receives no attention from her husband. To do so or to threaten to leave him against his wish, however, may affront her husband, leading to the injury or death of the woman.

To stress only the aggressive ideals of masculine character is to paint too one-sided a picture of Tairora morality. The Tairora are also, of course, concerned with reciprocities, with compensation, repaying favour for favour, gift for gift, as well as with balancing slight against slight, hurt against hurt. Hospitality and exchange are prominent. They mitigate somewhat the differences of status that develop among individuals and provide a means for adjusting debts and wrongs that occur. These various arrangements play no small part in the course of Tairora life, admittedly, and afford a motive for gathering together physically as well as for concluding agreements—e.g., for marriage or peacemaking—between groups of people.

It is possible to see in these usages a strong egalitarian thread in the life of the Tairora and one that might seem to contradict the arbitrary acts of a strong man. It could therefore be argued that the system would normally operate against the open or unmuted expression of power. On this basis a Matoto would be viewed as a moral anomaly. I wish to examine briefly the egalitarian emphasis of Tairora culture as expressed in reciprocal usages and expectations, as well as in the absence of numerous familiar symbols of superordination. In this light, whether Matoto is morally anomalous can be better appreciated.

Unless one rejects out of hand the authenticity of Matoto and other strong men of the Tairora vicinity, it is undeniable in the first place that strong men often and perhaps characteristically do use their power in clear and unilateral ways. Yes, it might be countered, but people speak ill of them for it. To that, I think the effective answer is that people's words and thoughts, though surely relevant, seem to belie some of their deeds—and deeds not only during the life of the strong man, be it noted, but, in Matoto's case at least, after his death. People may have called Matoto bad, but they proffered him brides. They still set great store by his bones and his ghost is helpful. People may not call a man of limited power bad, on the other hand, but they do him no comparable favours, pay him no post-mortem compliments. They are sometimes quick, in fact, to call attention to a small man's lack of a name or to describe him as a 'garden man' (formerly) or a 'rubbish man' if he irks them for any reason. They may infringe his rights if he is thought unlikely to protest effectively. The claims of strong men are naturally taken seriously; the unassertive risk being slighted or ignored. Tairora is thus a system in which the major rewards can go to men who are bad. They do not go, in any case, to the ones who least threaten the status of others or threaten equality. The egalitarian virtues in some important respects are therefore 'a custom more honoured in the breach than the observance'.

A second point can be put in the form of a question: if the overt and personal use of power is contrary to a Tairora ethic of equality, what is to be said of a hypothetical situation in which no men of a community at all evince strength in the forms recognized by the Tairora? To say nothing of its effect on the politico-military standing of the territory these men defend, their mildness would be counter to the ideals of masculine strength and aggressiveness. In matching one value, it seems, the other is contradicted.

In the third place, there appears to be a considerable margin of option and expediency involved in the practice of reciprocity. Reciprocal practices may well be a major expression of egalitarian values in Tairora, but they are not some iron law. The force behind them is the force of those who claim their rights and demand the fulfilment of obligations, on the one hand, and, on the other, the possible damage to name and reputation—shame—on the part of those who are indebted if they fail to acknowledge their debts in due course. The initial force is of course the fact that one party at least, and probably both, find it desirable or necessary— expedient—to institute or maintain a given relationship which is best or can only be done in the form of a reciprocity of some kind. As long as all parties concerned find it possible and profitable to comply to some degree; as long as the risks and costs of not complying seem greater than those of complying; as long as men with obligations do not wish to challenge men with expectations, or slight or hurt them; as long as both parties to a transaction wish or are content to appear or act as equals; so long do these usages serve the purpose of expressing balance and equality. But it is equality of the particular exchange, not an identity or equality of all exchanges and exchangers. Each reciprocator plays such a part as he can or wants to play, and with such individuals—and with as many—as he can or wants to be involved with—according to whether they wish to be involved with him.

Finally, I think it is clear that reciprocity in the form of giving and receiving goods offers little embarrassment to ambitious individuals in concentrating power in their hands. As patronage, in fact, it may well be a major device for increasing a man's influence. For a strong man, compliance in the giving and exchanging of material goods is typically much easier, as a result of his very strength, than for the ordinary men. He may in fact engage more lavishly in such giving and more often beyond the possibility of material equivalence. Perhaps it will be contended that this is therefore a corruption of the very principle. Indeed, it may be. But one-sided giving can easily be justified in the name of expediency, as in the case when Matoto gives large amounts of food to men who fight: they fight; he feeds them. Or, to take another suggestion, he fights and non-fighting men help his wives in the garden. I submit that reciprocity is a highly adaptable practice and no inherent brake, in any case, on the development of complementarity.

Even ruling out patronage—unbalanced or unilateral giving: there are still two dimensions to a strong man's reciprocities. His exchanges with a given individual may be larger than the exchanges of other men; and there is also the matter of how extensive a network of exchanges centres upon him. In other words, he might be a person whose reciprocal ties to any given person differ from those of that person to others, and he may also have ties to many more persons—as, in fact, the strong man typically does have. If power comes in part from the extent of a man's relationships and the number of people upon whom he has some claims, reciprocity alone cannot ensure an egalitarian society.

To be sure, the symbols of superordination are not well developed in Tairora life in some of the ways with which one is familiar. There are no sharp differences of housing, clothing, utensils—although there may be some of diet. There are no status terms—other than those like 'strong man'—to match the terms of some Melanesian societies. There is no visible inheritance of superordinate status other than that which may accompany the differentiation of an older, resident sib from the members of an immigrant group whose outside origin is still remembered. Nevertheless, among individual men, there is a considerable range of behaviour appropriate to the expression and the acknowledgment of prowess and strength. Some of the behaviour of others toward Matoto (pp. 238-9, 250, 252), though perceived as his intimidation of them or as their circumspection, seems *de facto* as deferential as one might please. Such behaviour, moreover, can still be observed in some of the newer, less contacted parts of the Tairora ethno-linguistic area, where the strong-man tradition remains closer to its origins.

As a final word on political morality, I return to the local account of Matoto. Since it is by no means bereft of moral overtones, it might shed some light on the question of the paramount Tairora virtues. Matoto is of course condemned for taking liberties with other men's rights, with being arbitrary in his exercise of power. In this condemnation, if anywhere in the tradition of Matoto, the ethic of equality is perhaps expressed. Yet here the analyst is confronted with a subtle interpretive problem: is Matoto bad because his intimidation of others, his killings, and his open adulteries intrinsically are bad, that is, are direct violations of the moral code? Or is he bad primarily because these are unilateral and superordinate rather than reciprocable acts toward others? I have tended toward the first opinion, but I recognize that the other view is logically possible.

There is no need, of course, to pose the question dichotomously. One could suggest that Matoto outraged morality both because his deeds were intrinsically bad and because they implied superordinate status. With present evidence, what disposition of the question is possible?

Intimidation, fear, and awe are, in Matoto's case, inherently unilateral responses proper to a complementary relationship, not a reciprocal one. Arguing that it is these relationships *per se* that violate Tairora morality, because it is an egalitarian and reciprocal morality, practically implies that the Tairora political order is an inherently leaderless ('acephalous') one, or one in which leaders can only seem to lead while really being but custodians of the *vox populi*. It is my impression, on the contrary, that the pre-contact Tairora are quite accustomed to strong men and that in essence their strength is necessarily expressed in some differentiation, through behaviour, from men of lesser strength. Surely, I do not say that Tairora politics is therefore *inherently* the politics of despotism. Indeed, I have argued above that despotism is rather a condition to which the political order is susceptible and occasionally succumbs, but for various reasons is not its constant state. I do, however, tend to reject the image of intrinsically headless political groups in the Tairora area except where headlessness occurs—as it often does occur—by default of adequate leader recruitment.

The issue may come down to whether a better case can be made that (1) Tairora have a leaderless political morality, though intermittently experiencing strong, even arbitrary leaders, or that (2) the political ideal rather calls for the leadership of men of strength but, when they arise, the Tairora often experience with them the moral conflict expressed in characterizing them as bad.

In either case there would be an incongruity between morality and real experience. In the first case, the community would sometimes get a sort of leadership that directly violates its egalitarian and acephalous ideals. In the second, it would sometimes get a leader who is extremely valuable, being in many respects almost ideally suited to the political field; but it would get him at a price, since adequate social controls are lacking against his aggressive behaviour among his own people. In either case, the problem can be recognized as one of frank conflict between moral expectations, on the one hand, and political and military needs or the consequences of their fulfilment, on the other. My view is that Tairora local groups like Abiera frequently stand in need of (or are capable of benefiting greatly from) the power of men like Matoto though they are far from being able to recruit such men regularly. Much of the education and ritual of indoctrination is explicitly designed to this end but, at the same time, the community risks moral violations when it succeeds too well of its purpose. Whether in Matoto's case the violation was more of egalitarian ideals or the practice of outrage or terror I cannot settle with finality, though I incline toward the second view.

In developmental terms, such a moral conflict could arise under conditions of increasing competition between territorial groups for space, manpower, and the other advantages of military strength while these groups (a) still lack the sociological and political inheritance to ensure some permanency of office and continuity of community position, i.e., against short-term fluctuations in the field of interterritorial relationships, and while they (b) cannot provide social controls sufficient to protect the moral expectations still held by their members at the same time as succeeding in the field of interterritorial relationships.

NOTE

1. In this paper 'q' = a glottal stop; 'x' = schwa: for example, Poreqorxntx, Ondaburx, etc.

REFERENCES CITED

BERNDT, R. M. (1962): *Excess and Restraint: social control among a New Guinea mountain people.* Chicago: University of Chicago Press.
BROMLEY, M. (1960): A preliminary report on law among the Grand Valley Dani of Netherlands New Guinea. *Nieuw Guinea Studien,* Vol. 4, No. 3: 235-59.

BROWN, Paula (1963) : From anarchy to satrapy. *American Anthropologist*, Vol. 65: 1-15.
CRIPER, C. (1966) : The politics of exchange (Upper Chimbu). Ph.D. thesis, Australian National University.
MEGGITT, M. J. (1964) : Male-female relationships in the Highlands of Australian New Guinea. In *American Anthropologist Special Publication*: New Guinea, the Central Highlands (J. Watson, ed.), Vol. 66, No. 4, Part 2: 204-24.
POLANYI, K., C. M. ARENSBERG and H. W. PEARSON (eds.) (1957) : *Trade and Market in the Early Empires*. Glencoe: Free Press and Falcon's Wing Press.
READ, K. E. (1954) : Cultures of the Central Highlands, New Guinea. *Southwestern Journal of Anthropology*, Vol. 10: 1-43.
READ, K. E. (1959) : Leadership and consensus in a New Guinea society. *American Anthropologist*, Vol. 61: 425-36.
REAY, Marie (1959) : *The Kuma*. Melbourne: Melbourne University Press for the Australian National University.
SALISBURY, R. F. (1964) : Despotism and administration in the New Guinea Highlands. In *American Anthropologist Special Publication*: New Guinea, the Central Highlands (J. Watson, ed.), Vol. 66, No. 4, Part 2: 225-39.
SCHAFER, A. (1938) : Kavagl, der Mann mit der Zaunpfahlkeule. *Anthropos*, Vol. 33: 107-13.
SCHWARTZ, T. (1963) : Systems of areal integration: some considerations based on the Admiralty Islands of Northern Melanesia. *Anthropological Forum*, Vol. 1, No. 1: 56-97.
STRATHERN, A. (1966) : Despots and directors in the New Guinea Highlands. *Man*, Vol 1, No. 3: 356-67.

DOUGLAS OLIVER

SOUTHERN BOUGAINVILLE[1]

ABSTRACT

The Greater Buin Plain of southern Bougainville provides a complex picture of similarities and diversity. From northwest to southeast, a clearly marked range in emphasis from maternal to paternal ties and descent is paralleled by a shift in the bases of the status hierarchy, from kinship and age (northwest) to greater stress on renown and a system of inherited class-status. These are considered in relation to differences in leadership. Defining 'political' broadly on the criterion of a group's corporate title(s) to the territory it normally occupies, the paper suggests that, in addition to cumulative change, all of these factors can be seen in terms of cyclical change between two sharply contrasting types of political unit.

INTRODUCTION

The publication of Leach's *Political Systems of Highland Burma* (1954) drew attention to a type of ethnographic landscape which anthropologists working in Asia and the Pacific have heretofore either ignored or misinterpreted. He described and analysed overriding 'political' ideologies throughout a large area of extreme linguistic and cultural diversity, where the traditional anthropological concepts of culture area, structural equilibrium, and the like, are said not to apply. The area I am going to describe, southern Bougainville, is less complex ethnologically than Highland Burma, but it may offer some instructive data on a kind of complexity probably found in many other parts of Melanesia as well. Some of this complexity results from the arbitrary imposition of an alien administrative organization by the Australian Government, and is therefore a common feature of many colonial dependencies. Some of it is cultural in the general sense—that is, within each of the several language areas of southern Bougainville there have developed many distinctive cultural, including 'political', traits. But in addition, there are also instances of indigenous political relationships crossing linguistic boundaries. And finally, one finds here contrasting types of 'political' groups existing side by side within uniform linguistic and ecological areas.[2]

THE SETTING

The Greater Buin Plain of southern Bougainville is a fairly distinctive physiographic province. It consists of thick alluvial deposits sloping seaward from a mountain range containing peaks up to 7300 feet above sea level. The eastern boundary of the Plain is formed by a smaller range stretching from the larger mountain range to the sea. A wide belt of swamp separates the inland Plain from the narrow beaches and the sea. These several natural barriers do not completely block Plainsmen's social links with the outside world but they have tended to discourage them.

Over 17,000 natives inhabit this Plain. Settlements are widely but not continuously distributed; in most cases the more extensive uninhabited areas constitute boundaries between languages.

Four distinct languages are spoken on the Plain. At the east is Rugara (about 7600 speakers), west of it is Motuna (about 4700 speakers), and northwest of Motuna is Sibbe (about 3700 speakers); these are very closely interrelated 'Papuan' languages. Along the western beaches and inland from there live people who speak Banone, a 'Melanesian' language totally unrelated to the Papuan tongues; about 500 Banone-speakers dwell along the coast, another 1000 live inland. It is probable that Banone language and culture are intrusive, from the islands to the south. For generations Banone-speakers have been moving inland and adopting many features of the inlanders' ways of life, and it is these latter cultures which will be the concern of this study.[3]

In several places on the Plain, language areas directly abut and one can find settlements in which many people speak two or even three languages; usually, however, every settlement can be safely included within a single language area— that is, there will be a preponderance of persons who learned one of the languages first and who speak it most.

The outside world impinges directly upon these people through missions and Government. Catholic and Methodist missions have been continuously active in this area for more than a decade; the former maintain European missionaries at four stations in the interior, the latter missionaries reside at the coast. Most natives past childhood are nominally Christian, and in nearly every village there is a chapel in charge of a native catechist; but in general Christianity has little discernible effect except upon the lives of a score or so of the more rigorously indoctrinated catechists. The influences of Government have been more apparent. Feuding and head-hunting were stopped by the mid-twenties, and except for a subsequent flare-up between over-zealous mission rivals, the Plains people have since then conducted their rivalries by sorcery or by feuding with property. Each village now has a Government Headman (*kukerai*) and interpreter-deputy (*tultul*), both appointed by the Australian Government representatives, and recompensed with small salaries and a few material privileges. These village officials are subordinate to official District Paramount Chiefs, who are responsible directly to the Australian Administration.

At the northern border of the Plain numerous streams flowing from the mountains have cut deeply into the alluvium, leaving long and narrow interfluvial ridges separated by steep canyons. Farther south these ridges flatten out; here the streams have shallow, broad and shifting beds, and many of them debouch into the swamps, which seem to be moving inland. Except where natives have cleared land for gardens, settlements, and roads—probably less than one-fourth of the whole swamp-free area—the Plain inhabited by the Papuan-speakers is covered with rain forest. The climate of this area is wet and tropical, having little seasonal variation.

Food technology is practically the same throughout the whole area. Everywhere the basic foods are taro, sweet potatoes, plantains, and coconuts—supplemented occasionally by a little sago, breadfruit, and canarium almonds. Nearer the mountains natives go hunting more often, for wild pigs and opossums; nearer the coasts their coconut groves are more extensive. Otherwise, natives throughout this whole area obtain and process the same foods in the same way. Gardening is by slash and burn technique; planting and harvesting are continuous. In fact, the only seasonal factor which appears to influence their lives significantly is the annual ripening of almonds; this has the effect of concentrating feast-giving in the months following nut harvest. Sibbe-speakers must in general work longer and harder hours in their gardens than the rest because of the more mountainous nature of their region; hence there is some ecological variation despite the uniformity of techniques.

Everywhere natives raise pigs in much the same manner, supplying them with garden produce for part of their food and allowing them to run free for the remainder; they also consume them for the same purposes, for ceremonies and special occasions rather than everyday meals. For ecological and historical reasons, however, these domestic pigs are more numerous in the Motuna and Rugara regions than in Sibbe.

Throughout this whole area nearly every person past childhood has a steel machete, and most men own steel axes or adzes as well; these, plus wooden digging sticks and shell scrapers, serve as their primary tools. Baskets of many shapes and sizes are everywhere used for carrying and storage, clay pots for cooking everyday meals.

Residences are everywhere about the same size and shape, being made of wood and sago-leaf thatch; some are built directly on the ground, some on piles, with no clear regional patterning discernible in this regard. Men's club-houses are everywhere larger and more elaborate than dwellings, and there are more of them nearer the coast.

Costume is uniform everywhere: calico lavalavas, and ornaments of shell and plait-work.

To purchase their calicos and steel tools, along with a few other foreign luxuries, these Plains people require Australian currency. And they also need such currency to pay the annual capitation tax demanded of most healthy adult males. Only those few nearer the coastal trade-stores choose to smoke-dry and sell their copra; the only other important source of Australian currency is work on the plantations of Europeans. Every year many youths go away to engage in such work, and return home three years later with a few shillings, a few luxury goods, and even fewer European ideas or values.

For native commercial and ceremonial transactions the people of the Plain use pigs and shell money, the latter having come from the islands to the south. In this respect there is some regional variation: people nearer the mountains own less shell money than those elsewhere.

In summary, the materials and techniques for getting a living are fairly uniform throughout the Plain of southern Bougainville, but there are some regional differences in productive effort and in per capita amounts produced or otherwise acquired. We shall consider later on the uses made of these 'surpluses'. There is also some regional and individual specialization in the production of pottery, ornaments, lime for betel mixture, etc.; and these items are consequently bartered or exchanged for shell money. This commerce, however, is very small in scale and is carried out directly between producer and buyer.

LOCAL GROUPINGS

Most households in this area own two residences, one in a small hamlet located off the main paths, the other in the 'line' villages, larger, more concentrated, and fenced settlements created by the Administration for sanitary and administrative purposes.

Throughout the whole area households consist of nuclear families; very rarely does one find a household containing persons other than spouses and their unmarried offspring, and occasionally the fiancées of unmarried sons. Most families are monogamous, although there are many bigamous households and some men have up to eight or nine wives. Everywhere the household is the principal productive unit. In some places members of neighbouring households co-operate in clearing garden sites or processing sago or conducting fish-drives, but such activities are exceptional. And in this connection it should be noted that there are very few subsistence techniques that *require* co-operative effort on a scale larger than could be accomplished by a single household, or, at most, a single hamlet. Fish-drives are one exception, and they are infrequent. The large-scale wild-pig hunts of former years are no longer carried out.

The nuclear-family household characteristic of the Plain is a distinctive kind of unit in other ways as well. Occasionally neighbouring households may prepare meals together, but they always eat separately; and this emphasis upon household separateness and privacy is everywhere the same. Also, the household is everywhere the unit of socialization. Children remain at home until they become betrothed or married, or until they go away to work at European plantations; save for the poorly attended mission schools for boys there are no institutions outside the family, formal or informal, for educating the young.

The uniformity characteristic of households does not apply to hamlets, the indigenous form of settlement. In the same neighbourhood may be found hamlets of widely different size and composition. There are isolated one-household 'hamlets' near larger ones of seven and eight. Some hamlets consist of houses concentrated around a central workshed; in others the houses straggle over several acres. Some hamlets are formed around interrelated males, or females; some around either matrilineally *or* patrilineally related males and females; and others are thoroughly composite in these respects. There is, however, a discernible regional patterning in household composition, a trend from a maternal-tie emphasis in the mountainous northwest to a paternal-tie emphasis in the southeast. With this is associated a similar trend in descent.

The whole population of this region is divided into named and totemic matrisibs. Some of these cross language boundaries; for example, members of the Kuuape Raruna (totem: parrot) live on both sides of the Mivo river, which approximately separates Motuna-speakers from Rugara-speakers. Apart from these common features, matrisibs differ considerably from region to region in sociological and religious import.

In the mountainous northwest, matrilineages form the nuclei of all the hamlets we encountered, and matrilineages claiming common descent from mythical ancestresses cluster in adjacent areas, so that natives speak of 'the territory of such and such a matrisib', although the sib itself is not a corporate body, nor in fact an interaction group.[4] These Sibbe-speakers also share a living tradition of moiety affiliation: in addition to each sib having its own totem, part of the sibs claim common descent from a single spirit ancestress, Poreu, while the other sibs claim descent from 'sibmates' of Poreu's spouse, Paramorun. Thus, Poreu people may marry only Paramoruns, and vice versa. These ancestral spirits are believed to exercise benevolent influences upon the lives of their descendants; and materializations of them are treated with affection-tinged respect.

In the southern part of the Rugara-speaking territory H. Thurnwald (1934: 146) informs us that matrisibship is evident only in totemic affiliation, and from the northwest to the southeast of the whole Plain there is an unmistakable cline between these two extremes. In the western Motuna-speaking region the tradition of moiety affiliation is retained only in the regulation that members of the large Eagle sib may marry members of any other sib having a different totem, but the latter may marry only Eagles. Eagles consider Paramorun (or rather, Horomorun, its Motuna cognate) one of their founders, but the other sibs share no common traditional origin. In the eastern part of the Motuna-speaking region, the moiety tradition is replaced by a multiplicity of intermarrying exogamous matrisibs and phratries.

The existence of regional differences was mentioned earlier in regard to amounts of food produced in excess of subsistence needs. There are also some marked regional differences in the uses made of such surpluses. Throughout the whole area these surpluses, plant foods and pigs, are consumed in connection with feasts held on the occasion of kinship and life-crisis rituals; in the northwest this is their principal use. Elsewhere they are utilized by ambitious men to achieve positions of authority and influence outside the context of kinship, and this brings us to the subject of *indigenous* concepts of social hierarchy.

TYPES OF AUTHORITY

With the exception of certain dyadic groups—for example, trade partners, sibling pairs, friends—every group we observed in southern Bougainville was structured hierarchically: one or two persons exercised authority more frequently than other members. This was the case not only with *actual* groups—groups whose existence we recorded on the basis of reliable observation or hearsay—but with normative and suppositional projections of groupings as well. For example, in actual households throughout the area father and mother share authority over other members, mother in connection with gardening and food preparation, father in connection with most other household activities. In suppositions (including myths) about household social structure—what people *imagine* usually happens, or happened, or will happen—relationships are conceived as being even more rigidly ordered: the supposition is that husband-father has supreme authority in all activities; and the same is true of *norms* (that is, rules) for behaviour among household members.

In hamlets throughout the area, authority in *hamlet* activities is usually shared by the older members, male and female, of the kin segment which possesses full or residual title to the land on which the most hamlet residents live and garden. These are the 'Old-ones'. Where matrilineages are important, hamlet Old-ones and matrilineage Seniors ('First-born') are usually the same. Kinship and age are the crucial qualifications for these positions, but a commanding or persuasive personality is also a factor. In connection with authority in this kind of grouping supposition and norms correspond fairly closely to empirical modes.

Toward the southeast of the Plain, where matrilineages are less important, factors of personality and of 'renown' sometimes override age and even kinship affiliation as qualifications for hamlet leadership.

Throughout the whole area, 'renown' is a very concrete concept; it means, literally, the kind of esteem enjoyed by the man who gives feasts frequently. The concept is most elaborately institutionalized in the northeast quarter of the Motuna-speaking region, which, significantly, is not the richest part of the Plain in material surpluses. Here, at the centre of this complex of ideas and practices is the *mumi*, the man of the neighbourhood who has most renown.

To become a *mumi* a man must own or control material resources. He can either accumulate these by his own hard labour, plus the labour of members of his household, or he can persuade kinsmen and friends to make him gifts or extend him loans. The usual method of accumulating wealth is by cultivating large gardens and converting the surplus produce into pigs, which can then be either distributed at feasts or sold for shell money. Another method is by making and selling pottery; another by practising magical skills for fees.

Accumulation alone does not however bring renown; wealth has to be distributed in the form of food and other valuables, usually at feasts. It is useful to have had a *mumi* father, to have begun life with some of the latter's reflected renown, together with what is left of his wealth after most of it has been given away in the form of mortuary distributions. Such an initial advantage prompts many informants to assert that 'Only the son of a *mumi* can become a *mumi*'. Actually, a *mumi*'s son is only slightly better off than an orphan. He has to increase his inheritance many times over, or have very liberal backers, before he can begin serious feast-giving.

It is little wonder that the feast-giver is highly esteemed. Feast food—roasted and steamed pork, boiled eel and opossum, tasty vegetable and nut puddings—provides a welcome break in the everyday monotony of a vegetarian diet. Also, natives keenly enjoy the excitement of milling crowds and the pleasure of dancing and pan-piping. However, the ambitious man does not merely invite a few of his neighbours and treat them to a banquet: that would be a waste of resources. He usually makes the feast the occasion for a house-raising or some other kind of work-bee; no one esteems him any less for that.

It is customary to begin a social-climbing, renown-seeking career by building a club-house. The club-house is a rectangular, shed-like structure built directly on the ground and without walls. Large wooden slit-gongs occupy most of the floor space. These are sounded to convene workers, to announce feasts, etc., and serve as benches for the men who gather in the club-house to gossip and sleep. Here among these Motuna-speakers only close kinsfolk visit one another's hamlet dwellings, so that the club-house is virtually the only public gathering place for men. Hence, the man who wishes to become a *mumi* must own a club-house; and to derive most renown for his ownership of one he must build it rather than inherit it. The most renown-bringing manner of building a club-house is to collect all the helpers available, draw out the work as long as possible, and reward the workers with such a bountiful feast that they will ever afterward remember the occasion and the club-house with pleasure.

There are many club-houses in the Motuna region—an average of one to about eight adult males—so that mere possession of one does not ensure for the owner lasting renown. To serve as a lasting symbol of the owner's renown the club-house must be the scene of almost continuous activity; and since nothing draws or pleases a crowd like a feast the ambitious owner gives as many feasts as he and his followers can afford. He has men cut down trees, fashion them into slit-gongs, and install them in the club-house; then he rewards them with a pork feast. When no more gongs can be crowded into the club-house he causes the roof to be repaired or the floor swept, and provides food delicacies for each occasion. After a while people will say of him: 'He is a true *mumi*: he gives large feasts.' And when they stroll about in search of amusement they will usually end up in his club-house. They are at pains to ingratiate themselves with the feast-giver, to defer to his judgment, to perform little services for him, laugh at his sallies of wit, praise whom he praises or scorn whom he scorns. In this manner the *mumi* assures himself of a following in his own neighbourhood and even extends his renown and influence beyond it.

Some *mumi*s stop here; others are led by their ambition to seek wider acclaim. Their lives turn into continual rivalries for renown. So long as they are active feast-givers they can count on exercising authority over their immediate neighbours and kinsmen, who line up behind them with patriotic pride in 'our *mumi*' and 'our place'. These rivalries between neighbouring *mumi*s culminate in competitive '*mumi-honouring*' feasts at which the host presents his rival with large quantities of pigs and shell money. The guest of honour then distributes these goods among his own supporters, as rewards for their support, and then sets about to accumulate an equivalent or more than equivalent reciprocal gift. If he cannot reciprocate within a year or two he forfeits much public esteem and is no longer considered a worthy rival by other *mumi*s. If he returns an equivalent amount of goods and no more, that is a sign that he wishes to cease competing with the initiating host; thereafter the two usually become 'trade-partners' and assist one another in competing with other *mumi*s. If, however, the debtor-guest reciprocates more than he received, the rivalry continues until one of the principals gives up in defeat. A supernatural sanction supplements the social sanctions connected with these exchanges: either the club-house demon-familiar or an ancestral spirit of the creditor *mumi* accompanies the 'gift' and tears out the soul of the debtor *mumi* if he does not repay in good time. (In our experience, however, this supernatural sanction provided less motive power than the social ones.)

A successful *mumi* is fortunate in a number of respects. He is singled out among his fellows by means of special beliefs about his personality and destiny—for example, the *mumi* has a better chance than most other mortals of attaining paradise. Also, he has the satisfaction—highly valued among these people—of hearing himself frequently praised. Others show great respect for his name and person and opinions, and in his own community he exercises considerable authority even in matters not directly concerned with feast-giving. Next to his material resources his most powerful weapon is his ability to focus praise or scorn upon friends or enemies.

There are also certain more material advantages in being a *mumi*. At pork distributions a *mumi* usually receives the best cuts. He has little difficulty in raising loans. And he has the tacit right to utilize land belonging to all those persons to whom he regularly distributes pork or other valuables. The term *tuhia* is applied to these persons and, derivatively, to the lands so utilized by them; it is in this connection that natives describe certain *mumi*s as having extensive *tuhia*s, which some Europeans have interpreted as 'kingdoms'.

There are also drawbacks in being a *mumi*. Such a man must be scrupulous in his everyday conduct and in his commercial or ceremonial transactions. Moreover, he is dangerously situated, being the potential victim of sorcery aimed at him by envious rivals.

Natives state that in the days before European control *mumi*s were primarily war-leaders, their renown having been mainly dependent upon their success in organizing and financing victorious head-hunting forays or pitched battles with rival *mumi*s. In those days, informants assert, a *mumi*'s authority was backed by physical force. How closely such assertions correspond to past actual events it is difficult to judge, but even according to these suppositions, feast-giving was the principal kind of reward given by a *mumi* to his warriors, and feast-giving was the most important factor during the early stages of a man's rise to affluence. Feast-giving rather than personal bravery or martial skill attracted followers who would then fight one's battles.

All the foregoing refers specifically to the northeast quarter of the Motuna-speaking region. There are some noteworthy regional variations on these themes.

In the mountainous Sibbe-speaking region feast-giving is less frequent, less lavish, and is mainly connected with life-crises. Club-houses there are smaller, fewer in number, contain only a few slit-gongs apiece, and are not restricted to males as is the case elsewhere in southern Bougainville. (This last situation utterly scandalized our Motuna-speaking companions.) The Sibbe word for feast-giver, *mumiako*, is cognate with the Motuna *mumi*, but Sibbe-speakers refer to such men as 'the *mumiako* of such and such a moiety' rather than, as among Motuna-speakers, 'the *mumi* of such and such a place'. Those *mumiako*s pointed out to us were usually venerable old men well past their physical prime, whereas Motuna *mumi*s are usually younger and more robust, qualities required in their active careers.

In the western part of the Motuna region, feast-giving for renown is almost as important a preoccupation as it is in the northeast, but there is one significant difference. In the northeast, sibship and feast-giving for renown are quite distinct institutions; a *mumi* attracts his adherents from among neighbours and friends no matter what their sib affiliations may be. But in the west, the *mumi* remains distinctly a matrilineage leader. Matrilineage mates tend to live closer to one another and men make a point of assisting a matrilineage mate throughout his career. Here, patrilineal succession to *mumi*ship is not even incipient, as is the case in the north-east. Mongko, the leading *mumi* of the western Motuna Eagles, explained their position in this way:

> The Kiap [Australian Patrol Officer] is trying to start a new custom among us. He is trying to have the son of a *mumi* succeed him. That is not our method. With us a man becomes a *mumi* if he is capable of giving large feasts; and our sib-mates, not our fathers, assist us to give feasts . . .

Finally, in the southeastern part of the Plain, in Rugara-speaking country, the institution of feast-giving for renown exists side by side with one of inherited rank. We turn to Richard Thurnwald for a description of this area.

R. Thurnwald (1934:134) speaks of "the traditional ethnic stratification", with *mumira* (cognate with Motuna *mumi* and Sibbe *mumiako*) families at the top. "These families are inter-related . . . and constitute an aristocracy" (*ibid*. 125). Under them are their bondsmen (*kitere;* cf. Motuna *kitoria,* children). "The *mumira,* members of the chief's stratum, claim the ownership of pigs and *abuta* [shell money] for their class, just as the pastoral tribes in Africa do with regard to cattle. They treat the 'bondsman' as the warden of the domestic animal." "The *mumira* family claims all the land of the district. This land is divided up for usufruct among its adult male members and is inalienable. Moreover, each *mumira* owns a number of *kitere* families; a big chief several dozens, a smaller one (second or third line) perhaps half a dozen, or one or two dozen. The head of each *kitere* family has received part of the land belonging to his *mumira,* transmitted perhaps from his ancestors. The *kitere* may sell the land if his *mumira* agrees. If a *kitere* family should die out, the land reverts to the *mumira* to be disposed of as he wishes" (*ibid.* 125).

Thurnwald then goes on to describe the main obligations of a *kitere* for his *mumira.* He raises pigs for him, assists him to clear ground for gardens, helps him repair fences, build houses, and the like. The daughters of a *kitere* are required to help their chief's wives in garden or house work; and occasionally they are chosen to contribute to the guests' pleasure when a big feast is held. In return for all these services the *kitere* and his family members are said to be remunerated by the *mumira,* in the form of food or shell money (*ibid.* 126).

Thurnwald also describes an intermediate class consisting of a *mumira*'s chief supporters, men who are not genuine *mumira* by descent through seniority in the paternal line but who may be of mixed parentage, or even commoners who have become affluent through their own skills in accumulating and distributing wealth, much as in the northeast Motuna region. In fact, Thurnwald notes that in some places these self-made leaders have superseded those aristocratic *mumira*s unable to compete with them in commercial and ceremonial transactions.

Summary

Summarizing all these findings on southern inland Bougainville: there is a clearly discernible cline, from northwest to southeast, in the devaluation of sibship. There is a parallel trend in emphasis upon 'renown' as a factor in determining social hierarchies, with the additional factor of inherited class-status in the southeast.[5] What accounts for these regional differences?

Ecological considerations certainly play some part. The Sibbe-speakers must work harder and longer to obtain their subsistence requirements, with the result that they produce fewer surpluses and have less time to devote to other activities. However, the mere existence of larger surpluses and more 'free' time does not necessarily determine the uses to which they will be put.

Population density and communication facilities may also play a role. One might argue on *a priori* grounds that the denser populations and better trails nearer the coast permit people, including non-kinsmen, to interact more frequently. But again, this does not determine that they *will* interact more frequently, nor does it determine what form that interaction will assume.

Outside influences cannot be overlooked. In pre-European times Sibbe-speakers undoubtedly had less contact, direct or indirect, with cultural influences from the islands south of Bougainville, whence came most of the shell money and the main stimulus to trade. And when that trade was interrupted at the end of World War 1[6] the resources that had been devoted to it were available for other uses; but this alone would not determine *what* uses. In this connection, Thurnwald's explanation (*ibid.*) for the class-stratified society of the Rugara-speakers is in terms of alien conquerors, Melanesian-speaking warriors from the islands to the south, who imposed their regime upon the more primitive and less organized aborigines. This may be so, but it is not the only possible explanation. An alternative hypothesis is that the Rugara institution may be viewed as an extreme but logical variation on the prestige-ranking theme, a crystallization in dynastic form of beliefs and practices present, incipiently, elsewhere. Frequent contact by the Rugara-speakers with aristocratically organized outsiders may have provided a reference-model for an otherwise local development made possible by larger surpluses and more shell money, traded directly from the southern islanders.

Perhaps all the above 'explanations' have some validity, but it is unlikely that we shall ever discover all the explanations for such phenomena as these.

POLITICAL GROUPS

The cline we have discerned in southern Bougainville has been characterized mainly in *spatial* terms; there is evidence that it also can be viewed as a series of cumulative changes through *time*. For, with the introduction of steel tools, which make men's work easier, and European breeds of pigs, which encourage pig-breeding, even Sibbe-speakers are beginning to compete for renown. And *cyclical* changes are also evident; for example, we are told by Thurnwald that Rugara-speaking commoners have begun (again?) to set up prestige hierarchies which compete with and even outrank the older aristocratic ones.

Before proceeding, we had best say a word about language and 'tribe'. First of all, in some hamlets in southern Bougainville there are bilingual or even trilingual individuals; this is especially true of the border zone between Rugara and Motuna, and of the so-called Baitsi region, between Sibbe, Banone, and Motuna. Secondly, there are some men of renown whose feast distributions, *tuhias*, extend beyond the boundaries of their own languages. Informants assert that in pre-European times this was also the case with war leaders' authority. On the other hand, no contemporary man's *tuhia* encompasses a whole language area; nor—as far as we could learn—was this true of a war leader's authority in the past. In other words, there is not, and probably has not been within the recent past, any correspondence between the boundaries of languages and actual social groups. Nor, for that matter, do natives assert that there *ought* to be such a correspondence in the future, or that there ever has been such correspondence in the past. In this respect, actual social behaviour, suppositions about social behaviour, and norms for social behaviour are all in perfect accord.

Up to now we have been examining a number of contemporary Bougainville institutions without identifying any one of them as 'political'. What relevance do these descriptions have in a series of contributions on 'Political Systems'?

As a matter of fact, if we were to adopt the usage most popular in Political Science circles, the only type of political unit in southern Bougainville today is the organization of the Australian Administration, including its various local officials. These alone are backed by penal sanctions, by the capability of applying coercive physical force. Native leaders—whether household parents, hamlet Old-ones, matrilineage Seniors, neighbouring *mumis*, or patriarchal aristocrats—have long since been denied the use of coercive force over any but their smaller offspring, and even these sanctions of theirs are subject to severe limitation. Happily, anthropologists appear to regard this usage as unnecessarily restrictive, not only with respect to colonial societies but for autonomous ones as well. There are societies in which coercive force does not operate as an organized sanction; moreover, societies differ widely in the relative effectiveness of penal as contrasted with other kinds of sanctions.

For comparative purposes we find it convenient to designate as 'political' any society's numerically more inclusive type or types of group possessing some kind of corporate title, or titles, to all the territory normally occupied by resident members of the group. To add to this definition statements about 'rule of law' or 'settlement of disputes' and such would be redundant, for all multi-member *groups* are hierarchically organized, and *hierarchy* implies procedures and sanctions for implementing authority.

Utilizing this very broad definition seriously complicates our analysis of southern inland Bougainville institutions, but it is a kind of complication which reflects complexities in the data themselves. For, in addition to the overriding political unity implicit in the Australian Government's rule over all this area, there are several other types of 'political' units here: matrilineages, hamlets, *mumi*-dominated neighbourhoods, and, in Rugara territory, feudal-type communities as well. We have already seen how these types vary in importance from region to region, because of ecological and other factors; we shall now examine the manner in which some of them exist side by side within a single region, where ecology and outside contacts and cultural tradition are about the same, and hence where quite different explanations must be sought for their varying importance from neighbourhood to neighbourhood.

CYCLICAL CHANGES IN POLITICAL TYPES

The northeast quarter of the Motuna-speaking area, bounded by the Mivo River on the east, uninhabited rain forest leading into mountains on the north, the Mopiai River on the west, and a belt of relatively unutilized forest on the south, covers an area of about sixteen square miles and contains about one thousand individuals. The hamlets and villages of this population are distributed fairly evenly throughout the central part of the region. In terms of social interaction, these northeasterners constitute something of a separate 'society': rates of communication are somewhat more frequent among themselves than with their Rugara-speaking neighbours to the east and their fellow Motuna-speakers to the west and south.

The northern hamlets and villages are located in rougher terrain than those in the southern part of this region, but these differences are not great enough to affect work loads or surpluses to any significant extent. There are some local differences in production of economic surpluses, but these are not attributable to environmental or technological factors.

Also, throughout the region contact with the outside world—with other Islanders and with Europeans—has been about the same; that is, all neighbourhoods have had equal access to alien influences, although settlements in the south of the region were the first to become organized into Australian Administration villages. Mission influence also has been about the same throughout this region; the population is preponderantly 'Catholic', but 'Methodist' enclaves are fairly uniformly distributed.

And finally, all persons in this region have access to the same body of cultural 'information', to the same suppositions and norms about man's relationship to nature and to other men. As we shall see, individuals in this region may choose among various sets of norms, but all socially mature individuals are aware of the full range of alternatives in this uniform cultural universe. Our object now is to describe some typical examples of how different neighbourhoods have followed different organizational patterns in carrying out activities not immediately concerned with subsistence. We can begin with Jeku.

The small line village of Jeku has 57 inhabitants, six of whom—young men —are absent working on European plantations. All its people are close relatives; the nucleus of the village consists of members of two intermarrying matrilineages, Cranes and Kingfishers, along with a few spouses from outside matrilineages. The houses are all located close together on land near the confluence of the Mopiai and Reraka Rivers, to which these Cranes and Kingfishers have possessed title for generations. Located on this land are nearly all the gardens of the Jeku people, along with sib shrines identified with their mythical ancestresses. Jeku territory is favourably located: there are large enough stretches of fairly flat and well-drained soil, extensive groves of bearing coconut and areca palms, and numerous almond trees. Also, there are rivers to provide prawns, and many good springs for drinking water.

A generation ago Jeku was united with several neighbouring hamlets into a cohesive war-making unit under leadership of the great *mumi*, Tokura. But Tokura was killed and the other Jekuans dispersed during the fighting that accompanied establishment of Australian rule. Eventually the Jekuans returned and rebuilt their homes, but not their 'political' ties with the neighbouring communities.

Kangku, a man of about 45, is the Senior of the Crane matrilineage here. His father was Senior of the Kingfishers, and now he is called the Old-one by both Cranes and Kingfishers.

The eleven households in Jeku each own an average of 4.5 pigs and 805 spans of negotiable shell money—about 15 percent more valuables than are owned by the average household of this region as a whole. Discrepancies among the Jeku households are slight in this regard, and they are socially unimportant because there is a general sharing of these valuables when crises arise. It is interesting to note that the Old-one, Kangku, has fewer pigs and less negotiable shell money than five other householders in the village.

Nevertheless, Kangku is undisputed leader of Jeku.

There are three large garden sites on Jeku territory, and a number of smaller isolated ones. All the households co-operated in clearing the three large sites and the men combined to fence them; then, as usual, each household planted, cultivated, and harvested from its own plot. Kangku made the decisions in connection with site clearing. Before his illness, which has now incapacitated him, he used to visit the old gardens every day to note the progress of the growing crops; and when he perceived that new land was needed he himself picked the new site, judging its readiness by the size of its secondary growth.[7] He set a day for all the able-bodied males to begin clearing, sending word about informally. Twice the day was postponed because it did not suit the convenience of some men; and this delay was concurred in genially by Kangku.

During clearing operations Kangku worked along with the rest, but it was noticeable that he rested more often than most. He issued no orders or exhortations that we could detect: certain Jeku men are stronger than others or better with axes or more expert at fence-making, and no foreman is needed to say who does what and when. The one garden clearing project we witnessed at Jeku proceeded leisurely and congenially. At one point, one of the younger men stopped work and slept for an hour. The only visible reaction to this was the others' ribald jokes, to the effect that he had spent his strength fornicating the previous night. Kangku himself is a good axeman and his self-assigned job was to ring-bark the larger trees.

The largest club-house in Jeku is Kangku's, but no feast was held there during our sojourn in this region. In fact, Jeku's only other large-scale enterprises we witnessed or heard about during our stay involved the building of a dwelling, participation in a communal fish-drive, the performance of a funeral, and the holding of a seance.

The dwelling belonged to Puipui, Kangku's brother's son. Puipui announced to Kangku his intention of building a new house and secured the latter's promise to lend him a small pig to help feed the house-builders. Eight men from Jeku assisted, along with five of Puipui's friends and relatives from neighbouring communities. They finished the construction in about four hours, the materials having been collected and prepared in advance by Puipui and his wife. Kangku attended this work-bee but did not join in the construction work. Instead, he supervised two boys in the cooking of the pork and taro meal, which was the workers' only material compensation for their labour. Later on, Puipui told us that although he had asked Kangku for the pig in the form of a 'loan', he probably wouldn't repay it: 'Kangku is our Old-one, my *father* [i.e., father's brother].'

Another time, a messenger from a distant village arrived in Jeku and invited Kangku 'and his people' to participate with them and several other communities in a large-scale fish-drive at the Mivo river. Kangku accepted, and on the appointed day he and 24 other Jeku men, women, and children trooped to the Mivo and joined in the sport. Once there, however, they no longer acted as a unit. Men joined other men in damming one branch of the river, women joined other women in plugging holes in the dam, and children played along the banks in small groups or accompanied their parents. Kangku, meanwhile, sat on the bank with some of the older men from other villages and talked. When the dam was finished he joined several other men in spearing fish left flopping in the dry river bed. Only at the end of the affair did he serve as leader of his people. When the last fish had been caught and laid on the bank, Kangku stood attentively by to watch and ensure that Jekuans received their just share of the catch. When the counters turned over to Kangku the Jeku portion, he motioned the women in his party to carry the fish back home, where each participating household received an equal share for separate cooking. Even the non-participating households received a little, at Kangku's instruction. Puipui later told us that some of the participants grumbled a little at this, but 'not very much; Kangku is the Old-one'.

Shortly after our arrival in northeast Motuna territory the orphaned daughter of one of Kangku's sisters died in childbirth. Throughout the arrangements for the cremation and the subsequent mortuary feast Kangku unobtrusively but firmly supervised proceedings. Even though the widower was on hand—he had married into Jeku from a neighbouring village—the Old-one took charge, set the date for the cremation, specified which outsiders should be invited, and decided upon the number of pigs appropriate for the mortuary feast. He talked this latter point over with the widower and other villagers, but held firm to his own estimate despite the widower's appeal for a smaller assessment, that is, three out of the five pigs required. Kangku reminded the widower that he was an outsider and intimated that he would no longer be welcome in Jeku unless he obeyed. (The widower complied. He later told us that he preferred Jeku to his own village, mainly because Kangku made so few demands upon Jekuans' labour and goods: 'He is a true Old-one; not always trying to build up his own renown with others' work.') Kangku himself contributed the fourth pig, the two surviving brothers of the deceased the fifth.

Mid-way during our stay Kangku became ill, complaining of fever, painful joints, and severe headaches. He remained in and around his dwelling for about a month, trying various herbal remedies. Then, when he did not improve he consulted a diviner from another village. The latter informed him that the ghost of his, Kangku's, mother's brother had smitten him as a sign that it wished to become his spirit-familiar. (Kangku may have encouraged this finding; we suspect that he wished to become a spirit-familiar magician, for the profit this practice would bring him.) Kangku then consulted a magician friend from a nearby village. The two agreed upon a date and a price for a seance, to establish rapport with the ghost. The price was set at two pigs and two hundred spans of negotiable shell money. Kangku himself supplied the money, but borrowed the pigs from two matrilineage mates in Jeku (a long-term loan, requiring no interest). In addition, he arranged for a small feast to be held on the occasion of the seance, killing his next-to-last pig for this but drawing upon his relatives for the taro. During all these activities Kangku quietly but decisively directed operations, from his sick-bed.

Later on during our stay, when the renowned *mumi* of nearby Turungum village (cf. below) gave a very large feast, Kangku was too ill to attend. His villagers attended in the train of the guest of honour, but did not go as a unit, nor did they receive a whole pig—as one of the Turungum men explained to us: 'There is no true feast-giving *mumi* at Jeku; Kangku is merely their Old-one.'

Kangku, then, did not participate in the renown feast-giving which pre-occupied so many other prominent men in this region. Nevertheless he exercised easy and amiable but decisive control over many of the actions and resources of Jeku villagers and no one questioned his authority. Also, as Senior of the local Cranes he was guardian over their small hoard of non-negotiable shell-money heir-looms, which he handed out to his matrilineage mates for ornamentation on festive occasions.

We spoke earlier of *Jeku territory*. This is precisely the way Jeku residents, and outsiders, refer to it; and it includes all the land around Jeku to which any Jeku people own title. But here as elsewhere there are different kinds of *title*, full, residual, and provisional. (See Goodenough 1951.) *Full* title implies undivided rights of use and of disposal. *Residual* and *provisional* titles refer, for example, to the rights of landlord and tenant, respectively. In Jeku all land is held in divided ownership: it is tacitly understood that Cranes extend generous provisional use-rights in their own matrilineage land to all other residents of the village, and so do Kingfishers. Normally it is not even necessary, say, for a Crane to ask a King-fisher for permission to plant on the latter's land. We observed that this tacit sharing of use of soil by all Jekuans also extended to fishing rights in waters and to the taking of coconuts for domestic use. (However, it stopped short of sharing of almonds, a source of money.) In connection with land *disposal*, however, lines of ownership are more sharply drawn. Normally, only full or residual title-holders have a say in this matter. But in Jeku the Kingfisher people assured us that they would consult Kangku before disposing of any of their own matrilineage land, even though he is a Crane.

Beyond these specified rights and duties of office, Kangku's authority reaches into many other aspects of everyday life. He does not choose spouses for all villagers, but he does occasionally veto a choice already made. He does not actively supervise food production in the separate household plots, but he admonishes the householder who does not clear enough land for his wife to cultivate. And, finally, he does not intervene in the everyday quarrels of others, except when they become chronic and threaten to lead to public disorder or social fracture.

As for the rest, Kangku eats no better than his fellows; and his house, though slightly larger, contains no kinds of comforts not found in other houses. Moreover, as Senior and Old-one, he must devote more than ordinary amounts of time and resources to the needs of his fellows.

When the Australian Government designated Jeku a village, they took cog-nizance of Kangku's status and appointed him Headman (*kukerai*), thereby increasing his duties slightly but adding little or nothing to the *effectiveness* of his authority. Kangku's native authority, backed by the moral sanctions of kinship and enhanced by the persuasiveness of his kindly but firm leadership, does not require the Government-backed sanction of coercive force. Nor does the continuance of his local authority depend upon renown feast-giving, at home or abroad. As an official in the Administration hierarchy, Kangku is responsible to the District Paramount Chief, Kope, whose village is in the central part of the Motuna-speaking region. But in all other respects the Jekuans are a separate and autonomous unit: Kangku and his fellow villagers do not regularly exchange pork or other valuables with any other place—that is, they form no regular part of any *tuhia*.

Though less than a mile from Jeku, the village of Turungum is a measureless distance away with respect to the ideology which governs its corporate life.

Turungum village contained an average of 95 persons during our sojourn there—25 more than in the average Motuna-speaking village. The 'official' houses of these Turungom people are clustered into two fenced villages; their native dwellings are scattered over eight hamlets. These residents fall into four extended families. One of these consists of the families of two brothers who sought refuge here during fighting times; each of the others is built around a matrilineage, and these three matrilineages own in full or residual title nearly all the land verbally identified with Turungum as a neighbourhood. Each matrilineage has one or two Senior members, male and female, but here in Turungum the title 'Old-one' is used more generally for any elderly person rather than being reserved for hamlet leaders. As a matter of fact, there are few occasions when hamlet members act as such. Matrilineages still function in connection with life crises and the use of matrilineage property, but in many other respects the *village,* as represented by all its adult male members, has superseded both hamlet and matrilineage as the unit of corporate effort and resource.

This emphasis upon *village* unity is a recent development. A generation ago the hamlets here were only occasionally united in common activities; and when Tokura, the war-leader of Jeku, once sent a punitive party here to avenge the murder of one of his kinsmen, there was no Turungum leader to mobilize the separate hamlets to oppose him.

Undisputed leader of contemporary Turungum is the renowned *mumi*, Songi, a solemn, slender man of about forty-five. Songi's life is utterly dominated by his driving ambition to become the most renowned man in southern Bougainville—that is, throughout the whole area where renown is measured in terms familiar to him. Moreover, he is well on the way to achieving his goal. During our stay he challenged, in the form of a lavish competitive feast, one of the two other Motuna-speaking *mumi*s at the apex of the prestige hierarchy, and few people anywhere—including his chief rivals—doubted that he would in time rank supreme.

This lofty eminence was reached almost entirely by giving feasts—feasts for the construction of club-houses, for the acquisition of slit-gongs, for rapport with his demon-familiar, for aid and comfort of his allies, and for social ruination of his rivals. These last, the competitive feasts, gained renown for him in several ways:

by dispensing hospitality to numerous guests, who repaid him in renown-making praise; by giving to his rivals large competitive gifts which, because not repaid in full, directly enhanced the giver's renown; and by publicly humiliating his rivals, thereby reducing them to a social position below his own in the prestige hierarchy.

We did not, of course, witness all these activities, but those we did observe— and we believe that they are typical of his procedures—left no doubt in our minds about this *mumi*'s way to success. After an initial push given him by his kinsmen, every step in the process was initiated and planned by Songi himself, and every step was supervised either by him directly or by some lieutenant acting on his explicit orders. He mapped and began implementing his strategy years in advance, by manipulating loans, granting credits, enlarging gardens, obtaining options on pigs, and tabooing his coconut groves to conserve nuts. He sought assistance from close kinsmen and affluent friends, but usually in the form of specific goods and services rather than in the form of advice.

When a job needed to be done he selected the villager with most technical ability to do it, regardless of the latter's kinship position or rank. One of his deputies was the Senior of his own matrilineage (and, incidentally, the official Headman of the village); another was the village buffoon, a man of very low prestige-rank but of superior technical ability.

Songi accomplished all this through versatile changes of tactics: sometimes he persuaded genially, sometimes he issued brusque commands; sometimes he cajoled, sometimes he threatened.

Turungum is not a rich village; the average number of pigs per household is only 3.5 (compared with the six to seven pigs per household in some villages). Nor is Songi a wealthy man.

What stands behind this authority of a man who is neither wealthy, nor Senior in his matrilineage, nor Headman in his village? What persuades nearly every youth and adult male in the village—including many who are only distant kinsmen at most—to spend whole months out of every year, contributing services as well as material goods, mainly to enhance the renown of one man? It is true that some of that renown is reflected toward them; but is that enough to motivate all this aid?

To begin with, *mumi*s usually get their start through the active assistance of sympathetic kinsmen, and that seems to have been the case with Songi also; but kinsmen will not assist unless they believe in the young aspirant's qualifications for this exacting enterprise. On the basis of our acquaintance with Songi and with several other almost as successful *mumi*s elsewhere, we believe these qualifications must include:

Intelligence: knowledge of his society and culture, and capacity to make long-range plans of action.
Industriousness: continuous application to the difficult job of feast-giving.
Charisma: ability to attract and keep adherents.

Executive ability: a faculty for delegating work and an adroitness in distributing rewards and credible promises of rewards.

Diplomacy: tact in dealing with persons outside his own community, and acumen in arranging and maintaining useful alliances.

All these qualifications may lead to positions of persuasiveness, of influence; but without sanctions they cannot lead to positions of authority. We have already noted some of the sanctions behind a *mumi's* authority, including his control over certain supernaturals; most important of all these, we believe, is his potentiality for focusing public opinion upon friends or adversaries so that they feel, respectively, flattered or shamed. There are numerous institutionalized devices for focusing praise and shame, including public discussion and dramatically symbolized contempt, and the greater the renown of the initiator the more effective the measure. Men shamed by a *mumi* do not destroy themselves but they may bear the mark of their embarrassment for months or even years.

But let us return to Turungum. Unlike some *mumi*s in other villages, Songi did not attempt to extend the domain of his authority beyond the activities connected with feast-giving. He left the affairs of his own matrilineage to his Senior, Siham, and he did not directly intervene in the kinship affairs of other villagers. Moreover, he even arranged for Siham to be appointed Headman, wanting no truck with the alien regime, and wishing to devote all his own efforts to renown feast-giving. Nevertheless, Songi's decisive authority over village affairs was there to exercise, if he wished. And, realizing this, Turungum villagers usually conducted themselves in accordance with their knowledge of his views concerning the whole range of domestic and public behaviour.[8]

The various matrilineage properties making up Turungum territory remain more separate than is the case in Jeku; for example, people in Turungum usually obtain the verbal consent of owners before they plant on their land, but that consent is always forthcoming and rent is never required. Turungum pigs rove freely around the whole village territory (outside the gardens, of course) without precipitating the howls of protest typical in some other places. In fact, Turungum differs from many other villages in its absence of inter-household quarrels and litigation, over land as in other matters. In other words, Turungum is a 'political' unit in the native as well as in the administrative sense. Within its boundaries all its residents enjoy liberal provisional use-rights in one another's land.

All this, we believe, comes about as result of Songi's activities, which have united separate hamlets into a self-conscious territorial whole. And, as Turungum's leading citizen, Songi's use-rights over any Turungum land is universally and proudly acknowledged.

Outside Turungum, Songi's authority loses much of its effectiveness, but he nevertheless has the satisfaction of hearing the whole northeastern region of Motuna, along with adjacent parts of the Rugara-speaking region, spoken of as 'Songi's *tuhia'*—an attenuated kind of title, to be sure, but one which he could probably make use of if he cared to do so.

Jeku and Turungum serve as examples of two contrasting kinds of native political units, both being relatively autonomous and hierarchically organized groups but one organized along principles of kinship, the other along those of prestige-ranking. At the same time, both of them are Administration units headed by appointed officials backed by the whole awesome coercive machinery of the Australian Government; but these alien organizing principles, although perhaps decisive in any critical show-down of powers, have little or no effect upon everyday life in these two villages.

There are several other tightly cohesive villages in this northeastern region organized on either kinship or prestige-ranking principles. And there are also officially demarcated villages held together only by the existence of Government coercive sanctions. Hinnu is one such village. It is composed of several extended-family hamlets which jealously guard the boundaries of their separate tracts of land. Formerly Hinnu was the residence of a very powerful war leader, Kupiraki, and under his leadership all the hamlets of this neighbourhood were united against communities to the north and west. But when Kupiraki died the unity disappeared, and now Hinnu acts as a unit only in connection with obligatory Government projects, such as road maintenance and village fence repair. Its constituent hamlets are also divided into mutually hostile congregations, Methodist and Catholic; but this denominational division is the result rather than the cause of inter-hamlet hostility, which goes back to pre-mission times.

The Hinnu Headman does his best to carry out Government orders, but he is not an active feast-giver and his authority is limited to official matters, being rather ineffectual even there. In fact, Hinnu lacks tight cohesion even though the two highest officials in the northeast district dwell there. Neither of these men, the Paramount Chief nor his Deputy, is a feast-giver, and even their *official* authority is weakened through their mutual jealousy and dislike.

Still another kind of native unit is exemplified in Moronei, a large and wealthy community divided into several hamlets but containing also a central village settlement. A generation ago Moronei was a tightly cohesive political unit, welded into an aggressive fighting unit by its warmaking *mumi,* Moki. The memories of those glorious days, and some of the social habits engendered during them, continue to draw together many residents of the separate hamlets to co-operate in clearing large communal garden sites; and on such occasions community spirit runs high. But no successor to Moki has yet appeared, to unite the community in feast-giving. In fact, denominational factionalism has already split the village and such fissures are likely to widen, until a new *mumi* begins to emerge.

Turungum also contains both Catholics and Methodists, but there no such fissures have appeared. But it is not unlikely that they will appear if the *mumi* Songi fails and no worthy successor takes his place. For here in this northeastern region we can witness *cyclical* phenomena in addition to the manifestations of *cumulative* change.

At one point in the cycle there are communities like Jeku, made up of two or three intermarrying lineages, where kinship ideology provides the cohesive factor. It is probable that there is a relatively low numerical limit to the size of communities of this kind.

Half-way around the cycle are the Turungums, relatively large communities composed of several kinship-based hamlets welded together partly through marriage but mainly through the feast-giving activities of renown-hungry men.

But Turungums will fall apart, first into Moroneis and later into Hinnus, if they lose the binding force of an active *mumi*. And finally, unless a *mumi*-less Hinnu kind of community is held together by an outside authority, it will return full cycle, becoming again a number of separate Jekus.

NOTES

1. This paper was composed in 1956 in response to a request for contributions to a projected volume on "Political Systems of Papua-New Guinea". Alas, the volume in question never materialized, and our contribution—such as it is—has been accumulating dust and obsolescence in some file-drawer of brave but unfulfilled plans. Now that it it is to appear, finally, in print, we are faced with the alternatives of 'bringing it up to date' (in the interest of more elegant, sophisticated topicality) or of 'leaving it untouched' (with the kind of sentimental feeling of integrity which archaeologists display toward the old things they excavate). For a number of reasons we have followed the latter course, and hope that the moss and patina that now encrust our simple moral will not obscure the ethnographic verities underneath.

2. The fieldwork on which this study is based took place in 1938-39; the present tense is used throughout this study to refer to that period. This study is an abridgement of portions of two works by the author (1943, 1955).

3. These population figures are based on the official census and our own survey. The Rugara-speakers are commonly called *Terei*, or *Buins*. Also, most of the Motuna-speakers are commonly called Siuai and most of the Sibbe-speakers *Nagovisi;* however, those Motuna-and Sibbe-speakers who inhabit the fairly isolated border zone between the Siuai and the Nagovisi are called *Baitsi*.

4. A discrete combination of individuals between or among whom social events take place recurrently and face to face, or equivalently, may be said to constitute a *primary group*. By *discrete* is meant that, while they are thus interacting with one another, the social events involving one another have a more frequent occurrence than social events with individuals outside the combination. *Secondary* groups are, according to my usage, those larger social units all of whose members do not necessarily interact face to face, or equivalently, but who are nevertheless interrelated in distinctively hierarchic patterns of interaction. These usages are based on definitions set forth by Chapple and Arensberg (1940).

5. For an informative example of suppositional projections of these different social structures see D. Oliver (1943).

6. The international boundary between the Territory of New Guinea and the British Solomon Islands Protectorate lies just south of Bougainville.

7. South Bougainville farmers usually garden on old gardening sites, after these have remained fallow for time enough to permit trees to reach fence-building proportions, that is, about six years.

8. Near the end of our stay, Songi yielded to public opinion and allowed himself to be appointed Headman over a newly consolidated Administration unit of Turungum and nearby Rennu village.

REFERENCES CITED

CHAPPLE, E. D. and C. M. ARENSBERG (1940): Measuring Human Relations. *Genetic Psychology Monographs*, No. 22. Provincetown, Massachusetts.

GOODENOUGH, W. H. (1951): Property, Kin, and Community on Truk. *Yale University Publications in Anthropology*, No. 46. New Haven.

LEACH, E. R. (1954): *Political Systems of Highland Burma*. Cambridge, Mass.: Harvard University Press.

OLIVER, D. (1943): The Horomorun Concepts of Southern Bougainville: A Study in Comparative Religion. *Peabody Museum Papers*, Vol. XX. Cambridge, Mass.

OLIVER, D. (1955): *A Solomon Island Society*. Cambridge, Mass.: Harvard University Press.

THURNWALD, H. (1934): Woman's Status in Buin Society. *Oceania*, Vol. V, No. 2.

THURNWALD, R. (1934): Pigs and Currency in Buin. *Oceania*, Vol. V, No. 2.

L. L. LANGNESS

BENA BENA POLITICAL ORGANIZATION[1]

ABSTRACT

Focusing on the Korofeigu 'district' of the Numuyagabo 'tribe' in Bena Bena census division, this paper considers the appropriateness of terms used to designate units of New Guinea Highlands social structure. Some terms have a certain utility, but not for understanding Korofeigu political organization—taking 'political' as referring primarily to public affairs. Marriage and warfare were not directly linked, and districts and clans rarely acted as single groups or polities. The key figures are Big Men whose status rested on ability in warfare. War relations were power relations with no notion of fair play and no opposition of balanced groups. A group's survival rested on the success of its Big Men in organizing and extending their personal networks, and on the balancing of competition and individual ambition between them in a complex interplay of security circles—the significant polities in political action.

I

In an earlier paper (1964), I suggested that although it was difficult to perceive the Bena Bena as having unilineal descent groups in terms of their behaviour, they nevertheless appeared to have an ideology or dogma of patrilineal descent. The problem, as I stated it, was to resolve the discrepancy between their ideology and their behaviour. I now believe that is at least misleading and could be quite incorrect. Although I do not intend to go into this in detail here, the problem will, hopefully, become clearer below.[2] This account of Bena Bena primarily describes some features of political organization, but I hope it will also help to clear up some of the controversy over New Guinea Highlands social structure (Barnes 1962, 1967; Brown 1962; de Lepervanche 1967; du Toit 1964; Langness 1964; McArthur 1967; Meggitt 1965; Watson 1965).

The name Bena Bena now applies to a census division of approximately 14,000 persons divided into approximately 65 subunits I have elsewhere referred to as 'tribes' (1963, 1964, 1967, 1969). This use of Bena Bena is an arbitrary, postcontact phenomenon which took the place name of one relatively small group and extended it, ignoring dialects, to include a larger number of people on the basis of language similarities. Similar census divisions now surround Bena Bena and, although these may be taking on political significance now, they were originally an administrative convenience reflecting no indigenous political reality whatsoever.

One of the 65 units of Bena Bena, in the extreme southeast corner of the census division, is called Korofeigu. Korofeigu is probably the name of a place only and not, precisely speaking, the name of a people. Thus a person is *from* Korofeigu but is not a Korofeigan. If you ask a man from Korofeigu who he is, or what he is, or what he or his people are called, he will most probably reply that he (or they) are Numuyagabo.

Numuyagabo appears to be the name of a dialect spoken at one time by several units similar to, and including, Korofeigu. It is almost impossible now to determine precisely who all of the Numuyagabo speakers were. I am reasonably certain Numuyagabo was spoken by the people who reside today at Korofeigu, Gitenu, Sirupa, and Kotomi, and it may have been spoken by as many as six other similar places, some of which have disappeared. Some men say that Numuyagabo was a man who lived long ago, and that he taught people how to make the clothing they wear which distinguishes them as Numuyagabo. Some men elaborate on this and say that he also showed people how to butcher, to make fire, and a few other ways of doing things. I was told by one man that when he shot arrows at his enemies he would call out, 'I shoot you now with the bow of Numuyagabo'. One other reports saying, 'Numuyagaboo! Help me now! Let my enemy die!' Other men, however, say that Numuyagabo was not a man and that the name refers only to a dialect. But all, without exception, deny that Numuyagabo was the ancestor from whom the people originated; they do not know whether he had children; and his name is not used to describe any relationships between individuals or groups other than as suggested. Indeed, so far as I know, they do not believe any particular relationships exist between the places that speak this dialect except the language and costume. This identification appears to have been stronger at one time and led one of the District Officers to report Numuyagabo as a 'clan' (Driver 1959); but in my opinion this is not a reasonable interpretation.[3] In this paper, I will refer to the Numuyagabo as a tribe.[4]

Approximately 750 persons reside at Korofeigu. They are clearly divided into four major groups which are named, exogamous, possess their own territory within the larger territory of Korofeigu, and are autonomous. I have referred to these as 'level I' groups (1964) but more frequently as clans (1963, 1965, 1967, 1969). Here I will refer to them as clans. The four Korofeigu clans, Nupasafa, Nagamitobo, Wai'atagusa, and Benimeto, occupy adjoining territories. Within each territory, there are from one to three villages immediately surrounded by gardens.[5] It is approximately two miles between the two most widely separated villages.

Korofeigu, the unit I originally called a tribe, is apparently similar to what Berndt has called a district (1962), Newman a phratry (1965), Read a sub-tribe (1952), Watson a local group (1967), and Glasse a clan-parish (1969).[6] Having designated the Numuyagabo a tribe, I will redesignate Korofeigu, in this paper, a district. In the case of Korofeigu, whatever it is labelled, when you ask men in any one clan why the four clans reside contiguously they reply simply, 'because our ancestors did'. There is no conception of a single ancestor, and there is no named ancestor for the four clans together. Nor is there any belief that the ancestors of individual clans were brothers. At this level then, there appears to be no genealogical link, no myth of common origin, and no conception of brotherhood. Further, the men of one clan cannot give any information about the ancestors of other clans.

There is less doubt about clan ancestors, and many but by no means all of the adult males in any clan will give the name of a particular individual who is said to have been the first man of that clan. A few men of the clan, particularly older men, will describe the situation in more detail, explaining that the first man had 'x' number of sons and that their particular 'line' is identified with one of the sons. In the case of Nupasafa clan, for example, not all men could tell you the name of the first man, Gooyi; still fewer could tell you that Gooyi had five sons. Rarer still would be a man who could actually name any of the sons. Five or six men could name two or three of the sons, perhaps, but not all of them; and perhaps two or three old men could name all five. The men who can name one or more of the sons of Gooyi, however, can always tell which of the sons is pertinent to their own line, but no one can give any precise genealogical link to any of Gooyi's sons. I suspect that I know this, limited as it may be, only because I spent a great deal of time asking about it. That is, they do not seem very concerned with it; and looking back in my notes, I can find no instance when this information was invoked. In a few cases of dispute, there are statements such as: 'so-and-so is not a Nupa'; 'you do not belong here'; 'your father did not plant this ground'; or 'go back to your own ground'. Although it is difficult to interpret the true meaning of these statements, and although I have doubts as to how well the term patrifiliation applies to the way the Bena Bena conceive of themselves, I believe that, as Barnes suggested (1962), they might be more accurately described in terms of cumulative patrifiliation than in terms of descent.

Nupasafa is a clan, then, in the sense that it is a localized, land-owning, exogamous group which 'explains' its composition, in part, by reference to remote male ancestors to whom no genealogical links can be traced. Nor can precise genealogical links be traced between all living members. Descent is not indicated or emphasized except in the rather nebulous manner described. This is little more than the recognition of continuity—there were people in the past and, if all goes well, there will continue to be people in the future. Indeed, many men cannot name even their own grandfathers and seem to have few occasions when they find such knowledge either necessary or useful. They emphasize more strongly that they are 'one', and that they are brothers, or brothers and sisters. They also emphasize the importance of males and male superiority in a variety of ways. Their sisters must marry out and go to reside elsewhere; children are the property of males; all rituals are male activities, and so on. Careful examination of the membership of such a clan, however, reveals a surprisingly large number of residential males (at least 30%) who reside in Nupasafa for reasons having nothing to do with ancestors or descent, and nothing to do with brotherhood either, in any biological sense. If you ask these men why they live in Nupasafa, they do not reply in terms of descent, either agnatic or cognatic. Most of them say their fathers lived there at one time and so they are 'brothers' or 'like brothers'. Some say their fathers were 'friends'. Some say they themselves are friends and have come to live there because of sorcery elsewhere. Only two of ten such men have Nupasafa wives, and even these men do not say they live there because of their wives. I cannot determine that these men are perceived as having anything but the same 'rights' as others, in spite of rare statements to the effect that they somehow do not belong. Most of the situations that might clarify the question of rights, such as disputes over land or the inheritance of other property, do not occur.

The people of Nupasafa clan have a tendency to deny there are any smaller 'groups' than the clan itself and, behaviourally viewed, this may be true, even though I have spoken in the past of subclans and lineages (1963, 1965, 1967, 1969).[7] It is clear there are no named subclans or lineages. It is equally clear that neither subclans nor lineages are land-owning groups. There is no very marked tendency for the members to plant gardens in direct proximity. There is a stronger tendency for them to reside together but, even here, there are a great many exceptions.[8] What primarily distinguishes the membership of a subclan is the obvious suggestion, in some situations, that certain people are members of one 'line' as contrasted with those who are members of another. The only Bena Bena term for these lines that I am aware of is *goguna,* and I am only able to translate that as a 'line of men'. Only one of the five Nupasafa subclans can actually trace precise genealogical connections for all of its members but, nonetheless, people do know they are members of one subclan and not another (Langness 1964a). Certain occasions bring the subclans into focus, albeit not always very clearly. Each of these lines, for example, possesses one or more sacred flutes. Marriage, to a certain extent, is identified with subclans, as is ritual cannibalism. Occasionally, one line is said to have helped another. The largest number of adult males in any one subclan is 12. The smallest has 7. Subclans seem no more interested in tracing genealogies than do clans. Members are quite clearly 'recruited' to these groups, using non-descent principles, just as they are to clans. What I find of particular interest, however, is the emphasis placed upon clanship, and the lack of it regarding subclans. There is, first, the denial that such groups exist, and there is no identification of these groups with land. The members of subclans do not significantly appear to prefer to work with one another rather than with others. My observations of the work habits of individual men indicate that they tend to prefer age mates or adopted brothers, to fathers or brothers. And although subclans are the 'core', so to speak, of marriage arrangements, they will deliberately ask outsiders for help and say, specifically, that if they do not, those others will be angry. This is true even when, financially, a subclan could easily by itself afford a brideprice (Langness 1969).

What I termed a lineage must be seen as merely an extended family, or as two or more brothers with their wives and children. The term *goguna* applies to a line of this kind as well as to subclans, and I doubt that the Bena Bena themselves make much distinction. They do distinguish between the line and the family, however, and there is a term, *pana'na,* which refers to a man, his wife, and children. I propose to drop the term lineage here altogether.

Thus, in this terminology, we can now speak of the tribe, district, clan, subclan and family. However, although these terms may correspond roughly to what is 'out there', I do not think they very accurately convey what is in the minds of the Bena Bena. The actual meaning of this, to them, must be somewhat more elusive. Nonetheless, let us now turn to political organization. *It is the general thesis of this paper that although it is possible to speak of Bena Bena society in terms of tribes, districts, clans, subclans and families, named and otherwise, it is not possible to understand their political organization in such terms. To attempt to do so is to greatly over-simplify Bena Bena behaviour.*

II

Let us say that the term 'political' refers fundamentally to public affairs, and that particular publics, as well as their particular affairs, must be empirically determined (Langness 1971). Political activity goes on between groups as well as within them. Thus a public is never itself a corporate group but always consists of a number of such groups which constitute its political units. The United States, for example, is a political unit within a public composed of the world. Korofeigu, traditionally, was a political unit in a smaller public, the boundaries of which were limited to considerably less than the world. Although I am unable to state with precision what the actual limits of this public were, it is reasonable to assume that Korofeigu had no knowledge of anything beyond a radius of approximately twenty to thirty miles.

The units which make up a public are termed 'polities'. These can vary in size, in number, in internal organization, and in the processes they employ to manage their external and internal public affairs. Any unit of social structure which at times acts as a group is a polity. Thus in the public of which Korofeigu was a part, the tribe (the Numuyagabo) was not a polity, as it never acted as a group for any purpose whatsoever. The district (Korofeigu) can be seen as a polity, as it apparently did, at rare times, act as a single group. The clan, likewise, was a polity and acted, but again only at times, as a single group. I doubt very much that a subclan ever truly acted as a single group although conceivably it could have. It is difficult to see the subclan as a polity at all, strange as that may seem. A family, aside from domestic tasks, would appear to have had no occasion for acting alone or as a single group.

When a polity cannot be seen at any time as a part of any larger entity than a public, it is called a jural community and is the largest political unit within that public. A jural community, like any other polity, however, need not be permanent. The political system of a public is never identical with the political system of any one of its constituent parts. Political systems of publics are systems of power relations, whereas political systems of polities are always systems of authority, in addition to those of power. It is the presence of authority of some kind that defines a polity. In the case of New Guinea, it is typically the district or some similar unit which is considered the jural community. This is usually because of the claim that such a group is the largest unit which acknowledges authority in the sense that the members of this group agree that disputes should be resolved by adjudication rather than warfare. And, indeed, this is one thing the Bena Bena are fairly clear and consistent about, at least verbally. War, called *luva*, is distinguished from fighting, which is called *nonogatna*. War involves killing, bows and arrows, spears, sneak-attacks and the like, whereas fighting involves sticks, fists, and no killing. War, they insist, could not and did not occur within Korofeigu. They make no such claim in any wider context. Districts, however, as will become clear, only rarely acted as a single group—for war or any other purpose—and the claim that warfare could not occur within them is probably not well grounded. In any case, to define a jural community in terms of the single criterion of the absence of war is to overlook a host of other public affairs.

Power, as it is used here, means the ability to impose one's will on another in spite of opposition. Authority is limited power. It is the legitimate right to influence, to make binding decisions, and to direct the affairs of polities within the rules recognized by the members of those polities. There is considerable variation in the extent to which different polities will allow the use of power as opposed to authority. In some systems, a great deal of compulsion is tolerated; in others, very little. In some the use of violence and physical coercion is considered legitimate, and in others it is not. Authority, no matter how diffuse, is always hierarchic. It may or may not be centralized. Power is hierarchic only in that it is relative. Political organization, then, is that organization which, through polities, uses power and authority to facilitate, influence, and regulate public affairs.

One of the difficulties in the controversy over New Guinea Highlands social structures results from the exclusive preoccupation with 'descent groups' as such, when, as Scheffler has recently made clear, "the important issue may be whether the groups compared are political, economic, or religious corporations, or all of these, rather than descent groups of one kind or another" (1966: 542). This has an even greater significance, however, in the study of political organization in Highlands societies because of the unique significance of specifically political functions for segmentary lineage theory:

> . . . the fundamental concepts of segmentary theory centre about the definition of a system of political relations, and on the basis of this, differentiate lineages from other kinship groupings in terms of segmentary principles and structures which reflect and discharge political functions (Smith 1956).

It was my concern with descent, I believe, which prevented me from going far enough in my original account (1964). What I wanted to say at that time was that, although I did not believe these could be unilineal descent systems, segmentary or 'African' in type in terms of their behaviour (i.e., they did not discharge political functions), they appeared to be ideologically of that type. But they appeared to be ideologically of that type because (1) I was concerned with descent, (2) New Guinea Highlands societies were regarded as quite homogeneous, (3) all known New Guinea Highlanders were reported to be patrilineal, (4) there is a strong emphasis in Bena Bena culture on male superiority, male ancestor cults, brotherhood, fatherhood, etc., which can fairly easily be interpreted as a concern with descent, and (5) the language of Social Anthropology is exceedingly difficult to apply to Bena Bena behaviour. What this implies, of course, is that (1) either the Korofeigu people are very different from the Bena Bena in general, (2) the Bena Bena are different in this respect from all other Highlanders, (3) others who have worked in the Highlands have in some measure been prey to the same assumptions and language as I, or (4) I do not understand the situation at Korofeigu. It would be relatively simple if only one of these was true. Unfortunately, it is almost certain that they are all true, in part.

III

To know that the Bena Bena can be described, however imperfectly, as having tribes, districts, clans, subclans and families—that these are in some sense units of organization—does not, in itself, tell you very much about the way they manage their public affairs. It should be clear that the tribe is not a political group but is defined simply in terms of dialect and minor cultural similarities. There was no loyalty on the part of the people of Korofeigu to the tribe, and there was no agreement, apparently, among Numuyagabo speakers even to settle disputes amicably. Nupasafa informants report, for example, they did not war against Sirupa and Kotomi, but the people of Gitenu were among their worst enemies. These were all Numuyagabo districts. Granted that oral histories of warfare are not too reliable, there are several accounts of warring with Gitenu, and there appears to be complete agreement that at one time, long ago (but within living memory), the people of Korofeigu lived much closer to Gitenu. Some people from Yagaria came to take refuge with Nupasafa clan. These Yagaria people wanted to burn some grass to get rats to eat, which they did. But while they were getting ready to cook them, some people of Gitenu surrounded and killed them (all of them, it is said). Three Nupasafa women and one man were also killed. Nupasafa, in conjunction with some other Korofeigu men (but not all of them) fought with Gitenu. The Korofeigu people moved farther away and there were several battles over a period of years (until European contact). The Numuyagabo tribe, then, cannot be said to have prescribed *nonogatna* or proscribed *luva*.

This raises the question of alliances, which is absolutely crucial in understanding the political organization of the Bena Bena, but which is by no means easy to understand. The Nupasafans very consistently give the names of six places, the people of which are said to have been their worst enemies: Forape, Gitenu, Katagu, Legeyu, Sakanuga and Upegu. Within memory, however, they are known to have allied with at least three of these places—Gitenu, Katagu, and Legeyu—to fight others. The *only* group with which they consistently specify they did not fight is Kapakamaligi district, which is now the closest group to them. But I have reliable accounts of a fight between Hofaga district and Kapakamaligi, in which men of Nagamitobo and Benimeto clans (of Korofeigu), as well as *some* men of Nupasafa clan, helped Hofaga, while other men of Nupasafa fought on the side of Kapakamaligi. I do not know the details except that at least one of the Nupasafa men who helped Kapakamaligi was not married to a Kapakamaligi woman.

Furthermore, although they consistently give the same 6 places as people they warred against, I have accounts of Nupasafans fighting against at least 9 other places. Two of these were Gahuku groups (a different language) approximately 20 miles to the northwest. And this is only from the point of view of Nupasafa clan members! If you interview members of other Korofeigu clans, you find similar accounts and, although there is considerable overlap, there are also differences. The list of places Nagamitobo men fought is not identical with that of the Nupasafans, nor is that of Wai'atagusa, nor Benimeto. From the point of view of Korofeigu district, *someone* appears to have fought virtually *everyone* reachable in approximately a day's walk. All of this is within *living* memory.

Although the Nupasafans report only Kapakamaligi as a consistently friendly ally, there are at least 12 other groups they are known to have allied with at one time or another. Three of these appear on their list of 6 worst enemies and one more is in the group of 9 against which there is an account of war. Thus there are 8 groups the Nupasafans allied with and have no record of fighting against. But they do not characterize these groups as friends or as permanent allies—they merely report being allied with them at certain times when they warred against others.

There are still other groups with which Nupasafa men had relationships and with whom they did not fight. Again, they do not usually describe these people as friends but mention trading with them. I am reasonably certain that Nupa men traded with at least 12 other places, 9 of which do not appear on either the list of those they fought against or that of those with whom they were allied. One does appear on the list of those they fought against, and 2 are on the list of allies. Finally, there is a list of people with whom one or more Nupasafa men at one time or another took refuge. There are 18 places on this list. Of these 18, 6 are places they fought against, including 3 of their worst enemies. Eight of these are also on the list of allies. Four are on the list of those they traded with; 4 others do not appear in any other context. Again, this is only from the point of view of Nupasafa clan—the others seem equally complex. This information is quite obviously incorrect in some measure, and it is most certainly incomplete. My examination of it is also incomplete. But, even so, I believe certain conclusions can be drawn.

First, the public of which Korofeigu was a part was not homogeneous with respect to language. Represented above are people from what are now classified as Gahuku, Kafe, Yavi Yufa, Yagaria and Bena Bena speakers. There are some cultural differences between these people as well. Second, it is clearly not the case that these are relationships between Korofeigu district *qua* district and other groups.

People in different clans, as well as those of different subclans, and even individuals, went their own way when it suited them to do so. There is no account of an entire district taking refuge, or trading, with another. They do not seem to have *typically* fought together as a district although it appears that at times they may have. The same thing is true of clans. No clan took refuge as a clan so far as I can determine. If it did, it was a very small remnant. Nor does an entire clan have a trade relationship with another entire clan. Subclans are said to have taken refuge at times, but in this terminology, subclans can easily be a very small number of men and their families (which seems always, in fact, to have been the case). Individual men and their immediate or extended families are the rule, at least when speaking of trade partnerships and refugees. There are also instances of a man leaving his children in other places while there was fighting near his own over a period of time. Warfare itself is even more difficult to comprehend.

Warfare, as one would surmise, was frequent. It ranged from a fairly large scale enterprise, involving men from several districts, to small scale attacks involving men from a single clan, perhaps even a single subclan, although I doubt this latter. Some idea of what was involved can be gained from the following descriptions:

> The people live in villages which were in most cases surrounded by a barricade of split slabs up to 12 feet high if timber were available; and in the country away from the timber-clad ranges, wild cane stalks woven together formed a very effective wall; at intervals along the barricades the wall extended outwards to allow the besieged villagers to protect the barricades against invaders. Getting in closer to it and protected by their wooden shields the invaders would cut the vine binding it together and let in their comrades to burn the rounded grass-thatched houses and kill all to whom they could get near enough (Leahy 1936: 229).[10]

> . . . and when the owners are unfortunate enough to be driven out of their villages the invaders do not consider that they have destroyed the village properly until they have ring-barked the trees [which are hand planted, individually owned casuarinas] and so destroyed it (Leahy 1936: 242).

> . . . One man has died a natural death and they can't quite understand it. Death by an arrow being the usual way out. The death rate in this area alone [the Bena Bena valley] from fighting is appalling and every day we are getting particulars of more deaths of people we knew when we were here before [this was only three years previously]. We are also being continuously invited to go with a friendly mob and wipe out another crowd whom they are at war with, the rewards held out to us being plenty of pigs and marys [women] but to identify ourselves definitely with any one tribe would be to court endless trouble later on (entry, Leahy diary, 22 February, 1934).

Some idea of the numbers of people involved can be roughly ascertained from other early reports. In an entry from a patrol report dated 5 June 1933 Bates (1932-33) records 150 Sigoiabu people—men, women and children—hurriedly taking food from the gardens of a place called Gafia, which had just been attacked and routed. On 7 June 1933 he reports passing 400 armed natives in war dress, accompanied by several women carrying arrows and supplies. Black (1934-35) mentions, on 20 November 1935, "interrupting a serious attack on the former place [Moheweto]". The following places (he refers to these as villages) are reported as being involved: Safanuka, Siguya, Kwahisipa, Giminarbi, Gorpogohi, Oyafuyufa, and Nayufa. I do not know precisely what groups all of these were but they are not all clans of a single district. Most of them are names of districts, so that people from several districts must have been involved. Giminarbi village, Black says, was "mainly responsible" for the attack.

These early accounts are quite consistent with the statements of informants. Very large battles are described in which, for example, three districts (Korofeigu, Mohebeto and Ketarabo) are said to have been involved in routing another district (Samegu). Sometimes two districts (Korofeigu and Moheweto) rout another (Katagu). There are also accounts involving only Korofeigu, apparently as a single district, routing another district (Forape); cases of three of the four Korofeigu clans fighting together, of two, and of one. But there are two serious questions to be raised here. First, although the descriptions are given in terms of districts or clans, I am personally satisfied that this means only 'selected men of' those places, and does not imply an activity between districts and clans acting as 'corporate' in the usual meaning of that term. Individual men could and did elect not to take part, and, as indicated above, even to take the opposite side at times. This appears to have been the case in other Highlands societies as well. For example:

. . . In warfare with a traditional enemy, every man in the parish could be conscripted to fight, whereas a group that was only temporarily hostile invariably included some men who were related to parish members through intermarriage, and these kinship links with obligations neither to kill nor to injure certain persons made the parish fighting force in some measure less effective (Reay 1959: 54).

The main difference between this Kuma case and the Bena Bena is the difficulty in distinguishing 'traditional' from 'temporary' enemies in the latter where, if the distinction exists at all, it is primarily verbal and not necessarily behavioural. The following description, from an area closer to Bena Bena, fits more precisely:

. . . there was a conflict of loyalties, but not of an equally balanced kind: one centred on the group, the other on the person. Individual consideration of kin and of trading partners, if these were distinguished, meant that in almost all fighting between two opposed groups . . . there were some persons who would hold their hand in regard to some other persons. This in itself had a moderating effect on warfare. Warfare was never "total". Even apart from the issue of neutrality, participation of adult males was rarely complete. Non-participation was in some cases a conventional matter, as among Mbowamb . . . In others . . . in any given encounter it was left very largely to individual choice. The apparent disregard for human rights in warfare outside a certain social range was, in fact, combined with a certain respect for such rights, and that respect was manifested in the provision for personal relationships even in the heat and excitement of actual combat. Flexibility, allowance for personal initiative within loosely defined limits, was apparent in this sphere of Highlands living no less than in others (Berndt 1964: 203).

This individuality, so characteristically described in New Guinea Highlands societies, is quite inconsistent with notions of "jural equality" and "corporateness" (Langness 1971). The second point here, related to individuality, is that the polity most typically at war seems not to have been a district or a clan, or even an alliance of such units, but, rather, an essentially unpredictable alliance of numbers of men from different places who joined together on a purely temporary basis. However, these temporary polities did co-operate; they did have a single goal; and they must have had some system of authority, however diffuse. What is so difficult to understand or explain are the motives involved in different cases, the specific personnel involved, and how they actually decided to ally as they so obviously did. This becomes somewhat more intelligible, perhaps, when it is realized there were no leaders with authority to command or speak for the district, or even the clan as a whole.

Small scale raids occurred fairly frequently, it appears, and could be precipitated by a number of things—suspicion of sorcery, theft of women or pigs, an argument over the ownership of trees, and personal disputes of various kinds. In these it appears that, if attacked, a clan would respond defensively as a single unit. It is not so clear that the clan acted very frequently as a single unit offensively, however. It was a rare man who could actually mobilize an entire clan for a raid, and in the cases I have heard described, the man who wanted revenge usually recruited only a portion of the clan to accompany him on his raid. These would be brothers, age mates, friends, and perhaps others acting from motives of their own. Sometimes men from other clans would go along also. It would seem that a Big Man could recruit a large following, and the Big Men, or *gipinas*, precipitated the larger wars even though the causes might still fundamentally have been personal revenge. For example:

A man from Benimeto, a *gipina*, was married to a woman from Gitenu. His wife died. He believed a man from Gitenu (presumably of another clan) had worked sorcery on her. A large funeral was held to which people from many places, including Gitenu, were invited. They all came in mourning and were given gifts of pork. The *gipina* had his bow and arrows but kept them concealed under his foot in some leaves. He called the man from Gitenu to come forward to receive some pork. But when he came near the *gipina* said, "You cannot eat this pig." He shot and killed him. Another man of Gitenu who was present ran and hid in a house. The Nupasafa men present started to tear it down and the man then ran into the tall grass. But they caught him and killed him. This precipitated a large war between men of Korofeigu and Gitenu.

Again, it is not clear just who was involved in this fighting except for Nupasafa men and Benimeto men. I do not know whether men of the deceased woman's clan became involved, or on which side they would have fought; but from other accounts of similar incidents they could have been involved at one point or another, and they could have fought on either or both sides. It is unlikely that a lesser man would have attempted anything quite like this. The *gipinas*, and there seem always to have been from three to ten in Korofeigu at any given time, were usually behind the major offensive actions:

When K and T's fathers were initiated [this would have been approximately 1920], the *gipina*s said, 'Now we are strong, there are lots of men in Korofeigu.' They decided whom they should fight. They said, 'All of the other places are small now. Only Forape is large.' So they decided to fight the Forape, which they did, surrounding them in their gardens and killing many of them. N and B, who were small then [they must have been about ten years of age] went along to watch.

*Gipina*s sometimes disagreed over fighting. One would want to fight against a certain place but one or more others might disagree. Sometimes a *gipina* would recruit followers and lead a raid anyway. *Gipina*s from one clan would consult with those of other clans and attempt to enlist their support. Men from one clan would sometimes follow a *gipina* from another. A *gipina* seems to have been assured of the support of his subclan, at least, but the more successful they were, the more easily they could draw others behind them as well. It would be a mistake to conclude from this that *gipina*s were subclan leaders. It is more reasonable to conclude that if a man could not lead his subclan, or most of it, he could not become a *gipina*.

In this area, it is almost exclusively ability in warfare that is stressed as prerequisite for the status of Big Man. There are no hereditary chiefs or claims to leadership as in Kuma (Reay 1959), although if a man's father was a *gipina,* he would be more likely to achieve that status than otherwise. Patronage is nowhere near as important as in Enga (Meggitt 1965), nor is entrepreneurship (Meggitt 1967), as the scale and preoccupation with exchange, when compared with Enga, is very small indeed, and land is not scarce enough to be as rigidly apportioned. Furthermore, although it has not yet emerged very obviously from the literature, there is no real functional equivalent to the huge Moka or Te exchanges of the Western Highlands (Bulmer 1960). To be a *gipina,* a man had to be able to organize a successful raid, to attack and take a village, to command a knowledge of terrain, strategy and weapons, and to be knowledgeable in the ways of war in general. *Gipina*s are said to have been able to send men out to scout and to detect weaknesses in an enemy barricade. They also deployed men in battle. They alone seem to have made decisions as to when the enemy was vulnerable or weak. Certainly to be a *gipina* a man would have to have killed. The only other important context in which *gipina*s are described has to do with pig exchanges. But these exchanges are held to pay back for help in warfare, which the *gipina*s were responsible for in the first place.

It is true that a *gipina* had to be able to 'talk well', but flamboyant oratory, as reported in Kuma (Reay 1959), is not very characteristic of the Bena Bena. Nor is there anything that could be described as formally as a "clan orator" (Read 1959). *Gipina*s did not necessarily possess any specialized knowledge of the clan ancestors. It is interesting to note in this connection that, when I asked one of the few surviving Korofeigu *gipina*s about his clan ancestors (Nagamitobo), he said he would ask the old men (he was himself approximately 45 years of age) so he could tell me about them. However, his knowledge of warfare was immense when compared with that of most men. It is also true that *gipina*s usually had more wives than other men, and thus more pigs and gardens. They also used this wealth to gain support; but even so, it appears to have been much less important than success in battle. Wealth was a way in which one could enlist and encourage men's support and not so much a way of validating the status itself.

The number of supporters and the amount of power a *gipina* could mobilize seem to have depended upon his position *vis-à-vis* other Big Men. *Gipina*s did command the following of men of other clans. At one time, for example, all of the truly Big Men of Nupasafa clan had been killed. K, a *gipina* of Nagamitobo, visited them and told them that since all of the Big Men were dead, they should listen to and follow him, which they did, and for some period of time. However, it was dangerous to be a *gipina* and to 'have a name'. *Gipina*s were particularly susceptible to treachery, sorcery, and physical attack from their enemies. For this reason, they say they did not often leave their own territory except to fight. For example:

> We wanted to kill a man at Forape, a *gipina*. He was strong and we had not been able to kill him. We took an arrow with a tanket leaf to the people at Kami who were friendly with Forape. We also took some shell and some pig. The Kami took the "pay" and divided it among themselves. They invited some people from Forape to Kami, telling them they would give them some pig. This *gipina* was there and they killed him. They pulled the arrow (Nupasafa had given them) out of the body and returned it to us with a tanket leaf. We killed pigs for them.

This sort of thing does not appear to have been unusual. It points up what I interpret as a relative lack of rules governing warfare. These were strictly relations of power. The alliances were brittle and impermanent. Allies of one day could be enemies the next. Sneak attacks were common and involved creeping up on people in their gardens, bribery, and ambush. Early morning raids were popular and were made on villages while people were asleep. The men's house 'door' was tied shut and the building set afire. Men who tried to escape were shot as they broke out. The Nupasafans are quite proud of having had three different techniques for dealing with this: either a secret weak spot in the back wall of the men's house they could easily kick out, or a hole in the floor leading out through a tunnel, or a false menstrual hut fifty or more yards away where two or three men would sleep so as to be able to counterattack. Once a men's house was routed, the women's houses were burned. Women, children, and even old people were killed. Gardens and trees were looted and/or destroyed. Pigs, sometimes women, and other goods were captured. There was no notion here of an 'underdog' or 'fair play', nor was there, so far as I know, any notion of 'equivalence'. Certainly warfare did not involve balanced groups in opposition to each other if that could be avoided.

The theme of fighting the strong is common. They say they lived well only at certain times—when Korofeigu was strong and other places were small. The accounts reveal that large groups were attacked and driven away and, as reported above, everything was destroyed so the routed did not quickly return. They did on occasion, it is true, invite people to return to their ground but only, it seems, when they were small in number and no longer considered a threat. Korofeigu was particularly successful at this, and, at the time of European contact (1930-31), dominated the entire Bena Bena valley, insofar as any one group could have done so entirely.

I am not certain that, from the point of view of Korofeigu as a whole, there were any groups within reasonable walking distance someone did not fight against. From the point of view of Nupasafa clan, however, there were several. Many of these were groups with whom they traded and upon whom they depended. The Nupasafans made salt which they traded for bows, black palm for making arrowheads, feathers, shell, wooden utensils, and materials for magic. They also traded pigs for these things. As the Korofeigu people are true grass dwellers, they have no wood for bows or arrowheads, and it was crucial, of course, for them to have these and to maintain good relations with those from whom they got them. But most of the places they traded with were quite a long distance away and trips were infrequent and dangerous. The trade relationships were strictly between individual men. Only 4 of the 15 groups mentioned as those they traded with are also mentioned as places where people took refuge. The Nupas themselves report that most of these groups were 'too far away to fight'. Thus, although these relationships were of great importance to them, they were specialized and only infrequently invoked.

As the only adequate information I have on marriage covers the relatively recent period, whereas the accounts of warfare extend much further back, it is not possible to link the one directly with the other. Because of the high 'divorce' rate and the insignificance of women, it is not possible to gather satisfactory data on marriages in the past. An examination of the marriage customs themselves, however, as well as the Korofeigans' attitudes and statements about marriage, leads one to the conclusion that there was no very direct relationship between marriage and warfare. They do not say, "we marry those we fight" (Elkin 1953), nor is there anything to suggest that "Hostility between clans is strictly incompatible with intermarriage" (Reay 1959). They are inconsistent about whether individual men would fight against their fathers-in-law or brothers-in-law. In general, I believe they would not, or they would spare such relatives in battle if they did participate in a raid against their group (Langness 1969).

There seems to be a strong tendency for wives to come from groups with whom they allied, traded, or took refuge, rather than from those with whom they fought. But as wives were sometimes taken by capture, were purchased from distant places as young girls, and as there are definite cases of clans having fought against clans from which they did have wives, I do not believe any great significance can be attached to this. The manner in which they go about finding wives indicates that it was a more or less random system. It also indicates that although marriages appear superficially to be arrangements between subclans, they really involve larger numbers of people, again in a somewhat random manner, but in the name of clans.

Warfare, leadership, and marriage are all public affairs and hence, by definition, political. But it is exceedingly difficult, in the Bena Bena, to see these as activities involving groups if defined as districts, tribes, clans or subclans. A Bena Bena district like Korofeigu, although a corporate entity in some sense, is in others a rather peculiar kind of organization. Although it is not itself part of a permanent larger jural community, some of its members sometimes ally with 'outsiders' to destroy others. During the period of that activity, there is some kind of 'group' or polity, sometimes even larger than a district, acting for a single purpose. Once that purpose has been achieved, the group disbands, probably never to form again with the same membership. The district is seen in action as a single group or polity only when the self interests of its collective members are threatened by a possibly overwhelming force, except that, as it believes 'the best defence is a good offence', it apparently can sometimes be mobilized as a single offensive unit also. Thus it rarely has relationships as a group with other such groups, and these relationships cannot be seen as either permanent or stable.

A district has no centralized authority—no single leader who can speak for it or represent it as a group (although it would seem to be theoretically possible for a single Big Man to do so). For a district to act as a single unit, two or more Big Men have to agree on a single course of action which is, in effect, another form of temporary alliance. Indeed, there is no good reason to assume that a district would not fight within itself and split, although they say they would not.[11] As the authority of Big Men is not usually over entire clans, or even subclans, there are no predictable combinations of like segments acting in opposition to others.

Finally, a district is unusual in that it seems to recognize and encourage the almost unlimited activity and ambition of individual men within it. It seems to allow its citizens the right of non-participation even when its own interests are at stake, and it allows its Big Men unlimited power if they can achieve it. Paradoxically, the kind of "despotism" described by Salisbury (1964) and Watson (1967) could probably only arise in such a system of "anarchy" (Brown 1963), and in societies with a relative propensity for recognizing physical violence and coercion as legitimate. Indeed, this may help a group to insure its survival. The success of the group depends upon the success of its Big Men which, in turn, depends upon their ability to extend their personal networks of power and influence. To do this, they must establish ties with as many others as possible—first within their own subclan, then their own clan, then within other clans of the district, and finally with others. They recruit members, maintain ties with affines and cognates, maintain trade partnerships, help others in battle, and give gifts and bribes. As success in battle is the primary criterion for the status of *gipina,* and as it is also the only guarantee of survival, the individual acts of men in competition promote the well being of the group. Thus to describe warfare as an activity between districts is to overlook the overwhelming significance of individualism and alliance.

The same thing is true of clans, although certainly clans act as polities more often than districts. However there do not appear to have been many times in the history of Nupasafa clan when there were not from two to five individuals striving to become *gipina*s. They did not always act together; they disagreed over where to fight, when, and against whom. Men of Nupasafa occasionally fought on different sides, just as men of different clans in the district did. Decisions to take one side rather than another, or to participate at all, seem to have hinged on factors of self-interest only—which relationships a man chose to activate and maintain, and which he did not; which relationships offered him the most security and which did not; and what his particular circumstances at the moment demanded of him. This is still true, although less so, at the level of subclans. A man generally supported his subclan, but not always.

Because of the emphasis on individualism, and because the acts of individuals were at times at variance with those of their district, clan and subclan, it is necessary to add another concept to describe Bena Bena political organization. Lawrence's notion (1965-66: 375) of the "security circle" comes the closest to being satisfactory:

> The organization through which political action is carried out is a system of interpersonal relationships, which collectively can be called the security circle. The people who belong to a man's security circle are neither a distinct social nor a distinct local group. They are merely those individuals—close kinsmen, affines, and persons tied to him in other special ways—with whom he has safe relationships and toward whom he should observe certain rules of behaviour.

It is difficult, indeed, to determine the limits of any individual's security circle, particularly in the case of Big Men, and in the same way it is difficult to determine the bounds of a public. Nonetheless, to understand any given public affair in Korofeigu—whether warfare, marriage, or whatever, it is probably necessary to begin from the standpoint of one or more 'egos' and proceed from there outward. What one finds is that the particular activity involves an exceedingly complex interplay of individual security circles. The security circles are the significant polities engaged in political action. Groups such as districts, clans and subclans tend to be involved by association, rather than as corporate, specifically political institutions. Individual members of districts, clans and subclans, in this situation, are not always 'jural equals', although they may well inadvertently suffer the consequences of the acts of others. This itself probably helps to keep the cycle of violence and revenge going. And, although one can define distinct social and local groups of one kind or another that somewhat resemble 'descent systems' or 'segmentary lineage systems', the New Guinea systems are, in fact, quite different. The problem, then, is not to resolve the discrepancy between ideology and behaviour, as I originally suggested (1964), but to try to find out more accurately what the ideology is, and how a society can feature so prominently the rights of individuals.

This problem is probably much less true of the Western Highlands than the Eastern Highlands. Whether Meggitt (1965) is entirely correct in characterizing the Mae-Enga as a segmentary lineage system, they are pretty obviously organized differently from the Bena Bena. Again, contrary to what I suggested earlier, they are probably not on the same continuum. They cover the land in a markedly different pattern and land has an entirely different significance. Warfare, quite probably has a different significance as well (Langness 1970). The groups differ in size and scale. They pursue different public affairs. They are part of a different and much larger public. They seem to emphasize genealogical criteria more heavily and have longer, more precise genealogical knowledge. They appear to emphasize agnation more importantly whether or not they, in fact, use it more rigidly in practice. Leadership seems to be achieved in substantially different ways and may be more directly linked to group membership and descent. They probably have wider and more generally acknowledged systems of authority with less emphasis on relations of power. Even if this could subsequently be shown to be incorrect, it is strategically important, I believe, to abandon the widespread notion of a continuum across the New Guinea Highlands, and to entertain, for a time, an assumption of greater heterogeneity.

NOTES

1. The observations upon which this article is based were carried out during the period 1 January 1961—15 May 1962, at which time I held a predoctoral fellowship and supplementary research grant from the National Institute of Mental Health, United States Public Health Service.

2. I hope to deal with these and other problems in more detail in a subsequent paper. The history of anthropological research in the New Guinea Highlands contains a most instructive lesson for all anthropologists.

3. It was also believed by several Europeans in the area, Patrol Officers and others, that Numuyagabo referred to Korofeigu and Kapakamaligi combined. This is quite definitely not so. Kapakamaligi spoke a different dialect entirely. Some of the men at Korofeigu will tell you that Korofeigu and Kapakamaligi were the Numuyagabo but this is the result of trying to please. See Langness 1963 for similar problems. I believe the identification as Numuyagabo is beginning to disappear entirely with contact and people now tend to identify themselves either as Korofeigans or as Bena Bena.

4. I fully realize that shifting terminology is undesirable. I also realize that to call the Numuyagabo a 'tribe' is questionable. But as the terminology that has been applied in the Highlands is so inconsistent and variable already, I doubt that my indecision will make a great deal of difference.

5. Formerly it was typically the case that each clan had only one village unless, perhaps, it was very large. Villages were fortified, the gardens immediately outside the fences.

6. The fact that six different investigators have arrived at six different terms for what appear to be, on the ground, very similar groups is probably of some significance. This is especially true when one recognizes the relatively close proximity of these people to each other and the recency of contact. It would seem to me that either these groups are very different indeed, which is difficult to believe, or else

it is a difference primarily in interpretation. If it is the latter it probably reflects two different things: (1) the indigenous ideology is not very clear and (2) the language being applied is not very appropriate.

7. I believed for a long time this was the result of working mostly in Pidgin English but now I am not so sure that is what is involved. I think there is a genuine attempt on the part of the people to minimize the significance of sub-groups.

8. See Howlett 1962: 160-1, for a map illustrating this.

9. Yagaria, to the people of Korofeigu, refers to all of the people to the south who speak a language they claim they do not understand. In this particular context, however, I believe it refers to some people from either Kami or Fore who would speak a dialect probably more similar to Numuyagabo than what is now classified as Yagaria.

10. In Bernatzik (1935: 80-3) there is a picture of what is said to be a burned Bena Bena village in which one can count the ashes of at least 18 houses.

11. I have no accounts in which a district—that is, a group similar to Korofeigu—is said to have split apart from fighting. It is quite possible, however, that Gitenu and Korofeigu were a local unit of just this sort and that the accounts of their split represent the division of what was once a district.

REFERENCES CITED

BARNES, J. A. (1962): African Models in the New Guinea Highlands. *Man,* Vol. LXII, No. 2, pp. 5-9.

BARNES, J. A. (1967): Agnation Among the Enga: A Review Article. *Oceania,* Vol. 38, pp. 33-43.

BATES, C. D. (1932-33): Patrol Report of Sofi Valley and Upper Purari. No. 25 of 1932/33, Morobe District.

BERNATZIK, H. A. (1935): *South Seas.* New York: Henry Holt and Co.

BERNDT, R. M. (1962): *Excess and Restraint.* Chicago: University of Chicago Press.

BERNDT, R. M. (1964): Warfare in the New Guinea Highlands. *American Anthropologist,* Vol. 66, part 2.

BLACK, C. (1934-35): Report of Patrol from Finentegu Base Camp. B16.

BROWN, P. (1962): Non-Agnates Among the Patrilineal Chimbu. *Journal of the Polynesian Society,* Vol. LXXI, pp. 57-69.

BROWN, P. (1963): From Anarchy to Satrapy. *American Anthropologist,* Vol. 65, pp. 1-15.

BULMER, R. (1960): Political Aspects of the Moka Ceremonial Exchange System Among the Kyaka Peoples of the Western Highlands of New Guinea. *Oceania,* Vol. 31, No. 1, pp. 1-13.

DRIVER, F. G. (1959): Area Survey for Establishment of Native Local Government Council, Bena Bena Census Division. Goroka.

ELKIN, A. P. (1953): Delayed Exchange in the Wabag Sub-District, Central Highlands of New Guinea, with Notes on the Social Organization. *Oceania,* Vol. 23, pp. 161-201.

GLASSE, R. M. (1969): Marriage in South Fore. In *Pigs, Pearlshells and Women* (M. Meggitt and R. M. Glasse, eds.), Englewood Cliffs: Prentice-Hall.

HOWLETT, D. R. (1962): A Decade of Change in the Goroka Valley, New Guinea: Land Use and Development in the 1950's. Ph.D. dissertation, Australian National University, Canberra.

LANGNESS, L. L. (1963): Notes on the Bena Council, Eastern Highlands. *Oceania,* Vol. 33, pp. 151-170.

LANGNESS, L. L. (1964): Some Problems in the Conceptualization of Highlands Social Structures. *American Anthropologist,* Vol. 66, Part 2, pp. 162-182.

LANGNESS, L. L. (1964a): Bena Bena Social Structure. Ph.D. dissertation, Department of Anthropology, University of Washington, Seattle, Washington.

LANGNESS, L. L. (1967): Sexual Antagonism in the New Guinea Highlands: A Bena Bena Example. *Oceania,* Vol. 37, pp. 161-177.

LANGNESS, L. L. (1969): Courtship, Marriage and Divorce: Bena Bena. In *Pigs, Pearlshells and Women* (M. Meggitt and R. M. Glasse, eds.), Englewood Cliffs: Prentice-Hall.

LANGNESS, L. L. (1971): Political Organization. In *Encyclopaedia of Papua-New Guinea,* Melbourne.

LAWRENCE, P. (1965-66) : The Garia of the Madang District. *Anthropological Forum*, Vol. I, Nos. 3-4, pp. 371-392.

LEAHY, M. (1934) : Diaries. Library, Australian National University.

LEAHY, M. (1936) : The Central Highlands of New Guinea. *Geographical Journal*, Vol. 87.

LEPERVANCHE, M. de (1967) : Descent, Residence and Leadership in the New Guinea Highlands. *Oceania*, Vol. 38, No. 2, pp. 134-58; No. 3, pp. 163-89.

McARTHUR, M. (1967): Analysis of the Genealogy of a Mae Enga Clan, *Oceania*, Vol. 37, No. 4, pp. 281-85.

MEGGITT, M. (1965) : *The Lineage System of the Mae Enga*. New York: Barnes and Noble.

MEGGITT, M. (1967) : The Pattern of Leadership Among the Mae Enga of New Guinea. *Anthropological Forum*, Vol. II, No. 1, pp. 20-35.

NEWMAN, P. (1965) : *Knowing the Gururumba*. New York: Holt, Rinehart and Winston.

READ, K. E. (1952) : Nama Cult of the Central Highlands, New Guinea. *Oceania*, Vol. 23.

READ, K. E. (1959) : Leadership and Consensus in a New Guinea Society. *American Anthropologist*, Vol. 61, No. 3, pp. 425-436.

REAY, M. (1959) : *The Kuma*. Melbourne: Melbourne University Press.

SALISBURY, R. F. (1964) : Despotism and Australian Administration in the New Guinea Highlands. *American Anthropologist*, Vol. 66, No. 4, Part 2, pp. 225-239.

SCHEFFLER, H. W. (1966) : Ancestor Worship in Anthropology: or, Observations on Descent and Descent Groups. *Current Anthropology*, Vol. 7, No. 5, pp. 541-51.

SMITH, M. G. (1956) : On Segmentary Lineage Systems. *Journal of the Royal Anthropological Institute*, Vol. 86.

TOIT, B. du (1964) : Filiation and Affiliation Among the Gadsup. *Oceania*, Vol. 35, No. 2, pp. 85-95.

WATSON, J. B. (1965) : Loose Structure Loosely Construed: Groupless Groupings in Gadsup? *Oceania*, Vol. 35, No. 4, pp. 267-271.

WATSON, J. B. (1967) : Tairora: The Politics of Despotism in a Small Society. *Anthropological Forum*, Vol. II, pp. 53-104.

CHERRY LOWMAN-VAYDA

MARING BIG MEN

ABSTRACT

Several types of Big Men in Maring society are described, as are the mode of their recruitment, their authority, and the checks on their authority. It is suggested that one type, the shaman who can issue directives affecting clan policy, can be considered to hold a political office but one which has become ineffectual with the achievement of pacification in the first phase of contact.

INTRODUCTION

The absence of traditional chiefs and the rise of political entrepreneurs in Melanesian societies have been popular subjects for theoretical discussion—for example, see Barnes (1962), Meggitt (1967), Sahlins (1963), and Schwartz (1963). Because Big Men in Maring society were first observed by anthropologists in 1962, shortly after effective contact and pacification of the Maring in the mid- and late 1950's, and because the authority for the Big Men's political role before contact was sanctioned by supernatural powers they are believed to possess, a description of Big Men in the context of Maring society can provide more fuel for the theoretical fires.

The Maring inhabit an environmental zone characteristic of the Highlands fringe in interior New Guinea. In contrast to the Highlands core area where valleys may be broad and relatively level, the fringe area is one of extreme topographic relief. The main Maring area is located at approximately 5° south latitude and 145° east longitude and is situated on the northern fall of the Bismarck Mountain range in the Simbai valley, Madang District, and the southern fall of the Bismarcks in the Jimi valley, Western Highlands District.

The Patrol Post in the Jimi valley was established at Tabibuga in 1956, and in the Simbai valley a Patrol Post was established at Simbai in 1958. The Simbai valley was not officially opened to Europeans until 1962. I was engaged in field research for a total of fifteen months between 1962 and 1966 among two different Maring local populations, the Fungai population in the Simbai valley and the Kauwatyi population in the Jimi valley.[1] The data presented here are based not only on reconstructions of precontact behaviour but also on observations of and interviews with Big Men during the period of field research.[2] According to informants, there was a continuity from pre-contact times to the ethnographic present in the Big Man's performance of certain roles. Because the Big Men were among the few figures representing the interests of local groups *vis-à-vis* other local groups in a society where many cultural conventions support a fragmentation and dispersal of local populations,[3] and because their decisions could influence public policies ultimately affecting the ability of clans to defend and thereby maintain their territories, Maring Big Men may be considered to have performed political roles before contact.

The Maring language is classified as belonging to the Central Family in the Eastern New Guinea Highlands Stock (Wurm and Laycock 1961; Bunn and Scott 1963), but the 7,000 Maring speakers cannot be readily stated to be culturally most similar to specific populations in the New Guinea Highlands or, for that matter, in the coastal area or on other Melanesian islands. Instead, Maring society is similar in some particular respects to societies, past or present, in each of these regions. For example, in the Highlands proper, the Maring resemble Middle Wahgi societies in many respects, at least two of which are relevant here. First is the presence in both areas of mediums, magicians, and diviners with important positions in "determining the policies of the clan and the behaviour of the individual" (Luzbetak 1958: 81). Second is the presence, although not after the early years of contact, of circular 'War-Magic Houses' where sacred sorcery stones (sometimes a pair of stones characterized as male and female), fight-magic leaves, and/or exuviae of the enemy were stored in a small net bag and guarded by a specialist (Aufenanger 1959). As regards societies on other Melanesian islands, it is noteworthy that Maring Big Men resemble, in a whole complex of features, 19th century 'chiefs' in the Solomon Islands, especially the island of Florida as described by Codrington (1891: Ch. 3). Thus, both the Maring Big Men in the 1950's and the 19th century Florida 'chiefs' had the power to implement decisions in spheres such as warfare and the sacrifice of pigs and, in both cases, the sanction for their authority was derived from their putative ability, said to be inherited frequently from their fathers, to determine the will of the ancestor spirits.

Because the Solomon Islands and Middle Wahgi societies were also observed during early years of acculturation, it may be that such cultural features were more widespread in Melanesia before contact. Missionization probably would undermine both the belief in the power of ancestor spirits and the authority of the mediums or diviners who depended on consensus in this belief for the sanction of their authority. Codrington himself (1891: 54, 57) indicated that missionized natives could not assume chiefly status which, if not for conversion, they might have inherited from their fathers.

The cessation of warfare was perhaps an even more fundamental factor in reshaping patterns of leadership. Oliver (1955: Ch. 12 and p. 440), who worked among the Siuai on Bougainville in the Solomons in 1938, sees Siuai leadership as having been greatly altered by the cessation of warfare and of "native-controlled physical coercion". Siuai leaders were originally "fierce and relentless war leaders".

Since contact, however, as one young Siuai Government-appointed official complained, "We fight weakly, with our mouths . . ." (that is, with oratory; *ibid.* 411). Bulmer (1961: 2-3), who studied the Kyaka not long after their area was opened to Europeans, found there were a number of Big Men (fourteen in the case reported) for a clan parish but that before contact apparently only one of these, a war leader, enjoyed pre-eminence. Watson's reconstruction of the career of a pre-contact Tairora Big Man of considerable reputation also presents a picture of a leader who was characterized by fighting competence and 'aggressive masculinity' rather than by an ability to acquire wealth (Watson 1967: 93). Citations such as these suggest that in some societies in which leadership was directly related to warfare, pacification (an early achievement of contact) may have had an immediate impact on the traditional system of leadership. This seems to have been the case in Maring society. Accordingly, a main object of this paper will be to present the attributes of the Maring Big Man as I understand them to have been before contact.

Ethnographic data on the Maring will be offered in three parts. Part I will provide an ethnographic context for the later presentation of a pre-contact picture of the Big Man in Maring society. In this part, data will be included on the location, subsistence, and demography of local groups as well as on social organization. Also, because it would be difficult to discuss the Big Man's political functions without describing his ritual duties, a brief discussion of ancestor worship will be included. Part II will describe the bases for recruitment to the position of Big Man and the powers, rewards, and checks on the authority of Big Men before contact. In Part III, the effects of European contact on the Big Man complex in Maring society will be briefly reviewed.

PART I

ETHNOGRAPHIC CONTEXT FOR A DESCRIPTION OF THE BIG MAN COMPLEX IN MARING SOCIETY

Location, Subsistence, and Demography

The environmental zone occupied by the Maring is between the coast and the Highlands and may conveniently be called the middle zone. On a vegetation map, this middle zone appears as a broad green band ringing the Highlands proper. The Maring area specifically is characterized by steep valleys, a dense cover of rainforest and secondary regrowth, and frequent cloud cover. The area ranges from an altitude of about 2,000 feet at the two major rivers, the Jimi and the Simbai, to about 7,000 feet at the top of the Bismarcks.

Within this altitudinal range, the Maring distinguish two different environmental zones, varying in altitude, which correspond to zones identified by geographers on the basis of floral associations (William C. Clarke, personal communication). Although both zones are occupied by many of the same faunal and floral species, some species are limited to one of these two habitats. Different soil types may also characterize the two zones. The upper association, *kamunga* (*ka*—'ridge'; *munga*—'rising'), is well established by 4,000 to 4,500 feet. The lower association, *wora* (*wor*—'soft ground'; *ra*—'becoming'), commences at a base elevation of about 2,000 feet and gradually grades into *kamunga* associations. Maring territorial units are vertically oriented land areas—strips running from mountain top to valley bottom —and therefore usually include within their boundaries the products of a diversity of habitats. Houses are generally put in the transition area, *kamunga-wora amang* ('*kamunga-wora* between'), where the climate is most equable and the resident population has more ready access to the products, floral and faunal, of both associations.

The Maring practise slash-and-burn or swidden farming. The altitudinal range within which they clear swiddens, about 3,000 feet to 6,000 feet, permits the cultivation of a wide variety of crops, most of them being interplanted except where altitude limits the growing of certain crops. For instance, yam gardens and *marita* pandanus (*Pandanus conoideus;* oily red seeds) are generally planted in the lower altitude zone, sweet potato gardens in the upper one. In addition to being cultivators, the Maring are also pig husbandmen, pigs being fed and housed by the women in most cases.

The Maring speakers are bordered on the north and west by Gants and Karam speakers and on the south by Narak speakers, to whom they are most closely related linguistically and culturally. The only substantial Maring group living south of the Jimi River, the Mindyi-Kumom of Wum, have Medlpa-speaking neighbours. In the east, Maring communities front on a no-man's-land of virgin forest which can be seen to drop eventually into the distant Ramu flats. The Maring do not think of themselves as a group distinct from other adjacent linguistic groups. A clan's most intensive relations are conducted with other territorial groups contiguous to its own territory. Neighbouring territories may include a clan's most bitter enemies and strongest allies. Since socio-political relations involve immediately adjacent clans, whether Maring or not, linguistic border communities are generally bilingual and linguistic boundaries grade into one another.

The approximately 7,000 Maring speakers are organized into at least twenty localized clan cluster populations (defined below under *Clan Clusters*), containing some eighty-eight clan populations. Air photographs of ten of the clan cluster territories have been measured with a planimeter and tentative estimates of territorial size have been made.[4] The ten clan cluster populations range in size from 130 to 850 people, include a total of 3,240 individuals, and occupy an area of fifty-five square miles. Primary forest characterizes 40% (approximately twenty-two square miles) of the total area, while 58% (about thirty-two square miles) is in secondary forest and cultivated land. Grassland constitutes only 2-3% of the total area measured. Population density for this total area is about 59 per square mile and ranges from 24 to 85 people per square mile in the specific clan cluster territories for which we have tentative areal estimates. Economic density, the number of people per square mile of secondary forest and cultivated land, for the ten clan clusters is about 101 per square mile and ranges from 62 to 250 per square mile within specific territories. The territory of the Fungai-Korama clan cluster has a population density of 24 per square mile and an economic density of about 74 per square mile, while the Kauwatyi territory has an overall density of about 77 per square mile and an economic density of around 100 per square mile.

Estimates on the range of present population density are probably not applicable to pre-contact populations. The population structure of several of the larger Maring clan clusters suggests that there was a decline in the population between 1930 and 1945. This corresponds to the time of the first European contacts made in the Highlands in the 1930's. There was one very early patrol through part of the Maring area in the 1930's. European diseases may have been introduced with the first steel axes along trade routes into the Maring area in the early 1940's. Both Andrew P. Vayda (unpublished field notes and census data) and Roy Rappaport (1968: 15) gathered evidence in 1962-63 which indicates that Maring populations may have been reduced by as much as 25% by epidemics reckoned to have occurred in the early 1940's. This means that, prior to these epidemics, overall population density may have averaged around 78 people per square mile or more in contrast to the present calculation of 59 per square mile. The period of contact and intensive development by the Australian Government and the Anglican Mission since the 1950's may correspond to an additional wave of epidemics and population decline, noted as having occurred within the last ten years or so.

Maring informants state a preference for nucleated settlements, but settlements are, in fact, often dispersed. In the event of epidemics (or epizootics affecting domestic pigs), people may move in order, they say, to escape the vengeance of angry ancestor spirits. When there is intraclan hostility, as in the aftermath of homicide or alleged sorcery, or in cases of fights between spouses or co-wives, the involved parties are likely to fracture off spatially. Also, if settlement is very dense and the pig herd does not appear to have access to good foraging areas, pig-owners may move into areas bordering on virgin forest where pigs may forage during the day. An increasing frequency of pigs invading gardens may also cause intraclan hostility that may result in dispersal.

Social Organization

Here I describe those features of the social context which will be relevant to a later discussion of Big Men in Maring society.

Structural Levels

The terminology used by Ryan (1959) to describe social units among the Mendi has been adopted by Vayda and Cook (1964) for describing structural levels in Maring- and Narak-speaking populations in the Bismarck Mountains. Vayda and Cook have distinguished five levels in the structural hierarchies of these local groups: the subsubclan, the subclan, the clan, the clan cluster, and the clan subcluster. The distinctions are convenient ones for purposes of the present paper.[5]

Clans. In this paper, I shall be consistent in defining clans as the largest exogamous groups in any given structural hierarchy. These groups among the Maring are generally land-claiming populations which have a Fight Magic House and Fight Medicine Man representing territorial interests and which also may claim to be related through patrilineal descent.[6] Structural levels included within the largest exogamous group will be designated subclans and subsubclans, while the larger groupings into which clans are organized will be designated clan clusters and clan subclusters.

I shall use the term 'clan population' to refer to all members of a local group associated with a clan, that is, to all persons sharing clan residence and gardening on clan land. The term 'population' can also be used to describe groups on other structural levels, for example, a 'clan cluster population'.

The core of the clan population are males who claim to be related through male ascendants, although they are often unable to demonstrate actual biological relationship. In cases where the clan includes several distinct but merging descent groups, the clan population may have several such cores. It will still, however, have only one Fight Magic House. Other members of the clan population include spouses who are members of other clans and female members of the local clan who have not yet married. Married females may also reside with their own clan and garden on clan land, in which case their husbands reside uxorilocally. Other non-agnatic males and their spouses may also share residence with a clan on the basis of cognatic or affinal ties.

First generation non-agnates in residence are usually considered members of other clans. Their children, however, appear to be considered members of the clan with which their father resides. The rationalization for this is that these children have been nourished by and grown on the products of local land and therefore may be claimed as members of the clan. We knew several young boys in the Fungai and Korama clan populations, about nine to twelve years of age, who claimed to be members of the clan with which their fathers, first generation non-agnates, were residing. The kinship terminological system, which is generational on the second ascending and first descending generations, facilitates the assimilation of non-agnates. Within two generations, members of non-agnatic origin would be addressed by the same terms as clan members.

Offences such as theft or murder committed against members of other clans, marriages contracted with other clans, and payments made to allies in war are made in the clan's name even though members of the relevant subclans are actually held responsible. Although most ritual activities are conducted by subclan members, there is generally only one Fight Magic House and Fight Medicine Man for the clan.

Subclans. The subclan is the basic ritual and economic unit in Maring society. Subclan members are expected to garden together, to share food, and to make sacrifices to common ancestor spirits in the subclan's sacred grove. Gardening and food sharing are activities that may also be engaged in with affines, cognates, or agnates. The ritual activities required by ancestor worship are, however, restricted exclusively to the subclan.

Subclans and even smaller groups, subsubclans, are said by Kauwatyi informants to be given names by other members of the clan population. Outsiders to the clan are not expected to be familiar with named groups at this level. Interpreters from other territories were often unable to give the subclan name for members of the local population unless they happened to have kinsmen in that group.

Subsubclans. Vayda and Cook (1964: 800-1) do not consider the subsubclans within subclans to be "functionally distinguishable" from the subclans and regard them as potential or incipient subclans.

Clan Clusters. Clan clusters result from the co-operation or amalgamation of two or more clans whose territories are immediately adjacent. Clans in the cluster almost always seem to have a higher frequency of affinal ties with one another than with clans outside the cluster. Statistics on this have been collected by Andrew P. Vayda but remain to be analysed. Alliances of any type between clans before contact seem to have been made primarily for the co-ordination of activities in times of war, clans in a cluster fighting the same battles. Before contact, most clan clusters were involved in hostile relations with at least one other neighbouring cluster. Frequency of warfare was in many cases (but not all) regulated by ritual cycles following truces (for details, see Rappaport 1968: Chs. 4 and 5).

There are two distinctions which can be made between types of clan clusters. First, they may or may not share a common territory. In one type of cluster, the constituent clans, usually a pair, co-operate in times of war, co-ordinating fighting and ritual activities. The clans have contiguous territories but do not claim to share a common territory, for example, they do not hunt on the same forest land. The alliance may be indicated by the compounding of clan names, for instance, the Fungai clan and its ally, the Korama clan, are referred to as 'Fungai-Korama'. On the other hand, when the clans share a common territory, a single, uncompounded name may be assumed by the local population, for example, the 'Tyenda' clan cluster or the 'Kauwatyi' clan cluster. It is possible that clusters with common territories develop as a result of extensive intermingling of swidden lands through clansmen's land grants to affines and non-agnatic cognates in other clans of a single cluster.

A second distinction between types of clan clusters is whether or not clans in the cluster claim common descent. Five of the six clans in the Kauwatyi cluster, the largest of the Maring clan clusters (850 people in the clan cluster population), do claim a common ancestor. Since it is relatively rare for groups on this level to claim common descent, it may indicate that the Kauwatyi represent an original population which has expanded without as much population dispersal and realignment as some local groups seem to have experienced or, at least, that it has not been dispersed in recent generations. The fact that only about one-tenth of Kauwatyi land is in primary forest is consistent with this possibility in that it suggests fairly long and continuous occupation of the territory. In contrast to the Kauwatyi cluster, the recently amalgamated Tsembaga cluster traces its origin to at least three other local groups.

Because of the occurrence of such variations, the term 'clan cluster' is more appropriate for describing Maring social structure than are other terms which have been offered in the literature. For instance, Brown's distinction (1960: 24-5) be- tween phratry, a group of clans claiming common descent, and tribe, an alliance of clans not necessarily claiming it, is not a useful distinction for Maring groups. The Fungai-Korama clan pair, which neither claims common descent nor shares a common territory, would in Brown's definition be labelled 'tribe', although the clan pair comprises only 160 people while the Kauwatyi, claiming common descent, sharing a common territory, and having 850 people in the clan cluster population, would be classified as a 'phratry'.

Clan subclusters. Vayda and Cook (1964: 800) define clan subclusters as clans within the cluster which have contiguous territories and share a dance ground where they may hold ceremonies excluding other clans of the cluster. In the Kauwatyi territory, one of the two clan subclusters resides in the lower part of the high altitude zone and the other in the upper part of it. In a territory as large as Kauwatyi's (about 10½ square miles), it makes sense to have at least two dance grounds so that people would be able to reach their own houses or the houses of their affines without having to walk for two hours.

Fission or fusion may take place on any of these structural levels. More often than not, groups shift from one structural level to another as a function of increase or decrease in size (*ibid.* 801). For instance, what was originally a clan may be dispersed as a result of warfare and segments of the clan may accrete to other clans as subclans, assuming the original clan name as a subclan name in the new population. For a discussion of these mechanisms, see Rappaport (1968: 23-4, and 1969).

It is notable that the Maring have no words for the structural levels described above. The main criterion they use to distinguish groups from one another is size, particularly with reference to the number of adult males (about 14 years of age and over) and sometimes to the number of children. Since there are imbalances in the structure of clan populations, imbalances not uncharacteristic of small groups in general, this does not offer an adequate means for estimating the total popula- tion size of a local group or a segment thereof. It could, however, be the most critical attribute of a population from the Maring point of view, since it provides a way of estimating the actual and potential military power of the group and its ability to defend and thereby maintain its territory. Estimating the number of children relative to the number of adults is not only a way of evaluating population growth and estimating fighting potential, but may also function as a statement about the health status of the population in indicating its survival rate.

The term most frequently used by the Maring themselves to designate local groups is *yu kai* ('men-root/base')[7] which refers to a group claiming comomn descent through males and more often than not is used to designate the clan. *Yu kai timblu* ('men-root/base-small') refers to the minimal hierarchical unit which is usually the subclan but may be the clan or the subsubclan. In a count of the total number of minimal units in the structural hierarchies of the twenty local groups surveyed by Andrew P. Vayda (unpublished census information), there were approximately twenty-eight clans without subclans, 140 subclans without subsubclans, and thirty-two subsubclans. This makes a total of 200 minimal structural units. Informants stated that each *yu kai timblu* has exclusive sacred groves for ritual offerings to ancestors. *Yu ming* (*ming* are small projections such as 'fingers' or 'buds' or 'fruit') is used to designate clans and clan clusters with relatively few adult males (15-20 adult males for a clan population of approximately 80 people or 35-40 adult males for a clan cluster population of 150). *Yu nim* (meaning unclear) denotes large clans or clan clusters with many adult males (40-50 adult males for the clan and at least 150 for the cluster in the local groups specified). *Yu kai* probably refers to clans of intermediate size. Fungai clan members did not refer to their group as *yu kai* but as *yu ming,* although informants would not deny that the group was a *yu kai. Yu kai* was most often heard to designate clans and clan clusters averaging perhaps 60 adult males, totalling over 200 people for the cluster population and about 30 adult males for the clan.

Affinal Networks

The subclan is the unit that makes and maintains contracts for wives from other subclans belonging to other clans. The affinal ties established specifically between subclans provide the basis for a network of personal ties that relate the clan as a whole to an informal, regional socio-political system. In times of war, the success of the clan or clan cluster in mobilizing allies for defence would depend largely on the success of the constituent subclans in maintaining their own specific affinal and cognatic contracts. These ties are sustained through repeated payments to the wife's clan, which include not only the initial brideprice but also payments subsequently made for her children (particularly her female children when they are old enough to marry) and for her bones when she dies if she has resided and is buried on her husband's territory. A son may assume responsibility for payment for his mother's bones if his father has died. Failure to reciprocate these payments in kind seems to function as a signal that the recipient clan is not interested in continuing an exchange of services. This requiting of payments appears, however, on the basis of present evidence, to be well developed only among Jimi valley Maring.

Payments made to affines comprise a number of items of wealth, perishable and non-perishable. These may include steel axes and bushknives, green sea-snail shells, pearl shells, strings of cowrie shells, bark head bands stitched with Job's tears, bird of paradise feathers, roast pork, and, sometimes, roast cassowary. The most highly prized item of exchange still seems to be roast pork, and payments may be judged as inadequate if what is considered an acceptable amount of pork is not forthcoming. Pigs can also be used as items of exchange for the non-perishable forms of wealth. A man's success in maintaining affinal contracts may therefore depend to a great extent on his success in pig husbandry and in trading. There are men, called *yu auwa* or 'men [who] give', who are noted for their generosity in affinal payments. However, the ability to acquire and distribute material wealth does not appear to be a requirement for eligibility for the position of Big Man.

Since the only relationships that a subclan has traditionally maintained outside of its own clan are with affines and cognates, the selection of affines may be economically strategic. There are two types of marriage in Maring society: contracted and romantic. The ideal form of marriage, at least from the standpoint of male members of the clan and subclan, is the contracted one where, characteristically, the parents select a location in which it would be economically advantageous to have affines. They then offer their daughter in marriage to a man in such a location. The romantic marriage is one in which the woman runs away to a man she is said to consider irresistibly attractive. This type of marriage is probably increasing in frequency because the original sanctions of beating an errant daughter or sister or attacking the man to whom she has run have not been practicable since the Australian Government's establishment of control in the area. Data on the frequency of different types of marriage were collected throughout the Maring area by Andrew P. Vayda but have not yet been systematically analysed. A young woman may also run away to a man in a nearby clan if she anticipates being sent in marriage to one far away, for she can be expected to want to remain near her own native territory.

Following are a few of the many possible motivations for offering a daughter or sister to a specific clan:

1. To have her in a proximate clan so that help may be exchanged in garden work or in warfare, and so that the daughter may be near by to bring food and firewood when her parents are ill or old;

2. To have access to the other clan's garden land;

3. To have a daughter or sister married into a nearby subclan with an impressive number of adult males so that there may be many affines to contribute aid in times of war. It is difficult, if not impossible, to co-ordinate fight schedules with geographically remote clans;

4. To send her to a clan noted for its ability (usually for geographical reasons) to obtain bird feathers;

5. To obtain in exchange for the bride a wife for her brother. Women, apparently, are said to run away only to men who are especially attractive. An ordinary or a homely man might not be able to acquire a wife except through sister exchange.

Before contact, there was every advantage in sending a daughter in marriage to nearby clans. Therefore, the network of effective relations did not extend very far for any particular clan. With contact, however, many men have been expected by Government officials to travel much farther from home than at any previous time in their lives to clear airstrips and roads. In the Jimi valley, many men stated that they were without sufficient food in these distant locations. Now, men may send a daughter or sister in marriage to distant clans (as well as nearby ones) in order to protect themselves against privation in the event of further development work in the area of a Patrol Post where they may consider the food supply to be inadequate or uncertain in the absence of relatives to provide it.

The maximal units of co-operation in Maring society are the coalitions which emerge in the event of warfare. When a territorially defined population becomes engaged in formal war, individual members of the population mobilize as many as possible of their affines and non-resident cognates to join them on the fight ground. Male members of this coalition may stand together and be observed on several occasions—on the battle ground and on a few occasions during the year-long festival held to reward allies for their help. Such festivals may be held from eight to twenty years after truce is established (Rappaport 1968: 156-7). The coalition is manifest only when these activities are co-ordinated. Membership of these loosely formed coalitions is shifting. For instance, since a man may not marry a woman from his mother's clan, the clan origin of affines may be expected to shift every twenty years or so. Members of a subclan may be members of several coalitions, and not necessarily the same ones.

Ancestor Worship

Because Maring Big Men are said to have certain attributes which indicate that they are favoured by the ancestor spirits, a brief discussion of Maring beliefs about ancestor spirits is in order.

When a Maring dies, it is believed that his spirit (*min*) continues to exist. The main distinction between living (*indok*) and dead (*raua*) persons is said to be that the living are perceivable while the dead are 'hidden'. There are some men who have a special ability to hear the talk of the ancestor spirits and to communicate their wishes to living men. Men with this supernatural ability are *ipso facto* Big Men, and are thus described by the Maring themselves. (There is, however, another type of Big Man who does not necessarily have this ability.)

There are two main classes of ancestor spirits which are stated to perform different functions and through which different kinds of knowledge are acquired: (1) Fight Ancestor Spirits (*raua mugi*: 'ancestor spirits-red/mature') include the spirits of people killed in battle and are believed to inhabit large trees and rocks in the upper part of a territory; (2) Ordinary Ancestor Spirits (*raua mai*—probably 'older ancestor spirits') consist of all other people (including men, women, and children) and are believed to inhabit the lower altitudinal zone.

The Fight Ancestor Spirits may include women and children killed in battle. This class is, however, stated to be primarily composed of males who died at or about puberty or when they were vigorous young adults who were still strong and could fight. Fight Ancestor Spirits are thought to be active defenders of clan territory and to give protection to living fighters. It is upon this class of spirits that the viability of the territorial group is believed to depend. The Fight Ancestor Spirits are believed to be inherent in fire and lightning, symbolizing their heat and strength.

Cold, wet foods (such as eel) are forbidden to warriors for fear that the fire em-
bodied within them, acquired ritually from the Fight Ancestor Spirits, might be
extinguished. Because the Fight Ancestor Spirits are also thought to be in the fires
in which men cook, people are not supposed to eat from the same fires as their
enemies for fear of enraging the Fight Ancestor Spirits who might strike them dead.
This fear sustains an elaborate network of food and fire taboos (*akek*) which,
among other things, may sustain a fragmentation of clan members' interests. For
instance, a woman whose agnates fought on the side of her husband's clan's enemy
would not be able to share fires with her husband's agnates. Also, because agnates
do not always fight on the same side in a battle, there may be agnates who cannot
share cooked foods. (See Rappaport in an unpublished manuscript for a compre-
hensive discussion of food and fire taboos.)

The ancestor spirits of the low altitude zone are thought to be cold, wet, and
weak. They inhabit a wet area where living things grow in abundance. However,
since moisture is noted to be conducive to rotting or moulding, the Ordinary Ancestor
Spirits are also believed to have negative as well as positive attributes. Living men
involved in fighting and fight magic must avoid associations with women and with
the lower altitudinal zone in order to maintain their strength. It is also believed that
women would be endangered by contact with the 'hot' warriors at this time.

Ancestor spirits are held responsible for phenomena that have no apparent,
observable cause, for example, fevers, epidemics, earthquakes, and lightning. In
order to control these unknown forces, living people are expected to appease the
ancestor spirits by making the appropriate exchanges, that is, the spirit of sacrificial
pork must be offered the ancestor spirits in exchange for their services and protection and their 'pigs'—the marsupials, wild cassowary, and birds hunted in the
forests. If men fail to make these sacrifices, it is believed that either the ancestor
spirits will turn their backs on living people, who will then succumb to the evil
effects of other types of spirits (*raua demi*: 'wild/harmful spirits'), or those persons'
own ancestors will call upon the spirits of dead cross-cousins (*wambe*) from
another clan to come and strike living clansmen and cause illness and perhaps
death. The Fight Ancestor Spirits, residing in the upper altitude zone, are said to
affect the upper part of the body (*mamb ke*: 'in the vicinity of the head'; head,
arms, and upper torso) and the Ordinary Ancestor Spirits, residing in the lower
altitude zone, to affect the lower part of the body (*ambo ke*: 'in the vicinity of the
buttocks'; legs, hips, and viscera).

The Maring also consider the ancestor spirits to be responsible for imparting
knowledge about Maring life. Such knowledge is believed to be clan-specific.
Nomani is a term meaning the knowledge of procedures for the performance of
certain clan-specific activities. This is not limited to knowledge of *how to do* something but also involves prescriptions on *how to relate* to other populations, that is,
with which clans one should exchange wives, food, and trade items. Thus, the
nomani of each clan is expected to be different because each clan has its own
diverse set of affiliations. Maring believe the collective *nomani* of the clan is

guarded by the ancestor spirits who impart it to living people. The different classes of ancestor spirits are said to provide information on different types of activity.

Among the activities for which the Fight Ancestor Spirits are responsible and about which they impart knowledge are those having to do with inter-territorial hostilities. They are said to impart knowledge of fight magic (*mbamp kunda*), fighting techniques (*wura rimbe*: 'fight-making'), and the ritual dance ceremonies in which allies and ancestor spirits are repaid for their help in war (*kaiko rimbe*: 'ritual festival-making'). They are believed to send fight magic in the form of powerful stones which clansmen may find in the upper altitude zone after a lightning storm. The Fight Ancestor Spirits are also said to be responsible for the success of certain varieties (usually those which are red in colour) of the following crops planted and tended by men only: banana, sugarcane, pandanus, and *pitpit* (*Saccarum edule*). These particular varieties are said to be ritually offered to the Fight Ancestor Spirits in order to ensure that they grow well. The Fight Ancestor Spirits are also a source of knowledge about the habits and whereabouts of various high altitude fauna.

For knowledge on how to plant all crops other than the varieties attended by the Fight Ancestor Spirits, the Ordinary Ancestor Spirits are appealed to. Further, they are said to impart knowledge of all kinds of magic (*kunda*) with the exception of fight magic. They also guard knowledge on the whereabouts of low altitude fauna, on making fences, on courtship techniques, on friends to visit, and on wife exchange, except in cases of marriage to an enemy clan—in which case both types of ancestor spirits are appealed to.

Children are not believed by the Maring to have acquired *nomani*. It is not until a person is mature enough to plant gardens and marry that he is considered to have knowledge. In childhood, a type of communion service is held. The child is directed to partake ceremonially of the head of a pig ritually dedicated to the ancestor spirits, thereby embodying the knowledge of the ancestor spirits believed to be inherent in the roasted head.

Only boys may partake of the pork dedicated to the Fight Ancestor Spirits, who impart knowledge on specifically masculine activities. Pork sacrificed to the Fight Ancestor Spirits is roasted in a bed of leaves and hot stones elevated off the ground. A stick may be placed behind this raised pit and a young boy directed to stand on it. The boy (eight to twelve years of age in the cases observed) is then asked to take a bite from the cooked pig's head and ears so that he may grow as tall as he is while standing on the stick. The adult male making the sacrifice may then address his Fight Ancestor Spirits and request them to protect the boy when he hunts in the woods, to show him where to find the fauna of the high altitude forest, and to see that he grows as strong as the warrior spirits. Following is a free translation of a text on consuming the heads of ritually slaughtered pigs as communion with both types of ancestor spirits (from a male informant about twenty-five years of age):

When we eat the head of the ancestor spirits, it stays inside of us. We eat the head and it stays in our skin and we travel with it in our skin. The opinion (*ngot'*) of the ancestor spirits is also here, in its ears. We know their opinion as well as acquiring their knowledge if we eat this pig's head and ears. Having perceived their knowledge, we know how to make fences, to make gardens, to plant crops, to visit people, to make festivals, to sing courtship songs, to travel to other clans, to fight, to build houses for hunting birds, and to look for marsupials. We live with this knowledge the pig's head gives us in our skin.

The Maring consider transactions with ancestor spirits necessary to ensure the continuing health and prosperity of clan members. To exact favours from the ancestor spirits, certain things need to be done:

(1) Men should behave in a manner that does not offend the ancestor spirits by violating the knowledge they have imparted. For instance, living men should not eat from the fires of their ancestors' enemies, nor should they cut down the trees that house the ancestor spirits. Such beliefs generally appear to provide fairly effective sanctions for the regulation of social behaviour. Although the prescriptions and proscriptions on social behaviour attributed to ancestor spirits are not universally heeded, they do appear to be upheld in the majority of cases. The Big Man who is a shaman seems to enjoy an authority that acquires a certain legitimacy on the basis of his ability to issue admonitions and directives in the ancestor spirits' name.

(2) Men must periodically make offerings of ritually slaughtered pork, or animals captured in the hunt, to their ancestor spirits in order to maintain their good will. Subclan ritual offerings are generally required on special occasions such as a marriage into an enemy clan, the initiation of a major battle, a declaration of truce, a ritual festival, or peacemaking ceremonies following intraterritorial homicide. The shaman may attempt to determine from the ancestor spirits how many pigs should be killed on each of these occasions. Individuals may also sacrifice pigs to their ancestor spirits in times of illness.

PART II

BIG MEN IN PRE-CONTACT TIMES

Physical and Behavioural Attributes of Maring Men:
Preconditions to the Status of Big Man

As already suggested, there are several traditional types of Big Man (Kauwatyi: *yu yondoi;* Fungai: *yu ruo*) in Maring society. Recruitment to the status of Big Man in adult life appears to be based on a number of criteria: age and physical strength, temperament, physical attractiveness, relationship to powerful clansmen who have died or who may die in the near future, evidence of support of the Fight Ancestor Spirits, and ability to communicate with the ancestor spirits. The final two attributes define the Big Man class, that is, a man who manifests one or both of these will be considered a Big Man. These two attributes are acquired later in life, after trial. Those men who manifest any combination of the first four attributes are the ones who may one day become Big Men. It is therefore relevant to discuss the Maring distinctions for men of different ages, temperaments, and physical attractiveness.

Age and Physical Strength

There are two lexemes in the Maring language which represent two broad classes denoting males of different ages: *wai* and *yu,* 'boy' or 'boys' and 'man' or 'men'.[8] Within these, the Fungai distinguish at least four subclasses that are relevant to our discussion: *wai* or pre-adolescent boys; *wai mer* or pubescent, incompletely developed males with sparse beard and slight musculature, about thirteen to nineteen years of age: *yu nga,* adult males about twenty to forty years of age; and *yu mai,* older men, usually over forty years of age. (The age ranges given are based on my estimates of the Fungai males stated by my informants to be in one or the other of these four categories.)

Wai mer are protected in warfare by elaborate ritual preparations and taboos forbidding them to associate with women. They are not fully developed (men seem to develop full musculature only after they have begun intensive garden clearing activities) and are considered weak and an easy prey for an enemy if extensive, ritual precautions are not taken. The future of the territory depends on them. They will produce the children of the future, the defenders of the future. They are put under the close supervision of a Fight Medicine Man during times of formal war. In times of peace, they spend much of their time hunting in the forest, and share the fruits of their hunts with other young clan brothers and sisters. Simultaneously, they develop the hunting skills upon which future business acumen may partly depend, since a young wild cassowary or the plumage of a prized bird can be traded for a sow, a profitable investment.

The category *yu nga* ('men-sharp') seems to coincide with *yu munga* or 'men-growing', 'still to reproduce'. The *yu nga* are said to be characterized by their strength and agility. They have developed not only the fleetness of the hunter but also the musculature of the horticulturist. They are said to be able to clear secondary forest for swiddens in one day, figuratively speaking. These are married men who have already begun their families, are involved in collecting brideprice and other types of payment, and in raising pigs and wealth. They are said to have *nomani* and, because they have a vested interest in many clan matters, are expected to speak frequently in public settings. This is the age group actively involved in acquiring and sustaining affines as clan allies. They are strong enough to help selected affines fight their battles or plant their gardens.

The *yu nga* are critical to the defence of a territory. Young boys very early acquire agility in dodging the reed arrows used in war games. The *yu nga* are often the archers (*tim yu*: 'bow-men') in formal war, their agility enabling them to dodge enemy arrows while taking part in the offensive vanguard unit. Very young men and older men are said to be protected by and to advance behind shields (the *ramp yu* or 'shield-men'). The success of offensives such as ambushing the enemy in their gardens, raiding villages, or initiating axe fights in formal war at a territorial boundary depends in part on the number and/or quality of *yu nga*.

The *wai mer* and *yu nga* categories overlap. A man in his mid-twenties who has fully developed musculature but is unmarried and has not yet assumed the responsibilities of pig-raising and debt-paying may still be called a *wai mer*. Both older *wai mer* and *yu nga* may travel from clan to clan on trading expeditions.

Yu mai are mature men, some of whose children are already grown and married (*ndukop mai*: domesticated plants which have already borne fruit). They have lost some of their strength and are not expected to be able to make long trips into the high altitude forest to gather materials required for war rituals although they are still able to engage in productive swiddening. These are men who have paid many of their debts, who have maintained long relations with affines, who have probably sent daughters in marriage to other clans, and who know more of the men who are now ancestor spirits than do other living clansmen. They seem to travel much less to other clans than their younger agnates do. The explanation given for this by Kauwatyi informants seemed usually to be that the people in other territories with whom they shared an active exchange of services had died. *Yu mai* are also expected to voice opinions in public settings, but seemed to speak less often and with less animation than the *yu nga* on the occasions I observed. Most *yu mai* are ordinary men, unable to communicate with ancestor spirits. However, some men in this age range may manifest that ability.

The age categories of *yu nga* and *yu mai* also overlap to some extent. A man seems to be designated as one or the other on the basis of his own specific attributes, such as vigour, agility, age of children, and behaviour in public settings.

Temperament: Fighting Men

Kauwatyi informants describe men of two contrasting types of temperament. These types can be used further to distinguish adult males within age classes. They are *mbamp yu* ('fight-men') and *yu amun* (probably 'quiet men'). *Yu amun* are said to be men who do not lose their temper when they are displeased. They are also described as being less strong than *mbamp yu*. They cannot endure long, hard walks. They are not physically vigorous. Some women are said to prefer marriage to this type of man because he is less likely to injure his wife should she annoy him. Many of my adult male Kauwatyi informants (about twenty-five *yu mai*) stated, however, that *yu amun* are not common and that adult Maring men are more typically *mbamp yu*. The more vigorous and responsive informants boasted that they had been *mbamp yu* before the Australian Government Patrol Post was established in the region. They would volunteer stories about their own acts of violence against wives or fellow clansmen.

Mbamp yu are said to be physically strong and vigorous men who can walk rapidly and great distances. They are quick to bursts of temper and quick to action, and they may commit acts of physical violence against those who antagonize them. Men who are *mbamp yu* may therefore depend on physical coercion to sanction and maintain their own vested interests. Males are said not to acquire a fighting temperament until they have *nomani,* knowledge about clan life, that is, until they have assumed the duties of adult clansmen. Angry *mbamp yu* have been known to beat persons offending them with the back side of a steel axe or to shoot an arrow or throw a spear. Such assaults within the clan are not considered serious unless blood is drawn. Maring informants say that people do not die of arrow or spear wounds unless the 'liver' is penetrated. The weapon that kills is said to be the axe. Despite the fact that relatively few intraclan assaults result in death, they do frequently appear to result in injury. It is not surprising therefore that Fight Men (*mbamp yu*) are stated to be feared and can be observed to be handled cautiously by their agnates and other residents in the territory.

This type of physical coercion was witnessed by me only among the Fungai, which, of all the populations studied, is the one most remote from Australian Administrative offices. When such hostilities did break out between brothers, brothers-in-law, husband and wife, or brother and sister, other clan observers generally feigned disinterest and uninvolvement by staring off into the distance or picking at the ground.

It is the Fight Men who are most likely to involve a clan in interclan or intercluster wars, initiating hostilities between groups by an assault on one or a number of a nearby clan's members. If a series of assassinations between the clans ensues, formal war may be declared. In this case, effective relations between the two groups may be discontinued for at least a generation, and clan members become subject to all the restraints and obligations involved in establishing truce and the ritual cycle which follows (for a description of these, see Rappaport 1968: Ch. 5).

There are some rewards for aggressive behaviour. For instance, a man may induce an affinally or cognatically related Fight Man to avenge for him the death of one of his own agnates. The Fight Man may then be rewarded with a wife or an axe and shells in exchange for his services. One Kauwatyi Fight Man told me of an occasion when an enemy of his cross-cousin (in another territory) had come to the Kauwatyi territory on a trading expedition. The Fight Man sought out the trader, asked him to display the items he had to trade, and then drew his own axe and killed him instantly. He had previously been requested by his cross-cousin to commit such a killing at the first opportunity. Men who have killed an enemy of their allies may also be given the prestige of having their name called at the allies' final festival in the ritual cycle so that they may be publicly presented with the prized reward of salted pork fat.

There are at least three indications that the Fight Man displays a culturally sanctioned form of behaviour over which there appears to be a certain amount of personal control. First, there is the statement by Kauwatyi informants that males without *nomani* do not manifest this kind of behaviour, the implicit statement being that one must have vested interests to have a legitimate basis for physical aggressiveness. Of the fourteen adult males in the Fungai clan, eight of these were observed on different occasions to manifest this type of aggressive, coercive behaviour in defence of their own interests. Only two of these were under twenty years of age, but both were over sixteen. No males under sixteen years of age were observed to behave in this manner, although young boys were seen to mimic this type of behaviour in jest with their younger siblings, to the amusement of onlookers of all ages.

The second indication is that there are men (informants from Tukumenga, Kauwatyi, and Tsembaga clan clusters) who considered themselves to have been Fight Men before contact but declare that they no longer behave in this way (*ndende murmbon*: 'quiet-we stay'). All of these informants live in territories which are closer to Australian Patrol Posts, less than a day's walk, in contrast to Fungai territory which is a two-day walk from the nearest Patrol Post. A threat from those being coerced by a Fight Man to report the issue to the Australian Patrol Officer can be more readily carried out in territories nearest the Administrative centres.

The extent to which Fight Men control this type of aggressive behaviour also appears to be related to the type of decisions and sanctions which Patrol Officers are known to apply. A Fight Man must carefully weigh the possible consequences of his behaviour. For example, if a father is irate over the fact that his daughter has run away to marry a lover when he had contracted to send her elsewhere, he would not now be wise to make physical threats, as he might have done before contact. It is known that Australian Patrol Officers tend to support the interests of young lovers rather than those of an abused father. If the father does actually inflict injury on any of the parties involved, he will no doubt face a gaol sentence if the case is taken to court. If, however, the father controls aggressive impulses but makes his displeasure apparent by other kinds of signals (for example, refusal to visit his daughter), he is likely to receive a larger brideprice than may have been originally planned so that his anger may be assuaged. It would pay him to remain quiet, without violence.

Although threats to take issues before the Patrol Officer were heard constantly from the Fungai clan, even concerning relatively trivial matters, they were carried out in only one instance in the period of a year and then only because visiting Europeans initiated the action. Fight Men in the Fungai clan appeared to run less risk in terms of outside intervention. This may explain why it was in the Fungai population that I found it difficult to elicit information from the more powerful men. Kauwatyi men were, in contrast, extremely co-operative informants. Although the Fungai were aware of the distinctions between anthropologists and Anglican Mission and Government personnel, they never fully accepted the view that the anthropologists were completely uninvolved in clan action—and understandably so, as there *was* intervention on an occasion when a young boy was seriously wounded by an angry Fungai male.

A third indication that the behaviour of Fight Men is culturally acceptable and something over which the actor seems to have some control is that there is a separate lexeme for the aggressive, violent male who has no control over his actions.

This is the *yu prim* ('man-deaf'; unable to reason or to hear reasoning), which any man may become for a brief period of time, perhaps two to three days. Such a man may run away into the forest, shoot people at random with his bow and arrow, do things inappropriate to his age-sex status, and may have to be physically restrained by his fellow clansmen until the fit has passed. He is considered a madman, and his actions are not treated as if they had any rational basis. He is not considered responsible for his actions during this period but is pitied and helped by his agnates. In 1966, Andrew P. Vayda observed one man who manifested this behaviour among the Marings on the Jimi side. It appears, however, to be relatively rare. The Fungai knew of only one man, a decade or so ago, who had had such a spell. The clear definition of this behaviour pattern and the fact that it is considered aberrant by Maring informants does suggest that the Fight Man is not a man who has lost control over his temper. Indeed, the more successful Maring men seem to be able to turn this type of behaviour on and off, depending on the risks involved and on the advantages it may bring. The Fight Man is held totally responsible for his behaviour. Women do not have the same power of coercion regarding their own property interests, probably because they are of inferior strength and because the only implements of assault available to them are pieces of firewood and rocks which they may hurl in a fit of temper at their male antagonists.

The above discussion should make it apparent that physical contests over property (for example, disputes over garden land and pigs) and rights (for example, to contract marriage for a daughter or sister) may have been fairly common in pre-contact times.

Physical Attractiveness

One further quality of Maring men needs to be discussed. This is physical attractiveness. A Splendid Man, or *yu piag* as the Kauwatyi call him, is a 'man on top' or a 'tall man', figuratively speaking. The Fungai expression, *yu wundi* ('man-good'), is probably synonymous. The Splendid Man is said to be a man who is so fine looking that he is 'held on top in the hands of his relatives' for all to see. He is, in other words, designated by the clan to represent them. He is likely to have a handsome face with a long nose (the nostrils of which do not show) and to be decorated with impressive feathers and marsupial pelts. *Yu piag* may also refer to a man who is, in fact, relatively taller than his fellow clansmen. Physical height is a greatly admired physical attribute. It is stated that taller men have the advantage in hand-to-hand combat with war axes where the intent is to kill the enemy rather than merely injure him. The Splendid Man who is not a relatively tall man may make a point of saying, 'Even though my arms and legs are short, women like my face and my finery and they run away to me.' Although the attributes of Fight Men and Splendid Men are not necessarily interdependent, men with a combination of physical attractiveness, vigour, and aggressiveness are not unusual in Maring populations.

The physically attractive man is an important lure for potential affines from other clans. Before contact, such a man is said to have been enhanced with love magic, adorned with the subclan's shells and plumage, and sent to travel from clan to clan to advertise the strength and magnificence of his own clan with the expectation that women from other clans would be tempted to run away to it. A woman may actually run away to such a man, or else may observe that a particular clan has strong, handsome men and ask her father to send her there in marriage. Two of the *yu piag* whom I interviewed about women who had run away to them said that one woman (in each case) had agreed to marry a clan brother instead and that these marriages became enduring ones. Such men do not need to depend on sister exchange in order to obtain a wife. They can attract their own women.

Particular clans may gain a reputation for having fine and strong men. This increases their prestige in their own regional network since they become very desirable as affines. Some clans are considered to have no Splendid Men. Both outside observers and male members of such unfortunate clans seem to agree on this. It is not simply a way of being derisive about a clan with which one is competing for other clans' women. Of one clan in the Kauwatyi cluster, it was said, 'None of the men have good faces, they do not make trips to other territories, they have trouble acquiring wives, and the wives they do have commit suicide because they don't like their husbands' penises.' Such clans would not be expected to be very successful in love and war unless they happened to be affiliated in a clan cluster with other clans of better reputation.

While Fight Men seem to have been fairly common in clan populations before contact, the incidence of Splendid Men seems to have been more variable. Splendid Men may, in fact, have always been at least relatively tall men. One man designated a *yu piag* in the Kekapagai clan of the Kauwatyi clan cluster was 63″ tall, while the average height of the forty adult males in his clan was 60.3″. The only exceptionally tall men in the Fungai population, stated to have no Splendid Men, were residing there uxorilocally and were considered to be members of another clan population.

Types of Maring Big Men

Maring speakers apply the term Big Man (*yu ruo/yondoi*) to at least the following three types of men: Unvanquished Men, who have been marked for assassination by an enemy but nonetheless survive; Ancestor Spirit Men, who are able to 'hear the talk' of clan ancestor spirits; and Fight Medicine Men, who are in charge of sacred fight objects and the care of young warriors in times of war. The following section presents a description of the types of Maring Big Men, their power, and the limitations on their power. In discussing a specific individual who is simultaneously an Unvanquished Man, an Ancestor Spirit Man, and a Fight Medicine Man, I use the term 'Big Man' to save space. Otherwise, the type is distinguished by the appropriate label.

The Unvanquished Man

A major distinction in types of Big Men is whether or not they are able to communicate with ancestor spirits. Many Big Men do have this ability, but some do not. One type of Big Man, the man who is observed to be undefeatable in battle, does not necessarily have it. I know of no special term in the Maring language for distinguishing this type of Big Man. I therefore offer the label 'Unvanquished Man' to designate his particular attribute.

Kauwatyi informants stated that Splendid Men, tall or handsome men, and Fight Men, the men noted for their aggressiveness, are often specifically marked for assassination by an enemy. The elimination of such men would weaken the clan's capacity to defend its territory by virtue of reducing both its effective fighting power and its ability to attract potential affines, some of whom, in addition to providing wives, may volunteer aid in war. Aggressive clans may be expected to seek aggressive allies. In war, only those males who have been formally marked for assassination (by procedures described below) are the object of co-ordinated manoeuvres on the part of an enemy. Because the enemy may, at the boundary between territories, announce whom it intends to kill, the marked man's clansmen are apt to know of the specific risk he must take when he engages in combat. When a man survives such attempts on his life, it seems evident to his fellow clansmen that he must be favoured by the ancestor spirits who, it is assumed, have been closely guarding him. Any adult male who has been marked by the enemy and who survives an extended period of fighting is said to be automatically regarded as a Big Man. Such Unvanquished Men may later be given the opportunity to become practising shamans. Since marked men are frequently handsome (*yu piag*) or aggressive (*mbamp yu*), men with these attributes are likely to be given the opportunity to become Ancestor Spirit Men.

The Ancestor Spirit Man

All adult men are believed to be capable of summoning the spirits of their own proximate ancestors to come and partake of the ritual pork being sacrificed to them. When the male head of a family group slaughters a ritual pig, he calls out to his ancestors, first addressing them by general classificatory terms (*ana, koka, nguige*: 'fathers-grandfathers/ancestors-brothers'; Fungai dialect) and then proceeding to single out by name those relatives whom he has known personally during his own lifetime. When the family head begins to cry, the ancestor spirits are said to have arrived. Married men preside over the ritual sacrifices they make. Pigs are sacrificed independently by brothers, each qualified to sing out to their common ancestors, each indebted to them.

Only a few adult men, however, are able to 'hear the talk' of the ancestor spirits (Fungai—*raua kep kaindim*: 'ancestor spirits-talk-they perceive'). These men are the Ancestor Spirit Men (*raua yu*). The seances they conduct take place in highly ritualized form, usually after dark when the ancestor spirits are believed to be abroad. The setting for the seance may be in a man's house, a sacred grove used for ritual pig slaughter (Tsembaga: *raku;* Fungai: *ngolik*), or in the Fight Magic House (*ringi ying*), a permanent structure for housing sacred fight objects. The Ancestor Spirit Man's male agnates join him there in chanting a chorus called *nde.* Twenty-five to fifty years ago, the agent for inducing the communication trance was a certain leaf (Fungai: *kom*), which was chewed. (I have not been able to identify this leaf.) Now, however, the Ancestor Spirit Man smokes tobacco as well as chews *kom* leaves. The ancestor spirits are summoned by the Ancestor Spirit Man and are believed to have arrived when he begins to perspire. He then addresses questions to them. If the Ancestor Spirit Man chokes on the smoke he has inhaled, the answer to his question is regarded as negative. If, however, there is no choking at all, the ancestor spirits have failed to come. Whether or not the smoke catches in the Ancestor Spirit Man's throat at any particular moment is not likely to be purely a matter of chance. He must have some control, be it conscious or subconscious, over the presumed responses of the ancestor spirits.

The three seances that I observed in 1962-63 were emotionally charged and dramatic. During the seance, the Ancestor Spirit Man might sometimes address particular ancestor spirits. Such ritual oratory usually includes rebukes regarding activities of fellow clansmen. For example, one Ancestor Spirit Man addressed a dead classificatory mother in the following way: 'Why have you turned your back on us? I cannot see your face. It must be because your son is not here to dedicate a pig to you but is off displaying himself with the other men on the festival grounds.' The Ancestor Spirit Man's discourse may be tinged with pathos or with humour. The few who were observed seemed to be effective orators in these respects. Women and young children may, on special occasions, sit outside the house where a seance is being held. They were observed on one occasion to form an audience, laughing at the more amusing passages. In times of war, however, women would not be allowed within hearing distance of such rituals.

Because the Ancestor Spirit Man is believed to be capable of communicating with the ancestors of all living clansmen, he represents the interests of all clan members. His is one of the few positions which operate on the clan level. Informants stated that clans normally have only one Ancestor Spirit Man. There are exceptions, however. Some clans have two Ancestor Spirit Men, true brothers in the instances known. In one case, a clan cluster was reported as having only one Ancestor Spirit Man to represent two of the clans in the cluster.

If a clan's Ancestor Spirit Man is not able to establish contact with the ancestor spirits, he may turn to the Ancestor Spirit Man of a nearby clan to which his own clan is closely related through affinal ties. This is done on the assumption that the spirits being summoned might be visiting the territory of the other clan. In 1963, the Fungai Big Man tried for three weeks, without success, to locate a sick clansman's ancestor spirits. He finally turned for help to the shaman in the other clan of the clan pair, Fungai-Korama. The Korama shaman was at last able to establish contact.

According to informants, a man is not considered eligible for the role of Ancestor Spirit Man until he is about thirty years old. The occasions for appointing a new Ancestor Spirit Man generally seem to be when there is peace and when the practising Ancestor Spirit Man is relatively old. Although an Ancestor Spirit Man is able to communicate with all clan ancestor spirits, it is nonetheless stated by informants that ideally this position should be assumed by his biological son or, if he has no sons, his paternal nephews. The position of Ancestor Spirit Man may therefore be limited to a particular subclan.

It is said that, ideally, the ancestor spirits should be transmitted by the Ancestor Spirit Man to his successor. From the few cases of such transmission described to me, it appears that a number of candidates may be assembled by the Ancestor Spirit Man. They all smoke tobacco (rolled in plantain leaves) and chew *kom* leaves together. The first person to choke on the tobacco smoke is said to become the successor to the Ancestor Spirit Man (there are probably clan- or cluster-specific variations on this). No doubt some significant steps are missing in this account. One would want to know, for example, whether all candidates smoke simultaneously, or whether they smoke in turn, in an order assigned by the practising Ancestor Spirit Man. Clansmen are said afterward to kill a pig for the designated successor, who continues to 'pull smoke' with the Ancestor Spirit Man for one week. This would appear to be an exclusive type of initiation. However, because other males may witness the seances and may participate in the chanting, smoking, and chewing of *kom* leaves, they (who might one day again be eligible for this position) are also instructed in the formalities.

Such initiations are probably planned well in advance. One Fungai informant, an unmarried man about twenty-five years old, told me only a day before I left the Fungai in 1963 that within the year, when two of his agnates would have returned from indentured labour on the coast, these two men, two other young agnates, and himself would slaughter a pig and become '*yu ruo*'. I was quite mystified by this at the time. I did not visit Fungai territory in 1966 and so was unable to pursue the matter. In retrospect, however, it seems to me that he might well have been describing the appointment of successors to the position of Ancestor Spirit Man, a procedure more clearly explicated to me by Jimi informants in 1966. The Fungai Big Man was a man of at least fifty years of age in 1963 and the young man who was my informant, as well as the other agnates then in residence, had already inherited knowledge of fight magic procedures (see below). Since there is no plural form in the Maring language, this use of the term '*yu ruo*' could have meant that all of them would become Big Men or that only one of them would do so. (I failed to note whether he used the verb form marking plurality.) At the time, I assumed it referred to all of them, but in the light of subsequently collected information I now suspect otherwise.

It is not known what happens if the Ancestor Spirit Man dies before having an opportunity to pass the ancestor spirits on to a successor. In one case, an eligible man was said to be simply possessed by the ancestor spirits, and was claimed by his fellow clansmen to be the incumbent Ancestor Spirit Man. His father had died without first formally transferring this position to him. It is possible that in other cases clansmen may turn to the Ancestor Spirit Man of another clan in their clan cluster to perform this function. Practising shamans are not believed to have exclusive rights to communication with a particular group of ancestor spirits. Two or more men are said to be able to communicate with the same aggregate of ancestor spirits.

At least three qualifications for the position of Ancestor Spirit Man can be specified: being an Unvanquished Man, being a biological descendant of the practising Ancestor Spirit Man, and having inherited fight magic formulae and procedures. A single individual may have all of these qualifications or only one or two of them.

Several Jimi valley informants (from two different territories) stated that, because the Unvanquished Man is clearly favoured by the ancestor spirits, he is given the opportunity after a period of warfare (some time after truce has been established, perhaps years after) to communicate with the ancestor spirits. He may simply be one of several candidates for the Ancestor Spirit Man's position.[9] If he is unable to establish contact with the spirits, that is, if the smoke does not catch in his throat, he still continues to be regarded a Big Man. If he survives yet another clan war, he is said to be given a second opportunity to communicate with the spirits. This is his final opportunity. If he survives a third war, he is said merely to offer pigs to his spirit *ana-ama* (Fungai: 'fathers-mothers') for protecting him.

Ancestor Spirit Men, in the cases known to me, occupy also the position 'Fight Magic Man' (*mbamp kunda yu*). Many types of magic may be inherited by a son from his biological father. Benign magic, such as that used to treat fevers, may also be inherited by daughters. Fight Magic may be inherited only by male descendants. It is considered malevolent because it involves some procedures for sorcerizing the enemy as well as others for protecting clansmen from enemy sorcery. There are several Fight Magic Men in the Fungai clan. Rappaport (1968: 120) also reports several Fight Magic Men for each of the Tsembaga clans. Biological sons are said to be the preferred inheritors of knowledge of fight magic. Because a Fight Magic Man must observe various taboos restricting his social behaviour and the foods he consumes, some informants suggested that few men would be eager to assume this role.

Fight Medicine Man

The positions of Fight Magic Man and Ancestor Spirit Man appear to be merged in the position of 'Fight Medicine Man' or *aram ku yu*. The meaning of *aram* is not entirely clear but, because the term was used by the Fungai in reference to all oral medication offered to them (anti-malarials, antibiotics, and aspirin which, perhaps significantly, were effective in all cases administered), 'medicine' seems to be an acceptable translation. *Aram ku* ('medicine-stones') are the sacred fight-magic stones which are used in times of war to sorcerize the enemy and to strengthen and protect clansmen. The Fight Ancestor Spirits are believed to provide these stones. Before major battles, the Fight Medicine Man presides in a ritual in which the stones are used to strengthen young warriors. For a description of these stones and the rituals surrounding them, see Rappaport (1968: Ch. 4). Each clan (or maximal exogamous unit by the definition given earlier) is said to have one pair of sacred stones and one Fight Magic House in which they are guarded. Some clans, however, may be without any such stones. One of the Kauwatyi clans had instead a fire-smoked, gourd-like object stated to contain the exuviae of ancient enemies and other magical materials. It was said to have been passed down from father to son for seven generations and to have been the property of the original founding ancestor. It was called an *aram ku,* and before contact had been guarded in a Fight Magic House. It was said to be used in exactly the same way as the fight stones were used by other clans.

Enemy clans are believed to be in a continual contest to sorcerize one another. The clan with the most powerful fight magic is believed to be able to conquer its enemy through sorcery, which is thought to have the power to cause illness and epidemic as well as to weaken warriors. Thus, the health and survival of the clan are thought to depend on the careful maintenance of the clan's sorcery objects. Since the cessation of warfare, most Fight Magic Houses have been destroyed and the fight-magic stones have been buried. At least one clan, however, is known to be considering building a new Fight Magic House because so many of its members have been dying. They believe that this is the result of enemy sorcery and that they must establish counter-sorcery, if not war, for the sake of their survival.

The Fight Medicine Man is the man who attends to the sacred fight magic objects during war and who assumes so many taboos in this role that he is sometimes referred to as a Taboo Man (*akek yu*). There is never more than one Fight Medicine Man (in the cases known) for any given clan. In addition to guarding the fight-magic objects and supervising the preparation of young warriors for battle, the Fight Medicine Man is instrumental in determining whom among the enemy should be killed. He is therefore valued, not only for his role in maintaining the viability of the clan population through magical prescriptions believed to insure the survival and vigour of clansmen, but also for his role as military strategist, since maintenance of the clan population as a local group will result from military success.

The position of Fight Medicine Man is probably one of the most important in Maring society. It seems, however, in some respects to be even more transient than the positions of Fight Magic Man and Ancestor Spirit Man: in times of peace, the duties, taboos, and powers of the position may be distributed among two or more individuals. For instance, during my period of residence among the Fungai, the Fungai Big Man's unmarried son, who had already inherited fight magic from his father, was the acting guardian of the fight-magic stones. The son had assumed the taboos associated with this role. He was not, however, a Fight Medicine Man. His father retained this title but had rid himself of some of the responsibilities. In one Kauwatyi clan, there was no apparent heir to the position because several of the younger descendants of the previous Fight Medicine Man, now dead, were either not interested in assuming the position or not trusted by their elders. An older Fight Magic Man was guarding the sacred objects until a successor could be found.

Since the Fight Medicine Man is generally a Fight Magic Man and an Ancestor Spirit Man, it is likely that the three positions may be transmitted within a particular subclan and to the same individual when possible. Jimi valley informants equated *raua yu* (Ancestor Spirit Men) with *aram ku yu* (Fight Medicine Men) as though being the first led inevitably to being the other. The statement cited previously, that a Kauwatyi clan's sacred gourd had been passed from father to son for six generations, epitomizes the Maring ideal. There are procedures, however, for transferring the positions to classificatory sons in another subclan. This is said to be done in the following manner. If a Big Man believes he is near death, he waits for his biological son to kill a pig for him as a gesture of respect and goodwill, indicating that he wants his father to enjoy pork before death. Should the son not kill a pig, it is concluded that he does not want to take on the responsibilities and limitations of action incumbent in these positions. The Big Man will then pass on the magical formulae and ancestor spirits to that classificatory son within the subclan who is genealogically closest to him and who does give him pork. If no sons

TABLE 1—CHARACTERISTICS DISTINGUISHING THE MARING MALE ELITE
BY ROLE AND ATTRIBUTES[1]

Role

Attributes	Fight Magic Man (mbamp kunda yu)	Ancestor Spirit Man (raua yu)	Fight Medicine Man (aram ku yu; akek yu)	Big Man (yu ruo; yu yondoi)	Spirit Woman Man (kunagage yu)
Possesses Fight Magic	X	X	X	y	y
Tends sacred fight magic objects	y	y	X	y	y
Can summon ancestor spirits	y	X	y	X/y	X
Unvanquished in battle	y	y	y	X/y	y
Father was an ancestor spirit man	y	y	y	X/y	y
Male agnates have been killed in battle	y	y	y	y	X

X: distinguishing attribute
y: may or may not possess the attribute
X/y : a Big Man must possess at least *one* of these attributes.
[1] Only those attributes are listed here which are distinguishing characteristics for at least one role. There are other attributes which are not defining characteristics of Maring élite males but which are often possessed by them. For instance, men in these roles may be Splendid Men or Fight Men.

within the subclan give pork, the positions may be transferred to a classificatory
son who belongs to another subclan and who does give pork. Whether or not these
positions are maintained within a particular subclan would probably depend on the
total number of classificatory sons within the subclan and on the predisposition of
those men eligible to assume the responsibilities and curtailment of activity associated with these positions. In some instances, two biological brothers may both
serve as Big Men. In one Jimi valley clan belonging to the Kundagai cluster at
Bokapai, two true brothers, sons of a Big Man, had both inherited fight magic from
their father, were both Unvanquished Men, and were both shamans who participated
jointly in the same seances. In a Tsembaga clan, two biological brothers had inherited fight magic from their father's younger brother, but only one of them was
a practising magician, the other serving as a passive repository for magical information.

The Ancestor Spirit Man
as
Public Policy Maker and Clan Representative

The Ancestor Spirit Man conventionally attempts to determine from the
ancestor spirits their wishes regarding the sacrifice of pigs, that is, how many and
what kind (colour, sex, and size) should be sacrificed on various occasions. Further,
if the Ancestor Spirit Man also functions as a Fight Medicine Man in wartime, he
must determine the ancestor spirits' wishes concerning warfare: whether or not to
resume it and whom among the enemy to kill. The shaman's authority is sanctioned
by the fact that the directives he issues on these matters are made in the name of
the ancestor spirits. According to informants, the shaman does have power to command the actions of clansmen in that his directives must be executed whenever
possible. His power is stated, however, to be confined to these matters. Because
military strategy and management of the clan's domesticated pig herd are both
spheres in which a shaman can affect clan policy, his role may be considered a
political one.

Because pigs are seldom slaughtered non-ritually and because occasions for
communicating with the ancestor spirits seem most often to be related to events
that may involve the sacrifice of pigs, directives from the Ancestor Spirit Man on
the number of pigs to be slaughtered would almost certainly have a long-range
effect on the size of the clan population's herd. Just what this effect might be is
impossible to determine on the basis of available data. One would have to know
the vital statistics of the clan's herd at the time the Ancestor Spirit Man made his
pronouncements, as well as whether other commitments had already been made to
slaughter a certain number of pigs on future occasions. Slaughter and distribution
of pigs are directed by the subclan, but because there is frequently one Ancestor
Spirit Man for the clan, his decisions affect the total number of pigs of the clan
population and not just of the subclan.

A number of Fungai informants remarked that they regard as quite uncanny the ability of an Ancestor Spirit Man to designate pigs of a certain size, sex, and colour belonging to specific clansmen. They asserted that this was evidence of the Ancestor Spirit Man's supernatural powers, and that it made people tend to fear as well as respect him. This suggests that at least some Ancestor Spirit Men may be careful observers of the composition of the clan's pig herd, while ordinary clansmen may not be. Whether such Ancestor Spirit Men use these observations judiciously is, of course, another matter.

Because roast pork is the most highly valued item of exchange, the viability of the clan's pig herd may be directly related to the ability of a clan to mobilize allies. For instance, at a time when the Kauwatyi population was to hold its festival to pay off allies in a previous war, there was said to be a serious epizootic in the domesticated pig population. Since invitations had been sent and the festivities of year-long duration had already been initiated, the festival had to take place as planned. A number of men reported that their herds were ravaged by disease at that time. One man, noted for his generosity in affinal payments, had planned to slaughter and present five pigs to his affines and cognates. Four of them had died in the epizootic. Not all Kauwatyi men had their herds seriously reduced, but those that did may have lost the ability to mobilize allies in the future since they had been unable to pay them for services already rendered. For example, a man from Tukumenga territory in the Jimi valley told me that, although he had been very close to his cross-cousin in Kauwatyi territory, he would never visit him again because he had not been given ritual pork at the time of the festival even though he had come to his cousin's aid in war. He himself had already given ritual pork to this same cross-cousin for his help in a Tukumenga war. His cross-cousin's obligations to him, however, had been unfulfilled and the relationship had been discontinued.

In matters of military strategy as in pig herd management, the effectiveness of the shaman can only be speculated upon. It does seem likely, however, that the Fight Medicine Man's assessment of the relative strength of his own clan and enemy clans and of the risk involved in formal war and in man-to-man combat would affect his directives on whether to resume war and whom among the enemy to kill.

In pre-contact times, the Fight Medicine Man was charged with the responsibility of determining from the ancestor spirits whom among the enemy to kill in ambush and on the battlefield. There were apparently two rituals for determining this. The Fight Medicine Man could hold a seance and address questions to the Fight Ancestor Spirits, asking them to designate who should be killed. An alternative, divinatory procedure was to place the head of a pig dedicated to the Fight Ancestor Spirits in a shallow depression in the Fight Magic House and cover it with stones. The spirit of an enemy male (or males) was believed to come and partake of the pig's head. (Maring belief is that the spirits of living men leave their bodies at night and wander abroad.) The Fight Medicine Man would then call out the names of enemy clansmen and, if the stones clattered or if the pig's head whistled, this was taken as a sign marking the man whose spirit was present and who was to be killed in battle next day. The Fight Medicine Man was also expected to determine whom among his own clansmen might be marked for killing by the enemy. He could then forewarn them and offer them supernatural protection.

Several types of men were said by Jimi valley informants to be marked among an enemy clan for killing. As noted above, these include Splendid Men, relatively tall or handsome, and the Fight Men, temperamentally aggressive. Other types stated by my informants to have been frequently singled out are the sons of a man responsible for the unavenged deaths of members of one's own clan, and the shamans of an enemy population. Rappaport reported his Tsembaga informants as stating that the shamans ask the ancestor spirits to name those enemies who "may easily be killed" (1968: 129). He does not qualify what kinds of men these are stated to be, and it appears that they may be 'easy marks' just because they have been marked by the ancestor spirits. I heard no statement of this sort from my Jimi informants.[10]

Whenever an enemy outnumbers the population under attack, it usually opts to rout that population from its land. The enemy warriors may, however, have to wait until they can round up a sufficient number of allies to guarantee that the rout will be successful. Attacks requiring the help of allies in other territories must be carefully co-ordinated. When populations are more equally matched in terms of fighting strength, formal war may be initiated. To be an effective strategist, the Fight Medicine Man would need to be familiar with the composition of the enemy population, and to assign for killing those men who could conceivably be killed so that the strength of the two populations could remain equivalent, in numbers at least. The rationale is retribution but the effect, if strategy is successful, is the ability to maintain one's own territory by maintaining a fighting force equivalent to the enemy's. If one of the enemy populations has an advantage in terms of physical size of warriors, the Fight Medicine Man might have to weigh the risks involved in killing one of the enemy strong men. If, however, enemy forces were matched in terms of size and number, it might have been more advantageous to attack and possibly eliminate one of the stronger enemy clansmen. Data on this subject can no longer be obtained through observation because, even though it is still possible to find surviving males marked in battle ten years ago, it is impossible to see them in the context of the clan population at that time due to the deaths of other males (some of whom may have been marked) in the meantime.

It is noteworthy that Maring Big Men appear to represent the interests of the clan population as a whole *vis-à-vis* other neighbouring populations. The Fungai Big Man was not heard to voice an opinion about intraclan disputes and his authority was said to be limited to the spheres discussed above. He did, however, occasionally make pronouncements about how clansmen should behave to please Australian Government officials, just as he might warn clansmen on how to relate to other clan populations in order to gratify the ancestor spirits. In this, he again seemed to represent the interests of the clan population as a whole rather than the interests of specific individuals. It may be instructive to describe here in detail an event that took place in 1963 during my stay with the Fungai.

Six women in the Fungai population had spent the day clearing the ground of weeds and debris around the Government Rest House. Four other women who had spent the day harvesting passed by the Rest House in the late afternoon. An older woman chastised her daughter-in-law (who had been gardening) for not bringing them any food. They had, she said, been working on the Government track all day, had no food, and were very hungry. The daughter-in-law, noted and nick-named for her sharp tongue, retorted angrily to one of the young women with her mother-in-law, 'Why didn't you get food? All you do is walk about idly and let men have sexual intercourse with you.' This initiated a public hearing in which testimony was presented by the parties involved. The husband of the accused had been away at the coast for almost two years and it was explained that, only a month before this incident, one of the unmarried clan brothers of her husband (from a different subclan) had in fact had sexual intercourse with this young woman. This appeared to be generally known. The older woman who had initiated this confrontation defended the young woman's good work in the gardens. A subclan brother of the young woman's husband also defended her and blamed himself for not looking after her better. He said that if he had not been to the coast to have a tropical ulcer treated, he could have prevented his clan brother from seducing her. Finally, about two hours later and after testimony had been presented, the Big Man made his first statement, a non-partisan one relating the issue to supra-local problems. He said:

> It is important that women sweep the track. If they do not, the Australian Patrol Officer will be very angry with them. There was a woman from the Karam area who was sent to prison. She was the only woman there. The men with whom she was imprisoned had sexual intercourse with her repeatedly until her backside was so heavy she had to walk like this [the Big Man then imitated a woman walking with her backside thrust out behind]. If you make the Patrol Officer angry, he will also kick you [then the Big Man made kicking gestures of the type a father uses when rebuking an errant son or daughter].

The point of this illustration is that, in this and other discussions, the Big Man seemed indirectly to support the position of any party which met requirements for relating successfully to Australian Government officials or ancestor spirits.

An additional indication that Big Men represent the clan population in a regional context is manifested in the response of clansmen to a Big Man's death. For two months after the death of a Kauwatyi Big Man, no people outside Kauwatyi territory were informed of his death. According to informants, when an ordinary person dies, mourning chants for the dead person may be heard at a great distance, even in enemy territories, on the day of his death. News of a Big Man's death would, however, bring great joy to enemy clans. The Big Man's clan brothers would not give the enemy that satisfaction. Additionally, the two-month period permitted the Big Man's clansmen to find a successor and to prepare themselves magically against any sorcery that might be used by an enemy eager to take advantage of the fact that the Big Man's clan had lost a powerful magician who had the full support of the clan's ancestor spirits. This particular Kauwatyi clan had already suffered considerable population decline, which the clansmen attributed to effective enemy sorcery.

Rewards of Big Men

Big Men have no special insignia designating their status, and their freedom of action seems to be curtailed by the taboos they assume with the position, particularly in times of war. These taboos may involve proscriptions on sharing the same fire with women, on consuming certain crops and animals, and on travel within as well as outside of the territory. As has been noted, the authority of shamans appears to be limited to those issues in which the will of the ancestor spirits is believed to be critical. There are nonetheless certain benefits that may accrue to a man in his role as Big Man.

It is said that, because a Big Man has powerful magic, people are afraid of him. If he should become angry with a fellow clansman and assault him with a weapon, informants claimed, the clansman would not recover, having been wounded by a man with strong magic. Because few men care to challenge him, a Big Man is more likely to be able to manage his personal affairs as he likes. Fight Magic Men are said to command the same respect. The ability of men with powerful magic to coerce fellow clansmen is probably even more effective than that of the aggressive men (*mbamp yu*) who do not necessarily have these special magical powers. It is also a Maring belief that if a shaman sits quietly by himself, the ancestor spirits may be near him. People are said to fear approaching the shaman at this time. This may explain why several of the Big Men whom I knew seemed to be strong, silent types. They may command greater awe and respect by silence than by verbosity. The occasions on which an Ancestor Spirit Man chooses to be silent may well be tactically selected.

Men who have knowledge of fight magic procedures generally practise other types of magic as well. They may be the curers, the clan's medicine men. For instance, there are at least five different types of magical formulae and practices for curing fevers. A Big Man may know all or most of these. An ordinary clansman may know one or two but, because the Ancestor Spirit Man also knows fight magic, it is believed that any magic he practises will be stronger than an ordinary man's magic. Thus, it is the Ancestor Spirit Man who might normally be called upon to perform magic when clansmen are critically ill. If the patient recovers and a pig is sacrificed for him or by him, a portion will be given to the magician as a gesture of thanks for his services and with the expectation that he will be induced to give aid again in the future.

If magical procedures fail, the Ancestor Spirit Man may be asked to determine from the ancestors how many pigs they require to be sacrificed to mitigate their anger with the patient so that his recovery may be effected. If pigs are promised to the ancestor spirits on the advice of the Ancestor Spirit Man, the latter will again be repaid for his services with salted pork fat and a generous portion of roast pork. Should an epidemic occur, the Ancestor Spirit Man may be asked to perform this service for a number of households. This could mean that he might receive a considerable amount of pork during the period of an epidemic. Since it is probable that the consumption of a high-quality protein, as in pork, has nutritional advantages (for example, for antibody production) for those under physiological stress, it is conceivable that a secondary reward to the Big Man who is a curer is that he (and members of his immediate family and subclan to whom he may distribute the pork) may enjoy better health than other members of the local population. For a discussion of the nutritional advantages of pork in times of stress, see Rappaport (1968: 82-7).

The Ancestor Spirit Man appears to be under no *a priori* obligation to perform such services for his agnates. He is said to refuse to do so if he so desires. It is possible that he may perform services only for those whom he knows to be able to reward him well. It is also conceivable that he may refuse to perform these services in households where he may be unfamiliar with the composition of the family's pig herd. His reputation could be impaired if directives he issued for slaughtering certain pigs reflected ignorance of the family's assets. His supernatural powers might be considered to be waning.

Contributing to the survival of the shaman in his role as Fight Medicine Man is the fact that he is, according to informants, well protected in times of war. If he joins warriors on the battleground, he is kept well to the rear and protected by many of his warriors. Sometimes he may even be hidden out of harm's way in the forest, near the battleground. The prospects of his survival in war would certainly be enhanced, if not assured, by these measures.

Polygyny is practised by some Maring men, and many Big Men (although by no means all) do have more than one wife and sometimes as many as four. Since there is a limit to the number of pigs any one woman can provide for, this means that the material assets, if expressed in numbers of pigs, of a Big Man may be twice or even four times those of ordinary men. But his affinal debts are proportionately increased. A Big Man's ability to acquire more than one wife may be at least partly related to his physical attractiveness to women if he is an exceptionally handsome man (a *yu piag*), as well as to the fact that other clans may desire to be related to such men in order to have their assistance in times of war and to have access to their magical curing powers. Because a Big Man's affinal ties may be more extensive than those of other clansmen, he is in a position to know more about the composition (age-sex structure) of a greater number of clans. He may also be able to acquire information from his in-laws about enemy clans that may be related affinally to his wife's clan or subclan. Access to this kind of information could be essential to his success as a military strategist.[11]

Pre-Contact Checks on the Authority of Big Men

The Big Man in Everyday Life

The fact that a Big Man is not relieved of any of the responsibilities of gardening and making affinal payments is a further check on his potential authority. He is as much involved in these activities as are ordinary clansmen. He must fence, plant, and harvest his gardens (banana, sugarcane, *pitpit,* and pandanus are male-tended crops), contend with his wife's interests in having payments provided to her natal clan, and collect wealth to make and return payments to other affines and cognates as well. Since the only payment he seems to receive for services performed in his role as Ancestor Spirit Man is a perishable one, that is, a leg or side of roast pork, he must, like other Maring men, depend on the health of his pig herd, his fortunes in hunting, his access to trade routes, and his business acumen to provide the wealth that enables him to meet his obligations to affines.

In addition to the Big Man's involvement in mundane affairs, there are also checks inherent in the social organization of local groups which restrain the emergence of a powerful local authority. The fact that the subclan functions as the unit that solicits and maintains affinal contracts and mobilizes allies in times of war contributes to the fragmentation of interests within local groups along subclan lines. The subclan also functions as the ritual unit for distributing pork to affines and cognates. Members of different subclans do not have access to one another's sacred groves and the rituals performed therein. The rituals observed in sacred groves seemed to me to be among the verbally most intense of Maring rituals, male heads of families reciting long prayers and asking the ancestor spirits to perform certain favours for them. Being excluded from the performance of subclan rituals may therefore mean being excluded from hearing articulated some of the more pressing concerns of a subclan, expressed in these addresses to the ancestor spirits. In general, people seem to pretend ignorance about the affairs of members of other subclans. Within the clan then, the Big Man is most intensively involved in the affairs of his subclan, a primary group frequently composed of no more than four to nine adult males. His everyday influence might well be limited to this group.

Conflict Regulations

Patterns for resolving intraclan and interclan conflict further limit the emergence of men with authority to mediate or adjudicate in local disputes. Physical aggression or strong argument betwen two individuals seems primarily to be regulated by ignoring disputants and by avoidance of communication between parties to the conflict. For instance, they may avoid one another by going to gardens and using village settings at different times or by actually moving to another location. In the Fungai clan, only a visiting, missionized native made any attempt to break up fights or arguments.

Disputes which are made public take the form of hearings in which the relevant parties present testimony. In cases of intraclan hostilities, the principle of

'It's their business, not mine' (*ngot' yenako aua*: 'opinion-theirs-alone') obtains, and the relevant parties are expected to iron things out among themselves. This, in effect, appears to localize the hostility and may prevent additional confrontations.

When the clan or a subclan is accused by outsiders of some wrong-doing, male interrogators do emerge. Rather than being Big Men, however, they were, on the occasions observed, men who were related by marriage to the plaintiff and who represented his interests rather than the interests of the accused. For example, in one instance an interpreter who was from another clan but was residing with the Fungai, claimed that a woman from the Fungai Wendakai subclan had sorcerized him by putting a small piece of skirt string in his food. A Wendakai man, to whom the accuser was most closely related affinally, conducted an inquisition of all the Wendakai women who presented their testimony before a Fungai clan audience.

On another occasion, a member of a nearby clan claimed that young Fungai men had killed and eaten one of his pigs that had run away into the forest. A Fungai affine of the claimant presented the issue to a public gathering and each young Fungai male gave testimony regarding his whereabouts during the previous days. The mothers of these young men also offered testimony on their sons' recent activities. The fathers were relatively silent. Their position may have been expressed in an anecdote one man told after the hearing, which related his own adventures in early manhood in killing and eating pigs that were found in the forest. Young men were noted on several occasions to consume secretly game which they had hunted during the night while the other villagers slept.

The phase of a public hearing during which testimony is presented was, on the four occasions observed, extremely tense. Only one person spoke at a time. This phase seemed to have a duration of one to two hours. Once the testimony was completed, however, the group fragmented into small enclaves of individuals enjoying relaxed conversation. In the case cited where a Big Man offered his comment (see above), it was only after the hearing was over and the group had begun to fragment that he contributed his remarks in the form of an anecdote. It is likely that such anecdotes are relevant to the issue at hand; for example, the admonition implicit in the Big Man's story about what might happen to women who do not sweep the Government tracks. The amusing comments made by Ancestor Spirit Men in their dialogue with the ancestor spirits may serve a similar purpose. That anecdotes are an acceptable form for the presentation of comments on social issues is almost certain. How effective these comments are cannot, however, be evaluated at this time. (I was not fluent enough in the Maring language to understand completely these highly stylized and rapid discourses.)

It is likely that a man cannot afford to become involved in heated disputes without risking some kind of physical contest which could result in group dispersal. With this in mind, it is worth mentioning that the only non-acculturated Marings whom I observed attempting to avert conflicts were adult, married females. They did not do this formally but through manipulation of situations. On several occasions, I observed older women whispering a warning to specific men that they should leave immediately because another man (or group of men), in a hostile frame of mind, was looking for them. In all cases, the men left promptly and a number of potentially serious conflicts seemed to have been avoided in this way.

The Kunagage Complex

An effective check on the authority of the Ancestor Spirit Man was the introduction to the Maring area of a spirit woman complex. In Fungai dialect, the spirit woman is called a *kunagage ambra* (*ambra*: 'woman/wife'), '*kunagage*' being untranslatable and probably not a Maring word (Tsembaga dialect: *kun kaze ambra*).

I shall refer here to the spirit woman as the *Kunagage* and to the man she possesses as the *Kunagage* Man. Kauwatyi informants explained that, because the *Kunagage* is said to represent the Fight Ancestor Spirits of the specific man she strikes and possesses, it is believed that, through communication with her, a man is automatically communicating with his Fight Ancestor Spirits. The *Kunagage* relays the messages of the Fight Ancestor Spirits, who in turn relay to the *Kunagage* the wishes of Ordinary Ancestor Spirits. This means that the *Kunagage* Man (a man struck by, possessed by, and able to communicate with a *Kunagage*) has essentially the same powers as the Ancestor Spirit Man. For instance, a *Kunagage* Man may ask his *Kunagage* to mark which people among the enemy are to be killed and, Kauwatyi informants said, his clansmen will execute these directives. He may also seek her advice for himself or his clansmen in times of personal misfortune. The limitations on a *Kunagage*'s behaviour also appear to be essentially the same as those on other shamans. For example, he may periodically observe the same taboos on travel to lower altitudes, consumption of certain foods, and social intercourse with women. While there are said never to be more than one or two Ancestor Spirit Men in a clan, there may be several *Kunagage* Men. Because the roles of the *Kunagage* Man and the Ancestor Spirit Man-Fight Medicine Man appear to be parallel, they must be in competition for whatever political power is embedded in these roles. A diffusion of authority must result.

The *Kunagage* is said to have come over the mountain tops, like the wind, about twenty-five years ago or about the time steel and tobacco were first introduced to the Maring area. A number of men in different clans in both the Simbai and Jimi River valleys said they were possessed by her at that time. Subsequently, these original *Kunagage* Men instructed apprentices in their own and cognatically related clans to become *Kunagage* Men.[12] In exchange for their supervision, they were and are still rewarded with ritual pork by their own clansmen or with payments of steel axes and valuable shells by non-agnates. Because the *Kunagage* Man may supervise initiates in clans other than his own, he, unlike the Ancestor Spirit Man, may have an opportunity for acquiring non-perishable wealth through his performance in this role.

There are a few characteristics that seem to distinguish the *Kunagage* behaviour complex from the Ancestor Spirit Man complex.[13] When a *Kunagage* Man is possessed by a *Kunagage,* his whole body shudders and he gibbers. The *Kunagage*'s speech is said to rise in his throat. He may speak in tongues (see Rappaport 1968: 119). Those words which are intelligible are thought to be the *Kunagage*'s words. It is possible that smoking may have been introduced at the same time as the *Kunagage* complex and then subsequently included in the Ancestor Spirit Man's ritual. Smoking is an important activity in the period of initiation of *Kunagage* Men (there is apparently no initiation of any duration for the Ancestor Spirit Man). Informants stated that, for five months, the five to eight initiates will be very thin, their eyes sunken, their breast bones showing, and their skin 'loose' because they may smoke for four days at a time without eating. Their fellow clansmen are said to avoid them during this period because they may behave irrationally. A final distinction of the *Kunagage* complex is that young as well as older men are eligible for initiation into the *Kunagage* cult. Several older male Kauwatyi informants complained that originally there was only one Ancestor Spirit Man. Now, they say, young and old alike think they too can hear the talk of the ancestor spirits.

Not all Maring clans have *Kunagage* Men. The Fungai clan has none, whereas the *Kunagage* complex is well-developed in the Tsembaga clan cluster. Members of several Jimi River valley clans report that they did have many *Kunagage* Men at one time but a number of these have died and are not currently being replaced by new *Kunagage* Men. In some cases, a man who had already become an Ancestor Spirit Man had subsequently been possessed by a *Kunagage* and then became a *Kunagage* Man.

It is difficult at the present time to account for the presence or absence of the *Kunagage* complex in different Maring clans. Nor are the bases for recruitment to the position of *Kunagage* Man entirely clear. At least two criteria can, however, be identified. First, because the *Kunagage* is believed to represent the Fight Ancestor Spirits of a particular man, some informants stated that in order to be eligible for possession by a *Kunagage,* a man must have relatives he has known personally who have been killed in battle. The cessation of warfare may then explain why there do not appear to be any new recruits. This does not mean, however, that this criterion might not be modified in order to meet changing circumstances.

A second criterion for participation in this behaviour complex might be the psychological predisposition to be possessed by a *Kunagage.* For a period of two (Tsembaga) to five (Kauwatyi) years, the novice is said to be continually possessed by his *Kunagage.* She is stated to be a companionable spirit who relates amusing stories to 'her man'. She is also believed to be very jealous and to strike down in anger any woman with whom the *Kunagage* Man might have sexual relations during this period. Several Kauwatyi informants told me that they had no children because they had been possessed by a *Kunagage* for five years and then, shortly afterward, their clan cluster had been engaged in warfare for an additional five years.[14] Initiation into the *Kunagage* cult does therefore defer the commencement of marriage and/or procreation. At the end of the period the *Kunagage* Man sends the *Kunagage* to reside in a sacred rock in the higher altitudes, and she returns only when he summons her.[15] The *Kunagage* Man may resume sexual relations at this time. A very similar complex among the eastern Kyaka has been described by Bulmer (1965: 148-51) who calls it the 'Goddess cult' and notes its similarity to a cult described by Vicedom and Tischner (1943/48) among the Metlpa speakers. The 'Goddess cult' became established in the Kyaka region in the late 1940's and early 1950's, only slightly later than it was adopted in the Maring region.

Because of the long period of sexual abstinence required by membership in the *Kunagage* cult, sexually active men might be expected to be less receptive to possession by a *Kunagage* than might inactive ones. It is notable that the Tsembaga clan cluster with a total population of about 200 has a disproportionate number of bachelors and a number of *Kunagage* Men (Rappaport 1968: 15-16, 119). The *Kunagage* is, in a sense, a wife substitute. She is considered an attractive and pleasing female by her *Kunagage* Man. One *Kunagage* Man told of having a vision of his *Kunagage* when she was pregnant and then later when she was carrying a small child which he assumed to be his own. The Big Man in the Fungai clan, a possible candidate for possession by a *Kunagage*, had three wives of his own and was engaged in wooing a widow on whom he lavished a considerable amount of time and attention. He had assigned one of his unmarried sons to take over his own magical duties so that he could be free of some of the restrictions on his own behaviour. Bulmer (1965: 150) reports that Kyaka informants also state that the 'Goddess cult' is "conceived as a marriage between men of the clan concerned and the Goddess". Rappaport (1968: 41), however, says that the *Kunagage* is not thought to be "antagonistic or dangerous to women" and that, even though she is "conceived as female, this conception does not seem to carry any implications of fertility". Although the sexual component of the *Kunagage* cult may not be present among the Tsembaga, initiates nonetheless must refrain from sexual relations for two years.

Regardless of the motivations of specific men which might be reflected in differential responsiveness to possession by a *Kunagage*, the effect of *Kunagage* Men on the power structure (as I have attempted to reconstruct it) in general is to diffuse whatever authority the Ancestor Spirit Man-Fight Medicine Man may have had. It is impossible at the present time to evaluate whether having a plurality of such specialists would make the services they performed even more effective, or whether possible loss of the overall view commanded by the Ancestor Spirit Man might make them less effective. Those male members of a clan cluster initiated together might perhaps be considered to constitute a 'supra-local age grade'. (Rappaport has suggested that this may be the case with Fight Magic Men [1968: 204].) If the *Kunagage* Men in a clan cluster population were to co-ordinate information from different clans in the cluster, they might be able to issue more informed directives.

It is in the context of the *Kunagage* complex that I would like to consider the differences in interpretation of Maring political organization between Rappaport and myself. Following is a quotation from his volume (1968: 28):

> There are no hereditary or formally elected chiefs among the Tsembaga, nor are there any named, explicitly political offices . . . . Among the Maring, to be sure, some men are recognized as *yu maiwai* ("big", or "important" men) and are especially influential in public affairs. They do not, however, compete in feast giving and do not command the obedience of others. The ability of such a man to effect compliance with his wishes depends upon his persuasiveness, and not upon his exclusive occupancy of a particular position in the social or political structure. Indeed, there is no limitation upon the number of big men that may be present in any subclan or clan: the Tsembaga are truly egalitarian in that there are as many big men as there are men whose capabilities permit them to be big men. Moreover, there is not on the part of men in general any abdication, either expressed or tacit, of decision making in favor of big men. Everyone has a voice in decision making, if he cares to raise it, and anyone may attempt to initiate action by himself proceeding to act and thereby instigating others to follow.

Rappaport did not hear the term *yu yondoi* (Tsembaga dialect) used to designate Big Men in the political sense. It was his impression that this was used simply to describe physically 'muscular' men (personal communication). I, however, heard the phrase used to describe leaders in the Fungai clan and Kauwatyi cluster. Male informants from the Tukumenga and Kundagai clusters on the Jimi River side of the Bismarcks also used the term in this manner. On the other hand, I did not hear the expression *yu maiwai* which Rappaport has translated as 'big' or 'important' men. *Yu mai* (older men without the ability to communicate with ancestor spirits) is the only similar expression used by the Fungai. The problems in comparing our interpretations may, then, be based in part on problems of semantic comparability. I suspect, however, that the differences in interpretation can be attributed largely to the presence of the *Kunagage* complex in the Tsembaga cluster, its absence in the Fungai clan, and its being on the wane in the Kauwatyi cluster. This would, for instance, explain the differences in our interpretations on the inheritance of political offices, on the number of Big Men in each clan, and on the degree of influence that Big Men exert.

These discrepancies indicate to me that there were in 1962-66 at least two alternative patterns for leadership in the Maring area: one in which authority is diffused among a number of individuals of various ages, and the other in which authority is concentrated in one or two older, adult males. It may seem remarkable that two patterns generally used to distinguish regions in Melanesia should co-exist in one small, geographic area and within a culturally fairly homogeneous population. There are insufficient data at the present time to provide sound bases for generating a hypothesis to explain these differences. Further research needs to be conducted in a number of Maring territories to elucidate the factors responsible for variations. These variations might, for instance, result from demographic factors (such as disproportionately large numbers of young adult males) or from acculturative ones. The only real problem confronting further enquiry is that it may be too late. Both of these patterns may have already been replaced by more acculturated ones.

In summary, for each of the Maring clans that I know best, it does appear that there was, before contact, a political position open for one adult male (rarely, two)—the position of Ancestor Spirit Man. I consider it a political position because it is one of the few offices representing the interests of the clan population as a whole and because the position holder has had the power to affect clan policy on war strategy and the sacrifice of pigs. The viability of the local population as a territorial unit before contact would have depended to some extent on its success in warfare and on its success in raising a pig herd of sufficient size to use as payments to maintain affinal and cognatic contracts for an exchange of services, including aid in war. The Maring Big Man who had the power to issue directives on when to initiate war, on whom among the enemy to kill, and on which pigs to sacrifice to the ancestor spirits, may well have affected, directly or indirectly, the success of the local population in holding its ground.

PART III

THE EFFECTS OF WESTERN CONTACT ON THE MARING BIG MAN COMPLEX

Western contact, although recent, has already exerted a considerable influence on Maring society. Here, I shall be concerned with describing only those aspects of acculturation which have been observed to affect the role of traditional authorities. Of direct consequence to the pre-contact role of Big Men were the cessation of warfare, decisions made by Australian courts penalizing natives for acts of physical coercion, the appointment of native headmen by Australian Government officials, and the acculturation of young men who served as employees in European households and as indentured labourers on coastal plantations.

Conventional warfare ceased entirely as soon as the Australian Government established Patrol Posts in the Jimi River and Simbai River valleys. Some populations, such as the Tsembaga, which had been dispersed as a result of warfare, were returned to their original territory by Australian Patrol Officers. The redistribution of populations through the mechanism of warfare is therefore no longer operative. There is thus no further need for local authorities to issue directives which might affect the maintenance of a clan's territory. Since contact, the Ancestor Spirit Man seems to have been primarily responsible for the health of the local population and for countering enemy sorcery. In this, he still represents population-wide interests but of a more limited and less political sort then previously. Today, the actions of an Ancestor Spirit Man primarily involve the performance of medical services through sorcery, magic, and divination.

The court decisions of Australian Patrol Officers have brought further changes in the traditional way of life. The fact that court decisions almost invariably seem to censure aggressive behaviour of Fight Men (*mbamp yu*) results in the fairly rigorous repression of this type of behaviour in areas closer to Patrol Posts. Men in the more intensively contacted areas therefore no longer have recourse to physical coercion as a means to secure or further their own interests. A secondary effect is that fathers and brothers are no longer able to protest against the romantic type of marriage. Thus, opportunities for selecting affines on sound economic bases are restricted. For these reasons, the ability of men in line for the position of Ancestor Spirit Man, to select politically significant affines or to implement their own interests through physical threat, has been curtailed. Perhaps, now, those who are able to influence public opinion through oratory are to become the authorities of the future. This is suggested by the above quotation from Rappaport (*ibid.*: 28).

Challenging the authority of traditional leaders are the local officials, luluais (headmen) and tultuls (assistant headmen), appointed by the Australian Administration to represent a territorial population.[16] In some cases, traditional authorities have assumed these new offices. In many cases, however, the identity of local Big Men was concealed with the expectation that they could continue to function in their roles as Fight Medicine Men—roles which, because of their relation to contests between populations, were assumed by the Maring to be subject to censure by the Administration. In some instances a competition for authority between traditional Big Men and Government-appointed officials has resulted. Thus, when an Australian Patrol Officer instructs a luluai to mobilize his people for carrying out a particular task, there can be serious retribution to the clan population by Government officials if they do not carry out the luluai's instructions. For example, on one such occasion in the Jimi valley, a large number of able-bodied men were taken away for a month's labour on the roads. When such action is taken, it is observed by the local group that the luluai does have an authority which is sanctioned by the potentially coercive action of Government officials. The luluai's sanctions are therefore more concrete and immediate than the Ancestor Spirit Man's sanction of threatening the retribution of angry ancestor spirits.

One of the most profound results of 'Westernization' is the schism it has created between older men and their sons. For example, because Europeans generally refuse to recognize the traditional patterns of enmity, any individuals who associate with Western personnel are put in situations where they must violate traditional restrictions on food- and fire-sharing with enemies and their allies. Because the few foreigners residing in the Maring area purchase food from all clans, store it in a common place regardless of the clan it came from, and prepare all foods in the same fire, the older Maring males refuse to share food with the Europeans. They believe that this indiscriminate mixing of foods from enemy groups contaminates meals prepared in European households. Since foreign residents, whether missionaries, Government officers or research workers, depend on local males, usually young boys and bachelors, to perform certain services for them and because household staff-members and interpreters share food and fires with their employers, such males are considered by their elders to be contaminated. Some Ancestor Spirit Men are known to refuse to share fires with their own sons. In the meantime, the young employees find that they are not avenged by the Fight Ancestor Spirits for the indirect sharing of fires with enemies or eating food from enemy territory. Instead, they enjoy relatively good health and prosperity while they are in the employ of Western households.

Some young men may even become critical of the magical beliefs and practices of their fathers. One young man, even though he had been appointed heir-apparent for the position of Fight Medicine Man, offered to sell me the sorcery gourd of his clan, presumed to belong to its founding ancestor. He stated that his elder clansmen would be very angry with him and might even try to kill him, but that it was all foolishness and now he wanted to follow the Western way. He undoubtedly knew that an effective threat would be to say that the Australian Patrol Officer would punish the elders if they did anything to him or if the officer came to know of their magical activities. These younger men are sometimes called by the Maring, 'Patrol Officer's babies' (*kiap umbaia*).

Young men who have spent two years on coastal plantations as indentured labourers develop similar attitudes. Some young men do still maintain respect for their fathers' values while also acquiring a desire to earn money and participate in a Western economic system. When indentured labourers return home they bring with them what, to the Maring, appears to be a tremendous amount of material wealth: beads, kerosene lamps, mats, cloth, soap, cooking pots, tinned food, and the equivalent of at least $25.00 in cash each. These young men find they have no difficulty in obtaining wives, for it is said that a woman will run away to any man who wears perfume and a *laplap* (sarong). Because the Maring area is characterized by such rough terrain, the Government has decided, at least for the present, not to develop the area economically. This means that there are few opportunities to earn money locally and that the pressure to leave the area to earn money will continue. The number of acculturated, pidgin-speaking natives will therefore continue to increase. These men have no interest in filling the role of traditional Big Men. Therefore, not only does the relevance of the Big Man's role to defence of a territory no longer obtain, but there are no recruits interested in filling the position, even if the criteria for recruitment were changed.

In the Maring area, there is an increasing shift to values favouring earning power and monetary wealth. Fathers in the Jimi valley await the return of their sons from the coast before making affinal payments so that trade goods and money may be included. The younger wage-earners have thus become strategic in the traditional system of affinal contracts and payments, and they may come to exert considerable influence in subclan and clan affairs. The leaders emerging in the present are, then, more similar to leaders described elsewhere in New Guinea—men without specific political offices who are skilled in oratory and in acquiring wealth. There is no longer a need for the Big Men of pre-contact times. As they die, knowledge of these patterns of behaviour will probably die with them.

NOTES

1. Field research was conducted for a period of twelve months between November 1962 and November 1963 among the Fungai population in the Simbai valley. This research was supported by a National Science Foundation Grant (No. G23173) to Columbia University for study of "The Human Ecology of the New Guinea Rainforest". My husband, Andrew P. Vayda, was the principal investigator under the grant. Also conducting research under the auspices of this grant were Roy and Ann Rappaport, who resided with the Maring-speaking Tsembaga population in the Simbai valley from 1962-63, and Allison Jablonko, accompanied by her husband Marek Jablonko, who shared residence with me in Fungai territory during the latter part of my field research. In 1966, I returned to the Maring area with my husband, who then had a grant from the Columbia University Council for Research in the Social Sciences. At that time I resided in Kauwatyi territory in the Jimi valley for a period of three months. Three geographers also studied the Maring area from 1964 on. They are John Street and Harley Manner of the University of Hawaii and William Clarke, who is joining the Geography Dept. at Australian National University. During 1966-67 and 1968-69 Georgeda Buchbinder studied the nutrition, health, and demography of Maring populations, particularly the Tuguma population in the Simbai valley, adjacent to and allies of the Tsembaga group.

2. The data presented here were collected among the Fungai and Kauwatyi populations. The Fungai, numbering around eighty individuals, is a clan population, occupying a territory of approximately two and a half square miles at the eastern end of the Simbai valley. Fungai territory is a two-day walk from the Simbai Patrol Post and was, of all Maring territories, among the most remote from Government and Anglican Mission influence. Field procedures among the Fungai stressed observation rather than interviewing and therefore many of the observations cited here were made during residence with the Fungai. I shall also refer to data collected among the Tsembaga by Roy Rappaport (e.g. 1968, 1969) during the period of my work with the Fungai in 1962-63. The Tsembaga are a one-day walk from the Simbai Patrol Post. The Kauwatyi clan cluster population, with whom I spent three months in 1966, numbers around 850 members and occupies a territory approximately ten and a half square miles in area. The Kauwatyi cluster comprises six clans. Its territory is about a two-hour walk from the Anglican Mission airstrip at Koinambe, and less than a day's walk from the Jimi valley Patrol Post at Tabibuga. Because my time and mobility were limited (our daughter, then two years old, was with me), I restricted field activities to intensive interviews with approximately thirty adult males over fifty years of age, most of whom were members of the Kauwatyi population. The only detailed observations made during this period concerned a funeral for a Big Man, a brideprice payment, and interaction between Australian Government officials and the local population. Because of the lack of commensurability in the data gathered in these two locations (i.e., in different valleys, at different times, and with different methods), I have taken care to specify the source of information where it seemed appropriate.

3. I hope to elaborate elsewhere the effect of the following in dispersing populations: warfare, frequency of and response to intraclan homicide, response

to epidemics in the human or epizootic in the pig population, the granting of land to affines and cognates, and meeting requirements believed to be essential for raising a healthy pig herd.

4. Preliminary estimates of the size of Maring territories were based on planimeter readings of air photographs taken of the Maring area. These estimates will probably be revised when more recent air photographs and better data on territorial boundaries are obtained. The estimates were made by the combined efforts of the three geographers who conducted research in the Maring area (see note 1).

5. It needs to be stressed that I am using these distinctions as a matter of convenience. Because the principle of cumulative patrifiliation (as used by Barnes to discuss social structure in some New Guinea societies [1962, 1967]) may be more appropriate than the principle of agnation for characterizing the basis for recruitment to and maintenance of Maring local groups, the term 'clan' should not be understood to refer necessarily to unilineal descent groups. The Maring clan is instead a descent group (as defined broadly in Davenport [1959: 557-8]) in which common patrilineal descent may be claimed but in which not all descent is, by more objective criteria (*ibid.*), unilineal.

6. The largest putatively patrilineal units and the largest exogamous units do not necessarily coincide. For instance, common descent may be claimed by a clan cluster which contains several exogamous groups but is not itself exogamous, or else the largest exogamous group may contain several separate descent groups claiming no common descent (see Rappaport 1968: 18-19).

7. In translations of Maring expressions, each English term between hyphens is a literal translation of its counterpart in the Maring sequence of words. Unhyphenated translations are not literal ones.

8. Nouns in the Maring language are not inflected for the plural form. Therefore, further translations into English will use whichever English form is relevant to the context.

9. This could be a significant point. Unfortunately, however, further field research would be necessary to clarify the processes of selection of Big Men.

10. It is possible that, in populations where men are relatively shorter in stature than their enemy counterparts, those enemy males may be marked for assassination who can readily be killed in man-to-man combat. If strong men are expected to be marked, then it might be good strategy to co-ordinate efforts to kill an ordinary or even a weak man, focusing strategy at an unexpected point in enemy ranks. The average height of Tsembaga males in 1962 was 58.1″ and the tallest man was 62.5″ (Rappaport 1968: 16) whereas the average height of Kundagai clansmen in the Tswenkai clan cluster in the Jimi valley, the Tsembaga's enemy, was 60.8″ and the tallest male was 65″ (Olive Robin, of the Anglican Mission at Koinambe and Cherry Lowman-Vayda, health survey in 1966). Rappaport reports that the Tsembaga killed only two of the enemy but twenty Tsembagas were killed (1968: 184). The Tsembagas were eventually routed from their own territory.

11. A polygynous Big Man may have more offspring than other men in the clan. The data previously presented suggest that Big Men may be recruited from among men of a certain physical and temperamental type. It is possible that at least the physical attributes tend to be maintained from generation to generation by virtue of the differential reproductive success of Big Men and other clansmen. Further, if a Big Man has more sons than do other clansmen, it becomes more likely that he will be able to transmit his power to one of his own sons.

12. Instruction in the *Kunagage* complex may have moved along affinal pathways as well as cognatic ones. My data on this are limited.

13. Actually, further research needs to be done to clarify the distinctions between these two patterns.

14. When a population is engaged in war, opportunities for procreation are more limited than in times of peace. Although some Kauwatyi informants said that older, married men could enjoy sexual relations with their wives in war-time (although such relations were forbidden to young men), many others stated that married men nonetheless tended to avoid women for fear of being coerced by them. For instance, a wife might say she had had a nightmare in which she dreamt her husband was killed by the enemy, and might implore him not to go to battle that day; or she might beg him to go to a garden near the border of enemy territory to get food for their hungry children, in which case he would have to risk being ambushed and killed. Both warfare and the *Kunagage* complex seem therefore to involve beliefs, proscriptions, and practices that deter procreation. This invites speculation about the possible overall effect that behavioural complexes such as the *Kunagage* cult and warfare have upon population growth and size.

15. The relationship of supernatural beings to sacred stones in the Maring area is reminiscent of the classical descriptions of *mana* which Codrington offers for Melanesians in the Santa Cruz, New Hebrides, and Solomon Islands in the 19th century, as is the stated preference for inheritance of supervision over fight-magic stones (cf. Codrington, 1891: 52, 119-20). So is the belief that larger stones characterize the abode of the *Kunagage* and of ancestor spirits. Bulmer (1962; 1965: 148) also reports that the 'Goddess cult' in the Kyaka region focuses on the ritual use of stone artifacts and natural stones, as did the cults which it replaced. Berndt (1954) too reports use of prehistoric stones in the Eastern Highlands for magical purposes.

16. At the time when the most extensive work was done in the Simbai valley (1962-63), there were luluais and tultuls but no councils had been elected. The council system had been adopted in the Jimi valley only shortly before our arrival in 1966 and there was insufficient opportunity for me to study it.

REFERENCES CITED

AUFENANGER, H. (1959): The war-magic houses in the Wahgi Valley and adjacent areas (New Guinea). *Anthropos*, Vol. 54: 1-26.

BARNES, J. A. (1962): African models in the New Guinea highlands. *Man*, Vol. 62, Item 2: 5-9.

BARNES, J. A. (1967): Agnation among the Enga: a review article. *Oceania*, Vol. 38, No. 1: 33-43.

BERNDT, R. M. (1954): Contemporary significance of pre-historic stone objects in the Eastern Highlands of New Guinea. *Anthropos*, Vol. 49: 553-87.

BROWN, Paula (1960): Chimbu tribes: political organization in the Eastern Highlands of New Guinea. *Southwestern Journal of Anthropology*, Vol. 16, No. 1: 22-35.

BULMER, R. (1961): Kyaka bossboys: post-contact leadership in a New Guinea highland society. Paper delivered at ANZAAS meeting, May 1961.

BULMER, R. (1965): The Kyaka of the Western Highlands. In *Gods, Ghosts and Men In Melanesia* (P. Lawrence and M. J. Meggitt, eds.). Melbourne: Oxford University Press.

BULMER, R. and Susan BULMER (1962): Figurines and other stones of power among the Kyaka of Central New Guinea. *Journal of the Polynesian Society*, Vol. 71, No. 2: 192-208.

BUNN, G. and G. SCOTT (1962): *Languages of the Mount Hagen Subdistrict*. The Summer Institute of Linguistics, Ukarumpa, Eastern Highlands, Territory of New Guinea.

CODRINGTON, R. H. (1891): *The Melanesians*. Oxford: Clarendon Press.

DAVENPORT, W. (1959): Nonunilinear descent and descent groups. *American Anthropologist*, Vol. 61, No. 4: 557-572.

LUZBETAK, L. J. (1958): The Middle Wahgi culture: a study of first contacts and initial selectivity. *Anthropos*, Vol. 53: 51-87.

MEGGITT, M. J. (1967): The pattern of leadership among the Mae-Enga of New Guinea. *Anthropological Forum*, Vol. II, No. 1: 20-35.

OLIVER, D. L. (1955): *A Solomon Island Society: Kinship and Leadership among the Siuai of Bougainville*. Cambridge: Harvard University Press.

RAPPAPORT, R. A. (1968) ["1967"]: *Pigs for the Ancestors*. New Haven: Yale University Press.

RAPPAPORT, R. A. (1969): Maring marriage. In *Pigs, Pearlshells, and Women: Marriage in the New Guinea Highlands* (R. Glasse and M. J. Meggitt, eds.). Englewood Cliffs: Prentice-Hall.

RYAN, D. J. (1959): Clan formation in the Mendi valley. *Oceania*, Vol. 29: 257-89.

SAHLINS, M. (1963): Poor man, rich man, big-man, chief: political types in Melanesia and Polynesia. *Comparative Studies in Society and History*, Vol. 5, No. 3: 285-303.

SCHWARTZ, T. (1963): Systems of areal integration: some considerations based on the Admiralty Islands of northern Melanesia. *Anthropological Forum*, Vol. I, No. 1: 55-97.

VAYDA, A. P. and E. A. COOK (1964): Structural variability in the Bismarck Mountain cultures of New Guinea: a preliminary report. *Transactions of the New York Academy of Sciences*, Ser. 2, Vol. 26, No. 7: 798-803.

VICEDOM, G. F. and H. TISCHNER (1943/48): *Die Mbowamb: die Kultur der Hagenberg Stämme in Ostlichen Zentral-Neu-guinea* (3 volumes). Hamburg: de Gruyter.

WATSON, J. B. (1967): Tairora: the politics of despotism in a small society. *Anthropological Forum*, Vol. II, No. 1: 53-104.

WURM, S. A. and D. C. LAYCOCK (1961): The question of language and dialect in New Guinea. *Oceania*, Vol. 32, No. 2: 128-143.

ROBERT GLASSE and SHIRLEY LINDENBAUM

SOUTH FORE POLITICS

ABSTRACT

This paper considers the South Fore political system with specific reference to the structure of local groups and their internal and external relations, focusing on warfare, sorcery and types of leadership. The 'parish', the widest political unit, is a volatile coalition of smaller units: the 'section', as the effective political body responsible for war and political alliances; and the 'line', as a complex of ties, the basis for interparish social networks. Big Men, of limited power, depend for support more on interpersonal networks than on solidary groups. Common descent nominally symbolizes parish unity, but the parish is actually a residential unit with a high personnel turnover and open recruitment.

INTRODUCTION

Since the publication of *African Political Systems* in 1940, the problem of how stateless societies achieve social order has engaged many anthropologists.

Field studies of tribal Africa have led to a notable series of monographs. From this work an important set of generalizations on the structure of unilineal descent groups has emerged (Fortes 1953). Without questioning the value for African studies, Barnes (1962) and Langness (1964) have shown that lineage theory contributes relatively little to the ordering of empirical data from the recently explored New Guinea Highlands. Other models are needed for this task. This paper is concerned with the political system of the South Fore of the Eastern Highlands. It focuses, not on statuses ascribed by unilineal descent, but rather on residential units and the networks that link individuals and groups. These connections are often based on genealogical kinship, but may also result from fictive kin ties, agemate bonds and military alliances. These ties are particularly important in the mobile, open communities found in many parts of the Highlands. It would seem that status is not embedded in any fixed frame of reference, but varies contextually. Open groups produce more ambiguous and fleeting ties among their members than do enduring corporate clans and lineages. From this perspective the local group is seen as a dynamic coalition of sub-groups, factions and individuals. What solidarity it possesses results primarily from the need for security and defence.[1]

The paper is divided into two main sections. Following a brief description of the setting, Part I describes the structure of the local group, its corporate functions, external relations and internal order. In this Part the emphasis is on the status of group members, particularly their obligations in warfare in the era before the advent of the Australian administration. Part II is more dynamically oriented and is concerned with sorcery and its consequences for political relations; it also discusses the pattern of leadership and the constraints inhibiting the powers of Big Men.

The Setting

The Fore are well-known to Anthropology from the work of the Berndts (see References Cited). They are also familiar to the medical world because they and their immediate neighbours suffer from a neurological disorder called *kuru,* a disease that has aroused wide interest (R. Berndt 1958, Gajdusek 1963, R. Glasse 1967). A discussion of *kuru* is relevant to politics not only because of its demographic impact, but because Fore attribute the disease to the malice of sorcerers employed by enemy groups. Despite the *Pax Australiana,* which became effective in the South Fore in the 1950's, continued deaths from *kuru* have kept hostility alive among local groups and undermined old alliances.

The Fore number about 13,000 and occupy an area of roughly 400 square miles in Okapa Sub-district of the Eastern Highlands. Compared with other Highlands language groups, the density of population is low, averaging only 33 persons per square mile (cf. Meggitt 1965, Bennett 1962). For administrative convenience, the populace is divided into two Census Divisions (C.D.), North Fore and South Fore. We are concerned here with the latter population only, a group of slightly more than 7,000 persons.[2] For a discussion of North Fore politics see R. Berndt's 1962 study and his contribution to the present symposium.

Census figures reveal a marked imbalance in the South Fore sex ratio. In 1963, 61 per cent of the population was male, a significantly higher proportion than among nearby language groups (Bennett 1962). *Kuru* is undoubtedly responsible, for females are subject to the disease much more frequently than males (for an epidemiological analysis, see Alpers 1966).

South Fore are greatly troubled by the shortage of women. Polygyny is now rare, and today there are more bachelors and widowers than married men in the adult population (R. Glasse, 1969). The status of women has been greatly affected by their diminished life expectancy. They now have a greater voice in decisions concerning whom and when they will marry. Family life too has been seriously disrupted, and many men must now care for their motherless children with little hope of finding new wives (S. Glasse 1964).

The South Fore live and garden at elevations ranging from about 4,000 to 7,500 feet above sea level. In this zone the climax vegetation is lower montane forest (Robbins 1961). The relatively small depredations on the forest suggest that Fore have been residing here for only a few generations; this is their own view, and it is supported in mythology. It is also possible that Fore have had a longer history in the region; if so, intensive horticulture may be a recent innovation, as

Watson has suggested (1965 *a* and *b*). Whatever their history, arable land suitable for Fore agricultural techniques is in good supply. The acreage in Imperata grasses and wild canes is not extensive, and competition for natural resources was rarely a cause of war. For the same reason, Fore had little interest in seizing enemy lands.

Subsistence is based on cultivation of the sweet potato (*Ipomoea batatas*) and other vegetables. Fore ordinarily reap good returns from fertile soils, and tend pigs, which are the major items of brideprice, mortuary and other payments. They also hunt for birds, marsupials and rodents. Game contributes little, however, to a predominantly vegetarian diet (for description of the fauna see Diamond 1966). Until the mid-1950's human flesh was another source of protein for the South Fore; not all the dead were eaten, and the custom was limited to women and children (R. Glasse 1967). Cannibalism appears to be of recent origin, arriving by diffusion from the north as recently as 50 years ago.

A bird's eye view of Fore territory in the pre-Australian era would have revealed more than 100 barricaded hamlets, and a scattering of small isolated huts near the gardens or at the edge of the forest. The latter were used for shelter when clearing new land, and provided overnight residence for families tending large pig herds. The hamlet was and still is the main residential unit. The principal dwellings consisted of one or two men's houses and a row of smaller women's houses, separated from the men's area by space for cooking pits. Boys under the age of about eight years lived with their mothers, but after initiation resided exclusively with the men. The traditional houses have today been largely replaced by single nuclear family dwellings. The barricades are gone and many of the outlying huts have fallen into disuse as a result of Administration emphasis on compact settlements.

The name 'Fore' has only recently come to refer to the present population and to their language and culture.[3] Fore previously had no collective name, though some people were aware of differences of custom in adjacent language groups. The largest named groupings that Fore recognized in the past were dialect units numbering several thousand of persons. The South Fore is divided into two such areas, namely Pamusa and Atigina, while the North Fore forms a third, Ibusa. Many people are fluent in two dialects and today there is much traffic between all three regions (Scott 1963). Fore attribute these differences to the isolation of the three regions in antiquity.

PART I

PARISH STRUCTURE

The largest local aggregate to form a distinct political entity is the *parish* (Hogbin and Wedgwood 1953). It may consist of a single hamlet, but more often comprises several hamlets situated on a single contiguous territory. It is the unit that R. Berndt calls the 'district' or 'big name' (1962).

There are 39 parishes in the South Fore. In 1962 they ranged in size from 41 to 525 persons. The mean was 180, 112 males and 68 females. Twenty-four parishes numbered between 100 and 200 members. Only one had less than 50 persons (the result of recent fission), while three exceeded the figure of 350.

The parish as a corporate unit

The primary Fore political value associated with the parish was unity in the face of the enemy. The parish ideally fought as a unit, and intentional homicide was prohibited within its ranks. Quarrels among members were to be settled peaceably, but failing this, only sticks should be used as weapons. If in the last resort arrows were fired at group members, the vital parts of the body were to be avoided. When a man was wounded, some of the participants in the fight would intervene and call for a ceasefire. All of these rules were aimed at conserving parish strength by limiting internal aggression and fragmentation of the group.

Yet the ideal of parish unity was not strong enough to prevent the eruption of serious clashes within the group. Segments of the same parish would on occasion align themselves as allies on opposing sides in a war. This meant that they might in fact face one another in direct combat. In general, we believe, these contradictions can be traced to the fact that parish loyalty was based on the idea of reciprocal support and mutual restraint of aggression among the subdivisions of the group, rather than upon a well-developed sense of common citizenship. We find, therefore, that there were no explicit sanctions to compel conformity with parish norms. Moreover, a dissident could always leave the parish and find sanctuary elsewhere. The parish then was not so much a solidary group as a coalition of factions united by the common need for security and defence.

The ideology of the parish

The notion of the parish as a coalition gains support from an examination of Fore terminology for group concepts. At the parish level, there is a conspicuous lack of any words that can be translated as 'clan' or 'lineage'.[4] Furthermore, Fore do not distinguish terminologically between agnates and other parish members, and name their groups not after forbears but from topographical features or botanical species associated with the territory. This is not the kind of nomenclature usually associated with unilineal descent.

The basic contrast in the lexicon of relationships is between *ka kina,* 'one people' and *togina,* 'other people'. While it would be tempting to regard this division as the boundary of the kin domain, it would be inexact to do so, for the terms may include larger or smaller ranges of persons according to context and purpose. 'We' and 'they' are elastic categories, not absolutes. It is significant that the widest span encompassed by 'one people' includes all persons linked together by mutual concern and reciprocity. This usage includes not only genealogical kin, but also fictive kin (*kagisa gina*), age-mates (*nagaiya*) and unrelated friends (*wagoli*). The term *togina* is defined negatively: all who are not 'one people' belong in this class. The image of 'one people' or 'my people' (*nei agina*) can also be used to describe the parish. Here the contrast is usually with *tupu gina*, 'enemy people'.

While Fore fail to distinguish between agnates and other parish members, they do draw distinctions in terms of residential stability and mobility. They speak of *tuba gina*, or *mago gina*, in contrast with *ambi gina* and *aguya gina*. *Mago gina* literally means 'ground source people', and like *tuba gina* conveys the idea of permanent or long-term residence. *Ambi gina* denotes 'those who gather' and can best be rendered as 'immigrants'. *Aguya gina* is more specific, referring to 'those who have been beaten', war refugees. Both terms clearly relate to shifting residence and not to status by descent.

While Fore vocabulary fails to reveal a clear concept of *unilineal* descent, it would be a mistake to assume that they have no concern with descent at all. Whenever Fore wish to stress the unity of the parish, they indicate that they possess 'one blood' (*ka kora*) and have descended from a common ancestor. In a sense they use 'descent' as a means of conceptualizing residence.[5] But their genealogies, seldom exceeding four generations in depth, are too short to be used to demonstrate extensive consanguinity. Women, as might be anticipated, are often overlooked or forgotten. Hence the pedigrees appear superficially to be patrilineal units. Their shallowness too fails to emphasize the fact that many subdivisions of the parish are in fact immigrant groups from other parishes.

External relations

The parish has been described as the political unit of widest span. It may, however, be linked to other parishes, forming a named grouping of higher order, on the basis of putative common descent. This association, similar in principle to a phratry, is not a political unit: it owns no property in common, and possesses no symbol of unity apart from its name. Since associated parishes occupy contiguous territories, they often fought against one another in the past. Such clashes, in fact, outnumbered those involving parishes from different associations.

Fore believe that their current parishes were formed by fission and segmentation from these broader units. Where segmentation has been recent, as among the Purosa parishes in the extreme south, the bonds among the newly formed units are understandably strong, provided of course that the splitting has been peaceful. The relations among associated parishes depend partly on historical, demographic and geographic factors. The specific cause of segmentation obviously influences the pattern of relationships. The greater the number of parishes involved, and the higher their rate of population increase following the division, the more tenuous their subsequent political relations are likely to be. Other things being equal, associate parishes occupying adjacent territories are more likely to have significant social relationships, of amity or enmity, than those which are miles apart.

To understand interparish relations it is necessary to comment briefly on the general character of war. First of all, in the pre-Australian era, fighting and warfare were part of normal life. Aggression and daring were instilled into boys from an early age (cf. R. Berndt 1962). At any given moment, a number of parishes were likely to be engaged in hostilities, while others waited for a favourable opportunity to renew contact with the enemy. Many men relished combat and today look back on the past with great regret.

War was not interminable, however, and peacemaking procedures existed. A fight could be ended by mutual agreement provided the losses on each side were even or nearly even. A truce could be arranged through intermediaries; formal prestations would later be exchanged to seal the agreement. Alternatively, a war might be terminated by the flight and dispersal of the losing side. When this occurred, the victors did not occupy the vacant land, for here the aim of war was not territorial conquest but the killing of the enemy and the destruction of his property. Retaliation for previous offences, real or imaginary, was the motivating force.

While destruction was the aim of war, the goal was seldom realized. Battles were never fought to the last man and no dishonour was heaped upon those who fled from a superior force. Equally matched opponents usually engaged in a see-saw struggle with neither gaining a decisive victory. We have seen that the parish is a relatively small group. It will be shown later that not all of its subdivisions could be counted on for support in time of war. Thus it was imperative to maximize fighting strength. This could be done by recruiting outsiders to parish membership and by forming interparish alliances.

The members of any one parish list at least three or four other parishes which they regard as friendly groups and potential allies. These links may be based on a wide variety of social relationships. For example, an asymmetric marriage connection may be the reason, though these links operate primarily at the subparish level (R. Glasse 1969). A history of food exchanges unconnected with connubial ties is often important. Other parish alliances may stem from the bonds between particular sections of two groups, or from the personal relations of prominent men on both sides. The latter may be kinsmen, age-mates, or friends. Any friendly parish will provide sanctuary in war time. Military assistance, however, usually involves an explicit agreement.

This arrangement could be made in advance of an attack or whenever the need arose. The host group offered a payment to secure a promise of support. This in effect established a contract making the hosts liable to pay damages and to exact revenge for losses sustained by the allies. When one of their number fell, the allies clamoured for retaliation. The man who satisfied this demand was accorded special honour and received a payment from the allies. A cordyline plant, symbolic recognition of the deed, accompanied the payment. Failure to avenge a death could in time undermine the relationship between the host group and the allies. In extreme instances this led to a reversal of the alliance—to war between the former allies.

Thus, interparish ties could be friendly, hostile, allied or neutral. The pattern was unstable, and it would be misleading to speak of either permanent alliances or permanent hostilities. This kaleidoscopic quality of parish relations was a characteristic feature of the Fore political system.

Internal Order

Analysis has so far focused on the widest political units in South Fore society. This allows us to perceive certain gross patterns of political behaviour. Yet within the parish there are subdivisions which act as distinct political entities. It is these subdivisions which are the elements that form the coalition called the parish. We turn our attention to them now.

Every parish is composed of two or more major subdivisions or *sections,* and these in turn are made up of a number of *lines.* The section, in fact, is the effective political and jural unit of Fore society. It is the section, rather than the parish, that actually enters into military alliances; inter-section bonds, rather than commitment to the parish, bring in other sections as allies. The section regularly supports a man confronted by an outsider. In the past, the section mobilized immediately when threatened or attacked. Now it usually settles internal grievances without resort to arms, and it has recognized Big Men, formerly fight leaders, who represent it in public affairs. Like the parish, it is not a genealogical unit. In terms of residence, it consists of one or two hamlets known by a single name (although a small percentage of its members may live elsewhere). As with the parish, the section name may be taken from a topographical or botanical species associated with section territory: the section Nabu, for example, refers to a species of Eugenia growing on Wanitabe ('Big Water') parish land.

The section is not represented in the lexicon by a single term. It may also be referred to as 'one people' or 'one blood'. To distinguish it from the parish, it may sometimes be called *amana kina,* 'small people', in contrast with *tabei gina,* 'big people'.

The smallest subdivision of the parish is the *runei* or *lunei,* literally a 'line'. It may be distinguished from the section on several grounds. Firstly, it is a genealogical unit, in that it is possible to assemble a line genealogy, though it may not fit together perfectly. Secondly, it is an exogamous unit, save that the rule may not apply to recent immigrants. Thirdly, it may enter into connubial relationships with other lines so that brides move in one direction and goods in the other (R. Glasse 1969).

The naming of lines in many instances is quite different from the naming of sections. It is true that some names refer to localities but they may also reflect the history of the group. Thus a line that has originated from another parish is identified by the name of its group of origin. Every parish in fact contains a number of lines named after other parishes. Not every immigrant group can be identified this way; some join with other lines to form a single new section taking a locality name; it may take a number of years before the line has sufficient numbers to be regarded as an independent entity. Often the critical factor in the emergence of an immigrant group as a separate unit is the establishment of connubial ties with other lines;

it is at this point that people decide whether an enclave line should be regarded as a unit capable of entering marriage transactions that will last for a long time. Immigrants may also be absorbed by a single line never to become independent again. What will actually happen depends upon a number of factors, such as the ratio of hosts to immigrants, their future reproductive and survival rates, and how well or poorly the two groups get along. Members of the section may also refer to lines as groups of men clustered around a particular Big Man. This is ambiguous to the outsider, for some Big Men at the same time may function as section leaders. It appears then that the term 'line' is capable of representing several kinds of unity: genealogical, spatial, and the unity of leaders and followers.

While it might be tempting to regard the line as a patrilineage, there are a number of reasons for not doing so. Agnates are not terminologically distinguished from other members, and the latter suffer no disadvantage in access to group resources. More importantly, the lineage concept obscures certain crucial features of the political system. By emphasizing descent, it fails to call attention to the myriad relationships between lines within and beyond the parish. The status of immigrant or enclave lines is particularly important in this respect. Enclaves possess in fact a kind of dual identity: absorption into the host parish does not cancel their former ties. Enclaves enjoy dual rights so long as they visit and maintain an interest in their former parish of residence. These bonds are extremely important in terminating war, providing avenues of communication among otherwise hostile groups. At the same time the second territory may be used as a place of refuge by those forced to flee their own territories.

There is no pressure or need for the South Fore to assimilate their lines to a fictional genealogy or to conceal those which originated as immigrant groups. We know of no parish, it should be stressed, that does not contain enclave lines. In a way, the concern of the Fore is to preserve the identity of immigrants—the reverse of lineage ideology—because of the political advantages that follow from doing so.

Thus, the political structure of the South Fore can be described at three related levels; at the level of the *parish,* which is the widest political unit; at the level of the *section,* the effective political body which is generally responsible for organizing war and for making political alliances; and at the level of the *line,* the smallest element possessing any sense of independence, and which provides a complex of genealogical and other ties forming the basis for networks of interparish social connections.

In sum, the central fact that emerges from the analysis is the conglomerate nature of the parish. It is not a unilineal descent group in indigenous concept, and it is not helpful to regard agnation as its recruitment principle. Yet it is true that common descent serves as a symbol of parish unity. In this respect the symbol opposes the divisive forces of section loyalty, parochialism and self-interest which at times threaten to undermine the group. It is noteworthy that members stress their common origin only in situations that have led or might lead to intraparish conflict. The parish then is essentially a residential and local group. Its members co-operate not primarily because of jural or moral sanctions associated with membership but because of the exigencies of their situation, the need for security and protection in a dangerous universe. It should be regarded, not as a hierarchy of genealogical segments, but rather as a volatile association of small independent political units. It is held together by a variety of networks based on kinship, affinity and propinquity. When these bonds prove insufficient, war within the parish, or segmentation, results.

PART II

DYNAMICS OF SORCERY AND LEADERSHIP

Sorcery

An examination of some aspects of sorcery in Fore society will give some insight into the motivation for activities between and within groups. We find in a sample of 457 deaths that 44.6 per cent are attributed to sorcery. Within the class of sorcery deaths, *kuru* accounts for 70.3 per cent of the total. About four times as many deaths are attributed to sorcery as to deaths from war injury, and only 3.5 per cent of deaths are assigned to old age. Sorcery then is an over-riding explanation for cause of death in Fore society.

Not surprisingly, therefore, Fore hedge themselves around with a myriad of protective devices to avoid part of their person falling into the hands of enemy sorcerers. Each hamlet traditionally digs deep pit latrines to hide excreta. Women burn or bury menstrual blood, afterbirth and the umbilical cord. When traversing territory outside the parish, care is taken to hide or throw scraps of food into running water.

Accusations of sorcery were a main cause of past fighting and the splintering of groups. Today the accusations continue, but 'court' gatherings and the hunt for a sorcerer have replaced warfare as a means of giving vent to suspicions and hostilities. Most present-day sorcery accusations concern *kuru,* and the appearance of a new victim mobilizes the woman's husband and five or six line and section members. Together they act as a group performing divination tests and visiting the hamlets of suspected sorcerers to confront the enemy and demand release of the victim.

In some cases, the hunt for a sorcerer is a re-enactment of old wartime hostilities, with a search party angrily challenging men of a parish with whom they have most enmity. Sometimes, the enquiry pursues an individual in a neighbouring but friendly parish, whose relationship with the victim and victim's husband is known to be abrasive.

Greatest activity results when the victim is the wife of a section or parish leader, for this is regarded as a challenge to the man himself. When the wife of a section Big Man at Akerakamuti showed symptoms of *kuru* in October 1961, the adult men of the section began a course of enquiry which involved them for the next 10 months in 10 separate actions against five different parishes. Initial investigations concerned men in enemy parishes, but by January 1962 their suspicions had turned to a section of their own parish. In July of the same year, they were again performing divination tests on men of a different, though friendly, parish. The adult men of this parish were called to assemble in front of the victim to shake her hand. If the guilty man was one of those present, the victim would break out in a sweat, faint, and fall to the ground. In contrast to challenge against enemy groups, the men of the parish were unarmed. The victim's section also acknowledged the friendly relationship between the two groups, yet the underlying truth was that the loyalty of allies could be deflected for pay, and beyond a certain limited span of kin lay feelings of uncertainty and mistrust.

An increased activity in the hunt for sorcerers also results when a parish section loses several members in a short period of time. The group becomes unnerved by the loss of numbers, and divination tests, court enquiries and the purchase of cures from the Keiagana, the Kukukuku, or the Gimi, people outside of Fore territory, occupy the attention of adult section men. In 1962, three new cases of *kuru* struck the Nabu section of Wanitabe parish. The luluai (government appointed headman), whose wife was one of the victims, called the men of the Akerakamuti section of the same parish to submit to sugarcane divination. Each man of Akerakamuti was called before the three seated women and given a portion of the sugarcane to eat. The remainder of each piece was then given to the women. As with the handshake test, a sorcerer is exposed if the woman sweats, urinates or faints. The luluai, a parish leader, addressed the gathering, pointing out that he had heard that men of Akerakamuti had stolen food scraps and shreds from the women's skirts to give to enemy sorcerers in distant parishes. Although certain men seemed to be under greater suspicion than others, the conversation always left an avenue open for final harmony. Many of the older men of the luluai's own line in fact stressed that they were all one group, that the young men talked too much, and they should turn together to face their common enemies, in particular, the parish of Waisa. This was in fact the conclusion at the end of the day, but it is interesting to note that before the enquiry began, the entire Akerakamuti contingent assembled in a tight ring while one of the members ran in a circle around them performing protective magic. They went unarmed, as men of the same parish should, but they were uncertain of the day's outcome. Several speakers following the test referred to past times when members of their lines had indeed fought against the men of the luluai's line, but that those days were over, and they now sat down in peace together. Under the luluai's direction, the men of Nabu did turn their attention to enemy groups, but by December 27, six months after the trial against a section of their own parish, they issued a challenge to a line within their own section.

Again the luluai stressed the fact that he did not think the sorcerer lived among them, rather, that they had been persuaded by their enemies to accept payment for supplying them with the necessary food scraps. Again, a theme of the speechmakers was that it was improper for them to be challenging one another, that they were one people, and should turn and accuse their enemies.

This is the wavering quality of life in the South Fore. On certain occasions parish members combine together in harmony to celebrate a ritual or to exchange food with friendly parishes. At other times, mutual suspicion is so intense that one parish section closes off the paths leading through the hamlets to divert traffic of suspected sorcerers. Social groups that are an expedient amalgamation of warriors may harbour enemies at close range. The high incidence of *kuru* helps to confirm this belief.

Leadership

Fore point to many kinds of Big Men (*tabei wai*) they consider necessary for group survival. As in other Highlands societies, they valued men with fighting prowess. After 10 years of peace, the deeds of war leaders are still remembered and their names respected. Their services to the community were marked with gifts of pork when the battles ended, to ensure their continued residence with the group. The most renowned war leader in the dialect region of Pamousa was awarded the daughter of the man whose death he had avenged, the brothers and parents of the girl foregoing brideprice. Such men were known as *wabai yagala*, men skilled with bow and arrow and 'hot' fighters. The term also applies to another aggressive role affording community protection—the sorcerers, especially those skilled in the art of *tokabu*. *Tokabu* is a form of attack in which the victim bears no outwardly visible marks of his lonely assault but returns to his kinsmen, his trachea apparently severed, and dies without further speech within three or four days. Group survival depends upon group strength, and, as has already been pointed out, there is a concept of equivalence concerning the deaths of all adult fighting men; loss of a member of one's own group must be matched by a death in the enemy camp, and the sorcerer is credited with enemy deaths at a distance. *Tokabu* sorcerers, when identified, are never old men. They are men of vigour, men the Fore classify as warriors. At Wanitabe, the *tokabu* man was one of two current polygynists in this time of an acute shortage of women.

A second kind of Big Man is the *agarantana yagala*, or *agara kina*, a curer and diviner. He has an extensive knowledge of the use of the barks, roots, and leaves which he uses in treating the ill, who are the victims of enemy sorcerers. With the aid of stimulants, often the bark *agara* (*Himantandraceae Galbulimima*), he divines the identity of a particular enemy sorcerer, and sometimes the location in a swamp or garden of the sorcerer's 'bundle' which is thought to be causing the ailment. He also performs surgery for the warriors, excising arrowheads from wounds after battle. He thus provides for the supernatural defence and well-being of the group's fighting men.

Fore describe a further character type recognized as performing a valuable role in intergroup affairs. This is the *kagi yagala*, the 'laughing man', also a notable fighter, but with the added quality of persuasiveness and 'sweet talk'. During a fight he slips out of hiding to confront an enemy warrior somewhat apart from the main battle area. He smilingly tells him that he has no intention of firing an arrow. He rubs the man's legs to evoke pleasure and offers a further enticement of cowrie shell and *tambu* shell if the man will see that sorcery is performed against a certain person on the enemy side. Several section and parish leaders were said to be *kagi yagala.*

The Fore also admit respect for the type of man they call *namagi yagala,* 'men whose mouths are fast'. A list of these 'silent men' includes many warriors, and again section and parish Big Men. The Wanitabe *tokabu* man too is a man of little apparent presence. The strategy of Fore warfare in fact requires men who carry out much of their work in secret; the sorcerer who relies on divination to disclose the identity of an enemy, and whose victim dies unable to accuse his attacker; the 'sweet talk' man who proposes secret alliances quietly persuading an enemy to carry out an action against his own parish. Even the avenger of an allied death is awarded 'cordyline payment' at night to keep his identity unknown to the enemy.

In the past, there was no need in Fore society for great orators, men who addressed large assemblies of fighting men. Allied forces were composed rather of small contracted groups. The present-day situation, however, does demand men of bold character who can assertively and forcefully argue the group cause at courts which have replaced combat as a solution of interparish disputes. This kind of man, the *kamana yagala,* or 'talk man', replaces the warrior leader of old, but even now is still a man with a fighting record. He acts as chief negotiator and arbitrator for the parish, always assisted by a group of at least four or five parish members, the warrior group of old. Indeed, when an issue between two parishes has aroused great hostility, the parish representatives come to court negotiations armed with bows and arrows.

As has been pointed out, significant political activity occurs at the level of the parish section, and an enquiry about leadership here elicits a surprisingly large number of respected men. In Nabu, for instance, a section of three lines with about 50 adult men, upward of six men are mentioned as exceptional warriors. In addition there is one curer, and at least one 'garden man' or 'pig man' whose food resources are a kind of group insurance. All eight are considered to be performing tasks necessary for group survival. In groups of such small size, the services of all men are valued to some extent. Of the eight valued men, however, one will be further regarded as headman or spokesman. The Australian government has appointed luluais one step above this, at the parish level, considering groups of this size (mean about 180) a minimal administrative unit. This is in fact the level at which the parish Big Man emerges in his role as organizer of interparish affairs. The Fore are aware, however, of the need for some political expression at the section level. A Wanitabe parish section with no resident government appointee refers to its most forceful leader by the honorary title of luluai. It is the section leader who oversees the daily activities of the group, directing behaviour toward currently hostile neighbours, advising participation in government roadwork or cash-cropping.

The parish leader is much like other members of the community except that he has a clustering of approved attributes. He will be a 'hot' fighter and will have an aggressive personality. R. Berndt notes that the child most admired by adults is the one who commands respect with tantrums, by a dominating approach to his fellows, and by bullying and swaggering, thus epitomizing the characteristics desirable in the 'strong' man (1962: 92). The Wanitabe parish Big Man recounts with some pride a story of his resistance to the severe discipline exerted on him at initiation. Twice he broke away from the adults holding him down and forcing sharp canegrass into his nostrils. He shouted and threw pebbles at the men as they tried to subdue him, thus earning the title of *yabakasu*, 'stone thrower', for some years to come.

The present-day parish leader will also be a 'talk' man, a spokesman in interparish affairs. But an aggressive manner and oratorical skill are not enough. The South Fore Big Man needs the additional powers of persuasion and the capacity to manipulate people and events.

The Big Man as Manipulator and 'Businessman'

The parish Big Man is often a man of superior intellect, whose speech is so lucid and authoritative that he is said to have a 'sharp mouth'. He directs the economic transactions of the parish, organizing payments to allies, and the meeting of indemnities and other group debts. He has authority to call in group assets; the 'garden men' contribute when the organizer demands it. This Big Man is a man whose perspective extends beyond his individual and local group affairs. He averts the total drain of capital from the group in piecemeal payments of pigs and valuables by individuals meeting kinship debts. He stands above the other men of the parish in his access to extra-local group information gained from a network of real and fictional kinship links with other communities. His own 'business' interests are wide-ranging, and the local community respects him as an investment adviser for the benefit it brings in attracting refugees, or the economic return which provides for the purchase of brides, or the means to attract allies.

The parish Big Man is skilled at adding new members to the group. He persuades a man quitting his last place of residence that he will find refuge in the parish. A single man may be given a woman of the parish as wife. A husband and wife, or a small line, are given assurance of ample garden land in the midst of the host group's territory. The Big Man affiliates the migrants to him as 'brothers' and 'sisters', sees that their food needs are met, and after several years of residence, when their gardens are productive and their pig herds have grown, they are expected to repay their debt to the host group and to the Big Man. The present-day Big Man acts as an arbitrator and judge in disputes concerning adultery or elopement for members of his own or neighbouring parishes. If the decision makes it impossible for the couple to remain living with their former kin, the Big Man invites them to take up residence with his group. If, on the other hand, the couple return to their original parish, the gratitude of the successful litigant is still remembered, and the debt paid in subsequent food prestations.

A Big Man's capital assets are not visibly different from those of other men in the community, but the economic transactions in which he is concerned may differ from those of ordinary men. As a contributor to payments for the death of his father's brother, for example, he may not be pressed to make an overly large donation. As a recipient, however, when his sister or sister's son dies, or of the brideprice for his daughter, he can demand high rewards. His public speeches at such payments emphasize his services as parish leader and enemy killer, and he demands that his name receive acclaim. He does not keep all the pay for himself, but distributes much of it again to kinsmen, thus confirming the lesson that association with him is of tangible benefit.

All men in fact regard certain of their kin as good investment possibilities. The fear of a pig epidemic that might wipe out an entire herd encourages the farming out of pigs to men in other localities. A man may choose to give his pig to an affine in the hope that this man's pig herd will increase, and he will be the benefactor of a well placed investment. Big Men attract more investments than other men, which they can turn to the improvement of personal or group positions.

Although economic transactions are carried out between existing kin, a new transaction may create a new 'kinsman'; an initial prestation establishes a tie which regulates future transactions between the two partners. Many men, for example, give prestations of food to a *kagisa anagu,* a fabricated mother's brother in expectation of later receiving the man's daughter as a bride (R. Glasse 1969). The mother's brother expects, in addition to further gifts of food, a brideprice, payments for the birth of children of the union, and a share in his daughter's husband's death pay. Or again, a man makes a gift of clothing or adornment to the daughter of a person he regards as a classificatory father,[6] and the girl becomes his 'sister'. On any future visits, he continues to take small gifts, and is assured of food in return. He may also give this 'sister' one of his pigs to tend, promising her a pig from a future litter. He in turn expects to receive a share of any payments made for his 'sister' at the time of her marriage or death. All men develop relationships of this kind, but Big Men maintain a larger number, extending their access to places of refuge and their network of 'business' ties. Thus Big Men tend to be more mobile than others, continually receiving messages to contribute to or share in prestations in surrounding and distant parishes.

Although leadership depends largely on qualities of personality, intellect and physique, and it is possible to arrive at a position of parish leadership in one lifetime, some advantages may be inherited. A Big Man may acquire a number of exchange relationships through the activities of his parents. The Wanitabe Big Man's father was a forceful man, a great fighter, and a man who earned widespread renown and goodwill. By choice, the Wanitabe Big Man maintains many exchange relationships with his father's age-mates, friends and the sons of these men. His mother, too, is remembered as a woman whose generous gifts of food to her husband's associates created a large scattering of 'brothers', which the Wanitabe leader now inherits as kinsmen who provide him with places of refuge, the fathers of possible wives. Thus he does not inherit a large body of capital so much as a reserve of potential exchange partners, and providers of essential services. It is up to him to maintain them or not. A true kin relationship which is allowed to lapse from failure to observe the expected economic exchanges is considered less valid than a newly activated one. The Fore social system is characterized by its adaptability to meet the needs of a mobile population.

The Big Man, more than ordinary men, moulds rules to suit his own needs. Faced with the death of his third wife from *kuru,* and with two children to care for, the Wanitabe luluai persuaded the men of his own line to give him one of their daughters in marriage. This would have been a breach of exogamy but they agreed to segment the line. As a result, it became possible for other men of the luluai's line to follow his path.

Limitations on the power of Big Men

Compared with leaders in other parts of the Highlands, Fore leaders may be described as 'Little' Big Men. The Fore Big Man commands respect for personal attributes recognized to a lesser degree in other men. He has a number of exchange relationships with kin and allies in other parishes, yet his network of ties is only more extensive than those of ordinary men. He provides the pivot around which extraparish affairs, such as defence and economics, may be co-ordinated. Yet his powers are limited.

An individual's ties beyond the parish are dispersed, scattered among surrounding groups; these ensure multiple exchange partners and places of refuge, rather than a force of fighting men which can be quickly drafted into service. The Big Man's renown exceeds his capacity to command support. There is no necessary relationship among his distant associates. He may be the only common link they have.

Loyalty within the parish is also limited by a lack of historical depth: in the course of a lifetime, men reside in a number of parishes and support the efforts of the host group. They give allegiance at that time to the group's most forceful spokesman. The repeated change in parish composition means that Big Men have no permanent body of supporters at the parish level. It also means that many parish leaders may be comparative newcomers in the parish, so that they lack the additional strength that might be provided by the presence of close kin.

The parish is thus an amalgamation of men of different lines who at times regard each other with mutual suspicion. There is no permanent attitude of friendship or hostility. Some years ago, a line of Wanitabe lived in one parish with the men of Waisa. Following the death of several Wanitabe men and women, they charged the Waisa with sorcery, fighting broke out, and the line departed for its present territory. Wanitabe and Waisa now regard each other with enmity, although there are Wanitabe men with wives from Waisa who engage in obligatory exchanges, and who still remember the years when the two groups lived together in harmony.

As already noted, despite the ideal of section unity, the extent of mutual trust sometimes narrows. Some years ago, four lines of Akerakamuti section accepted pay to join with the enemies of a fifth line living with them as refugees. In the battle that followed, the refugee line was forced to flee and combine with men of a neighbouring parish. This is an extreme instance of instability within the section, but a more common example of division of interest is indicated in present-day religious affiliation. Some lines within a section become members of the Lutheran Church, while others convert to Seventh Day Adventist. Intrasection rifts of this kind limit the effective power even of section leaders.

The exigencies of warfare have resulted in social groupings which readily amalgamate newcomers, but also allow for the maintenance of ties with original kinsmen and former co-residents. It is an ambiguous situation which not only limits the scope of leadership but also arouses uncertainty about the loyalty of migrants. Relative newcomers who commit an offence against section morality are reminded that they are free to return to their parish of origin. Older residents are always unsure of the intention of their hosts. A night-time speech of a Wanitabe section headman, an honorary luluai, expresses this ultimate insecurity:

I came here as a boy from the North Fore. I remained and grew up to lead you in battle after battle. Now my wife has *kuru*. If someone here has caused it, let him remove the poison 'bundle' so that she can recover. My legs pain from the distances I have walked searching for cures. In her lifetime she looked after the needs of visitors to our group. She saw that they had food and firewood. When she dies, there will only be rubbish people left here.

CONCLUSION

Our concern in this paper has been to develop a framework for understanding politics in the South Fore. The attempt to describe political relations systematically has led to a reassessment of unilineality as the basic principle organizing social relationships. We are not alone in making such a reappraisal, and have benefited greatly from the work of Barnes, Langness, de Lepervanche, Meggitt and Watson. It should be pointed out that our current view differs in some respects from that presented in other papers on marriage and age-mates; the latter were written before this paper, and touch on politics only incidentally. The change that has occurred mainly concerns the significance, or rather insignificance, of unilineal descent in structuring groups.

Given a culture strongly oriented toward physical aggression, it appears that the complex of low population density, small local groups and open recruitment has adaptive value. At the same time, the high turnover of personnel leads to status ambiguity among parish members, in turn reflected in sorcery beliefs and accusations. Mobility disrupts the group, and also constrains the development of powerful leadership. Forceful Big Men do emerge, yet are limited in their ability to attract and hold followers. Their activities tend to be manipulative and mediatory, rather than coercive. They depend more on networks of individuals than on solidary groups. The pressure to amalgamate for defence and security is thus opposed by suspicion, challenges of sorcery and the freedom to depart for residence in other groups. Sharpened by the impact of *kuru,* this contradiction seems to have led the South Fore to develop certain distinctive political forms.

Chief among them is the use of 'descent' or consanguinity as a means of conceptualizing relations of co-residence. To a certain extent they resemble the Bena Bena, as described by Langness (1964: 172):

> . . . the sheer fact of residence in a Bena Bena group can and does determine kinship. People do not necessarily reside where they do because they are kinsmen; rather, they become kinsmen because they reside there.

But South Fore go one step further. It is not simply that membership in the parish is equated with kinship, but that in addition it is conceptualized in terms of 'descent' or consanguinity. A similar situation has been reported by Robinson (1968: 148) for the Morapitiya of Kandyan Ceylon:

> . . . what really constitutes 'descent' from King Dutthagamani is not kinship but residence, although the relationship is conceptualized in terms of kinship. People who live in Morapitiya are 'descended' from King Dutthagamani. People who do not are not so 'descended'. And we find that women who marry into the village say they are 'descended' from the king. On the other hand, women who marry out and men who go to colonization schemes elsewhere gradually lose their claim to 'descent'; their children are not 'descended' from the king, unless they happened to return to Morapitiya to live.

In both Morapitiya and South Fore, 'descent' is not a principle of recruitment, but rather a symbol of group unity. The South Fore have no need to distinguish agnates from other members of the parish. If anything, the need is to avoid such discrimination, for a disgruntled man may leave, weakening the group. The comparison between Morapitiya and South Fore should not be overstated. When a South Fore joins a new parish, he does not relinquish rights and obligations in other groups; the occurrence of multiple claims is a general feature of New Guinea Highlands societies. What is particular about the South Fore political system is the combination of open groups with a high turnover in personnel, institutionalized means for attracting and incorporating outsiders, leadership of limited scale, and the use of 'descent' as a symbol of common residence.

NOTES

1. The importance of warfare in the New Guinea Highlands has been stressed particularly by R. Berndt (1964), Langness (1964), and de Lepervanche (1967) whose works should be consulted.

2. We carried out fieldwork in South Fore for 21 months between June 1961 and June 1963. The first period of work (nine months) was supported by the Department of Genetics of the University of Adelaide under the terms of a Rocke-

feller Grant. The second period was under the auspices of the Department of Public Health of the Territory of Papua and New Guinea. We are grateful to both of these institutions for support, and to the many individuals associated with them for generous hospitality and practical help.

3. We hope to give a fuller discussion of the name 'Fore' elsewhere. For the present it is sufficient to note that it can be used to refer (1) to a specific region bordering the Lamari River along the eastern border of Fore territory; (2) to the 'source' people and products, which according to myth originated there; and (3) to the hot, low-lying regions in contrast with the cooler, higher areas.

4. A clan may be defined as a group recruited by descent exclusively through members of one sex from a putative or known common ancestor. A lineage is similarly constituted but in this instance genealogical relationships among the members can be traced step by step.

5. This point is discussed further later; see at end of *Internal Order* and in the *Conclusion*.

6. Any man his father regards as a 'brother' in any sense may be counted as a classificatory 'father'.

REFERENCES CITED

ALPERS, M. P. (1966): Epidemiological changes in *kuru*, 1957 to 1963. NINDB Monograph No. 2, *Slow, Latent and Temperate Virus Infections*: 65-82.

BARNES, J. A. (1962): African models in the New Guinea Highlands. *Man*, Vol. 62: Article 2

BENNETT, J. H. (1962): Population studies in the *kuru* region of New Guinea. *Oceania*, Vol. 33: 24-46.

BERNDT, C. (1953): Socio-cultural change in the east central highlands of New Guinea. *Southwestern Journal of Anthropology*, Vol. 9. No. 1: 112-38.

BERNDT, C. (1957): Social and cultural change in New Guinea: communication, and views about 'other' people. *Sociologus*, Vol. 7: 38-56.

BERNDT, R. M. (1952): A cargo movement in the Eastern Central Highlands of New Guinea. *Oceania*, Vol. 23: 40-65, 137-58, 202-34.

BERNDT, R. M. (1954a): Kamano, Jate, Usurufa and Fore kinship in the Eastern Central Highlands of New Guinea. *Oceania*, Vol. 25: 23-53, 156-87.

BERNDT, R. M. (1954b): Contemporary significance of prehistoric stone objects in the Eastern Central Highlands of New Guinea. *Anthropos*, Vol. 49: 555-87.

BERNDT, R. M. (1954c): Reaction to contact in the eastern highlands of New Guinea. *Oceania*, Vol. 24: 190-228, 255-74.

BERNDT, R. M. (1958): A "devastating disease syndrome": *kuru* sorcery in the Eastern Central Highlands of New Guinea. *Sociologus*, Vol. 8: 4-28.

BERNDT, R. M. (1962): *Excess and Restraint: Social Control among a New Guinea Mountain People*. Chicago: University of Chicago Press.

BERNDT, R. M. (1964): Warfare in the New Guinea Highlands. *American Anthropologist*, Vol. 66, No. 4, Part 2: 183-203.

BERNDT, R. M. (1965): The Kamano, Usurufa, Jate and Fore of the Eastern Highlands. In *Gods, Ghosts and Men in Melanesia*. (P. Lawrence and M. J. Meggitt, eds.). Melbourne: Oxford University Press.

DIAMOND, J. (1966): Zoological classification system of a primitive people. *Science*, Vol. 151, No. 3714: 1102-4.

FORTES, M. (1953): The structure of unilineal kin groups. *American Anthropologist*, Vol. 55: 17-41.

FORTES, M. and E. E. EVANS-PRITCHARD (1940): *African Political Systems*. London: Oxford University Press.

GAJDUSEK, D. C. (1963): Kuru. *Transactions of the Royal Society of Tropical Medicine and Hygiene*, Vol. 57: 151-69.

GLASSE, R. (1967): Cannibalism in the *kuru* region of New Guinea. *Transactions of the New York Academy of Science*, Series II, Vol. 29: 748-54.

GLASSE, R. (1969): Marriage in South Fore. In *Pigs, Pearlshells, and Women: Marriage in the Highlands of New Guinea* (M. J. Meggitt and R. M. Glasse, eds.). Englewood Cliffs: Prentice-Hall.

GLASSE, S. (Lindenbaum) (1964): The social effects of *kuru. Papuan and New Guinea Medical Journal*, Vol. 7: 36-47.

HOGBIN, H. I. and C. H. WEDGWOOD (1953): Local grouping in Melanesia. *Oceania*, Vol. 23: 241-76 and Vol. 24: 58-76.

LANGNESS, L. L. (1964): Some problems in conceptualization of Highlands social structures. *American Anthropologist*, Vol. 66, No. 4, Part 2: 162-82.

LEPERVANCHE, M. de (1967): Descent, residence and leadership in the New Guinea Highlands. *Oceania*, Vol. 38: 134-58 and Vol. 39: 163-89.

MEGGITT, M. J. (1965): *The lineage system of the Mae Enga of New Guinea.* Edinburgh: Oliver and Boyd.

ROBBINS, R. G. (1961): The vegetation of New Guinea. *Australian Territories*, Vol. 1: 21-32.

ROBINSON, M. (1968): 'The house of the mighty hero' or 'The house of enough paddy'? Some implications of Sinhalese Myth. In *Dialectic in Practical Religion* (E. R. Leach, ed.). Cambridge: Cambridge University Press.

SCOTT, G. K .(1963): The dialects of Fore. *Oceania*, Vol. 33: 280-6.

WATSON, J. (1965a): From hunting to horticulture in the New Guinea Highlands. *Ethnology*, Vol. 4: 295-309.

WATSON, J. (1965b): The significance of a recent ecological change in the central Highlands of New Guinea. *Journal of the Polynesian Society*, Vol. 74: 438-50.

WURM, S. A. (1964): Australian New Guinea Highlands languages and the distribution of their typological features. *American Anthropologist*, Vol 66, No. 4, Part 2: 77-97.

RONALD M. BERNDT

POLITICAL STRUCTURE IN THE EASTERN CENTRAL HIGHLANDS OF NEW GUINEA

ABSTRACT

Focusing on a region that was just being brought under full Administration control, this paper looks at the question of social order in relation to warfare, sorcery, intermarriage, and leadership, including changes in leadership and authority in the new situation. The district is nominally the political unit, but its solidarity is weakened by internal dissension and by competition among Strong Men conforming with the ideal of aggressive self-assertion. Close social relationships include both antagonism and co-operation; and this is illustrated schematically in diagrams showing zones of interaction centring on one district.

At the time of my fieldwork, the part of the Trust Territory I am considering came within the jurisdiction of two Administrative Sub-districts, Kainantu and Bena. Some of its major social and cultural features have been discussed elsewhere.[1] Here I limit myself to a brief outline.

The area as a whole was only gradually being opened when my wife and I were there in 1951-53. The impact of the outside world, direct and otherwise, was very uneven indeed, a point that must be taken into account in respect of any general statements concerning it. This obviously raises problems in description, especially in a short account where local variation is treated only in the broadest terms. For instance, I cannot go into the subject of time differences in regard to the acceptance of introduced modes of behaviour and the modification of traditional ways. Our first and main base in Kogu (Usurufa) had first been visited by an Administration patrol toward the end of 1947 and declared 'controlled' at the end of 1949. Our second base in Busarasa-Moke (Fore) was first visited by the same patrol in 1947 but was not declared 'controlled' until the end of 1950. During our fieldwork, the country immediately to the south was still classified as restricted and still relatively unaffected by the southward spread of alien influence.[2] Although we visited other areas as well, these are the two main points of orientation I draw upon in this paper.

Four linguistic units occupied this region.[3] The Kamano (Kafe), about 12,000 in number, covered an area of approximately 320 square miles. Adjoining them on the south were about 900 Usurufa (Uturupa) in a small stretch of no more than 12 square miles. Farther south again the general label of Fore was applied to a somewhat more heterogeneous population of perhaps 10,000, made up of several fairly distinct regional-linguistic groupings and covering possibly 240 square miles of country. Another large constellation was the Jate (Iaté), on the western borders of the Kamano, Usurufa and Fore and extending west and south over a wide area with an overall population possibly exceeding 20,000. The groups that acknowledged the overall Jate label in varying degrees were named according to the dialect and territory that distinguished them as separate units. The most important were the Ke'jagana, the Kemiu and the Friganu.

Each linguistic unit was subdivided into a number of named regional groupings, or 'districts'. The expression I am translating as 'district' in each of these languages is 'big name'. The Usurufa comprised six districts, the Kamano approximately 67, the Fore perhaps 36; the Kemiu Jate subgroup 33, the Ke'jagana 41, and the Friganu at least 12. The districts were not uniform in size as regards either population or territory. Most of those for which figures were available contained about 200 to 600 people, but some had no more than 50 and a couple approximately 700. At least half the area formally occupied by each was normally unoccupied or uncultivated. Shifting cultivation was the rule. Even so, especially in the south, fairly large stretches of uninhabited bush were virtually no-man's-land. Within each district were 'small names' identifying sites or topographical features. At any one of these there might be a village or hamlet, conventionally situated on high ground such as a hill-top or ridge. In the south, some were still fortified with wooden palisades. As we shall see presently, in a general sense the political unit was the district. Nevertheless, a person could rely, ultimately, only on natal members of the same village. Just as the expression that I translate as 'district' was used for all such units regardless of size, so the term 'house-place' was applied to any occupied clearing, from the smallest hamlet (even, occasionally, one house) to the largest village. Scale was irrelevant in that context. All districts on one hand, all house-places on the other, whatever their size, were regarded as equivalent units of social structure.

There were other than linguistic differences between the four largest units, although some of the most striking of them could be accounted for primarily in terms of variation and spread of alien influence. Overall, however, we could identify a broad range of socio-cultural uniformities. Allowing for differences in terrain, ecological and economic features were very similar. The basis throughout was subsistence horticulture (with sweet potato the staple in the north, taro and yam in the south), supplemented by dry season hunting and the domestication or fattening for food of pigs, fowls, dogs and cassowaries. Close similarities became evident in the course of our research, in other fields too—mythology and songs, festivals and religious rites, age-grading and so on; and throughout the region there was the same emphasis on violence, warfare and fighting. In many respects we could, tentatively, make a number of general statements about the whole region, without glossing over local differences, but viewing them as part of a situation in which similarity was more apparent than diversity. The differences were increasingly numerous and important toward the outer fringes of the three larger linguistic units.

The point to be remembered, in this context, is that our most intensive fieldwork focused on the Usurufa, the Ke'jagana and Kemiu Jate, the southern Kamano, and the northeastern Fore. Inevitably, this shaped our regional perspective—or perspectives. But in surveys involving less detailed work we covered, partially, a much wider range, and supplemented these by regular and irregular contacts with people from other districts within this total constellation. (See Diagram One.)

At this juncture, a few words should be said about the possible use of the term 'society' for the linguistic unit.

There was little sense of unity between people just because they spoke one language. Frequently, indeed, they were on friendly terms with adjacent districts speaking a different language and at enmity with districts speaking the same language. (These languages were not mutually intelligible, but in most border districts and all through the Usurufa area there were people who could speak or understand at least one language other than their own.) From the standpoint of persons belonging by birth or adoption to any one district, everyone outside its boundaries (apart from certain kin) was potentially hostile. Nevertheless, they regarded these members of other districts as much the same sort of people as themselves—people with whom they fought, intermarried, joined in peace ceremonies, and so on. This recognition depended, in practice, on what could be called each district's zone of political influence (see below), usually although not invariably made up of a cluster of adjacent districts. It was not limited by linguistic boundaries. At the same time, regardless of external ties within the broader configuration, those speaking a common language were on that account assumed to be bound especially closely by common custom and practice; and the language name, rather than the district name, was a more widely understood clue to a person's social identity. District names were replicated, with slight variations, right through the region and possibly beyond it. The specific language names, however, remained relatively stable, and indicated in the broadest terms both cultural and local affiliations, as seen in contrast with other units of the same kind within and outside this constellation.

Whatever unit we isolate and call a society, there must always be a certain amount of arbitrary selection in making this classification. It is obviously not enough to define it in the terms of Hallowell's (1950: 601) minimum definition, which requires "organized relations, differentiated roles and patterns of social interaction, not simply an aggregation of people": or, to follow MacIver and Page (1950: 5ff.), as a "system of usages and procedures, of authority and mutual aid, of many groupings and divisions, of controls of human behaviour and of liberties", and so on. Nadel (1951: 95, 183-5) speaks of a "summation" of persons, and suggests that one can set out with some rough and ready criterion—a common language, for instance, or political allegiance, or an existing convention of referring to a certain population, known by a particular name, as a society. Nevertheless, he insists that we should be certain we are dealing with true groups and not merely with quasi-groups: we cannot merely assess which is numerically the largest and call that the society. A society is, to him, "the relatively widest effective group, regarding a certain kind of effectiveness as crucial".[4] For Firth (1951: 27), it is "an organized set of individuals with a given way of life", or "an aggregate of social relations".[5]

Clearly, none of the four broad linguistic divisions already mentioned could be regarded as a society in Nadel's or Firth's terms. Even the small Usurufa unit included people who did not consider themselves as really united or as possessing common interests. Its members *in toto* engaged in no corporate activity and manifested no political solidarity; representatives from its component districts and houseplaces never, it seems, came together collectively for any purpose in its name. They remained divided through interdistrict and intervillage suspicion, even while acknowledging the social and cultural regularities they held in common, an acknowledgment reinforced by use of a common language. According to Nadel's definition, the relatively widest effective group would be the district, which I have identified as the political unit. If we took Firth's, the limitation of the boundaries of aggregation would need to be defined, while the emphasis on relationship within the aggregate would bring us back to the concept of the 'effective group' and so, in our case, to the district.

To say, tentatively, that the unit which shares a common language and a common culture and is territorially bound to a limited and stipulated area,[6] can be regarded as a society is no more ambiguous than to call it a tribe, for instance.[7] However, I shall return later to this point, in identifying what I would classify as a social system for the purpose of this analysis. According to Nadel (1951: 185), the very word 'common' is misleading: we must distinguish the group proper from another, spurious, group, the "cultural group" so-called, for, he says (1951: 185-6), "Behaviour which happens to be uniform in a given population, and which the people concerned know to be uniform, is easily confused with behaviour which is intentionally co-ordinated". By 'common', however, I mean 'belonging more or less equally to' or 'sharing more or less equally in', according to context, and this can refer to language, ideology, and other aspects of culture. In the circumstances I do not consider it to be misleading, even if it raises, as it must do, further questions relating to co-activity between all individuals and sections within the groups concerned.

Use of the term 'cultural group' does give rise to some difficulties; but if we mean that the people so included recognize a 'uniformity', a 'likeness', a 'commonalty', then surely this involves also a recognition of boundaries, which in the present instance is at one level coterminous with the recognition of boundaries limiting the one language. On the other hand, when I speak of the Usurufa, Kamano, Fore and Jate as having a broadly common culture, do I mean that the people within each of those units were aware of this, or that it is my own assessment, based on a comparison of social and cultural features throughout the region? The answer, in each case, is a qualified affirmative. It is true that, as far as their active interest went, the people in any one district recognized only a certain vaguely conceived sphere of influence which underwent changes in the course of time. But this did not coincide with their recognition of the territorial and cultural confines of their linguistic unit because it ignored language boundaries and, in so doing, implied that linguistic factors were of secondary importance in practical considerations of cultural as well as social alignment. It is partly because of these linked spheres of influence, no two really coinciding, that we can say there was some awareness of this broader cultural identity.

That awareness was strengthened through interdistrict movements. From time to time, members of defeated villages and districts were driven away to other grounds in the course of fighting. Small groups of men moved about on raiding expeditions, and there were trading parties as well. Further, I have already mentioned the common mythological themes that extended through the whole area (see R. Berndt 1962: 39-58, 1965: 78-104; C. Berndt n.d.), and in varying degrees were explicitly acknowledged as such.

For instance, the two major creative beings were said to have passed through the region from south to north, and accounts of their activities and their journeys (by varying routes) came from the Fore around Busarasa, Moke and Ora up through the Jate, Usurufa, and Kamano. Over and above differences between individual narrators were local differences both in content and in social perspective, including the extent to which other linguistic units were taken into account. Nevertheless, verbal acknowledgment of a common origin, while varying in scope and emphasis, was one of the principal means of asserting and validating the basic cultural similarity of these four broad regional-linguistic groups. As 'children of Jugumisonta' (or whatever name was given to the creative mother), their behaviour was regarded as being more or less predictable; and although this implied siblingship was not spelt out explicitly in verbal terms or in practical situations, it provided a vaguely defined context within which interaction could take place between them and between their respective units.

THE NATURE OF THE POLITICAL UNIT

We return to the district, the 'big name', as being, functionally, the political unit. Any definition of political solidarity must rest not only on commonalty of interest, but on the co-operativeness of the members of the group in question. As Radcliffe-Brown has pointed out (1950: xiv et seq.), when we are dealing with political systems "we are dealing with law, on the one hand, and with war on the other". We are concerned with the maintenance of social order in the political unit, as a sub-system, and the structuring of its relations with other like units within the total system, or the total configuration. This brings in the question of authority, and the nature of leadership within that unit. Ownership of or title to the land that it holds is a subsidiary factor here. But before discussing any of these aspects we must consider the composition of the district.[8]

Within every district was a varying number of named house-places, each containing members of one or more patrilineages and their adherents. The patrilineage, the social unit based on genealogically traceable descent through males to a common, remembered (usually male) ancestor, was known by such figurative terms as 'vine' or 'rope' signifying its assumed continuity through time. Despite this conventional conception of it, it was always shallow in depth, incorporating no more than five or six generations at most in the perspective of any given person within it. It was the effective land-holding body, allocating and essentially controlling the garden lands. For everyday purposes, these lands were owned by its various members and their respective lineal descendants, and cultivated by them and by their female adherents—who normally had the right to dispose of a certain proportion of the crops in their own names, through the ordinary channels of food-giving at feasts and routine distributions.

Membership in the patrilineage rested primarily on direct patrilineal descent but also on the social fiction of quasi-consanguineal patrilineal descent—i.e., adoption. Children could be 'given' or exchanged at or soon after birth, especially between a brother and sister or between male patrikin. In several cases this took place also between non-kin belonging to different districts, but mostly in the course of interdistrict fighting, as captives or hostages, and mostly the children involved seem to have been well past infancy. The fact that adoption was conventionally accepted as a normal process, and that it was also practised to some extent, has obvious implications for intralineage solidarity and intradistrict loyalty, but I shall not discuss this question here.

Girls after marriage, at if not before puberty, normally moved out of their own house-places to live with their husbands, so that the core of the patrilineage was the cluster of co-resident males who acted, normatively, as a corporate body in such matters as offence and defence. They were jointly responsible for contributing bridewealth on the betrothal and marriage of any one of their male members, for co-operating in the heavier work connected with gardening (the routine work was carried out by women), and for performing, either as a separate body or in conjunction with similar units within the same district, rites associated with such matters as age-grading and initiation, the 'sweat-house' and the cult of the sacred flutes (see R. Berndt 1962: 73-80, 93-105).

These lineages were very small. Some had fewer than ten adult males and even, in the case of lineages which had recently split or segmented, only two or three. The relevant terms alone did not define or allude to the span of this unit. They included both the minimal patriline of two or three generations of males occupying a small communal men's house, and the larger named unit composed of a varying number of such 'lines' and not necessarily sharing the same men's house. (The membership of non-resident females did not lapse, whether or not they returned to their 'own' ground, but the active nucleus of the lineage was always the group of co-resident males.) On the other hand, among the Fore the same terms were used also for the combination of linked lineages, the clan. As in the case of the district, and the village or hamlet, the relevant term served as a label for a certain kind of social unit. The main factors to be considered, in local terms, were the nature of that unit, and the appropriate behaviour expected of its members— between themselves, and in relation to members of other units. There was, then, a fluidity about the concept of lineage in this region, insofar as its span and its internal differentiation into segments were concerned.

The unit that I am calling a clan (no specific local terms) differed between the southern Kamano, Usurufa and most of the Jate on the one hand and at least a certain proportion of the northern Fore on the other. Among the former it was co-resident and exogamous, comprising one or more patrilineages occupying the same village. Whether or not these were known by the one name, their members assumed an interrelationship which was not usually genealogically traceable. Lineages bearing the same name, but scattered through other districts in the same and different language units, acknowledged no special kinship or unity on that account. Among the northern Fore, however, the clan was not exogamous. The village or hamlet was still occupied by one or more patrilineages, but its members comprised a territorial rather than a kin-based unit. The assumption of common descent, not always genealogically demonstrable and in practice conceived of mostly in classificatory terms, linked members of lineages of the one name occupying different villages within the district. The clan thus cut across village membership, uniting lineages which were not co-resident, with the normative expectation of intermarriage to reinforce the ideology of close kin relations between them. It can be viewed, in effect, as a political sub-unit, having some sense of corporateness and commonalty of purpose and action.

The structural differences between Kamano, Usurufa, and Jate districts on the one hand and northern Fore districts on the other were not superficially noticeable. In the former the patrilineages, after dividing or splitting in a way which can be described as a form of segmentation, maintained relative independence from one another in this particular sense—although their members might be traceably related to one another and they might belong to the same district. If they did not settle down on an unoccupied house-site, they tended to align themselves with other lineages, forming (in my terms) a clan, which could be taken as synonymous with the patrilineal core of the smallest local unit, the house-place or village. In the Fore examples, patrilineages of the same name within a district aligned themselves dependently, in a parallel fashion, to form (in my terms) a clan, signifying a greater degree of co-operation between them even though they occupied several different villages or hamlets. It was primarily a matter of extending the degree of relative certainty, or expectation, of co-operation outside the village, whereas among the Kamano, Usurufa and Jate that certainty or solidarity remained largely in the village. In both cases the district as a whole was the political unit from which help could ideally be expected in crises, but in practice the provision of such help hinged largely on the relations between the political sub-groups, formed by the parallel linkage of lineages.

No evidence is available on how this difference developed, but it could represent two kinds of attempt to achieve security in the face of intermittent warfare. The Kamano, Usurufa and Jate built village strongholds, each relying primarily on the agnatic kin and quasi-kin within it. Attacks from outside were usually directed against a stockaded village rather than against the district as a whole, although it was district affiliation which counted in hostilities of this sort and other villages within the district might come to its help if, among other reasons, the matter seemed urgent. The Fore shared the fundamental assumption that aid in emergency devolved on co-resident male lineage kin, but in one sense they had widened the sphere of responsibility for immediate and more than nominal co-operation. An offence against a hamlet or village occupied by male members of one lineage was viewed as an offence against all the lineages of the same name within that district. An offence against one hamlet or village was also, at least nominally, an offence against the whole district, but the response of other segments of that district might be no more than nominal unless they themselves were directly implicated.

This particular difference between the two areas, then, lay in the relative degree of political action in an emergency. The Fore arrangement could be viewed as a development of political awareness, an endeavour to strengthen the political unit, the district, at the expense of the smaller local unit, the village or hamlet. Similarly, the northern Fore tended to marry predominantly within the district as well as within the clan. The Kamano, Usurufa and Jate showed verbal preference for intradistrict marriage as an ideal, but in practice the majority of such unions did not conform with this. Very few marriages among them took place within the same village or between lineages of the same name distributed through different villages within one district. Among the northern Fore, on the other hand, the majority of marriages we recorded took place not only between members of different lineages within the same district, but also within the linked lineages of the same name forming the clan. Whatever the origins of this practice, it did have the effect of enabling a district to be to some extent independent of others in respect of the obligations and commitments that betrothal and marriage imposed on the two kin-groups immediately concerned.

In both cases, however, members of the several clans within any one district looked on themselves as united by a common traditional bond and relations between them were phrased in kinship terms. They were expected to come together for age-grading and sacred rituals. Conventionally and generally, people often spoke as if all the adult men of a district would combine for purposes of offence, but from more specific reports it became clear that the position was much the same as in regard to defence: the particular action concerned might be carried out in the name of the district, but in practice it rested largely with the individual villages or local clans.

Marriage links were foci of strain as well as co-operation, because the field of marital and affinal relations was conceptualized as exemplifying the mixture of friendliness and enmity already mentioned in connection with interdistrict affairs. Intradistrict marriages therefore contributed substantially toward the incidence of the same pattern in intradistrict relations. Every marriage brought two groups of kin into a closer, but different, relationship. The rights and duties of the main protagonists were fairly well defined, but so was the patterning of dissension between them. Conventionally, distrust and suspicion between husband and wife and between a man and his affines were regarded as quite natural and proper. In regard to intradistrict, and especially intraclan, marriages people were prepared to qualify this expectation and to see it in balance. In interdistrict marriages, they tended to emphasize it at the expense of other equally significant features such as co-operation and mutual aid.

In practice, then, dissension centring on marriage and marriage arrangements could have repercussions in both intra- and interdistrict relations. Within the district, it could affect the provision of help and support in time of war. Outside the district, similarly, it could and sometimes did have a bearing on the formation of military alliances. Conversely, of course, since these influences worked both ways, the wider situation was reflected to some extent in local relationships, including interpersonal and other social facets of marriage and betrothal.

TRADITIONAL AUTHORITY AND THE POLITICAL UNIT

Traditionally in this region there was no formal social stratification in terms of a hierarchy of statuses. As a direct result of alien influence, however, new categories were being introduced—new, ranked positions which could, potentially, have served as spearheads for the development of classes with specified rights and powers. The new system included officially appointed headmen, native evangelists and so on. By 1953 there were certainly indications of this structural change, and since then, of course, there has been increasing diversification of occupations. In contrast, the traditional system, insofar as we can gauge this, appears to have been much more fluid and open, particularly in regard to leadership. Prestige and authority derived either from kinship positioning (i.e., ascribed status) or from wealth, prowess and physical strength (i.e., personally-achieved status). One road to achieved status involved, not so much the possession, but rather the display and distribution, of wealth—in this case, wealth in the sense of non-durable goods. Although other kinds of wealth were recognized, too (shells, arrows, birds' feathers and the like), they were much less important and their use was much less formalized than in the central and western Highlands.

A major item here was the holding of feasts on such occasions as marriages, initiations, deaths, pig-festivals, and peace ceremonies, or, at least, contributing substantially to such feasts. Whether or not the feast itself was acknowledged to have been personally instigated by a particular Strong Man, the names of donors of pig meat, vegetables and so on were always publicly known within their own environment; and the more generous the contribution, the greater the prestige. This conforms, in essence, with the accepted Melanesian pattern. But even more significant was a dominant, aggressive personality. This was of primary importance where authority was concerned. The position of headman of an agnatic descent group (one or more according to its span, and the amount of competition between them) depended on this; he had to be a fighter, a warrior leader. His elders might be better equipped to deal with the formalities of boys' initiation rites, or with magic and sorcery practices. Their kinship status might be higher than his, in terms of seniority, but the warrior leader usually took the initiative in coping with lineage and extra-lineage relations. Because his status rested so heavily on physical prowess, it was bound to fluctuate over a period of time. When his strength and energy waned, he was bound to give way. Any prestige he derived through the acquisition and distribution of wealth would dwindle rapidly unless it was bolstered by his reputation as a fighter. In this area, economics and warfare were two sides of the same coin (see R. Berndt 1964: 203): with the suppression of warfare, economics (and the development of entrepreneurial activities) could serve as a substitute. In the Highlands generally, there is ample evidence of this.

The ideal personality type for both men and women was based on the concept of strength through aggressive, forceful and often violent behaviour. It was considered both desirable and necessary for men, as men, to develop this particular emphasis. The process of socialization-enculturation was designed specifically along those lines and rested on that basic assumption. In practice, men approximated to it either more or less. At one extreme was the warrior, in the ideal stereotype— forceful, able to override the opinions of others when it suited him and to get his own way through bluff or threats in internal disputes, decisive in argument, expert with bow and arrows, quick to take and give offence without flinching and to follow this through with appropriate action, and ready to spring to the defence of his village or district and to help his co-lineage and certain other kin—when their interests did not conflict with his own. Very few men met all of these requirements. At the other extreme was the 'no-good' man, weak, erratic or physically inferior. The majority probably fell somewhere in between. But all men had passed through the same kind of socialization sequence and were assumed to strive in varying degrees toward reaching the standard exemplified in this ideal type. No prestige accrued to the man who could not use his bow to some purpose, who could not on occasion 'talk strongly'—who could not, in short, act as a man. All men were expected to engage in armed fighting from time to time if not more often and, at a minimum, to endorse, if only passively, the ideology of success-through-aggression.

Strength, therefore, was the only factor that really counted in any competitive situation and the principal means of acquiring prestige. A man who could maintain his ascendency over others, particularly but not necessarily if he also occupied a senior position in his lineage, would become its warrior leader more or less automatically; but he was liable to be supplanted at any time by someone else using the same techniques and fired with the same ambitions as himself. His position depended on his personal ability to maintain it in the face of continual competition. But while he was its main leader and organizer, the main planner of raids and ambushes, his chief rewards appear to have been the aura of prestige and personal satisfaction, the pleasure of dominating others. Generally speaking, a leader of this sort received few extra privileges, apart from gifts intended to ensure his goodwill or induce his support, and having a better opportunity to seize and keep loot obtained during fighting. Throughout one district there seem to have been as many warrior leaders as there were villages or hamlet-clusters, or even lineages. From all accounts, most of them had more or less equal status, but in rare cases an outstanding warrior was able to dominate an entire district.

This emphasis on self-assertion, manifested in the ideal type of the Big Man or Strong Man, the warrior leader, had implications for the maintenance of order within the political unit. It permeated the education of girls as well as boys. Commencing in early childhood, it was intensified during such occasions as initiation. For boys, training was more prolonged and far-reaching; it involved not just the techniques or arts of war but, even more important, the attitudes basic to the enjoyment of fighting as a natural occupation for men. Women were expected to be aggressive and forceful, but only in relation to members of their own sex. Men were not limited in the same way. Control of all behaviour within the political unit, apart from a mother's authority over her very young children, was actually in their hands, or rather in the hands of those who were able and willing to exercise it.

For both sexes, however, in some of the most important rituals, the welfare and interests of *individual* performers were explicitly stressed, rather than the collective welfare of the various social units to which they belonged. In any situation, a person was likely to be confronted with a choice between these two alternatives, but this was most pressing in regard to intradistrict affairs. The conception of normal behaviour was flexible enough, in most types of activity, to allow fairly wide scope for variation. Certain fundamental assumptions, on such matters as relations between the sexes and the maintenance of human and garden fertility, were largely unquestioned. But the moral code itself—as expressed, for example through myths, through informal statements, and through the injunctions given at initiation periods—embraced conflicting alternatives and took into account the situational pressures influencing decisions.

In general terms, certain wrongs were recognized and deprecated: for example, stealing, wounding, killing and sorcery between members of the same lineage, clan and district. In practice, however, when these took place within a district, and particularly between actual or adoptive members, a collective response on the part of the unit involved was very rare indeed. When they concerned outsiders (e.g., wives) resident in the district, the response was more straightforward and the affair was likely to be treated along interdistrict lines. Between district, clan or lineage members, division of opinions, loyalties and interests, with crosscutting kin alignments and obligations, tended to block any suggestion of majority action. Such action as was taken tended to be on a sectional or minority basis, largely controlled by individual members of the small subunits. If the culprit was a Strong Man his offence might not be openly criticized at all and in fact, because so-called wrongs were actually relative to the status of the person committing them, it might not even be viewed as an offence. Maintaining a show of strength meant that a man, especially, was not necessarily confined within the range of ordinarily tolerated or acceptable behaviour, and not necessarily subject to the rules which at least nominally governed those who were weaker or more submissive. Up to a point, such a man could make his own rules, but only provided he could continue to dominate his social situation. Fear of sorcery was not an effective check on the growing power of a Strong Man, since it was assumed to be virtually never employed between district members. But since a warrior leader could maintain his ascendency for only so long, there seems to have been little continuity in leadership.

Intradistrict offences, then, were settled between the individuals or the kin-units involved, with the relative strength of the parties influencing the nature and the outcome of the proceedings. When the matter was one between two districts, personal interests, kin and otherwise, were much less likely to complicate the issues. An injury to person or property committed by members of one or more districts against one or more members of another, was unquestionably an offence. The victim's co-members could normally be expected to stand by him, at least in name, and their opinion was likely to be more uniform, more obviously crystallized, and more readily translated into action. This was part of the expected form of interaction between districts as political units. Breaches between them, all fairly well-defined and straightforward, set in motion a system of retaliation whereby punishment and compensation were exacted either through direct force (as in warfare) or through indirect aggression (as, supposedly, in sorcery).

THE POLITICAL UNIT AND WAR

Warfare was the main activity that characterized the districts making up the whole region, separating one from another by emphasizing their distinctness as units in a total system of interaction. The training of boys underlined the desirability of interdistrict warfare and the benefits accruing to the Strong Man who could distinguish himself in that direction, but regimentation or coercion was minimal. Indirect pressures were strong and pervasive, stressing the kind of behaviour expected of males and legitimizing physical aggression and violence in an interdistrict context. Within this framework, however, responsibility for fighting, and generally for conforming to the ideal, was left to the individual participants.

Warfare was primarily retaliation, in the shape of "coercive action on the part of one group to exact compensation or revenge from another for a real or imagined injury" (R. Berndt 1962: 233, 1964: 183). Such an injury had to be 'backed' or reciprocated. The amount and kind of compensation required varied considerably. It might be simply a single killing to avenge a death; but quite often more was sought in compensation than the initial injury would seem to have warranted. For instance, in the event of a death attributed to sorcery, the nominal purpose of the response might be only to achieve the death of an enemy. On other occasions the ramifications were much wider. They could involve a number of deaths and more or less serious injuries, the devastating of crops, firing of villages and hamlets, rape and capture of women, and so forth. It was not unusual for people under attack to flee their home territory and become refugees. Generally speaking, interdistrict fighting consisted mainly of spasmodic raiding, in attacks and counter-attacks punctuated by peace declarations and festive gatherings. At any given time, one district might be on friendly terms with any number of others; but these relations could alter almost overnight, from friendship to animosity or from enmity to temporary friendship, perhaps, but not always, through the holding of a peace ceremony. There was no permanency in such associations, except in the expectation of interaction itself. 'Other' districts were potentially hostile as well as friendly. One did not normally fight with strangers outside one's interactory zone (see below). Strangers, in fact, were people with whom one did not fight. For one thing, they were too far away spatially, and for another they were an unknown quantity. This was not simply a matter of fighting people because they were categorized as enemies. Offensive fighting was normally a deliberate act, and defensive fighting a reaction against what could be called justified reprisal for injury. Whether the aggressors (i.e. the unit concerned) were really justified, retaliating because of a 'real' wrong, is beside the point. Normatively speaking, they could always expect a show of force in return. Conventionally, districts fought one another on that principle. Although only segments of each might actually be involved, it was nearly always described as an encounter between opposing districts, carried out in their names.

Political alliances between districts were mostly tenuous and designed to achieve some specific end. Direct requests for help involved either the payment of gifts or, as I would call them, bribes,[9] or less frequently an appeal to common fear of a stronger and threatening neighbour. The formation of these alliances had direct structural implications at the political level. Mostly they were brought about through bribery and therefore had no real continuity or consistency. But bribery did contribute toward the maintenance of the structure by widening the range of interaction. These shifting alliances need to be seen in conjunction with the interactory zone, from which their members were recruited.

Precipitating causes aside, in all acts of warfare and fighting the general aim was to achieve some kind of balance—to offset, in relatively equal terms, deaths, injuries and damages. This was not necessarily attained in one fighting sequence but rather over a fairly long period (of several years), if we take into account overall relations betwen the districts concerned. An immediate response, after an attack from a more powerful enemy, was not always possible. Members of a district might be dispersed and some time might elapse before they recovered their full fighting strength. In the interim period, that unit was not politically active. For practical purposes it lost its place in its original interactory sphere, at least until it returned to its home ground or engaged in some other, related, corporate activity. In the meantime, from the viewpoint of that unit or the segments acting in its name, a new sphere of interaction would develop in relation to each host district and its neighbours.

There seems to have been a fairly high degree of mobility among district segments, yet, because of the disadvantages of refugee conditions, they tended to come together again at the earliest opportunity. Some, however, became immobilized in refugee positions when warfare was officially suppressed in the northern part of the region. In 1953, for instance, two refugee Jate groups that had been caught in this way remained settled in Kamano territory. Similarly, members of the Fore-speaking district of Asafina remained in what had been regarded as Usurufa territory. Ordinarily, refugees nearly always had the expectation of returning to their own district, from which they had probably moved no more than a day's walking distance at most, occasionally only a couple of miles. They might have lost wealth, if not lives, in the course of their defeat, but they did not lose the right to their own land and gardens. And although they were dependent on the uncertain help of non-agnatic and quasi-kin, and always vulnerable to the threat of sorcery or of open attack from their hosts or neighbours, refugees in this situation were not among culturally dissimilar people. Nor were they obliged to make the same drastic psycho-social re-adjustment as if they had been faced with a markedly different environment. Nevertheless, to say this is not to minimize the personal stress and hardship involved, nor the structural ramifications. The problem of the refugee was significant throughout the New Guinea Highlands and had an important bearing on residential patterns and other organizational features (see R. Berndt 1964: 201, 203).

Before the region came under European control in the early 1950's, there seems to have been a fro-and-to movement of district segments. In a few cases, even, districts which had successfully driven away their opponents sent messages inviting them to return. The demand for social intercourse of this co-operative-antagonistic kind outside one's own district was built into the system—a system in which opponents were necessary as well as friends. In part, this is a straightforward example on a familiar theme—finding unity through opposition to a common enemy. But it illustrates, also, a demand for the kind of interaction in which hostility is both pervasive and conspicuous.

Closely connected with warfare was another feature that separated districts and set them against one another but at the same time, in broader perspective, drew them together in a relationship of actual or potential enmity. This was sorcery. One of its basic ingredients was mutual distrust, built up and sustained through living in a situation where the main emphases were on aggressive self assertion; and respect for strength found expression in two diametrically opposite ways—in readiness to yield to strength as well as practise it. Children were brought up to expect attack from others outside their own district, to see all outsiders as potentially hostile. This expectation was latent for much of the time, but came to the fore at crises. In local belief, within a certain range, sorcery was largely undiscriminating in its choice of victims. Although sorcerers were believed to be quite capable of singling out specific persons, the main criterion was seen as social affiliation—usually, district affiliation—with sex and age irrelevant. Even more than direct warfare, but certainly in conjunction with it, the patterning of beliefs about sorcery provides a useful social map of the conflicts which permeated intra- as well as interdistrict relations.

In other words, the two primary ways of dealing with situations which involved retaliatory action were a (direct or indirect) physical response, and sorcery. Choice of one rather than the other appears, in many cases, to have been more or less arbitrary. But choosing sorcery as a means of attack did not necessarily imply physical weakness or reluctance to engage in a direct confrontation. In local belief, both could be used simultaneously. However, when sorcery was brought into the open, with accusations and counter-accusations and threats, the presence of supposed victims and so on, fear and anxiety were most evident and could lead to direct physical aggression.

Sorcery was, normatively speaking, a weapon to be used against members of *other* districts, whether or not they were co-resident with the supposed sorcerer. This was regarded as entirely legitimate. Vulnerable persons included a man's own wife and other women married into his district unless they themselves belonged to it by birth or adoption. Although a few cases are available of sorcery being used within the district, this was not common and was generally regarded as morally wrong. Where women from other districts were concerned, the matter was not clear-cut. Conventionally they were regarded with suspicion and there was plenty of 'evidence' to suggest that they should be: they were obvious scapegoats when sorcery had been diagnosed as the cause of death, illness or injury. There are certainly many reported instances of sorcery being used (believed to be used) against them in these situations but, on the whole, direct physical action was preferred. Sorcery was believed to be especially appropriate in *inter*district relations.

Belief in sorcery capitalized on interdistrict dissension and distrust, and in fact exacerbated the situation. It provided a reason for warfare—which, in turn, proved also a congenial outlet for it. The death rate among young and middle-aged persons was fairly high, and even in warfare some deaths were attributed to sorcery. This meant that empirical evidence was always available to demonstrate to any sceptics (although they must have been rare) that sorcery did take place and could have disastrous effects.[10]

THE ZONE OF POLITICAL INFLUENCE

We are now in a position to discuss briefly the interaction of the district as the political unit within a constellation of political units, in terms of friendship and enmity.

Members of contiguous districts in this area were closely related to one another. This provides the setting or core from which may be constructed a range of *potential* co-operation-antagonism, extending from any one point (in this case, a district) and diminishing in intensity the further it is removed from that point. This structure of interaction remained, as far as we can gauge, fairly stable over a number of years, although alterations did occur as a result of interdistrict mobility on the part of refugees, for instance. This interactory zone, in each case, was made up of interdependent districts very closely linked through genealogical relationships and reciprocal obligations, along with others which surrounded them and with which relationships were not so precisely defined. This zone constituted the widest relevant frame of social reference, transcending linguistic boundaries. It could be seen as comprising the totality of actual and expected ties maintained by any one district and, also, the totality of ties maintained by its segments (that is, the villages and their patrilineages). This was the field in which interdistrict hostilities and friendships were activated. We can designate it as not simply a zone of social inter-action but, more significantly, a zone of political influence. It was not unlike what Lawrence has called a "security circle" (see P. Lawrence 1965-66: 379-85). In one sense, the situation here could lead us to speak of the zone of political influence as a security-*in*security circle. Within this range *both* order and disorder were expected and, what was more, accepted.

One significant point emerging from a brief comparative study of Highlands warfare (see R. Berndt 1964: 202) was that warfare was a co-operative under-taking involving all participants in much the same fashion as an economic venture: people must have partners, whether for economic, ritual or fighting purposes, and such partners were always found within the zone I have indicated. One might go even further in this context and suggest that, traditionally, security could be defined in terms of expected hostility almost as much as in terms of expected co-operation. This zone changed through time as, for instance, new alliances were formed, new marriages occurred, new oppositions emerged, and so on, but change was most noticeable in the relations between the units that made up the zone, fluctuating as they did between active friendship and active hostility. Taking every district as a central point, the corresponding zone marked the extent of its interactory perspective at a given period incorporating the same or different districts, but the patterns in each case differed. All such zones, however, were interconnected, providing a network of social and personal linkages of one kind or another through-out the region. Thus the zone centred on any one district at any point in time would show the extent of its interests, commitments, obligations and so on: but not its total social perspective. It reflected the dynamic quality of social living, with conflicting elements on both the structural and the organizational levels.[11] The co-ordinated activity within any one of these zones, from the point of view of any one district, differentiated them from one another, but the interrelationship of the zones themselves made up the wider social network.[12]

I shall illustrate, in summary, one way of delineating the zone of political influence, although the present example does not separate out the important feature of change through time. Attention is focused for the purpose on the Usurufa district of Kogu, mainly because it was relatively small and compact.[13]

Diagram One is a rough sketch map of the area. The linguistic units are demarcated by broken lines: five are noted. District names are referred to by numbers—thus:

0	Kogu	17	Busarasa	34	Jababi
1	Moiife	18	Ke'jagana	35	Etazena
2	Asafina	19	Amufi	36	Moke (No. 2)
3	Ofafina	20	Kimi'agumu	37	Kasa
4	Kemiu	21	Taramu	38	Numpagimi
5	Agura	22	Hafaru	39	Henagaru
6	Jumana	23	Jagu'	40	Jefanagumu
7	Anonana	24	Numparu	41	Haga
8	Irafu	25	Ki'o	42	Oka
9	Fomu	26	Tira'e	43	Ke'afu
10	Tiroka	27	Tebinofi	44	Wezu'epa
11	Numaga	28	Grufe	45	Mage
12	Ozana	29	Osena	46	Henganofi
13	Ifusa	30	Miarasa	47	Musa've
14	Emasa	31	Inivi	48	Sonofe
15	Ora	32	Tatagufa	49	Undefined:
16	Moke	33	Hogateru		Koga.

Kogu, in 1951-53, contained five villages or hamlet-clusters, with ten named lineages and their adherents. (See R. Berndt 1962: 20-1.) In this context the analysis is based on genealogies which purport to account for every male and female lineage member, mostly consanguineal but in a few cases adopted, dead or alive, over a period of approximately fifty years. Final checking and cross-checking of the genealogies was completed early in 1953, representatives of all ten lineages being used to compile them. There is always the possibility of deliberate or unconscious suppression of names and connections, as well as of falsifying or telescoping of data. In some cases, names were admittedly forgotten. Nevertheless, I went to a great deal of time and trouble in trying to ensure that they were reasonably accurate, without glossing over discrepancies or inconsistencies but using these as further sources of data. I shall not go into this last point here. The information contained in the genealogies was supplemented by case material, informal discussion and conversation, and so on.

In all, 514 persons of both sexes and all ages were accounted for, 175 of them living at the time of recording (adults: male, 69; female, 52; children:[14] male, 20; female, 34). Of 288 Kogu males whose names were recorded, 10 were said to have died naturally, 22 in a dysentery epidemic (between 1943-47), 91 shot by arrow or otherwise killed in fighting (11 by members of their own district), 47 from ordinary 'non-physical'[15] varieties of sorcery, 2 from 'kuru' sorcery, known in Jate as *guzigli*,[16] and 27 from another type of sorcery known in pidgin English as *sangguma*[17] (1 intradistrict case). Each death, whether attributed to shooting or

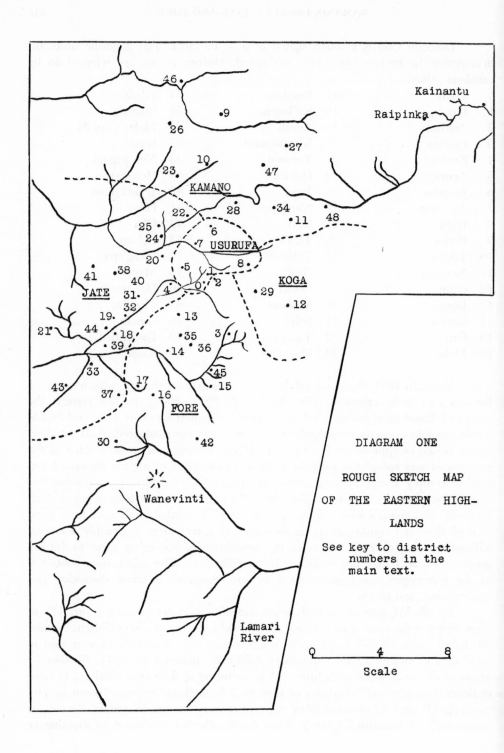

Kainantu

Raipinka

46

•9

•26

•27

10

23

47

KAMANO

22   28

•34

25   24   48   •11

6

•7 USURUFA

20   •5   8   KOGA

41   •38   1

40   •2   •29

JATE   31   4   0

32   •12

19

21   44   18   •13

39

•35   3

14   36

33   •45

43   37   17   15

16   FORE

30   •42

☼

Wanevinti

DIAGRAM ONE

ROUGH SKETCH MAP

OF THE EASTERN HIGH-

LANDS

See key to district
numbers in the
main text.

Lamari
River

0   4   8

Scale

to sorcery, was linked with the name of the district allegedly responsible for it. For the present rather limited purpose, this can be taken to indicate which districts, in our present analysis, formed an intensive interactory zone of opposition (four districts being primarily concerned here, all relatively close to Kogu: Ofafina and Asafina, both Fore; Kemiu, Jate; and Moiife, Usurufa), and which were of less significance.

Of 226 Kogu females, 13 were said to have died naturally, 21 in the dysentery epidemic, 5 by suicide, 2 shot by members of their own district, 31 from ordinary 'non-physical' sorcery, 10 from *guzigli'* sorcery, 33 from *sangguma,* and 25 shot in interdistrict fighting. The intensive zone of interaction in this respect involved two districts (Kemiu and Ofafina), with three others (Moiife, Asafina, and Ifusa) being of lesser significance as far as opposition was concerned.

Kogu men contracted marriages both within and outside their own district. The incoming women amounted to 170, from 28 districts. The districts with which most marriages were contracted were Moiife, Kemiu, Agura (Usurufa), and to a lesser degree Irafu and Anonana (both Usurufa), with corresponding weakening according to socio-geographic distance.

This information provides us with a relevant zone of interaction on the basis of deaths (in terms of oppositions), and marriages (in terms of co-operation and common interests) of Kogu men. There is a certain correspondence between the two kinds of material, and in totality we can take them as indicative of an immediate and primary zone of interaction for that one district.

Diagram Two is a conventionalized representation of Diagram One. Again, numbers stand for district names. The central box indicates Kogu (0), and it is from this perspective that we are viewing the situation. Linguistic units also are indicated.

Diagram Three provides us with a schematic picture of a complete elementary zone of interaction (as in Diagram Two), but shows further the relative intensity of interaction over a period of about fifty years. The pattern, it must be remembered, is as it were an assessment over that period, taking into account all violent action allegedly resulting in death and all cases of supposedly effective sorcery, in addition to all marriages contracted outside the Kogu district. It *does not* represent the pattern which could be depicted at any one point in time. But the boundaries of at least two interactory spheres within the zone seem to have remained fairly constant through time, while the third reveals considerable fluctuation, with spasmodic fighting and occasional marriages. In its totality it represents the summation of marital and various other ties existing between all Kogu men and the outside, in addition to fatal contacts in fighting. It *does not* reveal the frequency of warfare, for much fighting occurred without associated deaths. Nor does it show the districts involved in short-term alliances for fighting purposes, over this period. But it does provide one sort of gauge, showing the high percentage of deaths that were directly attributed to fighting. Approximately 32% of the total males whose names were recorded were said to have died in that way, or approximately 12%

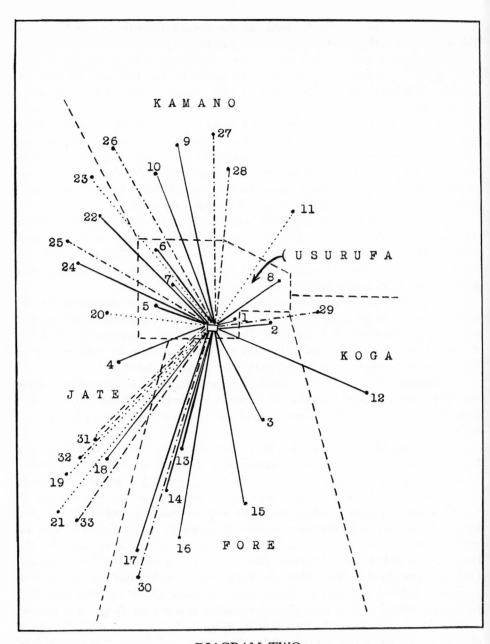

DIAGRAM TWO

Key: See main text, where district numbers are given.

——————— = opposition and co-operation;

—.—.—. = co-operation without obvious opposition;

.... = opposition without obvious co-operation.

of the total male deaths; but only approximately 12% of the total Kogu females were shot, and a little less than 12% of incoming wives of Kogu men.

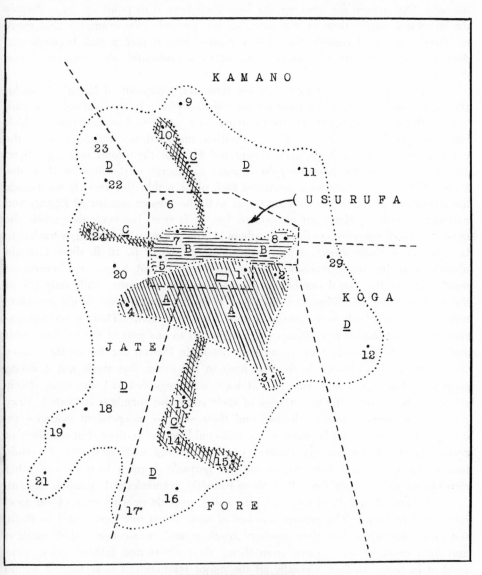

DIAGRAM THREE

Key: See main text, where district numbers are given.
A = major sphere of intensive interaction;
B = supplementary major sphere;
C = secondary sphere of interaction;
D = spasmodic occurrence of fighting and occasional marriages.

The interactory zone for the district may be translated in interpersonal terms, so that the extensions outward resemble it in part, with varying spheres of intensity. One reason for ignoring the individual here is to point up more sharply the structural implications of this zone, on the grounds (for example) that every marriage contracted outside the district represented in fact a link between two districts, and every act of warfare was, at least nominally, the concern of two districts.

Sphere A in the diagram signifies, from the viewpoint of Kogu, the socio-geographic area within which most interaction took place. In the available material, 66% of the total Kogu male deaths by arrow were attributed to this sphere, which involved four districts (Moiife, Kemiu, Asafina and Ofafina) and 62% of all the cases of sorcery, while Kogu men contracted 41% of their total marriages here. Moreover, 61% of the Kogu women (lineage members) were killed by these districts, while 41% of their total marriages took place within this area. If we include the secondary sphere of interaction (C) as well, the greater number of killings and marriages involving Kogu are accounted for. It is true, however, that while the majority of killings were confined to sphere A, the majority of marriages tended to be spread over both sphere A and supplementary sphere B. In B, three Usurufa districts were involved (Anonana, Agura and Irafu), and Kogu men contracted nearly 28% of their total number of marriages within this area, while only 1% of the total number of killings was ascribed to it. Yet the picture is not complete unless we include both these spheres A and B in our estimate. There is no explanation of the fact that so few killings were attributed to one part of the linguistic unit and so many to another. The answer does not lie in kinship ties, for on the surface these were no less obvious in the one than in the other. But there was a strong suggestion that Agura and Anonana, at least, were regarded as being more closely related to Kogu than the genealogies of their respective members indicated. Since genealogical memory was so shallow and there was no independent evidence relating to kin connections between them, this could not be verified; but members of certain of the Kogu lineages claimed nominal kinship with members of certain lineages in Agura and Anonana, as did not normally happen in respect of other districts, on the grounds that all of them formerly acknowledged common descent.

Spheres A and B, of intensive interaction, provide us with some of our most interesting problems. The greater number of male Kogu members found in them, not only their wives, but their mothers' brothers and cross-cousins; their mothers and their brothers' wives came from them; their sisters and fathers' sisters were resident in them. In fact, virtually all the major relationships were located within this relatively confined sphere. Within the district itself were predominantly agnatic and adopted kin, plus women from these adjacent districts. Of course, this is balanced by the consideration that 31% of the external marriages were distributed among 21 different districts, while 27% of all the Kogu women married members of their own district and so remained in Kogu.

The fact remains, however, that the primary area of tension included districts intimately connected by a close network of interrelationships, involving a (Kogu) person's nearest kin. Marriage and close relationships in this region were, clearly, somehow correlated with warfare. Affines were not wholeheartedly trusted. The expectation of conflict and disagreement was always present, and actual situations confirmed it. A simple but convincing framework on the basis of a 'self-fulfilling prophecy' had been developed and sustained in ideological terms. As I have suggested elsewhere (1962: 234), the more closely districts were bound by kin ties, especially affinal kin ties, the greater the possibility of dissension and overt hostility between them. There were more precipitating causes which could lead to warfare. Conversely, increasing distance between two districts, spatially and genealogically, diminished that possibility.[18]

Within this small sphere, then, most fighting is reported to have occurred. Kemiu, Moiife, Ofafina and Asafina were traditional enemies of Kogu as well as being its principal sources of marital partners. Additionally, they visited one another during festivals and ceremonies. At the time of our fieldwork they comprised the most intensive interactory zone focusing on Kogu. Because of their mutual accessibility, they relied on one another for a wide range of co-operative undertakings—which traditionally in the normal course of everyday living included fighting as well. In such circumstances, because they were thrown so closely together, common interests were likely to clash and real and imagined wrongs could easily be blamed on close neighbours and kin. Proximity as such was, however, only a contributing factor; it did not account for the form and content of the social relations involved. It does not of itself provide a sufficient 'reason' for the particular types of patterned conflict which characterized interaction between these social units.

The presence of sisters and male and female cross-cousins in other districts did not minimize strain between the districts concerned or rule out open manifestations of it. A man would not refrain from fighting on their account, and his lineage and district would be even less closely affected. But he would refrain from shooting them, because the sibling-of-opposite-sex and male cross-cousin relationships, especially, represented almost the strongest bonds of personal affection and mutual aid. A man would not knowingly kill or wound them; but he would not be so discriminating where their husbands and certain other kin were concerned, unless he acknowledged close ties with such men on his own account—for instance, if his sister's husband were his own cross-cousin. This virtual neutrality in respect of certain relationships was a normal feature of warfare. There was no demand for total participation overriding kinship ties. But the presence of such kin in another district, a sister or brother, a cross-cousin of the same or opposite sex, might aggravate any existing dissension. The bond between brother and sister, particularly, helped to underwrite conflict as well as co-operation. Further, in any district at least half the resident population (i.e., females from outside) was regarded as potentially disloyal to it, with interests in their own lineage, village and district.

This represented also an indirect threat to lineage solidarity, since there was always the possibility that a man might be influenced by his mother and her male kin, especially her brothers, to take their part against his own patrikin and district.

Even when there was strong affection between spouses belonging to different districts, this did not necessarily influence their attitudes toward their affines. On a personal level, in cases of interdistrict marriage there was said to be always a conflict of loyalties. On a district level, seen in terms of the interaction of the total population of which it was composed, it was much more intense, and primarily localized within two spheres (i.e., as in diagram, A and B); but a residue was diffused over spheres C and D. In other words, the interactory zone in its broader sense was significant functionally only at its centre and virtually non-existent at the periphery.

The major sphere of interaction, then, was criss-crossed with lines of distrust and conflict, potential hostility and outbursts of physical aggression, countered by ties of loyalty, affection, trust and co-operation. The two operated together, one tending to disturb the other through their interdistrict implications, because to each person within this constellation these ties of opposition and common interest meant different things, if only as attitudes and actions involving different people.

Each district had to contend with this framework of relationships that affected both interdistrict and intradistrict intercourse, as far as the presence of a large number of 'foreign' women was concerned. One consequence was an attempt to make the lineage or the clan a solidary unit in which a person could find refuge from outside disruption. On one structural level, this unit had the problem of maintaining a certain independence as against the wider district. At another level, the district was faced with the same problem in relation to the linguistic unit. Superimposed on this, the ephemeral sphere of political influence, as an interactory zone, on the one hand widened the significance of the linguistic units; on the other, it had the dual effect of splitting the district into factions, dividing while simultaneously integrating the respective segments, and strengthening the lineages.

The intradistrict situation showed the same concomitance of interdependence and conflict. The assumption that a man could rely confidently only on the members of his own lineage or clan, on his brothers, sons and fathers, did not obviate rivalry. Jealousy between elder and younger brothers—a popular conflict situation in myth and drama—was openly expressed. It was accentuated by pressures and influences from the zone of interaction and by the emphasis on aggressive self-assertion. The strain extended to classificatory and adoptive patrikin throughout the district and was manifested in intradistrict quarrelling. Further, Kogu men contracted at least 62 of their 232 marriages within their own district, including some polygynous unions, while 11 out of 91 male killings and 2 out of 27 female killings took place on this intradistrict level. This does not take into account quarrels resulting only in injury, nor does it concern Kogu men's dissension with resident 'foreign' women or ordinary fighting between co-wives, and so on. Nor is there any need to qualify this picture by pointing out again the strong co-operative bonds that continued to exist on a personal basis, for although they helped to ameliorate dissension they often helped to exacerbate it.

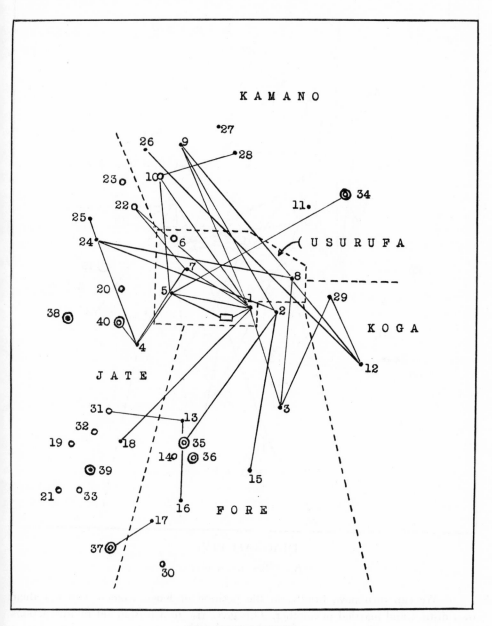

DIAGRAM FOUR
Key: See main text.

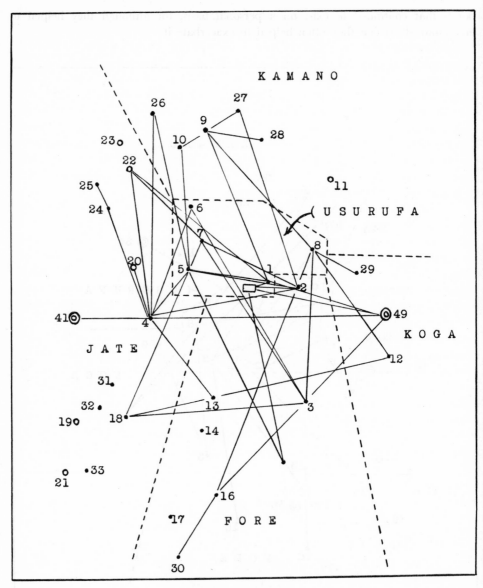

DIAGRAM FIVE

Key: See main text.

We can turn now, briefly, to the position of Kogu women who left their own district and married in another. This gives rise to a further set of interactions in relation not only to the marriage itself, but to the husband's oppositions and interests, providing connecting links between further districts. These are necessarily incomplete, but for our purpose they demonstrate how the various zones, each centred around a specific district, are connected. The interactory zone of a Kogu female (for example) who married outside the district was greater than that of a Kogu male: women resident in any district, but not lineal members of it, were for some purposes caught up in their husbands' interactory zone. For instance, Kogu women contracted 124 (or 66%) of the total marriages outside their district; the majority of these, as noted, were distributed among four districts (Moiife, Anonana, Irafu and Agura), but the total spread covered 23 districts. Of the 124 husbands accounted for, 34 were shot, 12 succumbed to ordinary sorcery, 11 to *sangguma*, and 13 died from natural causes (5), dysentery (7) and suicide (1): 54 were still living (at that time); only 2 from Moiife and 1 from Agura were reported shot by Kogu: the remaining shootings involved 13 other districts.

Diagram Four is set out socio-geographically. Linguistic group boundaries are conventionally noted, and a small box signifies the district of Kogu; darkened circles represent districts where Kogu women were located; light or open circles are districts within the Kogu zone of interaction, from which Kogu men had obtained wives (although some of these are also from darkened circles) or where oppositions were reported; shaded or light concentric circles refer to districts not specifically in the Kogu-centred zone: unbroken lines, between district points, signify oppositions in relation to the Kogu women's husbands.

Of Kogu men's wives who came from outside the district, 20 had been shot by arrow, 19 killed by ordinary sorcery, 13 by *guzigli'*, 11 by *sangguma*, and 33 died from natural causes (22), dysentery (10) and suicide (1), while 74 of the 170 were (at that time) still living. The majority of the women were from Moiife, Kemiu, Agura, Anonana and Irafu, although 28 districts are represented overall. In Diagram Five, we are concerned with the districts responsible for the 'killing' of 63 of them. Darkened circles signify the districts from which the women came: light circles represent districts within the Kogu zone of interaction; darkened or light concentric circles refer to districts not specifically in the Kogu zone; unbroken lines, between district points, signify the districts held responsible for the women's deaths.

IMPLICATIONS ARISING FROM THIS DISCUSSION

a. *The Structural Survival of the Political Unit*

In the first place, a problem arises in respect of an interactory zone of opposition and co-operation relevant to any district and spreading spatially in terms of intensity of interaction. It not only served to highlight the functioning of regulative aspects of behaviour within the district. It obviously involved the operation and functioning of forces over and above these, with the regulation of interpersonal behaviour.

Warfare is a key consideration in this context. The district, as the political and consequently also the war-making unit, was (if I can put it in this shorthand way without being accused of reifying) concerned with its own continuity and identity and also with the continuity and identity of its component segments. Structurally speaking, warfare did two things. It exposed the relative isolation of the district as a unitary element—and it emphasized the interdependence of units within a fluctuating zone of interaction, accepting this zone as being a 'security-insecurity circle'. At the organizational level, in the working out of actual events, warfare was a retaliatory mechanism ensuring that real or imagined wrongs were reciprocated or 'backed'. This took place mainly on an interdistrict basis; and traditionally, except for sorcery there was no other way of obtaining redress. Such procedure was assumed to have the support of the political unit as a whole, although not all members would necessarily participate.

Warfare (see R. Berndt 1962: 266-8, 1964: 193) was traditionally an important aspect of social control. It was primarily designed to re-establish an idealized *status quo*, which constantly fluctuated but, nevertheless, underlined the principle of continuity. In all retaliatory warfare compensation was sought, and the aggressive use of force was used to achieve this in much the same way as, in a different context, judicial procedure (see R. Berndt 1962: Chapters 15-16). But it could rebound unhappily on the unit or units involved. In the attempt to gain compensation for almost every death, the regulative qualities of a war-making unit could be strained to a point of imbalance and at least partial internal disorganization. For example, one of the two principal parties in any particular fighting sequence (i.e., excluding allies) might be forced either to sue for peace or to leave its home territory, or both.

In looking at the total picture, over time, an impression that emerges quite strongly is one of some form of balancing between the constituent units in any one interactory zone, in terms of a fluctuating range of opposition and co-operation. In a sense, members of any one district *as a whole* (i.e., excluding specific inter-personal relationships) viewed the members of other districts *as a whole* as 'outsiders', whether or not they were incorporated within the interactory zone. But they were not really outsiders unless they fell outside the recognized confines of the interactory zone. Within it, they constituted persons whose behaviour took expected and predictable shapes, within certain limits, and who *in toto* made up that particular social world. The dispersal of one unit within the zone did not necessarily upset its overall structure: its position (or status) within that system was retained although it might have to wait some time before it could actively re-enter the system. Because of the nature of warfare and the refugee problem as such, all zones varied in form over a period of years. And all zones, necessarily, overlapped.

b. *Identification of the Social System*

Under these circumstances, the interactory zone itself can be identified as a social system. This is an abstraction, which could be made at any point in time, and its content changes through time—but the variations fell within a range. Looking at the situation in this way is important for an understanding of the nature of social order in this region, in terms of conflicting and opposing elements, and in relation to the segmentary composition of the linguistic units. While the narrower zones of political influence overlapped if we look at them in wider perspective, nevertheless from the perspective of any one district each one of them was relatively self-contained, comprising all the major socio-cultural ingredients necessary to maintain and perpetuate it. Defining allies and enemies (R. Berndt 1964: 202), defined also the area of intensive interaction. This represented a 'community' of common interests, aims, and means of achieving these, where warfare was a co-operative undertaking and where the behaviour of others could be predicted with reasonable certainty.

c. *Conflict as an Inherent Factor*

Recapitulating, then, we have here both a considerable degree of basic conflict and, simultaneously, a strain toward order in terms of co-operation and 'balance'. These two features, of course, are present in any social situation anywhere; and study of the interplay between them is basic to the question that some writers claim is the central concern of social science generally—the question of social order. In the situation I am outlining, conflicting and unifying features are in almost constant interaction. This aspect is of primary importance in considering political structure and organization in this setting. Conflicting elements appear at different levels of any analysis, and give the impression of cutting across and militating against the processes that make for conformity. But in so doing they often serve a dual purpose, in reinforcing and maintaining the basic tenets of social living.

In considering the interactory zone centring on any one district, we have seen that the major area of tension incorporated districts intimately connected by a close network of interrelationships: that is, including many of a person's closest kin. Social distance in this context was therefore smaller between actively opposed and hostile groups than it was in the case of strangers who, although not actively hostile, were barely known and with whom little or no interaction took place. And the more closely a person was bound by kin ties with other persons in adjacent districts, the greater the likelihood of dissension, which could be intensified into open hostility. The people who were the main source of marriage partners were those with whom one not only co-operated but also fought.

With the political zone of interaction involving such a constant interplay between opposition and co-operation, the process of ordinary living included the expectation that one might oppose members of another unit while expecting help from them later, aiding them on one occasion and fighting them on the next. This would seem to bear out the point that Simmel (1955: e.g., 14-18) made, in speaking of what he called "the positive and integrating role of antagonism" and of conflict. (See also R. Berndt 1962: 413-18.) These particular groups represent perhaps a special case, in which the repetitive and in a sense self-balancing nature of this conflict is thrown into sharp relief. Nevertheless, conflict was embedded in any social situation composed of the interrelationship of persons, and modified or intensified according to cultural emphases. It was not necessarily correlated with inconsistency. Nor does its presence in a social system, as we see it here in contrast with counteracting elements, necessarily lead to social disorganization—provided that it takes place within a broadly common framework of agreed-upon values and expectations.

THE WEAKNESS OF THE POLITICAL UNIT

Districts were the nominal protagonists in each interactory zone. I have emphasized the term 'nominal', and now it is necessary to return to this point and consider the weakness of the district as a political body. The division of responsibility and authority within the district, in conjunction with the informal and competitive nature of leadership, is significant here, and so is the dispersal of its members in wartime emergencies. We cannot be sure how frequent was this shifting of groups from one area to another. Although fairly full (retrospective) data are available on the movements of some districts, they are incomplete for others; so we do not know whether such movements were due to population differences between districts, as a factor in inequality in fighting strength. Where we do have detailed information it would seem that, with a few salient exceptions, most districts were more or less evenly matched, and that any two engaged in a given series of fights appear to have had an equal chance of success. This may have been because, as already mentioned, only a certain number of the available fighting men would be actively engaged in any such event. Another factor was the general understanding that there would not and should not be more than half a dozen deaths in any one clash. A greater number of deaths was likely to provoke an outcry, invoking the norm—tantamount, almost to a 'rule of war'. The aim was never complete extermination of an enemy. Over and above any concern with justifying any specific encounter, there was an assumption that warfare itself was a good thing, an exciting and pleasurable activity for men. The means were 'good', and so was the generalized goal: success meant, essentially, assertion of superiority, of dominant status, over members of another unit. For the victors in any encounter, there had to be living opponents who could be taunted with defeat, or would acknowledge such defeat tacitly through their response. Warfare was no fun if no suitable opponents were available. Hence the occasional plea on the part of a successful district for the return of a defeated neighbour.

Ordinarily, only a series of hit-and-run fights, with the devastation of one house-place after another, could force an entire district away from its own ground. To achieve this, its opponents would have to engage in fighting over a period, be exceptionally fortunate in initial attacks (as sometimes happened), or bribe other districts to help as temporary allies. As the subject of their attacks became weakened, they would close in for the final decisive fight that would split and scatter it. In many cases collapse seems to have been sudden, when morale was weakened by a war of nerves and fear became predominant. In such circumstances there was no concerted effort to repulse the attacker at all costs. The ideal of the Strong Man rested on the assumption that there would always be people to submit to him unless and until they themselves became strong enough to defeat or supplant him. The patterning of warfare reflected the same understanding—that one response to displays of apparently superior strength was to beat a temporary retreat.

In some examples the routing of a village or series of hamlets was a time of confusion and panic, with individual adults and children escaping in the high grass or jungles and making their way as best they could to villages they hoped would be friendly. In other cases the exodus was rather more orderly, with previous discussion of possible destinations and small groups setting off in the directions they preferred. Sometimes the groups were larger, but the district as a whole, its members and adherents, never moved *en masse* from one locality to another.

Although the groups so dispersed were no longer able to make even a show of combined fighting, this did not deter some of them from attempting occasional sorties, still carried out in the name of the district; but usually they seem to have preferred not to fight until they were re-united. A small exiled group, unable to return to its gardens, having lost its major items of wealth (e.g., pigs), had to rely heavily on the kindness of others—'kindness' that had to be paid for. On the other hand, such happenings forced people into areas they might not normally have visited and widened their interactory perspective, bringing in new elements of common interest quite as much as of antagonism.

This relative mobility of district members, the relative ease with which they separated into groups bound for different destinations, points up the absence of central authority and the centrifugal pull of its component segments. The rate at which a district collapsed in the face of outside attack depended very much on the distribution of power and authority within it. The political unit, as such, existed only through the common consent and common interest of the leaders of each component hamlet and village. There was no authority independent of these, no central political body able by force or through constitutional means to insist on adherence to the ideal of political solidarity, and no 'office-holders' whose business it was to maintain unity as well as order. The symbols relating to district cohesion were no more powerful or persuasive than those of more limited reference. In rallying sentiment for the internal solidarity of a district the appeal was always to self-interest, the need to unite against a common danger—represented by other districts.

The weakness, in this respect, lay in the diffusion of power and authority, with the leader or Strong Man of each small segment of a district remaining such only until another took his place. Competition was keen, and the system as such flexible enough to permit interpersonal clashes even within the village, as well as within the district. Nevertheless, the unity of the district as a political entity was more than a verbal ideal. With few exceptions, the tendency of its scattered segments was always to re-unite, on their own ground or elsewhere; and in interaction with other like units, its members would assert their own identity by stressing their district affiliation, speaking for or taking action on behalf of that district even when no suggestion, or claim, of majority representation was made.

In the ordinary course of events, decisions on matters affecting the political unit in its relations with others were made by the various groups of male lineage kin, discussing them informally in their communal houses from which women were normally excluded. The leaders in each case tended to take the initiative, overriding or ignoring other opinions. When the issue was one of war or bribery or a request for a peace ceremony, all or most of the Big Men of a district would come together in one of its villages or hamlets, and decisions reached at such meetings would be treated as if they were binding on the whole district. Big Men who did not attend might in some cases have been deliberately excluded, perhaps because their loyalty was in doubt on a certain issue—e.g., if they had close and active maternal ties in a district against which offensive action was planned. This was possible, since such meetings were usually held at night in comparative secrecy. In any case, and especially if the Strong Men could not come to a satisfactory agreement, the district might 'break' temporarily into opposing factions, even to the extent of supporting hostile districts in active warfare. This was not usual, particularly in the north. Nevertheless such a possibility, among other factors, was sufficient to blur the contrast between 'warfare' as an interdistrict activity and 'fighting' as intradistrict. There was not a clearcut distinction in local terminology between the two (see R. Berndt, 1962: 233, note 4; 1964: 188-93). Nevertheless, according to the verbal ideal of district solidarity, any cleavages that threatened its identity as a unit should be resolved before they went too far; but dissension between districts was never deprecated in that way.

With alien contact, a centralized authority system based on overwhelmingly superior force made its appearance in areas where warfare was being suppressed or restricted. The key to the problem of political weakness rested primarily in the nature of the major cultural emphases, which ensured that both prestige and power depended on self-assertion through strength and aggressiveness, and that male dominance could be achieved and maintained only through a display of physical superiority, preferably involving the use of force and violence. Central authority as such was in fact antithetical to local ideology, although *temporary* domination of one district by another was a familiar state of affairs. The alien-sponsored appointments of luluai (village or district headman), tultul (subsidiary functionary or interpreter), bossboy or 'mouthboy' (subsidiary spokesman) and the rest, like alien Administrative authority itself, were not seen so much in their total context as part of a programme of unifying the whole region under central control. They were regarded as particular individuals or units temporarily possessed of superior strength. Each 'normal' adult male, trained to strive for just this kind of goal, saw himself as a possible rival of any leader who might emerge in his district or village. Rivalry between competing Strong Men was kept in check only by explicit stress on the need to present a united front to hostile outsiders, since none of them could survive without some kind of alliance that was reasonably secure over a period.

The demand for developing self-reliance and initiative at the expense of others emphasized the dimension of superordination-subordination in personal as well as in wider social relationships, and pulled against the contrary demand for co-operation and reciprocal aid except insofar as these were identified as promising certain advantages. But the tension between these two alternatives, self-assertion and self-interest versus the welfare of the wider unit, was explicitly recognized. One source of statements about it was a body of stories or secondary myths that included, among other things, a set of moral rules, a code of behaviour governing social relations. On this particular topic the code was that, although intradistrict dissension could lead to wounding or killing in the heat of a quarrel, once tempers had cooled the unity among its fighting men should be re-affirmed and the dispute settled without further bloodshed.

This was the setting, and the rationale, for what I have called bribery. As well as being used quite often in interpersonal affairs such as quarrels between co-wives, it was one of the conventional means a district could employ in trying to get the better of another. A member of one district would be approached secretly by members of another trying to persuade him to act against his own district. Or Big Men in one district would be asked by Big Men in another to join them in proceeding against a third—in effect, an attempt to weld together two or more districts as a fighting unit, even though this might be for only one encounter and in any event was always on a short-range basis. Two points seem to go together: the popularity of bribery in the sphere of interdistrict relations, and the smallness of the political unit in its struggle to assert itself against others. There was a desire —sometimes implied, sometimes spelt out in exhortations—to create a stronger group, and so to achieve greater security in a situation where there was always the possibility of attack from others.

Granted all this, bribery was an uncertain way of either securing political strength through alliance or achieving personal reward. The undertone of distrust in interpersonal relations, as well as its more overt expression in interdistrict affairs, not only accentuated the position—developed the practice, so to speak—but made this an extremely unreliable means of attaining the desired ends.

THE CHANGING AUTHORITY SYSTEM

We turn to alien-sponsored leadership and its influence on local affairs. I shall speak of such leaders mainly in relation to informal courts—informal, or un-official, as contrasted with the formal administrative courts. (See R. Berndt 1962: Chapters 15-16.)[19]

The informal court was not so much an attempt to imitate or copy the Administrative judicial system, although that must have had some connection with the way it developed. The process was more haphazard, more mixed, and less deliberate than that. It was a local adjustment to cope with a situation brought about by alien impact. Warfare and armed fighting were officially banned soon after the first Administration patrol came through the region late in 1947. This official stand, in sharp contrast to fundamental local views, was reinforced almost immediately by mission-sponsored native evangelists, Lutheran and Seventh Day Adventist.

The 'new rules' could not be strictly enforced all at once, and most of the new things and new ways infiltrated very slowly indeed, especially since there were so few direct lines of communication and actual contact with Europeans was, at best, extremely limited. Nevertheless, re-orientation in some forms of traditional behaviour was inevitable. The new era had been heralded by the alarming sight of aeroplanes (the local equivalent of Unidentified Flying Objects) and equally alarming rumours from the north of the area, with impressive eye-witness reports of the devastating power of firearms.[20] According to retrospective accounts, fear and anxiety were the dominant emotions at that time, and these provided a congenial atmosphere for the emergence both of 'cargo cults' and of informal courts. The switch-over from armed warfare to the kinds of aggressive action that became a feature of these courts was quite rapid, but for a time both forms of social control operated simultaneously and even in conjunction—although the informal courts eventually prevailed, at least until 1953. The process was uneven, however. When the informal courts were operating in the Kogu-Busarasa areas, armed warfare was the norm farther south in what was then (in 1953) officially uncontrolled territory.

The transformation was carried out, not by the people at large—that is, not by common consent—but by members of the newly established hierarchy of authority that emerged almost simultaneously with the establishment of alien control. Its members were informally nominated by Administration officers patrolling the region, and became, in effect, the new élite. These luluais, tultuls and 'mouthboys' were, nominally, the official representatives of their respective districts. They were not necessarily traditional leaders or Strong Men, although a few were, or were trying to be. In some cases they had no recognized affiliation, on the basis of either birth or adoption, with the districts to which they were allocated and their appointment was more or less arbitrary. Retrospective statements aside, if later events were any guide to what had happened earlier, a man who went to some trouble in helping a visiting patrol officer and his entourage or bustled about conspicuously with an appearance of doing so, especially if he spoke a few words of pidgin English, stood a very good chance of being nominated—even though he might have been only a visitor himself, come to see what the patrol was doing there. Under such circumstances, conflict between new and traditional leaders was bound to ensue. Occasionally the warrior leaders, remaining in the background, were able to manipulate the new leaders to their own advantage.

In any case, there was a precedent for this usurpation of authority within the traditional system itself. The prestige of any Strong Man or Big Man was derived and maintained through personal initiative and high-handed action in the face of constant competition. The new men depended on this too, and in many respects they did not differ from their predecessors. Foisted into power by an irresistibly superior force, they simply took advantage of the situation and behaved in a socially approved manner toward their subordinates in order to demonstrate their ability and justify their status. From the Administration's point of view, they were expected to serve as intermediaries between it and the local people. This meant that they were in a much better position than the warrior leaders had ever been. Within their districts they had less competition to contend with. The overall Governmental framework, up to the early 1950's, was still patchy at the local level, but one effect of the new moves was to centralize local authority within the district, bringing its villages more closely together. But although this spelt strength for the district as a political unit, Administration control set limits to the kinds of activity in which such a group could engage. Only two major avenues for the expression of overt aggression in anything like the traditional sense seemed to be left open. One was sorcery. The other was the informal courts.

As long as such avenues appeared to be available, it was easier for values from the traditional past to be carried over into the 'present'—in this instance, the 'present' of the early 1950's. And, to reinforce them still further, strength and self-assertiveness were not only still significant locally. They were, also, qualities commended by the Administration, which at that time was in the process of 'opening up' the country—or, at least, qualities commended by some of its officers who were personally involved in that process. The changes that were being thrust upon the local people were therefore much less traumatic than they might have been. Where there was an outright clash in values, this was handled largely through the medium of ritual action. The local 'cargo cult' or adjustment movements were attempts, not so much to adjust to alien ways, as to accommodate those ways to traditional forms. Likewise, the new leaders were little more than old leaders in a new guise, the guise of formalized authority. When rivalry between them did come to the surface, the only element lacking was the approved use of physical force.

Along with the 'officially' appointed leaders, expansion of mission influence brought other new men. Evangelists, self-styled and otherwise, claimed to act and speak with the authority and support of the Administration. In most cases, they saw no fundamental conflict between missionaries and government officials and initially regarded their aspirations as being virtually synonymous. At the interpersonal level, however, they did clash with the luluais and tultuls, especially as their respective spheres of interest became more sharply defined.

Both types of new leader drew their authority, their right to command others, from outside, and what local support they had was almost wholly a reflection of that. In both cases too their status rested in one sense on personal achievement even though it was validated by alien recognition. Generally speaking, this ensured greater stability and continuity than in the case of the warrior leaders as such, who were now forced to seek alien support or retire from the contest. In this respect the situation did not differ radically from its traditional counterpart: it represented simply a resorting of personnel in new positions of authority. And this was how the people perceived it at first. However, the changes were structurally significant. A new hierarchical system was in the process of crystallizing. Political control had widened considerably, and with it the rule of law. Moreover, the new leaders were the instruments of innovation, with both direct and indirect access to new areas of wealth and ideas, and they were in a position to assert their authority with alien support.

The most powerful of all the non-European leaders were the native police. They were the direct representatives of the Administration. All came from other parts of New Guinea, and none spoke any of the local languages. In 1951-52, apart from the main base at Kainantu no more than half a dozen all told were in the region, in charge of several scattered posts. But in 1952-53 there was an influx of police, moving through the districts and stirring up local men, women and children in an official drive to build motor roads through to the south and bring all the Fore areas under Administration control. Except on those occasions when they were with European officials, they gave the impression of having virtually absolute authority: their actions were rarely questioned by the local people. It was not that the local people did not realize the police were under European jurisdiction. It was simply that, particularly when they spoke no pidgin English and lacked the support of local leaders, they had no effective avenues of appeal against abuses of police authority. Pragmatically speaking, the native police were the real leaders in the new situation and all local dignitaries, officially appointed or otherwise, had to defer to them. Up to the early 1950's the Administration exercised control of the region through them and their interpreters, and many minor and some major decisions relevant to everyday affairs were left in their hands. The informal courts were a case in point.

These courts were under the direct jurisdiction of the new local leaders supported by the native police and by native evangelists. All such men were believed to have the power to enforce punishment and exact compensation. That recognition was extended to include leaders outside their own districts—and not only within the same interactory zone. This expansion of the rule of law, in spatial terms, was in marked contrast to the traditional picture, and is structurally significant. Superficially, at this level, there was an appearance of compliance with the imposed alien-inspired authority system. As in the past, acceptance rested primarily on the strength of the leaders concerned. Should that strength be reduced (and there are indications that it has been reduced in recent years), the likelihood of local interests predominating would be correspondingly greater: and with this a shift in focus from an Administration-centred situation, with implications for broader New Guinea political integration.

Much depends on how far traditional values are retained or translated into acceptable contemporary forms and whether informal law continues to be mediated through the new men—also on whether these new men must, to be locally acceptable, still dramatize, or over-dramatize, their role as Strong Men. In the early '50's they were certainly very much in the forefront of local affairs. Obviously the situation at that time was culturally congenial, even though the context was different from what it had been before. But structurally, as already indicated, crucial changes were taking place. The framework of the new authority system resulted in a hardening of public opinion, a narrowing of the range of action and tolerance in relation to certain wrongs. Public support, generally, was much more articulate than it had been in the immediate past, or than it was at the same period in areas farther south where the informal courts were not operating. In part, of course, this was in response to an outwardly new form. Although these people were oriented primarily toward their traditional past and the values and practices deriving from it, that orientation did not rule out the possibility of change, and the acceptability of change in certain fields.

Actually, although the models used in ordinary everyday life were undoubtedly derived from the past, the framework of social action emphasizing insecurity and conflict, and even spatial mobility (insofar as refugees were concerned), provided a congenial background for innovation and change. This is especially brought out in the adjustment movements which were fairly frequent from 1930 or so until at least the early 1950's. (See R. Berndt 1952-53, 1954; C. Berndt 1953, 1957.)

IMPLICATIONS OF POLITICAL CHANGE-OVER

In summary, these alterations in the power structure went hand in hand with the development and persistence of the informal court as a judicial mechanism, as part of a re-assembling of local control mechanisms in general. Important structural changes came directly from the reshuffling of the authority system, including the 'phasing out' of traditional warrior leaders, and from the continuing and increasing pressures of outside control. The outlawing of armed warfare made possible the emergence of the informal court as an institution linked at first indirectly with the Administration. Coercion was more clearly defined and regularized than it had been before. Traditional control mechanisms employed against other districts, with district independence as a major issue, became ineffective, and those that were substituted had the effect of establishing district *dependence* through the extension of legal space. The range of offences treated in the informal courts shows that radical alterations had taken place, not so much in attitudes as in the action through which they were expressed. No formal distinction now existed between such procedures within and outside the political unit.

Changes at the organizational level (re-organization of recruitment for authority, the extension of legal space, and crystallization of views concerning what constituted conformity) were inseparable from fundamental changes at the structural level. At the time of our fieldwork, there was a lag between structural and organizational change. The structural form of traditional social behaviour was still partly intact, but the system as such was marked by changes in emphasis at different points, each with its empirical linkage at the organizational level.

On the one hand, the establishment of defined authorities like the luluai, tultul and 'mouthboy' for each district strengthened the political unit at the expense of the interactory zone. On the other hand, a counteracting influence was the increase in legal space, extending far beyond the boundaries of the traditionally defined political unit—weakening that unit, but at the same time reinforcing and strengthening the interactory zone. This was, essentially, the traditional interplay between more or less clearly defined structural elements and those that were more ephemeral in form. Permeating both of them was a crystallization or hardening of certain controlling mechanisms, establishing a more positive and increasingly wider interactory zone, more stable and less dependent on overt oppositions and antagonisms. This unit, or quasi-unit, that developed as a result of external influence had implications in the sphere of social action—in relation to social oppositions and continuing distrust, but also in positively reducing these. The contemporary picture, as far as we can judge, has shown a gradual lessening of internal antagonisms, which had not been really erased but were now focused outward toward the Administration.

The judicial system as an institution, in the final count, depended on the individual authorities who were obliged to administer, interpret or even formulate the new rules and laws that were emerging and to translate them into action. In one sense they were the innovators, the new manipulators. In the immediate past, Big Men were not greatly influenced in their decision-making by those weaker than themselves. They were not dependent on any expression of collective opinion, nor did they take into account dissenting minorities that were not vigorous or strong enough to translate their wishes into action or effectively threaten to do so. Similarly, in the new situation control was still in the hands of adult men, with females formally subordinated and dependent on their male kin or their husbands for the assertion of their rights. It was only in the Administration courts and (during our fieldwork) in the informal courts in their immediate neighbourhood that a woman could bring a complaint against a man and expect to receive what could be considered as a relatively impartial hearing.

The authorities who operated the new system did so, as I have noted, with the support of the 'aliens', with the ostensible purpose of maintaining order. They had substituted new coercive controls although they had retained the indigenous content as far as possible, while the court system was the medium through which the new coercive measures could operate. Significantly, it did not interfere to any extent with one vital medium for expressing and reinforcing interpersonal and interdistrict antagonisms. Belief in the efficacy and the supposed practice of sorcery was largely unaffected by alien contact up to the early '50's. Indeed, there were indications that it could become even more strongly entrenched following the suppression of open warfare—because native police as well as evangelists openly expressed belief in it, and also because sorcery represented one of the few remaining means of self-help through which personal animosity could be expressed, where personal responsibility was still significant as long as it remained secret and did not come to the notice of the court.

The rapid and far-reaching changes that were taking place during our fieldwork, and the implications of these, were not completely realized by the local people. They envisaged them as being of short-term duration. That was probably why initial Administration control of the region took, on the whole, such a smooth uninterrupted course. The people were, up to a point, eager to co-operate with what they still regarded as a 'foreign' government. Because they hoped to obtain comparable power and wealth for themselves, they were interested positively in participating in the process of accelerating change.

Generally speaking (there were exceptions), up to the early '50's they apparently did not feel they were being controlled or forced to comply with foreign regulations and accept new ideas. They were still preoccupied with management of their own internal order, even though this had been re-adjusted to suit existing conditions. The more articulate among them, especially, recognized that the judicial system had formalized their code of rules, or their 'law', and that it was of 'foreign' inspiration, but at the same time they considered it to be their own peculiar adaptation that had emerged more or less gradually. And this was, more or less, what had in fact taken place. The underlying traditional patterns of belief had proved remarkably resilient in the face of organizational and structural changes. The process was one of re-assembling. What has happened since our fieldwork in this region is another matter. Enough has been said, however, to indicate some major local trends at this early stage of relations with the outside world, before the tremendous expansion in Administration, medical and mission contact that was to follow a few years later.

NOTES

1. See, for instance, R. Berndt (1962) and C. Berndt (n.d.).

Field research in this area was carried out in 1952-53 under the auspices of the Department of Anthropology, the University of Sydney. My wife accompanied me on both occasions, with an Ohio State Fellowship from the International Federation of University Women, and help from the Research Committee of the University of Sydney. The initial analysis of this material was undertaken while I was in receipt of a Nuffield Foundation Dominion Travelling Fellowship and (later) a Leverhulme Award at the London School of Economics and Political Science, the University of London.

The original version of this article was written in 1956 for the projected volume on 'New Guinea Political Systems' (to have been edited by Professor K. E. Read). The section on the 'Zone of Political Influence' was originally presented as part of a lecture to the Royal Anthropological Institute in 1955: a summary was published in R. Berndt (1955: 105-7). In the present instance, the 1956 version has been amended, with additional references, but I have kept the basic format. Also, sections of this paper have been used in other studies. In this case, however, I have tried to bring together a summarized statement of the political situation. I have restrained myself from presenting further material to support the contentions put forward here, and have avoided additional analysis. Particularly, I have not dealt with the matter of political decision-making which, it could be argued, is crucial to such a discussion. My main focus is on the political system *per se* and on the identification of the 'Zone of Political Influence' which, theoretically, is of some significance.

But I do want to comment on two points: (i) It is one thing to say that the empirical case-material set out in R. M. Berndt 1962, should have been annotated to show clearly which cases were observed at first hand and which rested merely on verbal reports. This is fair comment, and in fact the omission was unintentional and simply an oversight. But it is quite another thing to say that *therefore* I drew no distinction between the two kinds of evidence and to construct an edifice of incredible-fantasy around this. The study did not go into the matter of variation and (in)consistency in oral tradition and the theoretical problems this poses. I see that as an issue for separate discussion. But for references to it as asides in the course of the text, see e.g. R. M. Berndt 1962: xii-xiii, xiv, 151*n*, 181, 281, 295. (ii) My intention in that volume was to provide an overview covering a fairly wide field. The particularly interesting circumstance of that time and place, in a region which (in the south) was in the process of being and (in the north) had only just been brought under control, led me to believe that it was important to present it in that way—even though this meant highlighting the *quality* of belief and behaviour without concentrating on the 'microsociology' of the situation. But from the extensive and quite detailed case-material that I have, some of it based on verbal reports alone and some on such reports plus first-hand observation (*including* observation of aggressively violent behaviour), I suggest it is a mistake to suppose that a detailed following-through of specific persons and relationships will explain actions and events that otherwise appear to be quite arbitrary. (Cf. A. L. Epstein 1967.) This is just not so in a number of incidents I have recorded —again, including incidents that I personally witnessed. My wife came to the same conclusion independently, in regard to several such events which she explored in working with women. I am not saying that, if we knew *all* the facts, these would still seem to be simply 'arbitrary' decisions and actions, merely that it is not enough to claim that the answer lies in a detailed examination of social relationships through time in respect of specific persons.

The political situation in this particular area has been considered comparatively in relation to the Highlands of New Guinea as a whole (see R. Berndt 1964 in J. B. Watson, ed.: 183-203) but in that case the focus was on warfare. In another comparative study, within the field of social control (as in R. Berndt 1962), I have considered the Australian-administered Highlands focusing on Leaders, External Relations, Internal Order, Sorcery, and Suicide: see R. Berndt, 1971.

2. Our main centre was the 'small name' of Pintagori in Busarasa. For Administration purposes this is, apparently, now called Oka(pa); it is the site of the Kuru Research Centre. In 1951-53, Oka was a district to the southeast of Busarasa and Moke. Since that period, far-reaching changes have taken place, most notably the investigations into *kuru* sorcery, which has been diagnosed as a disease syndrome (see R. Berndt 1958: 4-28). Later, R. M. Glasse carried out fieldwork in the region south of where we initially worked: see his contribution (with S. Lindenbaum) on 'South Fore Politics'.

3. For a different perspective on language divisions in this overall region, see, e.g., S. Wurm 1964. The classification I use here is a summarized statement of the one my wife and I arrived at in the course of our fieldwork. In compiling it, we drew on a variety of local sources: e.g., the names people gave to the languages/ dialects that they themselves and others spoke, the range of mutual intelligibility when they communicated with one another or when we communicated with them, and so on.

4. See Nadel (1951: 187): "In doing so we assess two factors—the quantitive range of institutional activities entered into by the group, that is, the range of its corporate functions, and the nature and general relevance of these activities . . ." "Mostly, then, when we look for a society we find the political unit, and when

speaking of the former we mean in effect the latter . . ." See also I. Schapera (1953: 359), criticizing Nadel's definition.

5. R. Firth (1951: 27): "Society emphasizes the human component, the aggregate of people and the relations between them." See also G. P. Murdock (1949), I. Schapera (1953: 357-61) and A. R. Radcliffe-Brown (1952: 188-204).

6. Cf. A. R. Radcliffe-Brown's suggestion (1952: 193) of "any convenient locality of a suitable size" (i.e., territorially defined), plus a "network of social relations" (i.e., one assumes the widest effective group in Nadel's terms).

7. For a discussion of this concept in relation to an Australian Aboriginal area, see R. Berndt (1959: 81-107).

8. The concept of the district as a political unit is discussed briefly in R. Berndt (1962: e.g., 233-4, 267-8, 319-20). Specifically in connection with warfare, and viewed comparatively throughout the Highlands, see R. Berndt (1964: 188-93); in that same contribution Table II, p. 187, provides an equation of social units for the Highlands.

9. In its customary dictionary usage, this signifies an attempt to pervert someone by gift or other inducement, so that there is an element of dishonesty or illegality attaching to the transaction. My use of the word here is somewhat broader, embracing actions which, although involving gifts to solicit aid, do not always have that connotation. It covers two types of behaviour. In the first sense, where a bribe is accepted by a person for the purpose of doing injury to a member of his own district or betraying that district to an enemy (that is, outside the normal relationship ties in respect of which this is implicitly permitted or tolerated), then it can be described as an illegal procedure which if discovered is punishable, or at least open to censure. In the second sense, however, it is entirely an interdistrict affair. One or more members of another district are offered or promised payment for performing a specific task, such as killing some person belonging to a third district, or a request is made for help and payment given or promised to bring about a temporary alliance. We cannot use the term "pervert" in relation to it, nor is there in this context any element of illegality. However, I call this bribery, rather than payment for anticipated services, since once the bribe is given it may not be recovered if the agreed-on task is unfulfilled. There is no sanction, apart from physical force or sorcery, to ensure its recovery or the accomplishment of the task. No moral claim is involved, as there is in regard to (e.g.) the payment of bridewealth, and there is an uncertainty about the whole transaction.

It is true that hostile relations between two districts tended, in practice, to cancel at least temporarily any claims beween their respective members, even as regards such matters as bridewealth, so that here too physical force or sorcery offered the only means of obtaining redress—or compensation. Nevertheless, there was at least nominal insistence that these claims *should* be met, an acknowledgment of their validity. Failure to meet them was, admittedly, a hostile act. In the case of what I am calling bribes, there was no such assurance or assumption of normative validity. Acceptance of payment (or promise of payment) did not constitute an undertaking that the required task would be performed, and was not expected to do so. There was no security of satisfaction, nor any suggestion that there should be; and it is this connotation that I imply in using the term 'bribery' instead of the more neutral term 'payment'. (See R. Berndt 1962: 230.)

10. In a genealogical survey of four districts (one Usurufa, two Jate, and one Fore), involving 1,931 persons, 1,018 were still living in 1953; of the others, 392 were said to have died from sorcery, 275 from arrow wounds in fighting and the residue from natural causes, dysentery, suicide or cause unknown. These

genealogies covered a time-depth of approximately 50 years, the maximum memory-depth, in this respect, of adults participating in the survey. (See R. Berndt 1958: 17.)

11. For the purpose of this discussion, I use the terms 'structure' and 'organization' in accordance with Firth (1951: 30-5).

12. Up to a point, there are striking similarities here with K. E. Read (1954: 40-1). There are also significant differences. The Gahuku-Gama, for instance, entered into permanent alliances, as the groups discussed in this paper did not. (See also R. Berndt 1964: 193-9.)

13. Reference is made to this material in R. Berndt (1955: 106; 1962: 309-10; and 1964: 193).

14. I.e., in rough classification, those who had not yet reached puberty. It was not possible to be more exact here.

15. I.e., sorcery in which there was believed to be no direct physical contact of a face-to-face kind between sorcerer and victim, although the sorcerer might use substances that had been in direct association with his victim. (See R. Berndt 1962: 214-23.)

16. Here too the sorcerer was said to work at a relative distance from his victim. *Guzigli'* was sometimes known as shaking sorcery but is now more generally called *kuru,* from the pidgin English word *guria.* See Note 2. It was said to be common among the Fore, who specialized in it, to involve some loss of muscular control, and to be accompanied in its final stages by internal decay and increasing loss of sphincter control. (See R. Berndt 1958: 4-28.)

17. This form of sorcery (*tunakafia* in Jate) was said to include direct physical aggression, with the sorcerer performing a special operation on the victim. It is in the same general category as the well-known *vada.* (See R. Berndt 1962: 223-8; 1969.)

18. I have not framed this in operational terms; but that could readily be done, provided it is recognized that to cope with it satisfactorily much (though certainly not all) of the data would need to be retrospective.

19. When I mentioned these courts in personal discussions with Administration officials at the end of our fieldwork period, I was told (a) that this was the first time they had heard of such 'independent' courts in this region and (b) that such courts were officially 'illegal', whether they were conducted by native police or by local native officials.

20. This initial traumatic experience set in train the later 'cargo' movement manifestations in this region, which continued spasmodically up to 1952. (See R. Berndt 1952-53: e.g., 50-1; 1954: 193.)

REFERENCES CITED

BERNDT, C. H. (1953): Socio-Cultural Change in the Eastern Central Highlands of New Guinea. *Southwestern Journal of Anthropology,* Vol. 9, No. 1.

BERNDT, C. H. (1957): Social and Cultural Change in New Guinea: Communication, and Views About 'Other People'. *Sociologus,* Vol. VII, No. 1.

BERNDT, C. H. (n.d.): *Myth in Action.* Forthcoming. [Originally titled 'Mythology in the Eastern Central Highlands of New Guinea', Thesis for the degree of Ph.D. in the University of London, 1955.]

BERNDT, R. M. (1952-53): A Cargo Movement in the Eastern Central Highlands of New Guinea. *Oceania,* Vol. XXIII, Nos. 1-3.

BERNDT, R. M. (1954): Reaction to Contact in the Eastern Highlands of New Guinea. *Oceania,* Vol. XXIV, Nos. 3-4.

BERNDT, R. M. (1955): Interdependence and Conflict in the Eastern Central Highlands of New Guinea. *Man,* Vol. LV, No. 116.

BERNDT, R. M. (1958): A "Devastating Disease Syndrome": Kuru Sorcery in the Eastern Central Highlands of New Guinea. *Sociologus,* Vol. 8, No. 1.

BERNDT, R. M. (1959): The Concept of 'The Tribe' in the Western Desert of Australia. *Oceania,* Vol. XXX, No. 2.

BERNDT, R. M. (1962): *Excess and Restraint.* Social Control among a New Guinea Mountain People. Chicago: University of Chicago Press.

BERNDT, R. M. (1964): Warfare in the New Guinea Highlands. In *New Guinea: the Central Highlands* (J. B. Watson, ed.). Special Publication of the *American Anthropologist,* Vol. 66, No. 4. Part 2.

BERNDT, R. M. (1965): The Kamano, Usurufa, Jate and Fore of the Eastern Highlands. In *Gods, Ghosts and Men in Melanesia* (P. Lawrence and M. J. Meggitt, eds.). Melbourne: Oxford University Press.

BERNDT, R. M. (1971): Social Control in Papua-New Guinea. Section B. 'The Australian-administered Highlands'. In *The New Guinea Encyclopaedia.* Melbourne: Melbourne University Press.

EPSTEIN, A. L. (1967): The Case Method in the Field of Law. In *The Craft of Social Anthropology* (A. L. Epstein, ed.). London: Social Science Paperbacks and Tavistock.

FIRTH, R. (1951): *Elements of Social Organization.* London: Watts.

HALLOWELL, A. I. (1950): In *Anthropology Today* (A. L. Kroeber, et al., eds.). Chicago: University of Chicago Press.

LAWRENCE, P. (1965-66): The Garia of the Madang District. *Anthropological Forum,* Vol. I, Nos. 3-4.

MacIVER, R. M. and C. H. PAGE (1950): *Society.* London: Macmillan.

MURDOCK, G. P. (1949): *Social Structure.* New York: Macmillan.

NADEL, S. F. (1951): *The Foundations of Social Anthropology.* London: Cohen and West.

RADCLIFFE-BROWN, A. R. (1950): Preface to *African Political Systems* (M. Fortes and E. E. Evans-Pritchard, eds.). London: Oxford University Press. (1st published 1940.)

RADCLIFFE-BROWN, A. R. (1952): *Structure and Function in Primitive Society.* London: Cohen and West.

READ, K. E. (1954): Cultures of the Central Highlands, New Guinea. *Southwestern Journal of Anthropology,* Vol. 10, No. 1.

SCHAPERA, I. (1953): Some Comments on Comparative Method in Social Anthropology. *American Anthropologist,* Vol. 55, No. 3.

SIMMEL, G. (1955): *Conflict.* (K. H. Wolff, trans.). Glencoe: Free Press.

WURM, S. A. (1966): Australian New Guinea Highlands Languages and the Distribution of their Typological Features. In *New Guinea: the Central Highlands* (J. B. Watson, ed.). Special Publication of the *American Anthropologist,* Vol. 66, No. 4, Part 2.

THE CONTRIBUTORS

RONALD M. BERNDT

Department of Anthropology, University of Western Australia.

PAULA BROWN (GLICK)

Department of Anthropology, State University of New York at Stony Brook.

KENELM O. L. BURRIDGE

Department of Anthropology and Sociology, University of British Columbia.

ANN CHOWNING

Department of Anthropology, University of Papua and New Guinea.

ROBERT M. GLASSE

Department of Anthropology, Queens College of the City of New York.

WARD H. GOODENOUGH

Department of Anthropology, University of Pennsylvania.

PHYLLIS M. KABERRY

Department of Anthropology, University College, University of London.

LEW L. LANGNESS

Department of Anthropology, University of Washington, Seattle.

PETER LAWRENCE

    Department of Anthropology, University of Sydney.

SHIRLEY LINDENBAUM

    (care of) Department of Anthropology, University of Sydney.

CHERRY LOWMAN-VAYDA

    Department of Anthropology, Columbia University, New York.

MERVYN J. MEGGITT

    Department of Anthropology, Queens College of the City of New York.

DOUGLAS L. OLIVER

    Department of Anthropology, Harvard University.

MARIE REAY

    Department of Anthropology and Sociology, Australian National University.

JAMES B. WATSON

    Department of Anthropology, University of Washington, Seattle.

INDEX

Abelam (meaning northern Abelam), 35-73

Abiera, 224-74

Administration, 25-8; authority system, 413-19; boundaries determined by, 178; built roads and access, 246, 416; convenience of new units, 298; emphasized compact settlements, 364; influence in southern Bougainville, 276-7, 284, 286-7, 288; influence on Maring, 326, 327, 355-8, on Tangu 97, 98, 100, 106-10, 111n; influence so sorcery traps rot, 177; native reaction to, 26, 109; outlawed warfare, 66, 288, 355, 394, 413, 417; usurped local initiative, 251. *See also* House of Assembly; Local Government Councils; Native officials; Courts, administrative; Courts, informal

Alliances, 6, 116, 304, 313, 322-4, 327, 365, 367, 368, 373, 387, 389, 393, 396, 399, 408, 409, 422n. *See also* Warfare

Ancestor Spirit Man, 337-40, 341, 342, 343-4, 347-8, 349, 350, 351, 352, 353, 355, 356, 357

Ancestor Spirits, 327-30

Ancestor Woman Spirit complex, *see* Kunagage

Anglican Mission, *See* Missions

Assembly, place of (piazza), 45, 48, 49, 51, 52

Authority, 80, 303, 308. *See also* Leadership

Bagasin area (Garia), 74-93

Bena Bena, 221, 298-316

Big Man, 14-15, 16, 17, 193-5; attributes: ability in pig exchanges, 309; and hereditary succession, 3, 14, 209, 375-6; authority limited, 14-15, 16, 80-1, 91, 378; community prime mover, 155-63, 167-9, 172; curer and diviner, 372; laughing man, 372; magnetic attraction, 14; manager for *Br'ngun'guni*, 103, 105; manipulator and business man, 374, 375; medicine man, 356; *mumi*, 281-4, 287, 288, 292-3; not brave in war, 264; not merely elder but entrepreneur, 51-6, 59-63, 70; orator, 358; peacemaker, 168, 239-40; persuasive powers, 374; pivot, 376; prominent in political manoeuvre, 17; representative of hamlet 43-5; reputation as yam grower, 35; responsible for conduct of ceremonies, 43; set attacks in motion, 17, 391; silent man, 373; skill in ritual knowledge, 80; strong man, 410; 'talk' man, 374; warrior leader, 390-2, 412; of Bena, 308-10, 312; Chimbu, 216-18, 220; Mae-Enga, 194, 196, 199, 200-3, 204, 205n, 206n; Maring, 318, 319, 326, 327, 330-50, 354, 355-8. *See also* Leaders; Leadership; Manager; and individuals Matoto, Songi

Bribery, 312, 391, 393, 410, 412, 413, 421n

Br'ngun'guni, 94, 97, 100-6, 109

Buin Plain, southern Bougainville, 276-97

Cannibalism, 364

Cargo, 27, 28, 118, 171, 173n, 414

Catholic Mission, *see* Missions

Central authority: lack of, 6; people unable to understand principle of, 29

Central Enga, 222, 309; comparison with Kuma, 182-7. *See also* Mae-Enga

Ceremonies: create sense of cultural identity, 38. *See also* Br'ngun'guni; Feasts; Exchange(s); House-tamberan; Masks

Chiefs, *see* Big Man; Leaders

Chimbu, 189, 207-23

Clan: attempt to make it solidary unit, 319-20, 322-5, 404; leaders, 205n; organization Abelam, 56-63; Bena, 299-302, 313; Chimbu, 211-12; Mae-Enga, 196-9; support of, for Big Men, 202-3. *See also* Social structure

Coffee: in Waiye Council area, 215; land for, 175, 178, 180, 181, 182, 184, 187; plantation by Siune, 218

Cognation: role of in forming local groups, 6-13, 15. *See also* Kinship

Co-operative groups: clearing land, 279; co-ordination critical in group activity, 155; fish drives, 289-90; Lakalai 141-5. *See also* Pools

Courts, administrative, 413, 418

Courts, informal, 413-18, 422n

Cults, *see* Tamberan cult; Yam cult